# ETRUSCAN
# VASE
# PAINTING

# ETRUSCAN VASE PAINTING

BY

## J. D. BEAZLEY

# ETRUSCAN
# VASE
# PAINTING

BY
J. D. BEAZLEY

HACKER ART BOOKS / NEW YORK 1976

First published 1947 by
Oxford University Press, Cambridge,
in the Oxford Monographs on Classical Archaeology.
Reissued 1976 by
Hacker Art Books, New York.

Library of Congress Catalogue Card Number 75-11054
ISBN 0-87817-182-7

This reprint has been authorized by the Clarendon Press, Oxford.

Printed in the United States of America.

# PREFACE

THIS book contains less, and more, than the title promises. It began as a study of Etruscan red-figure, prefaced by a lecture on Etruscan vase-painting as a whole which was delivered to the Classical Association at St. Albans in April 1944. I then added appendices on Etruscan black-figure, vases with decoration in superposed colour, black vases, silvered vases, and other classes. These so grew that it seemed natural to rearrange the chapters and to call the book not 'Etruscan Red-figure' but 'Etruscan Vase-painting'. I have not dealt with the very earliest products of Etruscan or Italic vase-painting in the eighth and seventh centuries B.C.; and since there is already a good account of Etruscan black-figure I have not treated it at length. My title—not 'Vases' but 'Vase-painting'—dispensed me from touching bucchero. On the other hand, Latin pottery is included, besides a good many vases that are not what is generally understood by 'painted'.

The subject has never been treated on anything like this scale. Long ago Gerhard, Jahn, and Brunn made a good beginning; Furtwängler and others made brief but useful contributions; among recent writers two stand out: that very acute Milanese scholar Carlo Albizzati; and Tobias Dohrn.

I have often noticed in Greek scholars a real dislike of the Etruscans, which I do not share. The world owes the Etruscans an immense debt for admiring, treasuring, and causing to be preserved so many masterpieces of Greek art. Add their own splendid work in bronze and clay; their gay wall-paintings; their jewellery and engraved gems; their buildings and their bonifications;

> adde tot egregias urbes operumque laborem,
> tot congesta manu praeruptis oppida saxis,
> fluminaque antiquos subterlabentia muros.

Clay vases were not their forte: but even these may help towards the understanding of a people which had some touch of greatness; and with that hope this study goes forth.

I have done my best with the material at present available to me: my notes; some photographs; the imperfect reproductions in books and periodicals. Some of the originals I examined carefully while it was still possible; others more casually; much I neglected, and cannot now make good my fault. I might have postponed publication till I should have had the opportunity of going round some of the museums again; or at least of obtaining information from the authorities: but that would have meant years of delay.

The treatment may appear somewhat scrappy in places: the groups small, many isolated pieces, the relation of one group to another vague, the location of the fabrics uncertain, the dates not precisely determined. This is partly due to my not having been able to examine all the originals; partly to the scarcity of information about the circumstances of discovery, which are often unrecorded, or if recorded not published, or published only with slight descriptions and meagre illustration: but partly also it is due to the derivative character of the art. It would be vain to expect the majestic continuity of

Attic or Corinthian vase-painting, or of Attic stelai. A derivative art is apt to proceed by fits and starts.

The illusion of greater compactness might have been created by the omission of pieces that for one reason or another will not drop into place: but that would have falsified the picture.

Unexpected visits to America and Switzerland have brought me new material at the last moment. The printing was so far advanced that most of this, instead of being incorporated in the text, has had to find place as addenda at the end of the book. Had it still been possible I should have somewhat remodelled the chapters on Later Red-figure, VII, VIII and IX: for it has become plain to me that more of the late red-figured Etruscan vases are Faliscan than I had thought at first, so that a good many pieces now described in Chapters VII and IX should have appeared in Chapter VIII. I have made this clear, as occasion arose, in the addenda: but should have preferred to rearrange the text.

I venture to hope that my work, imperfect though it be, will at least lead to many Etruscan vases being brought out of their lurking-places, scrutinized, and published.

In the scantiness of my material, I am doubly grateful to those who have increased my slender stock of photographs and added permission to publish: to the late Dr. L. D. Caskey, and to Mrs. Sarah Glanville Downey of the Museum of Fine Arts, Boston; to Miss Gisela Richter of the Metropolitan Museum, New York; to Mrs. Dorothy Burr Thompson of the Royal Ontario Museum, Toronto; to Prof. H. R. W. Smith, University of California, and Prof. E. W. Gifford of the Museum of Anthropology, Berkeley; to Mr. G. Roger Edwards, Bowdoin College, Brunswick, Maine; to Prof. Bernard Ashmole of the British Museum; to Mr. Louis Clarke of the Fitzwilliam Museum, Cambridge; to Mr. D. B. Harden of the Ashmolean Museum, and Mr. T. K. Penniman of the Pitt Rivers Museum, Oxford; to the late Prof. A. D. Mainds, and to Mr. I. A. Richmond, King's College, Newcastle-upon-Tyne; to Dr. Paul Jacobsthal, Christ Church, Oxford. I owe a special debt to Paul Jacobsthal: it was he who urged me to enlarge my first version to the size of a book; he has read the manuscript twice and out of his wide range of accurate knowledge improved it in many places. Our conversations on Etruscan matters are of long standing. It is just that the book should be dedicated to him.

I wish to thank Mr. Andrew Gow of Trinity College, Cambridge, for reading the proofs and making many valuable criticisms; and Prof. P. N. Ure of the University of Reading for generously placing at my disposal his notes on Etruscan vases in the museums of France and Italy: it will be seen from the frequent references to 'Ure's notes' that they have been most useful. To thank also Miss Ethel Van Tassel for photographs of several vases in Berkeley and San Francisco, and for her notes on them; Prof. A. D. Trendall for photographs of three vases in Sydney; Dr. Adolf Greifenhagen for photographs, given me many years ago, of the Faliscan stamnos in Bonn; Dr. Hansjörg Bloesch for a photograph from Leipsic; Mr. J. A. Spranger for examining some vases in Florence, and for procuring me recent Italian fascicles of the *Corpus Vasorum*; Miss Barbara Bartle and Mr. W. S. Evans for notes on Faliscan vases in Berkeley; Mr. Oswald Couldrey and Dr. Otto Kurz for Indian facts; Prof. G. K. Braunholtz, Prof. Eduard Fraenkel,

Dr. Arnaldo Momigliano, and Dr. Dietrich von Bothmer for information specified in the text.

Even with the generous assistance of the friends I have named, the illustrations are not such as they would have been in other times. I have often had to use defective reproductions because no others were to be had; and many pieces which I should have liked to illustrate have never been photographed.

Nearly all the plates are devoted to red-figure. This is not a mere survival of the original plan. The fact is that a fairly representative selection of Etruscan black-figure, and of vases with added colour, has been published in other works; and the same is true of black vases, silvered vases, and the rest, which in any case tend to repeat with no great variation.

As to scale, I have tended, if I had a good photograph of a vase, to reproduce it large; if I had only a poor photograph, to reproduce it small; and to reduce the size of the illustrations that are taken from other books. These illustrations, therefore, are seldom equivalent to the original publication, which should be used if available.

Although owing to the troubles of the times they have had no immediate connexion with the present work, I am moved to express the gratitude which in common with all students of Etruscan art I feel to four Italian scholars: the late Raniero Mengarelli; Bartolomeo Nogara; Carlo Albizzati; Antonio Minto.

As usual I have consulted my wife on many questions to which a professional scholar might well have given a more conventional, a less fresh and trenchant answer.

J. D. B.

OXFORD, 1946

TO
PAUL JACOBSTHAL

# CONTENTS

LIST OF PLATES . . . . . . . x

LIST OF ABBREVIATIONS . . . . . xiv

I. ETRUSCAN VASE-PAINTING . . . . . 1

II. BLACK-FIGURE . . . . . . . 11

III. EARLIER RED-FIGURE . . . . . . 25

IV. FALISCAN . . . . . . . . 70

V. CLUSIUM . . . . . . . . 113

VI. VOLATERRAE . . . . . . . 123

VII. LATER RED-FIGURE: I . . . . . . 133

VIII. LATER RED-FIGURE: II. THE FLUID GROUP (LATE
FALISCAN). . . . . . . . 149

IX. LATER RED-FIGURE: III . . . . . 163

X. VASES WITH PATTERNS OR FLORAL WORK ONLY . 181

XI. PLASTIC VASES . . . . . . . 187

XII. VASES WITH DECORATION IN SUPERPOSED COLOUR . 195

XIII. BLACK VASES . . . . . . . 230

XIV. THE GROUP OF VILLA GIULIA 2303; AND VASES WITH
YELLOW SLIP . . . . . 281

XV. SILVERED VASES AND THE LIKE . . . 284

XVI. LATE RELIEF-VASES . . . . . . 294

ADDENDA . . . . . . . 295

INDEX . . . . . . . 311

# LIST OF PLATES

1, 1–2.    Vatican 231, neck-amphora. After phots. Alinari. See p. 1.

1, 3–6.    Munich 837, neck-amphora. After Ducati *Pont. V.* pl. 2, above, and pl. 1, above. See p. 1.

2–2a.    London B 64, neck-amphora. See pp. 2–3.

3, 1.    London B 63, hydria. See p. 2.

3, 2.    Baltimore, Walters Art Gallery, 48.7, neck-amphora. After *Journ. Walt.* 3, 110. See p. 2.

3, 3–4.    Vatican G 91, neck-amphora. See p. 2.

4, 1–3.    Paris, Musée Rodin, 980, cup. See pp. 3 and 25–7.

4, 4.    See Pl. 13a.

4, 5.    See Pl. 12.

5, 1.    Orvieto, Museo Faina, pelike. After phot. Alinari. See p. 37.

5, 2–3.    Vatican G 111, oinochoe. See pp. 49–50.

6, 1–3.    Oxford, Pitt Rivers Museum, kantharoid. See pp. 29–30.

6, 4.    Lost, stamnos. See pp. 27–8.

6, 5.    Leipsic T 952, column-krater. See Pl. 7, 2 and pp. 49–50.

7, 1.    Munich 3227, stamnos. See pp. 3 and 44.

7, 2.    Leipsic T 952, column-krater. See Pl. 6, 5.

7, 3.    London F 484, stamnos. See Pl. 8, 1–2 and pp. 3–4 and 43–5.

7, 4.    London F 482, pointed amphora. See pp. 45–6.

8, 1–2.    London F 484, stamnos. See Pl. 7, 3.

8, 3–4.    London 1927.10–10.1, bell-krater. See pp. 35–6.

9, 1.    Florence 4026, bell-krater. After FR. pl. 177. See pp. 33–5.

9, 2.    Vatican, cup. After phot. Alinari. See pp. 4 and 55.

10, 1–2.    Florence, stamnos. After Conestabile *Pitt. mur.* pll. 15–16. See pp. 5 and 52–3.

10, 3–5.    Paris, Cabinet des Médailles, 1066, cup. After *Gaz. arch.* 1879 pll. 3–5. See pp. 6 and 54–5.

11, 1–2.    Roman market (Basseggio), calyx-krater. After Micali *Mon. ined.* pl. 37, 2. See p. 46.

11, 3–4.    Paris, Cabinet des Médailles, 947, stamnos. After Micali *Mon. ined.* pl. 38, 1–2. See pp. 5–6 and 53–4.

11, 5.    Vienna, Oest. Mus., 448, stamnos. After *Annali* 1879 pl. V. See pp. 8 and 152–3.

11, 6.    Florence, stamnos. After Heydemann *Mittheilungen aus den Antikensammlungen in Ober- und Mittelitalien* 4. See pp. 146–7.

11, 7.    Roman market, stamnos. After Gerhard *Trinkschalen* pl. C, 4. See p. 46.

11, 8.    Rome, Prince Torlonia, pointed amphora. After *Bonner Jahrbücher* 120, 180. See p. 179.

11, 9.    Rome, Principe del Drago, skyphos. After Helbig *Untersuchungen über die Campanische Wandmalerei* 367. See p. 160.

12.    Vatican G 112, cup. See Pl. 4, 5 and pp. 4 and 55–6.

13, 1–2.    Toronto 427, stamnos. See p. 65.

13, 3–4.    Brunswick 268, cup. After *C.V.* pl. 44, 1–2. See p. 64.

13a.    Oxford 1917.4, stamnos. See Pl. 4, 4 and pp. 4 and 56–7.

14.    Boston 07.862, stamnos. See pp. 4–5 and 57–61.

15, 1–5.    Berkeley 8.989, oinochoe shape III. See p. 73.

15, 6–8.     Berkeley 8.998, skyphos. See p. 87.
15, 9–11.    Berkeley 8.997, skyphos. See pp. 84–5.
15, 12–13.   Berkeley 8.988, oinochoe shape VI. See p. 73.

16, 1.       Villa Giulia 1600, stamnos. See pp. 73–5.
16, 2.       Villa Giulia 3592, stamnos. See pp. 81 and 84.

17.          Oxford 1945.89, stamnos. See pp. 78–9.

18, 1–6.     Berkeley 8.984, hydria. See p. 101.
18, 7–8.     New York GR 641, stamnos. See p. 88.
18, 9–11.    Berkeley 8.999, skyphos. See p. 100.
18, 12.      Berkeley 8.2303, fragments of a cup. See p. 111.

19, 1.       Villa Giulia 6152, stamnos. See pp. 79–80.
19, 2.       Florence, stamnos. After Conestabile *Pitt. mur.* 161. See p. 78.

20, 1.       Villa Giulia 2491, volute-krater. See Pl. 24, 3 and pp. 7 and 81–4.
20, 2.       Berlin inv. 5825, stamnos. After *Ausonia* 5 pl. 5. See pp. 8 and 87–92.
20, 3.       Bonn 1569, stamnos. See Pl. 24, 1–2 and pp. 7–8 and 96–100.

21, 1–2.     London F 479, calyx-krater: 1, after Walters *B.M.Cat. iv*, pl. 13.  See Pl. **22, 1 and**
             pp. 7 and 92–4.
21, 3.       Rome, Principe del Drago, calyx-krater. After *Mon.* 10 pl. 51. See pp. 7 and 92–3.
21, 4.       Oxford 570, bowl. See p. 112.
21, 5.       Amsterdam inv. 2583, fragment of a calyx-krater. After *CV.* IV B pl. 1, 5. See pp. 92
             and 96.
21, 6.       Oxford 1927.4069, fragment of a cup. See p. 107.

22, 1.       London F 479, calyx-krater. See Pl. 21, 1–2.
22, 2.       Vienna University 499, cup. After *CV.* pl. 28, 4. See p. 110.
22, 3.       Vienna University 498, cup. After *CV.* pl. 28, 1. See pp. 109–10.

23.          Villa Giulia 1197, calyx-krater. See pp. 7, 92, and 94–6.

24, 1–2.     Bonn 1569, stamnos. See Pl. 20, 3.
24, 3.       Villa Giulia 2491, volute-krater. After *CV.* IV Br. pl. 7. See Pl. 20, 1.
24, 4.       Villa Giulia 43968, stamnos. See p. 97.

25, 1–3.     Berkeley 8.935, cup. See p. 107.
25, 4.       Villa Giulia 1674, cup. See pp. 7 and 106–7.
25, 5.       Tübingen F 13, cup. After Watzinger pl. 45. See p. 107.
25, 6.       Villa Giulia 3594, cup. After *Boll. d'Arte* 1916, 360. See p. 107.

26.          Boston 01.8114, cup. See p. 111.

27, 1–3.     Boston 01.8123, cup. See pp. 6 and 114.
27, 4–5.     Florence, cup. After *St. etr.* 12 pl. 57. See pp. 6 and 115.
27, 6.       Lost, fragment of a cup. See p. 114.
27, 7.       Louvre H 100, duck-askos. After *Enc. phot.* iii, 64, a. See pp. 6 and 119.
27, 8.       Orvieto 598, fragment of a cup. After phot. Armoni. See p. 113.
27, 9.       Florence, cup. After *RM.* 30, 132. See pp. 6 and 114.

28, 1–3.     Cambridge, skyphos. After phots. Marie Beazley. See pp. 6 and 117.
28, 4–5.     Villa Giulia, head-kantharos. See p. 118.
28, 6–7.     New York 07.286.33, skyphos. See p. 116.

29, 1.       Volterra, column-krater. After phot. Alinari. See pp. 10, 122 and 124.
29, 2–3.     Perugia, column-krater. After *Boll. d'Arte* 1922–3, i, 28–9. See p. 124, no. 4.

29, 4.      Volterra, stamnos. After phot. Alinari. See p. 121.

29, 5–6.    Berlin inv. 3986, column-krater. After *RM.* 52, 127 and pl. 27, 1. See pp. 122 and 124.

29, 7.      Berlin inv. 3996, column-krater. After *RM.* 52 pl. 28, 1. See p. 128.

29, 8–9.    Berlin inv. 3988, column-krater. After *RM.* 52 pl. 29. See pp. 10 and 128.

29, 10.     Berlin inv. 3989, column-krater. After *RM.* 52 pl. 30, 1. See p. 128.

30, 1–2.    Paris, Cabinet des Médailles, 918, volute-krater. After phots. Giraudon. See pp. 8–9 and 133–4.

30, 3.      Newcastle-upon-Tyne, King's College, fragment of a neck-amphora. See pp. 134–5.

31, 1–2.    Paris, Cabinet des Médailles, calyx-krater, 920: 1, after phot. Giraudon; 2, after *Mon.* 2 pl. 9. See pp. 9 and 135–7.

31, 3–4.    Oxford 1925.670, phiale. See pp. 181–2.

32, 1–2.    London F 480, calyx-krater. See pp. 136–41.

32, 3.      London F 486, stamnos. See p. 142.

32, 4.      London, sard scarab. See pp. 8 and 138 no. 4.

32, 5.      Boston, sard scarab. See pp. 8 and 138 no. 2.

32, 6.      Paris, Cabinet des Médailles, sard scarab. See pp. 8 and 138 no. 5.

32, 7.      New York, sard scarab. See pp. 8 and 138 no. 6.

33, 1–3.    Berkeley 8.3825, skyphos. See p. 143.

33, 4–6.    Berkeley 8.3399, oinochoe shape VII. See p. 143.

33, 7.      Carlsruhe 348, stamnos. See p. 142.

34, 1–3.    Cambridge AE 29, stamnos. See p. 142.

34, 4.      London F 487, hydria. See p. 172.

35, 1–3.    Bowdoin College, 13.9, stamnos. See p. 153.

35, 4–5.    Berlin inv. 30549, stamnos. See pp. 149 and 151.

35, 6.      Villa Giulia 1660, stamnos. After *Atti Pont.*, new series, 15, 258. See p. 152.

35, 7.      Vatican, stamnos. See p. 150.

36, 1–3.    London 1913.4–17.1, stamnos. See p. 153.

36, 4.      Berkeley 8.1000, skyphos. See p. 158.

36, 5–6.    Michigan 2609, oinochoe shape VII. After *CV.* pl. 24, 4. See p. 156.

36, 7.      Boston 80.539, phiale. See p. 158.

37.         Boston 97.372, skyphos. See pp. 166–7 and 303.

38, 1.      Formerly Munich, Dr. Adolf Preyss, cup. See p. 167.

38, 2.      Oxford 1914.37, fragment. See p. 37.

38, 3.      Oxford 1920.320, oinochoe shape VII. See p. 183.

38, 4.      New York 91.1.465, oinochoe shape VII. See pp. 169 and 303.

38, 5.      Oxford 339, duck-askos. See p. 192.

38, 6.      Oxford 259, oinochoe. See p. 186.

38, 7.      Oxford 1932.122, neck-amphora. See p. 14.

38, 8.      Oxford 1936.619, kantharos. See p. 232.

38, 9.      Oxford 258, duck-askos. See pp. 184 and 192.

38, 10.     Oxford 1874.403, kantharos. See p. 237.

38, 11.     Oxford 1874.431, 'salt-cellar'. See p. 245.

38, 12.     Oxford 1872.1269, oinochoe. See p. 261.

38, 13.     Oxford 381 A, oinochoe shape VII. See p. 268.

38, 14.     Oxford 1896–1908.G 520, oinochoe shape VII. See p. 268.

38, 15.     Oxford 1936.620, squat lekythos. See p. 270.

38, 16.     Oxford 1937.680, squat lekythos. See p. 271.

38, 17–19.  Providence 27.188, stemmed plate.  See pp. 10 and 175.

38, 20.      Berkeley 8.991, stemmed plate.  See p. 175.

38, 21.      Oxford 1878.146, plate.  See p. 177.

38, 22.      Oxford 1925.618, stemmed plate.  See p. 175.

38, 23.      Oxford 1872.1240, stemmed plate.  See p. 176.

38, 24.      Oxford 1872.1241, stemmed plate.  See p. 175.

38, 25.      Carthage, plate.  See pp. 10 and 176.

38, 26.      Oxford 454, stemmed plate.  See p. 175.

38, 27.      Oxford 1872.1242, stemmed plate.  See p. 175.

39, 1.       Villa Giulia 23949, plate.  See pp. 211–15.

39, 2–3.     Berlin, kantharos.  See p. 208.

40, 1–2.     Munich, head-mug.  After Hirth *Formenschatz* 1902 no. 2.  See pp. 188–9.

40, 3.       London E 803, lion-askos.  After Newton and Thompson pl. 11.  See p. 193.

40, 4.       New York GR 615, negro-head oinochoe.  See p. 187.

40, 5.       Boston 07.864, negro-head mug.  See p. 187.

40, 6.       Villa Giulia 16338, negro-head mug.  See p. 187.

40, 7–8.     Boston, plastic vase.  See pp. 189–90.

40, 9.       Vatican, plastic vase.  See p. 190.

# LIST OF ABBREVIATIONS

*ABC. Antiquités du Bosphore cimmérien.*

*ABS.* Beazley *Attic Black-figure: a Sketch.*

*AD. Antike Denkmäler.*

*AJA. American Journal of Archaeology.*

Albizzati. *Vasi antichi dipinti del Vaticano.*

*AM. Mitteilungen des Deutschen Archäologischen Instituts: Athenische Abteilung.*

*Annali. Annali dell' Instituto di Corrispondenza Archeologica.*

*Ant. cl. L'antiquité classique.*

*Anz. Archäologischer Anzeiger* (part of *Jb.*).

*ARV.* Beazley *Attic Red-figure Vase-painters.*

*ARW. Archiv für Religionswissenschaft.*

*Atti Pont. Atti della Pontificia Accademia Romana.*

Aurigemma. *Il R. Museo di Spina.*

*AZ. Archäologische Zeitung.*

Baur. *Catalogue of the Rebecca Darlington Stoddard Collection . . . in Yale University.*

*BCH. Bulletin de correspondance hellénique.*

Benndorf *GSV. Griechische und sicilische Vasenbilder.*

Bieńkowski *C. Les Celtes dans les arts mineurs gréco-romains.*

Bieńkowski *D. Die Darstellungen der Gallier in der hellenistischen Kunst.*

*Bildertafeln. Bildertafeln des Etruskischen Museums der Ny Carlsberg Glyptothek.*

*Boll. st. med. Associazione Internazionale Studi Mediterranei: Bollettino.*

*BPW. Berliner Philologische Wochenschrift.*

Brants. *Description of the Ancient Pottery preserved in . . . the Museum . . . of Leiden.*

Brunn *Rilievi. I rilievi delle urne etrusche.*

*BSA. Annual of the British School at Athens.*

*BSR. Papers of the British School at Rome.*

*Bull. Bullettino degli Annali dell' Instituto.*

*Bull. com. Bullettino della Commissione Archeologica Comunale di Roma.*

*Bull. Metr. Mus. Bulletin of the Metropolitan Museum.*

*Bull. MFA. Bulletin of the Museum of Fine Arts, Boston.*

*Bull. nap. Bullettino Napolitano.*

*Bull. Vereen. Bulletin van de Vereeniging tot Befordering der Kennis van de Antieke Beschaving.*

*CIE. Corpus Inscriptionum Etruscarum.*

*CIL. Corpus Inscriptionum Latinarum.*

*Cl. Rh. Clara Rhodos.*

*Compte-rendu. Compte-rendu de la Commission Impériale Archéologique.*

*CR. Classical Review.*

*CV. Corpus Vasorum Antiquorum.*

*Delt. Arkhaiologikon Deltion.*

Dohrn. *Die schwarzfigurigen etruskischen Vasen aus der zweiten Hälfte des sechsten Jahrhunderts.*

Ducati *Cer. Storia della ceramica antica.*

Ducati *St. Storia dell' Arte Etrusca.*

*El. cér.* Lenormant and de Witte *Elite des monuments céramographiques.*

*Eph. arkh. Ephemeris arkhaiologike.*

Essen *Did Orphic. Did Orphic Influence on Etruscan Tomb-paintings exist?*

Fairbanks. *Catalogue of Greek and Etruscan Vases in the Museum of Fine Arts, Boston.*

FR. Furtwängler and Reichhold *Griechische Vasenmalerei.*

*From the Coll. From the Collections of the Ny Carlsberg Glyptotek.*

Furtwängler *AG. Die antiken Gemmen.*

   *Beschr. Königliche Museen zu Berlin: Beschreibung der Vasensammlung im Antiquarium.*

   *KS. Kleine Schriften.*

Gerhard *AB. Antike Bildwerke.*

   *AV. Auserlesene Vasenbilder.*

   *EKV. Etruskische und kampanische Vasenbilder.*

   *ES. Etruskische Spiegel.*

   *TG. Trinkschalen und Gefässe des Königlichen Museums zu Berlin.*

   *Trinkschalen. Trinkschalen des Königlichen Museums zu Berlin.*

Giglioli. *L'arte etrusca.*

Graef and Langlotz. *Die antiken Vasen von der Akropolis zu Athen.*

Hartwig. *Die griechischen Meisterschalen.*

Haspels *ABL. Attic Black-figured Lekythoi.*

*Hesp. Hesperia.*

Heydemann *Ober. Mittheilungen aus den Antikensammlungen in Ober- und Mittelitalien.*

Holwerda. *Het laat-grieksche en romeinsche Gebruiksaardewerk . . . in het Rijksmuseum van Oudheden te Leiden.*

Hoppin *Bf. A Handbook of Greek Black-figured Vases.*

   *Rf. A Handbook of Attic Red-figured Vases.*

Inghirami. *Pitture di vasi etruschi.*

Inghirami *Mon. etr. Monumenti etruschi o di etrusco nome.*

   *Mus. Chius. Etrusco Museo Chiusino.*

Jacobsthal *ECA. Early Celtic Art.*

   *O. Ornamente griechischer Vasen.*

*Jb. Jahrbuch des Deutschen Archäologischen Instituts.*

*Jh. Jahreshefte des Oesterreichischen Archäologischen Institutes.*

*JHS. Journal of Hellenic Studies.*

*Journ. Walt. Journal of the Walters Art Gallery.*

*JRAI. Journal of the Royal Anthropological Institute.*

Körte *Rilievi. I rilievi delle urne etrusche.*

*Kunstbesitz. Kunstbesitz eines bekannten norddeutschen Sammlers.*

Langlotz. *Martin von Wagner-Museum der Universität Würzburg: Griechische Vasen.*

Lau. *Lau, Brunn, and Krell Die griechischen Vasen.*

Leroux. *Vases grecs du Musée Archéologique de Madrid.*

*LHG.* Beazley *The Lewes House Collection of Ancient Gems.*

Libertini. *Il Museo Biscari.*

Martha. *L'art étrusque.*

Matthies. *Die praenestinischen Spiegel.*

*Mededeelingen. Mededeelingen van het Nederlandsch Historisch Instituut te Rome.*

*Mél. Mélanges d'archéologie et d'histoire publiés par L'École française de Rome.*

Micali *Mon. ined. Monumenti inediti a illustrazione della storia degli antichi popoli italiani.*

   *St. Storia degli antichi popoli italiani.*

Milani *Mus. Top. Museo Topografico dell' Etruria.*

   *R. Mus. Il R. Museo Archeologico di Firenze.*

Mingazzini *Cast. Vasi della Collezione Castellani.*

*ML. Monumenti antichi pubblicati per cura della Reale Accademia dei Lincei.*

*Mon. Monumenti inediti pubblicati dall' Instituto di Corrispondenza Archeologica.*

*Mon. Piot. Fondation Eugène Piot. Monuments et Mémoires publiés par l'Académie des Inscriptions et Belles-Lettres.*

*MPAI. Monumenti della Pittura antica scoperti in Italia.*

*Mus. Greg. Museum Etruscum Gregorianum* (ed. 1842).

Neugebauer *ADP. Antiken in deutschem Privatbesitz.*

Noël Des Vergers. *L'Étrurie et les Étrusques.*

Nogara. *Gli etruschi e la loro civiltà.*

*NSc. Notizie degli Scavi di Antichità.*

Overbeck *KM. Atlas der griechischen Kunstmythologie.*

Pagenstecher *Cal. Die calenische Reliefkeramik.*

Passeri. *Picturae Etruscorum in Vasculis.*

Pellegrini *VF. Catalogo dei vasi greci dipinti delle necropoli felsinee.*

      *VPU. Catalogo dei vasi antichi dipinti delle collezioni Palagi ed Universitaria.*

Pernice *HKP. Die Hellenistische Kunst in Pompeji.*

Pfuhl. *Malerei und Zeichnung der Griechen.*

Poulsen *Kat. Etr. Katalog des Etruskischen Museums der Ny Carlsberg Glyptothek.*

Pryce *Cat. Sculpt. Catalogue of Sculptures in . . . the British Museum: Cypriote and Etruscan.*

PW. Pauly and Wissowa *Real-Encyclopädie der classischen Altertumswissenschaft.*

*RA. Revue archéologique.*

*REG. Revue des études grecques.*

*Rend. Pont. Rendiconti della Pontificia Accademia Romana.*

*Rev. arch. Revue archéologique.*

*RG.* Beazley and Magi *La raccolta Benedetto Guglielmi nel Museo Gregoriano Etrusco.*

Richter *Bronzes. The Metropolitan Museum of Art. Greek, Etruscan and Roman Bronzes.*

Richter *Etr. Handbook of the Etruscan Collection.*

Richter and Hall. *Red-figured Athenian Vases in the Metropolitan Museum of Art.*

Richter and Milne. *Shapes and Names of Athenian Vases.*

de Ridder. *Catalogue des vases peints de la Bibliothèque Nationale.*

Ritschl. *Priscae Latinitatis Monumenta.*

*Riv. Ist. Rivista del R. Istituto d'Archeologia e Storia d'Arte.*

*RM. Mitteilungen des Deutschen Archäologischen Instituts: Römische Abteilung.*

E. Robinson. *Museum of Fine Arts Boston: Catalogue of Greek Etruscan and Roman Vases.*

Robinson and Harcum. *A Catalogue of the Greek Vases in the Royal Ontario Museum of Archaeology, Toronto.*

Romanelli *T. Tarquinia: la Necropoli e il Museo.*

Schaal *Brem. Griechische Vasen . . . in Bremen.*

      *F. Griechische Vasen aus Frankfurter Sammlungen.*

Schumacher. *Beschreibung der Sammlung antiker Bronzen . . . zu Karlsruhe.*

Séchan. *Études sur la tragédie grecque dans ses rapports avec la céramique.*

*Sg. Vogell. Griechische Altertümer aus dem Besitze des Herrn A. Vogell.*

SH. Sieveking and Hackl, *Die Königliche Vasensammlung zu München. i.*

Sieveking *BTV. Bronzen Terrakotten Vasen der Sammlung Loeb.*

Solari. *Vita pubblica e privata degli Etruschi.*

*St. e. mat. Studi e materiali.*

*St. etr. Studi etruschi.*

Tarchi. *L'arte etrusco-romana nell' Umbria e nella Sabina.*

Tillyard. *The Hope Vases.*

*V. Pol.* Beazley *Vases in Poland.*

Wagner. *Antike Bronzen der Grossherzöglichen Badischen Alterthümersammlung in Karlsruhe.*

Watzinger. *Griechische Vasen in Tübingen.*

*WV. Wiener Vorlegeblätter.*

Zannoni. *Gli scavi della Certosa di Bologna.*

# CHAPTER I
# ETRUSCAN VASE-PAINTING

GREEK vases used to be called Etruscan: but there are plenty of Etruscan vases. They have not received much attention, and this is intelligible, for few of them are works of art. The Etruscans were gifted artists, but clay vases were not their forte. Bronze was their favourite material, and their best achievements were in bronze: statues and statuettes, candelabra, mirrors, and the rest. Yet many of their clay vases have great interest of subject. In style, they imitate Greek models, but they have a characteristic flavour which is sometimes agreeably racy.

I shall say nothing about the earliest Etruscan or Italic imitations of Greek vases, in the eighth and seventh centuries, and the first part of the sixth; the importance of these has been shown by Blakeway, Payne, and Mrs. Dohan.[1] Let us begin with an Etruscan black-figured vase from the middle of the sixth century, a neck-amphora in Munich of the so-called Pontic class ('Pontic' is only a conventional term).[2] It is a gay lively piece in an eclectic style with the Eastern Greek element predominating. The Judgement of Paris, one half of the picture on each side of the vase. Hermes is conducting the three goddesses to Paris, and he turns to give his last instructions. Hera, Athena, and Aphrodite are all well differentiated. Priam has guided the party to Paris. Here is Paris's dog with lolling tongue, Paris's herd, and their familiar the raven. The photograph shows that the modern copyist has not got the expression of number one, Hera, perfectly right: till now she has been smiling and chattering like the others; but when Hermes gives the word she becomes suddenly serious. These 'Pontic' vases were made in Etruria, but they are very Greek, and it is possible that the fabric was founded by a Greek immigrant. Another vase by the Paris Painter, as he has been called from the Munich vase, is a neck-amphora of the same shape in the Vatican.[3] This picture, too, is divided between the two sides of the vase: a cavalry engagement: on the one hand, Oriental archers, with high felt caps, using the Parthian shot; on the other, Western javelin-throwers. Hounds and hares form a kind of underplot. This is lively too, though it pales a little if it is compared with the sort of original from which it was imitated, an Attic vase-picture of about 560.[4]

In the later stage of the 'Pontic' fabric the non-Hellenic element, as might be expected, becomes somewhat stronger: but that need not be illustrated, and instead let us pass to a black-figure fabric which succeeds the Pontic and is the most important group of Etruscan vases in the last quarter of the sixth century and the early part of the fifth. The chief artist may be named the Micali Painter[5] in honour of an Italian scholar who published some of the vases a hundred years ago. This painter has a jolly, slogging

---

[1] Blakeway in *BSA.* 33, 170–208, and in *JRS.* 25, 129–49; Payne, see p. 11; Dohan *Italic Tomb-groups in the University Museum*; see also *JRS.* 33, 97–100 (Jacobsthal), and *C.R.* 1944, 30–1; and now Åkerström *Der geometrische Stil in Italien* (Lund, 1943).

[2] Munich 837, from Vulci. Pl. 1, 3–4, after Ducati

*Pontische Vasen* pll. 2 and 1. See also FR. pl. 21, and SH. pl. 33 and p. 99. On Pontic vases see p. 12.

[3] Vatican 231, from Vulci. Pl. 1, 1–2, after phots. Alinari: see also Albizzati pl. 25 and pp. 78–80.

[4] Athens Acr. 606: Graef pl. 31, whence *ABS.* pl. 4.

[5] See pp. 12–15.

style, and must have enjoyed himself. A neck-amphora of his in Baltimore[1] immediately transports us into what has been called 'that wonder-world of rushing men, women, satyrs, maenads, amidst all sorts of plants, trees, weeds, birds, beasts real and fantastic, in which the Etruscan, especially the earlier Etruscan, delights'.[2] The chief picture on his hydria in the British Museum[3] represents a dead man lying in state with the mourners about him, but the artist has not let that cast him down. There is nothing funereal about the winged youth, or the Pegasus, or the capering centaur. Big ugly birds like those that jostle the youth and the centaur are great favourites in Etruria and you find them everywhere in Etruscan art.[4] Here is a late work by the same painter, a neck-amphora in the Vatican with a Battle of Gods and Giants:[5] Herakles, Athena, and Ares on the Gods' side; the Giants assisted by a winged goddess—Eris or the like—and also by a second Athena, due to the excessive love of symmetry sometimes found in Etruria: the style is coarser and the movement more lumbering, but there is still plenty of life. A hideous bird has already alighted on one of the Giants. A fourth work by this painter, one of his earliest, is worth looking at more closely. A neck-amphora in the British Museum presents a sports meeting in the Etruria of the late sixth century B.C.[6] There are several scenes. First scene, a boxing-match. There are many such pictures on Greek vases, and amusing ones, but here it is not so much of Greek vases that we think as of those rude old prints, from the classic era of English boxing, in which the heroes of the prize-ring are shown confronting each other in bellicose attitudes: Tom Cribb, Jem Belcher, or Molyneux the Moor. The boy looks like a bottle-holder, but although he has the sponge in one hand, it is an oil-flask, a lekythion, that he holds in the other, and the water—or wine— is in a jug on the ground. They box to the flute, in Etruscan fashion. Then comes the umpire with his wand. This scene, and others on the vase, reappear on the walls of the Tomba della Scimmia at Chiusi.[7] Second scene, climbing the greasy pole. Third scene, at the end of the picture-band, under the handle: I always took these to be spectators, the countryman bringing his old father to see the fun; but there is a similar scene in the Tomba della Scimmia, where the couple seem to be performers, and it has been suggested that they are acrobats, and the little man a child in disguise.[8] Fourth scene, pentathlon—discus-thrower, javelin-thrower. Fifth scene, dance in armour: the youth is leaping up, on a springy platform. Sixth scene, chariot-race, the winner passing the post. Seventh scene, satyrs dancing. Are they real satyrs, in which case the artist in his excitement has left the sports ground and soared into another sphere? Or are they performers dressed as satyrs?—If so, the artist has used his privilege of making the performer more like what he is intended to be than would be possible in real life, and has depicted not the actors but the characters they represent. Eighth scene, a second team of dancers, veiled women. One of them turns and looks at you; and if we were told that these were

[1] From Castel Campanile: *Journal Walters Art Gallery* 3, 110 (D. K. Hill), whence Pl. 3, 2: see p. 14.

[2] Dohrn in *St. etr.* 12, 285 (slightly modified).

[3] B 63, from Vulci: Pl. 3, 1: *RG.* 78 no. 39.

[4] See pp. 96–7.

[5] Vatican G 91, from Vulci: part, Pl. 3, 3–4; *RG.* pll. 29–30 and pp. 76–83.

[6] B 64; Pll. 2 and 2a: Dohrn pl. 8: *RG.* 77 no. 1; see p. 12.

[7] The Tomba della Scimmia: *Mon.* 5 pll. 15–16; best in *MPAI. Etr. Clus.* i pll. 1–4, pll. A–B, and pp. 31–5.

[8] So Bianchi Bandinelli. The group: *Mon.* 5 pl. 15; *MPAI. Etr. Clus.* i, 10–11.

modern Italian women, in local costume, from the Abruzzi or Sardinia, I believe we should agree. Ninth scene, a third team, boys dancing in pairs and playing the castanets.

These were black-figured vases: Etruscan *red-figure* begins not much before the middle of the fifth century, that is to say long after red-figure had become the ruling technique in Attica. Before that, Etruscan painters had experimented with a kind of pseudo-red-figure, in which the figures, instead of being reserved in the native colour of the vase, were painted on top of the black background.[1] This easier and inferior technique was itself borrowed from Attica, where it was tried and soon rejected.[2] One of the earliest examples of true red-figure in Etruscan is a cup that was formerly in the collection of the sculptor Rodin and is now in the Musée Rodin, Paris.[3] If one had only heard of this vase and not seen it, one would have taken it for a forgery, but Nicolas Plaoutine, who brought it to light, saw that it was genuine. The outside is copied from an Attic cup: and by a strange coincidence the Attic original is preserved. It is the famous kylix in the Vatican with, inside, Oedipus listening to the Riddle of the Sphinx. The Etruscan painter has not copied the interior picture: but his exterior is a verbatim, somewhat heavy copy, even to the details of the floral decoration at the handles, of six out of the eight figures on the exterior of the Vatican cup. For the Oedipus and the Sphinx he has substituted a picture of two satyrs, one spinning round on the bottom of an empty wine-krater and clutching the other by the beard: after-dinner diversions. The date of the Attic cup, which is by a follower of the painter Douris, is between 470 and 460, and the Rodin cup cannot be much later. It is inscribed *Avles Vpinas*, a proper name, just possibly the artist's.

A large vase, a pointed amphora, in Perugia, with Dionysos, Ariadne, a satyr, and a maenad caressing a fawn,[4] is over a generation later than the Rodin cup. The style is very close to Attic, and the technique of the drawing is lighter and more accomplished than in the earlier vase. The Attic original has not been preserved (nor is it certain that the Etruscan is copying any single piece, and the design may be in part his own): but it is plain what he is imitating:—the style of the Meidias Painter and his companions. Vases in such a style were painted in Athens about 420 B.C. or 410, and the Perugia vase can hardly be later than the last decade of the fifth century.

The Perugia Painter has an accomplished hand: there is nothing provincial about him, or not very much. Other Etruscan vases of the same period are provincial: but they are not always the worse for that, and some of them have a flavour which pleases wherever one finds it—a perceptible tang of genuine popular art.

Perhaps not much can be claimed for the drawings on a stamnos in Munich,[5] but they are worth looking at because by the same hand as a vase of the same shape in the British Museum.[6] Apollo, it seems; a Lasa (an Etruscan goddess or daimon, with wings); Pan; a satyr. On the other side, a rider, Eros bringing him a wreath and sash in token of victory, and another Lasa, sitting on the ground, smelling a flower, and not heeding the

[1] See p. 195.
[2] Haspels *ABL.* 392 (index).
[3] Pl. 4, 1–3: see pp. 25–7.
[4] See pp. 36–7.

[5] Pl. 7, 1: Munich 3227: see p. 44 no. 2.
[6] Pl. 7, 3 and Pl. 8, 1–2: F 484: see p. 43 no. 1 and pp. 44–5. The old drawings in Gerhard, *AV.* pl. 321, may also be consulted.

others. These pictures remind one of a pagan scene by some very humble Italian painter of the fifteenth century: something between a vision and a valentine.

Let us pass on to the first half of the fourth century. We may begin with a cup in the Vatican which represents a god, probably Zeus, carrying off a goddess or heroine, either Hera or one of his other brides.[1] This has often been compared with a much earlier Attic cup of about 480 to 470 B.C., by Douris, in the Louvre: Zeus carrying off the sleeping Hera.[2] The Etruscan picture is not copied from the Attic, but the subjects are similar: and one sees how light and swift the Attic figures are, and how the Etruscan artist has stressed the labour and the effort. Something else has also been in his mind, something we have not met before: the notion of σεμνότης, seriousness or majesty: his god is kingly.

Another Etruscan cup of this period, a recent acquisition of the Vatican,[3] is not by the same hand as the Zeus cup, but has much in common with it besides the kind of subject. At first glance this would seem to be Eros carrying off a woman or rather bringing her to her lover, a subject best rendered on a Greek gem of the late archaic period in New York:[4] but the Etruscan cup is inscribed, and we learn from the inscriptions that the winged youth is not Eros, but *Zetun*, carrying off *Phuipa*. Phuipa is the Etruscan equivalent of the Greek Phoibe; and Zetun would correspond to a Greek Zeton. Zetes, the winged son of Boreas, is probably meant: this would become Zete in Etruscan, but one common termination has been substituted for another. The story is not known. Here again we notice the sense of effort, as if the winged one were trudging with his burden through heavy soil, and this sense is increased by the clogging garment, the blown hair, the starting eyeballs, and the open panting mouth. If this is Greek, it is Greek spoken with a strong accent. Outside, in each half, a merman, Tritun, seen from the front, ending in a pair of fish-tails, holding a rock in each hand: a favourite figure in Etruscan art.[5] We used to be told that the stories of mermaids arose from the half-human appearance, at a distance and in half-light, of the dugong or sea-cow: our monster, with his grave, long-lipped, subaqueous expression, looks like a progenitor of sea-cows. The heavy plant-work, too, makes one think of the bottom of the sea.

Another vase that is related in spirit to these two cups is a stamnos in Oxford.[6] The tone of the picture is very curious. 'Zeus and Ganymede' is a topic often treated in Greek art, but nowhere in this form. The chiefest of the gods, when Ganymede reveals his charms, sinks back in awe. Ganymede wears an Etruscan bulla round his neck, and holds a lyre. On the ground, the cock: in earlier art Ganymede holds this in his hand; here he has dropped it. Cock and lyre were white and have faded. Above, Eros suddenly appears from behind a rock, and looks at Zeus satirically. Here also there is σεμνότης: the figure of Zeus has a certain majesty, even at such a moment, and in such an attitude.

Ever since this vase came to Oxford, nearly thirty years ago, I have wanted to find another work by the same master: and here is one. A stamnos in Boston.[7] On one side,

[1] Pl. 9, 2: see p. 55.

[2] Louvre G 123: Hartwig pl. 68; Beazley and Ashmole fig. 57: *ARV.* 286 no. 83. See p. 297.

[3] Pl. 12 and Pl. 4, 5: Vatican G 112: see pp. 55–6.

[4] *Lewes House Gems* pl. A, 3; Richter *Cat. Engraved Gems* pl. 10: see pp. 55–6.

[5] See p. 56.

[6] Pl. 13a and pl. 4, 4: Oxford 1917.54: see pp. 56–7 and 295.

[7] Pl. 14: Boston 07.862: see pp. 57–61.

Polydeukes is binding Amykos to the stump of a tree. It is an episode from the adventures of the Argonauts. Amykos was a brute who refused to allow them to approach the fountain to draw water, and challenged them to a boxing-match: Polydeukes defeated him and bound him to a tree, and the Argonauts drew water and sailed away. The group on the Boston vase is an extract from a famous picture which was very popular in Etruria: the fullest and most faithful copy of it is engraved on the finest of bronze cistae, the Ficoroni cista by Novios Plautios:[1] many other monuments reproduce the central group: ours is one of the closest to the Ficoroni cista and, we may feel confident, to the original picture. In one point our version differs from others: Polydeukes is using not a leather thong but a withy. The picture on the other side of the Boston stamnos is still more interesting but very puzzling. In the middle stands a young hero—it cannot be an ordinary excavator —with a mattock in one hand, and in the other something he has found; an elderly satyr trots up with a pail and a patera; while Hermes, god of lucky finds, ἕρμαια, looks at the hero. I am inclined to think that this is a unique version of a subject which gave special pleasure to the Etruscans: the hero is Polydeukes; and what he has found, while loosening the ground of the boxing-ring with his mattock, is the Egg which will prove to contain Helen. Once more, the faces are very expressive, and Hermes, in particular, like Eros in the Oxford vase, has more expression in his face than an onlooker, especially a divine onlooker, would show in a Greek picture. This is not a matter of Greek artistic tradition only, but of Greek behaviour and bearing.

Σεμνότης, though in a ponderous form, distinguishes the work of another Etruscan artist of this period and vicinity: the Settecamini Painter, as he may be called from a Florence stamnos found at Settecamini just outside Orvieto.[2] Herakliskos: the infant Herakles and the Snakes. Stately Zeus and Hera watching from a window. Stately, unwieldy women: both Alcmena, and the maid or nurse who has been spinning. The artist has named the children, but instead of Viphikle (Iphikles) he has written *Vile* (Iolaos), not because he did not know the difference, but from carelessness: modern scholars also often make this mistake. We find the same exceedingly massive forms in another stamnos by the Settecamini Painter, in the Paris Cabinet des Médailles, for which I have to use the outline drawings published by Micali a hundred years ago.[3] On one side, not, as has been supposed, Paris making Helen a present of a mirror engraved with her name, *Elinai*, but Polydeukes (or Kastor) holding Helen herself, still ensconced in the Egg: he has found the object on the altar of Zeus, and is handing it over to Leda, who according to the version of the story given in the *Cypria*, and accepted in Attica, was not Helen's mother, but her foster-mother, the mother being Nemesis.[4] On the other side of the vase, Ajax, and probably Tecmessa: the hero holds spear and sword, and it is not any moment in his life that is represented, but hero and heroine standing, like saints in the wing of a triptych: beside Ajax is the hyacinth, inscribed with his name *Aivas*. The extraordinary position of the inscription, on the stalk of the plant, shows that the painter knew the legend, familiar from Ovid's *Metamorphoses*, that the hyacinth sprang from the blood of Ajax, and bore the words *Ai ai* on its petals. There is no evidence for the legend,

---

[1] *WV.* 1889 pl. 12, 1; Pfuhl fig. 628: see pp. 57–60.
[2] Pl. 10, 1–2: see pp. 52–3.
[3] Pl. 11, 3–4: Cab. Méd. 947: see pp. 53–4.
[4] See Bethe *Homer* iii, 27.

in extant literature, before the third century: but the Paris vase proves that it is at least as old as the middle of the fourth.

It is always said that whatever the ὑάκινθος was, it was not a hyacinth: but whatever the plant on the vase may be, it looks like a hyacinth.

One more vase by the Settecamini Painter: a remarkable cup in the Cabinet des Médailles, with a unique subject.[1] Pasiphae, nursing the infant Minotaur. The delightful little fellow has passed his hand round his mother's waist, between the two garments, where it is warm. Several episodes from the story are represented in antiquity. Etruscan cinerary urns of the Hellenistic period show Minos when he first sets eyes on the infant —a tense moment. In Euripides' play we hear him raging, and hear Pasiphae's tremendous defence. Then there is silence: but after all the Minotaur survived. Someone gave him a beautiful name, Asterios; and someone must have reared him: why not his mother? Here is a port-hole view, as it were, of an otherwise obscure period in the life of one whom some at least of my readers would probably describe as their favourite character in fiction.

Hitherto we have not attempted to answer the question in what part of Etruria these vases were made. One of the fabrics was probably in the great city of Volcii (Vulci), but there may have been others. We now come to two fabrics which can be localized: Chiusi,[2] and Falerii.[3] The nucleus of the Clusium fabric is a group of cups which are either by one artist or from one workshop. The technique of these cups is fine, the drawing more deft and sophisticated than in the vases we have been studying, the spirit less ambitious or more reserved. The subjects are either women at their toilet, as in a British Museum cup,[4] or satyrs and maenads, as in a Florence cup[5] (Dionysos, supported by a satyr, ready to play kottabos, while a maenad adjusts the disk on top of the kottabos-stand) and the Boston cup, where a maenad dances with the fingers held out stiff in the Etruscan manner of dancing, a boy satyr plays the flute, and a middle-aged satyr cools his hands in the laver.[6] The painter of these cups bestows all his care on the packed interior compositions: his outsides, both figures and patterns, are hasty and mechanical, but useful to us because they enable us to assign other works with certainty to the same fabric. Thus the exterior of a cup, from Monte San Savino, in Florence is almost a repetition of what we have seen: but the pretty interior is by another Clusine artist of whom nothing else seems to have been preserved.[7] Again, the Egg containing Helen: Hermes, this time, entrusting it to the foster-parents Leda and Tyndareos. Perhaps the most attractive vase in the whole group is not a cup, but a small skyphos, finely fashioned, in Cambridge, with a Triton and a Tritoness on each side.[8] There are several Clusine skyphoi of this shape, and also a good many askoi in the shape of ducks, the best being in the Louvre:[9] the figures, one on each side, are Lasas, holding sashes.

Falerii counted as an Etruscan city, although the Faliscans spoke a dialect of Latin. Faliscan vase-painting begins about 400 B.C., with close and elegant imitations of con-

---

[1] Pl. 10, 3–5: Cab. Méd. 1066: see pp. 54–5.
[2] Pp. 113–22.
[3] Pp. 70–112.
[4] London F 478: see p. 113 no. 2.
[5] Pl. 27, 9: see p. 114 no. 10.

[6] Pl. 27, 1–3: Boston 01.8123: see p. 114 no. 9.
[7] Pl. 27, 4–5: Florence 79240: see p. 115.
[8] Pl. 28, 1–3: see p. 117 no. 4.
[9] Pl. 27, 7: Louvre H 100: see p. 119 no. 5.

temporary Attic vases. The best-known Faliscan vases are three cups in the Villa Giulia at Rome, replicas one of another, with a picture of Dionysos embracing Ariadne.[1] Two of them bear the inscription, in large letters, *Foied vino pipafo cra carefo*, that is, *Hodie vinum bibam, cras carebo*. In one of them the first two letters of *pipafo* were accidentally omitted. The finest Faliscan vase is the volute-krater in the Villa Giulia from which the Aurora Painter takes his name.[2] Eos drives her chariot over the sea; Eros escorts her, and a boy beside her—Tithonos, or Kephalos—shares the reins. Dolphin, and monsters —a sea-horse, a pistrix—in the flood; stars in the sky, and a pair of ducks flying straight and fast, one with a blossom in its bill. The picture has a surge and lift that are rare in Etruscan art.

Less gifted than the Aurora Painter, but a true personality, is an artist who may be named the Nazzano Painter from the site, north of Rome, where one of his calyx-kraters was found.[3] It represents Ariadne, and Dionysos approaching her; and is really very like a moderate Attic vase of the early fourth century, at first glance. His calyx-krater in the British Museum represents, again, the infant Herakles and the Snakes.[4] There are some restorations. Athena stands by, holding her owl by the wings; Hermes and Artemis; right in the middle of the composition, Apollo, no doubt the Ismenian Apollo of Thebes; Zeus and Hera; Eros; another Eros, or one of his brothers, Pothos or Himeros; Dionysos; lastly, rather astray among all the deities, the children's white-haired nurse. In a later work, a calyx-krater in the Villa Giulia,[5] the Nazzano Painter has moved farther from his Attic masters, and the tendency to scatter the figures somewhat arbitrarily over the surface is more pronounced. The theme is the Sack of Troy. Neoptolemos, as usual, has seized the child Astyanax and is about to bring him down upon the aged Priam: but Priam has been shifted from his natural place, and almost looks as if he were being attacked by a Trojan warrior. The painter is not taking his tragic subject very seriously. Below, the familiar scene of Menelaos pursuing Helen to slay her: this is the most successful part of the picture, and the artist has drawn the group with relish and even, one might fancy, some personal feeling. Helen, in a himation only, trips away mincingly, with much white showing, and a perfect air of injured innocence; Aphrodite interposes on her behalf, with a stern look at Menelaos and a peremptory gesture; and Menelaos drops his sword.

A Faliscan stamnos, by another painter, in Bonn, has a very unusual battle-scene.[6] Two groups: a mounted youth and two opponents; a man attacking a naked youth who turns tail, a naked youth lying on his back dead. There is good reason for supposing that the naked youths, and probably also the two opponents of the horseman, are Gauls: and if so this must be one of the earliest representations of Celts in classical art.

Once more the Etruscan birds of prey: not certain what kind of birds, perhaps young vultures: in any case the artist has given them a cruel beak and an intent, wicked expression. The figure of the dead man is also typically Etruscan and recurs, with little change,

[1] Pl. 25, 4: Villa Giulia 1674: see pp. 106–7 nos. 1–3.

[2] Pl. 24, 3 and Pl. 20, 1: Villa Giulia 2491: see p. 81 no. 1 and pp. 81–4.

[3] Rome, Principe del Drago: Pl. 21, 2: see p. 92 no. 3 and pp. 92–3.

[4] Pl. 21, 1 and 3 and Pl. 22, 1, London F 479: see p. 92 no. 1 and pp. 93–4. The restorations have now been removed.

[5] Pl. 23: Villa Giulia 1197: see p. 92 no. 2 and pp. 94–6.

[6] Pl. 24, 1–2 and Pl. 20, 3: Bonn 1569: see pp. 96–8.

on the late-fourth-century relief sarcophagus from Torre San Severo[1] in the Slaughter
of the Trojan Prisoners, a favourite Etruscan subject which also appears on vases. One
of these is a Faliscan stamnos, not very well preserved, in Berlin.[2] The figures of Achilles
slaying a captive, and a second captive waiting his turn, are derived from the same
original as the corresponding figures on the sarcophagus from Torre San Severo—a
famous painting which was widely imitated in Etruria. In the Berlin stamnos the action
takes place at the tomb of Patroklos, a mound with armour laid on it and a monument
beside it: Patroklos himself, a shade, stands in front of it, watching. Two other figures,
a woman, Briseis, and a Greek warrior, complete the picture, or nearly: it is completed
by a couple of eager birds of prey. This is not a pleasant subject: but before finding
fault with the Etruscans, it should be remembered, first, that after all it is taken from the
*Iliad*; secondly that there *are* Greek representations; thirdly, that Virgil himself thought
it necessary to imitate Homer and make Aeneas sacrifice eight prisoners to a shade.

Against certain crude or brutal traits in the Etruscan there is something to set. I
cannot believe that the intense interest in the great heroic and tragic figures of Greece,
which is proved by their constant appearance in Etruscan art, was due to no more than
the love of exciting tales of adventure and violence; but must suppose that there was a
heroic strain in the Etruscan character to which these figures made a natural appeal.
Let four scarabs, engraved with the Death of Ajax, signets of Etruscans, bear witness
here.[3]

The last period of Etruscan vase-painting, in the later part of the fourth century and
the beginning of the third, is a period of decadence: but here also there is considerable
interest of subject. A new character appears on the stage: it is the Devil. Wherever we
look, not only in vases, but in wall-painting and sculpture, hideous demons meet the eye:
Charun with his hammer, Tuchulcha, and others whose names are unknown. This has
been supposed to be a symptom of a revolution in Etruscan religion: 'the old confidence
in a happy immortality', it has been said, 'is replaced by fear and despair'. I believe it
is possible to exaggerate the significance of the new subjects, and that the change may have
been not so much in religion as in taste.[4] Let us look at some of these devils.

On a stamnos in the Villa Giulia the demon is worsted.[5] A Fury-like female attacks
a woman, the dead: but is repelled by Hermes. The woman has a thyrsus in her hand,
is therefore a votary of Dionysos, which doubtless gives her additional protection. On
a stamnos by the same fluent painter in Vienna,[6] a woman, naked, sits holding a lyre,
and is attacked by two demons: yet she pays no attention, seems immune. On the other
side of the vase, two youths attack a dragon, one with a hammer, one with a spear: these
may be champions of the dead, but the interpretation is doubtful, and the subject may
also be some unknown myth. On the well-known volute-krater in the Paris Cabinet des
Médailles, *Atmite* and *Alcsti* (Admetus and Alcestis) are menaced by two demons.[7] It
is a feeble work; and from a Greek point of view the rendering of the situation is crude,

---

[1] See p. 90 no. 6.
[2] Pl. 20, 2: Berlin inv. 5825: see p. 88 no. 1 and
pp. 87–92.
[3] Pl. 32, 4–7: see pp. 138–9.
[4] So already van Essen, in *Studi e materiali di*

*Storia delle religioni* 4 (1928), 286, and Nogara 285–9.
[5] Pl. 35, 6: Villa Giulia 1660: see p. 152.
[6] Pl. 11, 5: Oest. Mus. 448: see pp. 152–3.
[7] Pl. 30, 1–2: Cab. Méd. 918: see p. 133 no. 1 and
p. 134.

but after all the ending was a happy one, and the Etruscan artist knew it. Another vase in Paris, a calyx-krater, has Charun in both pictures.[1] On one side, the Slaughter of the Trojan Prisoners. The hero is inscribed *Aivas*, but this is a slip for *Achle*, Achilles. The figure goes back to the same original as the Achilles on the Faliscan stamnos and the sarcophagus from Torre San Severo, but the attitude of the victim is different. In pictures like this it is often a relief to turn from the subject and fix one's attention on details: Achilles is wearing two uncommon pieces of armour, the vambrace and the rerebrace. The other picture on the calyx-krater is an extract from a Nekyia—a visit to the Nether World: and through the mist of the coarse style one divines, far off, a noble original. Charun has taken the place of an Odysseus: the phantoms of heroines drift up and past: ἦλθε Δ' ἐπὶ ψυχή. . . . Two of the women are shown by the bandages they wear to have died violent deaths. The third has her hair cut short in mourning, and the folded hands indicate suppressed sorrow. *Turmuca* should be an Amazon like *Pentasila* (Penthesilea), and it is mortifying that while for once we can translate the common noun (*hinthia* means shade, *imago*), we cannot translate the proper name *Turmuca*, although we are so strong on Greek names in their Etruscan equivalents. The first part ought to be Δορι-, but the rest is baffling. In both dreadful scenes Charun is in place: later Etruscan taste, but nothing to dismay the just man.

Three vases by one hand were found at Orvieto and are now in the Faina collection: a volute-krater,[2] and two neck-amphorae which are replicas one of another.[3] On the volute-krater the dead, an elderly man with paunch and bald head, lying in a mule-cart, arrives in the Nether World. Hades himself drives up in his chariot, escorted by a demon who holds a hammer—Charun—, and followed by a goddess whose name will appear later. The dead man raises his staff as if to ward off the demon—as if pressed: but Hades is already pulling up: it is alarming, but the powers are not ill disposed, and all will be well.

The two neck-amphorae repeat one another with trifling variations. On the left in the roll-out we see an aged man, warmly clad, conducted by two Charuns over ground infested by serpents, which do not harm him. On the right in the roll-out, Persephone, in a chariot drawn by a pair of monsters with legs of a bird of prey, heads and necks of a crested snake. Hades hastens to mount, followed by a goddess holding a scroll inscribed with her name: it is *Vanth*, Etruscan goddess or daemoness of death. The scroll probably contains the *record* of the dead: his deeds, the offices he has held, and his pedigree. Under the handle sits Cerberus, ugly, but inoffensive. It will be noticed that although there are terrors here, they are all *terrors of transit*: the Charuns are rough but friendly; and Hades himself turns out to greet his new guest. It cannot be said that 'the old confidence in a happy immortality is replaced by fear and despair'. There is nothing that need unduly frighten 'good people', people of standing and family and anything else that the Etruscans may have included in the term.

Not all Etruscan vase-fabrics succumbed to the fascination of the Devil. There is no

---

[1] Pl. 31, 1–2: Cab. Méd. 920: see p. 136 no. 1 and p. 137.

[2] *Mon.* 11 pl. 4–5, 3: see p. 169 no. 1 and p. 170.

[3] *Mon.* 11 pl. 4–5, 2, and ibid. 1: see p. 170 nos. 4–5 and pp. 170–1.

trace of him in the Clusium fabric; and when in the later part of the fourth century artists from Chiusi settled, as it seems, at Volterra in northern Etruria, the new Volaterrae fabric[1] remained free from demons. The favourite shape at Volterra is a version of the column-krater. Of the earlier examples it is hard to say whether they were made at Chiusi or at Volterra. The Lasa on a column-krater in the museum of Volterra[2] is very like the Lasa on the Clusian duck-vase in New York,[3] and the design of the floral decoration is typically Clusine. This floral design persists in the Volaterrae fabric to the very end. A favourite subject on the late Volterran kraters, which belong to the early part of the third century, is the human head: realistic portraits, or portrait-like heads, of very modern cut. Earnest matron; chubby maid; young man.[4] We need not suppose that all Etruscans of the period looked like this: but so some of them looked to one disillusioned Volterran. The human head, by itself, though not realistically conceived, is a favourite topic in the last phase of other red-figure fabrics, Apulian, Campanian, even Attic. Indeed, in the last phase of any art, the human head is apt to receive more than its proper share of attention. Roman art differs from others in having been obsessed by the human head, usually in a realistic form, throughout its history:

> So when they did design
> The Capitol's first line,
> A bleeding head, where they begun,
> Did fright the architects to run.

We may conclude with a glance at an inconspicuous fabric which yet has a certain importance: small plates decorated either with a star, or with a female head.[5] Some of these have been found in Etruria, others in Latium and in Rome; and one of them, now in Providence, bears a Latin inscription, painted in the potter's workshop before firing, *P(oplia) Genucilia*:[6] doubtless the name of the purchaser, of the lady on whose behalf the plate or set of plates was ordered. Where exactly these plates were made is unknown: possibly in Rome itself, possibly in some other Latin city, or in Etruria. There are other interesting proveniences besides Rome: a small plate, with a star on it, in Oxford, was found in Malta;[7] a plate with a female head on it was found at Carthage.[8] Etruscan vases are hardly ever found outside Etruria and Latium. Even in the great Etruscan outposts towards the north, Bologna, Spina, and Adria, there is little Etruscan pottery: Attic vases easily reached them by way of the Adriatic, and the inferior Etruscan vases were not required.

Every phase in the assimilation of Greek civilization by the peoples of Italy is of interest: and Etruscan vase-painting throws light on one stage in the slow, complex, and many-channelled process which culminated, centuries afterwards, and on other soil, for a brief stretch of time, in the perfect union of Italian and Greek in great Romans: Cicero, Lucretius, Virgil.

[1] See pp. 123–32.
[2] *RM*. 30, 155: see p. 122 and p. 124 no. 3.
[3] New York 19.192.14: Richter *Etr*. fig. 137: p. 119 no. 9.
[4] Pl. 29, 8–9 (Berlin inv. 3998): see p. 128. Pl. 29, 10

(Berlin inv. 3989): see ibid.
[5] Pl. 38, 17–27: see pp. 175–7.
[6] Pl. 38, 17–19: p. 175 no. 2.
[7] Pl. 38, 21: p. 177 no. 37.
[8] Pl. 38, 25: p. 176 no. 33.

# CHAPTER II
# ETRUSCAN BLACK-FIGURE

IT was said in the preface that Etruscan black-figure would not be treated at length, especially as there is already a good study of part of it by Dohrn (*Die schwarzfigurigen etruskischen Vasen aus der zweiten Hälfte des sechsten Jahrhunderts*). On Dohrn's localizations, see Riis *Tyrrhenika* 69–71. See also p. 1.

### ETRUSCAN IMITATIONS OF CORINTHIAN

Etruscan imitations of Corinthian: see Albizzati *Vasi antichi dipinti del Vaticano* 48–65; Payne *Necrocorinthia* 206–9 and 340–1; *CV*. Oxford ii, 67–74 (Payne); *RG.* 73–5; *Bulletin of the Fogg Museum of Art* ix, 3 (Nov. 1940), 44–9 (Hanfmann); Dohan *Italic Tomb-groups in the University Museum*; and *Cl. Rev.* 1944, 31.

### THE IVY-LEAF GROUP

Earlier contributions, see Dohrn 7. *BPW.* 1934, 682 (Rumpf). Dohrn 7–23 and 143–4. *St. etr.* 12, 284 and 289 (Dohrn). The amphora in New York (B, *Bull. Metr. Mus.* 20, 301) stands apart from the rest: by the same hand the Munich amphora 833 (SH. pl. 32 and p. 94). I cannot feel sure that the amphora Louvre E 723 (Longpérier *Mus. Nap.* pl. 59, whence (A) *JHS.* 14, 117 and (B) Weicker *Seelenvogel* 119 fig. 44: Dohrn no. 27) belongs to the Ivy-leaf Group. The small amphora in Leyden, K 94.9.5 (Brants pl. 15, 3: Dohrn no. 34c), looks Attic.

### THE LA TOLFA GROUP

Earlier contributions, see Dohrn 23. Dohrn 23–33 and 144–5; *St. etr.* 12, 284 (Dohrn). The group seems to divide into two: (α) the neck-amphorae Boston F 550 (Fairbanks pl. 60), Villa Giulia M 409 (A, Mingazzini *Vasi Cast.* pl. 35, 1–2), London (A, *BMQ.* 4 pl. 15, b; A, Dohrn pl. 2, 4), Goettingen J 4 (A, Jacobsthal *Gött. V.* pl. 2, 3), Goettingen J 5 (B, ibid. pl. 2, 4), Louvre E 724, Florence, Florence (A, Dohrn pl. 2, 1), Florence 84819, and the dinos Villa Giulia M 408 (Mingazzini *Vasi Cast.* pl. 34): (β) the neck-amphorae Carlsruhe inv. 2592, Geneva F 140 (phots. Giraudon, whence Dohrn pl. 3), Louvre E 731 (A, Pottier pl. 53), Louvre E 728 (A, ibid.), Louvre E 729 (A, ibid.), Conservatori 150 (A, Dohrn pl. 2, 3): that is (α) Dohrn's nos. 42, 41, 43, 35, 36, 54, 39, 38 and another, 53, (β) his nos. 46, 44, 45, 47, 49, 50. The neck-amphora in Philadelphia (A, *Mus. J.* 5, 225) is a crude imitation of (α). The Boston vase was found at Cervetri.

A small neck-amphora from Capua, New York 06.1021.43 (Richter *Etr.* figs. 111–12: A, young satyr sitting on the ground; B, youth sitting at an altar) has been attributed to the La Tolfa Group (ibid. 38): but it is Campanian black-figure, by the same hand as the Leyden neck-amphora GNV. 4 (Brants pl. 15, 1: A, symposion: B, woman running to an altar). New York 06.1021.44 (Richter *Etr.* figs. 113 and 116) and New York 06.1021.42 (ibid. fig. 117), both from Capua, are also Campanian black-figure. Hamburg inv. 1917. 989, from Capua (*Anz.* 1928, 343), is by the same hand as New York 06.1021.44; compare also Naples inv. 81045 (A, Patroni 30 fig. 26 = *St. etr.* 8 pl. 34, 2).

## 'PONTIC' VASES

I keep the old conventional name for this Etruscan group. Recent studies by Ducati *Pontische Vasen*, Mingazzini (*Gnomon* 11, 68–76), and Dohrn (33–89 and 145–51, 'Dümmler Class'; and in *St. etr.* 12, 283–4 and 287–9). On earlier contributions see Dohrn 33–4. Add the stemmed plate Vatican G 87 (*RG.* pl. 27), the lydion Vatican G 88 (ibid.); the four vases mentioned in *RG.* 75; a vase formerly in the Marshall Brooks collection at Tarporley and now in Oxford (1946.54) of the same shape as Munich 989 (SH. pl. 42), but earlier (on each side two sirens with a plant between); and a fragment of a kyathos, from the Castellani collection, in the Villa Giulia (siren, swan; on the offset lip, floral). I find it difficult to accept the column-krater Villa Giulia M 392 (Mingazzini *Vasi Cast.* pl. 32) as Pontic (Dohrn no. 167b). The outline technique is so rare in Etruscan that I wonder whether the stemmed plate Vatican 233 (Albizzati pl. 21: Dohrn no. 163) may not represent Selene: see *JHS.* 59, 150, compare also Tischbein 3 pl. 44. See also p. 295.

## THE MICALI GROUP

The nucleus of this group is due to Dümmler (*RM.* 3, 173–9), and additions were made by Gsell, Weicker, and Albizzati. In *RG.* 76–85 I put together a large number of late Etruscan black-figured vases under three headings: (1) Micali Painter; (2) school of the Micali Painter; (3) school of the Micali Painter, small pieces with floral decoration. This was done independently of Dohrn's classification, which did not appear until after my manuscript had been sent in. Dohrn (89–128 and 151–7) treats the same group of vases under six headings: (1) 'Siren Painter'; (2) 'Siren Painter, not from his own hand'; (3) 'Perseus Painter'; (4) 'same workshop as the Perseus Painter'; (5) 'Palaestra Painter'; (6) 'same workshop as the Palaestra Painter': the material is thus divided up somewhat differently. 'Perseus Painter' covers some of my school-pieces; 'Palaestra Painter' certain vases which I took to be very early work by the Micali Painter. I do not consider my own treatment final, and said so in *RG.* 77.

I do not mean to draw up a concordance between my list and Dohrn's. My list contains many vases that do not appear in his; his, many that do not appear in mine, and I ought to say something about these. It should be premised that the influence of the Micali Painter was wide, and it is not always easy to draw the line between 'school' and 'influence'. Dohrn includes a good many pieces that do indeed show the influence of the Micali Painter, but were deliberately excluded by me as too far from the centre: but it is often a question of degree only.

I have no knowledge of the Bonn vases mentioned by Dohrn, except his no. 213 (*RG.* 78 no. 32), the hydria-fragment figured on his pl. 5, no. 235, which is by the Micali Painter, and the oinochoe figured on his pl. 7, no. 287, which he rightly assigns to his Palaestra Painter, that is to say, as I believe, the Micali Painter in his earliest phase.

Of the Munich vases in Dohrn's list but not in mine, three are not figured and I have no notes on them, but I assume that I saw them and did not think them close enough to the painter for inclusion: they are Dohrn's nos. 218, 228, 233 (Munich 860, 874, 856): this is certainly true of his no. 252 (Munich 855: SH. p. 112; A, *Bulletin van de Vereeniging*

1939, 13) and his no. 251 (Munich 958: SH. pl. 42). Of the vases placed by Dohrn under the heading of 'Siren Painter, but not from his own hand', his no. 275a (Munich 857: A, SH. pl. 35) is in the manner of the Micali Painter but is much restored, his nos. 274 and 275 (Munich 873 and 875: SH. pl. 35) are on the outskirts of the group. His no. 273, a good little vase (Munich 977: SH. 148 figs. 188–9), is very like Naples 2508, on which see p. 17. As for the two late vases which Dohrn puts under the same heading in *St. etr.* 12, 289, Munich 883 (SH. pl. 37 and p. 118 fig. 132) and 882 (SH. pl. 37 and p. 118 fig. 131), I cannot consider them as any longer forming part of the group. On 883 see below, p. 21.

Dohrn's 'Siren Painter' takes his name from the Berlin hydria 2157 (*Jb.* 1, 211–12; *Jb.* 29, 240: Dohrn no. 168): I had examined this vase carefully and decided not to put it in my list: I was wrong, and should now set it in the neighbourhood of the Micali Painter, among the school-pieces.

Dohrn's no. 230, Hamburg 1156, now published in *St. etr.* 11 pl. 37, 3–4, is by the Micali Painter; or, if school-work, almost indistinguishable from him. Two more Hamburg vases are added by Dohrn in *St. etr.* 12, 289:—Hamburg 505 (*St. etr.* 11 pl. 35, 1–2), and 1193 (ibid. pl. 37, 1–2): I should count them school-pieces: Mercklin had already compared 505 with Würzburg 795 (Langlotz pl. 231: *RG.* p. 81 no. 19) and 1193 with the small floral neck-amphorae Vatican 277 and 278 (Albizzati pl. 28: *RG.* 85 nos. 5 and 3). The neck-amphora, with flaring mouth, Hamburg 1917.509, attributed to the 'Palaestra Painter' by Dohrn (no. 289), is now published in *St. etr.* 11 pl. 35, 3–4: it is by the Micali Painter. Another vase ascribed by Dohrn to his Palaestra Painter (no. 291) is a hydria formerly in the possession of Philipp Lederer (detail, Dohrn pl. 6, 2): it may be by the Micali Painter himself. Dohrn attributes a hydria in Hamburg (512: *St. etr.* 11 pl. 39, 1 and pp. 367–8: Dohrn no. 291c) to 'the same workshop as the Palaestra Painter', but I do not see any appreciable resemblance in the style of the drawing. As to the Tuebingen fragment with the same attribution (Dohrn no. 291a), I cannot judge it from the reproduction in Watzinger pl. 2, C 79. Similarly, it is not clear from the wretched drawing in Noël Des Vergers pl. 15 whether the lost neck-amphora Dohrn no. 236 can be by the Micali Painter or is not rather, as I should believe, on the edge of his sphere of influence. Dohrn's no. 261a, a fragmentary cup in Heidelberg (*St. etr.* 7 pl. 17, 1–2), is certainly from the school of the Micali Painter if not from his hand. Fragments of a neck-amphora in the Villa Giulia (Dohrn no. 257 and p. 96) did not seem to me very like the Micali Painter; nor did Florence 4200 (Dohrn no. 256) fit into the Micali Group as I conceived it. Dohrn's no. 255 is a neck-amphora in Florence with Tritons on the body and a polyp on the shoulder: Dohrn gives the museum number as 2079, but I wonder whether this may not be no. 26 in my list *RG.* p. 78, 'Florence 71005 from Pescia Romana', which has the same subject. Dohrn's no. 260, London B 67, is by the Micali Painter.

Some of the vases under Dohrn's heading 'Siren Painter, but not from his own hand' have been dealt with already. Of the rest, no. 268, the Breslau kyathos (*RM.* 3, 180 figs. 9–10) and no. 272, the fragment in the Oesterreichisches Museum (*AEM.* 15, 128) should have been in my list of school-pieces; and there no. 275c, the neck-amphora in Berkeley (*CV.* pl. 29, 1), might perhaps find a place: compare Munich 857 (above, line 2). No. 263, the Villa Giulia stamnos 25153 (*ML.* 24 pl. 25, 44, Cultrera; *CV.* IV Bn pl. 1, 1 and 3), as Dohrn observed, goes with no. 264, the Faina neck-amphora (phot. Al. 32467, whence Giglioli pl. 130, 3): they are in the Micali tradition, but I do not reckon them as belonging to the group in the strict sense. No. 265, the Louvre oinochoe E 772 (*Mededeelingen* 7 pl. 2, 2), is still farther from the Micali Painter, nor should I care to include the lost oinochoe from Chiusi, no. 266 (Inghirami *Mus. Chius.* pl. 161): see p. 22. I do not understand why Dohrn should think that his no. 284a, the amphora Yale 230, was 'from the same workshop as the Perseus Painter': it is East Greek, by the same hand as London B21, which was found by Salzmann at Camiros.

Of the vases without figures (Dohrn's nos. i–xii on his p. 156), nos. ii, iii, vii, and x are not in my lists. No. vii, Munich 823 (A, SH. 92 fig. 87) might well have been in *RG.* on my p. 85, and no. ii, Hamburg 1157 (*St. etr.* 11 pl. 36, 4) should be added. No. iii, Munich 821 (A, SH. pl. 38) is somewhat unusual. As for no. x, the neck-amphora Hamburg 1224 (*St. etr.* 11 pl. 36, 2–3 and p. 363), Mercklin (ibid. 362) has pointed out that it is by the same hand as Munich 871 (A, SH. 115 fig. 130; side-view, *St. etr.* 11 pl. 36, 1), which in *RG.* 81 no. 14 I described as a wretched imitation of the Micali Painter.

Dohrn's no. 267 remains: 'Goettingen, Jacobsthal no. 6, Pl. 1 no. 5–6, oinochoe, snake-footed giant.' This entry is a conflation of two vases in Goettingen:—(1) Jacobsthal no. 6, pl. 1, 5–6, oinochoe, satyr-face and youth between eyes; (2) Jacobsthal no. 8, pl. 3, 8, neck-amphora, on each side a snake-footed monster attacked by a youth. These are nos. 32 and 7 in my list of school-pieces, *RG.* 81.

Passing to my own lists in *RG.* 77–85, I make first a few corrections, and then some additions over and above what has already been added in the course of comparing Dohrn's lists with mine.

Corrections: p. 81 no. 31: Munich 926, not 936. P. 82 no. 36: Munich 995 not 925. P. 79 nos. 59 and 60, according to Dohrn (no. 262) are one and the same, which may well be.

On p. 77 no. 11 and p. 79 no. 65 see below, p. 17. P. 78 no. 19: Louvre CA 1901. P. 85 no. 6: Villa Giulia 3588. P. 77 no. 1: now published in Dohrn pl. 8. P. 77 no. 6: side-view Dohrn pl. 5, 2. P. 78 no. 12 bis: A, *St. etr.* 12 pl. 55, 5. P. 78 no. 38: Dohrn pl. 7, 3. P. 79 no. 44: shoulder, Dohrn pl. 6, 1. P. 79 no. 62: A, Dohrn pl. 7, 4. P. 80 no. 67 bis: Richter *Etr.* fig. 118. P. 81 no. 13: A, Dohrn pl. 7, 1. P. 81 no. 33: *St. etr.* 11 pl. 40, 3–4. P. 85 no. 7 (neck-amphora Oxford 1932.122): Pl. 38, 7. See pp. 295–6.

## ALSO BY THE MICALI PAINTER
### *Neck-amphorae*

1. Baltimore, Walters Art Gallery, 48.7, from Castel Campanile. A, *Journ. Walt.* 3, 110, whence Pl. 3, 2. Satyrs. On the shoulder, A, birds; B, the like. Flaring mouth. Correctly placed by Miss D. K. Hill (ibid. 137).

2. Once Tarporley, Hon. Marshall Brooks (*Cat. Sotheby May 14 1946* no. 76). Fight (two groups, each of two warriors fighting, with a third down on his knees between them; and a warrior leading a horse). On the shoulder, each side, a lion attacked by a panther. On the neck, each side, a sphinx walking. Much restored. Flaring mouth.

## Oinochoai
(exact shape uncertain:  trefoil mouth)

3. Once Rome, Campana. *AZ.* 1871, 61. Death of Ajax. See p. 139.

(olpe)

4. Brunswick 677, fr. *CV.* pl. 33, 7. (Satyr running).  Placed correctly by Greifenhagen (text to *CV.*: 'Siren Painter').

### ALSO FROM THE SCHOOL OF THE MICALI PAINTER

I owe my knowledge of the small neck-amphorae nos. 4–10 to Ure's notes: some of them may be by the painter himself; so may nos. 14 and 11.

## Neck-amphorae

1. Lost. A, Micali *Mon. ined.* pl. 36, 2. Bigae. On the shoulder, A, gorgoneion. Flaring mouth.
2. Tarquinia 857, from Tarquinia. Romanelli *Tarquinia* 132. Sirens.  Cf. the Hamburg neck-amphora 505 (*St. etr.* 11 pl. 35, 1–2: above, p. 13).
3. Louvre E 763. A, siren; B, the like.  The sirens wear chitons; they hold out garlands, and one of them a little ball or fruit.  They are very like the sirens on Munich 873 (SH. pl. 35: above, p. 13).  The neck-amphora is of a different model.
4. Orleans A 250. A, sphinx.  Small.
5. Once Rome, Dr. Signorelli, from Tarquinia.  Sirens.
6. Once Rome, Dr. Signorelli, from Tarquinia. Hounds. On the shoulder, ivy-leaf between birds.
7. Orvieto, Conte Faina, from Orvieto.  A, birds with three ivy-leaves, one above the other, between.  On the shoulder, A, similar ivy-leaves between eyes.
8. Orvieto, Conte Faina, from Orvieto.  A, fawn-bird;  B, hares.
9. Orvieto, Conte Faina, from Orvieto.  Floral.
10. Orvieto, Conte Faina, 332, from Orvieto.  Sirens.

## Hydria with two handles

11. Cambridge, Museum of Classical Archaeology, 13.  A, Gigantomachy: an extract consisting of two figures which repeat the Athena and Herakles of the neck-amphora Vatican G 91 (Pl. 3, 3–4 and p. 2). B, centaur rushing to left with a branch in each hand: this is probably another extract, from a Centauromachy.  On the shoulder, palmettes.

## Two-handled mastoid (the same type of vase as, in Attic, Richter and Milne fig. 171)

12. Cambridge, Prof. A. B. Cook. A, eyes; B, the like.

## Fragments

13. Munich, frr. (Naked youth mounting chariot, naked youth running.)  On the shoulder, hounds or the like.
14. Sèvres 1237.8, frr., from Chiusi. *CV.* pl. 30, 32.

## THE PAINTER OF VATICAN 238

In *RG*. 77 note 1 I assigned four vases to one painter. Three of these were subsequently put together by Dohrn (*St. etr.* 12, 286–7) and another (no. 5) added. I keep my own designation, rather than adopt Dohrn's briefer one, for the reason that I already have a 'Kaineus Painter', an Attic red-figure artist.

In Dohrn's view this is 'one of the more gifted of the Caere painters' (l.c. 287), whereas the Siren Painter (l.c. 285) is 'of poor quality, and has brought Etruscan vases into disrepute'. I do not find myself in agreement with his valuation: the 'Siren Painter' (Micali Painter) has plenty of vigour, while the Painter of Vatican 238 has a meagre, mincing style which disgusts me.

### Hydria

1. Vatican 238. Albizzati pl. 24. Youths. On the shoulder, hound attacking bull. On the neck, winged goddess.

### Hydriai with two handles

2. Louvre CA 2515. A, Herakles and Triton; B, Herakles and the Hydra. On the shoulder, naked youths running. On the neck, naked youths.
3. Vienna 406. Baur *Centaurs* pl. 9, 176; A, *Bulletin van de Vereeniging* 1939, 7; *St. etr.* 12 pl. 52, 1–2. A, Kaineus and the Centaurs. B, unexplained: a woman and a youth attacking a youth. On the shoulder: A, Centauromachy; B, woman attacking centaur. On the neck, women.
4. Villa Giulia 15539. *ML*. 24 pl. 24, 43 and pl. 25, 43 (Cultrera); *CV*. IV Bn pl. 1, 4–5 and pl. 2, 5; *St. etr.* 12 pl. 52, 4 and pl. 53, 1–2; A, phot. Al. 41165. A, satyrs; B, satyrs. On the shoulder, A, sphinxes, B, sphinxes. On the neck, youths with horses.

### Neck-amphora

5. Amsterdam inv. 1806. A, *St. etr.* 12 pl. 53, 3. Chariot-race (bigae). On the shoulder, A, sphinxes, B, sphinxes. On the neck, A, woman, B, the like.

Dohrn adds a vase which has some kinship with these but is not, so far as I can tell, by the same hand: it is the much restored hydria (with two handles) Munich 911 (SH. pl. 37 and p. 128 fig. 147; B, *St. etr.* 12 pl. 52, 3). As to the hydria (not 'stamnos') Villa Giulia 15538 *ML*. 24 pl. 24, 42, Cultrera; *CV*. IV Bn pl. 1, 2; phot. Al. 41178, whence Giglioli pl. 130, 5) which Dohrn considers 'related to the manner of the Kaineus Painter' (*St. etr.* 12, 289), even this cautious description is inacceptable. The drawing of the heads a little recalls the Berlin amphora 2154 (see p. 17). The influence of the Micali Painter is patent, as in many of these vases. There is some restoration.

### THE KYKNOS PAINTER

The nucleus consists of two good vases put together by Dohrn (130), and also by myself in *RG*. 77 note 3:—

### Hydriai

1. Leningrad inv. 3145, from Vulci. *JHS*. 43, 171–2 and pl. 6. Herakles and Kyknos (or rather Ares?). On the shoulder, panthers attacking hind.

2. Munich 897. SH. 122–3. Centauromachy. On the shoulder, panthers attacking goat. Dohrn attributes a third vase to the same artist, and mentions two others as probably by him: it seems to me very likely that all three are by the Kyknos Painter:

### Neck-amphora

3. Munich 870. SH. pl. 37 and p. 115 figs. 128–9. Bigae. In *RG.* 77 no. 11 I took this to be a late work of the Micali Painter, or perhaps a school-piece.

### Oinochoai
### (shape I, but with low handle and a collar)

4. Naples 2506, from Vulci. Herakles and a youth (Diomedes?); to left, two horses standing to left, side by side.
5. Naples 2508, from Vulci. *RM.* 3, 176 and 159. Satyrs. Above, panthers and bull. This was no. 65 in my list of vases by the Micali Painter, *RG.* 79.

With Naples 2508 I should put a good little vase which Dohrn classes under the heading of 'Siren Painter, not from his own hand':—

### Kyathos
### (of Attic type)

6. Munich 977. SH. 148 figs. 188–9. Satyrs and (maenad?).

Dohrn appends, as 'probably not from the master's own hand', the column-krater Bari 4305 (A, Herakles and Cerberus; B, fight), a hydria-fragment in Bonn, and the Hamburg hydria 511 (*Anz.* 1917, 105; Giglioli pl. 131, 2; *St. etr.* 11 pl. 40, 1–2: archers; on the shoulder, centaurs fighting). The centaurs on the shoulder of the Hamburg vase may somewhat recall the Kyknos Painter's satyrs, but I do not see any other resemblance. I have little information about the krater in Bari, and none about the fragment in Bonn.

### THE BERLIN AMPHORA 2154
One of the finest Etruscan vases is in Berlin:

### Amphora (type A)

Berlin 2154, from Vulci. Endt 29–31 and pl. 1; B, Neugebauer pl. 24. A, Hermes and three goddesses. B, unexplained subject: a youth and two women approaching a woman. On the shoulder, A, chariot-race, B, the like. The white parts are largely repainted, repainted also the face of Hermes.

Studniczka (*Jb.* 11, 268) rightly associated the Berlin vase with another masterpiece of Etruscan vase-painting:—

### Amphora (type B)

Würzburg 799, from Vulci. *Mon.* 2 pl. 50; Gerhard *AV.* pl. 194; *Jh.* 13 pll. 7–10; Langlotz pll. 232–4. A, Athena mounting chariot; B, Aphrodite mounting chariot. On the shoulder: A, fight (Diomed and Aeneas); B, fight.

These two amphorae are connected by the potter-work, by the type of decoration, by quality and precision, by the choiceness of the motives; and the distance from the Micali Painter is about the same. Dohrn (130) seems to have been the first to attribute the pictures to a single hand: his predecessors had been more cautious, and with reason: the style is different. In Munich there are fragments of a neck-amphora (or possibly a stamnos) which made me think of the Berlin vase: a winged horse galloping, a sejant sphinx, a siren; on the shoulder, an eye.

A third, very lively vase was connected with the Würzburg amphora by Studniczka (*Jb.* 11, 268 note 117), Klein (in Endt 32), and Dohrn (130), but must be by yet another painter:

### Hydria

Naples 2781. *Jh.* 13, 157–9. Fight (Achilles and Memnon?). On the shoulder, Centauromachy (Kaineus). Restored. The centaurs use celt-like stones for weapons.

Of three vases placed in the neighbourhood of those in Berlin, Würzburg, Naples by Dohrn (130), it is hard to judge the lost ones known only from the slight drawings in Micali's *Monumenti inediti*: I connect Micali's pl. 36, 2, more or less closely, with the Micali Painter (see p. 15); the other, the neck-amphora with Gigantomachy, pl. 37, 1, is also in the Micali tradition, but how far it is from the centre I cannot tell. Dohrn's third vase seems to be related to the Würzburg amphora:—

### Neck-amphora

Chiusi 577, from Chiusi. Phots. Alinari 37482–3, whence (A) *ML.* 30, 495, (A) Giglioli pl. 130, 2. A, fight; B, fight. On the shoulder, symposion (A, two youths reclining; B, youth reclining, and boy waiting).

A neck-amphora resembling Chiusi 577 is in Prof. A. B. Cook's collection, Cambridge: on one side two warriors, on the other a satyr and another male figure (apparently not a satyr); on the shoulder, eyes. See also p. 296.

### THE LOTUS-BUD GROUP

These three vases were put together by Dohrn (*St. etr.* 12, 290, E), and the group named after the floral band above the pictures.

### Neck-amphorae

1. Boston F 571, from Cervetri. Fairbanks pl. 73. A, satyrs; B, satyrs.
2. Rome, Conservatori. A, *St. etr.* 12 pl. 56, 3. A, satyrs and maenad.
3. Florence 4168. A, *St. etr.* 12 pl. 56, 2. A, satyrs.

Dohrn assigns a fourth neck-amphora to the same group, Copenhagen, Ny Carlsberg, H 148 (*Bildertafeln Etr. Mus.* pl. 49, 2) and speaks of two others, in Munich (892: A, SH. 120 fig. 133) and Viterbo (Giglioli pl. 131, 5) as close. These attributions are not clear to me.

## A LEKYTHOS

Paris, Petit Palais, 431, from Sala Consilina. *GV*. pl. 3, 1 and pl. 4, 3–6. Centauromachy. On the shoulder, floral between panther and lion. Restored.

This unusual vase, which Plaoutine saw to be Etruscan, is a copy or close imitation of an Attic lekythos from the beginning of the fifth century.

## THE CHIUSI PYXIS GROUP

*St. etr.* 7, 359–62 (Herbig); Dohrn 139–40 and 158.

## THE ORVIETO GROUP

One or two of these vases were put together by Baur, Scheurleer, and Herbig: but the first to study them as a class was Miss Calò, who showed them to be Orvietan (*St. etr.* 10, 429–30). Then came Dohrn's treatment (131–9 and 157–8 under 'the Painter of Vienna 318', and in *St. etr.* 12, 284–5 and 289); and Minto's in *NSc.* 1939, 18–24. The clay in the group is regularly white or whitish, the black glaze often fired to reddish-brown. The style of the drawing is wild but vigorous and lively.

Nearly all the vases in Miss Calò's list (*St. etr.* 10, 436–7) go together and are the work of one or two closely connected painters. I have not seen her no. 5, or the two vases in Florence, without figure decoration, at the end of the list. The Heidelberg fragment from Orvieto, her no. 25 (*St. etr.* 7 pl. 16, 3), belongs to the same fabric as the last, but the style of drawing is different. I can add something to Herbig's description in *St. etr.* 7, 356–8 no. E 40a–c. The leaf-pattern above the figures stops to the right of the left-hand warrior in pl. 16, 3, which suggests that this is the right-hand figure on one side of the vase, while the second warrior is the left-hand figure on the other side: the vase may have been a neck-amphora. I have a rough tracing of the lost fragment which Herbig quotes, from an old inventory, on his p. 358, no. E 40c: it joins pl. 16, 3 on the right, and gives, seen from behind, part of the opponent of the retreating warrior; what the inventory took for a second hat, worn on top of the helmet, is the sword, held in the right hand and passing on this side of the helmet. As to the fragment E 40b (*St. etr.* 7 pl. 15, 6), Dohrn thinks that it may not belong (158 no. 307a), and I am inclined to follow him.

In style of drawing, Heidelberg E 40a resembles a vase, of white clay, from Orvieto which Dohrn attributes, though with justifiable hesitation, to the Painter of Vienna 318: it is Berlin inv. 3212 (A, Dohrn pl. 9, 3: Dohrn's no. 307).

Another vase that belongs to our group, but is somewhat unusual in style of drawing, is the neck-amphora Copenhagen, Ny Carlsberg, H 147 (A, *Bildertafeln Etr. Mus.* pl. 49, 1; A, *St. etr.* 11 pl. 39, 3), which is no. 11 in Miss Calò's list, no. 307c in Dohrn's.

Of the vases attributed by Dohrn to the Painter of Vienna (Oest. Mus.) 318, no. 305, the neck-amphora in the Nederlandsch Lyceum at the Hague (A, *Mededeelingen* 7 pl. 2, 1: fight) is surely to be struck out. Whether it was made at Orvieto or not (I do not know whether the clay, which is of a greyish-yellow colour according to van Hoorn, is decisive), the style is very different from that of the Vienna painter and of the other vases in our group: it somewhat recalls the neck-amphora Chiusi 577 (see p. 18, lower middle). The only other item that seems out of place in Dohrn's list is no. 307h, the outline oinochoe, from Cumae, in Naples (*ML.* 22 pl. 70, 8): it is of the right period, as the objects found with it show (ibid. 455), and not fourth-century as Dohrn is disposed to opine (p. 136), but is no doubt Campanian.

On the other hand, the Berkeley olpe 8.920, of white clay, from Orvieto (*CV.* pl. 30, 1) may perhaps belong to our group as Dohrn conjectures (p. 139), although the style is unusual.  Perhaps also the Bonn neck-amphora 1226 (A, Dohrn pl. 9, 1: no. 307b).  Then there is the Bonn stamnos 501 (A, *St. etr.* 12 pl. 55, 4: A, two sphinxes; B, two panthers conjoined in head), which Dohrn is ready to attribute 'to the Orvieto workshop on grounds of clay and technique': the style, however, does not seem from the reproduction to have much in common with our group.

Valuable additions to Miss Calò's list and Dohrn's were made by Minto in *NSc.* 1939, 18–24: important not only the figure-pieces but the almost plain vases described in his pp. 22–4.  See also p. 296.

The following vases also belong to the Orvieto Group:

*Neck-amphora*

Florence.  Centauromachy.

*Pelike*

Florence 78785, from Orvieto.  Black (fired to red).

*Oinochoe*

(flat mouth, thin neck, high handle: type of Oxford *CV.* pl. 48, 13, text p. 40)
Florence.  Black (fired to red).

*Stemmed bowls*

(the bowl of kantharoid form)
Florence 75777, from Orvieto.  Dots on the rim outside.

(with offset lip: general shape as *CV.* Cop. pl. 217, 2, or Albizzati pl. 25, 248)
Oxford 1933.1564, from Orvieto.
Florence 76407, from Orvieto.

*Fragments*

Munich, frr.  Athletes (among them a discus-thrower).  A bird (cock?) (if from the same vase?).
Florence, fr., from Orvieto.  All round, swans.
Leipsic, fr. (Warrior running to right, looking round).
Leipsic, fr., from Orvieto. (Satyr bending).
Leipsic, fr., from Orvieto. (Woman, satyr, woman).

## LATE ETRUSCAN BLACK-FIGURE

The Micali Group is continued by a large class of black-figure vases many of which show the influence of late Attic black-figure, especially late neck-amphorae large and small.  The class has not received very much attention, and I cannot make good the neglect: all I can do is to distinguish a few small groups.

## THE GROUP OF MUNICH 883

Nos. 1–3 are no doubt by one hand.

### Neck-amphorae

1. Munich 883 (J 991), from Vulci. A and side, SH. pl. 37 and p. 118 fig. 132. A, rider; B, the like.
2. Copenhagen, Ny Carlsberg, H 149. *Bildertafeln Etr. Mus.* pl. 50. A, athletes; B, athletes.
3. Geneva. A, phot. Giraudon 4016, a. A, satyr and maenad.
4. Geneva. A, phot. Giraudon 4005, b. A, bull; B, the like.

Not far from these are the neck-amphorae

Munich 887 (J 992), from Vulci. A, SH. pl. 38. A, youth; B, the like.

Brussels R 270. A, Giglioli pl. 130, 4. A, satyr and maenad.

### THE PAINTER OF VATICAN 265

### Neck-amphorae

1. Vatican 265. Passeri pll. 246–7; Albizzati pl. 27 and p. 93. A, athletes; B, youths.
2. Copenhagen inv. 3837, from Orvieto. A, *CV*. pl. 217, 7. Komos? (A, youth; B, youth.)
3. Chiusi, from Chiusi. Ex Paolozzi. A, two youths (in himatia, one standing to right, one arm raised, the other standing to left, one arm extended downwards). Between them a double spiral.

Compare also the small neck-amphora of unusual shape

Vatican 292. A, Albizzati pl. 27. On the neck, palmettes. According to Albizzati, Vatican 293, which is not reproduced, is like 292, only shorter in the neck.

### THE GROUP OF NEW YORK GR 517

### Pointed amphorae

1. New York GR 517. On the shoulder, each side, two Erotes. The foot of the vase seems modern.
2. Florence 72711. On the shoulder, Erotes, like those on the New York vase. Below them, in black, the same broad band between two lines as there. On the shoulder, floral like that of the New York vase, but with a maeander above it. Drawing in silhouette.

The same large rosettes are used for filling in one or two other vases:

### Stamnoi

1. Barcelona. A, two athletes; B, the like.
2. Cambridge, Museum of Classical Archaeology, 24. A, youth on horseback hurling a javelin; B, centaur rushing to the attack, his weapon an uprooted tree. Compare the last.

*Oinochoe* (shape II)

3. Lost, from Chiusi. Inghirami *Mus. Chius.* pl. 161. Centaur.
   For the broad band between two lines just above the middle of the vase compare the
Vatican neck-amphora 267 (Albizzati pl. 26).


### THE GROUP OF MUNICH 912

*Stamnos*

1. Munich 912, from Vulci. A, SH. pl. 40. A, horse; B, the like.


*Oinochoai* (shape I)

2. Munich 930. SH. pl. 40. Horse.
3. Munich 929, from Vulci. SH. pl. 40. Two youths.


### THE GROUP OF MUNICH 878

*Small neck-amphorae*

1. Munich 878 (J 996), from Vulci. A, SH. pl. 38. A, satyr; B, the like.
2. Munich 877 (J 1011), from Vulci. A, SH. pl. 38. A, naked youth running (or dancing);
   B, the like.
3. Munich 825. A, SH. pl. 38. Floral.


### THE GROUP OF MUNICH 886

*Small neck-amphorae*

1. Munich 886, from Vulci. A, SH. pl. 38. A, fight. B, two naked youths.
2. Munich 885, from Vulci. A, SH. pl. 38. A, women dancing. B, naked youth running.


### THE GROUP OF MUNICH 891

*Small neck-amphorae*

1. Munich 891, from Vulci. A, SH. pl. 38. A, naked youth; B, youth.
2. Munich 890, from Vulci. A, SH. pl. 38. A, warrior. B, naked man.


### THE GROUP OF MUNICH 872

*Small neck-amphorae*

1. Munich 872, from Vulci. A, SH. pl. 38. Komos (youths running).
2. Munich 884, from Vulci. A, SH. pl. 38. A, woman; B, woman.


### THE GROUP OF COPENHAGEN ABC 1059

Small vases without figurework. Nos. 1–3 are counted Campanian by Blinkenberg and
Johansen, but I take them to be Etruscan.

*Small neck-amphorae*

(ordinary shape)

1. Copenhagen ABc 1059, part. *CV.* pl. 229, 1.

(special shape)

2. Copenhagen ABc 1059, part. *CV.* pl. 229, 2.
3. Copenhagen, no number. *CV.* pl. 229, 3.
4. Orvieto, Conte Faina, from Orvieto.

For the shape of nos. 2–4 compare the vase represented on a later monument, the Etruscan sarcophagus published in *Mon.* 1855 pl. 12–13.

### THE GROUP OF THE LEYDEN KYATHOS

*Kyathoi* (one-handled kantharoi)

1. Leyden K 10.2.11. *Kunstbesitz* pl. 19, 774; Brants pl. 15, 5. Sphinx and winged goddess.
2. Geneva. Phot. Giraudon 4005, c. Sphinx. On the front of the handle, (youth?).

### THE GROUP OF MUNICH 980

*Kyathoi* (of Attic type)

1. Munich 980, from Vulci. SH. pl. 43. Fight.
2. Munich 979. SH. pl. 43. Satyrs.

### THE GROUP OF VATICAN 246

*Skyphoi* (with offset lip)

1. Vatican 246. Albizzati pl. 25.
2. Florence 4174.
3. Chiusi (1914?), from Chiusi.
4. Florence V 80, from Chiusi or near. Ex Lunghini.
5. Orvieto 175, from Orvieto.
6. Florence 4185.
7. Florence V 78, from Chiusi or near. Ex Lunghini.

Patterns only: in nos. 1–5, maeander.

### THE GROUP OF THE DOT-WREATH PLATES

A brief allusion to this large group of plates will suffice. Some of them are stemless, others rest on a stout stem and foot. On the rim, a wreath, reduced to a line between two rows of dots; at the centre, a rosette consisting of dots and circles or the like; the rest of the upper surface is either reserved or black. A list is given in *RG.* 85–6 on nos. 95–106, and good examples figured there on pl. 1. Add the plate Harvard 3122 (*CV.* pl. 35, 6).

### THE SPURINAS GROUP

This chapter may conclude with a list of vases which bear inscriptions inside, painted in glaze before firing. They are plates, stemmed plates, stemmed dishes of various sorts; and I think they must be from a single fabric. There is no other decoration, except sometimes a circle or two, and a central dot. The shapes point to the fifth century, or at earliest the late sixth, and this date would agree with such slight evidence as there is from co-finds. The Denci plate (no. 3) came from a chamber-tomb at Pitigliano which yielded nothing later than Attic black-figured vases from the third quarter of the sixth century; the S. Giuliano fragment (no. 15) was found in the Tomba Ciarlanti, and in the left-hand chamber of it, with fragments of a late black-figured Attic cup from the beginning of the fifth century.

1. Vienna, Oest. Mus., 451, from Cervetri. The inscription only, Masner, inscr. plate, 451. *Larisal*: 'Plate'.
2. Vatican. *Ṣech* complete. Plate.
3. Once Pitigliano, Giovanni Denci, from Pitigliano. *NSc.* 1903, 276. *Spurinas*: 'Plate'.
4. Once Canino, from Vulci. Micali *St.* pl. 101, 7, above. *Spurinas*:
5. Florence, fr., from Populonia. *St. etr.* 6, 465; Buffa pl. 8, 624. *Unas*: Plate.
6. Florence 4203, from Tarquinia. *Venelus* complete. Stemmed plate.
7. Berlin 4091. The inscription, Furtwängler *Beschreibung* 1035. *Ṣachus*: Stemmed plate.
8. Berlin 4090, from Cervetri. The inscription, Furtwängler *Beschreibung* 1035. *Titeles*: 'Stemmed plate'.
9–10. Tarquinia, from Tarquinia. Several stemmed plates. *Avi* complete.
11. Once Canino, from Vulci. Micali *St.* pl. 101, 7, below. *Avi* complete. Stemmed plate.
12. Bonn, fr. *Vei* complete. Stemmed plate or stemmed dish (only the lower part remains).
13. Bonn, fr. . . . *e*: . . . (what remains of the inscription is the last letter of a word, and the interpoints). Stemmed dish, the upper edge flat and reserved: part of the bowl remains.
14. Cabinet des Médailles. *Kalnies* complete. Stemmed dish with cup-like bowl.
15. From S. Giuliano (E. of Tarquinia), fr. *ML.* 33 pl. 32 fig. 60, 3. . . . *s*: *sr* . . . (what remains of the inscription is the last letter of a word, the interpoints, and the first two letters of the next word). (Stemmed) dish: part of the bowl remains.
16. Once Canino, from Vulci. Micali *St.* pl. 101, 8. *Ḷap*[ ]*nas* complete. Stemmed dish.
17. Once Canino, from Vulci. Micali *St.* pl. 101, 9. *Ṣutnas* complete. Compare the last.
18. Berlin 4092. *Thenus*: Stemmed dish with torus lip.
19. Berlin 4093. [. . .] *falus* [.]. Said to be the same shape as the last.
20. Cambridge 200, from Vulci. *CV.* ii pl. 30, 10. *Specas*: Stemless dish.

A plate in the Villa Giulia, from Vulci, has the word *Vimarus* painted on the rim before firing, but I do not know if it belongs to our group.

## CHAPTER III

# EARLIER RED-FIGURE

PLENTY of black-figured vases were made by Etruscans in the first half of the fifth
century;[1] and a good deal of 'pseudo-red-figure' with decoration in superposed
colour:[2] but not much red-figure. The unpublished neck-amphora Florence 75689,
from Orvieto (A, fight; B, warrior mounting chariot), mentioned by Hartwig (*Jb.* 14, 161
note 14), is not Attic: I took it to be Etruscan, and if it is, it must be among the earliest
of Etruscan red-figured vases. Pale clay, poor hesitant drawing, no relief-lines. I do not
wish to insist upon this vase, because it is a long time since I looked at it, and there is
the possibility that it may not be Etruscan at all. I speak with more confidence of a vase,
from Chiusi, in Palermo, 1485 (Inghirami *Mus. Chius.* pl. 103). It is a column-krater of
Attic type, with two warriors on one side and on the other a horse-hoofed satyr followed
by a maenad. The only pattern is the band of rays round the base. The clay is a light
buff; and here again there are no relief-lines: the lines are all brown and flat. The style
is still archaic and the date, even allowing for an Etruscan lag, cannot be after the middle
of the fifth century.

The earliest Etruscan vase, so far as I know, in which relief-lines are used[3] is the extraordinary cup in the Rodin Museum of which Plaoutine was the first to see the importance.
It is essential, in Etruscan red-figure, to distinguish between the two techniques: that in
which the design, or the greater part of it, is carried out in relief-lines; and the poorer
technique in which the lines are flat. From this point of view, Etruscan red-figure may
be divided into three periods:

1. At first, the two techniques are used side by side, some painters using the one and
   some the other.
2. Before the end of the fifth century, the relief-line technique becomes dominant, and
   remains so for good part of the fourth century.
3. In the latest period, the relief-line technique is abandoned, and the other is universal.

It should be added that in the second period there are vases in which both techniques
are used: the nobler one for the chief picture (the interior of a cup, or the front of a
stamnos), the baser for the minor parts (the exterior of a cup, or the back of a stamnos).

Let us first examine the Rodin cup, and other early examples of the relief-line technique,
and then pass to some vases that lack relief-line.

Paris, Musée Rodin, 980. *JHS.* 50 pl. 1; *CV.* pll. 28–30; Pl. 4, 1–3. I, satyrs; A–B, satyrs.
On I, retr., *Avlesvpinas*, and below it, *naplan* (?). Dm. 232. The foot of the cup is
alien.

---

[1] Chapter II.

[2] Chapter XII.

[3] It might have been expected that in Etruscan
black-figure, or at least in its more elaborate products,
the relief-line would be used to the same limited extent
as in Attic black-figure from the middle of the sixth
century onwards: that is to say, for the uprights
dividing the tongue-pattern above the picture, for
spears, staves, and other details: but it is not so.

I quote Plaoutine's description of the interior.

The left-hand satyr totters forward in a dancing movement, carrying a large wine-skin on his back. He grasps the upper end with his left hand, just above his head, to prevent it sliding down. The right arm is lowered, with the fingers of the hand raised. His tail does not show, and his left leg is almost entirely hidden behind the krater on which his companion is seated; a bit of the calf appears to the left of the base. The second satyr, who wears a wreath of ivy, is sitting on the foot of a large calyx-krater which has been turned upside down: streaks on the uneven ground represent the remains of the wine: the feast is over. He stretches out his legs and arms and seizes the chin of his companion so as not to lose his balance.

I cannot add anything to this, but note that on the London stamnos F 484 (p. 43 no. 1; Pl. 8, 1) the terrain is rendered in the same way as here, and there it is clear that nothing has been spilt.

The exterior, as Plaoutine saw, is carefully copied, palmettes and all, from a famous Attic cup found at Vulci and now in the Vatican (Hartwig pl. 73; A–B, *JHS*. 50 pl. 2), which is by a follower of Douris[1] (*ARV*. 296 no. 12: by the same, the Oxford cup 1929.752, ibid. no. 13) and must have been painted about 470–460 B.C. The Rodin cup is smaller than the Vatican cup and there was not room for eight figures on the exterior, so the Etruscan copyist omitted one figure on each half. Plaoutine justly observes that 'the Rodin cup cannot have been painted much later than its Vatican model, for if it had been the artist would surely have betrayed himself, if not in the figures, then in the floral decoration; and the handles are of early type. If the date of the Vatican cup is about 470 or 460, ours can hardly be brought down past the middle of the century; and the probability is that it was painted soon after the arrival of the model in Etruria.' Allow a little longer, and it remains a very early example of Etruscan red-figure.

The head of the right-hand satyr in the inside picture may somewhat recall that of the satyr on the London stamnos F 484 (Pl. 8, 1 and p. 43), which has been quoted already for the similar rendering of the terrain. The big dots representing the hair between navel and pubes recur on vases by the Perugia Painter and the Sommavilla Painter (see pp. 38–9). It is only fair to mention these analogies, which might point to a later date than that adopted, but I do not think they should be pressed.

The painter has very slightly modified the Dourian palmettes of his original by adding small 'leaf-hooks', but these do not affect the dating.

The first inscription is a proper name, Avles Vpinas (= Vipinas): so Fiesel in *JHS*. 50, 24. The second inscription, in a line below the first, was not discovered by Plaoutine till after his publication in *JHS*., and I should like to check it.

De Witte adds the word 'Pouille' to his description of the cup in the Durand catalogue of 1836, no. 134 (see *JHS*. 57, 24). He must have meant by this that it was found in Apulia, which would be odd. What his evidence was we do not know. Jahn assumes 'Pouille' to be a stylistic judgement (*Beschreibung* ccxxxv, note 1466), but that is not the proper meaning of such phrases, and this is not the sort of vase that de Witte or any one else could have thought of as 'in Apulian style'. Moreover, de Witte did not

---

[1] There is some restoration on the exterior of the Vatican cup: in particular, the satyr who intercedes for the boy is much repainted from the waist upward.

belong to the great and irrepressible band of those who confuse provenience with place of origin: for example, on no. 6 of the Durand catalogue he writes 'Vulci. Style de Nola'.

When I said that de Witte added the word 'Pouille' to his description of the Rodin cup I was not quite accurate. To be precise, he prefaces his account of the *two* vases composing his lot 134 with the word 'Pouille': here is a possible source of error: 'Apulia' may have been the provenience of the other vase in the lot, a skyphos now lost, and the word may have been shifted from its place so that it came to cover the Rodin cup as well, the provenience of which may have been unknown.

The Vatican cup was found at Vulci. This renders it, if not certain, extremely probable that the Rodin cup was made there.

A vase known to me from a photograph only (the source of which I do not recollect) is not so old as the Rodin cup, but is still an early example of Etruscan red-figure carried out in relief-lines:

*Stamnos* (of special type)

Whereabouts unknown. A, Pl. 6, 4. A, warrior leaving home. On the neck, an ivy-wreath in added colour (white or red).

The handles are missing: the stumps show that they set off from the body as usual, but rejoined the vase on the neck. No other extant stamnos has such handles, and I cannot exactly picture them in my mind. The profiles of the lip and of the base-fillet are unusual. The ivy-wreath round the neck is not common in Attic stamnoi: Hermonax has it on all four of his signed stamnoi (Hoppin *Rf.* ii, 25, ii, 23, ii, 21, and *CV.* Florence pl. 52, 1–5 and pl. 48, 2: *ARV.* 317 nos. 1, 4, 5, and 6), but in added red;[1] a black ivy-wreath surrounds the neck of a black-figured Attic stamnos in the possession of Miss Joan Evans (above, komos; below, A, symposion, B, komos). The picture represents a young warrior leaving home: he stands with both legs frontal, naked, helmeted, a wrap over his left forearm, his shield on his left arm, his spear in his left hand and a phiale in his right, and looks at a woman (mother or wife) who stands in front of him, holding an oinochoe from which she has filled the phiale or is about to fill it; on the other side of the youth is his father, wearing chiton and himation, and holding a staff. This is a typically Attic treatment of the subject, although it was occasionally borrowed by South Italian painters:[2] and our picture is an imitation of some such Attic vase-painting, from the Group of Polygnotos, as those on the pelikai by the Lykaon Painter in London and the Vatican (Gerhard *AV.* pl. 150; *Mus. Greg.* 2 pl. 63, 2, phot. Moscioni 8570: *ARV.* 690, below, nos. 3 and 4). The date of such Attic vases is between 440 and 430 B.C., and our vase cannot be more than a few years later. The drawing of the eyes is old-fashioned for that period: it is a survival. Puppy-lions very like ours, reserved against a black background, are common shield-devices in Polygnotos and his group: stamnos by Polygnotos in Capua (Patroni *Mus. Camp.* pl. 3: *ARV.* 677 no. 6); calyx-krater, manner of Polygnotos if not by himself, in Bologna (Pellegrini *VF.* 134, whence Pfuhl fig. 557: *ARV.* 682 no. 5);

[1] The 'three-handled stamnos' Cambridge 249 (p. 44 no. 5) has a black ivy-wreath round the reserved neck.

[2] e.g. neck-amphora, by the Painter of the Berlin Dancing-girl, in Lecce, 571 (FR. ii, 29 fig. 11; *CV.* IV Dr pll. 1–2).

stamnos by the Hector Painter in Philadelphia (*Mus. J.* 5, 39: *ARV.* 684 no. 7). The Etruscan had made it more formal by the scale-like stylization of the mane: like other Etruscans (see below) he is fond of largish spots and has put plenty of them on the mane and on the band below the lion, as well as on the phiale. The animal on the cheekpiece is a griffin.

A small fragment of an Etruscan cup in Brunswick (*CV.* pl. 44, 3–4) may still belong to the fifth century. All that remains inside is part of the maeander. Outside, there is the knee of a male figure playing the lyre, and in front of him a satyr with a torch or a thyrsus in his hand. Big black dots below the navel. An Etruscan cup in Bowdoin College, with a lively picture of two young satyrs filling their water-pots at the fountain (I, *JHS.* 57, 26), borrows for the exterior a textile design used on Attic stemlesses, cups, and skyphoi between 440 and 425, and Plaoutine dates the cup 'not much after 420'. I find the style of the interior (for which I am now dependent on the reproduction) difficult to date exactly: the late fifth century seems possible, but the early fourth not excluded. With a fragmentary cup in Florence (*CV.* pl. F, B3; *CF.* p. 31) we are on surer ground. The picture on the exterior, a youth leaving home (*CV.* pl. 18B65), imitates Attic cups of the 'Sub-Meidian Cup-group' (*ARV.* 859–64 and 966), which were painted in the last two decades of the fifth century: compare, for example, cups by the Painter of London E 106 (*ARV.* 859–61), such as Oxford 1931.11 or the Heidelberg–Florence– Villa-Giulia cup (part, Kraiker *Kat. Heidelberg* pl. 44). For the interior the Etruscan artist had no Greek model, or stuck to it less closely. Eros approaches a woman, who seems to be seated and looking round at him: a large piece is missing, and the precise motive is not clear. The lavish use of big black spots, as here on wings and garment, is a favourite decorative device with Etruscan vase-painters: see, for example, the lost stamnos figured on Pl. 6, 4 (p. 27), the works of the Painter of London F 484 (pp. 43–5), the Pitt Rivers vase (Pl. 6, 1–3), the Phuipa cup (Pl. 12), the cup with Dionysos riding a panther (pp. 50–1). The Florence cup comes from the Campana collection and the provenience may be Vulci.

A small fragment of an Etruscan cup, Amsterdam inv. 3207 (A, the upper part of a woman, head turned to right), is very like the Florence cup. A cup in Erlangen also seemed to be an imitation of the Sub-Meidian Cup-group, but I have no particulars of it, only the subject: inside, a woman and a youth; outside, on each half, an athlete and women. Two cups from Chiusi, one in Florence, the other published by Inghirami (*Mus. Chius.* pll. 200–2), are imitated from the same group of Attic cups: but the technique of the first is added colour, not red-figure (see p. 204). What the technique of the second is, is not clear from the reproduction, whether red-figure, or added colour. The picture inside represents a youth leaving home—a youth and a woman; outside, on one half, the same subject—a youth with a woman and a youth; the other half shows three women, but is evidently restored.

The same question of technique arises over two small stemless cups, or a stemless cup and what is described as a 'tazza', which may be stemless:

Once Borghesi, from near Arezzo. Inghirami *Mon. etr.* 5 pl. 4, 2 and 4. I, woman.

Once Borghesi, from near Arezzo. I, Inghirami *Mon. etr.* 5 pl. 4, 1. I, woman. Said to have been found with the last and a black-figured neck-amphora. If it is red-figured, there are no relief-lines.

A small stemless in Orvieto, from Orvieto, seems from the description to be in added colour rather than red-figure (I, *NSc.* 1939 pl. 3, 3: I, Hermes).

A calyx-krater in Munich, from Vulci (3224; J. 526: A and side, Jacobsthal *O.* pl. 57, c–d), would seem, from the illustrations, to use relief-lines (A, Dionysos and satyrs; B, Hephaistos and satyrs; at each handle a vine). It is difficult to date, especially as it must be much restored: but the drawing has an early look, and the pattern below the pictures may point to the fifth century: at any rate the latest Attic vases with addorsed palmettes are by the Kleophon Painter (*ARV.* 785 nos. 11 and 12) and must be dated about 430–425. Jacobsthal placed our vase 'well on in the second half of the fifth century' (*O.* 82 and 157). On the vine-ornament see ibid. 82–3.

All these vases are at present, to me at least, isolated: but before the close of the fifth century we find small *groups* of Etruscan vases in the relief-line technique, each group consisting either of works by one artist or of closely interconnected works. One of these consists of four small squab vases more like a sort of kantharos than anything else:

### THE PITT RIVERS PAINTER
#### Small kantharos-like vases

1. Oxford, Pitt Rivers Museum, 'from Florence'. Given by Prof. E. B. Tylor in 1917. Pl. 6, 1–3. Nike between youths. Present height 0.104 (the foot is missing as well as the handles).
2. Florence, five frr. One of them, *CV.* pl. 21, 345. Nike between youths (not women, as Levi).
3. Florence. *CV.* pl. 21, 343. Athlete between youths. The foot is lost.
4. Florence, fr. *CV.* pl. 21, 344. (Athlete?) between youths. The left-hand figure is male, not female (as Levi).

The clay of the Pitt Rivers vase (no. 1) is a light buff. Inside, the vase is reserved. Inside the lip, and on the front of the vase (overlapping at the sides), there is ruddle, evidently laid on with a brush. Relief-lines are used for the drapery, for the feet of the left-hand youth (but not the outline), the right ankle of Nike, the creases at her elbows, the inner markings of her right hand, and her wings. The rest of the drawing, including the eyes, is in flat lines, so that the relief-technique is imperfectly carried out. For the big spots on the wings see p. 28. Below the picture, a rough reserved line. Picture and patterns cease half-way round the vase, and the back is simply covered with a yellow wash of strongly diluted glaze. The foot of the vase is missing and so are both handles. In no. 3 one handle is preserved, continuing the line of the mouth. I do not know any other vases of this shape.

According to Levi 'the lower half' of no. 3 'is left in the orange colour of the clay'. Should it be 'the back half'?

The style of these humble little objects is based on Attic vases of the late fifth century, sub-Meidian vases one might say, and the date will not be after 400.

Much more important groups, from the same period, will be discussed under the headings of Perugia Painter, Sommavilla Painter, and so on: but before passing to them we turn aside and look at some vases which are contemporary with those just studied, but executed in flat brown lines without relief: in the same base technique, that is to say, as the early neck-amphora in Florence, and the early column-krater in Palermo, with which we began.

### Column-krater

Arezzo, from Casalta in Val di Chiana. A, *Jh.* 12, 165. A, uncertain subject, two women and a youth standing at a chest; B, two youths and a woman.

Shape and patternwork are the normal Attic, except that the profile of the foot is a little unusual. The subject is uncertain. At first glance one thinks of Danae and the Chest, but that is obviously wrong. Engelmann (*Jh.* 12, 165–8) proposed Tennes and Hemithea: I suppose the youth would be Tennes, the woman on the right Hemithea, and she in the middle Phylonome reasoning with her stepchildren and inviting them to step quietly into the chest and be dropped into the sea. This is improbable. It may be that the scene is not mythical, but taken from ordinary life: the mistress at the chest, the maid, and the spouse: for chest and women, compare an Attic stamnos, by the Copenhagen Painter, formerly in the possession of Campanari (Gerhard *AV*. pl. 301: *ARV.* 193 no. 6).

The style is founded on Attic vases of about 440 to 430. The 'maid' wears the same garment as some of the Washing Painter's women (*ARV.* 742–7), a peplos with long overfold, overgirt, and ornamented with an unusually wide black border: hydriai in New York (22.139.25: Richter and Hall pl. 149, 147: *ARV.* 745 no. 58), London (E 206: *CV.* III Ic pl. 88, 6: *ARV.* 746 no. 72), Munich (2433: *ARV.* 746 no. 71).

Two column-kraters, from Volterra, in Volterra, are still of the fifth century: one has youths and a woman on one side, the other (phot. Alinari 34712, 1) two youths on the reverse. A column-krater in Copenhagen deserves a word more:

Copenhagen inv. 3842. *CV.* pl. 220, 2. A, komos (two ill-favoured men, and a woman); B, satyrs and maenad.

The shape is normal, except that the foot is not quite like the feet of Attic column-kraters; the patternwork unusual. A lively komos: a woman dances, or dances along, with one finger passed through the handle of a cup, or stemless cup, in the gesture of kottabizing; the men who dance round her are naked dwarfs, with all their parts realistically rendered. Each of them has a cord round his middle, with a pendant attached to it: in the left-hand dwarf, a couple of small rings, one fastened to the other; in the right-hand one, a crescent, the σεληνίς which was a popular amulet throughout antiquity.[1] Cords

---

[1] On σεληνίΔες see Stephani in *Compte rendu* 1865, 182 and Wickert in PW. s.v. luna, pp. 1811–12. Here are a few additions: Greek, 7th c. B.C., Cretan aryballos in Berlin, 307 (Pfuhl fig. 56; Neugebauer pl. 10, 1). Greek, 6th c. B.C., mirror in New York, *AJA.* 1938, 338–41 and 337 note 6 (Richter). Greek, mid 5th c. B.C., Attic rf. cup in Athens, Acr. 446 (Langlotz pl. 33). Etruscan, 4th c. B.C., mirrors in Leningrad (Gerhard *ES.* pl. 322) and Munich (Endell *Antike Gravierungen in deutschen Sammlungen*: Pan, two women, and a seated youth). Etruscan, 3rd–2nd c. B.C.: bronze oinochoe in Bologna (Ducati *St.* pl. 250, 603 and 605;

with beads or amulets attached to them were common enough in Greece and Etruria, but I do not remember seeing them worn round the waist. The vase can hardly be earlier than 420—the woman is of a Meidian plumpness—and is probably not much later, certainly belongs to the fifth century.

An Etruscan column-krater found at Lucignano between Arezzo and Chiusi and formerly in the collection of Francesco Aliotti at Arezzo (Micali *Mon. ined.* pl. 35, 2) is still of fifth-century shape and must belong to the late years of the fifth century or the beginning of the fourth. The technique would seem to be red-figure, rather than added colour, but whether relief-lines are used or not one cannot tell. On one side, two youths and a woman; on the other, three youths. The greater part of the drawing must be genuine: but it may be suspected that the objects in the hands have been improved by the restorer or the draughtsman; and there must be some restoration in the lower parts of the woman and of the youth behind her, for there is no sign of her chiton at her ankles, and he has no right foot.

Now a more important piece:

### Stamnos

Bologna 824, from Bologna. Zannoni pl. 24, 1–2 and 8; *St. etr.* 8 pll. 29–30 and p. 122.

A, Theseus and Periphetes? B, youths and woman. At one handle, a male dwarf, at the other a female dwarf. Over one handle, an owl, over the other a swan.

Ducati (*St. etr.* 8, 120) puts this in the first quarter of the fourth century: but the shape of the vase and the style of the drawing imitate Attic work of about 430. For the shape compare, among others, the stamnoi figured by Langlotz *Fruehgriechische Bildhauerschulen* pl. 14, 7–8 (*ARV.* 666 no. 5, and 696 no. 18); the drawing, broadly speaking, is such as is found on the outskirts of the Group of Polygnotos, and the figures on the reverse remind one of the column-krater, just mentioned, from Casalta, in Arezzo (p. 30).

Let us now look at the other contents of the grave in which the stamnos was found (Zannoni pl. 24). These are all of local work. The unglazed plate and the pair of small unglazed dishes are not very characteristic, but they are thoroughly compatible with a fifth-century date: for such plates see Zannoni pl. 43 and p. 170, tomb 86, and pl. 41 and p. 169, tomb 82; for such dishes pl. 61, 5 and p. 224, tomb 133. There remain the plain bronze pan and the unglazed kantharos. Now, first, bronze pans of this type are common in Felsinean tombs of the fifth century: Ducati himself says so (*St. etr.* 8, 119), gives references which need not be transcribed here, and adds that in our tomb he would regard the pan as an old-fashioned, traditional object. Second, the unglazed kantharos

Giglioli pl. 314, 3); fragment of a bronze statuette, from Orbetello, in Florence (*NSc.* July 1885 pl. 1, 11). Roman: Ara Pacis. Roman, marble statuette of a child in the Vatican, Galleria dei Candelabri 99 (Visconti *Museo Pio Clementino* 3 pl. 22, Clarac pl. 883, 2249; the amulets, Dölger Ιχθυς pl. 136). Antonine, statue of Aphrodite of Aphrodisias, in Athens (*AM.* 22, 362; Thiersch *Ependytes und Ephod* pl. 11 and pp. 65 and 72). Roman: terracottas from Nijmegen (*Bull. van de Vereeniging* v, 1, 5). Palmyrene, relief in Rome, Museo

Barracco (Dölger Ιχθυς pl. 135, 3). Modern Egyptian, *ARW.* 29 (1931) pl. 5, fig. 3 and p. 134 (Lassally). Modern Spanish, *Man* 42, 73–84 (Hildburgh). See also Robinson *Olynthus* x, 125–8.

According to Marcellus Empiricus (29, 52: quoted by Wolters *Faden und Knoten als Amulett* = supplement to *ARW.* 8, 20), a cord of nine differently-coloured strands, which has been threaded through the body of a puppy with a silver needle, cures the colic if worn round the waist as a girdle.

of the type Zannoni pl. 24, 4 is one of the commonest finds in Felsinean graves of the fifth century, in association with Attic black-figured vases and Attic red-figure of the period between 480 and 430: unnecessary to give examples: turn over the pages of Zannoni. I note only to complete the circle, that the graves just quoted for plate and dish contain such kantharoi as well. It looks, then, as if the stamnos belonged to the fifth century.

It seems to be agreed that the subject of the obverse is Hermes attacking Herakles: so at least Zannoni (90), Pellegrini (*VF.* 233), Ducati (*St. etr.* 8, 120–1), while Heydemann (*Mittheilungen aus den Antikensammlungen in Ober- und Mittelitalien* 62) speaks of 'a youth and Herakles'. But the youth is not characterized as Hermes: and as for his adversary, the pelt he wears has no mark of a lion-skin, the club is not confined to Herakles, and who has ever seen a Herakles with a bald head and a face like a satyr's? It is evidently a young hero quelling a middle-aged bandit, perhaps Theseus and Periphetes of Epidauros, 'the man with the club' (Korynetes), a contest depicted on an Attic cup by the Pistoxenos Painter in Munich (Gerhard *AV.* pl. 232–3: *ARV.* 575 no. 8), as well as in one of the metopes of the Theseum (Robert *Heldensage* 723–4).

Ducati is surprised that Hermes should be attacking Herakles, since they seem to have been such good friends, and thinks that the Etruscan painter must have been a very ignorant fellow: unless indeed the subject is not a myth at all, but a gladiatorial performance, a variant of the contest depicted on a wall of the Tomba degli Auguri at Tarquinia, where Phersu, wearing a mask, sets a large dog at a man who carries a club and has his head tied up in a bag.[1] Quite a variant.

The two dwarfs are 'handle-figures': each a small picture by itself, set under the handle, and not connected either in composition or in subject with the main pictures, any more than the owl is, or the swan. These dwarfs are said by Ducati to have that 'lively, vigorous feeling, that stamp of realism, which are the earmarks of Etruscan art': but they are copied from Attic dwarfs of the fifth century, which are far livelier and more realistic: see Caskey *Attic Red-figured Vases in Boston* 59; *RM.* 52, 44–7 (Lippold); *JHS.* 59, 11.

So much for the Bologna stamnos: we pass to two others:

### Stamnoi

1. Hamburg 658. Giglioli pl. 249, 4–5; *Anz.* 1928, 351 fig. 68. A, three warriors. B, Herakles, a woman crowning him, and a man.
2. Munich 3192 (J 1010), from Vulci. *Jb.* 43, 354–5; *Anz.* 1928, 351 fig. 69. Replica of the last. A good deal restored (the restorations are given by Mercklin in *Anz.* 1928, 353–4). The foot is modern; what of the handles?

The two stamnoi are replicas, and by a single hand. The Munich vase was published by Dragendorff as an example of the 'Praxias' technique—designs in superposed red: but Mercklin pointed out that the technique was red-figure (*St. etr.* 11, 374). To judge from the reproductions, the lines are all flat, without relief. The picture on A is more attractive than that on B: the proportions are better, and the formal patterns on the

---

[1] *Mon.* 11 pl. 25; Weege *Etr. Mal.* pll. 94–5; Ducati *St.* pl. 79, 228; Giglioli pll. 109–10.

clothes help to bind the figures together. Charlemagne's knights, or the Champions of Christendom, or their Paynim opposites, in an old book for children.

There is little to add to Mercklin's descriptions. As to the date, what he says is 'fifth to fourth century, after an Attic model'. Probably fifth century, though not before the twenties. It should be said that the latest extant Attic stamnos with handle-projections (like our two vases) is Cabinet des Médailles 388, by the Persephone Painter (de Ridder pl. 13 and p. 82: *ARV.* 652 no. 4), which is not later than the thirties, but that is not sufficient to warrant an earlier date.

The band of black palmettes round the neck does not occur in Attic stamnoi.

Another vase without relief-lines is the Würzburg stamnos 803 (Langlotz pl. 236): A, two athletes shaking hands, or perhaps rather, as Langlotz says, an athlete seizing a friend by the hand; B, two youths. According to Langlotz the left-hand youth on B holds a full basket: in the photograph it looks like the same cloak, laid over the left shoulder, as in the athlete on A. The vase is said to have been found in the Basilicata, but it must be Etruscan, as Langlotz recognized. His date is the middle of the fifth century, which seems somewhat early. The painter is a simple soul, and has an old-fashioned way of drawing eyes: but I doubt if his work is earlier than the thirties or even the twenties.

## THE ARGONAUT GROUP

The last vase to be considered before returning to the relief-line technique is the most important:

### Bell-krater

Florence 4026. A, Milani *R. Mus. Arch.* pl. 43, 2; A, Behn *Die Ficoronische Cista* pl. 2, 2; *Mél. d'arch.* 37, 141–7; FR. pl. 177 and iii p. 353, whence (A) Pl. 9, 1. A, warriors. B, youth and women.

There is a great contrast between the finely conceived figures and the shabby technique in which they are carried out. The patterns, too, are poor, and the potter-work miserable. The scene is not easy to interpret. Rocky ground. On the right, a naked man, holding a spear in the left hand, is having something tied round his right forearm by a naked youth who stands in front of him. It is one of those bands, with a bulla or the like attached, which Etruscans, men as well as women, sometimes wore on the right arm, very often on the left, and occasionally on both arms. The man already has three such bands on his left arm, and this will make the third on his right. He also has rings on his fingers. The youth wears a sword. Another naked youth stands to the left of these, in the middle of the picture; parts of his right hand and left arm are restored, but he is almost certainly adjusting a bulla-band on his left forearm. He wears boots. In the left half of the picture there are two youths and a man. One of the youths is sitting on the ground clasping his knee and looking towards the first three persons as if watching them. The man stands behind him and lays one hand lightly on nape and shoulder of the youth. The second youth pays no heed to the others, but sits on the ground, turned away from them all, resting, with his head bent and his face buried between his arms. These three wear chlamydes and two of them swords.

Behn called the vase early South Italian (*Die Ficoronische Cista* 26). He thought that a bell-krater in Oxford, 529, might be by the same hand: but was misled by the inferior reproductions which were all that were available when he wrote: the Oxford krater is Attic, and gives its name to a late member of the Mannerist Group who has left four other works (*CV.* pl. 24, 3 and pl. 25, 8; *ARV.* 393 no. 1). Buschor also called the Florence vase South Italian (FR. iii, 161), and attributed two fine Italiote calyx-kraters to the same painter, that with the Capture of Dolon in the British Museum (F 157: FR. pl. 110, 4) and that with Odysseus and Teiresias in the Cabinet des Médailles (422: FR. pl. 60, 1): but I do not believe he would maintain these attributions now. Milani (*R. Mus. Arch.* 154) and Albizzati (*Mél. d'arch.* 37 p. 112 no. 17 and p. 139) saw that our vase was Etruscan; and Watzinger offered the same opinion in a modified form: an Etruscan painter working in Campania. I do not myself see any connexion with Campanian art, and I count the vase Etruscan. Albizzati assigned it to the fabric of Vulci; and ascribed two other Etruscan vases to the same hand, in which I cannot follow him, nor could Watzinger: the two vases will be studied later under the heading of 'Perugia Painter' (p. 36).

The original model of the figures seems to have been a painting from the last decade or so of the fifth century: in Attica, the great white lekythoi of 'Group R' (*ARV.* 827–8 and 968) show the influence of the same current. How much later the vase may be is another question. Even if the current persisted for some time, and even allowing for a certain lag in Etruria, I should not be inclined to date the drawing much after the first decade of the fourth century; and shape as well as patternwork would suit.

To return to the subject-matter: these youths and men have always been taken to be Argonauts, owing to the resemblance between the picture and others which are Argonautic, for instance the lower frieze of the early Italiote volute-krater in Munich from which the Sisyphos Painter has his name (FR. pl. 98; Trendall *Frühitaliotische Vasen* pl. 19), and above all the Ficoroni cista. It seems very probable, if not certain, that these are Argonauts (rather than, for example, the heroes bound for Thebes).

Albizzati (*Mél. d'arch.* 37, 140–2) believes that the man with the spear is preparing for a contest in which mortal means will not avail: it is Jason, making ready to meet the Dragon, and the magic power of the talismans will bring him victory. This would be a new version of the legend: but Albizzati reminds us that the ancient representations of Jason in the Dragon's mouth have no counterpart in extant literature either. The most famous picture of Jason disgorged by the Dragon, on the Attic cup by Douris in the Vatican (*Mon.* 2 pl. 35; I, phot. Alinari 35830, whence Pfuhl fig. 467: *ARV.* 286 no. 93), gives warrant also for a bearded Jason. As to the spear in the hero's hand, Jason more often uses a sword in his fight with the Dragon, but on an Apulian mascaroon-krater in Leningrad (*Mon.* 5 pl. 12) he attacks with a spear: the vase is much restored, but according to Petersen (*AZ.* 1879, 16) the head of Jason and part of his spear are antique.

This interpretation raises certain difficulties. Albizzati does not mention the youth in the middle of the picture who, if our description is correct, is fastening an amulet to his forearm. If the man on the right is Jason, it was awkward of the painter to show another Argonaut taking the same precautions as the principal character; and it would not be sufficient defence to point out that in some pictures of Jason quelling the Dragon he is assisted by companions. Again, the subject as it stands is Etruscan: for the wearing of the arm-band with a bulla attached to it is an Etruscan custom. The vase-painter may have altered his model in one particular and substituted the Etruscan bulla-armlet for what was in the Greek original some other kind of periapt: but it must be said that I do not recollect any story in which Greek heroes secure themselves with talismans before an adventure. The alternative would be to suppose that the new version of the legend which Albizzati postulates was an Etruscan version: but this is not Albizzati's contention: he speaks of a Greek version, unrecorded in extant Greek literature, but Greek.

Watzinger holds a different opinion about the subject (FR. iii, 352). He believes the figures to be extracts from the same Greek picture as the 'Binding of Amykos' on the Ficoroni cista. Novios Plautios did not copy all the figures in the original painting, and among those not copied by him are the six on our vase: the painter of the Florence vase has changed one of the motives in his model, and the bulla-armlets are due to him; Watzinger does not say what he believes the original motive to have been.

I am inclined to think that Watzinger's explanation is correct in the main. Details are naturally problematical (to take only one instance, the original might have been a companion picture to the Chastisement of Amykos, say the decoration of another wall in the same building): but it seems likely (1) that these unusual and expressive figures were not invented by the vase-painter, were copied directly or indirectly from a work of monumental painting; (2) that as the composition suggests, the vase-painter has given only an extract and that there were more figures in the original; (3) that the characters in the original were Argonauts; (4) that the general sense of the vase-picture as it stands would be intelligible to an Etruscan beholder: two heroes adjusting their bulla-bracelets, and comrades looking on or resting; (5) that the Etruscan beholder would probably think of the bulla-bracelets as not mere ornaments but as possessing talismanic value; (6) that the motive of the bulla-bracelet is due to the vase-painter (or to another Etruscan artist preceding him); if we are to guess at what he found in his original, it may have been a group of a hero bandaging a slightly wounded companion (one may think of Sthenelos binding the right forefinger of Diomed on the Chalcidian neck-amphora formerly in the Pembroke collection, *Mon.* 1 pl. 51, whence Pfuhl fig. 163 and Rumpf *Chalkidische Vasen*, pl. 12), and a single figure of a hero adjusting his own bandage, or perhaps only rubbing his forearm like the athlete on the cup by the Kodros Painter in the British Museum, E 83 (Norman Gardiner *Athletics of the Ancient World* fig. 47: *ARV.* 740 no. 14): the vase-painter will have modified these motives and given them an Etruscan colour.

There is another vase in the same style as the Florence krater and surely by the same hand: but it will be found disappointing:

### *Bell-krater*

London 1927.10–10.1. Pl. 8, 3–4. A, two youths; B, the like. On the left of A, an altar, and another on the right.

This was formerly the property of Lt.-Col. C. J. de B. Sheringham, sold at Sotheby's

on July 27, 1927. It has a brass band round the foot stating that it was presented to
Bunsen by Platner, Kestner, Braun, Lepsius, Papencordt, Ulrichs, and two Abekens on
April 24, 1838; and is the only vase in the British Museum with a brass band round
the foot. No relief-lines, much incised sketch. These are more careful than ordinary
mantle-figures and parts of the drawing are rather good, but the technique is wretched and
the figures do not stand out from the background. The wreath on the mouth of the vase
is the same as in the Florence krater, with the berries tucked away between leaf and stem.

We now return to works in the relief-line technique, and begin with a puzzling vase:

*Calyx-krater*

Copenhagen inv. 8179, from near Soracte. *CV.* pl. 220, 1. A, bathing (naked women at
   the laver; woman seated; and two satyrs stealing up). B, three youths.

The subject, satyrs surprising women at the bath, is as old as the Phineus cup (FR.
pl. 41). Other good examples, Attic, a bell-krater by the Dinos Painter in the University
of Cracow (103: *CV.* pl. 9, 2; *ARV.* 791 no. 29), and another by the Nikias Painter in
the possession of Feuardent (Tischbein 1 pl. 59, whence *El.* 4 pl. 22; A, Tillyard pl.
25, 150: *ARV.* 847 no. 14). An unpublished 'krater' found at Nazzano, described by
Helbig (*Bull.* 1873, 118, 3) and Furtwängler (*Annali* 1878, 84 = *KS.* i, 215 note 4) has
women at a laver, with Eros, women, and satyrs: it might prove to be Faliscan.

The date of the Copenhagen krater must be late fifth century, perhaps about 420.
As to the style, it is more like Attic than anything else, but it is not Attic; nor can I
match it in any Italiote fabric. Blinkenberg and Johansen take it to be Etruscan, and are
probably right: but in Etruscan also, so far as I know, it stands alone.

The vases that follow are easier to place:

### THE PERUGIA PAINTER

Brunn saw that the two vases were by one hand (*Bull.* 1859, 28–9); so also Albizzati,
who attributed them to the fabric of Vulci (*Mél. d'arch.* 37, 107 no. 1, 111 no. 13, and
150).

*Pointed amphora*

1. Perugia, from Perugia. A, *Mon.* 6–7 pl. 70, whence *Mél. d'arch.* 37, 149; B, *Annali*
   1862 pl. O; detail of A, Jacobsthal *O.* pl. 55, b. A, Dionysos seated, with Ariadne,
   satyr, and maenad. B, youths, and woman with laurel-staff.

*Calyx-krater*

2. Florence V. 3, from Chiusi. A, *Mél. d'arch.* 37, 148. A, Dionysos and Ariadne
   reclining, with satyrs, maenad, and Pan. B, youths and woman. The foot of the vase
   is modern.

The Perugia Painter atticizes with ease and success. His pointed amphora imitates the
style of Attic vases from the last two decades of the fifth century: to be exact, the style of
the Talos Painter and of the Meidian circle: compare such vases as the Talos krater
itself, back as well as front (FR. pl. 38–9 and i, 197; *ARV.* 845, below, no. 1), the pelike

formerly in the possession of Raoul-Rochette (Jahn *Vasenbilder* pl. 2: *ARV*. 835 no. 9), the lost Panathenaic published by Jahn (*Vasenbilder* pl. 3, whence, A, Welcker *Alte Denkm.* pl. 13: *ARV*. 835 no. 11). The inspiration of the calyx-krater comes rather from such artists as the Kadmos Painter (*ARV*. 803–5 and 965).

## THE FAINA PELIKE

Orvieto, Conte Faina, from Orvieto. A, phot. Alinari 32752, whence Giglioli pl. 280, 4, Tarchi pl. 119, 3, and Pl. 5, 1. A, a woman holding a pomegranate, between two youths. B, (according to Körte, the heads of three youths remain, one of whom holds 'a palm-branch').

The vase is briefly described by G. Körte in *Annali* 1877, 138 no. 32, and mentioned by Furtwängler in *Annali* 1878, 88 note 2 (= *KS*. i, 218 note 2), who seems to have thought it Italiote. Much of it is missing. It is not by the same hand as the pointed amphora in Perugia, but it is contemporary and of like character, and depends on just the same late fifth-century Attic models: such models as the Raoul-Rochette pelike, and above all the lost Panathenaic published by Jahn (see above). On the drawing of the pubes see p. 39.

A fragment of a large vase, also from Orvieto, imitates the same sort of Attic originals, from the Meidian period, as the Faina pelike, and the style seems to me similar:

Oxford 1914.37, fr., from Orvieto. Pl. 38, 2. Aphrodite riding the Goose. Greatest length 0.115.

Inside, the vase is reserved. The chief lines of the drawing are in relief, but the lines of the drapery are brown and flat. Unfortunately I have no note on the clay of the Faina pelike. The clay of the fragment is typically Orvietan, a light drab. Outside, it is brought up to the proper colour by means of ruddle.

## THE SOMMAVILLA PAINTER

Heydemann saw (*Mittheilungen aus den Antikensammlungen in Ober- und Mittelitalien* 48 nos. 45 and 46) that these two vases were by one hand; so also Albizzati (*Mél. d'arch.* 37 p. 111 nos. 15 and 16, and p. 161), who ascribed them to the fabric of Vulci.

### Calyx-kraters

1. Parma, from Sommavilla Sabina. *Mon.* 2 pl. 55, a, whence Welcker *Alte Denkm.* pl. 11 and Gerhard *Ak. Abh.* pl. 5, 1; A, *Mél. d'arch.* 37, 168; A, *Histoire générale des religions*, Grèce-Rome 42. A, the Sun and the Satyrs. B, the Sphinx.
2. Parma, from Sommavilla Sabina. Jahn *Arch. Beitr.* pll. 5–6, whence (A) *Jb.* 40, 157 fig. 65; *Mél. d'arch.* 37, 169 and 171. A, Bellerophon. B, the Sphinx and satyrs.

These two vases must be founded on Attic originals of about 420 B.C.

On the front of the first vase Helios is seen: the disk of the sun, darting rays, and on it head, in profile, and breast, frontal, of a youth who wears an ornamental garment of the kind that becomes common in Attic painting from the middle of the fifth century onwards (*AJA*. 1939, 622); over it, crossbands. Below and in front of him, young satyrs in expressive attitudes. The subject must surely go back to an Attic satyr-play, and it is perhaps permissible to guess at the plot. A possible plot would be an eclipse of the Sun: dismay and despair of the Satyrs. But the Sun blazes out again: the Satyrs dazzled, amazed, and delighted. More likely because of the satyrs' attitudes, Helios is here the all-seeing detector of wrongdoers, and the guilty satyrs scatter before his face. In any case the picture would figure no moment of the stage-performance, but the gist of the plot.

The three dots on the knee of the right-hand satyr represent his knee, and have not the stellar significance which Deonna attributes to them (*Rev. ét. gr.* 1916, 2).

The back of the vase shows the Sphinx between two youths, one of whom flees in alarm, looking back and ready to defend himself with a stone; the other, who looks quietly on, with great composure, is probably Oedipus.

The chief subject of the second vase is Bellerophon quelling the Chimaera. A woman watches, with one foot on a rock and one hand resting on her knee; and a youth, seated, his pilos hung up behind his head. The picture on the back of the krater is again the Sphinx, but here accompanied by two satyrs, one holding lyre and plectrum, the other dancing. This also should be a reminiscence of the Attic Satyric drama, though not so vivid as in the other vase: the satyr-play of Aeschylus' Theban trilogy was a *Sphinx*, and other poets may have treated the same theme. Ilberg, it is true (in PW. s.v. Sphinx p. 1374), forbids us to think of a satyric play: the picture is 'merely another illustration of the connexion, found elsewhere, between the Sphinx and the Dionysiac circle'. But of the three works to which he appears to refer, two, the Vagnonville krater in Florence (*Jh.* 8, 145, and 10, 118; *Mon. Piot* 29 pl. 5; Buschor *Feldmäuse* 8: *ARV.* 184, Flying-Angel Painter no. 28) and the Paestan vase by Python in Naples (FR. pl. 180, 2; Trendall *Paestan Pottery* pl. 21, a), are in all probability derived from the Satyric drama: there remains the archaic Greek scarab in Boston (Furtwängler *AG.* pl. 63, 1; *LHG.* pl. 2, 17 and pp. 12–13), but that is not enough to establish a regular as opposed to a casual connexion between the Sphinx and the Dionysiac circle.

An unusual feature is the radiate nimbus—borrowed, one might almost think, from Helios—which surrounds the head of the Sphinx in the first vase, and the upper part of Bellerophon in the second. In Greek vase-painting certain deities and daimones are given such nimbi (see Keyssner in PW. s.v. nimbus), and, twice, the hero Perseus (see M. J. Milne in *Bull. Metr. Mus.* 1945-6, 126–30). Malten suggests, though with diffidence (*Jb.* 40, 157), that Bellerophon wears the nimbus because he was originally a heaven-god; so also Radermacher *Mythos und Sage bei den Griechen* 99. Nock (in *Bull. Metr. Mus.* 1945-6, 130), with more justice, recalls the supernatural light that sometimes plays round the heads of Homeric heroes (*Il.* 5, 4–8; *Il.* 18, 214).

The Sommavilla Painter is not so accomplished an Atticizer as the Perugia, but his style is still close to his Attic models. One or two details. The hair of the woman watching Bellerophon has the same dark dots on a lighter background as appear in many of the Perugia Painter's heads. The pubes of the satyrs in the Helios krater has a peculiar form, most pronounced in the right-hand satyr: a single long worm-like curl or wriggle, horizontal, with a row of largish dots running up to the navel: the same form may be seen on the reverse of the pointed amphora by the Perugia Painter, and also on the Faina pelike (pp. 36 and 37). The dots are used in the Rodin and Brunswick cups (pp. 26 and 28). The faces of the satyrs somewhat recall the Painter of Vatican G 111 (p. 48).

## THE PALERMO STAMNOS

Palermo, from Chiusi. *Annali* 1848 pl. K, whence (detail of A) Kekulé *Ueber ein griechisches Vasengemälde* 19, (A) Roscher s.v. Tyndareos 1422 fig. 5, (B) Daremberg and Saglio s.v. Charon fig. 1357, (B, redrawn) Séchan 130; better, *AZ.* 1871 pl. 47 and pl. 46, 1, whence (A) Kekulé op. cit. 16. A, Leda and the Egg. B, Death of Ajax.

I have no note of the technique, but think it likely that the relief-line technique is used and not that of flat lines.

The ovoid marks to the right of A and the left of B in the reproductions are the same sort of upright projections beside the handle as in the Hamburg stamnos (p. 33).

Near the middle of the picture on A is an altar, with windscreens. Leda bends, with her hands on the egg. She wears a peplos, open up the left side. Polydeukes and Kastor stand facing her, and watching. They wear cloaks laid lightly over their shoulders, and each holds a pair of spears. Behind Leda is Tyndareos, dressed in a himation, wreathed, and holding a sceptre. These are the principal characters, but there are two subordinate figures, one below each handle. On the left it is the young attendant of the Dioskouroi, with one foot raised and set on a rock. He wears chlamys and pilos; in his left hand he holds a short crooked stick to which a fardel is attached, and in his right a walking-stick. On the right it is Hermes: he has brought the egg and laid it on the altar, and now he runs off, looking back; he wears a chlamys and holds the caduceus. The altar is in the open, and the ground near it is rocky: Polydeukes, Tyndareos, and Hermes stand on a higher level than the other persons. In the background, between the heads of the two brothers, a Doric building is indicated by the upper part of a corner column with a piece of epistyle and frieze: the statue in Polion's picture of the subject (see p. 40) makes it likely that the building is the Temple of Zeus: the scene being laid in the precinct, round the altar in front of the Temple.

With the Tyndareos compare the man in the middle of the reverse on the calyx-krater by the Dinos Painter, Bologna 300 (*Mus. Ital.* 2 pl. 2, whence Pfuhl fig. 579: *ARV.* 790 no. 7). The arrangement of Polydeukes' garment, lying over one shoulder and held with one hand, is the same as in the Faina pelike (Pl. 5, 1 and p. 37). The Kastor resembles the corresponding figure on the Attic hydria by the Chrysis Painter in the Louvre (*CV.* d pl. 55, 2 and 4–7: see p. 40). The youth behind Kastor is called a shepherd by Eitrem (in PW. s.v. Leda, 1121) who is no doubt thinking of the ποιμήν said by Apollodoros (3, 10, 7) to have found the egg and brought it to Leda: but here it is Hermes who has brought the egg; moreover shepherds do not look like that, and a glance at the corresponding figure on an Attic pelike in the Paris market (Jacobsthal *Die melischen Reliefs* 87: *ARV.* 793 no. 18) and the other figures that Jacobsthal has put with it (*Die melischen Reliefs* 86–8) shows our youth to be an attendant carrying the hero's luggage.

A figure rather like the Hermes is the Philoktetes on an Attic bell-krater, by the Painter of London F 64, in the Mustilli collection (Gerhard *AB*. pl. 31, whence FR. ii, 257 fig. 90: below, p. 104 no. 4).

The picture as a whole is very Attic, and looks as if it had been copied, with little change, and at no long interval, from an Attic vase painted about 425 or not much later.

The representations of this subject on vases have been collected by Kekulé in two articles, *Ueber ein griechisches Vasengemälde im Akademischen Kunstmuseum zu Bonn* (1879), and *Die Geburt der Helena aus dem Ei* (1908), which I shall refer to as *U*. and *G*.[1] The following list includes some additions.

*Attic*

1. Bonn 78. Bell-krater by Polion (*ARV*. 797 no. 4). Kekulé *U*. pl. 1 and p. 21; *CV*. pl. 19, 1–2 and 4.
2. Boston 99.539. Stemless cup by the Xenotimos Painter (*ARV*. 752, foot). Kekulé *G*. 692–3 pl. 6 and figs. 1–2; Hoppin *Rf*. ii, 477.
3. Bologna 317. Bell-krater. *Atti Romagna*, 3rd series, 5 pl. 3, whence Kekulé *G*. 693 fig. 3.
4. Bonn 1216.1–14. Bell-krater. Kekulé *G*. 695; *CV*. pl. 29, 1.
5. Bonn 1216.15. Fragment of a bell-krater, replica of the last. *CV*. pl. 29, 2.
6. Louvre CA 2260. Hydria by the Chrysis Painter (*ARV*. 795 no. 3). *CV*. d pl. 55, 2 and 4–7.
7. Paris, Mr. Fernand Chapouthier. Hydria. *BCH*. 1942–3, 3 and pll. 1–2 (Chapouthier). This is by the same hand as a hydria with Apollo and the oracular head of Orpheus in the collection of Prof. A. B. Cook, Cambridge (Guthrie *Orpheus and Greek Religion* pl. 5; Cook *Zeus* iii pl. 16: restored).
8. Vienna 869. Bell-krater by the Kadmos Painter (*ARV*. 804 no. 9). A, Kekulé *U*. 12.
9. Vienna 2000. Bell-krater in the manner of the Nikias Painter (*ARV*. 848 no. 4). A, Kekulé *G*. pl. 7, 1.
10. Leningrad 852. Pelike by the Kiev Painter (*ARV*. 852 no. 2). A, Kekulé *U*. 13.
11. Oxford G 138.31. Fragment of a bell-krater. *CV*. pl. 50, 31.
12. Cambridge N 152. Fragment of a bell-krater. *CV*. ii pl. 27, 18.
13. Naples market. Bell-krater. *AZ*. 1853 pl. 59, whence Kekulé *U*. 14.

A fragment of a late fifth-century bell-krater, from Athens, in Leipsic, T 655, is probably from a 'Leda and the Egg': the upper half of a youth's head remains, turned to left, and his hand holding a pair of spears; on the left, an eagle flies downwards.

Kekulé (*G*. 702) dates the Attic vases too early: the earliest are not older than 430.

I do not know how to explain the Attic lekythos Berlin 2430 (*Annali* 1850 pl. L; Kekulé *G*. pl. 7, 2), where a woman stands gazing at a large egg (placed on an altar) which has a manchild inside it, or issuing from it. Kekulé observes that the child is just like the little

[1] My own account was written when through the kindness of Prof. Charles Dugas I received a copy of an important article by Chapouthier, *Léda devant l'œuf de Némésis* in *BCH*. 66–7 (1942–3), 1–21. I have not attempted to weave Chapouthier's results into mine, but have included the hydria he publishes, previously known to me only from the brief allusion in his *Les Dioscures au service d'une déesse* 347.

boys on contemporary choiskoi. He speaks (698 and 703) of 'a type misunderstood', which I am always loath to do. The date is about 430–425, not 450–440 as Kekulé.

### Italiote

14. Berlin inv. 4533. Campanian hydria. Kekulé *G.* pl. 9.
15. Naples, from Frignano Piccolo. Paestan bell-krater by the Caivano Painter (Elia: on the painter see Trendall *Paestan Pottery* 84–91 and 126; also *JHS.* 63, 80; and, below, p. 226). *NSc.* 1937, 105, xv, and 108. The finest work of this Campanizing Paestan. I cannot follow Miss Elia in thinking that the expressive gesture of Leda's left hand 'may be due to an error of drawing': there is something like it on Bologna 317 (Kekulé *G.* 693): the whole attitude signifies reflection, and calculation.

### Etruscan

16. Palermo, from Chiusi. Our stamnos.
17. Cab. Méd. 947, from Vulci. Stamnos by the Settecamini Painter (see Pl. 11, 3–4 and p. 53).
18. Florence, from Monte San Savino. Cup, of the Clusium Group (see Pl. 25, 4–5 and p. 115).

For the Etruscan mirrors with the subject see pp. 115–16. See also the Boston stamnos described on p. 60.

The Italiote bell-krater in Bari (*Ausonia* 2, 243, b, 252, and 257–9; Kekulé *G.* pl. 8; Bieber *Denkmäler zum Theaterwesen* pl. 80, 2; Bieber *Hist. of the Greek and Roman Theater* 271 fig. 365) stands apart from all these: it represents a stage-play which evidently had a novel plot.

Giglioli opined that an extremely crude fragment in the Villa Giulia, from Vignanello, might represent Leda at the altar (*NSc.* 1924, 198; Giglioli pl. 372, 3). He describes it in one place as from a vase 'imitating metal', in another as from 'a silvered vase', but does not explain how the technique differs from red-figure. In any case the subject is not Leda.

Robert mentions (*Heldensage* 341) 'a group of Attic vases which show Leda setting the egg down on an altar, while Hermes retires': but in none of the Attic pictures does Leda touch the egg, or Hermes move away; and Robert must be thinking of our Etruscan vase. When describing it just now, we spoke, for safety, of Leda 'with her hands on the egg'; and it is not easy to say whether she is picking it up or putting it down. In the Attic pictures Leda is not placing the egg on the altar; nor has she already done so: she evidently sees it for the first time, since she shows astonishment and occasionally even fear. To the question how it got there the answer is certain: Hermes put it there. Just what the Attic artists thought of as having happened after the discovery is doubtful. The Italiote painters of the Campanian vase in Berlin and the Paestan vase in Naples seem to have thought that it hatched out on the spot: at least they show Helen issuing from the egg, and the egg still on the altar. But there were many versions of the legend, and even in Attica there may have been more than one. In the Etruscan vase all that can be said is that Leda is either picking up the egg to carry it indoors and keep it warm (night as well as day); or setting it down, having received it from Hermes with instructions to place it on the altar of Zeus.

The picture on the other side of the Palermo stamnos is also based on Greek models, but seems to have more Etruscan in it. Ajax stands in the middle, and the sword is planted upright in the ground in front of him. He holds the scabbard in his left hand and raises his right, looking up. Athena stands before him with one foot raised and resting on a slaughtered ram: her spear is in her left hand, and with her right she makes a gesture towards Ajax. Behind the hero, a winged man steps forward, ready to lay hands on him. It is a death-demon, whether Charun, as is generally thought, or some Etruscan counterpart of the Greek Thanatos. The better reproduction (*AZ.* 1871 pl. 46, 1) shows that he has a hooked nose and a scrubby beard, but he has not the monstrous aspect of later representations of Charun.

Heydemann, who was the first to recognize the subject (*AZ.* 1871, 60–5), was reminded of Sophocles' *Ajax*: he did not claim that the picture was derived from the play, but only referred to the monologue in lines 815 ff. as 'the best commentary on the picture'. Von Mach, equally cautious (*Harv. St.* 11, 95), saw the influence of the epic version followed by Sophocles rather than of Sophocles himself. Séchan (130–1) seems inclined, on the whole, to admit the influence of the play.

The action of the winged demon is clear: he steals up behind Ajax and is ready to catch hold of him when he expires. Robert sees in this figure the δαίμων who in the Aeschylean version pointed to the vulnerable spot (p. 140), but the gesture is not appropriate, and, besides, we shall find reason for supposing the δαίμων to have been Athena (ibid.). The action of the Athena on the left of our picture is also clear: she orders the suicide: it is the only way. The meaning of Ajax's attitude is not so certain. Heydemann thinks that he is speaking to Athena; von Mach that he is chiding and arguing with her; Séchan that he is bidding farewell, as in Sophocles, to light and life. I wish I could interpret the gesture of Ajax. It is not, I think, arguing or chiding; it might be, whether he sees the goddess or not, greeting or acceptance: but I find it difficult to exclude the notion of farewell. The figure most like this is perhaps the huntress—Atalanta rather than Artemis—on an earlier vase, an Attic oinochoe by the Niobid Painter, somewhat before the middle of the fifth century, in the Louvre (*Bull. Nap.* new series 6 pl. 5, 1: *ARV.* 423 no. 72), but there also the significance of the gesture is uncertain; possibly awed greeting of a deity suddenly descried far away. An Attic lekythos with a somewhat similar figure does not help (Neugebauer *ADP.* pl. 71, 167).

On the attitude of Athena, with the left leg raised and set on an elevation, the left arm laid, foreshortened, across the left thigh, see pp. 60–1. I cannot recollect any other figure of Athena in which the aegis is brought up to hood the head: what Heydemann adduces is not to the point.

### A NECK-AMPHORA

Once Noël Des Vergers, from Chiusi. A, Noël Des Vergers *L'Étrurie et les étrusques* pl. 4, whence *Sitz. Bay. Ak.* 1881, 110 = Brunn *Kleine Schriften* iii, 65.

Noël Des Vergers was not a careful man: I am not sure that any of the vases he figures are wholly apocryphal, but many of them are largely modern. The neck-amphora from Chiusi has several suspicious features, and one might be tempted to dismiss it as a falsification. Noël Des Vergers spoke of 'Herakles bringing the apple of the Hesperides to Zeus', and that is the subject of the picture as it stands: Herakles, holding an apple, faces Zeus; behind them, the apple-tree; Apollo and Artemis present. Brunn saw the hand of an Etruscan and attributed the peculiarities of the picture to the artist's having misunderstood his original: on the fragment of an Apulian Panathenaic amphora in Berlin (3245: Gerhard *Akademische Abhandlungen* pl. 19) Herakles is seen presenting himself before King Atlas, and Brunn surmised that this had been the subject of the Etruscan painter's model and that the Atlas had been transformed into a Zeus by placing a thunderbolt in his hand. Furtwängler, in Roscher s.v. Herakles p. 2228, rejected Brunn's theory: the vase, he thought, was not Etruscan but Attic; the subject was what it appeared to be, Herakles bringing the apple to Zeus, and the suspect features were the fault of Noël Des Vergers's draughtsman, who had changed the lion-skin of Herakles into a bull's hide and given Zeus sleeves. Furtwängler found nothing impossible in the subject, and believed that he could point to another representation of it, on an Attic stamnos of the early fifth century in Leningrad (640: *Annali* 1859 pl. G–H: *ARV.* 433, Providence Painter no. 41). This vase, however, is very much restored: the subject is Herakles entering Olympus and received by Zeus, but the restorations include the hand of Herakles with the apple.

I take the vase published by Noël Des Vergers to be genuine in the main, but a good deal restored, either in fact, or on paper by the draughtsman. Among the restorations must be the hand of the seated figure, part of his himation, and part of the seat. If the hand is modern, then so perhaps is the thunderbolt. The king would then be Eurystheus, and not Zeus. The alternative would be that the thunderbolt is genuine, and the sleeves a restoration: this seems to me less likely, but I am doubtful.

The vase is Etruscan, imitating an Attic original of the late fifth century. The handle-palmettes recall those of the Leipsic column-krater by the Painter of Vatican G 111 (Pl. 6, 5, Pl. 7, 2, and p. 49), and, especially in the use of 'acanthized leaf-hooks', the Painter of London F 484 (p. 45).

### THE PAINTER OF LONDON F 484

Albizzati assigned the Cambridge vase, no. 5, to the same hand as the Vatican, no. 4 (*Mél. d'arch.* 37, 108 no. 4, 110 no. 10, and 156–7); and the London vase, no. 1, to the same centre, Vulci (ibid. 110 no. 9). In *RG.* 89 I assigned the two Munich stamnoi, nos. 2 and 3, to the painter of no. 1, the London vase; and connected no. 5.

### *Stamnoi*

1. London F 484, from Vulci.[1] Gerhard *AV.* pl. 321; Pl. 7, 2 and Pl. 8, 1–2. A, Apollo (?) and Lasa, with Pan and satyr. B, horseman with Eros and Lasa.

[1] Walters, in the British Museum catalogue, sets a question-mark after the provenience Vulci given by de Witte in the Durand catalogue: but the only reason for his scepticism is probably a mysterious sentence in the older catalogue of the British Museum vases under no. 1681: 'Durand no. 429, where this vase is said to be from *Vulci*, but the style seems rather that of *Orbitello*.'

See p. 3. The figure in the middle of A must surely be Apollo: but it is odd that the flesh should be painted white and a bracelet worn round the wrist. A figure in a somewhat similar attitude, and holding a laurel-staff, on a mirror from Orvieto, formerly in the possession of Riccardo Mancini, is Leda (Gerhard *ES.* suppl. pl. 76). Apollo is not 'climbing up hill' (Walters), but standing with one foot on an elevation. The left forearm rests on the thigh, wrapped in the himation. The left foot was drawn, with relief-lines, but was inadvertently covered over when the background was filled in. Pan holds a flute in one hand (one of Gerhard's alternatives), not 'castanets' (as Walters). Strange composition: Pan echoing Apollo, and the satyr the Lasa. Lasa has the face of a mournful doll. On B, Gerhard's drawing gives the leg of the horseman, which is preserved, but hardly comes out in the photograph, the relief-lines having lost their black. On B, the creature flying to crown the victorious horseman is male—the penis was omitted by mistake when the relief-lines were being added.

The surface of the vase is very strongly ruddled. The watery white used for the flesh of Apollo and both Lasas was laid on after the relief-lines had been put in, and overlies them. The white of Apollo is so thin as to be hardly noticeable.

2. Munich 3227 (J 525), from Vulci. B, Pl. 7, 1. A, a youth (Apollo) leading a woman. B, a youth riding one horse and leading another. The drawing is unfinished: on B, part of the background between the led horse's legs has not been filled in, and on A collar-bones and hand of the youth, folds, and much else are given by sketch-lines only. The palmettes have relief-outlines.

3. Munich 3228 (J 521), from Vulci. A, Overbeck *KM.* pl. 26, 7 (wrongly called a kalpis). Replica of the last, but finished. The youth on A holds an arrow and must be Apollo; the woman holds a sprig in her hand, and is not led, but looks as if she were floating down.

4. Vatican. *Mél. d'arch.* 37, 152–3. A, Apollo and Artemis. B, two warriors, one mounted, one on foot. For the subject see on no. 5.

#### *Stamnos* of special type
(with three handles like a hydria, but otherwise the vase is simply a stamnos)

5. Cambridge 249, from Vulci. E. Gardner pl. 41; *CV.* pl. 44, 3 and pl. 45, 3. Two warriors, one mounted, one on foot. Buff clay, with remains of ruddle. In the handle-palmettes, most of the small buds at the top are restored.

The youths on the Cambridge vase are very like those on the Vatican stamnos, no. 4, in costume as well as in other respects. In the Vatican vase the youth on foot wears a short chiton with sleeves reaching to the elbows, and over it a corslet of peculiar make, closely set with vertical lines (so that at first sight it looks like a chiton), and furnished with shoulder-flaps: the material seems to be long strips of leather stitched together. The horseman wears the same corslet: his sleeves, too, are the same, but there is no sign of the chiton at the thighs. He holds a whip, his comrade spear and long oval shield with midrib. Both have thick fair hair, blown back. In the Cambridge vase the horseman wears the same corslet as the Vatican youths, but no chiton; also a cloak which flies back from his shoulders. His companion wears the short chiton with sleeves reaching to the elbows, but no corslet; and a belt, set with large studs, to which a sword is attached at the *right* hip (see pp. 97–8). He carries a shield as well as a spear, the horseman a spear only. Both have thick fair hair.

How are these vases to be dated? The female figure on the Munich stamnos, no. 3 (Overbeck *KM*. pl. 26, 7), can hardly have been painted before the twenties of the fifth century. The shapes of the vases, and much in the drawing, look earlier: but it is the most advanced features that must determine the date.

A *terminus post quem* may be furnished by the 'acanthized leaf-hooks' terminating the handle-palmettes at the sides in London F 484 and the Munich stamnoi. 'Acanthus' appears in Greek ornament from the middle of the fifth century onwards (Giustiniani stele in Berlin, K 19, Blümel pl. 27, Jacobsthal *O*. pl. 139, a, and pp. 195–7), but the acanthized leaf-hook not until the twenties (stele from Aegina, in Athens, 715, Möbius *Orn*. pl. 5, b and pp. 17–18, Diepolder *Die att. Grabreliefs* pl. 6 and p. 14),[1] and on vases I do not remember it much before 410 (squat lekythos London E 701, Nicole *Meid*. 141–2, *ARV*. 838 no. 56; pyxis London E 782, Panofka *Cab. Pourt*. pl. 33, 3–4, *ARV*. 840 no. 82).[2] The line of arcs running parallel to the engrailed edge in London F 484 and the Munich stamnoi occurs on Attic squat lekythoi: Athens, private possession (*AM*. 62 pl. 28: see p. 72), last decade of the fifth century; Berlin 2691 (Jacobsthal *O*. pl. 127, c), not earlier than 400; another in Vienna (exhibition number 629), not much older if at all. In the Attic vases, however, the engrailed edge faces in, not out. The engrailed contour, with its border, appears in a side-acroterion from the later Temple of Poseidon at Sunium (*Delt*. i, 24), which is usually dated about 425: there, however, the thing is not a leaf, but a fancy edge to the whole piece of stone.[3]

It looks as if our vases were not earlier than the last decade or so of the fifth century.

Another vase belongs to the same fabric as the five by the Painter of London F 484:

### *Pointed amphora*

London F 482. A, Pl. 7, 4. A, man and woman. B, two youths.

One handle is modern. The contours on B, and parts of those on A, are without relief-line. The lid mentioned by Walters is no longer with the vase, and there is no reason to suppose that it belonged (see *JHS*. 63, 91 note 6). The drawing of the patterns links the vase with the Painter of London F 484. The inverted egg-pattern on the lip, the tongues on the shoulder, the maeander with chequer-squares below the pictures, and the floral designs at the handles are not only like those in his vases, but must be by the same hand. The figurework is different: the style of the figures is deplorable, and so old-fashioned that one would be inclined to date the vase much farther back: but a *terminus post quem* is given by the 'acanthized leaf-hooks' of the handle-design, for we have seen that they cannot be earlier than the last decades of the fifth century. The artist must have copied

---

[1] Jacobsthal tells me that he no longer maintains the early date assigned to the stele Athens 715 in his *O*., 191 and 146.

[2] See also Jacobsthal *O*. 191.

[3] The cut in *Deltion* is faulty in some respects but seems reliable in this.

the figures from a work painted many years before, or formed his figure-style long before he painted the vase: one cannot help recalling the Owl-Pillar Group of fifth-century Campanian red-figure (*JHS.* 63, 66–9). In any case it is certain that the pointed amphora comes from the same workshop as the five vases by the Painter of London F 484, and that the patternwork is by the same hand as there. The solid shape, moreover, might be by the same potter.

A vase decorated with patterns only has already been placed by Albizzati in the same general neighbourhood as the vases which we have attributed to the Painter of London F 484 (*Mél. d'arch.* 37, 114 no. 28):

### Oinochoe (shape VI)

Vatican, from Etruria. *Mus. Greg.* ii pl. 95, vi, 7; *Mél. d'arch.* 37, 175.

The connexion is close: and I do not hesitate to recognize in tongues, inverted egg, maeander and chequer-squares, palmettes and flowers, the same hand as in the pattern-work of the London pointed amphora, and of the five vases by the Painter of London F 484.

Two lost vases, evidently by one hand, are intimately related to the Painter of London F 484, and might even be slight works from his hand, but of this one cannot be sure from the old reproductions:

### Stamnoi

1. Roman market. Gerhard *Trinkschalen* pl. C, 1. A, Aphrodite seated, and Eros; B, Lasa bringing her a sash and a cup. The group on A recalls an Etruscan mirror formerly in the Borgia collection and said to have been found at Praeneste (Raoul-Rochette *Mon. inéd.* pl. 76, 3; Gerhard *ES.* pl. 117).

2. Roman market. Gerhard *Trinkschalen* pl. C, 4–5 and 13, whence (A) Pl. 11, 7. A, Herakles seated, and Eros; B, woman seated, and Eros. The Munich stamnos 3227, by the Painter of London F 484 (p. 44, no. 2: Pl. 7, 1), gives the explanation of the things to left and right of A, and to right of B, in the reproduction; they are the 'acanthized leaf-hooks' of the floral decoration at the handles, detached from it in error by the copyist. In the other stamnos a similar leaf-hook has perhaps influenced the outline of Aphrodite's garment below her right hand. Albizzati speaks with contempt of the Vatican stamnos by the Painter of London F 484 (*Mél. d'arch.* 37, 157): but I find there and in other works of the same hand that rude charm of popular art which he finds in a later Etruscan vase and I do not (ibid. 134). The same quality appears, to my feeling, in a vase which though earlier than those of our painter should be somehow connected with them:

### Calyx-krater

Roman market (Basseggio). Micali *Mon. ined.* pl. 37, 2, whence Pl. 11, 1–2. A, Herakles, Athena, and Iolaos. B, Zeus seated, Apollo seated, and a youth (or woman).

## THE PAINTER OF THE VATICAN BIGA

The three vases constituting the group are very much alike in style and are in all probability by one hand. They are closely connected with the Painter of London F 484, but freer, or looser. The volute-krater was attributed by Albizzati to the same hand as the hydria, the stamnos placed in their vicinity, and all three assigned to the fabric of Vulci (*Mél. d'arch.* 37, 111 no. 13, 109 no. 8, 108 no. 3, and 157–8, where for 'fig. 9–10' read 'fig. 17–18'). In *RG.* 89 I noted the kinship between the stamnos and vases by the Painter of London F 484.

### Stamnos

1. Vatican, from Vulci. Gerhard *AV.* pl. 240, whence (A) Overbeck *KM.* pl. 18, 14; *Mél. d'arch.* 37, 154–5. A, Hades and Persephone in a chariot. B, see below.

### Hydria

2. Vatican, from Vulci. *Mus. Greg.* ii, pl. 95, vi, 4; Gerhard *Festgedanken an Winckelmann* pl. 2, 1; *Ber. Sächs. Ges.* 1867 pl. 5, 5 (Jahn); *Mél. d'arch.* 37, 159. Man driving a biga; boy painting a tomb.

### Volute-krater

3. Vatican. B, *Mél. d'arch.* 37, 158. A, Dionysos, and youths preparing sacrifice. B, a boy riding one horse and leading another. Parts of the handles are missing.

First, the stamnos. Hades, according to Albizzati, has 'one of those foul and frightful mugs that are among the strongest things in Etruscan art'. It is disputed whether the subject of A is the Rape of Persephone; or not rather the peaceful annual return of Persephone to the shades (so Stephani in *Annali* 1860, 307: against, Foerster *Raub der Persephone* 235–7). The escort of the quadriga would certainly be called Hermes, were it not that a very similar figure appears on the left of B, and on B the youth in the middle is Hermes. Gerhard conjectured (*AV.* iii, 165–6 and 173) that the Etruscan artist may have thought of Hermes-Turms ψυχοπομπός and Hermes-Turms in a more cheerful, terrestrial aspect, as two different persons, and it is not easy to banish this notion from one's mind: on a famous mirror in the Vatican (Gerhard *ES.* pl. 240) the Hermes who ushers the shade of Teiresias, *hinthial Terasiaś*, is inscribed *Turms Aitas*, 'Hades's Hermes', almost as if there was more than one Hermes—a nether, servant of Hades, and an upper, servant of Zeus. Others discern in the left-hand figure on the Vatican stamnos an Etruscan demon, janitor of Orcus; or Charun: see Foerster *Raub* 235–7; Reisch in Helbig and Amelung, 349; Albizzati in *Mél. d'arch.* 37, 109, and 157. The youth on the right, with axe, spear, and shield, is thought to be a dead warrior, on whose behalf Hermes is parleying: if so, the self-satisfied air would be repugnant to a Greek. On the chariot see Nachod *Der Rennwagen bei den Italikern* 80 no. 98.

The interpretation of the picture on the hydria is not free from difficulties either. Albizzati is probably right in explaining the erection which the boy is decorating as a tomb in the semblance of a round tempietto, like the tomb of Thanchvil Masnia, from Vulci, in the Vatican (Ducati *St.* pl. 175, 447). Who is the charioteer? Three answers have been given to the question: a competitor at funeral games; the dead himself, heroized; Hades. The third answer is perhaps the most plausible. In any case, the chariot is not 'moving towards the boy': two funeral subjects have been juxtaposed in one picture, and the spatial relation between them does not correspond to anything in fact.

The charioteer is an empty form, and the horses are ludicrous: but the boy painter is a rare and unexpected glimpse of a vanished age, and one might search long in Roman art before finding so fresh a figure.

The chariot is of the same type as in the stamnos, and drawn in the same way. Gerhard's draughtsman has omitted the blacks in the lozenges of the car. The artist himself forgot to black in the background between the spokes.

The following vase bears the same relation to the Painter of the Vatican Biga as the London vase of the same shape did to the Painter of London F 484 (p. 45):

### Pointed amphora

Vatican, from Etruria. *Mus. Greg.* ii pl. 95, iii, 3; *Mél. d'arch.* 37, 173, 1. The same relation, or an even closer: for there the figures were not in the style of the Painter of London F 484: here there are no figures, but patterns only, and Albizzati has justly observed that the ivy and tongues look as if they had been drawn by the same hand as those of the Vatican hydria with the biga: we may add the inverted egg-pattern on the lip, which is exactly the same as in the Vatican stamnos (p. 47 no. 1: *Mél. d'arch.* 37, 154–5) as well as in the Vatican hydria.

The shape of the two pointed amphorae, the London (Pl. 7, 4) and the Vatican, is not the same, but there is a distinct resemblance in proportions and essential features, for instance in the form as well as the decoration of the lip.

Albizzati compares a pattern-skyphos in the Vatican (*Mél. d'arch.* 37, 173, 2) with the Vatican pointed amphora. A large skyphos in London (no number: ex Campanari) is in the same style as the Vatican one, and links it to the pointed amphora: ivy above; below, the same tongues as on the lower part of the amphora; a black palmette at each handle.

Another vase in the same style as the Vatican pointed amphora is an oinochoe of shape II, but with high handle, in Dresden (ZV. 2889: *Anz.* 1925, 136): Walter Müller calls it South Italian, but I take it to be Etruscan.

The black ivy on the pointed amphora in the Vatican makes one think of a vase to which I do not know any parallel:

Philadelphia 1754, from Tarquinia. *Museum Journal* 5, 216. I, gorgoneion. Outside, ivy in black.

It is a bowl, well made, and shaped in the main like a stemless cup, but without handles: roughly, therefore, the same sort of vase as those discussed on pp. 112 and 210. It has been spoken of as South Italian, but must be Etruscan. Relief-lines are used both for the gorgoneion and for the stalks of the ivy. I am far from wishing to insist on the likeness of the ivy-wreath to that on the pointed amphora, or on its being accompanied in both by a wave-pattern, but I think the vase ought to be mentioned here.

### THE PAINTER OF VATICAN G 111

*RG.* 88–9. I said there that the Leipsic vase was in the same style as the Vatican oinochoe, but at the time I knew it from a photograph only and had forgotten that it was in Leipsic and had been published by Studniczka.

*Column-krater*

1. Leipsic T 952. *Jh.* 6, 140; A, Pl. 6, 5; side-view, from a photograph kindly sent me by Hansjörg Bloesch, Pl. 7, 3.  A, two mounted warriors meeting.  B, Dionysos and a young satyr at an altar.

*Oinochoe* (shape II)

2. Vatican G 111, from Vulci. *RG*. pl. 34; Pl. 5, 2–3.  Apollo driving a biga drawn by horses, and Hyakinthos meeting him in a biga drawn by swans.

The Leipsic vase was given to the museum by Edward Warren, who bought it in Rome 'at a time when excavations were taking place in Southern Etruria' (Studniczka), or to quote Warren's note, which is more precise, 'in the territory of Falerii'.  It does not follow that Falerii is the provenience, much less that the vase is of Faliscan fabric. Studniczka calls it South Etruscan; Albizzati (*Mél. d'arch.* 37, 115) is disposed to assign it to the fabric of Vulci, and may well be right.

The light patch to the right of the picture on A, beside the horse's tail, must be a chip or flake.

Studniczka (*Jh.* 6, 139–41) thought that the horsemen were attacking each other, but the way the right-hand one holds his sword is surely against this: perhaps they are exchanging greetings before combat, perhaps rather meeting on the parade-ground.  The right-hand rider is smaller than the other, looks indeed like a boy.

The bodies of the horses are black, except for a sort of 'crust' near the contour: compare the horse on an Etruscan mirror, from Bomarzo, in Berlin (Gerhard *ES*. pl. 118). The horses are *phaleris insignes*: the strings of studs round their necks are common in Etruscan pictures of horses, and we have had examples already (Pl. 7, 1 and Pl. 7, 3). The long, unkempt manes have an old-fashioned look.

The costume and equipment of both riders are peculiar.  The left-hand one wears a sleeved and trousered combination garment, which is not, I think, chain-armour as Studniczka conjectured;[1] a chlamys; a helmet of pilos-like shape but with a nick as if for the ear; and, lastly, a sword-belt with the scabbard attached to it at the *right* hip (see p. 97).  He carries a spear, and a shield which seems to be oval.  The helmet is

---

[1] Studniczka compares the costume of the Triumphator on the Praenestine cista in Berlin (*Mon.* 10 pl. 29, whence *WV*. E pll. 9–10; Neugebauer *Führer: Bronzen* pl. 57; Giglioli pl. 293, 2; Goldscheider *Etruscan Sculpture* pl. 58), but the Triumphator is not wearing chain-armour: he sports fancy trews of striking pattern, with knee-pieces, perhaps of leather, sewn on. Knee-guards, doubtless of leather, are worn by Etruscan archers: together with trews, in the wall-painting of the Tomba dei Tori at Tarquinia (*AD.* ii, pl. 41 and supplementary pl. 41, 1a), and in the statuettes of a Capuan bronze dinos in London (560: *Mon.* 5 pl. 25); with stockings, the thighs being bare, on a black-figured olpe of the Micali Group (see p. 12) in the Vatican (mentioned in *RG*. 80 no. 68); with bare legs, it seems, on the bf. amphora Würzburg 799 (Langlotz pll. 232–3) and the bf. hydria Hamburg 462 (*Anz.* 1917, 105 fig. 34; Giglioli pl. 131, 2).  These are all archers: the curious couple in the Tomba della Scimmia—the 'big man and the little man' (*Mon.* 5 pll. 15–16; *MPAI. Etr., Clus.* i, p. 10: see p. 2)—also wear knee-guards with anklets, but their legs are bare.  The only bronze knee-caps preserved, or the only ones known to Hagemann, a pair from Magna Graecia in Brussels (Hagemann *Griechische Panzerung* 132 and 149 figs. 162–3), are quite different.

The leg-gear of the Amazons in the handle-group of the Chrysippos cista, from the Barberini collection, in the Villa Giulia, quoted by Studniczka, is different again (*Mon.* 8 pl. 31; *Boll. d' Arte* 1919, 179–83; Giglioli pl. 291, 2): the knees are bare: cuishes are worn; the right-hand Amazon wears leggings of the same material as the cuishes; the other probably wears leggings too.

painted white and decorated with a snake, and something else, perhaps a leaf. The equipment of the other horseman will be described later (pp. 98–9).

The altar on B is of an old Etruscan and Italian type which has been treated by Studniczka (*Jh.* 6, 139–45); compare also a tombstone in Copenhagen, Ny Carlsberg, H 212 (Poulsen *Bildertafeln* 83, 3) and another from Orvieto (*NSc.* 1939, 10, 1). Firewood is laid on it. The youth on the right, who wears a short himation, and round his neck a bulla on a cord, holds a phiale (drawn in three-quarter view, so that the omphalos is seen) in his right hand, for the libation, and in his left an oinochoe of 'shape VI'. Studniczka compares the figure of Apollo on the Semla mirror in Berlin (Gerhard *ES.* pl. 83, whence Ducati *St.* pl. 211; Giglioli pl. 296, 1–2). The wreath is not of ivy but of laurel or some other long-leaved plant; the wreath of Dionysos is not always of ivy (see pp. 87 and 109, and *AJA.* 1939, 631). The young satyr holds a cithara; and I suppose a plectrum. His hair is bobbed like his master's and his wreath is the same.

Studniczka dates the vase at the beginning of the fourth century and is probably right. It is not a canonical column-krater: the Attic vases it stands nearest are the latest column-kraters, those that belong to the beginning of the fourth century, but the shape of mouth and foot is different, and the manner in which the neck is joined to the body. On the other hand, some of these late Attic column-kraters have a maeander below the pictures (see p. 66), and many of them laurel or olive on the neck. Jacobsthal judges that the drawing of the palmettes points to a date after 400 rather than before. The figurework may look older: but it is the latest features that must determine the date.

I may be wrong, but I fancy I see a faint likeness between the style of the Leipsic krater, especially the altar scene, and that of certain Boeotian red-figure vases. This may be accidental, or it may be partly due to the Boeotian and Etruscan artists standing at the same distance from their Attic models and being similarly equipped.

As to the Vatican oinochoe, I have discussed it at length in *RG.* 89. The shape is a top-heavy version of the oinochoe type II: I do not know any other vase just like it. The subject is unique. There are other representations of Hyakinthos (a list in *RG.* 88–9, see also the subject-index to *ARV.* under the name), and he often rides a swan, but this is the only place where he is shown driving the swan-drawn chariot which seems to be referred to by Philostratus Minor (*Imagines* 14): ἐρῶν ὁ τῆς Λητοῦς τοῦ μειρακίου πάντα δώσειν αὐτῶι φησιν ὅσα ἔχει, τὸ ξυνεῖναί οἱ προσεμένωι, τοξείαν τε γὰρ καὶ μουσικὴν διδάξειν καὶ μαντικῆς ἐπαΐειν καὶ λύρας μὴ ἀπωιδὸν εἶναι καὶ τοῖς ἀμφὶ παλαίστραν ἐπιστήσειν, δώσειν δὲ ὑπὲρ κύκνων αὐτὸν ὀχούμενον περιπολεῖν χωρία ὅσα Ἀπόλλωνος φίλα.

## A CUP IN THE VATICAN

Vatican. I, *Mél. d'arch.* 37, 165. I, Dionysos riding a panther. A–B, tongues.

Albizzati (*Mél. d'arch.* 37, 160) attributes this to the school of Vulci: the picture, he adds, is copied from contemporary Attic cups, and 'as model we may consider the identical medallion of which we have a fragment in Jena, published in *AZ.* 1857 pl. 108, 1'. This statement is acceptable in the main, but requires modification. The painter is imitating Attic cups from the early years of the fourth century, cups by the Jena Painter (*ARV.*

880–3 and 966) and his contemporaries (ibid. 883–7 and 967); but the imitation is free: not to speak of Etruscan traits like the superabundance of big black spots (p. 28), the panther and the upper part of his rider are far more rigid than would be possible in Attic work of the time, and for the animal, which is really an abomination, the painter either had no Attic model before his eyes, or, if he had, neglected it.

When Albizzati writes that the Jena cup may be thought of as the model of our picture, he does not of course mean exactly what he says: he means a cup *like* the Jena (which never left Athens). When he speaks of the two medallions as identical, he is also exaggerating, as is clear from the fragment published, and clearer if we add the other fragments which join it, for there are more (*ARV*. 880, Jena Painter no. 2). The Jena animal is not a panther but a griffin; the rider, who wears chiton as well as himation, holds a pair of torches in the left hand (which also grasps the griffin's neck), and sits with legs turned towards the animal's hindquarters; the sex is uncertain. A variant of the same design appears on the cup Vienna 202 (I, La Borde 2 pl. 26, 2; *RM*. 42, Beilage 24, below), where the rider is Apollo: this is somewhat later than the Jena cup, and by an artist whom I have named the Painter of Vienna 202 (*ARV*. 887, no. 1). Fragments of a second cup in Jena, by the same painter as the first (384: *ARV*. 880 no. 11), are nearer the Vatican cup in one respect, for Apollo sits with his legs forward; so also on a fourth cup, in the Mouret collection at Ensérune (*CV*. pl. 11), which resembles the work of the Painter of Vienna 202 (*ARV*. 887, middle), but here Apollo is naked. Something like all these, but not just like any of them, will have been in the mind of the Etruscan artist.

### A BELL-KRATER IN TARQUINIA

Tarquinia, from Tarquinia. A, phot. Moscioni 8620. A, maenad on swan. B, draped figures.

There is a brief reference to this vase by Pallottino in *ML*. 36, 484. The subject is curious. A woman dressed in a peplos sits on the back of a swan, holding a thyrsus in her right hand, and raising her left hand towards the lower part of her face with the forefinger separated from the others as if imposing silence; the swan meanwhile has found some live fish in a rough cylindrical receptacle on the ground and is scrutinizing them with its beak. The head of the thyrsus is black, the shaft brown. The swan, the flesh of the maenad, her frontlet, and the sash that hangs in the field on the left are white. The picture is carried out in relief-lines. The floral decoration at the handles is un-Attic: it includes three-dimensional axillary convolvulus-flowers of the same general type as in the Phuipa cup, for instance (Pl. 12), and in many Etruscan and Campanian vases, but not exactly like any others; and 'acanthized leaf-hooks', both simplified, and elaborated with veins and the same relief-line border as in the Painter of London F 484 (p. 45). The drawing of the figures is rather heavy-handed but not unattractive or inexpressive: I should not mind seeing other vases in the same style, but have not found any up to the present. As for the date, a *terminus post quem* is provided by the foot of the vase: in Attic bell-kraters this form of foot does not appear until the early fourth century: of the bell-kraters mentioned in *ARV*. 866–79 some have it, while others keep the older foot: it cannot have appeared earlier in Etruria than in Attica.

## THE SETTECAMINI PAINTER

Albizzati attributed no. 3 to the same artist as no. 1 (*Mél. d'arch.* 37, 109 no. 6, 110 no. 12, and 136–9, and thought that no. 2 was probably also from his hand (ibid. 109 no. 7, and 139). He ascribed all three vases to the fabric of Vulci.

### *Stamnos* (special shape, with upright handles)

1. Florence, from Orvieto (Settecamini).[1] Conestabile *Pitt. mur.* pll. 15–6, whence Pl. 10, 1–2, and (A) *Jh.* 16, 167; A, Milani *Mus. Top.* 49, iii, 1 = Milani *R. Mus. di Firenze* pl. 92, iii, 1; *Mél. d'arch.* 37, 126 and 132; A, Ducati *Cer.* ii, 472 = Ducati *St.* pl. 218, 535. A, the infant Herakles and the Snakes. B, Ransom of Hector. On A, on cartellini, retrograde, *Hercle* and *Vile* (by mistake for *Viphicle*).

The shape is unusual: an Etruscan stamnos of the same type, but plain, is in the Vatican (*Mus. Greg.* ii pl. 99, 3).

On the subject of A, the infant Herakles and the snakes, see Watzinger in *Jh.* 16, 166–75, Robert *Heldensage* 619–21, Brendel in *Jb.* 47, 191–238, Richter in Richter and Hall 98–9, Lippold in *RM.* 51, 96–103, Philippart *Les coupes attiques à fond blanc* 19–21. Add the stemless cup, early Campanian red-figure, Würzburg 885, from Capua (Langlotz pl. 249), and see pp. 93–4.

With most writers I take the woman on the left to be Alkmene, and the woman with distaff and spindle (Brendel's Alkmene) to be a maid. On the 'window' at which Zeus and Hera sit see Herbig in *RM.* 42, 128.

Hera raises the end of her himation at her shoulder with a time-honoured gesture which Albizzati finds ridiculous: 'all the answer she can give to the rating of her divine spouse is to twitch the corner of her mantle': but, first, Zeus is not addressing Hera: the movement of his hand is directed towards Herakles: it is his will that his son shall overcome the dragons; and, secondly, the artist thought he knew how Saturnian Juno would bear herself if thwarted: not like a squalling scold.

The Ransom of Hector, on the other side of the vase, is no less carefully executed than the Herakliskos. Bulas has recently collected the representations of the subject, in his *Illustrations antiques de l'Iliade* (add the fine calyx-krater fragments, by the Kleophrades Painter, in the Ceramicus Museum, *Anz.* 1937, 185, and 1938, 612: *ARV.* 124 no. 38). The Settecamini vase is described on his pp. 68–9. Achilles, seated in the middle, turns towards Athena, who bids him yield the body of Hector to Priam: the gesture of Achilles' left hand is of one who listens and attends. Briseis approaches Achilles, holding kantharos and oinochoe, to serve him with wine. From the left of the picture Priam comes up with a pair of phialai, part of the ransom, in his hand. This portion of the picture is not very happy, and I am not sure whether the boy is an attendant of Achilles, or, as is more likely, of Priam. His left hand seems to lean on something behind Achilles' knees, but it is not clear what. He sees Athena and raises his right hand. Above, a glimpse, through a window, into Achilles' stable: the heads of his four chariot-horses, and head, arms, and shoulders of a groom bringing them water: water rather than oats, which would be

---

[1] According to Milani (*Mus. Top.* 49) this vase was found in one of the famous painted tombs, the Tombe Golini: but Conestabile, who ought to have known, says it was not (*Pitt. mur.* 157).

rendered differently. On this portion of the picture see Herbig in *RM.* 42, 122. Bulas feels sure that the painter misunderstood the model he was copying—substituted a boy for Priam, and Priam for one of his followers; added the figure of Athena 'in order to motive the gesture of Achilles turning his head': I have a somewhat higher opinion of the painter's intelligence. I follow Albizzati in calling the woman Briseis: Bulas thinks that she belongs to the retinue of Priam. I see a kantharos in her right hand, and not an amphora on her shoulder.

### *Stamnos* (of ordinary type)

2. Cabinet des Médailles 947, from Vulci. Micali *Mon. ined.* pl. 38, 1–2 (reversed), whence Kekulé *Ueber ein griechisches Vasengemälde* 23, and (corrected) here, Pl. 11, 3–4. A, Leda and the Egg (one of the Dioskouroi has found it and is offering it to her). B, Ajax and Tecmessa. On A, on the egg, ΕLΙΝΛΙ (*Elinai*), retr. On B, on the stalk of the plant, ΑΙ𐤥ΑΜ (*Aivas*) retr.

See p. 5. The picture on A was correctly explained by Kekulé (l.c.), in spite of which de Ridder follows de Witte and Micali and describes it as 'Paris offering Helen a mirror' engraved with her name. (Stephani, in *Compte-rendu* 1861, 139, had recognized the egg, but took the youth for Ajax: Ajax was one of Helen's many suitors, and here, according to Stephani, he is wooing her by offering her the very egg from which she had once emerged, a tasteful and ingenious gift.) The subject of the egg containing Helen is a favourite in Etruscan: see pp. 39–42, 60, and 115.

Kekulé noticed that the same couple of themes (Egg of Helen, Death of Ajax) recurred on a stamnos in Palermo (above, p. 39) and inferred an original in which they were already combined: but they are so frequent in Etruscan that no inference can be drawn.

On B, see pp. 5–6 and 137–41. It might perhaps be contended that the hero was Teucer, with his own spear in one hand, and the sword of Ajax in the other: but his scabbard is empty and it must be his own sword.

The extraordinary position of the inscription, on the stalk of the plant, makes it almost certain that the painter knew the story, familiar from Ovid's *Metamorphoses*, that the hyacinth sprang from the blood of Ajax, and bore the words *Ai ai* on its petals. Robert (*Heldensage* 1206) calls this a Hellenistic saga, and adds that it appears to have been related in a Greek lyric poem of which fragments are preserved in the Berlin papyrus 6870 (Schubert *Ein griechischer Papyrus mit Noten* in *Sitzb. Berl. Ak.* 1918, 765–8): but all that remains is, after an address to Telamonian Ajax, the words αἷμα κατὰ χθονὸς ἄπο..., and then the fragment ceases, so there is really no saying whether the hyacinth was mentioned or not; and in any case the date of the poem is unknown, and there is nothing to show that it is much earlier than the manuscript which records it, which is dated about A.D. 200. Robert does not mention the lines of Euphorion which are the earliest extant authority for the story in literature, and I owe the reference to Dr. Pfeiffer (Powell *Collectanea Alexandrina* 38 no. 40):

> πορφυρέη ὑάκινθε, σὲ μὲν μία φῆμις ἀοιδῶν
> Ῥοιτείηις ἀμάθοισι δεδουπότος Αἰακίδαο
> εἴαρος ἀντέλλειν γεγραμμένα κωκύουσαν.

In other Hellenistic allusions to the scriptured petals of the hyacinth it is not stated whether the blood of Ajax was the cause, or the blood of Hyakinthos. It follows from the words of Euphorion (μία φῆμις ἀοιδῶν) that the story had already been related in literature before he wrote: the Paris vase shows that it is at least as old as the earlier part of the fourth century B.C.

3. Parma, from Vulci. *Mon.* 5 pl. 41, whence (A) Roscher s.v. Kirke, p. 1195 fig. 2, and (coarsened) Overbeck *Gall.* pl. 32, 1–2; *Mél. d'arch.* 37, 127 and 133. A, Odysseus and Circe; B, Return of Odysseus.

The Parma vase shows the painter at his worst.

The interpretation of the second picture is disputed. Braun called it the Return of Odysseus (*Bull.* 1838, 28; *Bull.* 1853, 75–7), and was followed by Franz Müller (*Die antiken Odyssee-Illustrationen* 88) and Albizzati (*Mél. d'arch.* 37, 138 note 1). Overbeck saw Odysseus welcomed by Circe (*Annali* 1852, 230–41); so did G. Körte (*AZ.* 1876, 191) and Heydemann (*Ober* 48). One argument against this is that Odysseus has a spear instead of a sword. I follow Braun; and I take the woman to be Penelope, not, with most, Eurykleia. This is a very generalized version of the homecoming, not corresponding to any passage in the *Odyssey*. The painter remembered that Odysseus reached home, and was welcomed by his wife, and by his dog.

*Cup*

4. Cabinet des Médailles 1066. *Gaz. arch.* 1879 pll. 3–5, whence Pl. 10, 3–5, and (detail of I) Hadaczek *Ohrschmuck der Griechen und Etrusker* 35 fig. 62; A, Philippart *Iconographie des 'Bacchantes'* pl. 13, b. I, Pasiphae with the infant Minotaur on her lap. A, maenad and satyrs; B, the like.

The cup has a lip, inside only. The palmettes recall the Jena Painter (*ARV.* 880–3 and 966).

On the inside picture see p. 6. To right, a pet swan. A cylindrical cista hangs on a peg, which is carefully rendered. According to de Ridder 'Nymph (Maenad, Nysa, Persephone, Pasiphae??)' and 'Dionysos Zagreus (Minotaur?)'. The correct interpretation had been given by Braun (*Bull.* 1847, 121 = *AZ.* 1847, *Anz.* 9).

The Minotaur is not new-born as Robert states (*Heldensage* 363), but between two and four years old. It might be thought that the woman was not Pasiphae but a nurse: the much jewellery, and the large wreath (the same as is worn by Hera on the Settecamini stamnos, Pl. 10, 1) make this most unlikely.

The infant Minotaur appears on Etruscan cinerary urns: four in Volterra and one in Perugia (G. Körte in *Historische und philologische Aufsätze zu Ehren von E. Curtius* 197–208, and *Rilievi* ii, pl. 28, 3,[1] pl. 29, 4, pl. 29, 5; pl. 29, 5a, pl. 30, 6, and pp. 79 ff.; also Türk in Roscher s.v. Pasiphae). The heated scene—Minos in high rage, Pasiphae held prisoner, or taking sanctuary, the Minotaur in the nurse's arms—goes back to the

---

[1] The Volterra urn 299 (Körte *Rilievi* ii, pl. 28, 3) is figured in Roscher s.v. Telephos p. 298, 3 as 'Aleos threatening the infant Telephos'. This was Jahn's interpretation on the basis of the old drawing in Raoul-Rochette (*Mon. inéd.* pl. 67, A1) where the child was given a human head. Later Jahn himself found a more accurate drawing and gave the right explanation (*Arch. Beiträge* 249).

*Cretans* of Euripides. It is usually assumed that Pasiphae took her own life at the end of Euripides' play, but there is no evidence for this, and we do not know how long she survived.

Outside, one maenad brandishes a human leg, the other a human arm: not 'scenes of omophagy' (as Lenormant), or 'homophagy' (as de Ridder, and Séchan, p. 310), but extracts from a 'Death of Pentheus', as Panofka proposed (*AZ.* 1847, *Anz.* p. 23): see also Hartwig in *Jb.* 7, 163. The bones of the severed arm and leg protrude, which caused Lenormant and de Ridder to take them for artificial limbs, 'provided with a tenon, symbol of the Dionysiac homophagies'.

## THE ZEUS CUP IN THE VATICAN

In this well-known cup I find the same character—massive, majestic figures—as in the work of the Settecamini Painter, although it is by a different artist:

Vatican, from Vulci. *Mus. Greg.* ii, pl. 83, 2, whence (I) Overbeck *KM.* pl. 18, 12, whence *Jh.* 9, 100; I, phot. Alinari 35833, whence *Mél. d'arch.* 37, 116, Giglioli pl. 275, 1, and Pl. 9, 2; A, *Mél. d'arch.* 37, 114. I, a god (Zeus?) carrying off a woman. A, a man (or god) seated, between two naked youths; B, the like.

See p. 4. The restorations can be made out in the photograph: part of the woman's nose and of her forehead, repainted fractures in legs and drapery of Zeus. The headbands, armlets, necklace are gilt. Gilt details are very rare in Etruscan, though common in Attic vases of the late fifth century and the fourth, and found occasionally as early as the end of the sixth. The god is probably Zeus: Hades has also been suggested. Albizzati ascribes the cup to the fabric of Vulci (*Mél. d'arch.* 37, 108–9 no. 5, and 130); and attributes the stamnos Berlin 2954 (ibid. 117 and 119: see below, p. 62) to the same artist, an attribution which I confess I cannot understand.

## THE PHUIPA CUP

The Zeus cup naturally brings to mind another good Etruscan cup from the same site, which is not by the same hand, but has something of the same character:

Vatican G 112, from Vulci. *RG.* pl. 32; Pl. 12 and Pl. 4, 5. I, Zetun and Phuipa. A, Triton; B, the like. Dm. 220. On I, in white, retr., *Zetun, Phuipa.* The phi is diamond-shaped.

I have discussed the subjects and style in *RG.* 89–90; see also above, p. 4. The general layout of the group inside is much as in the Zeus cup, and here also, although the woman does not struggle, the male evidently feels the weight. The right hand of Phuipa does not connect very well with her arm. For the big spots (wings of Zetun, tails of Tritons, buds at the handles) see p. 28; for the garment of Zetun, caught on his thigh, *JHS.* 59, 20, and p. 95. There were several Phoibes, and it is possible that *Phuipa* is not the daughter of Leukippos, but a Phoibe not recorded elsewhere.

On the late archaic Greek scaraboid, from Cyprus, in New York, quoted in *RG.* 89, and above, p. 4, Eros may be carrying the maiden off for his own pleasure, but more probably a lover has begged the god to fetch her to him: compare Lucian *Philopseudes* 42 τέλος Δ' οὖν ὁ Ὑπερβόρειος ἐκ πηλοῦ ἐρώτιόν τι πλάσας, 'ἄπιθι', ἔφη, 'καὶ ἄγε Χρυσίδα.' καὶ ὁ μὲν πηλὸς ἐξέπτατο, &c.

On the snake-tailed monsters compared in *RG*. 90 with the fish-tailed of whom our Tritun is one, see also Dohrn 102–4. In *RG*. 90 there should be no asterisk against the Etruscan word *Tritun*, as it occurs on a fragment of a red-figured cup formerly in Volterra (p. 68: Inghirami *Mon. etr.* 5 pl. 55, 8).

In *RG*. I described the style of the cup as 'Campanizing', and I still seem to see Campanian influence in the floral part of the exterior and in the figure of Phuipa.

## THE BERLIN CUP 2947

I do not know anything like this cup, and if I mention it here it is because the huge figure of Herakles, dwarfing its companion, seems to reflect the same ideal as the Settecamini Painter's creatures and the Zeus of the Vatican cup:

Berlin 2947, from Chiusi. Gerhard *TG*. pl. 9, 1–2. A, Herakles and a seated maenad. A, two youths; B, the like.

## ˉ THE PAINTER OF THE OXFORD GANYMEDE
### *Stamnoi*

1. Oxford 1917.54. Given by E. P. Warren. Pl. 13a and Pl. 4, 4. A, Zeus and Ganymede. B, Gigantomachy (Athena and a Giant). A brief description was given in the *Report of the Visitors of the Ashmolean Museum* for 1917, 5–6. Height 0.368. See p. 4, and below.

2. Boston 07.862. Pl. 14; side-view, Shepard *The Fish-tailed Monster in Greek and Etruscan Art* pl. 13, 82. A, Polydeukes and Amykos. B, see below. A brief description is given in *Museum of Fine Arts, Boston: Thirty-second Annual Report for the year 1907*, whence *Anz.* 1908, 432. Height 0.368. See p. 57.

In both stamnoi the handles are in the form of sea-monsters (kētē) with tails intertwined; only one of the kētos heads is ancient in each vase.

The Oxford stamnos (Pll. 13a and 4, 4). The form of the foot is the same as in the Boston stamnos. The colour of the clay is a good light brown. The drawing is fully carried out in relief-line, but the palmettes are without relief. Fractures are slightly repainted, and the lower line of Ganymede's upper eyelid may have disappeared in a break. The cock, the lyre, the wings of Eros, the middle and ends of the thunderbolt were white: the white was laid directly on the clay and has disappeared. The arms of the lyre terminate in swan's heads: so also, for example, in the mirror in the Palazzo Bargagli at Sarteano (Gerhard *ES*. pl. 119, 1), and the Campanian hydria Berlin 3031 (FR. iii, 57). Eros appears from behind a rock (not a cloud), as might be shown, if necessary, by comparison with the rock on the Boston stamnos (Pl. 14), which is rendered in the same way. A band of brown marks off Ganymede's himation from the rock. The spaces between his waist and his garment, and again between his thigh and his garment, are filled in with brown to suggest shadow. Zeus and Ganymede have brown hair, Eros' hair is darker. Ganymede has put down his cock, and it stands on the ground between him and Zeus, as in the black-figured amphora, Munich 834 (SH. 95 and pl. 33). The use of a sash to fill in a space like that above the head of Zeus is not uncommon in Etruscan: compare the stamnos Villa Giulia 27134 (p. 163: *ML.* 24, Cultrera, pl. 26).

The branch, of fir as it seems, depending from the upper edge of the picture, is seen on later Etruscan vases, of the Alcsti Group (p. 134): both the volute-krater in the Cabinet des Médailles (Pl. 30, 1) and the calyx-krater in Trieste (*Ausonia* 10, 91).

The picture on the reverse is much less careful. The Athena and Giant is one more version of a group that is very common in Greek and Hellenizing battle-scenes from the third quarter of the fifth century onwards: a fleeing warrior falls on his knees, the pursuer sets one foot on the other's leg and stabs him downwards through the hollow beside the collar-bone. On this group see Löwy in *Jh.* 28, 63–7 and Zahn in *Festschrift für August Oxé* 54 note 22. There are naturally many variants of it, but we can speak of a *type*. An early example is on the Attic dinos London 99.7–21.5 (FR. pl. 58), which belongs to the group of the vase-painter Polygnotos (*ARV.* 697 no. 26) and was painted about 440 B.C. or not much later; there, as in our Athena, the sole of the pursuer's foot is seen from underneath. The finest and most elaborate version is on the Alexander sarcophagus (Hamdy Bey and T. Reinach *Une nécropole royale à Sidon* pl. 29, whence *Jh.* 28, 67 and Winter *Kunstgeschichte in Bildern* 337, 1); a Roman one is the bronze cut-out in New York, *Bull. Metr.* 6, 213 fig. 6; Etruscan, on urns in Volterra and Chiusi (Körte *Rilievi* ii, pl. 114, 4 and p. 149, and pl. 126, 8). A variant of the type presents the two figures in three-quarter view, nearly frontal, instead of in profile: as for example at Trysa (Benndorf *Das Heroon von Gjölbaschi-Trysa* pl. 10, above, right), and often in Etruscan (calyx-krater, from Monteluce, in Perugia, see p. 165: oval cista from Vulci in the Vatican, *Mus. Greg.* i, pll. 40–1, Ducati *St.* pl. 208, 516, Giglioli pl. 284;[1] alabaster sarcophagus from Vulci in Boston, Ducati *St.* pl. 197; nenfro sarcophagus, from the Tomba delle Bighe at Tarquinia, in London, D21, Pryce *Cat. Sculpt.* i, ii, 189 fig. 40). The painter of the Oxford vase has forgotten how the left arm of the pursuer should go, and it dangles as if broken. The face of Athena, on the other hand, is expressive—frowning, tight-lipped. The helmet is of the tiaroid form which is common from the fifth century onwards and is given to Athena, as well as to others, without special significance: see Wolters in *Festschrift H. Wölfflin* 13 ff. The peplos is kilted well up, revealing half-boots.

The artist has not forgotten to add a typically Etruscan stroke, the bird swooping down in quest of carrion: see pp. 96–7.

The seated youth must be Hermes. In his left hand he holds a sword in its scabbard, and a shield stands beside him. He extends his left arm as if giving directions, or at least following the execution of a manœuvre he has suggested. This is an unusual role for Hermes in the Gigantomachy.

For the filling-ornament between Athena and Hermes see p. 61.

The Boston stamnos (Pl. 14). See pp. 4–5. The shape is the same as in the Oxford vase, and the two vases must be the work of one potter. The style of the patternwork,

---

[1] The cista is also figured in *Monumenti* 1855 pl. 18, and with it the objects said to have been found inside it (text by Braun, pp. 64–5). The Attic lekythos said to have been found in the same niche as the cista must belong to a previous interment.

too—egg, tongues, palmettes—is the same in both.  The figure-style is the same: needless to go into particulars: note only the marcato character of the relief-lines.  The group of Polydeukes and Amykos on one side of the vase goes back to the same famous picture as the drawing on the Ficoroni cista (*WV.* E pl. 12, 1) and other Etruscan representations of the same subject: moreover, our version is one of the two that most closely resemble the group on the cista and, it may confidently be said, the lost original.  The other, later, is on the cinerary urn of Vel Vesini in Perugia (Dempster *De Etruria regali* 1 pl. 9, 1; *WV.* 1889 pl. 12, 6; Giglioli pl. 407, 1): there and in our vase Polydeukes' left leg is not set on a rock as in the cista, but presses against the tree-trunk with the knee.  The engravings on four mirrors go back to the same original, but are not so close to the Ficoroni cista as the vase and the urn: (1) formerly in the Sarti collection (*Vendita Sarti* pl. 12 no. 104, misprinted 107, whence Matthies 79: Praenestine); (2) Tarquinia, from Tarquinia (Gerhard *ES.* suppl. pl. 91, 2: Etruscan); (3) formerly in the Sarti collection (*Vendita Sarti* pl. 12 no. 105: Praenestine); (4) formerly in the Fillon collection (Gerhard *ES.* suppl. pl. 90, whence *WV.* 1889 pl. 12, 4 and Matthies 73: Praenestine).  In the Fillon mirror only the *Amucos* is taken from our original: *Polouces* is not binding him, but reading him a lesson.  How close the group on the unpublished Praenestine cista in Berlin, inv. 3528, may be to ours I do not know, for the descriptions are not sufficient (Schoene in *Annali* 1866, 181–2 no. 62; Behn *Die Ficoronische Cista* 12–13; Matthies 61 and 71–2).  The same applies to a Praenestine cista, now in the Villa Giulia (Weege in Helbig and Amelung 324 no. 1769e), published in *Collezione Gagliardi* pl. 3, 1; I have the plates of the sale catalogue, but they show hardly anything: there may be a line-drawing in the text, which I do not possess.  In any case only the Amykos is in question, for the Polydeukes, according to Matthies's account (61 and 71–2), is not binding but standing in the same attitude as on the Villa Giulia mirror Gerhard *ES.* pl. 171.

To return to the group on the Boston stamnos itself.  Here alone, as was noted earlier, Polydeukes uses a withy instead of a thong, and this was probably so in the original account.  In the *Iliad* (11, 105) Achilles binds Isos and Antiphos with withies; in the *Odyssey* Odysseus uses withies to tie the sheep of Polyphemos together (9, 427), and to truss up a stag (10, 166); in the *Cyclops* of Euripides, Silenos ties the lambs up with withies (225), in the *Aigeus* of Sophocles Theseus prepares withies to bind the Marathonian bull (fr. 25 Pearson).  The withy, and the spout, are white, and as in the Oxford stamnos the white, laid direct on the clay ground, has faded.  The tree is an aged willow. In most of the other representations it might be a willow, but might also be an olive. In the first Sarti mirror (Matthies 79) the engraver has drawn a branch of olive to left of the figures, and his tree is probably an olive too.  In the Fillon mirror (Gerhard *ES.* suppl. pl. 90) the trunk has much the same marks on it as in the Boston vase.  Neither olive nor willow, however, is what the literary tradition would lead one to expect: for the tree, famous in after time, under which Amykos was believed to have been buried was a laurel; and it was to a laurel, according to Apollonius Rhodius (2, 160), that the Argonauts tied their hawsers when they landed in the territory of Amykos (see Robert *Heldensage* 844).

As in the Ficoroni cista, the penes of both boxers are tied up with the κυνοδέσμη, Greek custom, but long familiar in Etruria, as may be seen from the boxers and wrestlers in the Tomba della Scimmia (*Mon.* 5 pll. 15–16; *MPAI.* Etr., Clus. i, pll. 1 and A–B) and those on the neck-amphora by the Micali Painter in London (B 64: p. 2 and Pl. 2).[1] The lips of Polydeukes are pursed, not parted as on the cista: this is expressive too, and so is the left foot of Amykos, here touching the ground with the heel only. It is a pity that the greater part of Amykos' face is missing, for it would certainly have added another to the painter's 'draughts of passionate looks'.

We have already mentioned the unusual plants at the rock and on the ground near Polydeukes; from the wet rock, a fern; on the ground, what looks like a poppy. The rendering of the stream that issues from the spout, twisting as it falls, is also unusual: it recurs in the Poseidon and Amymone on an Etruscan mirror in the Vatican (Gerhard *ES.* Pl. 64). This in its turn has two features that recall the Ficoroni cista: one is the lion-head spout, drawn in three-quarter view: the other is the kylix that hangs on a nail driven into the rock beside the spout. In modern times such public drinking-vessels are usually chained. The Etruscan is fond of showing kylikes hanging up, and unlike the Greek he regularly adds the nail on which they hang, for example in the reliefs of the Tomba dei Rilievi at Cervetri (Giglioli pll. 341–3). The water falls into a rough cylindrical or oval basin, no doubt of stone. The spout is a plain tube, not a lion's head as in the Ficoroni cista.

One of the pleasantest passages of the Ficoroni cista is the little boy, servant (temporarily?) of Polydeukes, who sits on the ground at the foot of the tree and looks up at him: he holds his master's sandals and strigil, has the chlamys over his shoulder, and the lekythion fastened to his forearm by a thong; beside him there is a mattock for loosening the soil of the palaestra: the contest no doubt took place not on the rocks but in a more or less well-prepared ring near by. In Attica a pick with two prongs is used for this purpose, but a mattock would also serve: see p. 80. Amykos' chlamys lies on the rock beside him, and his boots on the ground near his feet. Of all this gear only a lekythion and a chlamys appear on the stamnos. The lekythion or aryballos is of the same type as in the cista but much plainer, the only decoration being a band down the side and another parallel to the bottom: the other lines on the lekythion represent the ends of the thong tied round the neck. The chlamys is folded even more neatly than that of Amykos on the cista. Both garments are folded square: so also on two Etruscan mirrors, that with Peleus and Atalanta in the Vatican (Gerhard *ES.* pl. 224; Giglioli pl. 226, 4) and that with Peleus and Thetis in New York (Gerhard *ES.* suppl. pl. 96).

Other representations of Amykos are not connected with ours. *Amyche* is being bound on an Etruscan scarab which was formerly in the Tyszkiewicz collection (Furtwängler *AG.* pl. 61, 22), but there is little resemblance to our group. The early Italiote hydria in the Cabinet des Médailles, from which the Amykos Painter takes his name, also depicts the binding, but certainly does not go back to the same original as the Ficoroni cista, nor has it even borrowed anything from that original. A Faliscan stamnos in the Villa Giulia

---

[1] In the view of religious experts (such as Halliday in *CR.* 1926, 41) the origin of this practice 'may lie in the supposed magical efficacy of continence, of which chastity taboos in ritual are a different expression'. I should rather have thought that the prime object was to protect the mucous membrane from the hot sun and other irritants; and that a contributory cause was the liking for εὐπρέπεια.

(Pl. 19, 1, and p. 79) represents the preliminaries of the contest, and so does a Praenestine mirror in the Villa Giulia (Gerhard *ES*. pl. 171). The earliest extant picture of Amykos is on fragments of a magnificent Attic volute-krater, from Spina, in Ferrara (T. 404: part, *NSc*. 1927 pl. 19, 2; part, Aurigemma[1] 205 =[2] 237): this vase belongs to the group of Polygnotos (*ARV*. 696 no. 25) and was painted between 440 and 430: but the interpretation of the fragments is very difficult: *Amykos*, fastening his gloves on, stands on the right of one picture, (A), under the handle; then come, from right to left, *Hippomenes*, Atalanta, *Kleomolpos*, and . . . *os*. A second fragment seems to come from the left of A: a man seated to right, holding a wreath; behind him, . . . *as* crowning *Polydeu[kes]*. How all these persons came together I cannot tell, and above all what Amykos is doing in the company.

The picture on the other side of the Boston stamnos is not very easy to understand. The youth with the mattock, in the middle, as we said above, cannot be an ordinary mortal, must be a hero. Hero, satyr, Hermes suggest an Attic satyr-play as the original source. Pictures of Herakles in the service of Syleus (*ARV*. index, s.v.) show him plying a pick or a double axe: a mattock would also be appropriate; and *Syleus* was the title of a satyr-play by Euripides. But what is the hero holding in his left hand? It reminds one of the egg containing Helen, a favourite object, as we have seen, in Etruscan art (pp. 39–42): in several of the Etruscan representations it is one of the Dioskouroi who holds the egg. In our stamnos, also, the hero is perhaps a Dioskouros: Kastor, or rather Polydeukes.

In his other hand he has a mattock. It will be remembered that on the Ficoroni cista (*WV*. 1889 pl. 12, 1: see p. 59), and probably on a Faliscan vase as well (Pl. 19, 1 and p. 80), a mattock appears, not indeed in the hand of Polydeukes, but close to him. This may not be of any significance: but it is certain that in the palaestra the mattock served the same purpose as the pickaxe, to loosen the soil (p. 59). On Attic vases athletes are often shown either using the pick, or standing still and holding it, as for example the Euaion Painter's Atalanta on his stemless cup in the Louvre (CA 2259: *Enc. phot.* iii, 8b; *Die Antike* 16, 25: *ARV*. 530 no. 94) or a youth on a cup by the Eretria Painter, also in the Louvre (G 457: *Mon.* 1856 pl. 20; Pottier *Vases antiques du Louvre* pl. 148: *ARV*. 728 no. 65).

It may be, then, that in the version followed by the painter of our stamnos, Polydeukes, while loosening the soil with his mattock in the palaestra, came upon the egg, which had previously been planted there, just below the surface, by Hermes. This would account for the figure of the hero, and for the figure of Hermes, whose attitude and expression would be very suitable. The part played by the old satyr is not clear. He trots up with a situla in his right hand and a phiale or a small dish in his left. Perhaps he is acting as water-boy, and at a sign from the hero comes up to wash the egg.

I do not count this interpretation as certain: but it is the best I can do, and I now leave the problem to others.

The Hermes is one of countless figures, painted or sculptured, which lean forward with one foot raised and set on a rock or other elevation (K. Lange *Das Motiv des aufgestützten Fusses*; Horn in *Anz*. 1938, 657). In many of these, as here, the forearm is laid, foreshortened, across the raised thigh. An early example of this is the satyr on an Attic calyx-krater in the University of Vienna, painted in the manner of the Dinos Painter

(551c: *CV.* pl. 25, 4–6: *ARV.* 793 no. 15) and datable about 425 or 420 B.C.; some Etruscan figures are not much later: the maenad on the pointed amphora by the Perugia Painter (p. 36), the Athena on the stamnos in Palermo (p. 42). In those the head looks straight forward, in our Hermes it looks back and is in three-quarter view: compare the Hephaistos (Sethlans) on the Bologna mirror with the Birth of Athena (Gerhard *ES.* pl. 66); among many statues the Lansdowne athlete; and especially one of the Argonauts on the Italiote volute-krater by the Sisyphos Painter in Munich (FR. pl. 98; Trendall *Frühit.* pl. 19). I do not know any other figure just like our Hermes. The energetic movement of the right arm gives it a characteristic colour. The expressiveness of the face, indeed of all three faces in the picture, was noted above (p. 5).

The painter likes folds and creases of flesh: the satyr has a paunch; and the back of his neck is creased. The creases recall the Ficoroni cista (*WV.* 1889 pl. 12, 1), in which the folds of fat flesh on the satyr's arms and thighs have actually been mistaken for tattooing. Another satyr with puckered neck and shoulders is on the mirror in Florence with Herakles sucking the breast of Hera (Gerhard *ES.* suppl. pl. 60; Giglioli pl. 299, 5 and pl. 300).

The spots on the satyr's body are unintentional: a shower of tiny drops fell from the brush, and there are some on the hero and on the left leg of Hermes as well.

The thing between the satyr's legs is a filling-ornament, I suppose, of the same shape as one on the reverse of the Oxford stamnos. The thing to the left of the hero's head is no doubt vegetable: it recalls the long triangular branch on the obverse of the Oxford vase (p. 57). Hard to be certain whether the black parts are what is represented, or the light parts.

A word about the situla. Many situlae of this shape ('bell-pail', with bail or bails) have been preserved, some of bronze, others of clay (Schröder *Griechische Bronzeeimer im Berliner Antiquarium*; *Jb.* 35, 84–96 (Pernice); Pernice *HKP.* iv, 15 and 21–30; Züchner *Der Berliner Mänadenkrater* 18–25), and there are many pictures of them on Italiote vases. For Etruscan examples see p. 250. The 'bell-pail' is sometimes said to be peculiar to Italy or at least non-Attic, but although it does not seem to have been adopted by Attic vase-painters it was known in Attica, for it appears in the well-scene on an Attic column-krater of about 430 B.C., by the Naples Painter, in Madrid (11039: Ossorio pl. 30, 2; Leroux pl. 29, 1: *ARV.* 705 no. 15). It was known in Boeotia too, for it is part of Kadmos' luggage on a Cabirion skyphos in Berlin (Lücken pl. 26). As to the drinking-vessel, the position of the satyr's fingers is consistent with its being a phiale mesomphalos.

The Boston vase has hitherto passed for Faliscan: and it has much in common with Faliscan stamnoi. The shape is not unlike Faliscan; nor is the drawing of tongues and egg-pattern (p. 150); nor is the floral decoration at the handles (Shepard *The Fish-tailed Monster* pl. 13, 82), which may be compared with that of Faliscan stamnoi (*CV.* Villa Giulia IV Br. pl. 9).

### THE BERLIN STAMNOS 2954

In shape, the two stamnoi in Oxford and Boston approximate to a numerous class of Faliscan stamnoi (e.g. Pl. 17), although the model is not the same. Another stamnos that bears a certain resemblance in shape to our pair is Berlin 2954, from Bomarzo (Ambrosch *De Charonte etrusco* pll. 2–3; *Mél. d'arch.* 37, 117 and 119). The drawing of the tongue-pattern, too, is like. The style of the figurework is different. Albizzati (*Mél. d'arch.* 37, 108 no. 5, 130, and 134–5) attributes the Berlin vase to the same hand as the 'Zeus' cup in the Vatican: I do not see why, but I ought to say that I have only the very imperfect reproductions to judge from. The subjects show this to be a sepulchral vase—made for the tomb. On one side Charun, with his hammer, goes in front, then comes a youth on horseback, sounding a trumpet, and then a woman holding a box and a sash. On the other side an elderly man, well wrapped up, rides in a cart drawn by a pair of mules: this must be the same subject as in a later work, the volute-krater, from Orvieto, in the Faina collection (see p. 169), which represents the progress of the dead to his new home in the Nether World. The other picture refers to the funeral procession. The two pictures are not continuous, for the mule-cart faces the wrong way: and the interpretation of the second is disputed. Is the scene laid on earth, as the trumpeter and the woman with box and sash would suggest; or in Hades, as the Charun? The answer surely is that two figures from the earthly pageant are joined with one from the infernal, the notion of passage from one life to another fusing them together. A different explanation was offered by Albizzati (*Mél. d'arch.* 37, 134–5 and *Atti Pont.*, new series, 15, 251–2), and adopted by Giglioli (*Ausonia* 102–3). They believe that what is depicted is 'the funeral masquerade', and that the demon is a mortal in disguise. The idea of such funeral masquerades goes back to Martha (*L'Art étrusque* 417–20), although he does not apply it to this vase. The only evidence for the presence of a man impersonating Charun at Etruscan funeral processions is a sentence in Tertullian's *Ad nationes*, which is repeated with little change in his *Apologeticum*:

Risimus et meridiani ludi de deis lusum, quod Ditis pater, Iouis frater, gladiatorum exsequias cum malleo deducit, quod Mercurius, in caluitio pennatulus, in caduceo ignitulus, corpora exanimata iam mortemue simulantia e cauterio probat. (*Ad nat.* 1, 10.)

Risimus et inter ludicras meridianorum crudelitates Mercurium mortuos cauterio examinantem, uidimus et Iouis fratrem gladiatorum cadauera cum malleo deducentem. (*Apol.* 15.)

It is pointed out that Isidore identifies the Greek Charon with Orcus, and Orcus with Ditis pater: 'Pluton graece, latine Diespiter uel Ditis pater; quem alii Orcum uocant, quasi receptorem mortium. unde et orca nuncupatur uas quod recipit aquas. ipse et graece Charon' (*Et.* viii, xi, 42).

The theory is that the Roman custom which so amused the Christian father was adopted, together with the gladiatorial contests themselves, from Etruria; and that the mock funeral in the Etruscan arena was imitated from real Etruscan funerals. The theory is somewhat more plausible than might appear from Martha's paraphrase (op. cit. 420), for Tertullian does not say that 'a slave disguised as Charon came and removed the corpses lying in the arena', but that Ditis pater led the funeral of the gladiators with a hammer. Even so the element of conjecture is considerable. Further, even if it were established that a man disguised as Charun took part in the Etruscan funeral, it does not follow that the painter of a vase like ours would depict the actual funeral procession; that he would represent the impersonator of Charun rather than the demon himself. It is at least as likely that he would short-circuit the actor and portray the character.  I do not find any Etruscan monument which necessitates the hypothesis of a 'funeral masquerade': in particular, where there is any ground for supposing that the Charun is an actor and not the demon himself. Martha himself put forth his suggestion as an alternative only: and had already stated in clear and well-chosen terms the explanation which we have preferred (op. cit. 419).

We have said that the passages in Tertullian stood alone.  Other arguments have been adduced: but it should be evident that the curious masquerades at Roman funerals,[1] even if their Etruscan origin were proved, have no bearing on the question whether Charun was ever impersonated; that the Faliscan and Tarquinian priests, whose appearance on the battlefield in the guise of Furies, armed with snakes and burning torches, is said to have caused consternation in the Roman army, have nothing to do with funerals;[2] and that while the *Phersu* of the Tomba degli Auguri[3] is justly popular with archaeologists, the only reason for referring to him in this connexion[4] is the somewhat inadequate one that he wears a mask.

According to Albizzati the objects serving as filling in the field, which Furtwängler could not explain, are a greave and three round shields, recalling the things that hung on the walls inside tombs.  This may well be so: and on a cinerary urn in Chiusi pieces of armour—targe, helmet, spear, sword, and greaves—are scattered over the background in much the same way as here (Körte *Rilievi* pl. 112, 5).  Further, the left-hand thing looks like a greave; the others, however, are not so like shields (seen in three-quarter view) as might be wished, and shields when hung on walls are hung flat so that the whole round is seen.  The thing above the left handle in B is the box held by the woman on A and the end of the sash.

### THE CAMPANIZING GROUP

Many of the floral motives in Etruscan vases of the fourth century have something in common with Campanian: one or two resemblances in figurework have been noted above, or will be noted: there are a few vases in which the correspondence is closer.  The three that follow go together, and may even be by one hand:

### *Calyx-krater*

1. Bonn inv. 83.  *Annali* 1878 pl. H (=Furtwängler *KS.* i, pl. 8); part of A, *Jb.* 25, 132. A, Dionysos and Ariadne with satyrs and maenad.  B, komast and youths.

[1] On these, Zadoks-Jitta *Ancestral Portraiture in Rome*, 22–31.

[2] Livy 7, 17. According to Messerschmidt (*RM.* 45, 176) this passage furnishes a *terminus post quem* for representations of Charun with snakes in his hands and of Etruscan demons in the guise of Furies: the year 399 B.C. But the second consulate of M. Fabius Ambustus was in 356, not 399. Moreover, although the war with the Faliscans and Tarquinians is no doubt a historical fact, the story of the new weapon is obviously mythical trimming. I am indebted to Dr. Momigliano for guidance in this matter. He also refers me to De Sanctis (*Storia dei Romani* ii, 255), who points out that the story is a slightly more elaborate version of an episode related by Livy (4, 33, 2) as having taken place in an earlier war.

[3] The Tomba degli Auguri: *Mon.* 11 pl. 25; Poulsen *Etr. Tomb Paintings* figs. 4–5; phots. Alinari 26107–9, whence Giglioli pll. 109–10.

[4] Giglioli in *Ausonia* 10, 102–3, after Keck. The Roman funerals and the Etruscan stratagem had already been quoted by Martha (op. cit. 419–20), but only to show that the Etruscans liked dressing-up.

*Stamnos*

2. Villa Giulia 15540. *ML.* 24 (Cultrera) pl. 27, 46. A, satyr and woman. B, two youths. The foot of the vase, according to Cultrera, is probably alien.

*Cup*

3. Brunswick 268, fr. *CV.* pl. 44, 1–2, whence Pl. 13, 3–4. I am indebted to Miss Richter for a photostat. I, warrior and king. A, naked youth (athlete?) and two males; B, the like. The cup has been pared round; it may be in antiquity—this was often done.

Furtwängler saw (*Annali* 1878, 86–7 = *KS.* i, 216–17) that the group of Dionysos and Ariadne on the Bonn vase went back to the same late-fifth-century Greek original as that on the reverse of the volute-krater by the Pronomos Painter in Naples (*FR.* pl. 145: *ARV.* 849 no. 1); Salis added two other Attic derivatives (*Jb.* 25, 132–3), Buschor two more (*FR.* iii, 144–5). The Etruscan artist no doubt had the group, directly or not, from an Attic vase.

Behind Dionysos a satyr dances; and in front of him there is a group of a satyr bending right forward, looking round, and supporting a naked maenad who sits on the small of his back and plays the flute, while he dances—or at least staggers round, flourishes his arms, and makes uncouth movements with his rump. Furtwängler aptly compares the group on an Attic black-figured neck-amphora by the Andokides Painter in Oxford (*CV.* III H pl. 10, 3 and pl. 7, 3; *ARV.* 3 no. 19), but goes on to charge the painter with making 'a characteristically Etruscan confusion by combining archaic originals' (the group of satyr and maenad) 'with later ones' (the group of Dionysos and Ariadne). I do not admire the Etruscan picture: but I must say I see no confusion in it. I do not understand why there should be anything intrinsically archaic in representing a woman sitting on the small of a man's back while he waves his arms, or why the motive should be forbidden to a fourth-century artist.

Miss Fraenkel (in *Jb.* 25, 133) pointed to a somewhat similar group on a sigillata vase in Berlin (inv. 3130: *Jb.* 3, 252), but there the satyr holds the leg of the maenad with both arms, and she brandishes a thyrsus.

On the reverse a bearded reveller, naked, strolls along, jug in hand, and two stolid youths looks on as if disapproving. The jug is decorated with a figure and a tendril in silhouette.

Among the Campanizing features in the three vases two may be specified, the flat form of the groins in Dionysos—approximating to a horizontal line—and the crude little arcs used for the minor folds of the drapery in the stamnos and the cup.

The Brunswick cup, no. 3, has a certain affinity with the work of the Settecamini Painter (pp. 52–5).

Another stamnos goes with Villa Giulia 15540 in shape and in handle-palmettes: the figures, partly repainted, look earlier:

Baltimore, Walters Art Gallery, 48.62, from Castel Campanile. *Journ. Walt.* 3 (1940), 134. There are drawings in the Roman Institute (22,119). A, youth with spear, attended by two women. B, satyrs and maenad dancing. The skirt of the dancer, flying up in front, recalls Italiote vases—a volute-krater in Taranto (Trendall *Frühit. Vasen* pl. 26), an amphora of Panathenaic shape in Naples (3219: *Mon.* 4 pl. 16); and the Campanari vase to which we now come. It is only known from a poor illustration, but it must be closely connected with our Campanizing Group:

### Calyx-krater

Roman market (Campanari). Gerhard *AV.* pl. 89, 1–2. The obverse is also figured in *Mus. Greg.* ii pl. 95, vii, 3, but I do not think the vase is in the Vatican. A, Perseus, stag-headed woman, Nike. B, man (Dionysos?) and woman, satyr and maenad. I do not understand the subject of A: the vase is doubtless restored, and I am not inclined, without seeing it, to hold, with the writer in Roscher, s.v. Perseus, p. 2039, that the painter did not understand his subject either. Among the Campanizing traits are the drawing of the peplos, the flat form of the groin, and the straggly locks at the back of the head. On the maenad's skirt see above.

Another vase may be placed in the neighbourhood of these Campanizing works:

### Stamnos

Toronto 427. Robinson pl. 80; Pl. 13, 1–2. A, warrior and woman. B, youth and woman. On a cartellino, an inscription of which I can make nothing. Mrs. Homer Thompson kindly sent me, besides photographs, a tracing of the letters, from which it appears that the facsimile given by Robinson is correct, except that the fourth letter is a sigma, and the first (on the right) looks more like a Greek four-stroke sigma than it does in the catalogue. The woman on A seems to be giving instructions to the young warrior: she holds a spear, but I do not know if she can be called Athena. The youth on B holds a strigil, the woman a cushion, and there is a second cushion in the field behind the youth. The drawing of the peploi, the many small crude arc-like folds, the straggling locks behind the head, and the floral decoration, are reminiscent of Campanian. The female figures recall the maenad of the Villa Giulia stamnos 15540, no. 2 in our Campanizing Group (p. 64), and the little arcs occur there also.

Not much of the following vase can be made out from the minute reproduction, but it would seem to be connected with the Campanizing Group:

### Stamnos

Florence, from Populonia. A, *NSc.* 1905, 57, left. According to Milani the subject is 'a youth and a woman', on each side: one would guess the youth on the side reproduced to be a satyr. With the woman compare the maenad on the Villa Giulia stamnos (p. 64).

Of two other stamnoi, from the same site, and acquired at the same time, one is of the same shape as the last and is doubtless by the same potter; and so, probably, is the other, for the foot, which is different, looks modern in the reproduction:

1. Florence, from Populonia. A, *NSc.* 1905, 57, right. On each side, 'a youth and a woman'.

2. Florence, from Populonia. A, *NSc.* 1905, 58 fig. 6, left. On each side, 'a youth and a woman'. On A, I seem to make out a woman seated to right, and a male with his foot raised and set on a rock or the like, both naked or nearly. This vase is said to have been found in the same tomb as three Attic vases (ibid., below, middle, and to right of the middle): a glaux, and two squat lekythoi: the glaux is fifth-century, the squat lekythoi very early fourth: if they really come from the same tomb as the stamnos, there were probably two interments.

Lastly, there is a vase that campanizes strongly, yet cannot be said to form part of our Campanizing Group:

*Column-krater*

Berlin inv. 30042, from Falerii. *Sumbolae De Petra* 166–7. A, Telephos and Orestes. B, unexplained: a youth meeting a woman at a fountain.

There are a good many representations of Telephos with the infant Orestes: see Pollak *Zwei Vasen aus der Werkstatt Hierons* 1–20; Johannes Schmidt in Roscher s.v. Telephos 303–7; Nicole in *Sumbolae De Petra* 165–9; Séchan 121–7 and 503–18; *ARV.*, index, s.v. Telephos. Add the calyx-krater Berlin inv. 3974, Attic, beginning of the fourth century, described by Neugebauer *Führer: Vasen* p. 127.

In design, the group of Telephos and Agamemnon on the Berlin vase, as Séchan has already observed (*Trag.* 512 note 4), is much like that on a Campanian bell-krater in Naples (2293: Jahn *Telephos und Troilos und kein Ende* pl. 1, whence Roscher s.v. Telephos p. 305; Patroni 86, whence (redrawn) Séchan 511.

The picture on the reverse is not connected with that on the obverse, nor is there any reason why it should be, and Nicole's complaint (*Sumbolae* 168) that the persons pay no attention to what is taking place so near them is unwarranted. A young traveller arrives at a fountain, and meets a girl who is approaching it or rather leaving it, hydria on head. A woman with one foot raised and resting on an elevation looks on. The story must be taken from Greek mythology. A woman carrying water in a hydria on her head, a young traveller approaching: that is the situation at the beginning of Euripides' *Electra*; and possibly Electra and Orestes are represented here: but if so the artist might have made his meaning clearer; and I am far from insisting that this is the subject.

The same flat groin-line, and the same small arcs for the lesser folds, as on the stamnoi in Villa Giulia and Toronto (pp. 64 and 65).

The Campanian artist whose work both this vase and those of our Campanizing Group most resemble is the Errera Painter, on whom see *JHS.* 63, 82–3.

Shape and decoration of the Telephos vase differ from those of the standard Attic column-krater. In two of the very latest Attic column-kraters, from the early fourth century, the proportions are nearer ours, and the foot is not unlike, but the base does not reverse its curve as here: these are Bologna 197 (A, Pellegrini *VF.* 175) and Ferrara T 597 (A, Europa: B, satyr and youths). In Attic column-kraters the pattern below the picture is never, I think, a maeander until the last stage of the shape: but those of the end of the fifth century and the early fourth have it, and it is the rule in Italiote column-kraters. There seem to be no column-kraters in Campanian red-figure: excluding, of course, the very early 'Owl-column' Group (see *JHS*. 63, 66–9), which does not concern us.

A foot of the same type occurs in two Etruscan stamnoi, from Populonia, mentioned above (pp. 65–6) as apparently connected with the Campanizing Group.

Two column-kraters bear some resemblance to the Telephos vase in shape and ornament:

Florence, from Populonia. A, *NSc*. 1905, 58 fig. 6, middle. A, fight (Greeks and Trojans according to Milani). B, 'maenad between women'. On the neck: A, satyrs and maenad; B, 'maenad (?) between women'.

London F 481, from near Populonia. A, Gerhard *Trinkschalen* pl. C, 10 and 14.

I cannot tell from the minute illustration if the figurework on the Florence krater has any connexion with ours; as to London F 481, the vase is ancient, but the picture on the obverse is almost wholly modern, and much of the picture on the reverse.

### THE GROUP OF VATICAN G 113

Put together in *RG*. 90–1.

#### *Stamnos*

1. Vatican G 113, from Vulci. *RG*. pl. 33. A, Grypomachy. B, Nike seated. See *RG*. 90–1. Nike sits on a laver-stand (*RG*. 91: see also Deonna *Délos xviii* 73–8 and pll. 21–5: ὑποστάτης Paus. 10, 26, 8): for the use of laver-stands as seats see Pernice *HKP*. v, 39; and compare p. 135.

#### *Oinochoai* (shape III)

2. Tarquinia RC 1645, from Tarquinia. *ML*. 36, 482, 2; phot. Moscioni. A youth sits on a rock, to left, looking round; another youth lays his hand on the seated youth's arm; a woman, wearing a himation only, which leaves the breasts bare, leans on the second youth with her right hand on his shoulder and her left arm akimbo. Behind her, a heron or the like. I do not know who these are.

3. Tarquinia RC 1644, from Tarquinia. *ML*. 36, 482, 1; phot. Moscioni. Amazonomachy. A mounted Amazon strikes down a Greek with her spear.

The two jugs are a pair, by one hand. The stamnos is more laboured, and inferior. All three are carried out fully in relief-line. There is a little hatching at the base of the woman's left breast in no. 2: see pp. 103 and 116. The youth on the stamnos already bears a certain slight resemblance to one of the satyrs on the Alcsti vase in the Cabinet des Médailles (Pl. 30, 2, and p. 133).

Jacobsthal provides me with the following note on the shield in no. 3:

'The "Boeotian" shape of the shield has no analogies in Italic and Celtic art, but the midrib and the device across it between the scollops are Celtic. Celtic shields often have a midrib with a spindle boss, which has lateral wings, hammered out of the same sheet of bronze as the boss, or wrought separately and riveted on; the side pieces are often given ornamental form. The drawing becomes clear by comparison with the Gaulish shield on the Etruscan urn in Chiusi, Körte *Rilievi* pl. 118, Bieńkowski *Darstellungen der Gallier* pll. 8–9, Doro Levi *Il Museo Civico di Chiusi* 46. See also the painted stelae from Sidon, *RA*. 1927, 313, figs. 77–9 (not quite accurate); Pergamene balustrade, *Alt. v. Perg.*

2, pl. 46, 2 (Reinach *Rép. des reliefs* i, 213, 1); armour frieze, Augustan, at Antioch in Pisidia, *Art Bull.* 9 (1926–7), 35 fig. 51; arch at Orange, Tiberian, shield inscribed Boudillus Avot, Espérandieu *Recueil des bas-reliefs de la Gaule romaine* I, 199. And others.'

In *RG.* 91 I quoted a vase in London for the sake of its floral decoration, which bears a certain resemblance to that of the stamnos and the oinochoai. I think the reference is worth repeating; and add that the marks on the rock are the same, and that, although there can be no question of the same hand, the general character of the drawing, which is fully carried out in relief-lines, is not unlike. These four vases are already veering towards the softer style of the succeeding period.

## Oinochoe (shape II, with high handle)

London F 100, from Vulci. *Annali* 1845 pl. M, whence *El.* 4 pl. 81. The floral is not given in the reproduction. A wild medley. In the middle, a young satyr embraces a naked maenad, stans cum stante. To the left of this group, a youth sits on a rock, tuning his lyre: it is probably, as Walters says, Apollo. He pays no attention to the couple, but an old satyr who rushes up on the extreme left of the picture would appear to have caught sight of them and to be moved. To the right of the couple, a pair of swans draw a chariot in which a youth sits with a naked woman, who embraces him, on his knee: Adonis and Aphrodite according to Walters, although the Aphrodite is rather small-size for a goddess. It is possible that the youth is Apollo again, with one of his favourites: and that there are two scenes on the vase, not one: Apollo tuning his lyre, in the midst of satyrs; and Apollo in his chariot, embracing. The group in the middle of the picture is merely adumbrated in the reproduction. There is a somewhat similar symplegma on a later vase, a calyx-krater in Brussels (*CV.* IV. Be pl. 1, 11: p. 154, no. 2). I ought to have said that a small animal climbs up the satyr's leg: Walters calls it a panther with a human face, but it looks more like a Manx cat, and behaves like a cat: or could it be a tailless ape? The foot of the vase is carefully finished on the underside, which is decorated—a rare feature—with a thick black ring, surrounded by dots.

### VARIOUS CUPS

These are oddments.

Goettingen J 55. Acquired at Bomarzo. I, Jacobsthal *Gött. V.* pl. 21, 59. I, satyr and maenad. A–B, near the rim, a reserved band with a black wave-tendril. The couple are dancing. The drawing is fully carried out in relief-lines. The picture shows the influence of Clusium tondi (pp. 113–14): the maenad, of the female figures there; the satyr, of figures like the Boston satyr (p. 114, no. 9: Pl. 27, 1); for the uneven ground-line like a rumpled carpet compare the Florence cup (p. 114, no. 10: Pl. 25, 9), for the inverted egg-pattern on it the cup in London (p. 113, no. 2).

Volterra (?), fr., from Volterra. I, Inghirami *Mon. etr.* 5 pl. 55, 8. The reproduction is very crude. I, goddess riding a kētos, escorted by Triton. See *Jb.* 2, 116 (Winter) and Dressler in Roscher s.v. Triton, 1191. Inscriptions *Alacẹa, Tritun*, both retr. Schiassi supposed that an initial sigma was missing and read [S]alacea. The Roman goddess Salacia was wife of Neptunus and mother of Triton; the form Salacea occurs in a Roman inscription of A.D. 279. But it is very unlikely that a letter is missing; the epsilon may be a digamma; and the reading is in fact uncertain. Pauli preferred *Alaiva* (in Roscher s.v. Tritun); but it is not clear that he had seen the original. The fragment probably came from a cup, but a stemless cup is no doubt possible.

Florence, fr. *CV*. pl. 17B32. I (satyr). Relief-lines. Recalls the Clusium Group (pp. 113–22).

Cortona, fr., from Cortona. *NSc*. 1929, 165, h. I, a foot remains, and a small owl perched on a rock. Neat work.

Before leaving these earlier Etruscan vases I ought to say that I take three bell-kraters which Albizzati counts Etruscan, from the fabric of Vulci (*Mél. d'arch.* 37, 112–13 nos. 18–20, 160, and 162–3 figs. 21–22), to be Campanian: see *JHS*. 63, 103–4 (Riccardi Painter).

# CHAPTER IV
# FALISCAN

THE favourite shapes in Faliscan are the cup and the stamnos. There are also skyphoi, calyx-kraters, bell-kraters, one important volute-krater, and other shapes. It might be expected that the same artist painted now a cup and now a pot, and this may very well have been so: but I have found only one certain instance: a hydria in Berkeley is by the same hand as a cup in the Villa Giulia (p. 101). We take the pots first, then pass to the cups.

Faliscan vase-painting seems to have begun about 400 or not much later. The cups, in shape and in decoration, figural as well as floral, are based on the Attic cups of the Jena Painter (*ARV.* 880–4 and 966) and his contemporaries. The earlier pots, or many of them, as will be seen, go back to Attic vases of the early fourth century and sometimes approach them very closely. The 'purity' of the style in some vases (that is, absence of non-Attic flavour) and the complete mastery of the relief-line technique, raise the question whether the early Faliscan masters may not have been Athenian immigrants. If, as I believe, the vases of my 'Fluid Style' (pp. 149–62) are late Faliscan, the fabric lasted through the greater part of the fourth century: but only the earlier and finer phase of Faliscan will be treated in this chapter.

The discreditable reproductions in the Roman *Corpus Vasorum* can sometimes be supplemented by earlier publications in *Notizie degli Scavi*.

## A. FALISCAN POTS
### α. WITH RELIEF-LINES

#### THE NEPI GROUP

*Calyx-kraters*

1. Villa Giulia 8359, from Nepi. A, *Boll. d'Arte* 1916, 363; A, Giglioli pl. 237, 1. A, Athena in her chariot. B, maenad, satyrs, and women. See below.
2. Genoa, from Genoa. A, *Ausonia* 5, 33. A, Zeus in his chariot. B, woman seated, Lasa, and satyr. See below.

*Bell-krater*

3. Villa Giulia 6364, from Corchiano. A, Mingazzini *Le rappresentazioni vascolari del mito dell' apoteosi di Herakles* (= *Mem. Lincei*, 6th series, vol. i) pl. 9, 1. A, Herakles resting, with Athena. B, athletes and woman. See below.

Nos. 1 and 3, from the reproductions, might be by one hand. No. 2 is closely connected, but whether by the same painter can hardly be told from the very faint illustration. All three are extremely like Attic vases from the beginning of the fourth century; and in particular, kraters of the 'Plainer Class' (*ARV.* 866–9 and 966), especially those by the Painter of London F 64 (*ARV.* 867). The bodily forms, as in the 'Plainer Class', are sturdy, fleshy, the relief-lines thick, even coarse; and there is none of the elegance that marks the Diespater Group and most Faliscan vases of the spring and the prime.

The obverse of no. 1, the Villa Giulia calyx-krater 8359, shows Athena in her chariot, with the horses in full movement. She turns her head towards her charioteer Nike, who holds the reins. Eros flies towards Athena, and Hermes goes in front. Behind the car, Pan, small and bearded, with one hoof raised and resting on a rock, holds his club in one hand and raises the other towards his shoulder. A hound accompanies the horses. Behind, two columns represent a building. The procession is said by Della Seta (*Museo di Villa Giulia* 108) and Giglioli (49) to be advancing towards Zeus: Zeus is not visible in the reproductions, and it is not expressly stated that he is represented on the vase.

According to Savignoni (*Boll. d'Arte* 1916, 358) the animal in the upper left-hand corner of the composition is a winged lion, man-headed and bearded, a symbol of Persia; and the subject of the whole picture is Athena returning to Olympus after the victory over the Persians at Marathon. Unfortunately the animal is not very clear in the illustrations and looks more like a griffin. The presence of Pan is said to confirm the interpretation. If Pan were really on the point of mounting the chariot, as Della Seta and Giglioli allege, the case would perhaps be stronger: but there is no indication of that: he stands with one foot on a rock and watches. The building in the background is thought by Savignoni to be the Temple of Athena Nike: his reason is that the columns are Ionic: but the identification is not essential to his theory, which rests on the presence of Pan and the nature of the winged animal. Pan is such a favourite in fourth-century vase-painting that his presence here may have no special significance: on the other hand it may, and I do not feel that the theory is to be rejected absolutely.

Della Seta's notion that the picture 'might be a parody of the Apotheosis of Herakles, drawn from a satyric drama' is echoed by Giglioli, but unless I am greatly mistaken has no other claim to consideration.

The chief picture on the calyx-krater in Genoa, no. 2, is of the same description. Zeus stands in the car, holding the reins, while Nike mounts. Athena raises her hand to them; Hermes is also there, and below, Aphrodite, seated, with Eros, and a swan. It seems that there is a seated woman on each side of the picture, and Eros flying towards one of them.

On the third vase, the bell-krater in the Villa Giulia, Herakles, youthful, is seated, holding a kantharos. His lion-skin is under him, and his club rests on it. One might expect the club to be under his armpit, but it is not. He looks round in the direction of Athena, who stands to right of him, with spear and shield; Nike stands to left of him (holding a wreath or a sash?). To the left, a woman seated, playing with a goose. Farther to the left, a large tripod. To the right, Iolaos with a pair of spears. According to Mingazzini (op. cit. 476) the seated woman is a second Nike, but it is doubtless Aphrodite.

This picture is almost indistinguishable from many similar ones on Attic kraters of the early fourth century: Herakles sitting, often with a kantharos in his hand, among his well-wishers—Athena, Nike, Hermes, Iolaos, satyrs, maenads. Such subjects also occur on fourth-century Italiote vases: it is not with them, however, that the Faliscan vase agrees, either in style or in typology, but with the Attic. Many of these pictures, Attic, Italiote, and other, are collected by Mingazzini in his *Rappresentazioni vascolari del mito dell' apoteosi di Herakles*, pp. 453, 458, and 470–6, but not all under one heading, as his classification is made from a different point of view.[1] The motive is pictorial not sculptural: the fourth-century reliefs that show Herakles seated have no special connexion with the vase-paintings.[2]

The kantharos held by Herakles on the Faliscan bell-kraters and on many of the Attic pictures of the same subject is of the 'Sotadean' type,[3] so called because a vase of this shape in Goluchow is signed by the Attic potter Sotades; another, in the Cabinet des Médailles, bears the signature of a later potter, Epigenes (*ARV*. 727, Eretria Painter no. 33). On the shape see *V. Pol.* 28 and 80, Caskey *B.* 18, Haspels *ABL.* 139 and 248. To the examples given there add Agora P 9469 (Dinsmoor *Hephaisteion* 133 fig. 59); Agora P 9471 (ibid. 138, 22); Ferrara T 308, fragments by the Penthesilea Painter (*ARV.* 588 no. 110); Agora P 2322 (*Hesp.* 4, 501, 480, 8, and 502, 8). The Agora vase is probably somewhat later than the last of the red-figured specimens, the date of which is about 425; and it replaces the stout torus foot which is canonical by a foot borrowed from a type of cup-skyphos which first appears a little after that date (see *BSA.* 41, 18 note 2).

The 'Sotadean' shape of kantharos can hardly have any special connexion with Herakles, to whom all kantharoi are appropriate: but it may be worth mentioning that Herakles is shown holding one on an Attic white lekythos, of archaic style, formerly in the Barre collection (Froehner *Collection de M. Albert B.* 45),[4] and that there is a bronze one in the Museum of Thebes which was found on Mount Oeta and was probably therefore dedicated to Herakles. The kantharoi depicted on our kraters are doubtless of metal: but the only other metal kantharos of the shape or near it preserved is the 'proto-Sotadean' silver one from Trebenishte adduced by Caskey (op. cit. 18: Filow *Die archaische Nekropole von Trebenischte* 30). A full history of the shape would have to take into account first the varieties, secondly the geometric forerunners, and thirdly a good many more representations on vases than space can be found for here. I mention only the representation on an

---

[1] His no. 248 is Attic, not Faliscan, and so is his no. 261 (*ARV.* 867, Painter of London F 64, no. 7); his no. 251 is Attic, not Italiote (*ARV.* 871, Meleager Painter no. 16), and so is his no. 252 (*ARV.* 868, top). His no. 258 is *ARV.* 867, Erbach Painter no. 3; his no. 262 *ARV.* 868, Painter of Louvre G 508, no. 1; his no. 259, Athens 14902, is now published in *AM.* 62 pll. 25 and 27. In his no. 250 there is no Herakles, in his no. 175 Herakles is not seated. Add an Attic squat lekythos, late fifth century, in private possession at Athens (*AM.* 62 pl. 28: see p. 45); also the following Attic bell-kraters: Paris, Musée Rodin, 1 (*CV.* pl. 23, 1–2 and pl. 25, 3–5: *ARV.* 869 no. 2, by the Painter of Louvre G 508); lost (Passeri pl. 216); Vienna 1142 (La Borde 1 pl. 60); Madrid 11017 (L 224: A, Ossorio pl. 23, 1: *ARV.* 879 no. 2, by the Oinomaos Painter); London F 74 (Moses *A Collection of Antique Vases* pl. 13); and the following Attic pelikai: Louvre MN 734 (*CV.* d pl. 48, 3–5); Berlin 2626 (Furtwängler *Coll. Sabouroff* pl. 67 and text); Odessa (*Zapiski Imperatorskago Odesskago Obshchestva* 19 pl. 1, 3 and 1): bell-kraters and pelikai are fourth century, the pelikai later

than the kraters and farther from our Faliscan vase. The Herakles on a stemless cup in Tarquinia (note 3) is an extract from such pictures, or rather a minimal version of the subject: compare the squat lekythos mentioned above.

[2] (1) Naples R 140, from Andros (*EA.* 527: with the Herakles compare the relief in the Cabinet des Médailles, Louis Robert *Collection Froehner, i: Inscriptions grecques* pl. 22, 50); (2–4) Athens, Acr., Small Museum (Walter *Beschreibung der Reliefs im Kleinen Akropolismuseum* 72–4); (5) once Kaki Thalassa (described in *AM.* 12, 293); (6) Rome, Museo Barracco, from Athens (*RM.* 45 pl. 82). See also Walter in *AM.* 62, 41–51.

[3] For example, on a stemless cup, from the beginning of the fourth century, in Tarquinia (*ML.* 36, 487, left: see p. 210 note 1); on the calyx-krater Athens 14902 (*AM.* 62 pl. 25, whence *RA.* 1941, 103) a satyr is bringing the kantharos to Herakles.

[4] This belongs to the series of white lekythoi studied in Haspels *ABL.* 111–12.

Attic vase-fragment of the fourth century in Rhodes (*Cl. Rh.* 6–7, 176), where a metal kantharos is certainly intended.

Two smaller Faliscan vases must belong, I think, to the Nepi Group: certainly have the same character, and stand in the same relation as they to Attic work of the 'Plainer' style:

### Oinochoai

### (shape III: chous)

1. Berkeley 8.989, from Narce. Pl. 15, 1–5. Woman seated, Eros and woman. Eros brings the seated woman box and sash; the maid or companion turns to caress a waterbird. Ht. .174, dm. .136.

### (shape VI)

2. Berkeley 8.988, from Narce? Pl. 15, 12–13. Woman. Ht. .239. The surface is not well preserved. The lower part of the vase is large in proportion to the upper: see p. 266. An oinochoe of this shape is represented on a stamnos by the Aurora Painter (p. 81 no. 2 and p. 84: Pl. 16, 2).

### THE DIESPATER GROUP

This group, which I name after the inscription on a vase in the Villa Giulia, includes most of the finest Faliscan pots. The drawing is highly accomplished and elegant. I divide the group into six sections:

### i. *The Diespater Painter*

These vases are very like Attic work of the early fourth century (*ARV.* 866–79 and 966), and in quality hold their own with most of them.

### Stamnoi

1. Villa Giulia 1599, from Falerii. *RM.* 2 pl. 10 and p. 234; A, *Boll. d'Arte* 1916, 356; A, Ducati *St.* pl. 252, 615. A, Zeus, and Athena. B, satyr and maenad. On A, CANVMEDE, [DIE]SPATER, CVPICO, MENERVA. Mouth and neck of the vase are modern.
2. Villa Giulia 1600, from Falerii. A, phot. Alinari 41183, whence Pl. 16, 1; side-view, *Boll. d'Arte* 1916, 352, left. Replica of the last, without the inscriptions. Part of the lip of the vase is ancient, but I do not know if any of the neck. The photographer has retouched the negative, to remove a high-light, in the region of Eros' wings, Athena's face, and the forepart of her helmet and crest.

### Calyx-krater

3. Berlin 2950, from Cervetri. *AZ.* 1884 pll. 5–6, whence (A) Overbeck *KM.* pl. 25, 1. A, Apollo and Marsyas. B, Zeus seated, with maenad and satyr. See p. 75.

The two stamnoi by the Diespater Painter are of a broad-based type found sometimes in fifth-century Attica and common in Italic bronzework: a list is given by Jacobsthal in *Early Celtic Art* 137. A pair of stamnoi by the Painter of Villa Giulia 1755 (Villa Giulia 1755 and 1756, p. 77, nos. 1–2) are of the same model and must be by the same potter.

A stamnos in Copenhagen, Ny Carlsberg H 152, is of the same type and make, but the neck is a little shorter (see p. 150). A sixth stamnos of the type is in Colmar, and is connected with that in Ny Carlsberg (see p. 153).

No. 1, the stamnos Villa Giulia 1599, is noted for its inscriptions. They are included in the *Corpus Inscriptionum Latinarum* (1 ii 1² no. 454), but not in the Faliscan volume of the *Corpus Inscriptionum Etruscarum*. They may be Latin: but I think there is nothing to show that they are not Faliscan, and Prof. Braunholtz, whom I consulted, agrees. The first inscription seems to have had no final *s*: this may be due to Etruscan influence, like the *Hercele* on a Praenestine mirror in New York (Gerhard *ES.* pl. 147: see Matthies *Die praenestinischen Spiegel* 52), or it may be a slip. The *Corpus* reads *Cupido* with an inverted D, but all other authorities give *Cupico*. If this is right, the artist probably meant Cupigo (rather than Cupico), the same sign of course serving for C and G: he has carelessly substituted one common termination for another, the ending of *robigo, impetigo, scalpturigo* for that of *cupido* and *formido*. The position of the inscriptions, on a narrow band above the pictures—it is the lower border of the tongue-pattern, broadened a little for the purpose—is very unusual. The only other vase I remember with inscriptions so placed is much earlier, an Attic black-figured hydria in the Louvre (F 287: *CV.* III Hd. pl. 69, 4). Such inscribed bands are on the verge of the uses collected by Jacobsthal in *Charites Friedrich Leo dargebracht* 453–65.

Many white details omitted by the draughtsman in *RM.* 2 pl. 10 are visible in the photographic reproductions published by Savignoni and Ducati.

On the front of the stamnoi Athena appears before Zeus, who is waited on by Ganymede and crowned by Eros. Ganymede lays his hand on Zeus's shoulder, and is evidently no new-comer to Olympus. On an Attic volute-krater, by the Syleus Painter, from Al Mina, in Antioch (*JHS.* 59 pl. 1) and on the fragment of an Italiote skyphos, by the Amykos Painter, in New York (*Bull. Metr. Mus.* 7, 97 fig. 5; *Jb.* 52, 61; Trendall *Frühitaliotische Vasen* pl. 11, c), Eros flies towards Zeus, as here, with a wreath. Other examples of Eros in the proximity of Zeus are given in *JHS.* 59, 5–6. The sceptre of Zeus has rings round it, each consisting of two relief-lines and a white line: so also in the replica (Pl. 15, 1) and in no. 3. For his wreath see p. 77. Athena's aegis is slung round her shoulder. A white thong winds about the middle of her spear both here and in the replica (Pl. 15, 1): but the small fylfots on her apoptygma above the waist are absent there. This is not a successful figure. Below, on the left, a duck and a ram.

There are good descriptions of the calyx-krater, no. 3, by Gustav Körte (*AZ.* 1884, 80–90), Furtwängler (*Vasensammlung* 824–6), and Overbeck (*Apollon* 428–31). An unusual version of a popular subject. This is not the only picture of the Contest between Apollo and Marsyas in which Zeus is present, for so he is, as Körte noted, on an Italiote pelike in Naples (3231: *AZ.* 1869 pl. 17): but it is the only one in which Zeus is set right in the middle of the composition as if he were the principal character. Zeus is also larger than the other figures. Marsyas, seated to right of him, holds not the flute but the lyre, and in his other hand the plectrum. Apollo, on the left, with one foot raised and set on a rock, seems to have handed the lyre over to Marsyas and to be inviting him to play it. Behind Apollo, a second satyr, with a flute, holds up one of the auloi towards Marsyas as if begging him (it is Körte's suggestion) to keep to his own instrument and not to meddle with Apollo's lyre. Behind Marsyas, a third satyr, not discouraging him. Below, Aphrodite seated, with a mirror, and Eros (or Himeros or Pothos) kneeling: both are present, as Körte observed, on the Italiote pelike in Naples already mentioned. The youth below Marsyas is thought by Körte to be Olympos, pupil of Marsyas, but Olympos does not appear elsewhere in the guise of a traveller, wearing a chlamys and carrying a pair of spears, and the identification though possible is not certain. Over the left handle, a centaur, holding a torch over his right shoulder and extending his left arm in greeting: for centaurs in such contexts see p. 100. Over the right handle, Eros (or Pothos or Himeros), seated, offering a sprig of bay to a fawn, which clambers up to eat it. The flesh of Aphrodite and her Eros is in white.

On the reverse, Zeus is again seated in the middle: a maenad stands in front of him holding a tympanon in each hand, and Dionysos approaches.

Side by side with a good many Attic vases on which Marsyas plays the flute, there are three on which he plays the cithara or the lyre, and these indicate a version of the legend (not known from extant literature), in which Marsyas not only played the flute, but also essayed the cithara, whether at Apollo's instigation, or of his own accord. This was divined by Michaelis (*AZ.* 1869, 41–2) at a time when only one of the four vases—three Attic, a Faliscan—was above ground; see also Rizzo in *ML.* 14, 61–2. The three Attic are the following:

1. Ruvo, Michele Jatta, 1093. Volute-krater. *Mon.* 8 pl. 42, whence *WV.* 1 pl. 2 and Roscher s.v. Marsyas p. 2454; detail, *ML.* 14, 34. Attic, by the Kadmos Painter (*ARV.* 803, below, no. 1).
2. Syracuse 17427. Calyx-krater. *ML.* 14 pl. 1 and pp. 31 and 38 (where for 'Bologna' read 'Camarina'). Attic, by the Kadmos Painter (*ARV.* 804 no. 2).
3. Heidelberg 208. Bell-krater. Kraiker pl. 41. Attic, by the Pothos Painter (*ARV.* 802 no. 15).

In the Ruvo and Syracuse vases Marsyas has the cithara, in the Heidelberg the lyre.

On another Attic vase of the same period and group the lyre beside the fluting Marsyas may point, as Jessen perceived (in Roscher s.v. Marsyas, p. 2454), to a second performance, lyre following flute:

Paris market (Feuardent). Calyx-krater. Tischbein 3 pl. 12, whence (A) *El.* 2 pl. 66; A, Tillyard *Hope Vases* pl. 19, 122. By the Painter of the Feuardent Marsyas (*ARV.* 803, lower middle, no. 1).

For representations of the contest in which Marsyas plays the *flute* see Overbeck *Apollon* 420–39; Jessen in Roscher s.v. Marsyas; *V.Pol.* 76; *JHS.* 59, 35–42. The earliest of them are contemporary with those in which he plays the cithara or lyre, and most of them belong to the same stylistic group as they, come indeed from the same workshop or workshops. The Attic list is as follows:

About 425–420 B.C.: *ARV.* 791, Dinos Painter no. 21; *ARV.* 802, Pothos Painter nos. 16–18; *ARV.* 803, middle, near the Pothos Painter; *ARV.* 803–4, Kadmos Painter nos.

1 (neck), 3, and 11; *ARV.* 806, top, no. 2, Kadmos Painter or very near; *ARV.* 803, lower middle, Painter of the Feuardent Marsyas, no. 1.

Late fifth century: *ARV.* 851, above, Semele Painter no. 2; *ARV.* 853, Suessula Painter no. 7.

Early fourth century: Fragment of a bell-krater, from Chersones, in Leningrad (*Otchët* 1904, 68); fragment of a calyx-krater in Sarajevo, Bulanda *Kat. der gr. Vasen . . . Sarajevo* 39 (= *Wissenschaftliche Mitteilungen aus Bosnien* 12, 291) fig. 54. The despondent Marsyas on these vases recalls the figure on the Italiote pelike in Naples mentioned above (3231: p. 75: *AZ.* 1869 pl. 17).

Fourth century: Pelike in Leningrad, FR. pl. 87, Schefold *Kertscher Vasen* pl. 18 and *Untersuchungen* fig. 59 and pl. 32, 4; bell-krater formerly in the possession of Lady Cavendish-Bentinck, Tischbein 3 pl. 5, Tillyard *Hope Vases* pl. 27, 169: the youth on the right is Hermes (Overbeck), not Ares (Tillyard).

There is a Faliscan picture of the subject on a cup in Berkeley (Pl. 25, 1; see p. 107).

Myron's group of Athena and Marsyas—the prelude to the contest—is earlier than any extant representation of the contest itself. The Myronian subject is represented on two Attic vases of about 430–425: a fragment of a Nolan amphora, recalling the Phiale Painter, in Athens, Acr. 632 (Langlotz pl. 49), and the well-known chous in Berlin (2418: Hirschfeld *Athena and Marsyas* pll. 1–2; Mirone *Mirone d'Eleutere* fig. 48).

Even earlier than this, Attic vase-painters give the name Marsyas to satyrs, usually playing the flute, but not in competition with Apollo: *ARV.* 401, Villa Giulia Painter no. 3, *c.* 450 B.C. or somewhat earlier; *ARV.* 685, manner of the Hector Painter, no. 1, *c.* 440–430 B.C.; *ARV.* 684, Midas Painter no. 4, same group and period as the last.

Until recently there were no Attic vases extant with the *Punishment* of Marsyas: now there is the great calyx-krater, of about 330 B.C., from Al Mina, in Oxford (1939.599; *JHS.* 59, 35–42 and pll. 2 and 4).

Returning to the Faliscan krater. The figure of Zeus seated in the middle of the obverse divides the Apollo from the Marsyas; and perhaps also the Eros from the Aphrodite, for one might expect to find him at her feet, as in many vases, for instance the hydria by the Washing Painter in New York (Richter and Hall pl. 148: *ARV.* 745 no. 59) or the Italiote squat lekythos in Leipsic (*Jb.* 11, 194). One cannot help fancying that the painter had a model before him in which these pairs were close together and that the Zeus has been moved from the outskirts of the picture to the middle.

On both sides Zeus wears the same wreath as in the Diespater stamnos and its replica. It is ivy or ivy-like, and on an Etruscan mirror in Munich (Gerhard *ES.* pl. 74) Zeus is crowned with ivy. On the reverse of our vase, the sceptre of Zeus has loose rings round it, as in the stamnoi, so that the shaft looks like a thyrsus-shaft, especially as it is not straight but has a slight cast. The head of the sceptre, however, is not like a thyrsus-head, and the sceptre is not meant for a thyrsus: see p. 171.

Another vase was mentioned above, on which Zeus was present at the contest. He also appears at the chastisement of Marsyas, both on the Apulian calyx-krater in Brussels (*CV.* IV Db pl. 7, 7) and on the Attic calyx-krater in Oxford (*JHS.* 59 pll. 2 and 4 and

p. 40); besides, in an earlier episode of the story, on the Italiote bell-krater in Boston (*Annali* 1879 pl. D) where Athena, playing the flute, catches sight of her distorted face in the mirror. On the Brussels vase Aphrodite and Eros are there too, as on the Faliscan krater.

## ii. *The Painter of Villa Giulia* 1755

These vases are close to the Diespater Painter.

### *Stamnoi*

1. Villa Giulia 1755, from Falerii. A, *Boll. d'Arte* 1916, 352, right; *CV*. IV Br pl. 8, 1 and 3 and pl. 9, 1; A, Giglioli pl. 274, 5. A, Dionysos and Ariadne. B, athletes. On the shape of the vase see p. 74. The left-hand youth on B seems to hold a mirror, which is strange.
2. Villa Giulia 1756, from Falerii. *Boll. d'Arte* 1916, 357, and 352, second from right; *CV*. IV Br pl. 8, 2 and 4–5 and pl. 9, 2. Replica of the last. The left-hand youth on B holds a discus (rather than a tympanon, as Giglioli). To the right a really damnable bird, perhaps an owl.
3. Villa Giulia 3593, from Falerii. A, Giglioli pl. 274, 1; a little of B is visible, I think, in *Boll. d'Arte* 1916, 352, behind the volute-krater. A, Dionysos with satyrs and maenads. B, Nike and athlete.

In 1755 and 1756, Ariadne, naked, sits on a panther-skin; Dionysos approaches her; and, above, Eros holds out a phiale towards her (according to Giglioli a stick). Behind Dionysos, a heron, stork, or the like. In 3593 there are two groups, or three. To the left sits a maenad; a satyr embraces her, and Dionysos looks on. Below, Eros kneels, tying a bandage, it seems, round his shank; a duck watches him: I do not understand this figure. To the right, a maenad sits on a chest tuning her lyre and looking back at a satyr who appears to be indicating a tune; Eros flies towards her with a sash. Unusual motives. For chests as seats see p. 111.

Near these:

### *Stamnos*

Villa Giulia 3600, from Falerii. A, *Boll. d'Arte* 1916, 352, third from the right. A, Dionysos seated, with Erotes and maenad. B (according to Della Seta *Mus. Villa Giulia* 76), 'dwarf (?) and woman with tympanon'. Perhaps the 'dwarf' is only an ill-proportioned figure like the youth on Villa Giulia 26017 (*CV*. IV Br pl. 1, 2: see pp. 101–2).

## iii. *The Marcioni Group*

1. Oxford 1945.89, from Orvieto. A, *Cat. Sotheby Dec. 1, 1913* pl. 2, 78; Pl. 17.
   From the Marcioni collection. A, Dionysos seated with Ariadne; B, satyr and maenad. Ht. 0.36. Replica of the next two.
2. Florence, from Orvieto (Settecamini). A, Milani *Mus. Top.* 49, i, 3. The drawing in Conestabile *Pitture murali* 161 (whence Pl. 19, 2) is a contamination of this vase and the replica from the same tomb (see next). A, Dionysos seated with Ariadne.

3. Florence, from Orvieto (Settecamini). A, Milani *Mus. Top.* 49, i, 1. Replica of the last
   two. (See the last.)

Albizzati mentions the two vases from Settecamini in *Mél. d'arch.* 37, 175 note 2 and
says that they are 'identical with several in the Villa Giulia'.

These three stamnoi are replicas one of another, at least as regards the figurework and
the handle-palmettes. As to shape, the Oxford stamnos (no. 1) is so like the Berlin Captives
(p. 88 no. 1) and New York GR 641 (Pl. 18, 7–8: see p. 88) that it must be by the same
potter. For the shape of the two vases in Florence I have only the cuts in Milani's *Museo
Topografico* to judge from, which are exceedingly minute and obscure: I should guess,
however, that it was the same as in the Oxford vase. The drawing of the maeander-band
and of the patterns on mouth and shoulder is the same in Oxford as in Berlin and New
York. The figurework of the Oxford vase and its replicas is not so like, and stands closer
to the Diespater Group than that of Berlin and New York does.

In the Florence stamnoi, or one of them, the left-hand Eros holds a large alabastron in
his left hand and in his right a spattle with which he is anointing Ariadne's hair. The
alabastron is covered with pairs of transverse wavy lines, and is probably of glass: compare the alabastron held by the Lasa on the Villa Giulia cup 43609 (p. 111, μ: *CV.* IV
Br pl. 14, 3). On the left of the picture, an owl, standing on one leg, with head in profile,
reasonably well drawn; in front of it, a sucker of olive (see p. 107).

There has not been time to clean the Oxford vase thoroughly: the restorations in the
picture-zone, seen in the sale-catalogue plate, have been removed, but stretches of the
tongue-pattern, of the egg-pattern, of the maeander are also modern; so are parts of lip
and foot, and the left handle. Surface damage has spoilt the nose of the Eros on the left
of the picture. The restorer placed a phiale in his right hand, and scraped away a little
of the background to conform with this restoration, but there is no evidence for a phiale,
and nothing to show that the object was not a spattle as in the Florence replicas. The
other Eros looks as if he had just let the bird fly out of his hands towards the couple. In
the Florence stamnoi the motive is different: Eros catches Dionysos by the elbow: that
is, unless the hand in Conestabile's drawing is a restoration. Whether there was an owl
in the Oxford picture one cannot say. There is an owl on the reverse, between the legs
of the satyr. The left hand of the satyr is an 'Etruscan-dancer' hand (see p. 114). The
obverse is carried out in relief-lines; there are none on the reverse. The handle-palmettes
are typical early Faliscan, with 'trefoil' and 'heart-loop' (see pp. 150–1).


### iv. *Near the Painter of Villa Giulia* 1755

Compare especially Villa Giulia 3593 (p. 77 no. 3).

### *Stamnos*

Villa Giulia 6152, from Corchiano. A, *Boll. d'Arte* 1916, 364; A (from the same photograph), Giglioli pl. 274, 4; and Pl. 19, 1. A, Polydeukes and Amykos. B, satyrs and
   maenads.

The patternwork above and below the picture is very like that of Villa Giulia 3593.

Preparations for a boxing-match. A naked athlete stands in the middle with the thongs on, his left arm raised above his head, while Nike anoints him, holding the alabastron containing the oil in her left hand and rubbing his chest with her right. She wears chiton as well as peplos, the sleeves showing on the arms. To the left sits a winged youth, a torch in his left hand, and something in the right which I cannot make out in the photograph. A garment is under him and over his left thigh. Lower, on the left, the other boxer, thonged, sits on a rock looking round and up towards his opponent. His right forearm lies along his thigh and his left hand rests on a mattock. He also is being anointed, by a boy who lays one hand lightly on the athlete's shoulder and pours oil from an alabastron held in the other. To the right of this, and below the chief group, is a fountain consisting of an upright slab with a lion-head spout and a rectangular platform for standing the hydria on. A bearded satyr approaches to fill his pointed amphora. Another pointed amphora, broken, lies on the ground in front of the fountain.

The comparative sizes of the figures are unhappy. The seated athlete is perhaps thought of as in the background: at least his forearm is drawn as if on the far side of his adversary's foot. Similarly the fountain may be thought of as in the background, since the Nike's foot and shin cut across in front of it. But fountain, satyr, and seated youth look as if they were in the foreground and are too small. And in fact no inference can be drawn from the apparent arrangement of the planes: for while the legs of the winged youth are drawn as if behind the chief athlete's arm, his torch seems to pass on the hither side of it: compare pp. 93, 96, 154.

There is a noticeable resemblance between the chief group in our picture and that of a boxer being anointed by a companion on a Praenestine cista formerly in the possession of Franz Peter and now in the Vatican (Gerhard *ES.* pll. 6–7, whence, these two figures, Norman Gardiner *Athletics of the Ancient World* fig. 48; *Mus. Greg.* i pl. 37, 1). There the boxer pours oil on his body from a round aryballos and his companion rubs it in with both hands. Norman Gardiner figures the group after Gerhard's very inaccurate drawing in which oil and oil-flask are ill seen: the drawing in *Museo Gregoriano* shows them plainly and makes it clear that the action is not strictly massage, as Gardiner calls it, but anointing. On the stamnos it is Nike herself who oils the athlete, augury of success. The ointment may have been thought of as magical. Medea gave Jason a magic, 'Promethean' salve to anoint himself with before encountering the fire-breathing bulls (Pindar *Pyth.* 4, 221, &c.: see Robert *Heldensage* 795 and Pearson *Fragments of Sophocles* ii, 20): but the scene on the vase is more like that described by Virgil (*Geo.* 4, 415), where Cyrene anoints her son with her own hands before his struggle with Proteus:

> haec ait, et liquidum ambrosiae diffundit odorem,
> quo totum nati corpus perduxit: at illi
> dulcis compositis spirauit crinibus aura,
> atque habilis membris uenit uigor.

Savignoni, who first published the picture (*Boll. d'Arte* 1916, 364), was reminded of the Ficoroni cista (Pfuhl fig. 628), but hesitated to recognize Polydeukes and Amykos in the two boxers, and Della Seta echoed his doubts (*Guida* 85). The identification though not certain is quite probable. These cannot be ordinary mortals: and the moment before the contest between Amykos and Polydeukes is represented on a Praenestine mirror in the Villa Giulia where in attitude the two boxers are not wholly unlike ours (Gerhard *ES.* pl. 171, whence *Festschrift für Benndorf* 149) and the names, *Poloces, Amuces,* are inscribed. That Amykos is beardless is no objection, for so he is on the mirror, and elsewhere. It is in favour of the identification that the scene is laid at a fountain. The presence of a satyr at the fountain connects the picture with the Chastisement of Amykos on the Ficoroni cista; so do the amphora on the ground, and the mattock (see below). The winged figure is a difficulty. It does not look like Eros. If it could be certified as one of the winged sons of Boreas it would clinch the interpretation: but the torch is hard to explain.

Another figure, besides the Amykos of the Praenestine mirror, that recalls the seated boxer on the stamnos is the bronze statue by Apollonios son of Nestor in the Terme, which has been plausibly conjectured by Rossbach to represent Amykos (*Festschrift für Benndorf* 148–52: see also P. L. Williams in *AJA.* 1945, 330–47 and Rhys Carpenter ibid. 353–7).

It should be noted that this is naturally not the only seated figure on a vase that looks round and up: others are the satyr Tyrbas on an Attic Panathenaic in the manner of the Meidias Painter, Naples 3235 (*Mon.* 2 pl. 37; Minervini *Illustrazione di un vaso ruvese del Real Museo Borbonico* pll. 1–2, whence Roscher s.v. Olympos p. 862, whence *AJA.* 1938, 500: *ARV.* 835 no. 10, where the publication by Minervini, the best, should have been mentioned), and the maenad with the lyre on the Faliscan stamnos Villa Giulia 3593 (above, p. 77 no. 3).

A word about the mattock under the hand of the seated boxer. A bronze mattock of this very type was found at Talamone with other reduced models of implements and weapons, and is now in the Museum at Florence (*St. e mat.* i, 137 fig. 37, no. 24); and just such an object is represented among the athletic gear which the little boy is looking after in the Amykos scene on the Ficoroni cista (Pfuhl fig. 628; see p. 59). On an Etruscan scarab in the Thorvaldsen Museum, Copenhagen (Furtwängler *AG.* pl. 19, 34; Fossing *The Thorvaldsen Museum: Catalogue of the Engraved Gems and Cameos* pl. 2, 64), an athlete, bending to pick up his aryballos, has an implement over his shoulder which is not a two-pronged pick and may be a mattock.

## v. *The Aurora Painter*

### *Volute-krater*

1. Villa Giulia 2491, from Falerii. *Boll. d'Arte* 1916, 354–5, and 352 middle; A, Della Seta *L'It. ant.*[1] 243 fig. 276; A, Ducati *Cer.* ii, 467; *CV.* IV Br pll. 5–7, whence (A) Pl. 24, 3; A, Ducati *St.* pl. 216; A, phot. Alinari 41207, whence Pl. 20, 1, Giglioli pl. 271, 1, *Enciclopedia Italiana* s.v. Etruschi pl. 95, Nogara 151, and (neck) *RM.* 52, 185; side, Giglioli pl. 271, 2. A, Eos in her chariot with a boy (Tithonos or Kephalos). B, Peleus and Thetis. On the neck, A, griffins attacking bull, B, griffins attacking deer. At the base of the handles, plastic snake-bodies terminating in plastic fawn-heads (not horse-heads as Giglioli). See below.

2. Villa Giulia 3592, from Falerii. *CV*. IV Br pl. 9, 3–5; A, phot. Alinari 41205, whence Pl. 16, 2. A, naked women at laver. B, naked youth, and maenad. The photographer has retouched the negative, to remove a high-light, in the region of the bird, the egg-pattern above it, the right hand of the woman seated to the right, the right arm of the bather near her. See p. 84.

The volute-krater is one of the best Faliscan vases. Brizio, Savignoni, Weege, Della Seta interpreted the two chief figures as Eos and Kephalos. Giglioli preferred Aurora with the young Sol: it is a pretty thought, and he might have referred to the picture described by Johannes of Gaza (55), in which the Sun was represented by a disk charged with the figure of a child:

ἀλλ' ἐνὶ μέσσωι
ἀνδρομέη μόρφωσε φύσις βρέφος· Ἀντολίη γὰρ
πρώϊος ὠδίνουσα πυριτρεφέων ἀπὸ κόλπων
ξανθοφαὲς μαίωσε φάος νέον· ἐκ δὲ λοχείης
ὄρθριος ἀντέλλων ἀναπάλλεται ὠκὺς ὁδίτης,
καὶ πάλιν ἡβήσαντα παλίμπορος ἠθὰς ἀνάγκη
ἐς δύσιν οἷα γέροντα μεταλλάξαντα κομίζει.

He might have proceeded to quote Herakleitos (fr. 6 Diels):

ὁ ἥλιος νέος ἐφ' ἡμέρηι ἐστίν

with Manilius (1, 182):

nam neque fortuitos ortus surgentibus astris
nec totiens possum nascentem credere mundum
solisue assiduos partus et fata diurna.

Or perhaps Aeschylus (*Ag.* 279):

τῆς νῦν τεκούσης φῶς τόδ' εὐφρόνης λέγω.

Or Sophocles (*Trach.* 93):

ὃν αἰόλα νὺξ ἐναριζομένα
τίκτει κατευνάζει τε φλογιζόμενον
Ἅλιον Ἅλιον αἰτῶ . . .

Or even Shakespeare's seventh sonnet.

But the fact is that the notion of Helios as a child or a young boy, as will be seen from Friedländer *Johannes von Gaza* 170–1, though familiar to the Egyptians, is not very firmly rooted in Greek mythology, and the companion of the amorous goddess is probably either Kephalos or Tithonos: which of the two, it is hardly possible to be quite sure. Both were well known to the Etruscans. On an Etruscan mirror in Florence (Gerhard *ES*. pl. 290, whence Roscher s.v. Tithonos p. 1028 and Cook *Zeus* iii, 258 fig. 171) *Thesan* embraces *Tinthun*. There are several Etruscan examples of a favourite Greek group, a winged goddess running with a boy in her arms, who in Attica at least, as is shown by inscriptions on vases, were understood to be Eos and Kephalos:[1] clay akroterion in Berlin

[1] On Greek representations of Eos pursuing a youth or boy, or carrying him off in her arms, see Furtwängler in *AZ*. 1882, 335–9 and 349–56, Robert *Bild und Lied* 32, Rapp in Roscher s.v. Kephalos pp. 1100–4, Johannes Schmidt ibid. s.v. Tithonos, Jacobsthal *Die melischen Reliefs* 21–3 and 56–7, H. R. W. Smith *Der Lewismaler* 10. Smith alone among these writers mentions the Attic red-figured skyphos in the Cabinet des Médailles (846: de Ridder 497: *ARV*. 694, Pantoxena Painter no. 1) in which the youth is inscribed *Tithonos* (Jacobsthal

(*AZ.* 1882 pl. 15); mirrors in Berlin (Gerhard *ES.* pl. 363, 1), in the Vatican (ibid. pl. 180; Giglioli pl. 134, 1), in Berlin (Gerhard *ES.* pl. 362); and so forth. On a Praenestine mirror in Brussels (ibid. suppl. pl. 74, whence Matthies *Die praenestinischen Spiegel* 87) Eos assaults the hunter Kephalos. But there is no other representation like ours.

Giglioli calls the winged boy preceding the chariot Phosphoros: thinking, no doubt, of Homer:

> ἦμος δ᾽ ἑωσφόρος εἶσι φόως ἐρέων ἐπὶ γαῖαν,
> ὅν τε μέτα κροκόπεπλος ὑπεὶρ ἅλα κίδναται ἠώς.
>
> (*Il.* 23, 226)

and of Virgil:

> Iamque iugis summae surgebat Lucifer Idae
> ducebatque diem.
>
> (*Aen.* 2, 801);
>
> Qualis ubi Oceani perfusus Lucifer unda,
> quem Venus ante alios astrorum diligit ignis,
> extulit os sacrum caelo tenebrasque resolvit.
>
> (*Aen.* 8, 589);

and, in art, of an Apulian vase in Munich (FR. i, 51): but there the winged boy who may be Phosphoros is distinguished from Eros by the aureole round his head. In the Villa Giulia vase the youth may be Eros.

On the type of chariot, see Nachod *Der Rennwagen bei den Italikern* 78 no. 93. A good view of the underside of the car is given, with the axle.

The stars and birds above, the sea-creatures below, recall Apulian vases, the volute-krater in Munich just quoted, or the neck-picture of Pelops and Oinomaos on Naples 3256 (*Mon.* 2 pl. 32, middle).

The animals, described by Giglioli as 'a fish and two monstrous sea-horses' are a dolphin, a sea-horse, and a kētos.

In many Etruscan vases the animals are not fully digested and incorporated into the design: but here the sea-creatures and the flying geese are caught up into the total movement, and I am reminded of the grandiose lines of Nonnus (5, 178):

> . . . πόντος ἔην, γλαυκῆς δὲ λίθος χλοάουσα μαράγδου
> δεξαμένη κρύσταλλον ὁμόζυγον εἴκελον ἀφρῶι
> εἶχε φαληριόωντα μελαινομένης τύπον ἅλμης·
> τῶι ἔνι δαίδαλα πάντα τετεύχατο, τῶι ἔνι πάντα
> χρυσοφαῆ μάρμαιρεν ἀλίτροφα πώεα λίμνης
> οἷα περισκαίροντα, πολὺς δέ τις ὑγρὸς ὁδίτης

is only concerned with Kephalos). The Melian reliefs Jacobsthal pl. 7 and p. 22, nos. 10–13, probably represent Eos and Kephalos, as well as the later relief pl. 37 no. 75. Jacobsthal (22–3) hesitates between this and the alternative—a death-goddess—proposed by Zahn and adopted by Furtwängler. He thinks that the smallness of the boy is an objection. But, first, the early artist exaggerates the size of the goddess; and secondly, he may have thought of Kephalos as a young child; Adonis, too, became the lover of a goddess, but was caught young, ἔτι νήπιος (Apollodorus iii, 14, 4).

It was probably in this form that Eos and Kephalos were represented on the Throne of Apollo at Amyklai: at least the language of Pausanias suggests it, iii, 18, 12 Κέφαλος δὲ τοῦ κάλλους ἕνεκα ὑπὸ Ἡμέρας ἐστὶν ἡρπασμένος.

μεσσοφαὴς ἐχόρευεν ἐπιξύων ἅλα Δελφίς
ψευδαλέην Δ' ἐλέλιζεν ἑὴν αὐτόσσυτον οὐρήν,
καὶ χορὸς ὀρνίθων ἑτερόχροος, ὧν τάχα φαίης
ἱπταμένων πτερύγων ἀνεμώδεα Δοῦπον ἀκούειν.

The subject on the other side of the vase was at first supposed to be Boreas and Oreithyia (Brizio, followed by Weege and Della Seta), but Savignoni saw that it was Peleus and Thetis and that this is one of the few pictures in which Peleus surprises Thetis while she is bathing. So also, he noted, in the fourth-century Attic pelike from Camiros in the British Museum (G 424: FR. pl. 172), where the apparatus of the bath is not detailed in such a matter-of-fact way as here, but where the goddess is in the traditional attitude of Greek women bathing, from the Phineus cup onwards (FR. pl. 41; Attic red-figured pelike in Leningrad, FR. pl. 87, 2; Praenestine mirror in Berlin, Gerhard ES. suppl. pl. 154, whence Matthies *Die praenestinischen Spiegel* 113, q.v.; *Venus lavans sese* of Doidalses; wall-painting in Pompeii, Maiuri *La Casa del Menandro* pl. 14 and pp. 154 and 157). Schefold added (FR. iii, 334) the inscribed Etruscan mirror in New York (799: Gerhard ES. suppl. pl. 96; Richter *Cat. Bronzes* 275, below). Although the scene is the same in all three works the composition and treatment are different. On the Villa Giulia vase there is a vigorous struggle, and among all the many groups of Peleus wrestling with Thetis there is none like this. The cista containing the alabastra is knocked over and its lid falls off. The maids flee, one holding a box, the other a mirror. Thetis' himation lies on a column. The scene is not laid on the sea-shore, as in the London pelike, but at a fountain: two plain spouts project from a rock above. Birds in the air.

There is much that is remarkable in the patternwork of the vase. The handle-palmettes are very like those of the Diespater Group. As in the Diespater stamnos itself and its replica (Pl. 16, 1), three white dots to each side of the mid-petal, and a white dot in the centre of the volute. The loop-shaped mark on the palmette-hearts recurs in the stamnos Villa Giulia 1755 (*CV*. IV Br pl. 9, 1): more will be said about this later (p. 151). The drawing of the maeander is much as in the stamnoi Villa Giulia 1755 and 1756. The pattern-squares have a peculiar form which appears in three other Faliscan vases, perhaps four (see p. 86).

Passing to the neck, we find four unique patterns. We begin with the cavetto moulding on the back of the vase (*CV*. IV Br pl. 6, 1). The pattern here consists of an alternation: from below, a sort of palmette-like reserved space, which is charged with a black palmette; from above, a black space (of similar cut to the reserved space), which is charged with a sort of white palmette. The outline of the reserved space is not exactly that of any palmette, but (as Jacobsthal tells me) more like an aracea (see Eduard Jacobsthal *Araceenformen in der Flora des Ornaments*): he compares, for the *outline* only, clay antepagmenta from Falerii in the Villa Giulia (Giglioli pl. 326, 5) and the gold kōnos-helmet from Ak-Burun near Kerch in Leningrad (*Compte-rendu* 1876 pl. 2, 1; Minns *Scythians and Greeks* 391; Lipperheide *Antike Helme* pl. 154; Pernice *Griechische Pferdegeschirr* 11, above): the *filling* is different. On the front of the vase, aracea-like spaces, reserved, and charged with black *sprung* palmettes (see p. 183), alternate with white lotus-flowers of normal type, both elements starting from below. These two patterns, so far as I know, are unique: but I recognize the same principle in certain *cyma*-patterns on Apulian mascaroon-kraters of the 'A.P. Style', that is, the style of the Persians vase and what goes with it (see *JHS*. 63, 91). In the Persians vase itself (FR. ii, plate at p. 142, fig. 43) the downward-pointing cyma-leaf is reserved, and charged with a black palmette, while the upward-pointing one is black, and charged with a white flower; in the Munich Medea vase (ibid. fig. 45) and the Munich Hades vase (Lau pl. 35: this part is not given in FR. pl. 10) the cyma is similar, but the charge on the downward-pointing leaf is an arrow-head-like leaflet; in the Naples Archemoros vase (phot. Sommer 11104: this part is not given in the publication *Mon. nouv. annales* pll. 5–6) the downward-pointing cyma-leaf is red, with a white bud on it, while the other is black and charged alternately with a palmette and a rosette.

Another decorative motive that recalls Apulian red-figure is the small human face, frontal, in white, set within each coil of the handle-snake: such faces are used in the neck-decoration of the Persians vase (FR. ii, pl. at p. 142, fig. 43); but are not confined to Apulian, for they also occur in the upper band of the Ficoroni cista (*WV*. 1889 pl. 12, 1; Giglioli pl. 287) and are a favourite motive in Campana reliefs (Rohden and Winnefeld *Architektonische römische Tonreliefs*, passim). Jacobsthal adds to my instances an Etruscan bronze bottle, with relief decoration, in Como; two fragments of marble friezes, Roman of the first century A.D., in the Lateran, 149 and 146; a fragment of Gaulish sigillata (Jacobsthal *ECA*. pl. 219, c).

Turning to the patterns on the echinus moulding, we find on the obverse a curious 'black-figure' band through which now a tongue-pattern, and now palmettes, seem to loom. On the reverse it is a monster astragalos, drawn in three dimensions: the beads have been transformed into tympana (not shields as Giglioli thought). The tympana have tassel-like ornaments in the middle: compare those on the Etruscan calyx-krater formerly in the Hasselmann collection (*Kunstbesitz* pl. 18, 819: see p. 135 no. 1).

The nearest approach to this tympanon-pattern is perhaps on an Etruscan urn in Volterra (Brunn *Rilievi* i, pl. 32, 1.)

We now pass to the stamnos by the Aurora Painter, Villa Giulia 3592 (Pl. 16, 2). In the middle a laver, and two naked girls at it. Above, a rock, with a lion-head spout. To the left, a naked woman seated, looking into a mirror which she seems to hold by a ring at the top. Her reflection is seen in profile. To right, another naked woman, also seated, playing with a water-bird—heron or the like—which stands on the edge of the laver (see *JHS*. 59, 34). Beside the laver a cista of the same shape as in the Aurora vase but with handles on the lid, and an oinochoe of shape VI (see p. 73). On the left, a rock; on the right, a hydria, with the himation of one of the bathers rolled up and lying on it—recalling the Cnidian Aphrodite. The maeander is very like that of the Diespater stamnos and its replica (Pl. 15, 1: p. 73, nos. 1–2).

A smaller vase resembles the work of the Aurora Painter, and might be his:

*Skyphos*

Berkeley 8.997, from Narce (?). Pl. 15, 9–11. A, Apollo and Artemis. B, Dionysos and maenad. Ht. 0.287. The surface is in bad condition.

Apollo sits on a rock, tuning his cithara. Artemis approaches, with a torch in her hand. Behind Apollo a young girl, naked, stands on a low platform which is attached to a pillar over which a garment hangs. White was probably used for her flesh, and perhaps for that of Artemis too, but no trace remains.

The composition of the hasty reverse picture is much the same as in other Faliscan vases, see for example *CV*. Villa Giulia IV Br pll. 1–4 and 8–9.

The female figures on the obverse have the same lax attitudes as the bathers on the Villa Giulia stamnos by the Aurora Painter (Pl. 16, 2: pp. 81 and 84). Compare also the hands. The floral designs at the handles of the two vases are much alike.

On the pattern-square see p. 86.

### vi. *The Corchiano calyx-krater*

I think I am right to include this in the Diespater Group.

#### *Calyx-krater*

Villa Giulia, from Corchiano. *NSc.* 1920, 22–3 and 25. A, Aphrodite and Adonis? B, young satyr and maenad, with Nike and a seated male.

The picture on the obverse, though not well preserved, is one of the prettiest in Faliscan. It is divided into two parts by a tall plant in the middle. To right of this, a woman moves quickly forward and embraces a boy who rises towards her as if on wings—but there are no wings—and returns her embrace. Above them Eros, hovering horizontally, draws their heads together with one hand and with the other holds the boy's himation out behind the heads. The three heads nestle close together, encircled by a zone of hands and arms. Head and foreleg of a boar are seen behind the base of the plant. To the right, a satyr sitting on a rock, on which he had spread his panther-skin, looks round at the pair, shading his eyes. To left of the plant, a naked woman sits holding her himation away from her head with both hands and looking down at a swan. Hermes, with one foot raised and resting on a rock, holds his caduceus in his left hand and extends his arm, whether towards the chief pair or towards the naked woman is uncertain. Above the woman a bird flies with a tortoise in its beak.

It is a very unusual representation: the woman and boy embracing remind one of a passage in Aristophanes (*Ach.* 991). They are explained by Bendinelli as Aphrodite and Adonis, and his explanation is probably correct. Bendinelli takes the naked woman, with the swan at her feet, to be Leda. This is possible: there are other fourth-century representations of Leda and the Swan, notably the statue preserved in many copies, the most nearly complete in the Capitoline (*Cat. of the Museo Capitolino* 184-5); and the Attic statuette-vase in the Louvre (*RA.* 1912, ii, 108). Hermes, he thinks, is concerned with Leda, not with Adonis: there are two scenes, separated by the plant. One might prefer to connect the gesture of Hermes with Aphrodite and Adonis, and to suppose that the naked woman is a nymph or the like, and the swan no more than one of those many water-birds in which Faliscan and other Etruscan vase-painters delight.

I do not remember any other ancient monument where a bird carries a tortoise in its beak. The well-known legend of the death of Aeschylus comes to mind, a legend which, although the more circumstantial records of it are not earlier than Valerius Maximus, is at least as old as Sotades of Maroneia (fr. 11 Diehl). The 115th fable of Babrius is about the tortoise who wished she had wings: the eagle heard her, took her up, and let her fall. Bendinelli says that the bird on the Villa Giulia vase is a water-fowl: from the illustration one could not be sure.

The reverse of the vase is described somewhat summarily in the publication. The two chief figures are like many on Faliscan reverses. According to Bendinelli a plant rises from the ground in front of the woman. From the illustration it would have seemed to be a thyrsus, and she to be holding it. The shafts of Faliscan thyrsi often become very broad at the base: see, for example the Villa Giulia cup 1674 (Pl. 25, 4), the New York stamnos (Pl. 18, 7–8), or Villa Giulia 1607 (*CV.* IV Br pl. 2, 3). The youth with the tympanon might have been expected to be a satyr. Not much of the Nike on the left appears in the photograph. The seated male on the right is omitted in the description.

The drawing is at the same stage of development as in Attic vases of the early Kerch style, and the general character is similar. This would indicate a date not later than the third decade of the fourth century. The shape of the vase would agree: it is still short and compact, not tall, slender, flaring, and top-heavy like the later calyx-kraters.

Bendinelli finds Italiote influence, and in the satyr on the obverse a non-Greek 'ethnic type': I cannot detect either. The only definitely non-Attic element is the form of the plant.

The pattern below the picture on the obverse consists of slanting palmettes; on the reverse, of a maeander with pattern-squares. The pattern-square preserved is of an uncommon type. It recurs on three or four other vases with the slight difference that the central dot is sometimes voided. These are, first, the Faliscan Aurora krater in the Villa Giulia (Pl. 20, 1 and p. 83); second, a cup in Goettingen (J 52: Jacobsthal *Gött. V.* pl. 19, 56); third, a Faliscan cup in the University of Vienna (498: Pl. 22, 3 and p. 109); fourth, probably, the Faliscan skyphos Berkeley 8.997 (Pl. 15, 9–11), but here the surface is ill preserved and the form of the pattern-square not absolutely sure. The Goettingen cup was called Faliscan by Jacobsthal (l.c. 29), and the pattern-square would support his attribution. The picture inside shows a satyr sitting on a rock and receiving a large phiale from a maenad who has just filled it from an oinochoe. The style is not very like anything among the other Faliscan vases known to me, and appears to imitate earlier models than they—some Attic cup of about 425 or 420. The exterior is undecorated.

Before leaving the Diespater Group we should perhaps glance at a skyphos which seems to be nearer to it, for example to the work of the Aurora Painter, than to any of the Faliscan cups, although it is rather among the cups that one would expect to find analogies:

### Skyphos

Copenhagen, Ny Carlsberg, H 159, from Chiusi. A, *Bildertafeln Etr. Mus.* pl. 55, 1. A, seated woman (Aphrodite?) and Eros. B, maenad. Large (ht. 0.225).

The woman sits on a chest: see p. 111. Poulsen has already assigned this vase to Falerii. For the attitude of Eros, compare such fourth-century Attic vases as the pelike in Ferrara,

T. 250 (*NSc.* 1927, 155), or that in Copenhagen, Ny Carlsberg, H. 155 (A, *Bildertafeln Etr. Mus.* pl. 54, 1).[1]

A Faliscan stamnos, from the Sabina, in Berlin should perhaps be examined at this point (2953: A, Neugebauer pl. 86; side, Jacobsthal *O.* pl. 144, a), but it is so much repainted that I may be excused from discussing it.

### THE MUNICH NECK-AMPHORA
#### *Neck-amphora*

Munich 3225. A and side, Jacobsthal *O.* pl. 115, c–d. A, Dionysos, satyr, and Eros; B, youth. On the neck, A, Eros; B, the like.

This is no. 296 in Pollak's *Vendita Sarti* (May 7, 1906). Dionysos sits, holding sceptre and kantharos; a satyr approaches him, holding thyrsus and tympanon; Eros kneels or rather crouches on his hams, beating a tympanon. For other examples of Dionysos bearing sceptre instead of thyrsus, see p. 93. His wreath is of long leaves, not ivy: see p. 50. On B, according to Pollak, 'a youth holding in his left hand a drinking-horn and leaning on a tympanon with his right'.

Jacobsthal cautiously describes the vase as South Etruscan; Pollak must be right in calling it Faliscan. The floral ornament, though not the same as in any of our groups, is thoroughly Faliscan in character; and the figurework stands in the same relation to Attic models of the early fourth century as the vases of the Nepi Group or the Diespater Painter. Neck-amphorae are not common in Etruscan red-figure, and there is no exact parallel, so far as I am aware, for the shape.

### A SKYPHOS

Berkeley 8.998, from Narce? Pl. 15, 6–8. A, Herakles; B, satyr.

The surface is in poor condition, and part of Herakles' middle is missing. He sits on a rock, wreathed, with his lion-skin under him, and holds a phiale. His quiver hangs behind him, and a horn lies near his feet. The phiale is drawn in a sort of perspective. The young satyr hastens up to serve him, holding a thyrsus and a large horn. Behind him, a tympanon; before him, a sash. Typical Faliscan floral at the handles, with loops in the hearts (see p. 151).

### THE CAPTIVES GROUP

One of the best-known Faliscan vases is the Berlin stamnos with Achilles slaying the Trojan captives. The New York stamnos GR 641 is connected with it, first, by the shape: it must be by the same potter: characteristic, the ugly handles. See also below, p. 92. Secondly by the drawing of the ornament on mouth, shoulder, below the pictures, and at the handles. The handle-decoration is more elaborate in the Berlin vase, but the likeness is great, even in such details as the palmette-hearts and the axillary flowers.

---

[1] Beginners should notice that most of the clay vases figured in *Bildertafeln des Etruskischen Museums* are not Etruscan. Apulian: pl. 19, 1 (see *ARV.* 968 no. 4); 19, 2; 19, 3; 20; 21; 22; 23, 1; 23, 2; 25, 1; 25, 2; 26, 1; 27 (Canosan); 53, 2; 55, 2. Paestan: pl. 24. Attic: pl. 54. Alexandrian: pl. 26, 2.

Thirdly by the figurework: the hand may be the same, although the preservation of the Berlin stamnos is so poor that one can hardly be certain.

### *Stamnoi*

1. Berlin inv. 5825, from Savona. *Ausonia* 5 pl. 5 and p. 122 fig. 4, whence (A) Ducati *Cer.* ii, 466, (A) Ducati *Storia* pl. 215 fig. 531, (A) Bulas *Illustrations antiques de l'Iliade* 60 fig. 27, (A) *Jb.* 45, 69 fig. 6, (A) Pl. 20, 2; A and side, Jacobsthal *O.* pl. 147; A, Nogara 360; A, *RM.* 52, 129. A, Achilles sacrificing the Trojan prisoners; B, satyr riding panther, and satyr.
2. New York GR 641, from Falerii. A, *St. etr.* 1 pl. 70, 4; A, Richter *Etr.* fig. 140; Pl. 18, 7–8. A, naked maenad and satyr; B, satyr and maenad.

A word about the New York stamnos before turning to the more important vase in Berlin. White is used for the flesh of the maenads, for the thyrsus, and for the duck, but most of it has perished, and with it the inner markings. The fractures have been repainted. On the obverse, part of the maenad's hair is restored. Between it and the thyrsus there is also some restoration: originally there seems to have been a bunch of grapes, in black, with the contour reserved. The maenad on the reverse appears to be holding a garment. The garment she wears is let down to the waist. This motive occurs on several Etruscan vases: an oinochoe in the Vatican (p. 173, θ), a stamnos in the British Museum (F 485: p. 146, λ); compare also a stamnos in Florence (p. 146, 3). In Attic, on a pyxis of about 400 B.C., akin to Meidian, formerly in the Poniatowski collection (Stackelberg pl. 24, 4); in Italiote, on a situla, from Locri, in Reggio, which imitates Attic work of the Meidian school (*NSc.* 1913, suppl., 42 figs. 55–6).

When seen by Galli (*Ausonia* 5, 120) the Berlin stamnos was at Florence in the possession of the dealer Merlini, and the provenience was said to be unknown. According to Neugebauer (*Führer: Vasen* 166) it was found at Savona. I do not remember hearing of any pre-Roman antiquities being found there, but if Faliscan vases have appeared at Genoa I suppose there is no reason why they should not appear at Savona, and nothing would be gained by conjecturing Sovana.

The surface of the stamnos is in very bad condition: many of the details are hard to make out and are not given correctly in the drawing reproduced in *Ausonia*, which can be controlled, to some extent, from the photographs published subsequently by Jacobsthal (*O.* pl. 147) and Dohrn (*RM.* 52, 129). White was used freely, and is ill preserved. Most of the uncertainty, however, is in minor matters. Achilles slays one Trojan captive, and another Trojan stands waiting, his hands bound. Behind Achilles are the tumulus of Patroklos and a sepulchral monument consisting of a column tied with a fillet and supporting a rectangular block topped by a sort of pigna. The Shade of Patroklos stands beside the tumulus and looks on. Head and breast are bandaged. These are the principal figures: on the second plane, to left, a woman, Briseis, standing or moving forward, pointing with one hand, and holding an oinochoe in the other; to right, a Greek in armour seated, looking round at the scene, one hand raised to his chin in a gesture of doubt and concern. Two birds of prey, one in the air, the other perched on a rock, watch intently.

The mound is wreathed with ivy; a shield leans against it, and it is surmounted by a helmet and probably a corslet and a greave. A broken cup hangs by the remaining handle from a nail driven into the mound near the top: it has served, with the oinochoe that hangs below it, for the libation, and has then been broken. Savignoni has already explained this particular. The cup recalls those that hang beside the tomb-doors on the sarcophagus of Torre San Severo (*ML.* 24 pll. 1–2 and p. 42)—the tomb of Patroklos, the tomb of Achilles.

The bandages of Patroklos indicate the wounds of which he died. The motive occurs in other Etruscan representations of shades: on the walls of the Tomba dell' Orco at Tarquinia, *Memrun* and *Eivas V[ilatas]* are both bandaged (*Mon.* 9 pl. 15, 2); so are *Turmuca* and *Pentasila* on the calyx-krater in the Cabinet des Médailles (p. 136 no. 1: Pl. 31, 2), Achilles and Patroklos on the sarcophagus from Torre San Severo (p. 90 no. 6), Patroklos on the sarcophagus of the Priest in Tarquinia (p. 90 no. 5), and in two Italiote Nekyiai, on the volute-kraters in Munich (*FR.* pl. 10) and Naples (3222: *Mon.* 8 pl. 9, whence *WV.* E pl. 2), the sons of Herakles by Megara. Such bandages are not expressly mentioned in extant literature: but the notion that the shades still bear the marks of wounds and mutilation is familiar from the poets: the Deiphobus of Virgil (*Aen.* 6, 494) is the most fearful example, but already in the Nekyia of the *Odyssey* (11, 40–1) many wounded, with blood-stained armour, throng round Odysseus at the trench:

πολλοὶ Ǝ' οὐτάμενοι χαλκήρεσιν ἐγχείῃσιν
ἄνƧρες ἀρηΐφατοι βεβροτωμένα τεύχε' ἔχοντες.

Lines 38–43 were athetized by ancient critics, but must be of great age: perhaps they occurred in another epic—the Nostoi?—and were believed to have been transferred thence.

An erection very like that in the middle of the picture—a column supporting a pear-shaped or pigna-like stone—is figured on an Etruscan skyphos in Boston (Pl. 37: p. 166), and both belong to a class of Etruscan sepulchral monuments—many of which remain—consisting of a hemispherical, oval, or piriform stone, and a support: see Poulsen *Kat. des Etr. Mus.* 94–6 and pl. 83. The form of the support varies: the essential part is the head. The pear shape and the oval are not quite so common as the hemisphere: there are examples from Bologna (*ML.* 20, 471, middle), Orvieto (*NSc.* 1938, 9; and in Copenhagen, Ny Carlsberg: *Bildertafeln des Etr. Mus.* pl. 83, 2), Praeneste (Nogara 58 fig. 20), Marzabotto (Ducati *La città di Misa* 13; Nogara 54). For the column-support, Jacobsthal refers me to the travertine monument inscribed *La. Cnevi. au sacrial* in Perugia (the inscription only, *CIE.* no. 4307: hemispherical head), and to the representation on an urn in Florence, with two persons taking each other's hands, and three onlookers. On the Berlin vase the pigna is not plain, as is usual, but sits in a sort of floral cup: I do not find another instance of this, but note that the pigna from Praeneste stands on a neck ornamented with acanthus.

The representations of Achilles immolating the Trojan Prisoners have often been studied: by Furtwängler (in *FR.* ii, 156–60), Robert (*Heldensage* 1114), Galli (in *Ausonia* 5, 118–27, and *ML.* 24, 36–50), Savignoni (in *Ausonia* 5, 128–45), Bulas (*Les Illustrations antiques de l'Iliade* 57–64), Messerschmidt (*Nekropolen von Vulci* 153–60, and in *Jb.* 45, 64–75).

Seven of these representations go back to a single lost original. The seven are all

Etruscan: the only Greek representation, on the Apulian mascaroon-krater in Naples (3254: FR. pl. 89), is not derived from this source. Two other monuments that must be excluded are the cista Napoléon in the Louvre (1663: *Mon.* 6–7 pll. 61–4, whence *Ausonia* 5, 120–1 and Bulas 56 fig. 24; part, *Encyclopédie photographique* iii, 103–7) and the 'Palermo krater' mentioned by Messerschmidt (*Jb.* 45, 74). On the Paris cista a different moment in the story is chosen—and the engraving on the cista is, in part at least, false. The 'Palermo krater' is the early Paestan bell-krater by the Dirce Painter in Syracuse (*ML.* 28 pl. 2; Trendall *Paestan Pottery* pl. 2, b), which represents not the Slaughter of the Trojan prisoners, but Dolon seized by Diomed and Odysseus (Dohrn in *Gnomon* 14, 588).

The seven that remain are:

1. The Berlin stamnos.
2. London 638, from Praeneste, Praenestine bronze cista (the Révil cista). Raoul-Rochette *Mon. ined.* pl. 20, whence *Ausonia* 5, 122 fig. 3, whence Bulas 58 fig. 26; Walters *Cat. Bronzes* pl. 31; *Jb.* 45, 72–3.
3. Cab. Méd. 920, from Vulci, red-figured calyx-krater of the Turmuca Group, see p. 136, no. 1. *Mon.* 2 pl. 9; Pl. 31, 1.
4. Rome, Museo Torlonia della Lungara, wall-painting from the Tomba François at Vulci. Noël Des Vergers pll. 21 and 28, whence *Ausonia* 5, 119, whence Bulas 62 fig. 29; Garrucci *Tavole fotografiche delle pitture vulcenti* pl. 2, whence (part) *Ausonia* 5, 145; Messerschmidt *Nekropolen von Vulci* 155 (=*Jb.* 45, 65) and pll. 27–39; Giglioli pll. 266–8.
5. Tarquinia, from Tarquinia, painting on the stone Sarcofago del Sacerdote. *Jb.* 45, 67 fig. 4.
6. Orvieto, stone sarcophagus from Torre San Severo (com. Orvieto, on the slope of the Lake of Bolsena). *ML.* 24 (Galli) pl. 1 and pp. 35–50, whence Bulas 60 fig. 28, *Jb.* 45, 67 fig. 3, Giglioli pl. 348.
7. Volterra, from Volterra, alabaster cinerary urn. Brunn *Rilievi* 1 pl. 61, 2, whence *Ausonia* 5, 127, *ML.* 24, 38 fig. 21, Bulas 62 fig. 30, *Jb.* 45, 67 fig. 5.

These seven works had already been put together by Galli, and treated as if derived from a single original. So also Bulas, although, following Furtwängler and Robert, he adds the Apulian vase in Naples, which, as we said before, has no place here. Messerschmidt distinguishes two groups: (1) Sacerdote, San Severo, Volterra, derived from the same original as François; (2) Berlin stamnos, Révil cista, derived from another source; as for the krater in the Cabinet des Médailles, it is but loosely connected, he says, with the picture from the Tomba François. I cannot agree with this division: it seems to me impossible to deny that Achilles, his victim, and the other captive, on the Berlin stamnos; Achilles, his victim, and the right-hand captive on the Révil cista; Achilles (misnamed Ajax) on the Paris krater go back, directly or indirectly, to the same original as the corresponding figures in the painting from the Tomba François and the three monuments permitted to remain with it by Messerschmidt. Messerschmidt's four may descend from a single hyparchetype, but the archetype is the same as that of the stamnos and the cista.

Messerschmidt also states (*Jb.* 45, 71) that the picture on the Berlin stamnos, though painted within the Etruscan sphere of influence, does not presuppose the Etruscan version of the scene, but evidently depends on South Italian models. He mentions four features as showing Italiote influence: the bandage of Patroklos; the figure of Briseis; the figure of the seated Greek; and 'the swan on the rock'. We have spoken of the bandage; in the figure of the Greek I see nothing Italiote; nor in the bird on the rock—such birds are thoroughly Etruscan (p. 96); the figure of Briseis may possibly show the influence of Italiote vases (compare, for example, *CV*. Lecce pl. 31, 4, pl. 31, 6, pl. 31, 8, pl. 46, 5), but this does not prove that the picture as a whole is taken from a South Italian original.

A few words about certain features of the archetype. (1) If there was a structure near Achilles, Bulas is no doubt right in judging that it was a pyre, as in the Révil cista, rather than a stone tomb, as in the Sarcophagus from Torre San Severo, or a tumulus with a monument beside it, as in the Berlin stamnos: these will have been Etruscan substitutes for the Greek pyre. (2) Walters, in his description of the Révil cista, took the figure to the left of Achilles to be 'a female deity, perhaps an Etruscan Fury or Lasa'. Bulas saw that it was male, a companion of Achilles; but went on to conjecture that the Praenestine artist had 'misunderstood his original': did not recognize the Shade of Patroklos for what it was, and transformed the figure into a Myrmidon. I do not find this supposition desirable or necessary. (3) On the Révil cista, besides Achilles, another Greek is slaying a Trojan captive: Savignoni and Bulas think that this was so in the archetype, and see a confirmation of their view in the group on the Paris krater, where the slayer is inscribed *Aivas*, not *Achle*. I take the inscription to be a mere slip (p. 136); and cannot believe that the original artist was so false to the spirit of the Homeric narrative as to give Achilles a partner. (4) In the Berlin stamnos the captive on the right of the picture is not held, but the corresponding figure in the other versions is held by a Greek warrior, and this was no doubt so in the original. In the Tomba François the warrior is named *Aivas Tlamunus*, Ajax son of Telamon. (5) Achilles always wears a bronze corslet, the lower edge of which follows the line of the iliac furrows and the groin, whereas nearly all the other warriors depicted wear a different type, of leather, with pteryges: in the original also, Achilles probably wore a bronze corslet. (6) In most of our representations the hair of Achilles is cropped for mourning,[1] and this is probably an original trait. (7) François, Severo, Sacerdote, Volterra (Messerschmidt's 'François group') agree in (*a* and *b*) the presence and general aspect of Patroklos and of the two Greeks named the Ajaxes in the Tomba François, (*c*) the wearing of vambrace and rerebrace by Achilles,[2] and what is still more remarkable on both arms instead of the right only: it is reasonable to infer that in these points features of the hyparchetype are preserved. They also agree in the presence of

---

[1] *Il.* xxiii, 141 (κείρασθαί τε κόμην), 140 (στὰς ἀπάνευθε πυρῆς ξανθὴν ἀπεκείρατο χαίτην τήν ῥα Σπερχειῶι ποταμῶι τρέφε τηλεθόωσαν), 152 (ὣς εἰπὼν ἐν χερσὶ κόμην ἑτάροιο φίλοιο θῆκεν). Achilles 'polled his head' and did not merely 'shear off a golden lock' as Lang, Leaf, and Myers translate. In Philostratus' picture of the Greeks mourning for Antilochos (*Imagines* ii, 7, 4), Achilles is distinguished from the rest by his short hair: τὸν Ἀχιλλέα μὴ ἀπὸ τῆς κόμης, οἴχεται γὰρ τοῦτο αὐτῶι μετὰ τὸν Πάτροκλον, ἀλλὰ τὸ εἶδος αὐτὸν ἐνδεικνύτω καὶ τὸ μέγεθος καὶ αὐτὸ τὸ μὴ κομᾶν.

[2] Patroklos is missing in the abridged version on the Volterra urn. In the damaged painting on the Sarcofago del Sacerdote there seem to be no remains of vambrace or rerebrace. In San Severo and Volterra Achilles wears vambraces and rerebraces, in François vambraces. It is natural that these protectors should be worn on the right arm only, since the left was protected by the shield. See also pp. 136–7.

Charun: but the figures of Charun are so different that no inference can be made as to his aspect in the hyparchetype, and it is not even certain that he appeared there at all.[1]

The reverse of the Berlin stamnos is reproduced in *Ausonia* 5, 122 fig. 4, but little attention has been paid to it. Galli and Neugebauer (*Führer: Vasen* 166) do not mention any restorations, but from the small photograph with which Jacobsthal has provided me it is clear that much is modern: unless I am mistaken, the whole of the right-hand satyr (except part of the left leg); the pointed amphora; head and forelegs of the panther, left arm, left leg, right foot of the satyr riding it.

Oxford 1945.89 (Pl. 17) of the Marcioni Group (p. 78 no. 1) must be by the same *potter* as the stamnoi in Berlin and New York.

### THE NAZZANO PAINTER

Walters noticed that no. 3 was of similar style to no. 1 (*BM. Cat. iv.* 209).

#### *Calyx-kraters*

1. London F 479, from Falerii. A, Walters, *BM. Cat. iv.* pl. 13, whence Pl. 21, 1; A, phot. Mansell 3258; A, Pl. 22, 1; B, Pl. 21, 3. A, the infant Herakles and the snakes. B, maenads and satyrs.
2. Villa Giulia 1197, from Falerii. A, *Studi e mat.* 3, 176–7; A, *Boll. d'Arte* 1916, 365; *CV.* IV Br pl. 10; A, phot. Archivio Fotografico, whence Giglioli pl. 273, 2, and Pl. 23. A, Iliupersis. B, Apollo and maenad.
3. Rome, Principe del Drago, from Nazzano (N. of Rome).[2] *Mon.* 10 pl. 51 (= Furtwängler *KS.* i, pl. 7), whence Pl. 21, 2. A, Dionysos, and Ariadne sleeping; B, satyrs and maenad.
4. Amsterdam inv. 2583, fr., from Falerii. *CV.* Scheurleer IV B pl. 1 (Pays Bas pl. 87), 5, whence Pl. 21, 5. (Seated male, satyr; satyr, maenad). The first two figures may be from the obverse, the second two from the reverse.

First, the krater from Nazzano, no. 3 (Pl. 21, 2). The picture has been studied by Furtwängler (*Annali* 1878, 80–102 = *Kleine Schriften* i, 213–26) and after him, more briefly, by Salis (*Jb.* 25, 138). Dionysos seems to be thought of as some way off, while a forerunner, a satyr, has already come upon Ariadne asleep. The satyr extends his arm towards her, but the hand is missing and the gesture uncertain. One naturally thinks of the Pompeian wall-paintings in which a satyr draws aside Ariadne's garment for the benefit of Dionysos (Curtius *Die Wandmalerei Pompejis* 311 and 313), but such correspondence as there is may be accidental, nor is there any special resemblance between our picture and any of the other representations of the subject (Watzinger in *Eph. arch.* 1937, 449–53, with references, on p. 451, to previous accounts; see also *ARV.* index 979 s.v. Ariadne and

---

[1] In the sarcophagus from Torre San Severo all that is seen of Charun is a head thrust into the right-hand corner as an afterthought: Galli thinks that the right-hand captive is turning away from Charun in horror, but surely this is not so. Another small error: Hades is not holding a shield. For the dead Trojan lying on his back see pp. 7–8.

[2] The Attic bell-krater mentioned by Furtwängler in *Annali* 1878, 101 (= *KS.* i, 226) and already by Helbig in *Bull.* 1873, 122 is Yale 129 (A, Baur 86 and pl. 7, above, whence *AJA.* 1939, 627: *ARV.* 851, Painter of Louvre G 433, no. 2), which is therefore from Nazzano.

985 s.v. Theseus). The general aspect of our picture is the same as in many Attic kraters of the early fourth century, the more ornate of them, work by the Meleager Painter for instance, or the Oinomaos Painter (*ARV*. 870–4, and 879), and it is likely enough that the painter took one of these for his model: I do not suppose that he has gravely misunderstood it, or altered it very much.

A few matters of detail. Dionysos, here as in the London krater, no. 1, holds both a sceptre and a vine in his left hand. Dionysos is rarely given a sceptre, but one or two Attic instances are quoted in *AJA*. 1939, 629, and there are other Faliscan (pp. 87 and 111). The right hand of the god is missing: it may have held a kantharos. The hand, with tympanon, above his wrist belongs to the maenad on his left. The attitude of Ariadne, as Furtwängler noticed, recalls the sleeping maenad on a very poor Attic calyx-krater of the early fourth century in Würzburg (523: *Mon.* 10 pl. 3; Langlotz pl. 192: *ARV*. 871, Meleager Painter no. 6). To the left of the woman with the fan there is a sort of filling-ornament, hanging from the upper border, which if it had been in an athletic scene or even among the draped youths on a reverse picture would have been taken for a discus. The foot of the satyr who follows Dionysos is drawn on this side of the maenad below: it is another example of uncertainty in the arrangement of planes (see p. 79). What Furtwängler calls the lid of the basket held by the left-hand woman in the lower range is really its contents—the usual low, domed loaf or cake, with a central knob, and at each side a conical or pyramidal loaf. Two rocks. The kalathos on the ground does not seem appropriate.

The London Herakliskos krater (no. 1: Pl. 21, 1, Pl. 22, 1, Pl. 21, 3), one of the most amusing of our vases, has been described by Alexander Murray (*Cl. Rev.* 2, 327) and by Walters in his catalogue: see also Watzinger in *Jh.* 16, 169–70, Robert *Heldensage* 621, Brendel in *Jb.* 47, 201; and above, p. 7. Walters does not mention the restorations, nor is there any indication of them in the drawing he publishes (Pl. 21, 1). They included the left buttock of Herakles and the greater part of his thighs, parts of the snakes, and of the egg-pattern below them; the breast, waist, left arm of Artemis (but not her left hand), and small pieces of her bow; in Hermes, part of the left breast and of the left hand, with nearly the whole of the caduceus-head; in the woman beside Zeus, a small part of the chiton at the feet; the greater part of Athena's left foot. Prof. Ashmole kindly had the restorations removed before the new photograph was taken (Pl. 22, 1).

Below, in the middle, Herakles and his foster-brother, Iphikles. Above them, Apollo, seated. He has been thrust by the artist right into the middle of the composition, just as Zeus was in the Apollo and Marsyas of the Diespater Painter (p. 75). A knotted fillet of wool is fastened to his laurel-staff. The same pretty attitude, and the same drapery, will be found on another vase by the same artist (p. 94, foot). Alexander Murray was no doubt right in speaking of the Ismenian Apollo: Apollo Ismenios was a great god at Thebes, and in his sanctuary there Herodotus saw a tripod which according to an inscription in Cadmean letters had been dedicated by Amphitryon from the spoils of the Teleboans. To right of the children is Athena, holding a bird by the wings: Murray thought that this was 'probably an offering in connexion with the birth of the twin infants', and Walters followed him: but the children are not represented as new-born, and I take the bird to be Athena's owl, with the head in profile, not very accurately observed. To left of the children, Hermes and Artemis. The draughtsman has omitted the arrow mentioned by Walters as in the right hand. To right of Apollo, and shifted a little from her natural place, a white-haired nurse bends towards Iphikles, ready to help him: a nurse (as Murray) and not 'an old paidagogos in stage costume' (as Brendel, *Jb.* 47, 201). True that the flesh is not painted white, but neither is Athena's. Above, on the left, Zeus with sceptre and thunderbolt, and a female beside him with her left arm passed round him—the fingers show, in white, at his left shoulder—and pointing towards the children with her right hand. This is Alcmena according to Murray, Walters, and Robert, but according to Brendel Hera, who had already been suggested as an alternative by Watzinger (*Jh.* 16, 170). The chronological objection is naturally not cogent. Nevertheless it is difficult to think of Alcmena being shown in such intimate connexion with Zeus: possibly our artist had no very keen sense of τὸ πρέπον: but on the whole I incline to Hera rather than Alcmena. Compare the Settecamini Painter's picture of the same subject (Pl. 19, 2 and pp. 5 and 52). The Erotes might be supposed to speak for Alcmena rather than Hera, but perhaps they are not to be taken very seriously, and even if they are, the case could be argued. There are two of them, one flying up with a basket of delights— cakes, it seems, and fruit—the other approaching with a sash. On the other side of the picture, corresponding to Zeus, Dionysos sits watching, with sceptre and vine in the crook of his right arm and a kantharos in his left hand. For vine and sceptre see p. 93. Beside him is a maenad with thyrsus and fan. The fan is just like that on the Drago vase. That the thing below her is meant for a flower, seen from above, is suggested by the flower beside the kalathos on the Drago krater. On the extreme left of the picture there is another maenad answering to the first. The maenads and the Eros with the sash are wing-like extensions thrown out from the main mass of the composition into the region of the handles; and the maenads form a sort of transition to the Dionysiac scene on the reverse (Pl. 21, 2), three large figures, a maenad seated, holding a tympanon, and two satyrs hastening towards her. Between the legs of one satyr, a pointed amphora over-turned. Above, the same discus-like object as in no. 3 (p. 93).

For other representations of the infant Herakles and the Snakes see p. 52.

On the third vase, no. 2 (Pl. 23), the Iliupersis krater in the Villa Giulia, see Tosi in *St. e mat.* 3, 176–7, Della Seta *Mus. di Villa Giulia* 56, Robert *Heldensage* 1262, Giglioli in *Corpus Vasorum*; and above, p. 7. The group of Menelaos, Helen, and Aphrodite is clear, but the rest of the picture, if not crazy, is somewhat confused. Neoptolemos swings Astyanax by the leg—it is an old, traditional group—but the aged Priam, on whom he should be bringing the child down, is well out of range. Again, it really looks as if the warrior on the right were attacking Priam: but from his tiara he must be meant for a Trojan. The fact is that the artist's ingredients included one Trojan with a sword and one Trojan with a bow, and he has dropped them in at random. The bearded man sitting on the left, above, turned away from the scene, should be Zeus, but one could wish that the sceptre were clearer. Nike flies to him with an oinochoe and a sash. The seated or reclining figure corresponding to Zeus on the right is hard to name. Attitude and drapery are very like those of Apollo on the Herakliskos vase, but the man is bearded and holds an object which ought to identify him. Tosi (*St. e mat.* 3, 176–7) took it for a sickle and called the figure Kronos: but it is not like a sickle, though it might pass for a pruning-hook; and Kronos is hardly ever represented on vases—never as a spectator—very seldom indeed in earlier art at all.[1] If it were Kronos, the question why he should be interested in the Sack of Troy would call for an answer. Tosi says that as 'god of death' he would be quite in place: but he was not god of death. Giglioli describes the figure as Pan, holding a pedum: but does not look like Pan, and the thing is not a pedum, as it has a handle. The figure corresponding to Nike at this end of the picture is Eros, who rushes up with a sort of round box in one hand and the lid in the other. Below him, a satyr dances along in the same direction. Eros does not seem very appropriate here, as the group of Menelaos and Helen is far away; and the satyr has nothing to do with the Sack of Troy. Both figures, of course, like the Nike, are already on the reverse: and it is as if they had been lured away from their own setting by the excitement of what is taking place on the other side of the vase. Their defection cuts the reverse picture down to two figures only, Apollo and a maenad. With the maenad one would expect Dionysos, and Giglioli calls him Dionysos, but it is more probably Apollo, as Della Seta saw. There are a good many Attic bell-kraters of the early fourth century in which Apollo, sometimes accompanied by Artemis or another goddess, is surrounded by satyrs and maenads: London F 65 (*AZ*. 1865 pl. 202, 2; *ARV*. 866, Erbach Painter no. 4); Vienna (La Borde 1 pl. 56, whence *El.* 2 pl. 68); Berlin 2645 (*AZ*. 1865 pl. 203); Ferrara T. 187 (Apollo with Artemis, Hermes, and satyr); Ancona (Apollo with Nike, satyr, Hermes, and woman); Villa Giulia 18543 (Apollo with woman, Eros, satyrs, and maenad). On the Faliscan vase the crowd has melted away, leaving only Apollo and a maenad. She holds a thyrsus, and a box, with a pomegranate and a small calyx-krater precariously balanced on the lid. The owl that flies above them is another slight surprise. It might be said in favour of Giglioli's interpretation as Dionysos that on the Faliscan stamnos Villa Giulia 26017 (see p. 101) Dionysos holds what one would take for a laurel-staff.

A word more about certain particulars of the chief picture. The figures are ill assorted as to size. Neoptolemos and Menelaos are purposely made tall, and Menelaos has a mild, overgrown appearance which one has often seen in life (in a picture described by Philostratos, *Imag.* ii, 7, 2, Menelaos is said to be recognizable among the rest of the Achaeans ἀπὸ τοῦ ἡμέρου). But there is no reason why the archer should be much larger than the Trojan with the sword, the satyr tiny, the Nike outsize, and the Zeus little. The artist has a favourite drapery-motive, not a novel one, for it is as old as the second quarter of the fifth century: the garment, falling off, is caught momentarily over one shoulder and one thigh: this appears thrice, in Neoptolemos, in Eros, and in the Trojan swordsman. The motive is discussed in *JHS*. 59, 20. Helen is 'not dressed', wears a

---

[1] On representations of Kronos see Max.Mayer in Roscher s.v.; Richter and Hall 100–1; Cook *Zeus* iii, 929–35. The two vases are *ARV*. 396, Undetermined Mannerists no. 27, and 385, Nausicaa Painter no. 9 (what Cook takes for a child's cap in this is the upper edge of the garment above the embattled border: compare the 'child's nightcap' which Robert saw in a piece of cushion on a cup in Munich (*Hermeneutik* 264–6)). Among the treasures in the sanctuary of Athena at Lindos—according to the dishonest Timachidas (Blinkenberg *Chron. Lind.* 27)—there had been a krater decorated by Daidalos with a representation of Kronos receiving his children from Rhea and swallowing them.

himation only, but has bracelets and a frontlet. She was at her toilet when Menelaos surprised her, and he knocks over her cista as he runs. It contains a mirror and an alabastron. Aphrodite's sceptre has the same shape as that of Dionysos on the Drago and London kraters. She wears peplos and himation. The lower part of the apoptygma is decorated with a broad band of pattern, probably sewn on to the body of the garment. The patternwork inside the shields is probably textile too—round pieces of stuff glued to the shield (Lorenz in *RM*. 52, 186–90). The right shin of Neoptolemos passes behind Helen's head but in front of Aphrodite's: another example of uncertainty in the arrangement of planes (see p. 79).

We have spoken already of Helen's gait, referred also to the look of injured innocence on her face, and of stern reproof on Aphrodite's: this interest in facial expression though recurrent in Etruscan is rare in Faliscan.

Lastly, the fragment in Amsterdam, no. 4 (Pl. 21, 5). The two large figures on the right belong to the reverse of the vase; the two figures on the left to the picture on the obverse, the seated male occupying part of the space above the handle. The maenad has a very Attic appearance.

### THE GROUP OF THE BONN FALISCAN

The drawing here lacks the elegance of the Diespater Group. The figures are more solid, and there is no floral decoration at the handles.

#### i. *The Painter of the Bonn Faliscan*
##### *Stamnoi*

1. Bonn 1569. Pl. 24, 1–2 and Pl. 20, 3. No. 290 in Pollak's *Vendita Sarti* (Rome, May 7th, 1906). A, fight; B, satyrs and maenads (a satyr pursues a maenad; a satyr sits on a rock and talks to a maenad who faces him resting one foot on an elevation). Neck, mouth, foot, handles of the vase are missing. White was used for horses, shields, birds on A, thyrsus and female flesh on B, but most of it has disappeared. We noticed above (p. 7) that the figure of the dead youth lying on his back must be derived from the same original as a similar figure in the Slaughter of the Trojan Prisoners on the relief sarcophagus from Torre San Severo in Orvieto (*ML*. 24 pl. 1 and p. 20 fig. 7, a; Giglioli pl. 348, 1: p. 90, no. 6).

Sinister birds, especially carrion-eaters, are popular in Etruscan art, both in battle-scenes and elsewhere: see above, pp. 2 and 57 and *RG*. 83. Etruria depicts, like Mesopotamia, what Greece expresses in words only. Egypt goes with Greece: a slate palette (part in the Louvre, part in Oxford) shows birds attacking prisoners (cast into a pit?) (Capart *Primitive Art in Egypt* 240, whence Curtius *Antike Kunst* i, 24): but this very early representation seems to stand alone in Egyptian art.

In Greek art the only examples that Studniczka could find (*AM*. 11, 87–92) were both very early—seventh century: a fragment of a clay relief-pithos, from Tenos, in Athens (*AM*. 11, 87; Kunze *Kretische Bronzereliefs* pl. 54, b), and an island gem in the British Museum (*AM*. 11, 92; Furtwängler *AG*. pl. 5, 34; Walters *Cat. Gems* pl. 5, 211). Kunze, many years later, could not add to these (op. cit. 250–1). At most one might say that birds like that which swoops down towards a falling warrior on a Chalcidian vase in Leningrad have a meaning look (Rumpf *Chalk. V.* pl. 88). A parallel motive occurs, of course, in the stories of Tityos and Prometheus. The figure on an ivory plaque in Sparta is probably mythical (Dawkins *Artemis Orthia* pl. 100), and Tityos rather than Prometheus: but it is so badly damaged that one cannot be sure.

Very ancient and drastic examples in Etruria, not later than 600 B.C., are on two Etrusco-Corinthian oinochoai in the Villa Giulia (*Boll. d'Arte* 31, 1937–8, 149 left and 150; ibid. 149 right and 151).

2. Villa Giulia 43968, from Vignanello. *CV.* IV Br pl. 4, 1, 3, and 5–6, whence (B) Pl. 24, 4. A, Dionysos seated, with maenads and naked youths; B, satyr seated with maenads. The youths on A are not characterized, it seems, as satyrs. The youth under the right handle is not falling (Giglioli), but stealing rapidly forward, keeping low. He and his companion are good examples of handle-figures (see *RG.* 29), bending to clear the handles, but natural enough in their attitudes.

We return to the battle-scene on the stamnos in Bonn (Pl. 24, 1–2). A mounted youth, wearing a chlamys, and holding a spear, is faced by two opponents. The upper parts of these two figures are missing, but enough remains to show that they wore chlamydes. In the foreground a dead youth lies on his back, naked: a bird stands on his armpit and pecks at his entrails. To the left of this group, a man, dressed in a chlamys and armed with sword and round shield, attacks a naked youth who turns tail. The youth too has shield and sword. The shield is longer than the man's, but it is hard to be sure that an oval shield is meant and not simply a round shield seen in three-quarter view; and the same may be said of the shield carried by the two warriors on the right of the picture. The naked youth wears a belt; a long scabbard is attached to the belt, close up to it, and hangs at the *right* thigh. We are reminded of the Gauls who were said γυμνοὶ καὶ περιε-ζωσμένοι καταβαίνειν εἰς τὸν κίνδυνον (Diodorus 5, 29, 2, cf. 5, 30, 3; after Poseidonios: Jacoby *FGH.* iia, 303–4). Gauls are often represented with belts: see Bieńkowski *Die Darstellungen der Gallier in der hellenistischen Kunst* [*D.*] and *Les celtes dans les arts mineurs gréco-romains* [*C.*], both passim; Kekulé *Bronzestatuette eines Galliers* 10–11. The belts of the Gauls are mentioned, with their swords and shields, by Callimachus (*Hymn to Delos* 183). On the Faliscan vase the belt seems to be made of small roundels, whether leather or metal, overlapping like scales and no doubt sewn to a strap. The length of the scabbard, and the form of the chape, as Jacobsthal tells me, agree with Gaulish usage (see Déchelette *Manuel* ii, 1110 and 1112). He also points out that according to Diodorus (5, 30, 3: Jacoby *FGH.* iia, 304) the Gauls wore the sword at the *right* thigh (ἀντὶ δὲ τοῦ ξίφους σπάθας ἔχουσι μακρὰς σιδηραῖς ἢ χαλκαῖς ἁλύσεσιν ἐξηρτημένας, παρὰ τὴν δεξιὰν λαγόνα παρατεταμένας): and so it is in several representations of Gauls (Bieńkowski *D.* 107; 109; pl. 8, b; *C.* 86; and *D.* 147 fig. 157, if, as Bieńkowski thinks, this is a Gaul, which is probable though not certain). He adds, however, that according to Polybius 6, 23, 6 Romans, in early times, wore the 'Iberian machaira' at the right side. There are in fact many representations, from many periods, of Romans wearing the sword on the right side (so-called 'base of Domitius Ahenobarbus', *AD.* iii pl. 12, last

4912·1                                                       O years of the second century B.C., as has been shown by Goethert *Zur Kunst der römischen Republik* ii ff.; Arch of Orange, Espérandieu *Bas-reliefs de la Gaule romaine* i no. 260; Adamklissi, Ferri *L'arte romana sul Danubio* 374, 378, 381, 382; Rhenish tombstones, e.g. Rostovtzeff *History of the Ancient World: Rome* pl. 76 and Ferri *L'arte romana sul Reno* 61, 63, 64, 65.

I note that the naked warrior on our vase, and his dead companion, are sharply distinguished from their opponents by their stiff hair; and Diodorus tells us that the Gauls daubed their hair with gypsum until it was as stiff as horses' manes (5, 28, 2; Jacoby *FGH*. iia, 303): the effect is shown in the Dying Gaul and many other sculptures and terracottas. True that one of the maenads on the reverse (Pl. 19, 3) has rather stiff hair too.

That the dead man is a barbarian is suggested by the very un-classic cut of his features; camoys nose, dewlap neck. The face of the other is unfortunately lost: except the chin, which recedes more than that of the mounted warrior, but I do not insist on this.

I think it should be considered whether the naked warrior and his dead companion may not be Gauls: if so, this would be one of the earliest representation of Gauls in classical art: for the Volterran krater in Berlin (p. 128: Bieńkowski *D*. 30) is much later: the Bonn stamnos cannot be after the middle of the fourth century and might still belong to the first quarter. The only other representations that might be as early are the terracottas Bieńkowski 146, and 147 fig. 157.

We have spoken of the two fragmentary figures on the right of the picture as opponents of the mounted youth, and such they must be: the group—a horseman with levelled spear riding at two foot-soldiers and they running to meet him—stands in an old pictorial tradition (compare for example the Attic stamnos, by the Christie Painter, London 98.7–16.1, *CV*. pl. 25, 1, *ARV*. 693 no. 27) and could not be interpreted otherwise in antiquity. The two may be Gauls, for Gauls sometimes wore the chlamys (e.g. Bieńkowski *D*. 109); but there is also the possibility that they are Italians with whom the Gauls have made common cause, or who have taken Gauls into their pay.[1]

There are two other warriors on Etruscan vases who wear a sword, closely attached to a sword-belt, at the right thigh: one is on the column-krater, by the painter of Vatican G 111, in Leipsic (Pl. 6, 5, and p. 49 no. 1), the other on the three-handled stamnos, by the painter of London F 484, in Cambridge (above, pp. 44–5 no. 5: *CV*. pl. 44, 2).

In the Leipsic picture both figures are peculiar. The costume of the left-hand horseman is unusual (see p. 49), but there is nothing that might be Gaulish about it except the shape and length of the scabbard, and the wearing of the sword at the right flank. Studniczka took the youth to be an Italic warrior.

Now the curious thing is that the outfit of the right-hand horseman has certain features that might be Gaulish: Studniczka took him to be a Gaul, and Ducati agreed with Studniczka (*La Sedia Corsini* in *ML*. 24, 450). The head is normal, and the body is almost hidden by the shield—all one can say is that the chest was bare: but, first, the sword is held upright, and so, as Jacobsthal reminds me, is the sword of the Gaul on the Volterran krater in Berlin (p. 128: Bieńkowski *D*. 30); and, secondly, although large oval shields

---

[1] Dionysios I of Syracuse sent Celtic and Iberian mercenaries to help the Spartans in 369 B.C. (Xenophon *Hell*. vii, i, 20 and 31: Beloch iii, i, 120 and 126).

with spine and spindle-shaped boss are not confined to Gauls, this particular shield has
Gaulish traits. We distinguish on it (1) the spina, broadening to a spindle-shaped umbo
in the middle; (2) crossing the spina, two crescents, back to back, one above and one
below; (3) three dots to left and three to right; (4) dots along the rim; (5) a bow: compare
the rendering of the bow on coins of Populonia (*B.M. Cat. Coins Italy* 5 no. 74, whence,
restored, Nogara *Gli etruschi* 153 below, right). So far my own modest observations:
Jacobsthal has provided me with the following learned note:

'The three dots on either side of the umbo probably signify stars.

'Crescents and stars are common Celtic shield-devices, but not entirely wanting in Italy:—

'Samnite shield on a Capuan wall-painting, *Jb.* 24 pl. 9 and p. 104 fig. 3 (stars). Umbria: Aes grave
of Iguvium, Haeberlin *Aes grave* pl. 79, 12–6 (a crescent above, a star to right of the umbo and another
to left);

'Celts. Augustan: Tomb of Caecilia Metella, *Bull. Com.* 23 (1895) pl. 1, A; Loewy *Jb. der kunsthist.
Sammlungen Wien*, n.s., ii, 32 fig. 69; Hülsen *Neue Heidelberger Jahrbücher* 6 (1896), 52: crescents
beside the umbo, facing inwards (misinterpreted as anchors by Hülsen and referred to a naval victory).
Tiberian: Arch at Orange, Espérandieu i, 193 (foot) and 200. Flavian (?): weapon pillars in Florence,
formerly part of the armilustrium on the Aventine, *RM.* 48 pll. 1–18, passim, see especially pl. 16 no.
661 and pl. 18 no. 744. First century A.D.; altar from Nîmes, dedicated to Jupiter Heliopolitanus and
Nemausus, Espérandieu i, 297, Déchelette *Manuel* fig. 496, Cook *Zeus* i, 569, fig. 436; *CIL.* xii, 3072;
Dessau 4288.

'Numerous examples on the Column of Trajan (see Cichorius passim: who the bearers are, and
how their shields are connected with the Gaulish ones, is a question that need not be discussed here).
Add the relief in the Vatican, Sala a croce greca 574A (Lippold *Vat. Kat.* iii, 1 pl. 76, 4).

'It is worth noticing that the crescents in the Leipsic krater are larger than in any other representation.'

Jacobsthal also draws my attention to a terracotta in the Cabinet des Médailles published by Bieńkowski (*C.* 138 fig. 208; Winter *Die antiken Terrakotten* ii, 256, 3), in
which a sword is fastened to the outside of an oval shield: this may explain the bow in
the Leipsic vase: it would be a real bow, fastened to the shield. Bieńkowski takes the
terracotta to represent a Gaul: the shape of the sword, he says, is Gaulish, recalling La
Tène swords between the fourth and the second century B.C., and Jacobsthal agrees. I
imagine that this is a soldier's servant, holding his master's armour, and waiting for him,
wrapped up in the cucullus, in the cold. His master is within, drinking, or clipping, or
roaring native songs.

Jacobsthal further points to the lid of the Celtomachy sarcophagus in the Capitoline
(Bieńkowski *C.* supplementary plate 4; Stuart Jones *Catalogue of Sculptures in the Museo
Capitolino* pl. 14), where the quivers are laid against the insides of the shields and possibly
fastened to them. (It would be natural to pass the quiver through the armlet and hand-
grip, but these are not indicated.)

It will be seen that these Leipsic horsemen do not seem to be ordinary Etruscans:
parts of their equipment may be Gaulish: but the case is not so strong as in the Bonn
stamnos; and here I leave the problem.

The third example of a sword-belt with the sword worn at the right thigh is on the
three-handled stamnos in Cambridge (pp. 44–5: *CV.* pl. 44, 2). Although the costumes,

as we saw above (pp. 44–5) are unusual, there is nothing else in them that could pass as Gaulish.

## ii. *Stamnos*

Philadelphia 4854, from Orvieto. A, *Mus. J.* 11 (1920), 65. A, centaur and naked woman, with seated satyrs; B, satyrs and maenads.

Neck, foot, and one handle are missing. The handle preserved is in the shape of a pair of snakes intertwined. The style is close to the Painter of the Bonn Faliscan.

The centaur pursues the woman, while the satyrs sit and look on. This is an early example of centaurs taking part in the Dionysiac thiasos. Another is on the Faliscan calyx-krater by the Diespater Painter in Berlin (p. 74 no. 3 and p. 75): for it is probably as an associate of the satyrs and maenads that the centaur there has found his way to the scene. A third is on an Italiote oinochoe in Goettingen (J 50: Jacobsthal *Gött. V.* pl. 20, 54), where the centaur attacked by Herakles carries a thyrsus over his shoulder. Much earlier than these is the fragment of a plastic vase (perhaps a ram-head), from the Cabeirion, in Athens, 10461, where a centaur rushes to attack a satyr with his fir-branch: it is related to the Sotades Painter, and belongs to the second quarter of the fifth century: for the style compare a fragment, of a kantharos or a plastic vase, in the Villa Giulia (50328: *Boll. d'Arte* 1927, 320 fig. 23). Still earlier, about the beginning of the fifth century, is a small Etruscan black-figure vase in Munich (985: Sieveking and Hackl pl. 41 and p. 150 fig. 195) where two centaurs are accompanied by a satyr.

## iii. *The Painter of Villa Giulia* 43969
### *Stamnos*

1. Villa Giulia 43969, from Vignanello. A, *NSc.* 1924 pl. 6, b–d; *CV.* IV Br pl. 3, 1–4; A, Giglioli pl. 274, 2. A, male in chariot, escorted by Hermes; under one handle, a woman seated on a rock, with two birds; under the other, Pan seated on a rock, holding a torch. B, naked maenad seated, with satyrs and maenad. The foot of the vase is missing. It is not certain who the driver of the chariot may be: Giglioli conjectures Helios: the head is lost. Nor is it clear what kind of bird the artist meant to draw: they look more like monstrous chickens than anything else.

### *Skyphos*

2. Berkeley 8.999, from Narce? Pl. 18, 9–11. A, satyr and maenad. B, Nike. Ht. 0.243, dm. 0.25. White for female flesh, for wings, for the satyr's pelt. Awkward drawing.

On a fragment in Tuebingen, F 15 (Watzinger pl. 45), I see the same long-backed satyr with short ears, fat arms, white pelt; and conjecture that this also may be by the Painter of Villa Giulia 43969. Watzinger thinks that the vase may have been an oinochoe.

A stamnos found in the same tomb as Villa Giulia 43969 should be by the same *potter*, and the drawing also is not at all unlike:

### *Stamnos*

1. Villa Giulia 43970, from Vignanello. A and side, *NSc.* 1924 pl. 6, e and pl. 7, a; *CV.*

IV Br pl. 3, 5 and pl. 4, 2 and 4. A, naked women at laver, with Eros, women and satyr. B, Dionysos with Ariadne, satyr, and maenad. Under one handle, Pan, frontal, and a goose pecking at his fundament: similarly, on a Boeotian black-figured skyphos of the Cabirion class in Berlin, no. 3159 (Lücken pl. 29, reversed; better, Licht iii, 92) a crane alights on a pigmy's back and attacks him at the same spot; worth mentioning that in the adjoining group the pigmy is sitting frontal like our Pan. Under the other handle, according to the description, one of the large human heads often placed under handles in Apulian and Campanian red-figure. Eros stands on the laver between the two bathers and offers one of them an alabastron. In Attic bathing-scenes, too, Eros is seen standing on the laver: so, for example, in the bell-krater by the Nikias Painter in the possession of Feuardent (Tischbein 1 pl. 59; Tillyard *Hope Vases* pl. 25, 150; *ARV.* 847 no. 14), and a cup by the Jena Painter in Marzabotto (*ML.* 1 pl. 9, 20; Ducati *La città di Misa* 17, above: *ARV.* 881 no. 37). On the reverse, Dionysos gives his hand to Ariadne. The foot of the vase is missing.

## iv. *The Painter of the Berkeley Hydria*

### *Hydria*

1. Berkeley 8.984, from Narce? Pl. 18, 1–6. Satyrs and maenad; under each side-handle, a naked youth watching (one squatting, the other seated on a rock, beckoning to a duck). On the shoulder, palmettes. The foot and base of the vase are in great part modern plaster. Relief-lines are used, but not in the left-hand youth or in any of the patternwork. Poor work.

### *Cup*

2. Villa Giulia 43791, from Vignanello. *CV.* IV Br pl. 15, 5 and pl. 16, 1–2. I, naked youth (Dionysos?) seated, and satyr. A, athlete and woman; B, the like.

### THE STAMNOS VILLA GIULIA 26017

Villa Giulia 26017, from Vignanello. A, *NSc.* 1916, 58; *CV.* IV Br pl. 1, 1–2. A, Dionysos, and a boy waiting on him. B, athlete and woman.

The vase is described by Giglioli in *NSc.* 1916, 58–9, as well as in the *Corpus Vasorum.* Neck, mouth, and foot are wanting. Relief-lines are used in the chief picture, but not, it seems, in the picture on the back. On the style see p. 299.

A youth sits holding a tympanon in his left hand and a long branch, of laurel it would seem, in his right. A naked boy faces him, with one foot on a rock, holding a kantharos ready for him, and in the other hand a thyrsus. Behind, in the field, a horn. To left, a woman, smaller, sitting on the ground with a horn in her hand. In spite of the unusual staff, the chief figure is probably Dionysos, as Giglioli hesitatingly suggests. For the boy, the name of Oinopion comes to mind when one remembers the inscription on the London neck-amphora by Exekias (*WV.* 1888 pl. 6, 2, whence Hoppin *Bf.* 95; *CV.* III He pl. 49, 2).[1] On the other hand, three naked youths are grouped with Dionysos and

[1] The 'red-figured vase with a figure of Oinopion', Durand 389, mentioned in *CIG.* 7451 and in Roscher s.v., p. 794, is really the black-figured vase by Exekias. On Oinopion see also *Annuario*, n.s., 1–2, 71 (Magi).

maenads on another stamnos of the same group, Villa Giulia 43968 (p. 97), and if neither these, nor the youth facing Dionysos on the cup in Amsterdam (p. 111, v) can be named, it may be prudent here also to leave the identification open.

The picture on the back of the vase is a degenerate version of the usual pair, a naked youth (here holding up a headband) and a woman. Both are underset and ill-proportioned, and the 'sawn-off' appearance of the female has led Giglioli (in *CV.*) to make a curious conjecture, that the lower part of her is concealed in the earth, and that the subject is the Anodos of Kore. The figure, however, is complete, peplos-hem, feet, and all.

Giglioli (*NSc.* 1916, 58–9) mentions two stamnoi, from Falerii, in the Villa Giulia, of which I have no note, as so like Villa Giulia 26017 that they must be by the same hand. They are 2349 (A, Nike and youths; B, satyrs and maenads) and 2350 (Giglioli gives 2340: A, Hermes bringing the infant Dionysos to Zeus and Hera; B, Dionysos with satyrs and maenads). There are descriptions of both by Cozza and Pasqui in *NSc.* 1887, 315 and by Della Seta, *R. Museo di Villa Giulia* 72.

### FRAGMENTS IN TUEBINGEN

Tuebingen F 16, fragments of a large vase, an 'amphora' according to Watzinger. Watzinger pl. 46. On the shoulder, part of a female figure (maenad) and part of an animal (panther?) remain. On the body, two rows. Above, remains of at least two subjects: (1) Centauromachy (the disturbance at the wedding of Peirithoos); (2) Dionysiac (satyrs, maenads); Watzinger thinks that fragment (*g*) is from a third subject. It is not clear who the youth in Oriental costume on fragment (*a*) may be. Below, Dionysiac (satyrs).

### A POINTED AMPHORISKOS

New York 26.60.18. A, Richter *Etr.* fig. 139. Red details.

This little vase was attributed by Miss Richter to the Clusium Group (ibid. 46). It has no figurework. The excellent floral design on the body makes one think at first sight of the Clusian skyphoi in New York and Leipsic, or the Castellani head-vase (p. 116 nos. 1 and 3 and p. 118 no. 9: Pl. 28, 4–5); but looking closer one sees that the style is different: this is not the Clusium Group.

The tongues and egg-pattern on the shoulder of the New York vase approximate to the 'Faliscan' type: see p. 150. On the other hand, I do not know anything like these tendrils, palmettes, flowers, and buds in Faliscan. It should indeed be remembered that the *subject* does not occur on any other Faliscan vase: these are not handle-palmettes, traditionally two-dimensional and flat, but a three-dimensional vision of the vegetable world, forming not a subordinate but the principal decoration of the vase. Perhaps the painter is emulating such Clusine vases as those mentioned above. There is one particular that can be matched in Faliscan, and that is the trefoil or 'shamrock' leaf: it is like Faliscan trefoils (p. 150), especially those of the Marcioni stamnos in Oxford (Pl. 16 and pp. 78–9). I do not hold our vase to be certainly Faliscan: but place it here, conjecturally, with a warning.

This is not a wine-vessel, it must be a perfume-vase. The pointed-amphora shape, and the kindred panathenaic, were used for little perfume-vases in many fabrics and at different periods: see *BSA.* 41, 10–14.

In Heidelberg I saw long ago a miniature pointed amphora, E 48, from Falerii, with a satyr and a seated maenad on each side: I thought it Faliscan at the time, but do not know if I was right. It bore no special resemblance to the New York vase either in patternwork or in shape.

### β. *WITHOUT RELIEF-LINES* (except in the tongue-pattern)
#### THE GROUP OF VILLA GIULIA 1607

These stamnoi represent a later and poorer phase of Faliscan. Relief-lines are used in the tongue-pattern above the pictures, but in the first pair it seems likely from the reproductions that there are no relief-lines in the figurework, and in the second pair it is clear that there are none. In the figure of Dionysos on nos. 3 and 4 there is the same use of hatched lines for certain details of the body as in other late Etruscan vases (see pp. 116, 121–6, 135, 166). Giglioli mistook the hatching for hair (*NSc.* 1924, 196, and *CV.*: cf. p. 124).

All four vases are fragmentary: none of them has preserved its neck or mouth, and only no. 2 its foot.

In style the second pair is very like the first.

#### *Stamnoi*

1. Villa Giulia 1607, from Falerii. A, *NSc.* 1924, 197; *CV.* IV Br pl. 2, 1 and 3. A, nymphs quenching the pyre of Herakles. B, maenad. See below.
2. Villa Giulia 1609, from Falerii. *CV.* IV Br pl. 2, 2 and 4. Replica of the last.
3. Villa Giulia 43794, from Vignanello. A, *NSc.* 1924 pl. 7, b; *CV.* IV Br pl. 1, 3–5. A, Dionysos, and women fetching water. B, athlete and woman. See below.
4. Villa Giulia 43795, fr., from Vignanello. A, *CV.* IV Br pl. 2, 5. Replica of the last.

In the middle of Villa Giulia 1607 and 1609 is a rough representation of a pyre that has collapsed. Two women with hydriai are quenching it. On top of it there is a bronze corslet. It is the pyre of Herakles, and the subject is known from several other monuments, mostly vases. These have been collected by Furtwängler in Roscher s.v. Herakles, pp. 2240–1; see also Hauser in FR. ii, 254–6, Robert *Heldensage* 599–600, Mingazzini *Rappresentazioni vascolari del mito dell' apoteosi di Herakles* 441–2, Cook *Zeus* iii, 512–16. The vases are the following:

1. Villa Giulia 11688, from Conca. Fragments of an Attic bell-krater. Described by Della Seta *Mus. di Villa Giulia* 320, and mentioned by Mingazzini op. cit. 442 no. 110. I add a few particulars. One fragment gives (1) part of Herakles lying on the pyre; then to right of it (2) the legs of a male running to right, wearing a short chiton, and stockings of the kind explained by Miss Richter in Richter and Hall 99; then, farther to the right, (3) part of another figure running to right; either (2) or (3) held a hydria, presumably (3): (2) might be Philoktetes, (3) was no doubt a woman. A

second fragment gives part of Athena, bare-headed: a third, part of the lip of the krater, with the patterns. Large style of about 460 B.C., the same sort of thing (I say no more) as the best work of the Boreas Painter.

2. Leningrad. Fragment of an Attic bell-krater. What remains is the lower part of a naked male on a pyre, turned to left, resting on right sole, left knee and the ball of the left foot, left palm; on the right, the fingers of another figure, and perhaps part of the calf; if so it was male. Probably still before 450 B.C. There is no saying whether there was a woman with a hydria or not.

3. Munich 2360. Attic pelike. FR. pl. 109, 2, whence Cook *Zeus* iii, 514; *ARV.* 805, below, no. 1: manner of the Kadmos Painter and very close to him. Late fifth century.

4. S. Agata de' Goti, Dr. Domenico Mustilli. Attic bell-krater. Gerhard *AB.* pl. 31, whence FR. ii, 257 and Cook *Zeus* iii, 516; *ARV.* 867 no. 5, Painter of London F 64. Early fourth century. The man in the right-hand top corner, wearing chlamys and petasos, may be Iolaos (Gerhard) and is certainly not Zeus (Welcker, Mingazzini, Cook). Cook evidently felt a little uneasy about the identification, for he says that 'the peculiar garb implies some confusion with Hermes—perhaps a changed intention on the part of the vase-painter. Was the ground-line originally a caduceus?'

5. Rome, Marchese De Luca Resta. Apulian volute-krater. *Bull. Nap.*, new series, 3 pl. 14, whence Cook *Zeus* iii, 513.

6 and 7. Our pair of Faliscan stamnoi.

It would have been natural to keep apart those works in which Herakles is shown as still on the pyre; but in the earliest of them Herakles is still on the pyre, and yet a woman with a hydria is at hand. Apart from vases, the subject occurs on three monuments only: the first and second have the single figure of Herakles sitting on the pyre; in the third, he lies on it, and Poias or Philoktetes is lighting it:

8. London. Etruscan scarab of banded agate, from near Viterbo. Roscher s.v. Herakles, p. 2241; Furtwängler *AG.* pl. 16, 64; Lippold *Gemmen und Kameen* pl. 37, 8; Walters *Cat. Gems* pl. 11, 622). Second half of the fifth century.

9. Villa Giulia, from Todi. Etruscan mirror of the 'Z Group' (see p. 131 no. 3). *ML.* 23 pl. 3. Bendinelli (ibid. p. 623) saw that the figure at the base of the disk was Herakles on the pyre.

10. Leipsic. Fragmentary marble relief. *Annali* 1879 pl. E, 2. Roman.

In the Munich pelike the women who quench the pyre have their names inscribed: they are Arethousa and Premnousia. Roulez explained the names when he published the vase (*Annali* 1847, 271–2), observing that Πρεμνουσία is mentioned by Hesychios as κρήνη ἐν τῆι Ἀττικῆι, that several springs besides the famous one were called Arethousa, and that the painter, whether he had authority for these particular names or not, must have thought of the women as nymphs of springs: and so they will be on the other vases where they appear. Reinach (*Rép.* i, 481) and Trendall (*Paestan Pottery* 56) call the women on the Apulian vase 'Hyades', but without reason: nor do I understand why Cook describes the woman on the Mustilli krater as 'a mere handmaid' (*Zeus* iii, 516). Similar figures in the two pictures of the Rescue of Alcmena (Paestan bell-krater by Python, London F 149,

*JHS.* 11 pl. 6 whence Cook *Zeus* iii pl. 41, Trendall *Paestan Pottery* pl. 15; Campanian neck-amphora London F 193, *Annali* 1872 pl. A whence Cook *Zeus* iii, 511, *CV.* IV Ea pl. 6, 7) have usually been called Hyades (Engelmann in *Annali* 1872, 8 in Roscher s.v. Hyades, and in *Archäologische Studien zu den Tragikern* 54–7; Murray, Walters, Reinach, Séchan, Cook, Trendall), but there is no evidence for the identification: Engelmann and Séchan quote the words παρθένοι ὀμβροφόροι without reference, but no doubt from Aristophanes *Clouds* 299, where they are applied to the Clouds, not to the Hyades. See also Paul Maas in *JHS.* 62, 38 note 25. Robert (*Arch. Hermeneutik* 50) proposed to call the women on the Alcmena vases Clouds, and this is more likely.

The picture may be thought of as an 'extract' from a many-figured 'Apotheosis of Herakles': on the other hand, it is intelligible as it is, for the corslet, which recurs in the Munich pelike and the Mustilli krater, is sufficient to identify the pyre as that on which Herakles was consumed. Furtwängler quoted Diodorus 4, 38, 3, who says that Herakles sent Likymnios and Iolaos to Delphi to consult Apollo: ὁ Ζὲ θεὸς ἔχρησε κομισθῆναι τὸν Ἡρακλέα μετὰ τῆς πολεμικῆς Ζιασκευῆς εἰς τὴν Οἴτην, κατασκευάσαι Ζὲ πλησίον αὐτοῦ πυρὰν εὐμεγεθῆ· περὶ Ζὲ τῶν λοιπῶν ἔφησε Διὶ μελήσειν.

In 43794 parts of the taller woman's hand and vessel seem to be restored, but that may be the fault of the reproduction. In 43795 the vessel has rather a wide neck, and no back-handle is indicated: it may be a stamnos, as Giglioli suggests, rather than a hydria, although hydriai with no back-handle exist (see p. 103). In 1607 also (p. 103, no. 1) the right-hand vessel seems to have no back-handle, and has a wider neck than the other: it is serving, however, the same purpose as the hydria; and so probably here. One expects to see the spout of a fountain above, but instead there is a bird flying upward.

Giglioli conjectures (*NSc.* 1924, 196, and *CV.*) that this picture also, like Villa Giulia 1607 and its replica (p. 103), is an extract from an Apotheosis of Herakles, and that the women are the same as there. This does not seem very likely. The presence of Dionysos makes one think of the fountain-scene on an Attic black-figured hydria, by the painter of the London Hydria, in the British Museum (B 332: *CV.* III He pl. 88, 4: see Dunkley in *BSA.* 36, 157–8), and also of the inscription Διονυσια κρενε on the fountain-hydria with the signature of Hypsis in the Torlonia collection (*AD.* 2 pl. 8, whence Hoppin *Rf.* ii, 123: *ARV.* 30 no. 2).

It is an old habit to make the woman carrying a hydria on her head smaller than her companions: so for example, about 480 B.C., on the Attic hydria by the Berlin Painter in Madrid (*BSA.* 36 pl. 23: *ARV.* 140 no. 130).

### A PHIALE

Toronto 600. I, Robinson and Harcum pl. 95. Thin fabric. Outside, 'black with a band of egg-and-dot pattern round the lip, and a slightly different band of egg-pattern near the centre'. Inside, heart and eight petals; between each pair of petals, a palmette pointing towards the centre: this is a pleasant re-elaboration of a time-honoured phiale-design: see Luschey *Die Phiale* figs. 17–21, and in *Anz.* 1938, 768. Relief-lines, apparently, for the ribs of the quatrefoil on the heart, and in the egg-pattern of Faliscan type outside the quatrefoil. The palmettes have heart-loops (see p. 151). There is a good deal of painting, but the design is certain.  The only question is whether to place the vase here or in the 'Fluid Group' (p. 149).

### SKYPHOS IN GOETTINGEN

Goettingen J. 54. A, Jacobsthal *Gött. V.* pl. 20, 58. A, youth (satyr?) with a naked woman on his lap, and two women watching; B, satyr pursuing woman.

This much restored vase is Faliscan, and I place it here rather than in the Fluid Group. No relief-lines.  On the rendering of drapery see p. 162.


## B.  FALISCAN CUPS

Faliscan cups may be divided into two classes: (α) those in which relief-lines are used, and (β) those in which there are no relief-lines.  In class (α) the relief-lines are confined to the interior: the exteriors, so far as I am aware, never have relief-lines.

The cups of class (β) are later than the others, but the difference is slight, and there is no gap between.  It is useful to compare, on pl. 237 of Langlotz's Würzburg catalogue, a cup of class α (Würzburg 818) with a cup of class β (Würzburg 820).  The reverses of the two cups are very like, only 820 is more mannered than 818.  (Würzburg 819 on the same plate is not Faliscan, see p. 143, no. 18.)

In class (α) it is hard to distinguish earlier from later: all these cups were probably produced in close proximity and within no long spell of time.  Some small stylistic groups can be made out, but many cups remain unassigned.

### α. *FALISCAN CUPS WITH RELIEF-LINES INSIDE*
#### THE FOIED PAINTER
*Cups*

1. Villa Giulia 1674, from Falerii.  I, *NSc.* 1887, 273, 2; I, *Boll. d'Arte* 1916, 359, 1; I, phot. Alinari 41200, whence Giglioli pl. 272, 1, and Pl. 25, 4; I, *CIE.* no 8180.  I, Dionysos embracing a naked girl (Ariadne).  A, 'youth and women'; B, the like.  On I, retr., *foied · vino · pafo · cra · carefo ·*  Little remains of the last two letters but one.
2. Villa Giulia 1675, from Falerii.  I, *Boll. d'Arte* 1916, 359, 2; I, *CIE.* no. 8179.  Replica of the last.  On I, retr., *foied · vino · pipafo · cra · carefo ·*
3. Villa Giulia 17956, from Monte Cerreto in the territory of Stabia, modern Faleria. I, *NSc.* 1912, 74; I, *Boll. d'Arte* 1916, 359, 3; I, replica of I in the last two.  A, 'naked male and two draped figures'; B, the like.  No inscription.

See p. 7.  Savignoni figures the three replicas together in *Boll. d'Arte* 1916, 359.  In no. 1 the painter has omitted the first two letters of *pipafo*.  The girl leans back to be kissed, her hands clasped round Dionysos's shoulder.  There are similar groups on a mirror in Perugia (Gerhard *ES.* suppl. pl. 31, whence Ducati *Storia* pl. 244, 592) where Lasa embraces a boy lyre-player, and on a fine mirror in Berlin (Gerhard *ES.* pl. 83, whence Ducati *St.* pl. 211, Giglioli pl. 296, 1; Giglioli pl. 296, 2), where the names are inscribed, *Semla* and *Fufluns*. Neither group is a mere repetition of ours, and in the Berlin mirror especially the spirit is different.

The owl is drawn without relief-lines. Where an owl is, in antiquity, olive is apt to be; and the question always arises, whether the artist was conscious of the connexion: often he is. Is he in this picture? or in the stamnoi of the Marcioni Group (p. 78)?

Unfortunate that none of the reverses have been published.

### THE MARSYAS CUP

Berkeley 8.935, from Narce? Pl. 25, 1–3. I, Apollo and Marsyas: the Challenge. A, athletes and woman; B, the like. Dm. 0.253. Full use of relief-lines inside, none outside.

On the subject see p. 76. Good style, of an elegance that recalls the Diespater Group. The style of the following is less elegant, but the drawing of the forms is like:

Oxford 1927.4069, fragment. Pl. 21, 6. I, male seated (Dionysos holding a thyrsus?), and a woman running with a basket in her hand. A (all that remains is a frontal foot). Greatest length 0.108.

### THE PAINTER OF THE TUEBINGEN FALISCAN

#### *Cups*

1. Villa Giulia 3594, from Falerii. I, *Boll. d'Arte* 1916, 360, and 352, the third cup, whence Pl. 25, 6. I, Dionysos seated with Ariadne on his lap, and satyr. A, athlete, woman, and youth; B, the like.
2. Villa Giulia 3595, from Falerii. I, *Boll. d'Arte* 1916, 352, the second cup. Replica of the last.
3. Tuebingen F 13.[1] I, Watzinger pl. 45, whence Pl. 25, 5. I, Dionysos seated, and satyr: the satyr fills the kantharos from a pointed amphora. A, athlete, woman, and youth; B, the like.
4. Paris market. I know this cup from a small collective photograph. Only half the interior picture gets into the photograph, but it suffices to show that the cup is a replica of Tuebingen F 13 by the same hand. There is no branch to left of the satyr's leg.

### THE GROUP OF VILLA GIULIA 3597

#### *Cups*

1. Berlin 2946, from Bomarzo. I, *El. cér.* 3 pl. 25. I, Poseidon, and Amphitrite seated. A, 'athlete and two draped figures'; B, the like.
2. Villa Giulia 3597, from Falerii. I, *Boll. d'Arte* 1916, 352, the fourth cup. I, replica of the last. A, athlete, woman, and youth; B, the like.

---

[1] The cup-fragment Tuebingen F 12 (Watzinger pl. 45, the exterior misprinted E 12), counted Faliscan by Watzinger, seemed to me Attic of the early fourth century.

Perhaps also

Villa Giulia, from Vignanello.  I, *NSc.* 1916, 60.  I, Dionysos seated and satyr.  A, athlete, woman, and youth; B, the like.

According to Della Seta (*Museo di Villa Giulia* 76), Villa Giulia 3596, from Falerii, is a replica of 3597.

### THE GROUP OF WÜRZBURG 818
#### Cups

1. Villa Giulia 26013, from Vignanello.  I, *NSc.* 1916, 59; *CV.* IV Br pl. 14, 4–5, pl. 15, 3, and pl. 17, 6.  I, satyr and Lasa.  A, athlete, woman, and youth; B, the like.
2. Würzburg 818, from Falerii.  I, *Amtliche Berichte* 38 (1917), 301; Langlotz pl. 237. I, Artemis on a fawn, and Eros.  A, athlete, woman, and youth; B, the like.  Note that on I the head of Artemis from the pupil downwards, and the neck, shoulders, upper part of the breast, are modern.

Langlotz compared the two cups.  The outsides are in the same style.  The insides are not so easy to compare, but the drawing of the maeander, and the bold style of the sturdy figures with big hands and loose hair, make it likely that they too are by a single painter.

### THE GROUP OF VILLA GIULIA 1664
Akin to the last group in character.  Probably by one hand.

#### Cups

1. Villa Giulia 3602, from Falerii.  I, *Boll. d'Arte* 1916, 361; *CV.* IV Br pl. 15, 1–2 and 4 and pl. 17, 4.  I, Dionysos seated and Lasa embracing him.  A, athlete, woman, and youth; B, the like.
2. Villa Giulia 44502, from Sant' Oreste.  I, *NSc.* 1924, 330; I, *CV.* IV Br pl. 13, 5. I, Dionysos seated and Eros.  A, athlete, woman, and youth.  The motive of I is explained by Bendinelli (*NSc.* 1924, 331), but misunderstood by Giglioli in the text to the *Corpus*: Eros is filling a phiale at a fountain, the spout of which is in the form of the upper part of a vessel.  Dionysos takes hold of him by the forearm.
3. Villa Giulia 1664, fr., from Falerii.  I, *CV.* IV Br pl. 13, 4.  I, replica of the last.  A, athlete, woman, and youth.
4. Villa Giulia, from Vignanello.  I, *NSc.* 1916, 61.  I, Poseidon seated and Amphitrite. A, athlete, woman, and youth; N, the like.

### THE PAINTER OF VILLA GIULIA 43800
#### Cups

1. Villa Giulia 43800, from Vignanello.  I, *NSc.* 1924 pl. 5, a; *CV.* IV Br pl. 13, 1–3 and pl. 17, 3.  I, satyr and woman; A, satyrs and woman; B, the like.  See p. 299.
2. Villa Giulia 1614, fr., from Falerii.  *CV.* IV Br pl. 12, 4.  I, replica of the last.

3. Villa Giulia 1615, fr., from Falerii. *CV.* IV Br pl. 12, 5. I, replica of the last. A, (woman). Unfinished: the background is not filled in and the white has not been added. See pp. 299–300.

4. Goettingen J 53, fr. Jacobsthal *Gött. V.* pl. 21, 57. I, Dionysos. A–B, (remains of palmettes).

### UNASSIGNED CUPS

α. Vienna, Univ., 498, from Orvieto. *CV.* pl. 28, 1 and pl. 29, 1–3, whence (I) Pl. 22, 3. I, Dionysos and satyr. A, athlete, woman, and youth; B, the like. See the next.

β. Vienna, Univ., 497, from Orvieto. *CV.* pl. 28, 2 and pl. 29, 4–6. Replica of the last by the same hand. On the right of I, the same oinochoe as in the last: the 'chair-leg or table-leg' is due to restoration. Restored also the left knee of the satyr with much of his shank, part of his hair, in Dionysos part of the himation and of the right shank. The 'beard' of the satyr seems to be a chance stain on the vase. In 497 the left hand of the satyr catches the breast of Dionysos instead of being held behind him as in 498. The faces are a little less expressive than in 498. Dionysos, drunk, is helped over rocky ground by a boy satyr. As early as the Amasis painter's amphora in Würzburg (265: *JHS.* 19 pl. 5; Langlotz pl. 73) Dionysos, like his satyrs and maenads, is shown *dancing* under the influence of wine: but Zeus himself might dance, and did so in the *Titanomachy* (fr. v Allen), no doubt after the victory over the Titans—

μέσσοισιν δ' ὠρχεῖτο πατὴρ ἀνδρῶν τε θεῶν τε—

and it is not until the middle of the fifth century that Dionysos is shown the *worse* for liquor, and has to be helped along by a satyr. Miss Pease has collected the earliest examples (*Hesp.* 6, 267): about 450 or not long after on a bell-krater by the Methyse Painter (*ARV.* 410 no. 1) in New York (07.286.85: Richter and Hall pl. 109); about 430 on a fragment of a bell-krater in Corinth (C. 34.379: *Hesp.* 6, 264, 10) which recalls, as Miss Pease saw, the Phiale Painter); about 425 on a pair of oinochoai in Athens (1219 and 1218: *BCH.* 1895, 98 figs. 3 and 4, whence Pfuhl fig. 568; Deubner *Attische Feste* pl. 33, 1 and pl. 8, 3: *ARV.* 757, below). Add a fifth Attic vase, of about 440–430 B.C., a calyx-krater in Tarquinia, belonging to the Group of Polygnotos (*Jb.* 34, 133, Studniczka: *ARV.* 698 no. 59), where Dionysos, though not supported, walks unsteadily. In extant full-size sculpture groups of Dionysos supported by a satyr first appear in the early Hellenistic age (see Arndt, text to Brunn Bruckmann pl. 620), but in work on a small scale Miss Pease points to a fourth-century example, an Attic plastic vase from the North Slope of the Acropolis (*Hesp.* 4, 301 fig. 49).

Dionysos has a fat or distended belly in the two Faliscan cups. I do not remember another example of this till the gross figure in the Hellenistic relief, preserved in many copies, of Dionysos visiting a poet (Hauser *Neuatt. Reliefs* 15, 148, and 189–99; Schreiber *Die hellenistischen Reliefbilder* pll. 37–40; Merlin and Poinssot *Cratères et candélabres* 78; *AJA.* 1934, 137–52, Picard: see also *Rassegna d'arte* 9, 235).

The wreath of Dionysos is not of ivy, but of laurel or the like: see p. 50. For the pattern-squares in 498, p. 86. Two 'heart-loops' (p. 151) in the palmettes on the reverse of 497, but none in 498. For the drapery on the reverses see p. 162. See also below, on Vienna 500.

γ. Vienna, Univ., 499, from Orvieto. *CV.* pl. 28, 4 and pl. 30, 1–3, whence (I) Pl. 22, 2. I, satyr and goat. A, athlete, woman, and youth; B, the like. See the next.

δ. Vienna, Univ., 500, from Orvieto. *CV.* pl. 28, 3 and pl. 30, 4–6. Replica of the last, by the same hand. The subject of the interior is the same as in a later vase in the Drago collection (see Pl. 11, 9 and p. 160 no. 1): a butting contest. On the Vienna cup the satyr clasps his left forearm behind him with his right hand, which was evidently the rule of the game—no handing-off allowed. The satyr's dog, a Maltese, at his master's side, jumps up towards the goat much interested. In the field, between satyr and goat, a drinking-horn. On the right a sash. The figure of the satyr is carried out in relief-lines, but there is no relief in the animals, in the panther-skin, or elsewhere. 'Heart-loops' (p. 151) on the reverses. The two cups are quite like Vienna Univ. 498 and 497, but not by the same hand as they. All four are central pieces, resembling many other Faliscan cups, but not certainly by the same painter as any of those in our lists. The reverses are typical.

ε. Munich (ex Loeb), fragmentary. I, Sieveking *BTV.* pl. 53, 2. I, maenad and satyr. A–B, athletes and women. See p. 300.

ζ. Amsterdam inv. 2674, fr., 'from Rome'. I, Scheurleer *Cat.* pl. 46, 1; *CV.* IV B pl. 2 (= Pays Bas pl. 88), 2. I, male seated with lyre, and satyr dancing. Good style. 'Etruscan-dancer' hand (see p. 114). Scheurleer thinks of Apollo and Marsyas. The satyr cannot be Marsyas; but it is not impossible that the lyre-player should be Apollo. There is another comparison that should be indicated though not pressed: with the pictures of Hermes playing the lyre, and Pans dancing, on an Attic bell-krater by the Dinos Painter in Gotha (*Mon.* 4 pl. 34: *ARV.* 791 no. 26) and of Hermes playing the lyre, a satyr fluting, and satyrs capering round, on an Attic cup of early classical style in Oxford (1943.52: *Ashmolean Museum Report* 1943 pl. 1).

η. Villa Giulia 43608, from Vignanello. I, *NSc.* 1924 pl. 9, a, whence *Anz.* 1926, 75; *CV.* IV Br pl. 12, 1–3; I, Giglioli pl. 272, 2. I, Silenos, naked girl, and woman playing the flute. A, athlete, woman, and youth; B, the like. Inside, a hairy old satyr holds up with his right hand, against his forearm, a young girl, who dances to the woman's flute-playing. She makes 'Etruscan-dancer' gestures with her hands (see p. 114). Silenos supports a thyrsus against his left waist and arm, but the hand is open and is not grasping the thyrsus. He looks like a showman manipulating a puppet. The girl has been dancing, is caught up by Silenos, continues her movements in the air, and will be set down again in a moment, then caught up again, and so on, like a top going on spinning in the palm of the hand. The motive recurs on an Etruscan oinochoe in the Vatican (p. 173, θ). For the attitude of the dancer compare the handle of a bronze oinochoe, from Cerotolo, in Bologna (Ducati *St.* pl. 250, 603 and 605; Giglioli pl. 314, 3). The satyr's ears droop like those of the old Silenos on the Ficoroni cista (*WV.* 1889 pl. 12, 1, Pfuhl fig. 628), which do seem to be pig's ears: according to Weickert (*Festschrift für Loeb* 103) the earliest satyr with pig's ears is on the Midas stamnos London E 447 (*Annali* 1844 pl. H; *CV.* pl. 22, 2: *ARV.* 684, top, no. 3), an Attic work of 440–430 B.C.: but the ears there still seem to be those of a horse.

θ. Villa Giulia 6163, from Corchiano. I, woman washing at fountain, and woman. A, athlete, woman, and youth; B, the like. Brief description in Della Seta *Mus. di Villa Giulia* 86. A naked woman bends to left, forearms extended, at a fountain (lion-head spout as in the stamnos by the Aurora Painter, p. 84); behind her a woman standing to left, head in three-quarter view, holding a garment ready for her. The drawing is pretty, and I regret that I have no more particulars.

ι. Copenhagen, Ny Carlsberg, H156. I, *Bildertafeln Etr. Mus.* pl. 51, 2. I, Zeus. A, athlete and woman; B, the like. Zeus sits with a sceptre in his hand. Behind him, his thunderbolt. Before him his altar, and on it his eagle. Beside him a plant (olive?). Between altar and sceptre, a drinking-horn.

κ. Boston 01.8114. Pl. 26. I, Zeus. A, athlete and woman ; B, the like. On the altar in front of Zeus, a pomegranate, and instead of his eagle, the cock of Ganymede.

λ. Berkeley 8.2303, fragmentary, from Falerii. Pl. 18, 12. I (woman). A, athlete, woman, and youth; B, the like (the upper part of the woman remains). What is preserved of I is part of the right-hand figure-head and bare shoulders of a woman facing left; to right of her, in white, a branch of olive—probably growing, as in the Villa Giulia cups 1614 (p. 108, foot) and 43608 (p. 110, η). Unusual pattern-squares. On the drapery outside, see p. 162. It is thought that the fragment to left of the interior on our plate may belong.

μ. Villa Giulia 43609, from Vignanello. I, *NSc.* 1924 pl. 9, b; *CV.* IV Br pl. 14, 1–3 and pl. 17, 2. I, Lasa. A, athlete and youth; B, the like. For the alabastron in the Lasa's left hand see p. 78. The thing in her right is not an arrow (Giglioli) but the usual spattle (σπάθη) which was dipped into the alabastron, drawn out with oil on it, and applied to the hair (see p. 78 and passim).

ν. Amsterdam inv. 479, from Falerii. *CV.* IV B pl. 2 (Pays Bas pl. 88), 1, 3, and 5. I, Dionysos and youth. A, athlete, woman, and youth; B, the like. Poor style. Dionysos holds a vine and a sceptre, wears a himation (not a chlamys, as Scheurleer), and sits on a box (not 'a stool'). Behind him, his altar. Facing him, a youth, a votary. In the field to the right, a kantharos, fallen or falling. Chests were often used as seats, both in antiquity and in the Middle Ages: in the East pediment of the Parthenon, Demeter and Kore sit on chests (Studniczka in *Jb.* 19, 3–9; A. H. Smith *The Sculptures of the Parthenon* 10); another good example, one of many, is on the hydria by the Jena Painter in Berlin (inv. 3768: Jacobsthal *O.* pl. 84: *ARV.* 883 no. 72); see also pp. 77 and 86. On Dionysos with a sceptre see p. 93; on the attitude of the youth, p. 112.

ξ. Villa Giulia 44500, from Sant' Oreste. I, *NSc.* 1924, 329; *CV.* IV Br pl. 16, 3–5 and pl. 17, 1. I, Herakles and Athena. A, athlete, woman, and youth; B, the like. The oblong below the left hand of the athlete on B may be due to the painter not having filled in the background, compare p. 109 no. 3.

ο. Villa Giulia, from Rignano Flaminio. I, *NSc.* 1914, 271. I, satyr and maenad. A, athlete and woman; B, the like. Unusual style. The maenad has 'Etruscan dancer' hands (p. 114) and may be dancing, but the satyr is not, as his right foot is planted on a rock.

On Villa Giulia 43791 (*CV*. IV Br pl. 15, 5 and pl. 16, 1–2) see p. 101.

### THE GROUP OF OXFORD 570

These are not cups, but are decorated in the same manner as cups, and so are placed here. The shape is like a sort of stemless cup, but without handles: much the same as in the Volcani Group (p. 210); see also p. 48. The make is thin and fine. Relief-lines are used.

#### *Bowls*

1. Leipsic, from Rome. *Jb.* 11, 196 no. 51. I, a naked youth filling a pointed amphora at a fountain. The figure recalls the Amsterdam cup inv. 479 (p. 111, *v*), and so do maeander and pattern-squares.
2. Leipsic, from Orvieto. *Jb.* 11, 196 no. 52. I, head of Athena.
3. Oxford 570. I, Pl. 21, 4. I, head of Athena. Dm. 0.170, ht. 0.047. White details. Replica of the last.

### β. *FALISCAN CUPS WITHOUT RELIEF-LINES*
#### THE SATYR-AND-DOLPHIN GROUP

The outsides of Faliscan cups are regularly without relief-lines: here the inside as well. On the subject, a satyr riding a dolphin, see Amelung in *Strena Helbigiana* 1–9.

#### *Cups*

1. Würzburg 820. Langlotz pl. 237. I, satyr on dolphin. A, athlete, woman, and youth; B, the like.
2. Oxford, no number. Replica of the last. The surface much damaged.
3. Villa Giulia, fr., from Vignanello. I, *NSc.* 1924, 224. I, replica of no. 1. A, athlete, woman, and youth; B, the like.
4. Roman market, from Falerii? I, replica of no. 1. A–B, 'rough figures'.
5. Villa Giulia, fr., from Sant' Oreste. I, *NSc.* 1924, 331. I, replica of no. 1.

The Würzburg cup is the most mannered of the five. Langlotz does not mention the faded white details: fillet round the satyr's head, bandolier round his left shoulder, dots round the rosette below his left hand, dots edging the border against the background good part of the way round, a trio of dots above the sting-ray.

What appears to be the later phase of Faliscan will be treated under the heading of 'the Fluid Group' in Chapter VIII (pp. 149–62).

# CHAPTER V
# CLUSIUM

ALBIZZATI'S studies of this and of the Volaterrae Group which as he saw continues it, will always remain fundamental (*RM.* 30, 129–54; *Atti Pont.*, new series, 14, 221–32). I follow him in speaking of 'the Clusium Group';[1] many of the cups belonging to it were found at Chiusi, and the cups may have been made there. If they, then the whole group. It should be stated, however, that the dividing line between the Clusium Group and the Volaterrae is not easy to draw, and more will be said about that later (pp. 121–4).

## A. CUPS

Nos. 11, 12, 14, 15 were put together by Brunn (*Bull.* 1859, 137–8), nos. 1–5, 8 and 10 added by Albizzati (*RM.* 30, 129–54, see also *Atti Pont.*, new series, 14, 221–32). Walters saw the likeness between nos. 2 and 14 (*BM. Cat. iv*, 208).

The interiors are carried out in relief-line; the exteriors, so far as I know, never have relief-lines.

1. Vatican, from Chiusi. I, phot. Alinari 35812, whence *RM.* 30, 137, Ducati *St.* pl. 217, 534, Giglioli pl. 276, 1, Nogara 147. I, naked woman and satyr. A, naked woman and woman; B, the like. Fractures repainted, with a good deal of restoration (in the woman on the left, part of face and of hair; forearms and hands with most of the sash; navel, right thigh; in the middle woman, part of breasts and of mirror; forehead of the satyr). Some of the white has been gone over.

2. London F 478, from Chiusi? (rather than Falerii, according to Albizzati in *Atti Pont.*, new series, 14, 223 note 3). I, Walters *BM. Cat. iv* pl. 12, 2, whence *RM.* 30, 135. I, three naked women. A, naked youth, and woman; B, the like. The white details do not come out in the reproduction. There are two alabastra in the cista. Walters says that a taenia is twisted round the aryballos, but what one sees is a pair of strigils, and round the neck the usual arrangement of thongs, perhaps not quite accurately rendered (see Haspels in *BSA.* 29, 219–23). The peg may be of the same kind as in no. 9.

3. Florence. I, *RM.* 30, 134; I, Solari fig. 54. I, two naked women. A–B, ?. Much restored: the legs of both women are modern from the knees down, with the feet; modern also part of the right-hand woman's left arm.

4. Volterra, fr., from near Volterra. Inghirami *Mon. etr.* 5 pl. 55, 7. I (naked women).

5. Orvieto 598, fr., from Orvieto. I, phot. Armoni, whence Pl. 27, 8. I (satyr and naked woman: behind her, a laver; the arm of a third figure shows behind her right arm). For the laver compare no. 9.

6. Florence PD 150, fr. I (woman: what remains is the head of the right-hand figure, in three-quarter view to right). A–B (parts of the palmettes are preserved).

---

[1] I write 'Clusium' and 'Volaterrae' rather than 'Clusine' and 'Volaterran', as being a little less question-begging.

7. Where ?, fr. Pl. 27, 6. I, naked woman and two satyrs. I found this rough tracing in my copy of Albizzati's *Due fabbriche* and do not remember where I got it.

8. Rome, Prince Torlonia, from Vulci? I, two naked women and a satyr.

9. Boston 01.8123. Pl. 27, 1–3. I, woman dancing, boy satyr fluting, and satyr at laver. A, naked woman and woman; B, the like.

This is one of the best of these cups. The white and brown details do not all come out in the photograph. The satyr seems to be cooling his hands in the laver. The peg on the left must be a goat's horn tipped with a ball in modern fashion; an alabastron hangs from it by a thong, and above the mouth of the alabastron there is something that I do not make out, perhaps the head of a spathē. Behind the laver a thyrsus. Fine examples of the 'Etruscan-dancer hand': for others see pp. 79, 110, 111, 120, 121: I know an Italian family (a mother and two daughters) who can make Etruscan-dancer gestures with their hands, but judge the faculty to be uncommon even in Italy. For the pattern on the ground-line compare the Bucciosanti mirror Gerhard *ES.* suppl. pl. 35, from Castelgiorgio near Orvieto. The thing held by the naked women on the reverse should be a large horn, the upper part of it cut off by the rim.

10. Florence, from Montepulciano. I, *Annali* 1868 pl. B; I, *RM.* 30, 132 and 144, whence Pl. 27, 9; part of I (=*RM.* 30, 144), *Il Primato artistico italiano* ii, 5 p. 12; I, Giglioli pl. 275, 2. I, Dionysos, a satyr, and a maenad putting the plastinx on the kottabos-stand. A, athlete and woman; B, the like. The maenad holds a flute in her left hand. Σεμνότης in the figure of Dionysos here and on the next vase.

11. Berlin 2943, from Chiusi. I and A, Gerhard *TG.* pl. 10, 3–4; I and B, Montelius pl. 235, 7; I, *RM.* 30, 142; I, Neugebauer pl. 88, 2. I, Dionysos and maenad. A, one naked, and a woman; B, the like. Much restored.

12. Lost, from Chiusi. Inghirami *Mus. Chius.* pl. 88. I, Dionysos and naked maenad. Evidently restored. The maenad held a phiale as in the last vase.

13. Florence V 49, from Chiusi. I, male between naked women. Much restored.

14. Berlin 2944, from Vulci. Gerhard *Trinkschalen* pl. 16, 3–4; I, *RM.* 30, 139. I, mistress and maids. A, one naked, and a woman; B, the like.

15. Berlin 2945, from Chiusi. I and A, Gerhard *TG.* pl. 10, 1–2; I, *RM.* 30, 141. I, woman playing flute and satyr and Papposilenos dancing. The Papposilenos wears the woollen costume of the Satyric and other dramas. A, one naked, and a woman; B, the like. Much restored.

16. Volterra, fr., from Volterra. A (the upper part of the right-hand figure, a naked youth; and one of the palmettes).

17. Lost, from Orvieto. Once in my possession. A (part of a female figure, clothed, just like the left-hand woman in Pl. 27, 2–3). I mention this for the provenience.

I do not know the two cup-fragments in Arezzo mentioned by Albizzati (*RM.* 30 p. 131); nor the following, which according to Bianchi Bandinelli (*Sovana* pp. 60 and 130) belong to this group:

Florence ?, frr., from Sovana. I (satyrs).

Florence ?, fr., from Sovana.  I (two women).
Florence, fr., from Val d'Elsa.


The 'Clusium cups' are closely interconnected.  According to Albizzati those in his list are from one hand: and this may be so.  Nos. 10, 11, 14, 15 perhaps stand a little apart from the rest, but might be nevertheless by the same artist as they.  For safety, however, we speak, within the 'Clusium Group', of a 'Tondo Group' rather than of a 'Tondo Painter' as others have done.

A good cup-fragment in the collection of Prof. A. B. Cook, Cambridge, to whom it was bequeathed by Sir John Sandys, probably belongs to the Clusium Group, although the style seems not quite the same as in any of the cups in our list.  Part of the interior remains: the upper half of a naked woman, wreathed, stands with head in three-quarter to right; on the left, a second person, not much of whom remains, lays a hand on her shoulder; on the right of the naked woman, at the level of her breasts, there is part of a bird, probably an eagle.  Perhaps it was perched on a laver, but nothing of a laver is preserved.  Prof. Cook is reminded of Aelian's Cinderella-story about Rhodopis (*VH.* 13, 33).

The following cup, as De Agostino saw (*St. etr.* 12, 291–5), is from the same fabric as those of the Clusium Group: the exterior, both figures and floral, is indistinguishable from those of the Tondo Group, but the picture inside is by a new artist:

Florence 79240, from Monte San Savino in Val di Chiana (E. of Siena, W. of Cortona).
  *St. etr.* 12, 293 and pl. 57, whence Pl. 27, 4–5.  I, Hermes presenting the egg containing
  Helen to Leda and Tyndareos.  A, one naked, and a woman; B, the like.

The picture inside has charm, although the figures are not very well adjusted to the circular space: the heads overlap, and two of the feet are cut off.  The clothes, and the terrain, are fully shaded.  Tyndareos wears a necklace, Leda a torc and a bandolier.

This is the third or fourth Etruscan vase that figures the story of the Egg containing Helen.  One of them, the Palermo stamnos already described, shows Leda at the altar on which the egg lies, and agrees, in essentials, with the Attic pictures (see pp. 39–42): but the moment that most interested the Etruscan, to judge from the extant representations, a list of which follows, was the *Delivery* of the Egg, for that is the subject not only in two other vases but also in most of the mirrors:

### Vases

1. Cabinet des Médailles 947, from Vulci.  Stamnos by the Settecamini Painter.  Pl. 11, 3–4.  See p. 53, no. 2.  Kastor (or Polydeukes) offers the egg to Leda.
2. Florence, from Monte San Savino.  Our cup.  Hermes brings the egg to Tyndareos and Leda.

### Mirrors

3. Berlin, from Vulci.  Gerhard *ES.* suppl. pl. 75.  Tyndareos (*Tuntle*) has received it from Hermes (*Turms*), who gives him instructions.

4. Lausanne, from Aventicum (Avenches, canton Vaud).[1] Gerhard *ES*. pl. 370. Hermes offers it to Tyndareos, in the presence of Leda, and of two winged goddesses who lean on Hermes' shoulders.

5. Once in the possession of Mancini at Orvieto, from Orvieto. Gerhard *ES*. suppl. pl. 76. Leda has received it from Hermes, in the presence of Kastor (or Polydeukes).

6. Perugia, from Porano. Gerhard *ES*. suppl. pl. 77. *Kastur* gives it to *Tuntle*, in the presence of *Latva*, and of *Turan*, a woman (handmaid of Turan ?), *Pultuce*. The mirror belongs to the great group of late Etruscan mirrors referred to on pp. 130–1.

7. Berlin. Gerhard *ES*. pl. 189. Hermes gives the egg to Leda, in the presence of Tyndareos. The mirror is a poor specimen of the same group as the last.

8. Louvre. Gerhard *ES*. pl. 410, 2. The Dioscuri are seated facing each other: one of them holds the egg, and they seem to be wondering what to do with it.

## B. SKYPHOI
### (i: ordinary shape)

Florence, from Volterra. Inghirami pl. 185. A, satyr and naked maenad; B, the like. This goes with the column-kraters in Volterra (Passeri pl. 139) and Florence (Inghirami *VF*. pl. 67) mentioned on p. 122; and the Florence vase, of uncertain shape (Inghirami *VF*. pl. 271) mentioned on p. 120.

Here we find for the first time a treatment of the female breasts which is common in the Clusium Group: in the frontal breast the upper part of the base, and in the profile breast the whole visible part of the base, are indicated by brief hatched lines: 'Clusium breasts': compare pp. 120 and 122.

I cannot be sure from the illustration whether relief-lines are used or no, but I should guess not.

### (ii: a special type)

These are small finely-fashioned vases with exaggerated cyma reversa profile: evidently by one potter. This stage in the development of the skyphos is not quite reached in Attic red-figure (London, *CV*. pl. 31, 6; Agora P 8270), but in Attic black ware it practically is: e.g. in Agora P 1829 (*Hesp*. 3, 320, 6), Leyden 118 (Holwerda *Gebruiksaardewerk* pl. 1), Alexandria (Breccia *Sciatbi* pl. 56, 120): the last was found at Alexandria, and is probably therefore, if not certainly, later than 331 B.C.

These vases use relief-lines.

### (ii a: glaukes)

1. New York 07.286.33. B, *Hdbk. Class. Coll.* 186; Pl. 28, 6–7. A, head of maenad, amid floral; B, the like. On A, full-face, on B in profile.

2. Berlin 4096, from Bomarzo. A, Genick pl. 25, 2. A, two lions with a bull's head between; B, two panthers with a fawn's (?) head between. For the drawing of the rocks compare the Vatican cup, p. 113 no. 1, and the calyx-krater in Volterra, p. 120.

3. Leipsic, from Orvieto. *Jb.* 11, 197. Floral.

[1] On Etruscan bronzes found in Haute-Savoie and Western Switzerland see Jacobsthal in *Préhistoire* ii, 50, with references to Deonna *Cat. des bronzes figurés du Musée de Genève*.

## (ii b: both handles horizontal)

4. Cambridge (ex Hermann Weber, *Cat. Sotheby 22–3 May 1919* no. 93, 1: given by Miss Winifred Lamb). A, *Coll. Alessandro Castellani* (*Rome 17 mars 1884*), 22, whence Roscher s.v. Triton, p. 1170; Pl. 28, 1–3. A, Triton and Tritoness; B, the like, but the Tritoness holds a dolphin and a cushion (see p. 121), the Triton's hands are empty. The rosettes under the hands have white hearts, and white dots round about. Height 0.088. On female Tritons—mermaids—see Dressler in Roscher s.v. Triton p. 1170, Greifenhagen in *Anz.* 1935, 475, Shepard *The Fish-tailed Monster* 23–4, Haspels *ABL.* 250 nos. 23 and 24, Buschor *Meermänner* 35.

5. Villa Giulia 2775, from Todi. A, *ML.* 23, 638, 3, and 639. A, panthers with dove between; B, the like.

6. Villa Giulia 2781, from Todi. Floral. Found with the head-kantharos D no. 1, and a jar (see p. 185, ii).

The New York vase, no. 1, belongs to the Tondo Group, and the Leipsic, no. 3, goes with it. The Cambridge vase, no. 4, is one of the prettiest in the whole Clusium Group, but does not seem to be of the Tondo Group.

A glaux of much the same shape as nos. 1–3, but black, was found in the same tomb at Torre San Severo as the famous sarcophagus (*ML.* 24, 12, 2: see p. 90).

### C. PHIALAI MESOMPHALOI

It might perhaps be considered whether a pair of phialai, from Spina, in Ferrara, T. 1078 (Aurigemma[1] 125, 5 and 6 =[2] 149, 5 and 6), may not belong to the fabric of Clusium or Volaterrae. The wave-pattern recalls the duck-askoi, and the leaves above it the type of handle-palmettes peculiar to these fabrics.

### D. HEAD-KANTHAROI

Nos. 1–3 and 10 were ascribed to the Clusium Group by Albizzati (*Atti Pont.*, new series, 14, 221–32).

#### (janiform, head of satyr and head of maenad)

1. Villa Giulia 2769, from Todi. *ML.* 23 pl. 4 and p. 635; *Atti Pont.* 14 pl. 10 and pp. 224 and 226; Ducati *St.* pl. 220 and pl. 247, 598, 3; Giglioli pl. 281, 4–6; Tarchi pl. 103, 3 and pl. 105. Palmettes. See above, B ii a no. 6, p. 174, and p. 185, ii.

2. Rome, Prince Torlonia, from Vulci? I dare say this is the vase mentioned by Albizzati (*Atti Pont.*, new series, 14, 222) as in private possession.

3. Louvre H 75. Side, Rayet and Collignon 261, whence Hadaczek, *Ohrschmuck* 35 fig. 63. Palmettes and flowers. Gilt earrings.

4. Louvre H 77. Patterns (wave, egg).

5. Tarquinia, from Tarquinia. *ML.* 36, 486. Wave. I take this to be the vase ('phot. Moscioni 10029') mentioned by Albizzati (*Atti Pont.*, new series, 14, 223) as near Villa Giulia 2769 (our no. 1) but from another workshop.

6. Louvre H 78. Patterns (wave, maeander).

7. Louvre H 76. Patterns (egg, tongues).

(janiform, head of youthful Herakles and female head)

8. Villa Giulia, from Cervetri. Ex Augusto Castellani. Pl. 28, 4–5. Floral. The woman wears what at first glance looks like a lion-skin, but seen closer turns out to be the two halves of a split ram's head, with part of the skin: I do not know the meaning of this.

(one-handled—mugs—: head of satyrs)

9. Paris, Petit Palais, 356. *Coll. Alessandro Castellani (Rome, 17 mars 1884)* pl. 3, 1; *CV*. pl. 42, 1–2. Floral. Relief-lines.
10. Louvre H 80. Patterns (egg, maeander). The face is black.

Nos. 8 and 9 are connected with the best of the small skyphoi (p. 117) by the style of the floral. Nos. 1, 3, 8, and 9 use relief-lines: I am not sure about the rest.

Two good plastic vases, in one style and found in the same tomb, perhaps belong to the Group and are at least akin to it:

### One-handled kantharoi (mugs)

(head of satyr-boy)

1. Ferrara, T. 608, from Spina. *Rivista del 'Popolo d'Italia'* 6 (1928), 44; *Boll. d'Arte* 29 (1935–6), 248, 1; Aurigemma[1] 101, 6 and 102=[2] 113, 6 and 114. Floral (vine).

(head of negro girl)

2. Ferrara, T. 608, from Spina. Aurigemma[1] 101, 7 and 103=[2] 113, 7 and 115. Pattern (rows of triangles). The hair is confined in a tight sakkos or kerchief.
No. 2 seems to use relief lines, no. 1 not.

An oinochoe in the Torlonia collection (from Vulci?) appeared to belong to the Clusium Group; the plastic part is in the form of a youth's head, with black flesh; the mouth is flat, the handle high: tongues, and maeanders separated by black rectangles.

In another Etruscan plastic vase the satyr-head bears a distinct resemblance to those of the Clusium Group, but there is nothing particularly Clusine in the decoration—tongues and egg-pattern, without relief-lines:

### Head-kantharos

(janiform: head of satyr and head of maenad)
Paris, Petit Palais, 398. *CV*. pl. 43, 4–6.

### E. OINOCHOAI

(i: shape VII: beaked jug)

1. Volterra, from Volterra. Inghirami *Mon. etr.* 5 pl. 3, 1–2 and 5. Heads of satyr and of maenad; floral; on the neck, female head. This is like the New York glaux (Pl. 28, 5–6 and p. 116 no. 1) and belongs to the Tondo Group.

(ii: epichysis)

2. Florence 2048 (4027). Heads of Dionysos and of a maenad. Assigned to the Group by Albizzati. Style of the cups (Tondo Group).

### F. DUCK-ASKOI

Nos. 1, 15, and 16 were assigned to the Clusium Group by Albizzati in *RM*. 30, 152, nos. 3–6, 8, 10–12, 17–20 by myself in *JHS*. 56, 92, no. 7 by D. M. Robinson, no. 9 by Miss Richter. No relief-lines.

1. London G151, from Vulci. Panofka *Cab. Pourt.* pl. 39. In relief, A, naked youth with lyre and plectrum, B, naked woman with alabastron. Between them, not in relief, a maid.

2. Leningrad (St. 834). A, Stephani pl. 6, 289. A, in relief, Eros flying; B, the like. He holds his garment out behind him with both hands: for this motive see p. 164. The foot of the vase has the form of a wheel, as in Louvre H 97 (no. 8).

3. Once Naples, Bourguignon, from Orvieto. A, *Vente 18–20 mars 1901* pl. 5, 81. A, in relief, naked youth with lyre. Evidently much restored. The head of the duck must be modern. The plumage is not rendered in the usual way, and the vase may not be quite a regular member of the group.

4. Louvre H 98. In relief, A, Lasa, B, the like. Restored: of the duck, head, breast, and feet modern; modern also the base and the handle. Poorer work than usual.

5. Louvre H 100. A, Pottier *Le Dessin chez les Grecs* pl. 13, 40; A, *Enc. phot.* iii, 64, a, whence Pl. 27, 7. A, Lasa; B, Lasa. 'Apulian style' (Pottier); 'South Italy' (Massoul); 'un amour hermaphrodite' (Massoul):[1]

6. Ferrara, T. 224, from Spina. A, *NSc.* 1927 pl. 13, 1; A, Aurigemma[2], 109. A, Lasa; B, Lasa. See p. 258.

7. Baltimore, Prof. D. M. Robinson. B, *CV*. iii pl. 38, 2. A, Lasa; B, Lasa.

8. Louvre H 97. A, Lasa flying with shield; B, Lasa flying with corslet. The bottom of the base is openwork, in the form of a wheel: so also in the Leningrad vase, no. 2.

9. New York 19.192.14 (ex Hermann Weber). A, *Cat. Sotheby 22–3 May 1919* pl. 2, 103; A, Richter *Etr.* fig. 137. Part of the spout is lost. A, naked woman; B, the like. The woman might be a Lasa although not winged: the inscribed Lasa on the mirror Gerhard *ES*. suppl. pl. 24 is also wingless.

10. Orvieto, from Orvieto. A, phot. Armoni. A, young satyr.

11. Orvieto, from Orvieto (Settecamini). A, *NSc.* 1932, 96, r. A, female head; B, the like. Restored.

12. Louvre H 101. A, female head; B, the like. The base is modern.

13. Florence 74690, from Todi. A, *St. etr.* 9 pl. 41, 5. A, female head; B, the like.

14. Brussels. A, head of man; B, female head. The spout is modern.

15. Florence 4231. A, female head; B, the like.

16. Florence 4232. A, female head; B, the like.

---

[1] Cf. p. 227; and see *JHS*. 63, 99. In the Tomba delle Leonesse, too (*Mon. Pitt.* i Tarqu. i, 19), I find a plump youth, not a 'hermaphrodite' (Ducati ibid.; *Rev. arch.* 1940, i, 98).

17. Louvre H 99. A, head of young satyr; B, female head.
18. Orvieto, from Torre San Severo (found in the sarcophagus). *ML*. 24, 11 fig. 3, 7 and 17, 12. A somewhat different model. No figure decoration.
19. Once Naples, Bourguignon, from Città della Pieve. A, *Vente 18–20 mars 1901* pl. 5, 78. No figure decoration.
20. Cabinet des Médailles. I have noted no particulars.

The finest of these are the Louvre duck no. 5, and the Ferrara no. 6, which is very like it. The figures on the London duck, no. 1, are poor. The Lasas on nos. 5 and 6 have 'Clusium breasts' (p. 116).

For weaker duck-askoi, from other fabrics, see pp. 191–3 and 305.

### G. CALYX-KRATER

Volterra, from Volterra. *RM*. 30, 147–51, whence (B) Ducati *Cer*. ii, 471; A, Ducati *St*. pl. 217, 533; B, phot. Alinari 34712, 2, whence Ducati *Cer*. ii, 470 and Giglioli pl. 278, 1; detail of A (floral), *Atti Pont.*, new series, 14, 225 fig. 3. A, Athena and warriors (Athena, warrior, and Nike; goddess and warrior; warrior); B, warriors, goddess, and Nike. Below, floral. On the mouth, floral with female heads. On B, the mouth of the vase is restored.

Albizzati attributed this fine vase to the Clusium Group; further, to the same hand as the Clusium cup-interiors in his list (*RM*. 30, 146), which it certainly resembles closely, though that the hand is the same does not seem to me certain from what evidence I have.

Relief-lines are used. The proportions of the vase suggest that it is not earlier than the third quarter of the fourth century: see *JHS*. 59, 35–6. The shortening of the picture-field by cutting off a strip and filling it with floral or animal decoration occurs in other late Etruscan calyx-kraters (p. 154). The floral work connects the vase with the glaukes in New York and Leipsic (p. 116 nos. 1 and 3) and the head-vases (p. 117). For the alternation of 'sprung' palmettes and the older kind see p. 183. The figures have grandeur, must have been influenced by monumental painting, and make one think, for all the difference of style, of fifteenth- or early-sixteenth-century tapestries. The proportions of the figures point to a date well on towards the end of the fourth century, and recall a very late Etruscan vase, the Fould stamnos (p. 179): moreover, the chief warrior on the reverse of the Volterra vase resembles the Fould Achilles (Jahn *Telephos und Troilos und kein Ende* pl. 3, whence Roscher s.v. Troilos p. 1227).

The floral heads of the sceptres are reminiscent of thyrsi, but it is not certain that the painter intended the women who hold them for 'maenads and Bacchic Lasas' as Albizzati calls them: see p. 171.

### H. SHAPE UNKNOWN

Florence ?, from Volterra. Inghirami pl. 271. A, satyrs and naked woman; B, the like. 'Etruscan dancer' hands (see p. 114).

This joins the Florence skyphos (p. 116) and the vases connected with it.

J. STAMNOI

(i)

1. Perugia, from Perugia. Vermiglioli *Le Erogamie di Admeto e Alceste*, whence *Annali* 1832 pl. G, Inghirami pl. 13, *Berl. Ak.* 1851 pll. 1–2 (Panofka), (B) Gerhard *ES.* pl. 19, 3; B, Giglioli pl. 280, 5. A, a youth with spear and shield, a youth and a naked woman watching. B, a satyr embracing a naked woman, and a naked woman watching.

This stamnos was assigned to the group by Albizzati (*RM.* 30, 152). In *drawing* it resembles the cup-interiors: the reproductions hardly enable one to say which of the cups are nearest to it. The *shape* is of the same type as in many Etruscan stamnoi of the fourth century. On A, a boar's head is fastened to the pillar on which the woman leans: this caused Zannoni to call her Atalanta: but the elaborate head-dress is perhaps against this interpretation. In the field of each picture the same rosette as in the cup Berlin 2944 (p. 114 no. 14) and the two stamnoi presently to be described. The youth in the middle holds his garment spread out with both hands: for this motive see p. 164.

(ii)

2. Florence, from Populonia. B, *NSc.* 1934, 414. A, two naked women dancing; B, naked woman dancing. 'Etruscan dancer' hands (p. 114).
3. Florence, from Populonia. *NSc.* 1934, 412–13. A, naked woman; B, the like.
4. Volterra, from Volterra. A, phot. Alinari 34714, 3, whence Pl. 29, 4. A, naked woman and naked boy. The woman holds an alabastron and a spathē. The short negroid figure might be expected to be a maid, but seems to be male. Wretched drawing, without relief-lines, but much use of hatching for inner markings.

These three vases are of a special model and must be the work of one potter. In drawing, the Florence stamnoi are related to two column-kraters—a Volterra vase published by Gori and Passeri, and Florence 4132 (p. 122 nos. 3 and 4): these in their turn, as will be seen, are closely connected with the *reverses* of the Clusium cups. The Volterra stamnos may be compared with a third column-krater, in Volterra (p. 122 no. 2: a naked woman and a satyr dancing), but is of even poorer quality and is farther removed from the Clusium cups: it stands in fact on the border between the Clusium Group and the Volaterrae; and so do the two Florence stamnoi.

K. COLUMN-KRATERS

From a numerous class of column-kraters, about which more will be said presently, Albizzati has picked out a few which he associates, on good grounds, with the Clusium Group (*RM.* 30, 153–4, and 146 note 31):

1. Volterra, from Volterra. A, phot. Alinari 34714, 1, whence *RM.* 30, 154 and Pl. 29, 1. A, centaur. In his left hand he has the big branch which centaurs carry from geometric times onwards; but that he should hold a cushion in his other hand is somewhat surprising. There are many cushion-bearers in Etruscan vase-painting: maenads carry cushions (p. 142); so do satyrs (ibid.); so does a Tritoness (p. 117); and here a centaur.

2. Volterra, from Volterra. Inghirami pl. 131; A. phot. Alinari 34713, 3, whence *RM*. 30, 152, Ducati *St*. pl. 251 fig. 611,3, *Enciclopedia Italiana* s.v. Etruschi pl. 96, 3. A, naked woman and satyr dancing at laver; B, the like. Some hatching for inner markings.

3. Volterra, from Volterra. A, Gori *Mus. Etr.* iii pl. 32; Passeri pl. 139. A, two naked women.

4. Florence 4132, from Volterra. Inghirami pl. 67. A, naked woman and woman; B, the like.

According to Albizzati (*RM*. 30, 153) a column-krater in the Vatican is a replica of no. 2.

The Florence krater, no. 4, repeats, on a larger scale, the exteriors of the Tondo Group cups and the Leda cup from Monte San Savino. No. 3 matches it, and the naked women have 'Clusium breasts' (p. 120). No. 2 is based on the satyr-and-woman scenes of the Clusium Group. The earliest of the series, judging by the sturdy, unaffected shape of the vase, is no. 1. All these vases have characteristic Clusian handle-palmettes, which indeed persist throughout the whole class of column-kraters to the end and form one of their principal characteristics.

Albizzati includes another column-krater:

Volterra, from Volterra. A and side, Passeri pl. 42; A, phot. Alinari 34714, 2, whence *RM*. 30, 155. A, Lasa on dolphin. Some hatching; 'Clusium breasts' (p. 120).

This is by the chief artist of the Volaterrae Group (see below, p. 124), the Hesione Painter: but it is connected with the Clusium Group and particularly with the duck-askoi; and the same may be said of another column-krater by the same hand:

Berlin inv. 3986, from Monteriggioni. A and side, Jacobsthal *O*. pl. 149; A, *St. etr.* 2 pl. 29, 45 (doubtless this vase and not a replica): *RM*. 52, 126–7 and pl. 27, 1, whence (side and A) Pl. 29, 5–6. A, head of youth. B, Eros flying with a swan. A good deal of hatching.

There is continuity, in fact, between the Clusium Group and the Volaterrae; and the eight column-kraters just mentioned are transition pieces.

None of these vases have relief-lines. In the use of hatched lines for inner markings several of them go beyond anything in the Clusium group. In the Volaterrae Group, also, the relief-line has been abandoned; and other vases by the Hesione Painter are no less free with hatching than the Volterra Lasa and its companion in Berlin.

# CHAPTER VI

# VOLATERRAE

*Bull.* 1858, 151–7 (Brunn); *RM.* 30, 154–60 (Albizzati); *St. etr.* 2, 149–52 and 174 (Bianchi Bandinelli); *St. etr.* 8, 122–8 (Ducati); *RM.* 52, 119–39 (Dohrn).

THE column-kraters described at the end of the last chapter belong to a large class of such vases, inseparably interconnected in shape and ornament. The proveniences of the class (most of which are known) are all North Etruscan. One vase was found as far south as Montediano near Montefiascone at the south-east corner of the Lake of Bolsena, but apart from that the most southerly provenience is Montepulciano, and Volterra with its neighbourhood predominates. The half-dozen column-kraters that have been considered under the heading of the Clusium Group (pp. 121–2) stand at the beginning of the series. According to Albizzati, these were made at Chiusi, but the rest of the column-krater class at Volterra by immigrants from Chiusi. It is quite likely that Volterra was the home of what we have called the Volaterrae Group: Perugia was suggested by Brunn (who was followed by Galli and others), but is less probable. It is a question whether the six vases already mentioned may not also have been made at Volterra, by the first Clusine immigrants, especially as two of them are by the chief painter of the Volaterrae Group. As we said before, there is continuity between the Clusium Group and the Volaterrae, and the dividing line is hard to draw. Indeed the whole series of vases, 'Clusium' plus 'Volaterrae', viewed as a whole, has all the look of a single fabric; and but for the proveniences one would be inclined to locate the series in a single city. Nor is the evidence of the proveniences unequivocal. Indeed, considering that two of the thirteen 'Clusium' cups whose provenience is known, and no fewer than twelve of the other 'Clusium' vases, were found at Volterra, while no 'Clusium' vases except cups have been found at Chiusi, it should be pondered whether Volterra may not have been the home of the whole series —'Clusium' as well as 'Volaterrae'. The great city of Volterra, owing to the destruction of all but its latest cemeteries, is an unknown quantity, a 'dark planet', in the history of Etruscan art.

A relevant factor in the discussion would be a number of trifling cups in the Museum of Chiusi which according to Albizzati (*RM.* 30, 153–4) represent the output of the Clusium fabric *after* the emigration of the better Clusium artists to Volterra: I regret that I do not know these cups and cannot form a picture of them in my mind.

Brunn was the first to recognize the existence of what we call the Volaterrae Group (*Bull.* 1858, 151–7), but once again it was Albizzati who filled in the outline. Bianchi Bandinelli followed with an important contribution, and recently Dohrn, in a valuable article, distinguished four artists, the Hesione Painter, the Painter of the Pigmy Trumpeter, the Nun Painter, and the Painter of the Tuscan Column. I find his attributions, where I can check them, correct. I feel doubt only where he himself has hesitated, that is, in the vases which he attaches loosely, as 'uncertain', or 'related', to one or other of these four groups.

The many column-kraters from Monteriggioni (with the exception of the fragments referred to on p. 126) were all found in a single chamber-tomb, the tomb of the family Calinii Šepuś in the field of Malacena near the village of Monteriggioni between Volterra and Siena. A careful description of the finds is given by Bianchi Bandinelli in *St. etr.* 2, 133–76. The tomb contained many interments and was in use for a long time. Numismatic evidence points to 217 B.C. as a *terminus ante quem* for those interments of which Volaterrae column-kraters formed a part (l.c. 174).

Relief-lines are not used in the Volaterrae Group.

Dohrn compares the kraters with Faliscan vases (l.c. 126–30), but when he speaks of 'Faliscan' he includes, for some reason, the Clusium cups of the Tondo Group. From the language used by Dohrn the reader would probably assume that Albizzati had already classed the Clusium cups as Faliscan: but this is not so, and Albizzati has attacked Panfaliscanism more than once with his customary vigour. Dohrn also follows Langlotz in counting Würzburg 819 as Faliscan, which it is not (see p. 143 no. 18).

### THE HESIONE PAINTER

The earliest of the four artists and the best is the Hesione Painter, who has a free, large style and sometimes a certain grandeur. Five vases are assigned to him by Dohrn (*RM.* 52, 120–1).

#### Column-kraters

1. Perugia, Museo del Palazzone all' Ipogeo dei Volumni, from Perugia. Conestabile *I monumenti di Perugia etrusca e romana*, Atlas iii pll. 6–22; (A) *Mon.* 5 pl. 9, 2, whence Welcker *Alte Denkmäler* pl. 24, 2; (shape), *Annali* 1849 pl. A; Galli *Perugia: Il Museo Funerario del Palazzone all' Ipogeo dei Volumni* 147 and 150–1; *Boll. d'Arte* 1922–3, i, 31 and 34–5; A, Ducati *Cer.* ii, 473 = Ducati *Storia* pl. 219; A, Giglioli pl. 277, 2. A, Herakles and the Kētos; B, Herakles and Hesione. On the neck: A, head of a winged deity; B, the like: the head on B seems male, on A female. The himatia are fully shaded; and it looks from the reproduction as if there were some shading on the body of Herakles on A, but of this I cannot be sure. The vase has a lid with a pomegranate knob.
2. Berlin inv. 3986, from Monteriggioni. See p. 122.
3. Volterra, from Volterra. A, Lasa on dolphin. See p. 122.
4. Perugia, from Perugia (Monteluce outside the city, to the East). *Boll. d'Arte* 1922–3, i, 28–9, whence Pl. 29, 2–3; A, Tarchi pl. 127, 3. A, Dionysos supported by a boy satyr; B, Dionysos and Ariadne. On the neck, A, head of woman (no doubt Ariadne) between swans; B, the like. Hatching is used to shade the nude parts, and there is a little in the drapery. According to Galli the satyr is shaggy, but what he takes for shag is shading (cf. p. 103). The vase has a lid with a pomegranate knob.
5. Volterra, fr., from Volterra. *RM.* 30, 157; part, *RM.* 43, 157. On the neck, head of a woman (Ariadne?).

We return for a moment to the Hesione krater in Perugia (no. 1).

The identification of the front picture as Herakles entering the maw of the sea-monster that threatened Hesione is due to Flasch (*Angebliche Argonautenbilder* 24–9). Previous writers had thought of Jason in the Dragon's jaws, a subject not found in extant literary record but represented in a good many works of art. The story of Herakles is given in two passages:

Schol. Hom. *Il.* 20, 146. Ἡρακλῆς Δὲ παραγενόμενος ὑπέσχετο τὸν ἄθλον κατορθώσειν, καὶ Ἀθηνᾶς αὐτῶι πρόβλημα ποιησάσης τὸ καλούμενον ἀμφίχυτον τεῖχος εἰσΔὺς Διὰ τοῦ στόματος εἰς τὴν κοιλίαν τοῦ κήτους αὐτοῦ τὰς λαγόνας Διέφθειρεν . . . ἡ ἱστορία παρὰ Ἑλλανίκωι (Jacoby *FHG.* i p. 114, 26, b, and p. 444). (The τεῖχος ἀμφίχυτον which had been made for Herakles on this occasion by the Trojans and Pallas Athene is described in *Il.* 20, 144.)

Schol. Lycophr. 34. χωστὸν τεῖχος ποιήσας καὶ στὰς ὡπλισμένος παρὰ τὸ στόμιον, ὡς κεχηνὸς ἐπηίει τὸ κῆτος ἀθρόως τῶι τούτου ἐμπέπτωκε στόματι· τρισὶ Δὲ ἡμέραις ἔνΔοθεν κατατέμνων αὐτὸ ἐξῆλθεν, ἀποβεβληκὼς καὶ τὴν τῆς ἑαυτοῦ κεφαλῆς τρίχωσιν.

Ours is the only representation of Herakles entering the kētos, although other episodes in the legend are illustrated: a fourth-century Etruscan mirror in Perugia shows Telamon leading Hesione away, and the kētos, or its head (Gerhard *ES.* suppl. pl. 65); Antiphilos painted a *Hesione nobilis*; for other representations see Robert *Heldensage* 553 and 556.

Albizzati (*Mél. d'arch.* 37, 140 note 3) returns to the old interpretation, Jason and the Dragon. But as Flasch pointed out (op. cit. 27), and as Braun had already noticed although he did not draw the proper conclusion (*Annali* 1849, 111), the monster is not a dragon (that is, a serpent), but a fish-like, shark-like creature, a kētos. Albizzati objects that if Herakles were represented he would be shown in armour, but this seems to be based on a misconception of the ὡπλισμένος in the scholion to Lycophron: ὡπλισμένος does not mean 'in full armour' as Frazer translates it (*Apollodorus* i, p. 208) but 'armed', and Herakles is armed, with a sword.

Albizzati affirms that the text of the Homeric scholion is very doubtful, but it is not. True that Welcker changed τεῖχος to τεῦχος (*Alte Denkmäler* iii, 378) and that the emendation was accepted by Flasch, whose words may be quoted (op. cit. 28):

'The wide cloak which Herakles wears round his body is no haphazard addition by the artist: it has mythological significance and justification. The story ran that Herakles in his encounter with the sea-monster was given a preservative by Athena: schol. *Il.* 20, 145 καὶ Αθηνᾶς αὐτῷ πρόβλημα ποιησάσης τὸ καλούμενον ἀμφίχυτον τεῖχος. Welcker pointed out that the original expression was doubtless τεῦχος, a protective envelope which was later understood as an actual defensive wall. We can immediately make use of this excellent conjecture, because in fact it is correct. The preservative of which the writers speak is represented by the painter in the form of a cloak which covers Herakles like a shield from head to foot and wraps him round.'

It is not necessary for us to examine this 'excellent conjecture' at great length: enough to observe that the notion of a *wall* is at least as old as *Il.* 20, 144, which is pretty old. The field of pre-Homeric 'misunderstanding' is a productive one, but the tillers are many, and we note only that if on our vase Herakles has a special reason for holding his cloak in front of him, it is to protect himself from the noxious reek that issues from the monster's throat.

The subject on the reverse of the Perugia vase is also unique: Herakles is known to have passed Hesione on to Telamon, by whom she became the mother of Teucer: here

the transfer has not yet taken place. Robert thought that Seneca *Her. Oet.* 363 might
point to an amour of Herakles and Hesione:

> dilecta Priami nempe Dardanii soror
> concessa famula est.

But the words are also consistent with Herakles having yielded her to his friend intact;
and even if Seneca were insinuating otherwise, it would not prove that the tradition was
anything else.

Let us now glance at some vases that may be connected with the Hesione Painter.
Dohrn does not mention the column-krater Florence 4084 (A, Pigmy and crane; B, the
like: on the neck, head of a youth—Helios ?—and the heads of his horses; B, head of a
woman—Eos ?—and the heads of hers): only part of it has been published (neck of A,
*RM.* 42, 120), but enough to show that it is close to the Hesione Painter, even if it should
prove not to be from his hand. Hatching is used to shade the horses' heads near the mane.
For the subject of the pictures on the neck of the vase see p. 130.

Another Pigmy vase, from Volterra, seems to have disappeared, and all that is known
of it is the group of Pigmy and crane published by Inghirami (pl. 357, whence
Roscher s.v. Pygmaien p. 3293 fig. 2), but the drawing of this connects it with the Hesione
Painter: look for instance at the hatched lines on the thighs or below the iliac furrows,
and compare them with those in his krater from Monteluce, no. 4 in the list (p. 124).

Fragments from Cortona, in Cortona, are said by Minto to be from a bell-krater: only
one of the sherds has been figured (*NSc.* 1929, 165, c), but the details of the floral, and the
use of hatching for the furrow of the calf, link it with the Hesione Painter, and it may be
his work. I do not know of bell-kraters in this class, and wonder if a column-krater may
not be possible. Bianchi Bandinelli mentions 'fragments of several red-figured bell-
kraters in Volterran style, with remains of female figures between palmettes and spirals',
as found in Tomb 21 at Monteriggioni (*St. etr.* 2, 141, c): but on p. 153 he speaks of his
pl. 30, 89 as a bell-krater, whereas it is a calyx-krater, and on p. 154 of his pl. 31, 93 as
a bell-krater, so he uses the term in rather a wide sense. Moreover the Cortona fragments
have 'reticulated decoration on the neck', which would be odd in a bell-krater, but in a
column-krater natural: I hazard therefore that these fragments also may be from column-
kraters rather than bells, although I should wish them, for the sake of variety, not to be.

Another column-krater that may recall the Hesione Painter is in Volterra (A, phot.
Brogi 13657, ii, 3): it bears the head of a fat satyr looking upward with an intense
expression.

Dohrn appends four kraters to his list, one (*RM.* 52, 121 no. 6) as 'uncertain', the others
(ibid. nos. 7–9) as 'related'. His nos. 6 and 7 have been mentioned above (pp. 121–2):
they are the vases in Volterra with a satyr and a maenad, and with a centaur. His no. 9 is

Bologna PU 410 (from the Marsili collection: not found at Bologna). A, Pellegrini
*VPU.* 69, whence Ducati *Cer.* ii, 474=Ducati *St.* pl. 251, 610. A, Pigmy, armed; B,
the like. On the neck: A, head of an Amazon, with a corslet hanging from a column
on each side; B, the like. Some shading, but it seems no hatching.

The Bologna vase bears a certain resemblance to work of the Hesione Painter: but

Dohrn's no. 8, although the artist was no doubt emulating the Hesione Painter, is in a strange, inexpert, fluttering style that is very unlike the master: it is

Florence 88160, from Perugia (Monteluce outside it, to the east). *Boll. d'Arte* 1922–3, i, 23–5, and 27 fig. 5. A, a satyr fluting at a thurible; B, a woman between two plants. On the neck: A, head of a youth (Helios ?), between two foreparts of horses; B, head of a winged deity (female ?). Herbig says that the vase is also published in Paoletti *Studi su Perugia etrusca*, which I have not seen.

There seems to be some repainting along the fractures in the main picture on B, and the photograph looks as if it had been retouched in places.

For the subject on the neck of A see p. 130.

There is a little dog to the right of the winged head on B: according to Galli (l.c. 31) 'its connexion with Hades is as obvious as can be' and it is intended 'to stress the demoniaco-funereal idea of the picture'. I do not take this little dog so seriously.

The vase has a lid, with black patterns on it, and a knob which Galli believes to be 'symbolic' of something: it looks like a peeled fig.

In a Perugia krater (A, Tarchi pl. 127, 4) the heads of Helios and his horses on the neck somewhat recall the Hesione painter; while the patternwork on the neck is the same as in two other vases, one, from Volterra, in Volterra (?) (Inghirami pl. 358, whence, part, Roscher s.v. Pygmaien p. 3294 fig. 3: A, Pigmy and crane; B, the like; on the neck, two heads of horses with a column between), the other Florence 4035 (neck of A, *RM.* 42, 121), which has the same subjects as the Volterra vase and must be very like it. On all three vases see p. 130.

The masterpiece, as it would seem to be, of the whole class of column-kraters has never been published: there are drawings of it in the German Institute at Rome (xxiii, 41). It was found in a tomb at Montediano and was later in the possession of Marchese Patrizi in the neighbouring town of Montefiascone: bare mention in *NSc.* 1879, 135 and *Bull.* 1880, 67. It is of great size, 71 cm. with the lid. The handle-palmettes are of the usual Clusium-Volaterrae type. Palmettes on the neck, wave above the pictures, maeander below. On A, a woman holding a balance, and Hermes watching her; the woman is inscribed TALNIOⱾ (*Talnithe*), retrograde, downwards.[1] On B, Herakles standing at a fountain, and Apollo (?), with laurel-branch, approaching him. The faces, except Apollo's, in three-quarter view; the figures fine and expressive. I did not recognize the subjects, and refrain from speculating about them on the basis of my summary notes. A head published by Albizzati (*RM.* 30, 153), from an oinochoe in Volterra, makes me think of the Apollo.

### THE PAINTER OF THE PIGMY TRUMPETER

Dohrn (*RM.* 52, 121–2) attributes two vases only to the Painter of the Pigmy Trumpeter: the name-piece from Monteriggioni in the Terrosi collection (A, *St. etr.* 2 pl. 29, 41; A,

---

[1] Not Talmithe. *Talmithe* is the regular Etruscan equivalent of the Greek Παλαμήⱥης (Pauli in Roscher s.v. Talmithe; Fiesel *Namen des griechischen Mythos im Etruskischen* 40–3 and 118), but does not help us. It seems not to have been noticed that a by-form Ταλαμήⱥης need not be *postulated* to account for the Etruscan form, since it actually occurs: on the Attic rf. calyx-krater New York 08.258.21 (*Metr. Mus. St.* 5, 125–7; Richter and Hall pll. 135–7 and pl. 170, 135: *ARV.* 717 no. 1) the hero is inscribed TALAMEⱭEⱾ.

*Scritti Nogara* pl. 2, 6) and a Berlin vase (inv. 3991, also from Monteriggioni) which I cannot control.  To these he attaches a vase in Volterra as 'uncertain', and, as 'related', Berlin inv. 3987, from Monteriggioni (A, Bieńkowski *Darstellungen der Gallier* 30), which is supposed to represent Gauls, but the figures are plainly dwarfs in the guise of Gauls.[1] It is not clear to me that the Volterra krater is connected with the Pigmy Trumpeter (A, phot. Alinari 34713, 2, whence *RM.* 30, 158 fig. 19 and Ducati *Storia* fig. 611, 2; A, phot. Brogi 13657, ii, 2: A, naked woman drawing a himation about her shoulders): the drawing of the palmettes recalls the Painter of the Tuscan Column (see p. 129).  On the subject see p. 164.

### THE NUN PAINTER

The Nun Painter, so called from a nun-like head on one of his vases, almost confines himself to large profile heads, and his work has a portrait-like quality which wins the applause of Dohrn.  See p. 10.  Eight vases are assigned to the Nun Painter, six of which have been published:

*Column-kraters*

Berlin inv. 3996, from Monteriggioni.  *RM.* 52 pl. 27, 2 and pl. 28, 1, whence (B) Pl. 29, 7.  A, female head; B, head of youth.  This would seem to be the same vase as that published in *St. etr.* 2 pl. 29, 40, where it is said to be in the Terrosi collection: the alternative is that it is a replica.

Berlin inv. 3988, from Monteriggioni.  The neck, *RM.* 52 pl. 28, 2 and pl. 29, whence (the women ) Pl. 29, 8–9.  A, youth seated; B, youth running.  On the neck: A, heads of woman and of youth; B, heads of women.

Berlin inv. 3989, from Monteriggioni.  A, *RM.* 52 pl. 30, 1, whence Pl. 29, 10.  A, male head; B, head of woman.

Berlin inv. 3997, from Monteriggioni.  A, *RM.* 52 pl. 30, 2.  A, head of boy.  B, head of woman.

Berlin inv. 3995, from Monteriggioni.  A, *RM.* 52 pl. 31, 1 (not pl. 30, 1).  A, head (of a woman according to Dohrn).

Berlin inv. 4001, from Monteriggioni.  A, *RM.* 52 pl. 31, 2.  A, head of man; B, female head.

Those that I cannot test are Berlin inv. 3993 and inv. 3994.  A ninth vase, in Volterra, described as 'uncertain' (*RM.* 52, 124 no. 30) is doubtless by the Nun Painter (A, phot. Alinari 34713, 1, whence *RM.* 30, 158 fig. 20 and Ducati *Storia* pl. 251 fig. 611, 1; A, phot. Brogi 13657, i, 2: A, male head).  Probably, too, a tenth, also in Volterra (A, phot. Brogi 13657, i, 1:  A, male head).

I am less certain about the precise relation of two other 'portrait-head' kraters to the Nun Painter: Dohrn speaks of them as 'related' (*RM.* 52, 124 nos. 31 and 32).  They are a vase from Monteriggioni in the Terrosi collection (A, *St. etr.* 2 pl. 30, 52), and Tuebingen F 17 (A, Watzinger pl. 45), which is also from Monteriggioni, for it must be the vase mentioned by Bianchi Bandinelli in *St. etr.* 2, 135.  Compare with it one in Volterra (A, phot. Brogi 13657, i, on the right, behind).

[1] Compare the children playing at Gauls on Calene stemless cups (Pagenstecher *Cal.* 88 and pl. 16).

### THE PAINTER OF THE TUSCAN COLUMN
This is another painter of portrait-like heads, and the poorest artist of the four. Dohrn attributes seven vases to him (*RM.* 52, 122–3), four of which have been published.

*Column-kraters*

Würzburg 804. Langlotz pl. 236. A, head of youth. B, column.
Berlin inv. 3990, from Monteriggioni. A, *RM.* 52, 132. A, head of youth. B, 'naked youth with lituus?'
Berlin inv. 4000, from Monteriggioni. A, *RM.* 52, 133. A, male head; B, the like.
Florence, Terrosi, from Monteriggioni. A, *St. etr.* 2 pl. 30, 57. A, male head; B, the like.
These are nos. 14, 15, 17, and 20 in Dohrn's list; the other three are Berlin inv. 3999, inv. 4002, and inv. 4003, which I cannot test; he adds Berlin inv. 3992 as 'uncertain'.
Two column-kraters seem to me to be near the Painter of the Tuscan Column:

1. Florence, Terrosi, from Monteriggioni. B, *St. etr.* 2 pl. 29, 60. A, head of youth; B, male head.
2. Volterra, from Volterra. A, phot. Brogi 13657, i, 4. A, male head.

In conclusion, here is a list of column-kraters which are of the Volaterrae class, but either do not belong to our groups, or from lack of information cannot be attributed to any of them. Nos. 1 and 2 are cited by Albizzati, nos. 2–10 by Ducati, no. 19 by Dohrn, nos. 20 and 22 by Bianchi Bandinelli.

1. Volterra. A, phot. Brogi 13657, i, 3. A, a woman (rather than a youth) holding a sash.
2. Volterra. A, phot. Brogi 13657, ii, 1. A, dwarf. Restored. The treatment of the space below the palmette-volutes recalls the Painter of the Tuscan Column.
3. Volterra, from Volterra. Inghirami pl. 358, whence (part) Roscher s.v. Pygmaien, 3294 fig. 3. A, Pigmy and crane; B, the like. On the neck, A, heads of two horses with a column between; B, the like. See p. 130.
4. Florence 4035. Neck of A, *RM.* 42, 121. A, Pigmy and crane; B, the like. On the neck, A, heads of two horses with a column between; B, the like. Compare the last, and see p. 130.
5. Florence 4121, from Volterra. Inghirami pl. 130. A, dwarf dancing; B, woman. Same treatment of the space below the palmette-volutes as in no. 2.
6. Florence 4136, from Volterra. Inghirami pl. 100, 2. A, Pigmy armed; B, the like.
7. Florence 4090. A, Pigmy with hammer; B, Pigmy.
8. Florence 4105. A, Pigmies fighting; B, female head.
9. Florence 4122. A, Pigmy with sashes; B, the like.
10. Florence 4108. A, Pigmy with sashes; B, the like.
11. Bologna 876, frr., from the province of Bologna. A, naked male running; B, the like.
12. Bologna 875, frr., from Monzuno (province of Bologna)? A, naked youth running; B, female head.
13. Cortona? A, Passeri pl. 46, 1. A, naked youth running with sashes.

14. Cortona? A, Passeri pl. 46, 3. A, naked youth running with sashes.
15. Cortona? A, Passeri pl. 46, 2. A, Eros running with sashes.
16. Where?, from Volterra. Inghirami pl. 100, 1. A, woman; B, the like.
17. Perugia, fr., from S. Galigano (west of Perugia). *NSc.* 1914, 243. On the neck, A, Grypomachy; B, the like. An unusual piece.
18. Florence, from Volterra. A, Inghirami *Mon. etr.* 5 pl. 5, 3 and 5. A, head of youth.
19. Bologna 825, from Bologna. A, *Atti Romagna*, 3rd series, 5 pl. 5, 7, whence Montelius I pl. 111, 8. A, female head; B, the like. Found in a Gaulish grave, Tomb 954, with an Etruscan mirror (see p. 132), a kylix, and fragments of a small bronze vase.
20. Florence, Terrosi, from Monteriggioni. A, *St. etr.* 2 pl. 30, 67. A, (female ?) head; B, the like.
21. Siena, from Montepulciano. A, *NSc.* 1936, 243, 2. A, laver; B, the like. Doro Levi notes that the subject is the same as in the next.
22. Florence, Terrosi, from Monteriggioni. A, laver; B, the like. Described by Bianchi Bandinelli in *St. etr.* 2, 150 no. 48 but not figured.
23. Siena, Marchese Chigi, from Casale Val d'Elsa. A, column; B, the like. Described by Pellegrini in *St. e mat.* 1, 3, 7 no. 251.
24. Volterra. A, phot. Brogi 13657, behind to left. The subject not visible in the photograph.

Bianchi Bandinelli also mentions, in *St. etr.* 2, 149–52, several such column-kraters found in the Tomb of the Calinii Śepuś at Monteriggioni and not identical with any in our list.

The long necks of Volaterrae column-kraters are usually decorated with patternwork, but often with human heads or heads of horses. Some of these have been studied by Reinhard Herbig in *RM.* 42, 117–28. Florence 4084 (p. 126 : *RM.* 42, 120) has the head of a youth between two horse-heads flanked by a pair of columns to which the horses are attached: the columns represent the stable, and the heads may be thought of as seen at a window. The youth, who wears a necklace, and round his head a fillet and a band of jewels, may be Helios. In the Perugia vase published by Tarchi (pl. 127, 4: p. 127) the subject is the same. In the Florence vase from Monteluce (88160: p. 127: *Boll. d'Arte* 1922–3, i, 24) the strings of the puppets, as it were, have been loosened, and the subject has become almost unrecognizable. Two more vases, Florence 4035 (*RM.* 42, 121 : p. 129) and another very like it (Inghirami pl. 358: p. 129), show a pair of horses' heads with a column between them: this is certainly the stable-window, divided by a mullion, with a glimpse of one horse at each half. Outside Etruria, a good view of horses in the stable, as Herbig noted, is given in the background of the Apulian situla, with Pelops and Oinomaos, in the Villa Giulia (*Ausonia* 7, 117 and pll. 2–3; *CV.* IV Dr pl. 1; phot. Alinari 41161).

These pictures are not unconnected with the lunettes of certain Etruscan mirrors, although there the subject is different: it is a quadriga—the heads of four horses, and of a young charioteer, seen from the front. The charioteer is sometimes Helios and sometimes Eos. We give a list of these mirrors, adding two to Herbig's list (*RM.* 42, 118) and rearranging. Eight of them belong to the large and important group of late Etruscan mirrors to which I alluded in *Num. Chron.* 1941, 7,[1] and on which Bendinelli (*ML.* 23, 664–70) and Becatti (*St. etr.* 9, 296–8) have matter of importance: I shall call it 'Group Z'. The other three are contemporary but not of the group.

1. Florence 74781, from Todi. *St. etr.* 9 pl. 37. See Becatti, ibid. 296–8.
2. London 627, from Cervetri. Gerhard *ES.* pl. 398.
3. Villa Giulia, from Todi. *ML.* 23 (Bendinelli) pl. 3. On the right, as Bendinelli observes, an Ethiop greets the rising sun:[2] cf. Eur. *Phaëthon* fr. 771 Nauck, Arnim *Suppl. Eur.* p. 67.
4. Once Borgia. Gerhard *ES.* pl. 196 (misprinted 116 in Herbig). (On the inscriptions see Bianchi Bandinelli in *ML.* 30, 548.)
5. Once Orvieto, Ravizza. Gerhard *ES.* pl. 257B. As the last.
6. Perugia, from Porano. Gerhard *ES.* suppl. pl. 77.
7. Villa Giulia, from Palestrina. Gerhard *ES.* pl. 378. (The woman on the right is not *Irisis* but *Prisis* = Briseis: see Pauli in Roscher s.v. Prisis.)
8. Florence, private. Gerhard *ES.* suppl. p. 220.
9. Florence, 77759, from Tuscania. Ducati *St.* pl. 241 fig. 589; Giglioli pl. 299, 2–3.
10. London 700, from Castelgiorgio near Orvieto. Gerhard *ES.* suppl. pl. 34.
11. Vatican. Gerhard *ES.* pl. 381.

In an eleventh mirror (not belonging to group Z) the subject of the lunette is different: Perugia, from Perugia. Gerhard *ES.* suppl. pl. 78.

An architectural framework below and at the sides signifies, as Herbig has explained, sill and reveals of a stable-window, at which the upper parts of two horses' heads are seen, with the head of a groom, inscribed *Aur*, between them, and reins laid over a nail. Herbig compares the stable-window, with Achilles' horses and their groom, on the Settecamini stamnos in Florence (p. 52 no. 1); Castor's two horses at a stable-window on the Praenestine cista in the Morgan Library, New York (*Mon.* 9 pl. 22–3; *RM.* 30 Beilage 13); and the pictures on the necks of our column-kraters.

The use of horse-heads is not the only link between the Z group of late Etruscan mirrors and the Volaterrae column-kraters. A favourite motive in the kraters is the woman with face in three-quarter view, hair dressed high in front, the himation veiling the back of the head, hood-wise, and so arranged that it comes up to a point over the middle of the hair, producing a triangular effect. Similar heads occur on nos. 1, 2, 4, 5 in our list of mirrors; and in other mirrors of the same group Z (Florence, from Volterra, Gerhard *ES.* suppl. pl. 60; Leningrad, Gerhard *ES.* pl. 402).

---

[1] I ought to have observed there, when speaking of a favourite border in these mirrors, that rings or slides were not used on 'bakchoi' only, but also for securing wreaths or festoons (Roscher, suppl., s.v. Sternbilder, 893; *ML.* 8 pl. 5).

[2] The girl attending *Turan* is inscribed, retr., *Snenathturns*. On a mirror in Berlin (Gerhard *ES.* pl. 111) a similar attendant is called *Snenath*. Snenath might be taken, with Deecke and Bendinelli, as a proper name, a secondary deity belonging to the circle of *Turan* (like the Greek Peitho, for example): compare *Turms Aitas* (p. 47), but it might also be a common noun meaning 'handmaid': *snenathturns* = 'handmaid of Turan': so Vetter in *Glotta* 15, 227, and Cortsen ibid. 18, 187. Compare *acila* (= ancilla) on the Praenestine mirror in Corpus Christi College, Cambridge (Gerhard *ES.* suppl. pl. 151).

A third point of resemblance is the treatment of the hair: in the Z group of mirrors the hair, especially over the forehead, is rendered very formally by clusters of concentric arcs, and this is one of the most obvious characteristics of the group. Something like this appears in Berlin inv. 3986, by the Hesione Painter (p. 122 and p. 124 no. 2: *RM.* 52, 126–7 and pl. 27, 1), in the Volterra fragment by the same artist (p. 124 no. 5: *RM.* 30, 157; *RM.* 43, 157), and in Florence 4084 which we associated with him (p. 126: *RM.* 42, 120).

If we extend our purview to take in the Clusium Group of which the Volaterrae Group is an offshoot, we find that this treatment of the hair already occurs on the calyx-krater in the Museum of Volterra (p. 120: *RM.* 30, 147–51). Further, I think there is a distinct resemblance between the principles of composition in the Clusium cup-tondi and in our mirrors: the tondi are earlier and in general simpler, but the relation of the figures to the circular space is much the same.

It is not known where the Z Group of mirrors was made: Chiusi stands at the head of the proveniences, although Cervetri runs it close.

It may be worth mentioning that a mirror of our Group Z—one of the mass-produced specimens that swell its muster—was found at Bologna in the same Gaulish grave as the Volaterrae column-krater Bologna 825 (above, p. 130, no. 19: the mirror, Gerhard *ES.* suppl. pl. 80, 1). Another was found at Orvieto (Settecamini) in a chamber-tomb which contained a duck-vase of the Clusium Group (p. 119, no. 11) and other vases, among them those described on pp. 150, middle and 154, below, no. 2, but it does not seem certain that there was only a single interment (*NSc.* 1932, 88–99).

Before leaving the Clusium and Volaterrae Groups it should be said that sepulchral subjects, as far as is known, never occur in either. True, as already mentioned (p. 127), that a 'demoniaco-funereal' significance has been attributed to the picture on the neck of a krater from Perugia (p. 127), but without evidence. Bianchi Bandinelli conjectured that the heads on two vases from Monteriggioni (*St. etr.* 2, 151 nos. 60 and 68) might possibly represent Charun: the head illustrated is coarse and caricatural, but need not be other than human, and Bianchi Bandinelli would probably not press his point.

All these vases were red-figured: but Bianchi Bandinelli mentions, although he does not figure and appears not to have seen, a column-krater of unusual technique which was found in the Tomb of the Calinii Śepuś, and was formerly in the Terrosi collection, but is now lost (*St. etr.* 2, 151–2 no. 73). The vase is black, the decoration white, with pink for the flesh. On A, Dionysos, it seems, with sash and thyrsus; on B, a Lasa with a sash in her right hand and her left arm akimbo; at the handles, palmettes; on the neck, the usual diamond-pattern with crosses in the diamonds.

## CHAPTER VII

# LATER RED-FIGURE, I

THE Volaterrae Group formed one important branch of later Etruscan red-figure. Later Etruscan red-figure, apart from Volaterrae, will be considered under three headings, with a chapter corresponding to each. The division is a rough-and-ready one, but may serve for the present.

The painters in the first chapter attempt a more forcible style. The work has a strong provincial flavour; and the character is more Etruscan, or more in accordance with earlier Etruscan tradition, than in the vases grouped under the other two headings. The proveniences suggest that the centre of the art may have been Vulci.

The second chapter is devoted to what may be called the Fluid Group. A smooth, rounded, easy, characterless style with hardly anything in it that is not Hellenic: indeed, almost the only other ingredient is plenty of water. The Fluid Group is probably late Faliscan, the continuation of what was collected in Chapter IV.

The third and last chapter will be found more desultory than the others. It contains those later red-figured vases that have not been dealt with in the preceding chapters. Most of them, in character, are nearer to the Fluid Group than to the would-be forcible style.

## LATER RED-FIGURE, I

### THE ALCSTI GROUP

Nos. 1 and 2 are closely connected. Giglioli thinks that they are probably by one hand (*St. etr.* 4, 368), but this seems uncertain. No. 3 is very like no. 1. No relief-lines.

#### *Volute-krater*

1. Cabinet des Médailles 918, from Vulci. Dennis ii, frontispiece and i, 437, whence (A) *AZ.* 1863 pl. 180, 3, whence (part) Daremberg and Saglio s.v. Alcestis p. 179 (redrawn), Séchan 241; B, de Ridder pl. 27; phots. Giraudon 8147–9, whence *St. etr.* 4 pl. 29 and (A) Giglioli pl. 275, 3, (A) *Art Bulletin* 25, 296 fig. 2; phot. Giraudon 16300, whence Pl. 30, 1–2. A, Admetos and Alcestis, with Charun and another demon. B, satyrs and maenad. On A, *Alcsti* and *Atmite*, both retr.; and *eca: ersce: nac: achrum: flerthrce.* The long inscription is very popular: recent studies of it: *St. etr.* 1, 291–301 (Pasquali), *AJA.* 1936, 134–5 (Fiesel), *Glotta* 25, 203 (Runes), *St. etr.* 11, 24–7 (Goldmann) and 438 and 485 (Leifer), Elderkin as quoted in *AJA.* 1942, 455. *Eca* is 'this one', ' she', haec; *ersce* is the third person singular of a verb, past tense indicative; *flerthrce* also, but some think that it also contains an object; *achrum* is generally thought to be ᾽Αχέρων. *Nac* is disputed. The handles end below in heads of kētē.

#### *Calyx-krater*

2. Trieste. *Ausonia* 10, 89–93; A, Giglioli pl. 277, 1. A, Charun and another demon leading a woman away. B, satyr with donkey, and maenad. On A, on a cartellino, *sa:ş . . . . . i. csnai.* See p. 134.

*Neck-amphora*

3. Newcastle-upon-Tyne, King's College, fr.. Pl. 30, 3, from a photograph kindly sent me by Mr. I. A. Richmond. On the shoulder, ?. Then a band of scale- or feather-pattern. Then, all round, chariots. On the left of the photograph, above, traces of a handle. The vase must have been a neck-amphora, approximating more or less to the Panathenaic shape. See below, pp. 134–5.

On representations of Alcestis see Robert *Heldensage* 33. One of the finest has come to light since he wrote: the limestone relief with Herakles and Alcestis, from Cyrene, in Benghazi: [Micacchi] *Sculptures antiques en Libye* pl. 14 (catalogue of the sculptures shown at the Colonial Exhibition, Paris, 1931). Perhaps one should mention, since Robert does not, the picture of Alcestis, as a bride among her maidens, on the onos by the Eretria Painter in Athens (*Eph. arkh.* 1897 pl. 10, whence Pfuhl fig. 561; Beazley and Ashmole fig. 108; *ARV.* 726 no. 27)[1]; and because it is Etruscan, the New York mirror with *Atmite* and *Alcestei* (802: Gerhard *ES.* suppl. p. 217; Richter *Cat. Bronzes* 279, left; *Anz.* 1925, 283–4). See also p. 8.

If the woman on the Attic neck-amphora Louvre F 60 (*CV.* He pl. 31, 9), by the Swing Painter (*BSA.* 32, 15 no. 47), is Alcestis, it is the earliest representation of her: but the identification, though possible, is not certain.

The subject of the picture on the krater in Paris has been well explained by de Ruyt (*Ant. cl.* 1, 1932, 70–3). The demons have come to fetch Admetos (not Alcestis): Alcestis interposes, and is ready to offer her life for his.

Lesky and L. Weber think that the picture records an earlier, simpler version of the story than the Euripidean (*Sitzungsberichte Wiener Ak.* 203, 52; *Rhein. Mus.* new series 85, 135–7): this is more than can be said. It is true that no particular scene in the Euripidean tragedy is represented, but only the central fact of the story, the willingness of Alcestis to devote herself for her husband.

De Ridder says that the demon on the right is wearing white winged shoes like Charun. Giglioli points out that this is not so: the rendering of the feet is nearly the same as in the right-hand demon on the Trieste vase: they are the feet of a bird of prey, and have a projection behind like the spur of a cock. From the ankle up the legs are human. The artist painted the feet white and then went on to paint the legs white too. This had caused Giglioli to ponder whether the demon may not be wearing tights and whether the whole picture may not have been inspired by an Etruscan dramatic performance. Surely not.

The Trieste vase (no. 2) was formerly in Tuscania (in the Valeri collection), but is not certified to have been found there. A good account of it is given by Giglioli in *Ausonia* 10, 88–101.

The palmettes below the picture are red-figure, but give place to a black palmette between the roots of each handle. Above one handle there is a large black leaf or spray, of the same kind as in the Alcestis picture on the Paris vase; see also p. 57.

The subject of the chariot frieze on the Newcastle fragment (no. 3), is uncertain. One

---

[1] In the companion picture the painter has probably interchanged the names of Harmonia and Peitho, and the subject is another famous bride, Harmonia.

of the galloping quadrigae is well preserved. Two of the horses are white; white also the reins, the sleeves of the charioteer, his sash, and the woollen cap on his head—for it must be a cap rather than white hair, although I remember no such head-gear in charioteers. Part of the next team remains; one of the horses being white. It is preceded by a youth running, flourishing his sword in his right hand and holding his flying cloak with his left. He wears a tiara, and boots with flaps. The hilt of his scabbard is white. Above, a shield, half-seen, and a garment, suspended. The style is very like that of the Alcsti vase: perhaps the same hand. See also p. 172.

In the following three vases I find some similarity to the style of the Alcsti Group:

(i)

*Calyx-krater*

1. Once Hasselmann. *Kunstbesitz* pl. 18, 819. A, woman seated and winged youth. B, satyr and maenad. Either the original, or the photograph, seems retouched in places. Ht. 0.32. See p. 84.

(ii)

*Bell-kraters*

2. Roman market. Gerhard *AV.* pl. 320, 3–4. A, Apollo on a swan, with satyr and maenads; B, satyrs and maenad. The swan, and the women's flesh, were no doubt white.
3. Copenhagen, Ny Carlsberg, H 153. B, *Bildertafeln Etr. Mus.* pl. 53, 1. A, naked maenad seated, and satyrs; B, satyrs and maenad.

There are no relief-lines in no. 1. Nos. 2 and 3 go together and seem to be by one hand (see p. 161). I cannot be sure of the technique from the illustrations, but conjecture that there are no relief-lines.

To compare the Hasselmann calyx-krater with that in Trieste, the shape of the upper part is different, but the lower parts are much alike. Under the pictures, red-figure palmettes 'breaking into silhouette', as there (p. 134). The pattern above the picture is a black laurel: these *black* patterns are common, as will be seen, in later Etruscan vases.

The lady on A sits on a laver-stand: see p. 67. Eros, who wears a chitoniskos, which is unusual for Eros, brings her an alabastron, and the σπάθη for applying the ointment it contains. Spathē and alabastron are favourite objects in Etruscan, especially on mirrors. To the right of the lady there is said to be a large swan on a rock.

The legs of Eros, and his white chitoniskos, recall the demons of Paris and Trieste; the attitude of the satyr, that of the left-hand satyr on the back of the Paris vase. The drapery of the woman on the Trieste vase has something in common with the system seen on the Hasselmann krater, especially in the maenad: groups of short, straightish, radiating folds, recalling Faliscan (p. 162).

### THE TURMUCA GROUP

No relief-lines; much use of hatched lines for details both in bodies and in garments. The style is more forcible than in the Alcsti Group.

These two, though unusually elaborate pieces, are akin to the vases of the Funnel Group (pp. 141–5), and may well have been made in the same city as they or even the same factory.

### Calyx-kraters

1. Cabinet des Médailles 920, from Vulci. *Mon.* 2 pl. 9, whence Inghirami pll. 398–9, Rayet and Collignon 324, and (B) Pl. 31, 2; (A) Giglioli pl. 279, 2; phots. Giraudon 8050–1, whence (A) Pl. 31, 1. A, Achilles slaughtering a Trojan prisoner, with Charun. B, Nekyia (Charun, shades of heroines). On A, *Aivas* (by mistake for *Achle*), *Charu*. On B, retr., *hinthia Turmucas*, and *Pentasila*.
2. London F 480, from Vulci. *Mon.* 2 pl. 8, whence Inghirami pll. 396–7 and (A) *El.* 2 pl. 102; B, Walters *HAP.* pl. 58, 2, whence Giglioli pl. 279, 3; Jacobsthal *Aktaions Tod* 15; Pl. 32, 1–2. A, Death of Actaeon. B, Death of Ajax. On A, *Ataiun*; on B, *Aivas*, both retr. Short upright handles. The poor, lead-like, metallic glaze has turned brown in parts. The inside of the vase, except for part of the mouth, is reserved.

The two are closely connected, although they need not be by one hand. On the krater in the Cabinet des Médailles (Pl. 31, 1–2), which is the better of the two, see p. 9. The hero on A wears a short chiton, a corslet, greaves, and arm-protectors. The painter has written *Aivas* against him, but this is only a slip for *Achle*. The figure goes back, as was seen above (p. 90), to the same original as the Achilles in six other representations of the Slaughter of the Trojan Captives. The figures of Charun and the victim are not derived from this original. Charun wears a chitoniskos and holds his hammer ready. Aquiline nose, animal ears, long fangs.

The wearing of vambrace and rerebrace is one of the links between the figure of the hero and those that correspond to it in the painting from the Tomba François, the relief on the sarcophagus from Torre San Severo, and the cinerary urn in Volterra (see p. 91). In these, however, both arms are protected, and not only the right, as here and almost always. Vambrace and rerebrace are comparatively rare pieces of armour. Greeks some-times wore them in the sixth century: lists of the few Greek specimens preserved, and of representations on two Attic black-figured vases and in an archaic Italiote bronze, are given by Furtwängler in *Olympia* iv, 161–2 and Hagemann *Griechische Panzerung* (1919) 125–8. To these we may add a fine Greek rerebrace from the cemetery at the foot of Monte Sannace three kilometres north of Gioia del Colle in Apulia (Gervasio *Bronzi arcaici e ceramica geometrica nel Museo di Bari* pl. 16, 1 and p. 55);[1] a very similar one found in the recent excavations at Olympia (*Jb.* 52, *Bericht über die Ausgrabungen in Olympia* pl. 5, 1 and p. 54); and, quoted by Gervasio, the representation of both pieces of armour in one of the metopes from the great sixth-century temple in Corfu (*AM.* 39, 163–4). Hagemann does not mention the Etruscan representations: four of these have been cited already; and a fifth, earlier than the others, is on a mirror in the British Museum (623: Gerhard *ES.* pl. 389); but far the earliest Etruscan representation is on a rough black-figured neck-amphora of the early fifth century in the University of Reading, where

[1] According to Hampe and Jantzen it was found in the same grave as the shield Gervasio pll. 16–17, but Gervasio does not appear to say so.

one of the warriors wears vambrace and rerebrace on his spear-arm: the rerebrace is decorated with a satyr-like head. Jacobsthal draws my attention to a Samnite set, fourth century, and quite plain, from Alfedena and in the museum there (*ML.* 10 pl. 13, a, below, whence Duhn *Italische Gräberkunde* 563). For others, not Greek or Etruscan, and mostly late, see also Furtwängler loc. cit., *Anz.* 1898, 139 (Herrmann), Daremberg and Saglio s.v. manica (Saglio), *Amtliche Berichte* 31, 265 (Köster), Aurigemma *I mosaici di Zliten* 156 ff., Neugebauer *Führer: Bronzen* 17 and 32.

On B, see p. 9. Turmuca and Pentasila wear the himation only, which veils the back of the head. Pentasila's hair is mounded high in front and bound with a fillet: the veiled head, in three-quarter view, somewhat recalls those on Volterran column-kraters and late Etruscan mirrors (see p. 131). On their bandages see p. 89. The woman on the left wears a peplos, with overfall, overgirt; under it a chiton, which shows on the arms; and a necklace. The hair is cut short, as if in mourning, and encircled by a broad bandeau. The hands are joined:

εἱστήκει Κλύτιος μὲν ἀμήχανος· εἶχε δὲ δοιὰς χεῖρας ὁμοπλεκέας, κρυφίης κήρυκας ἀνίης.

(Christodoros in *Anth. Pal.* 2, 254)

The mood, however, is perhaps gentler and more resigned when, as here, one hand is simply laid on the other than when the fingers are pectinated.

Charun leans not on a stick (de Ridder) but on his hammer.

Now the London krater (Pl. 32, 1–2). Above each handle and extending into the picture-field there is a garment hanging on a pair of pegs. In the reproduction *Mon.* 2 pl. 8 one garment is put in the Ajax picture and one in the Actaeon, but I take it that both belong to Ajax (a chlamys and a himation), and so already Walters. This gives (A) a broad picture consisting of a single large figure flanked by gear, (B) a narrower picture consisting of a triangular group.

According to Heydemann (*AZ.* 1871, 61) and Walters the suspended garment shows that the scene is laid in the tent of Ajax. On the other hand, the rock on the right of the picture points to the scene not being laid in the tent, and cancels out the argument from the garment. Heydemann calls the upright thing a club, Walters a tree-stump, but it is evidently of the same nature as the rocky ground below: the artist, rather awkwardly, discontinued the rock so that the left leg of the hero should come out clear.

On representations of the Death of Ajax see von Mach in *Harvard Studies* ii, 93–9; Milani in *Boll. d'Arte* 2 (1908), 361–8; *Lewes House Gems* 33–4 and 37–8; Robert *Heldensage* 1201–2 and 1206; Payne *NC.* 137 and 340. As to the Greek representations, I add only that one of the chief, on a black-figured amphora by Exekias in Boulogne, has been republished in *ABS.* pl. 7 and in Technau *Exekias* pl. 24; that one of the earliest, the seventh-century gem of the Melian class, from Perachora, in New York, mentioned in *LHG.* 38, is now figured in Richter *Ancient Gems from the Evans and Beatty Collections* no. 141;[1] and that this is the subject, as Kunze saw (*Gnomon* 9, 14), of the relief on an ivory comb from Sparta (Dawkins *Artemis Orthia* pl. 130, 1 and pl. 131, 3). Of the Etruscan representations I give a full list.

---

[1] The gem should surely be poised with the sword upright?

*Stone*

1. Tarquinia, from Tarquinia. Stone relief. Giglioli pl. 157, 2. Ajax falling on the sword, which passes right through his middle. Early sixth century B.C.

2. Tarquinia, from Tarquinia. Nenfro relief. *NSc.* 1907, 345. Ajax falling on the sword, which has pierced his middle. Early sixth century B.C.

On reliefs of this kind see Levi in *NSc.* 1931, 223–7, Åkerström *Studien über die etruskischen Graeber* 57–9, Riis *Tyrrhenika* 66–7.

*Gems*

1. Boston. Sard scarab from Corfu. *LHG.* pl. 3, 37. Ajax lies dead, fallen on his sword, which passes through his left side. A winged daemoness approaches and covers the body with a large cloth: see *LHG.* 33–4. (Another representation of a corpse being covered: Attic rf. fragment by the Copenhagen Painter, Athens Acr. 780, Graef pl. 69, *ARV.* 194 no. 19). Beginning of the fifth century.[1]

2. Boston. Sard scarab. *LHG.* pl. 3, 41, and pl. 9, 41, whence (badly reproduced) Ducati *St.* pl. 129, 339 and Giglioli pl. 218, 5; *Bull. MFA.* 26 (1928), 47, 9; Pl. 32, 5. Ajax throws himself on his sword. It will enter below the breast. Behind, his scabbard. The hair hangs over in front of the head. There is no indication of the soil in which the sword is fixed. About 480 B.C.

3. Copenhagen, Thorvaldsen Museum, 41. Sard scarab. Fossing *The Thorvaldsen Museum: Catalogue of the Antique Engraved Gems and Cameos* pl. 1. 'The nude, bearded hero is turned to l., with bent legs and upstretched arms; before his body a sword, horizontally placed, and behind it a bird flying upwards' (Fossing). Bad work, but, so far as can be seen from the wretched reproduction, not late.

4. London 635, from Chiusi? Sard scarab. Furtwängler *AG.* pl. 17, 32; *LHG.* pl. A, 19; Walters *Cat. Gems* pl. 11; Pl. 32, 4. Ajax throws himself on his sword, which enters near the left armpit. Blood spirts. The hero is beardless. The sword is fixed in a mound. Bead border. Early fourth century.

5. Cabinet des Médailles 1820 bis. Sard scarab. Pl. 32, 6, from a cracked electrotype in my possession. ΑΙϹΑϹ, *Aivas*, retr. Ajax has flung himself on his sword, which has entered the right side at the level of the waist. Blood spirts. Beardless; blown hair. His left hand behind his back, the right hand behind his head. The right shank foreshortened away; the foot showing in profile. The ground in which the hilt is fixed has a sandy look. Early fourth century.

6. New York 41.160.489. Sard scarab. *Burl. Cat.* 1903 pl. 110, M 127; C. Smith and Hutton *Cat. Wyndham Cook* pl. 2, 41; *LHG.* pl. A, 20; Richter *Ancient Gems from the Evans and Beatty Collections* no. 42; Pl. 32, 7. Ajax falls on his sword, the hilt of which is planted in a mound. His breast touches the point. The sword will enter below the

---

[1] A battered gold plaque from Vulci, formerly in the Campana collection, and now in Leningrad (?), is believed to represent Eos tending the aged Tithonos: so Gerhard (*Akademische Abhandlungen* pl. 8, 4), Johannes Schmidt (in Roscher s.v. Tithonos p. 1029), and Cook (*Zeus* iii, 247): 'Eos pouring the contents of a jug (?) over Tithonos, who lies on a concave couch or cradle' (Cook). I do not see the cradle, or the jug, and should have thought that the subject was of the same kind as in the Boston gem: a goddess covering a dead man. The goddess seems to be winged, but according to Gerhard she is not.

pit of the stomach. He is bearded, and wears a chlamys. The head is bare (not helmeted as stated in the Cook catalogue). Behind, his shield. The artist has thought out the attitude: Ajax, to make sure that he will not spoil his fall by involuntary movement of his arms, has passed his left arm behind his back so as to grasp the right forearm with the fingers. A youth on the Attic cup Boston 10.193 (Hartwig *Meister-schalen* pl. 26: *ARV.* 917 no. 13, near early Douris) locks his arms in a similar way, though without, it seems, special reason. Early fourth century.

7. Copenhagen, National Museum. Sard scarab. Furtwängler *AG.* pl. 64, 38. See also ibid. iii, 193–4. Globolo style, very rude: late fourth century B.C. or early third. The exact attitude is not easy to make out. The arms are extended, perhaps praying (as Furtwängler). The torso looks, in the reproduction, as if it were seen from behind: but one leg seems to be frontal. The head is upturned and faces to right. On the right, the sword, fixed in a rectangular mound. On the left, shield and spear. Inscription AIAX VIET. Furtwängler, with the approval of Wölfflin, took *viet* to be subjunctive of the verb *vio* (= eo): 'let Ajax go' (into the under world) [Greek ἴτω], but Eduard Fraenkel, whom I have consulted, will not allow the verb at this date.

An unhappy suggestion is made by Lommatzsch in *CIL.*,[2] 576: 'fortasse Aiax viet(us), de elanguescente et morituro.'

### *Bronze statuette from a vessel*

Florence, from Populonia. *Boll. d'Arte* 2 (1908), 361; *NSc.* 1908, 207; *AJA.* 1909, 208; Ducati *St.* pl. 104, 277–8; Lamb *Greek and Roman Bronzes* pl. 41, b; Giglioli pl. 217, 1–2. Ajax, helmeted, grasps the blade, and is about to fall on it. About 480 B.C. See also Jantzen *Bronzewerkstätten* 5 note 1 and Riis *Tyrrhenika* 91.

### *Bronze mirror*

Boston. *Harv. St.* 11 pl. 2. Early fourth century. See below, p. 140.

### *Vases*

1. Formerly in the Campana collection. Bf. oinochoe with trefoil mouth. *AZ.* 1871, 61, after a drawing in the Berlin Apparatus. This is by the Micali Painter and should be added to my list of his works in *RG.* 77–80; see also above, p. 15. The woman running up is probably Tecmessa, as Heydemann proposed. Heydemann thinks that the warrior on the left in the reproduction has been escorting Tecmessa but has been so panicked by the satyr-face on the shield of Ajax that he draws his sword and rushes at it. The fact is that the modern draughtsman has divided the figures wrongly in his roll-out. Shield and warrior should be on the right of the picture, not the left: the shield goes with the rest of Ajax's belongings; and the warrior is an unfriendly or cautious Greek, who in the search for the missing hero is taking no risks.
2. Palermo, from Chiusi. Rf. stamnos. See pp. 39 and 42.
3. Cabinet des Médailles 947, from Vulci. Rf. stamnos by the Settecamini Painter. See pp. 53–4.
4. London F 480, from Vulci. Rf. calyx-krater, Turmuca Group. See pp. 136–7.

According to G. Haupt (*Commentationes archaeologicae in Aeschylum* 117–18) the London vase represents that version of the Death of Ajax which was given by Aeschylus in his *Thracian Women*; and Robert followed Haupt (*Heldensage* 1203). The Aeschylean version of the story, or something of it, is recorded by the Laurentian scholion to Sophocles' *Ajax* 833:

παραδεδομένον δὲ κατὰ ἱστορίαν ὅτι κατὰ τὸ ἄλλο σῶμα ἄτρωτος ἦν ὁ Αἴας, κατὰ δὲ τὴν μασχάλην τρωτός, διὰ τὸ τὸν Ἡρακλέα τῆι λεοντῆι αὐτὸν σκεπάσαντα κατὰ τοῦτο τὸ μέρος ἀσκέπαστον ἐᾶσαι διὰ τὸν γωρυτὸν ὃν περιέκειτο· φησὶν δὲ περὶ αὐτοῦ Αἰσχύλος ὅτι καὶ τὸ ξίφος ἐκάμπτετο, οὐδαμῆ ἐνδιδόντος τοῦ χρωτὸς τῆι σφαγῆι, τόξον ὥς τις ἐντείνων, πρὶν δή τις, φησί, παροῦσα δαίμων ἔδειξεν αὐτῶι κατὰ ποῖον μέρος δεῖ χρήσασθαι τῆι σφαγῆι· ὁ δὲ Σοφοκλῆς ἐριθεῦσαι μέν τι ὡς πρεσβυτέρωι μὴ βουληθείς, οὐ μὴν παραλιπεῖν αὐτὸ δοκιμάζων, ψιλῶς φησὶ
    πλευρὰν ἀναρρήξαντα τῶιδε φασγάνωι,
κατὰ τί τὴν πλευρὰν μὴ εἰπών.

Haupt's only reason for connecting the London picture with Aeschylus was the many marks of wounds on Ajax's body, tokens of his vain efforts to pierce it: but, as Séchan pointed out (*Études sur la tragédie grecque* 130), there are no such marks: what Haupt took for blood is shading. Séchan is ready nevertheless to associate the London vase with Aeschylus because 'the sword enters at the right armpit and issues at the left shoulder'. This is hardly an exact description of the course of the sword, and even if it were, it would not be sufficient to connect the vase with Aeschylus rather than Sophocles or another.

Robert and Séchan have overlooked a monument which as both John Marshall saw, and Edmund von Mach who published it as long ago as 1910, gives the Aeschylean version of the Death of Ajax. It is the fine Etruscan mirror in Boston figured in *Harvard Studies* 11 pl. 2. *Eivas Telmunus* kneels with a crumpled sword held by the blade in his left hand, and looks round wildly at *Menarva* who has hastened towards him. Her right arm is extended, not I think pointing to the vulnerable spot, but with a preliminary gesture—'Stop: let me show you how.' Von Mach is careful to speak of 'the myth *adopted by* Aeschylus'. We do not know how old the tradition of Ajax's invulnerability was, but it is unlikely to have been invented by Aeschylus.[1] Probably the design on the mirror is derived not from Aeschylus but ultimately from the epic source which Aeschylus used. In this it will have been Athena who showed the hero the vulnerable spot; Aeschylus, on the other hand, may have left the identity of the goddess vague, or at the very least not said in so many words that the δαίμων was Athena.

What was in the δαίμων's mind was no doubt pity: so in Virgil (*Aen.* 4, 693) Juno comes to the assistance of Dido:

Tum Iuno omnipotens, longum miserata dolorem
difficilisque obitus, Irim demisit Olympo,
quae luctantem animam nexosque resolveret artus.

Another *bent sword* appears in pictures of Herakles and the Nemean Lion. It will be remembered that the invulnerability of Ajax was due to contact with the Lion's hide

---

[1] Pindar alludes to it in an ode which is thought to be somewhat earlier than 480 (*Isthm.* 6, 47–8): he gives his own, somewhat rationalized, version of the encounter between Herakles and Telamon.

(above, p. 140).[1] Herakles first used the sword; but found that the Lion had proof of metal and was forced to strangle it (*JHS*. 54, 90, and Haspels *ABL*. 117). Attic vases show him attacking it with the sword; and on an Attic black-figured amphora in the Villa Giulia (Mingazzini *Vasi Castellani* pl. 65) the sword is seen falling from his hand, bent.

On B of the London calyx-krater (Pl. 32, 2), Actaeon, attacked by four hounds, lays about him with his lagobolon. Two of the hounds have collars. White details. The representations of the Death of Actaeon are collected by Jacobsthal *Aktaions Tod* (in *Marburger Jahrbuch für Kunstwissenschaft* 5). See also *Pan-Maler* 9–10 and 16, Jacobsthal *Die melischen Reliefs* 31–2 and 74–6, Bock in *Anz*. 1935, 498, Haspels *ABL*. 169 and 183. Jacobsthal compares our picture with the relief on a Volterran cinerary urn (Brunn and Körte *Rilievi* 2, 1 pl. 3, 1).

### THE FUNNEL GROUP

A large group of later Etruscan vases may be so named from the shape of the tongue-pattern: the inner part of it, whether above the pictures or below, is broad and flat at one end, and tapers strongly, with the sides nearly straight, suggesting a funnel: see Pl. 32, 3 and Pl. 33, 7. Each 'funnel' is separated from the next by a pair or sometimes a trio of upright lines. Another mark of the group is a rosette which presents itself as a disk, quartered, with a small white tag or feeler at the parting of each pair of quarters. There are no relief-lines. Hatched lines are used for some of the inner details of the body in the Munich cup, no. 19. There are some pretty attitudes, but the drawing is weak. The group can be subdivided. The stamnoi nos. 1–3, the calyx-krater no. 10, and no doubt no. 11, are by one hand; the calyx-krater no. 12 and the neck-amphora no. 15 are very like them; so are the oinochoe no. 16 and the skyphos no. 17, which are by one hand. The patternwork joins no. 5 to no. 4, but the style of the figures seems somewhat different; the figures of no. 7 approximate to those of no. 5. No. 19 is joined to no. 4 by the palmettes, no. 18 to no. 19. But the whole group is closely interknit. No. 8 may stand a little apart from the rest.

Several of these associations have already been made by Mercklin (*St. etr.* 11, 375–7): who saw that Hamburg 1912.1909 (no. 2) was by the same hand as Cabinet des Médailles 950 (no. 1); compared the Berlin calyx-krater with them (no. 10), and with the Berlin the Dresden (no. 12); assigned the Munich cup (no. 19) to the same fabric as the Berlin vase. H. R. W. Smith ascribed nos. 16 and 17 to a single hand.

The two vases of the Turmuca Group, as was noted above (p. 136), are related to the Funnel Group.

*Stamnoi*

1. Cabinet des Médailles 950. B, de Ridder pl. 29. A, satyr and naked maenad. B, woman with wreaths.
2. Hamburg 1912.1909. *St. etr.* 11 pl. 42, 3–4, pl. 43, 4–5, and p. 376. A, centaur. B, woman with wreaths.

---

[1] What exactly took place I do not understand: I cannot make head or tail. Robert gives an explanation (*Heldensage* 1047) of which

3. Vatican ? B, *Mus. Greg.* ii pl. 95, ii, 4. B, woman with wreaths.

4. Hamburg 661. *St. etr.* 11 pl. 41, 4–5 and p. 375. A, Nike. B, satyr fetching cushion. For the Nike see below, p. 146, γ.

5. Baltimore, Walters Art Gallery, 48.61, from Castel Campanile. *Journ. Walt.* 3 (1940), 138. A, naked woman and youth; B, naked woman and naked youth.

6. Carlsruhe 348, from Vulci. Side-view, Pl. 33, 7, from a photograph kindly given me by Jacobsthal. A, Hyakinthos on a swan. B, Lasa. See p. 148.

6 bis. Cambridge AE 29, from Cervetri. Pl. 34, 1–3. A, naked woman sitting on a rock and holding a cushion; B, woman sitting on a rock and holding a sash. The foot of the vase is modern: present height 0.29.

7. Hamburg 662. *St. etr.* 11 pl. 43, 1–2 and p. 378. A, naked woman leaning on a pillar; B, youth leaning on a pillar.

8. London F 486, from Vulci? (ex Campanari: 'volcente' according to Braun in *Annali* 1837, 272; 'probably from Orbetello' according to the old British Museum catalogue, no. 1682; but compare p. 43). A, Pl. 32, 3. A, a youth seated on a rock, holding a sword on his knee; a winged woman lays her left hand on his shoulder and raises her right hand with a torch in it. B, a naked man attacking another with a hammer. See below, p. 143.

8 bis. Cambridge, Prof. A. B. Cook. Gerhard *Trinkschalen* pl. C, 2–3 and 11. A, Athena and Eros. B, Herakles. There is much incised sketch. This is one of the many Etruscan stamnoi in which the picture-space is so narrowed by the handle-palmettes that there is only room for one figure or at most two. The statue on the tall pillar recalls Campanian vases, the Athena the austere female on the London stamnos F 486 (Pl. 30, 3). The Herakles has a statue-like appearance: compare, for example, a marble in the Terme (Cultrera *Una statua di Ercole* pll. 1–4). The club rests on a stone, as often in statues: it seems to have been agreed in antiquity that Herakles' club, when held down in the hand, was not long enough to reach the ground.

### *Calyx-kraters*

9. Cabinet des Médailles 921. B, de Ridder pl. 27. A, Amazonomachy. B, a youth attacking another. One of the groups in the wall-paintings of the Tomba del Cardinale at Tarquinia resembles B (*Ephemeris Daco-Romana* 6, 176).

10. Berlin 2952, from Vulci. Ambrosch *De Charonte etrusco* pll. 1–2; *Atti Pont.*, new series, 14, 196–7; A, Neugebauer pl. 87. A, Charun. B, woman with thyrsus and wreath. Albizzati is quite likely right in supposing (*Atti Pont.*, new series, 14, 180–1) that the woman forms part of the same subject as the Charun, and is the dead. The thyrsus shows her to be a votary of Dionysos, like the woman on the Villa Giulia stamnos 1660 (see p. 152).

11. Vatican? B, *Mus. Greg.* ii pl. 95, i, 3. A, ?. B, woman.

12. Dresden 395. A, *St. etr.* 11 pl. 42, 2. A, satyr fetching cushion; B, the like.

13. Munich 3222 (J 523), from Vulci. A, *St. etr.* 11 pl. 42, 1. A, satyr fetching cushion. B, dove.

14. Tarquinia, from Tarquinia. I descry this on the table to the left, in the view of the

Stanza Quinta in the old Corneto Museum, phot. Moscioni 8259; and make out the shape, the black laurel above the picture and at the sides, the tongues below, the presence of red-figure palmettes at the handles, but not the subject.

### Neck-amphora

15. Cabinet des Médailles 875. A, de Ridder pl. 25. A, a satyr and a naked maenad. B, a swan and a cushion (not an egg, as Gerhard, *AZ*. 1864, *Anz*. 254, and de Ridder). On the neck, in black silhouette, A, a naked woman; B, a naked youth. The woman bends to pick up a winged phallus which flutters towards her like a young pigeon. The next moment is represented by the Cerberus Painter on his cup in Villa Giulia, Florence, and Heidelberg (*Campana Fragments* pl. Y, 1 and p. 7 on pl. 1 B 8: *ARV*. 56 no. 10); but there the creature is not a winged phallus, it is a phallus-bird with legs as well as wings. On a fine fragment of an Italiote calyx-krater, with pictures in added colours, in the collection of Dr. Ludwig Curtius, Rome, a phlyax bends to pick up a winged phallus which scurries away from him. The youth who hastens up on the reverse of our vase is ithyphallic. In the fourth century silhouette tends to usurp the place of red-figure in floral patterns; but human figures in silhouette, side by side with red-figure pictures, are very rare.

### Oinochoe (shape VII: beaked jug)

16. Berkeley 8.3399. Pl. 33, 4–6. Head of a man, between two geese. On the neck, in white, a sprig of olive, and plants.

### Skyphos

17. Berkeley 8.3825. Pl. 33, 1–3. A, head of a satyr; to left of him, a sprig of olive in white. B, goose.

### Cups

18. Würzburg 819. Langlotz pl. 237. I, youth with horse, and satyr. A, seated youth; B, the like. Each youth has a panther-cub beside him; one of them has an affectionate dog, and a large bird perches on the shoulder of the other—this time it is a pet bird.
19. Munich inv. 8349. A, *St. etr.* 11 pl. 41, 3. I, woman with sash; A, woman with cushion; B, the like.

### Cup or the like

20. Orvieto, Conte Faina, from Orvieto. I, phot. Alinari 32471, whence Tarchi pl. 125, 4. I, woman and youth. Restored: the feet of the youth with the lower half of the shanks seem to be modern, and part of the face. I do not understand the subject.

To return to the London stamnos, no. 8. The youth on the obverse (Pl. 32, 3) wears boots with flaps, but is otherwise naked; his chlamys is under him. His sword, in its scabbard, lies across his thighs and his right hand rests on it lightly. The winged woman wears a long peplos, girt, but without overfall; a necklace; and bracelets. The short torch has a ring round it to catch the drips: the drip-catcher is rare except in racing-torches, but occurs also in the torch held by Lyssa on the Apulian volute-krater with

Hippolytos in the British Museum (F 279: *AZ*. 1883 pl. 6; phot. Mansell 3271). The rings are shaded where the upper edge turns over. I take the scene to be laid in the Nether World; the youth to be Theseus, or rather Peirithoos; and the woman Poine, Erinys, or the like.

In the late-fifth-century three-figure relief with Theseus, Peirithoos, and Herakles, preserved in fragmentary copies, Theseus and Peirithoos both hold walking-sticks, and Theseus a sword in its sheath (*RM*. 53 pll. 34–5 and pp. 207–220). In the Nekyia of Polygnotos at Delphi, Theseus held two swords, his own and his companion's (Paus. 10, 29, 9): . . . ἐπὶ θρόνων καθεζόμενοι Θησεὺς μὲν τὰ ξίφη, τό τε Πειρίθου καὶ τὸ ἑαυτοῦ, χερσὶν ἀμφοτέραις ἔχει, ὁ δὲ ἐς τὰ ξίφη βλέπων ἐστὶν ὁ Πειρίθους· εἰκάσαις ἂν ἄχθεσθαι τοῖς ξίφεσιν αὐτὸν ὡς ἀχρείοις καὶ ὄφελός σφισιν οὐ γεγενημένοις ἐς τὰ τολμήματα. This would be an elaboration of some such simpler motive as is preserved on our vase.

In three of the Apulian vases with scenes in Hades *Dike* is shown watching Peirithoos: sitting beside him, or standing with one foot on higher ground, and holding a sword, drawn or sheathed: an inscription on a fragmentary vase in Carlsruhe gives her name (258: *AZ*. 1884 pl. 19, whence *WV*. E pl. 6, 3; *Jh*. 10 pl. 7). The other two vases are in Munich (*WV*. E pl. 1; *FR*. pl. 10) and Naples (Stg. 709: *AZ*. 1884 pl. 18, whence *WV*. E pl. 3, 2): all three are volute-kraters of 'A.P. style' (see *JHS*. 63, 91). In the Carlsruhe vase Peirithoos, though bound, retains his sword, but it hangs at his side, does not rest on his knees. In the few Attic pictures of the subject Dike does not appear (Jacobsthal in *Metr. Mus. St*. 5, 124).

The long clothes of the woman on the Etruscan vase would suit Dike: but she is winged; and holds a torch, not a sword: the painter probably intended her for some daemon corresponding to a Greek Poine or Erinys.

The scene on the reverse of the London stamnos is also set in Hades. The man with the hammer is Charun, or possibly some other demon, and the fallen one is a transgressor. Charun has rough stiff hair, aquiline nose, beetling brow, lean shanks. His victim is small, bald, paunchy, wears a wreath, and has fallen on rocky ground. Both are ithyphallic, which I do not understand: nor, I think, does van Essen (*Did Orphic* 4–5).

In the Tomba del Cardinale at Tarquinia demons attack naked transgressors with hammers (*St. etr*. 2 pll. 19 and 22). On an Etruscan red-figured skyphos from Tarquinia, formerly in the possession of the brothers Marzi, a dead man rides in a cart drawn by two dogs and followed by Charun, who holds a hammer and is ithyphallic: the vase is lost and is only known from the description in *Annali* 1879, 304.

For the floral decoration at the handles compare nos. 1, 2, and 18.

A vase from Vulci formerly in the collection of Lord Swansea at Singleton Abbey is known to me from a minute reproduction only (*A Catalogue of the Contents of Singleton Abbey, Swansea, 13–19 October 1919*, plate, no. 714): it has tongue-pattern of the characteristic form on the shoulder, and may belong to the Funnel Group. It is a sort of stamnos, but the photograph shows small volute-like handles which may or may not be antique. The height is 8¼ inches. The subject is a chariot-race, and to quote the catalogue, 'this crude but vigorous drawing is archaeologically important, as giving not only a picture of the race, but also of the goal keeper, who is depicted in the act of putting up or removing a horizontal bar between the two winning posts'. Unfortunately, neither goal nor keeper is visible in the reproduction.

From Ure I have a note of a calyx-krater in the Faina collection at Orvieto which looks as if it might belong to the Funnel Group: on one side, a naked male with one foot raised, and a woman, naked from the middle up, standing full-face; flanking them, black patterns; below, egg-pattern.

According to Jahn the following, of which I have no note, are in the same style as the Munich calyx-krater 3222, no. 13:

### Stamnoi

1. Munich (J 522), from Vulci. A, woman; B, naked youth.
2. Munich (J 524), from Vulci. A, woman; B, naked youth.

A group of phialai, with floral decoration only, probably belong to the Funnel Group: they will be treated later (p. 181).

### A CALYX-KRATER IN BOSTON

Boston 08.201. A, a woman, a winged goddess (?), and a naked youth. B, a youth and two women. The vase is very much restored. The foot is modern. Tongue-pattern below the pictures; then, on the cul, red-figured palmettes. Above the picture, black laurel of the same type as at the sides of the pictures in Berlin 2952 (p. 142 no. 10). No side borders. No relief-lines. Very feeble style.

This calyx-krater must be put somewhere in the neighbourhood of the Funnel Group. The style of the drawing connects it with another vase which seems earlier and not so abject:

### Stamnos

Baltimore, Walters Art Gallery, 48.63, from Castel Campanile. *Journ. Walt.* 3, 136. A, satyr and seated maenad: he holds a tympanon. B, youth and woman. Slightly repainted according to Miss Hill. No relief-lines, except, apparently, for the uprights in the tongue-pattern above the pictures.

### SUNDRY STAMNOI

The stamnoi that follow do not form a single group, but they have the same general character as the Funnel Group, and belong to the same wing of later Etruscan red-figure. London F 485 (λ) is the only vase in the list about which I am properly informed: it might almost find a place in the Funnel Group.

α. Berlin 2956, from Etruria. The figures, Gerhard *ES.* pl. 19, 7. A, a maid holding a cista and a necklace; to left, a cushion. The cista contains an alabastron (the mouth seen from above), with a spathē stuck in it; B, the like. Miserable drawing, but still carried out in relief-lines. The palmettes recall the cup Würzburg 819, of the Funnel Group (p. 143 no. 18).

β. Berlin 2955, from Vulci. A, winged youth, seated, and winged woman. B, griffin. I have no note of this, but according to Furtwängler it is 'as 2956'.

γ. Berlin 2957, from Vulci. *El.* 1 pl. 88. A, Gigantomachy (Athena and Giant). B, Nike. For the subject of A (Athena has wrenched the giant's arm off) see Körte in *Bull.* 1885, 5–7; compare also an Etruscan black-figured neck-amphora published by Micali (*Mon. ined.* pl. 37, 1); on a mirror in Perugia the giant is inscribed *Akrathe* (Gerhard *ES.* pl. 68). For the Nike on B compare the Hamburg stamnos 661 (p. 142 no. 4) and a mirror in Parma (Gerhard *ES.* suppl. pl. 143, 2).

δ. London F485, from Orbetello. A, satyr and maenad. B, Nike. The maenad is naked above the waist (see p. 88), and holds her garment up with one hand.

ε. Cabinet des Médailles 948, from Vulci. A, de Ridder 568. A, youth and woman. B, winged woman; on the sash she holds, *Acnaine*, retr. No relief-lines, at least in the figures. The thing held by the woman on A is a necklace or armlet with pendents.

3. Florence, from Orvieto. A, Heydemann *Mittheilungen aus den Antikensammlungen in Ober- und Mittelitalien* 4, whence Pl. 11, 6. A, 'the Leaky Jar' (ὁ τετρημένος πίθος). B, Herakles and a seated woman. All I know about this vase is the picture published by Heydemann and his description ibid. 92–4 no. 40. There seem to be no relief-lines. On A, three women are emptying water into a pithos. One stands behind it, takes a full stamnos which is handed her by a second, and looks round to a third who is also bringing a full stamnos which she will hand to the first. The first woman seems to be naked, the second wears a short chitoniskos not reaching the knees, the third has let down her garment—probably also a chitoniskos—so that she is bare from the waist up as well as from mid-thigh down. The flesh is white. The pithos has a hole in it, and the water escapes. A lusty plant grows from the moist ground on each side. A sash hangs from above, and something else, fragmentary—a garment or the like.

The scene is in Hades. The women in such pictures used to be called Danaids: but it is pointed out that the earliest evidence for the Danaids as water-carriers in Hades is in the pseudo-Platonic *Axiochus* (573 e, Δαναΐδων ὑδρεῖαι ἀτελεῖς), which is assigned to the Hellenistic period; and that the water-carriers in the Nekyia of Polygnotos were not Danaids but in the words of Pausanias 'those who had held the Eleusinian rites of no account', that is, the uninitiated (Plato *Gorgias* 493 b). The question when the identification took place is not easy to answer; in particular, whether in Greek fourth-century representations the women are to be called Danaids. It is sometimes supposed that they are not, but there is no proof one way or the other. These fourth-century representations are as follows:

*Fragment of a limestone relief from the decoration of a sepulchral building*

1. Munich, from Taranto. *AD.* iii, pl. 35; Klumbach *Tarentiner Grabkunst* Beilage A, 42; Cook *Zeus* iii, 424 (drawn from a photograph). Tarentine work.

*Vases*

No. 2 is a Campanian hydria by the Danaid Painter (Trendall *Paestan Pottery* 109; *JHS.* 63, 74, foot, no. 1); nos. 3–6 are Apulian volute-kraters of 'A.P.' style (see *JHS.* 63, 91).

2. London F210. *CV.* IV Ea pl. 8, 15.

3. Leningrad (St. 426). *Bull. Nap.*, new series, 3 pl. 3, whence *WV.* E pl. 6, 2 and Cook *Zeus* iii, 423.
4. Leningrad (St. 424). *AZ.* 1844 pl. 13; Raoul-Rochette *Mon. inédits* pl. 45; *WV.* E pl.4.
5. Naples 3222. *Mon.* 8 pl. 9, whence *WV.* E pl. 2.
6. Carlsruhe 388. *Mon.* 2 pl. 49, whence *WV.* E pl. 3. (The woman in the lower right-hand corner holds a hydria, see Heydemann op. cit. and Winnefeld *Vasen in Carlsruhe* 103.)

From the assured bearing of the women in these six works one would guess that they were heroines, and that the identification as the daughters of Danaos had already taken place.

It is agreed that the water-carriers in Nekyiai on Attic black-figure vases, a neck-amphora of about 525 B.C. in Munich, and a lekythos of about 500 in Palermo (see Haspels *ABL.* 66), are not Danaids: but what is true of them need not be true of the fourth-century representations, which differ in important respects.

The reason for the identification has often been sought but remains obscure.

Ours, as Heydemann noted, is one of the two representations in which the leak in the pithos is actually shown, the other being on a marble well-head of the Roman period in the Vatican (Visconti *Museo Pio Clementino* iv pl. 36, whence Roscher s.v. Danaiden p. 951: Helbig-Amelung 231 no. 359). It is the only one in which the women are scantily clad. Heydemann puts their very practical costume down to what he calls 'Etruscan sensuality'. The well-planned group may be an extract from a many-figured Nekyia, but it has no special connexion with any of the Greek representations in our list.

Of a red-figured stamnos from Vulci, formerly in the Canino collection, I have no more information than is contained in Gerhard's *Rapporto volcente* (73 no. 678) and *Annali* 1834, 55: on each side, Nike writing in a volume the word *Lasna*.

## THE ORBETELLO GROUP
### No relief-lines.    Debased style.
### *Oinochoai* (shape VII: beaked jugs)

1. Vatican, from Orbetello. Inghirami pl. 189, whence *El.* 1 pl. 15; phot. Moscioni 8591, 2, whence Giglioli pl. 277, 4. Seated woman and young satyr. On the neck, Zeus seated and Nike.
2. Volterra, from Volterra. Phot. Alinari 34715, 2. Naked youth running, and (?). On the neck, woman running.

The woman on the neck of the Volterra vase recalls those on an oinochoe of the same shape from Populonia (p. 168: *NSc.* 1934, 415 fig. 69), or on vases by the Painter of Brussels R 273 (p. 167), and may be imitated from some such figure.

## THE GENEVA GROUP
### *Stamnos*

1. Geneva. A, phot. Giraudon 4017 F, b. A, female head.

*Oinochoe* (shape VII: beaked jug)

2. Louvre K 480. Female head.

Ure notes that 'the stamnoi Louvre K 415 and K 416 plainly go with the beak-jug K 480'.

No relief-lines. The drawing of the Geneva stamnos is miserable, worse than in the Ferrara vases which from the type of decoration it recalls (p. 177), for they have a certain dash. The female head, with earring and necklace, is in red-figure, but is flanked by a 'black-figure' floral pattern: see p. 135. Degraded tongues on the shoulder of the vase; the decoration on the mouth is reduced to a row of white uprights, as in the Carlsruhe stamnos 348 (Pl. 33, 7, and p. 142 no. 6) and three stamnoi of the Clusium Group (p. 121 nos. 2–4).

### TWO 'LEBETES'

Two small vases of peculiar shape go together and make one think of the Geneva Group, but cannot be said to come from that factory. One of them is Toronto 471 (Robinson and Harcum pl. 84: heads of a youth and a woman: height 0.178). The general form is that of a 'nuptial lebes', but it has also something of a situla; in addition to the two upright handles there is a back-handle, and besides, in front, a small lion-head spout of a type used in situlae and askoi. The lid is missing, but is preserved in the other vase, which is in the Vatican, from Etruria (*Mus. Greg.* ii pl. 95, iv, 1: a female head—or two of them facing ?). The Vatican spout seems from the illustration to be plain. The floral decoration in both vases is red-figured. Berlin 2963 and 2964, both from Bomarzo, have the same shape as Toronto 471 (Furtwängler *Beschreibung* pl. 7, 309), and would seem, from Furtwängler's description, to go with it: on one, a female head with the flesh in white; on the other, a laver and two swans. With all these we should perhaps compare an askos, of unusual shape, in Tuebingen (F 36: Watzinger pl. 44) which is said to be 'probably from Teano', but may be Etruscan rather than Campanian.

There are no relief-lines in these vases.

# CHAPTER VIII
# LATER RED-FIGURE, II

### THE FLUID GROUP (LATE FALISCAN)

I HAVE chosen the term 'Fluid Group', which explains itself, to designate a branch of Later Etruscan red-figure. It will be noticed that the name of Vulci hardly appears among the proveniences recorded in this chapter: and wherever the vases were produced it can hardly have been in Vulci. One of the difficult questions, for me at least, has been to determine the relation of the Group to Faliscan: I now think that these are late Faliscan vases.

There is an earlier phase in the Fluid Group, and a later, but the one passes gradually into the other. The vases with which we shall begin—stamnoi and a neck-amphora—illustrate the transition. The earliest vase in our whole list is probably the stamnos Ny Carlsberg H152; the stamnos Berlin inv. 30549 is connected with it; the next stage is represented by a stamnos in the Vatican and a neck-amphora in Vienna which are later work of the same painter as the stamnos in Berlin; a pair of stamnoi in Orvieto follow them without a break; these in their turn are inseparable from a bell-krater found in the same tomb; and this belongs to a group of bell-kraters and skyphoi which are right at the core of the Fluid Group in its later phase.

### I
### *Stamnos*

Copenhagen, Ny Carlsberg, H152. A, *Bildertafeln Etr. Mus.* pl. 52. A, Nike seated; B, Nike running.

In the greater part of the vase there is no relief-line; but relief-lines are used in the patterns—tongues, egg-pattern—on the shoulder, and in the egg-pattern on the lip. The flesh of the Nikai, or at any rate the Nike reproduced, is reserved, not white, but there is some white detail in the floral decoration at the handles, and the filling-ornaments are edged with white dots. On the shape of the vase, and the drawing of the patterns, see below, p. 150.

### II
### The Painter of Vienna, O[esterreichisches Museum] 449.
### (i)
### *Stamnos*

1. Berlin inv. 30549. A, and a side-view, Pl. 35, 4–5, from photographs kindly given me by Jacobsthal. A, young satyr and naked maenad; B, the like. The use of relief-line is the same as in the Ny Carlsberg stamnos just described. On the palmette-hearts see below. The maeander has the 'soft' form common in the Fluid Group. The handles are in the form of sea-monsters, kētē, with their tails intertwined.

## (ii)

### *Stamnos*

2. Vatican, from Etruria. A, *Mus. Greg.* ii pl. 95, v, 4; A, phot. Moscioni 8590, whence Giglioli pl. 274, 3; B, Pl. 35, 7. A, fight. B, Dionysos seated and naked maenad. No relief-lines. Much white detail. 'Soft' maeander. The shape of the stamnos is the same as in the last, and so are the plastic handles.

### *Neck-amphora*

3. Vienna, Oest. Mus., 449, from Cervetri. A, Masner pl. 9. A, a satyr embracing a naked maenad; B, a maenad. The shape is a unique version of the neck-amphora. The foot of the vase is of the same type as in the two stamnoi. At the lower junction of each handle, a bearded head in relief. On the shoulder (one side only), plastic, a satyr reclining, hugging a pot, the mouth of which forms a spout. No relief-line. 'Soft' maeander. On the palmette-hearts and the trefoils see below. The lid has tongue-pattern, and on the knob an olive-wreath in black.

The neck-amphora and the Vatican stamnos go together, and are later than the Berlin stamnos, which is close to that in Ny Carlsberg.

A pair of stamnoi, replicas, are just like the Vatican vase in shape and patternwork, and the style of the figures is at least close:

1. Orvieto, from Orvieto (Settecamini). B, *NSc.* 1932, 99, 1. A, mounted Amazon. B, Eros seated.
2. Orvieto, from Orvieto (Settecamini). A, *NSc.* 1932, 99, 2. Replica of the last.
   There are no relief-lines.

This pair of stamnoi, as was said above, is inseparable from a bell-krater found in the same chamber-tomb (*NSc.* 1932, 97–8: see pp. 154–5).

Other vases connected with the stamnoi and neck-amphora will be mentioned later: for the moment we may pause and consider, in those already described, certain features that link them with Faliscan.

First the Ny Carlsberg stamnos H 152. (1) The *shape*—work of an excellent potter——resembles Faliscan stamnoi of the broad-based variety (see p. 74). (2) The drawing of the *tongue-pattern* on the shoulder is characteristically Faliscan: no need to cite instances: most Faliscan stamnoi, and the volute-krater by the Aurora Painter, have such tongues. (3) The drawing of the *egg-pattern* below the tongues, and on the lip of the vase, is also Faliscan: in the Marcioni stamnos (Pl. 17 and p. 78) and the two stamnoi of the Captives Group (p. 87) the 'Faliscan' tongues are accompanied by just such eggs. (4) The big '*trefoils*' in the floral decoration at the handles are also Faliscan: compare the Aurora krater (Pl. 20, 1 and p. 81 no. 1), the stamnos by the same painter (Pl. 16, 2 and p. 81 no. 2), the Marcioni stamnos in Oxford (Pl. 17, p. 78 no. 1) and its Florence replicas, the skyphos Ny Carlsberg H 159 (p. 86).

In the stamnos Berlin inv. 30549 (Pl. 35, 4–5: p. 149 no. 1) the tongue-pattern on the shoulder is of the same 'Faliscan' type as in the Ny Carlsberg vase. The egg-pattern below them is of a commoner type than in Ny Carlsberg: it occurs, of course, in Faliscan as everywhere else: in combination with 'Faliscan' tongues, on the stamnoi Villa Giulia 3592, 43968, and 26017 (p. 81, p. 97, p. 101). The more characteristic form of egg-pattern appears on the lip of the vase. Another Faliscan feature may be seen in the floral decoration at the handle: a loop-like mark on the heart of the palmette (e.g. Pl. 17). Such 'heart-loops' are extremely common in Faliscan: I have noted them on the following Faliscan vases (and have no doubt that they occur on others the floral decoration of which I do not know):

Stamnoi: Villa Giulia 1755 (p. 77 no. 1); 3592 (p. 81 no. 2); Berlin inv. 5825 (p. 88 no. 1); New York GR 641 (p. 88 no. 2); Oxford 1945.89 (p. 78 no. 1).
Volute-krater: Villa Giulia 2491 (p. 81 no. 1).
Hydria: Berkeley 8.984 (p. 101 no. 1).
Skyphos: Berkeley 8.998 (p. 87).
Cups: Villa Giulia 43800 (p. 108 no. 1); 43609 (p. 111, μ); 43608 (p. 110, η); 43791 (p. 101); Berkeley 8.2303 (p. 111, λ); Würzburg 820 (p. 112, no. 1); Vienna, Univ., 499 (p. 110, γ); 500 (p. 110, λ); 497 (p. 109, β).
Phiale: Toronto 600 (p. 105).

Several other vases among those grouped under the heading of the Fluid Group have Faliscan traits: thus the 'Faliscan' tongue-pattern occurs on two beaked oinochoai (p. 155 nos. 1 and 5), and on one of them it is accompanied by the 'Faliscan' egg-pattern; the Faliscan 'heart-loop' appears on the calyx-krater in Brussels (p. 154 no. 2), and in white, as on the Vienna neck-amphora, on a stamnos in Bowdoin College (p. 153). A column-krater of the Volaterrae Group in Berlin (p. 128: Bieńkowski D. 30) has a loop, but on a petal, not on a heart. Again, a beaked jug in Michigan (Pl. 36, 5–6: p. 156 no. 10) has a way of rendering the folds of drapery which occurs on many Faliscan vases (see p. 162).

To sum up: the vases here attributed to the Fluid Group form a branch of late Etruscan vase-painting. They are linked with Faliscan; and they are very probably Faliscan— late Faliscan. The possibility, however, of vases being made in other cities by Faliscan emigrants is to be borne in mind. The matter will doubtless be settled when more is known about the finds already made at Falerii and near it.

Our sequence of stamnoi (Carlsberg–Orvieto) was in the nature of a trial-sinking: we now consider the whole group of stamnoi to which they belong, then pass to vases of other shapes.

### Stamnoi

Nos. 1–5 are early.

#### (i)

1. Copenhagen, Ny Carlsberg, H 152. See p. 149.

#### (ii: by the Painter of Vienna O.449)

2. Berlin inv. 30549. See p. 149.
3. Vatican. See p. 150.

(iii: two by one artist, the Painter of Villa Giulia 1660)

4. Villa Giulia 1660, from Falerii. A, *Atti Pont.*, new series, 15, 258, whence Pl. 35, 6. A, Hermes defending a woman, who holds a thyrsus, from an Erinys. B, naked maenad and satyrs. The head of Hermes, according to Albizzati (l.c. 257), is retouched.

5. Vienna, Oest. Mus., 448, from Cervetri. *Annali* 1879 pl. V, whence Pl. 11, 5. A, naked woman seated with lyre, between Charun and a demoness (Erinys or the like). B, two youths attacking a dragon.

There are no relief-lines. The Vienna stamnos has kētos-handles like the two by the Painter of Vienna O.449 (p. 151); the handles of the Villa Giulia vase are missing. The figurework is closely connected with the Painter of Vienna O.449. Although the Villa Giulia vase was found at Falerii, Albizzati described the style as 'not related to Faliscan but singularly akin to vases with Etruscan inscriptions from Orvietan tombs' (*Atti Pont.* 15, 25): by these he must mean the three Faina vases of our Vanth Group (pp. 169–70).

In the Villa Giulia vase the type of tongues and egg-pattern above the pictures is the same as in the Carlsberg stamnos (p. 151 no. 1), except for the absence of relief-lines.

The chief subjects of both vases are sepulchral, which is rare in this neighbourhood. A brief description of them was given above (p. 8), and some particulars may be added here. In the Villa Giulia vase the woman on the right used to be called Eurydice, and Albizzati was the first to interpret the picture aright (*Atti Pont.*, new series, 15, 257–9; see also volume 14, 180–1). Hermes defends the dead woman from a demoness: he wards off the attacker with the butt of his caduceus, and she turns and flees, looking round reproachfully; the dead woman stands firm and undismayed, laying her right hand on Hermes' shoulder, while in her left hand she grasps the thyrsus which doubtless gives her additional protection. Albizzati observes that the demoness with the snakes is Etruscan, and the same as is paired with Charun on the sarcophagus from Torre San Severo (Galli, *ML.* 24, pl. 1); but the Hermes protector of the dead is a Greek idea, and the thyrsus in the hand of the dead is Greek also—Italiote. This is one of the few monuments that bear witness to the cult of Dionysos as lord of the dead in Etruria, or at least to the belief that his votaries might hope for a privileged position in their passage to the Nether World. Albizzati adds a calyx-krater in Berlin (see p. 142 no. 10); and mentions unpublished vases in the Torlonia collection as combining Dionysiac elements with infernal. On a nenfro sarcophagus-lid in London (D 22: Pryce *Cat. Etr. Sc.* 191) an elderly woman holds a thyrsus in one hand and in the other a kantharos: this is evidence for the cult of Dionysos in Etruria, but not for any connexion between him and the grave, since the woman may be a priestess.

In the Vienna vase, Gustav Körte (*Annali* 1879, 305–7), and after him Masner, took the figure with the lyre to be male—perhaps Orpheus. The breast, they say, is masculine: but in many of these vases women's paps are quite small, for instance in the Berlin stamnos and the Vienna neck-amphora; and the white flesh, the earring, the broad frontlet, the absence of any hint of a penis, all these things point to the figure being female, even if one cannot say who it is. The demon who fronts her is also white, and, as Körte saw, female: there are other representations of Etruscan demons in the guise of old women;

for instance on a sarcophagus-lid, from Chiusi, in Perugia (*Annali* 1860 pl. N; Ducati *St.* fig. 635; Giglioli pl. 346, 2; better, *Dedalo* 6, 26); see also p. 170.

Our demoness looks more like an Anglican vicar: the frightful is not our painter's forte: his Charun, also, and the Fury on his other vase, seem harmless creatures. Nor is there anything very terrifying about the picture on the reverse of the Vienna vase: Körte thought that it 'alluded to the torments suffered by sinners in Hell': but it is not clear that the scene is Hades; and in any case the Dragon is getting the worst of it.

(iv)

6. Bowdoin 13.9. Pl. 35, 1–3. A, sea-god between naked maenads; B, naked maenad between two satyrs who sit on rocks and beat the tympanon. Agreeable designs both. The sea-god, seen from the front, holding up a rock in each hand, is the same sort of figure as those on the reverse of the Phuipa cup in the Vatican and the others compared with them (Pl. 12 and p. 56). He wears a fillet round his head, with the ends showing on both sides of his face, and over his shoulders a long string of beads like a chain of office. Close white lines below all three figures indicate the surf. The women are slenderer than on the stamnoi in Copenhagen, Berlin, and the Vatican. No relief-line. Much white detail. The filling-ornament to the right of A is the same as in the Vatican stamnos; those to left and right of the sea-god, variants of it, recur on a Faliscan cup from Rignano Flaminio (*NSc.* 1914, 271: p. 111, o); compare also the phiale in Boston (Pl. 36, 7 and p. 158). The palmette-hearts have white loops on them, as in the Vienna neck-amphora (p. 150). The shape of the vase is much the same as in the Berlin and Vatican stamnoi (pp. 149–50), apart from the plain handles.

(v: two by one hand)

7. Orvieto. See p. 150.
8. Orvieto. See p. 150.

(vi)

9. Colmar. A, *Anz.* 1904, 54, 2. A, old satyr; B, maenad. The stamnos is of the same broad-based variety as the Ny Carlsberg vase (p. 150) and the earlier Faliscans compared with it (p. 74), but the fabric is not so fine and precise. No relief-line. Much white detail. 'Soft' maeander, just as in the Vatican stamnos.

(vii)

10. London 1913. 4–17.1, from Falerii. Pl. 36, 1–3. A, Nike and satyr; B, Nike hastening with a sash and a tympanon. The shape of the vase is the same as in the Berlin, Vatican, and Bowdoin stamnoi (pp. 151 and 153 nos. 2, 3, and 6), but the handles are twisted and reserved. There are no relief-lines. A lid goes with the vase, but I do not know that it belongs.

*Calyx-kraters*
(no relief-lines)

1. Toronto 410. Robinson and Harcum pl. 78. A, a naked woman, with a lyre, riding on a dolphin, with a youth and a satyr. B, Apollo riding on a swan, with a woman and

a satyr. The satyr on A is not, I think, 'standing on the dolphin': the planes of the representation are somewhat vague (see p. 79). For the subject of B, see p. 161 no. 1.

2. Brussels R 254, from Sette Cannelle near Montefiascone (seven miles south of it: see *Bull.* 1876, 215). A, Giglioli pl. 278, 3; *CV.* IV Be pl. 1, 11. A, Dionysos seated, with satyr and maenads; B, satyr making love to a maenad, between two satyrs seated watching. Above: A, swan between panthers; B, the like. For the subject of B compare the oinochoe London F 100 (p. 68: *Annali* 1845 pl. M). Dionysos on A is not, I think, 'sitting on a bed'. The seated satyrs, as in the Copenhagen skyphos from Ferento (p. 161 no. 2: *CV.* pl. 220, 4), look as if they wore stays, which is a stage beyond the satyrs of the Bowdoin stamnos (pl. 35, 1–3: p. 153 no. 6). The palmettes have heart-loops (see p. 151). The base and foot of the vase are of the same shape as in the Toronto krater, no. 1.

3. Viterbo. From the Rossi-Dainelli collection, so probably from the neighbourhood of Viterbo. A, Giglioli pl. 278, 2. A, naked maenad seated, with satyr and maenad. Below, A, owl between swans. There are points of resemblance to the Hamburg skyphos 1220 (*St. etr.* 11 pl. 44, 1–2: p. 158 no. 2). The base is the same as in the last two vases, but the foot as in the Volterra calyx-krater of the Clusium Group (p.120: Giglioli pl. 278, 1).

4. Roman market. Gerhard pl. 320, 1–2. A, Apollo riding on a swan towards a seated woman. B, satyr and maenad. At each handle, a huge altar (see Studniczka in *Jh.* 6, 141 no. 4). The reproduction is poor, but through it a fourth vase to the last three looms. The naked woman, the swan, and the wreath in its bill were no doubt white. For the woman, the garment she sits on, and the filling-ornament, compare the skyphos Hamburg 1220 (p. 158 no. 2: *St. etr.* 11 pl. 44, 1–2) and the bell-krater Hamburg 659 (below, no. 1: *St. etr.* 11 pl. 45); for the attitude of the satyr on the reverse, the Viterbo krater just described.

   Gerhard thinks that the seated woman is Aphrodite, but she is more probably a paramour of Apollo's, hardly to be named, any more than in the Ny Carlsberg mirror (H 244: *Bildertafeln* pl. 108, 1) or in certain vases.

5. Lost, from Orbetello. Inghirami pl. 188. A, Dionysos seated, with two naked maenads. B, Nike. Compare the Hamburg skyphos 1221 (p. 158 no. 4: *St. etr.* 11 pl. 44, 3–4).

I am not sure how a calyx-krater in Florence, known to me from a very small reproduction, may stand to ours: should it perhaps head the list? It is figured, without comment, by Doro Levi in *Il R. Museo Archeologico di Firenze nel suo futuro ordinamento* pl. 8, 4 (extract from *1° Convegno Nazionale Etrusco, Firenze, 27 aprile–4 maggio 1926*).

Nos. 1–4 correspond to Attic calyx-kraters of the later Kerch period. No. 5 is later or at least laxer.

### *Bell-kraters*

1. Hamburg 659. *St. etr.* 11 pl. 45. A, Lasa seated; B, Nike. On B a repainted fracture. No relief-lines.

2. Orvieto, from Orvieto (Settecamini). *NSc.* 1932, 97–8. A, satyr and Lasa embracing,

both seated; B, seated satyr. No relief-lines. Two stamnoi (ibid. 99) were found in the same chamber-tomb, and it is possible that there was only one interment: see p. 150.

These two bell-kraters are very like one another. With them go the calyx-krater from Orbetello (p. 154 no. 5), the skyphoi nos. 2–4 on p. 158, and the fragments in Cuxhaven (p. 157 no. 1).

### Neck-amphora

Vienna, Oest. Mus., 449. By the painter named after the vase. See above, p. 150. Early.

### Oinochoai
### (oinochoai shape VII: beaked jugs)

1. Hamburg 1917.657. *Anz.* 1928, 354. Dionysos seated, with naked maenads and satyrs; on the neck, naked maenad. The upper part of the neck-figure, and the mouth of the vase, are modern. On the shoulder, tongues and egg, of Faliscan type, with relief-lines.
2. Berkeley, from Narce? Dionysos (?) and satyrs; on the neck, woman?
3. Berkeley, from Narce? Satyr and another. On the neck, ?. This and the last are mislaid, and known only from a tiny photograph.
4. Villa Giulia, from Falerii. All I can make out in the background of a collective photograph is one seated, and a satyr prancing towards him from the right.
5. Paris market. *Coll. B. et C.* pl. 24, 200. Satyrs and maenad; on the neck, satyr. On the shoulder, tongues of Faliscan type, with ordinary egg-pattern below them. Relief-lines for tongues and egg-patterns. Seems repainted.
6. Villa Giulia 26053, from Vignanello. *NSc.* 1916, 55–7; *CV.* IV Br pl. 11. Very large (ht. 0.58). On the right, Dionysos and Ariadne in a biga, with Eros approaching them, and a satyr serving them; on the left, Dionysos seated, with a maenad serving him, and behind him a woman undressing; on the neck, Dionysos seated, with two naked women. The chief figure in all three scenes is probably to be called Dionysos. The youth in the chariot holds a sceptre, the two other youths an ordinary stick: but Dionysos sometimes holds stick or sceptre instead of thyrsus (see p. 93). The style is akin to that of Attic vases in the later Kerch period. The horses recall those of the two Tombe Golini. The satyr, and the maeander, bring to mind a cup from Rignano Flaminio (*NSc.* 1914, 274: p. 158 no. 1) and the other cups of the Foro Group to which it belongs. The tongues and egg-pattern above the picture are of Faliscan type (p. 150), but there are no relief-lines either here or elsewhere on the vase. For the drawing of the palmettes compare Munich inv. 7440 (below, no. 9). This is a somewhat unusual piece, but must belong to our group.
7. Villa Giulia, from Rignano Flaminio. *NSc.* 1914, 275. Satyr with swan, and maenad; on the neck, Lasa with thyrsus. No relief-line.
8. Villa Giulia, from Rignano Flaminio. *NSc.* 1914, 273. Owl; on the neck, dolphin. No relief-line. For the owl, compare the oinochoe of shape VII in Toronto, 493 (below, no. 11), the squat lekythos Toronto 487 (p. 157 no. 2), and the skyphos from Ferento (p. 158 no. 6).

9. Munich inv. 7440, from Bologna (Jacobsthal gives no provenience: but this must be the vase mentioned in [Hackl and E. Schmidt] *Sammlung Arndt: kurzer Führer* 9, above, as from Bologna). Jacobsthal *O*. pl. 148. Eros and swan. On the neck, naked youth (satyr?). Restoration in the figure of Eros? No relief-line.

10. Michigan 2609. *CV*. pl. 24, 4, whence Pl. 36, 5–6. Woman and swan; on the neck, swan. No relief-line. Related to the Painter of Ny Carlsberg H 153 (see p. 161): on the drapery, and the 'cauliflower' tendrils, see pp. 162 and 161. The drawing is perhaps not quite finished: the triangular space to left of the woman was either meant to be filled in black or made into a bud; and the small reserved space to right of her swan ought to have been filled in. See also p. 157.

11. Toronto 493. Robinson and Harcum pl. 85. Owl. On the neck, palmette.

(oinochoe shape II, but with high handle)

Villa Giulia, from Vignanello. *NSc*. 1916, 72, 2. Swan. No relief. Found with two epichyseis and a ring-askos (see below and p. 158).

(epichyseis)

1. Villa Giulia, from Vignanello. *NSc*. 1916, 72, 1. On the shoulder, wave; on the neck, tongues.

2. Villa Giulia, from Vignanello. *NSc*. 1916, 72, 3. On the shoulder, wave. The mouth restored?

These small vases with simple decoration and no relief-lines were found with a single skeleton in one loculus of a chamber-tomb, and together with them a ring-askos of the same style (p. 158) and an oinochoe of shape II (above).

A finer epichysis, red-figured, resembles our two in shape though not in decoration, and may be from the same factory:

Villa Giulia 1761, from Falerii. Giglioli pl. 278, 4. No relief-lines.

The epichysis is a favourite shape in Apulian (see for example *CV*. Lecce IV Dr pl. 51), but appears occasionally in Attic (Salonica inv. 8. 158, R. 270, Robinson *Olynthus* v pl. 122 and p. 152; Salonica inv. 505, R. 84, ibid. pl. 57; variant, with a foot added, Salonica inv. 8. 41, R. 92, ibid. pl. 60), and in Campanian. Ours are nearer to earlier Apulian epichyseis (for instance one in Marburg) than to those of the later, 'A.P.' style but nearest to the few Campanian ones: London F 397 (*CV*. IV Ea pl. 12, 9); Capua 8378 (*CV*. IV Er pl. 46, 7 and 13). In origin, the epichysis is probably a compound shape; an imitation of a squat oinochoe standing in a concave-sided dish.

### Plastic vases

(oinochoai: the upper part of the vase is that of an oinochoe shape VII; the lower is in the form of a female head. In nos. 2–4, flesh and hair are painted black; in no. 1 the flesh is reserved. No relief-lines.)

1. Northwick, Capt. E. G. Spencer-Churchill. On the neck, owl.

2. Paris, Petit Palais, 355, from Vulci. *CV*. pl. 42, 3–5. On the neck, owl. All above the

forehead-hair and the hair-sling is treated as if it belonged to the body of an oinochoe shape VII.

3. Paris, Petit Palais, 391. *CV*. pl. 42, 6–7. On the neck, a bird, the upper part of which is missing with the mouth of the vase. In front of it, a horn.
4. Vatican, from Etruria. *Mus. Greg.* ii pl. 95, vi, 3 and 5; *Atti Pont.* 14, 231; phot. Alinari 35817, 3. The non-plastic part of the vase is badly damaged: the wave-pattern on the lip can be made out, and the egg-pattern just above the hair.

These four vases go together. The painted decoration of nos. 1–3 connects them with the oinochoe, shape VII, in Michigan (Pl. 36, 5–6, and p. 156 no. 10).

## Hydria

Villa Giulia 6369, from Corchiano. *Jh.* 7, 73. The fox and the goose: Aesop's fable, as Savignoni saw (ibid. 72–81). This vase makes it certain, I think, that the picture on an Attic red-figured pyxis-lid (shape D) in Athens (Acr. 576: Benndorf *GSV*. pl. 12, 7; Langlotz pl. 44) is an earlier representation of the same fable, from the first half of the fifth century. On later representations see Bormann and Benndorf in *Jh.* 5, 1–8, and Savignoni, l.c.; add a fragment of a Roman lamp, from Smyrna, in Oxford, 1884.642.

The animals are white; black palmettes on the neck of the vase.

## Squat lekythoi

1. Arles, Musée Lapidaire. Satyr and owl. A white owl on the ground, to right, and a satyr running towards it, to left, as if to catch it. The satyr is something like the one on the London stamnos (Pl. 34, 1–3, and p. 153, no. 10).
2. Toronto 487. Robinson and Harcum pl. 85. Bird. See p. 155, foot.

## Fragments of large vases

1. Cuxhaven, three frr. (Young satyr holding a necklace and grasping the back of a naked maenad; young satyr seated; naked maenad seated.) No relief-lines. Compare specially the Hamburg bell-krater (p. 154 no. 1) and the Hamburg skyphos 1220 (p. 158 no. 2).
2. Rome, Museo del Foro, fr., from Rome (Cloaca Maxima). Ryberg pl. 23 fig. 121 b. Compare the three calyx-kraters pp. 153–4 nos. 1–3, the skyphoi p. 158.
Another fragment from the same site (ibid. fig. 121 a) is in much the same style: I do not know whether it can be from the same vase or not.

## Askoi

(i: of the favourite Attic shape, Richter and Milne fig. 112, *CV*. Oxford pl. 45, 1–4 and 6–9 and pl. 48, 28)

Villa Giulia, from Corchiano. *Jh.* 7, 74. A, fox? B, goose. No relief-lines.

### (ii: ring-askos)

Villa Giulia, from Vignanello. *NSc.* 1916, 72, 4. Wave-pattern. No relief-lines. Found with two epichyseis of the same style and an oinochoe of shape II: on these see p. 156, middle.

A ring-askos in Harvard (2264: *CV.* pl. 35, 5) is Etruscan, and may be late Faliscan: the egg-pattern which forms its sole decoration may be compared with that on the beaked jug Munich inv. 7440 (p. 156 no. 9). No relief-lines. Untidy work.

### Skyphoi

No relief-lines. Nos. 3 and 6 were compared with nos. 2 and 4 by Mercklin (*St. etr.* 11, 380).

1. Brussels R 282. *CV.* IV Be pl. 1, 7. A, winged satyr; B, satyr. Parts of the legs on both sides seem to be restored. The things in the hands are tympana, not 'shields'. The figures are not recognized as satyrs in the *Corpus*, and a winged satyr is of course a monstrosity. Other satyrs with wings are also due to idle whims: inside a Calene bowl in Yale (326: *Jb.* 27, 154; Baur 192), and on a relief in the Villa Albani (Zoega pl. 88). Messerschmidt (*Beiträge zur Chronologie der etruskischen Malerei* 41) finds a winged satyr on a much earlier monument, an archaic Clusian sarcophagus in the Louvre (*Mon.* 8 pl. 2), but must surely be in error.
2. Hamburg 1220. *St. etr.* 11 pl. 44, 1–2. A, naked maenad seated. B, Nike.
3. Viterbo? (or Florence?), from Ferento. A, *NSc.* 1905, 34, b. A, naked maenad seated. As the last; compare also the bell-krater in Hamburg (p. 154 no. 1).
4. Hamburg 1221. *St. etr.* 11 pl. 44, 3–4. A, Nike. B, griffin. Compare the calyx-krater from Orbetello (p. 154 no. 5).
5. Berkeley 8.1000. A, Pl. 36, 4. A, owl; B, owl. The owl on B is white.
6. Viterbo? (or Florence?) from Ferento. A, *NSc.* 1905, 34, a. A, owl. Compare the beaked jug from Rignano, p. 155, no. 8.
7. Michigan 2614, from Chiusi. *CV.* pl. 24, 3. A, head of satyr; B, head of woman. Much restored.

### Phiale

Boston 80.539 (R 521). I, Pl. 36, 7. Thin make. No relief-lines. Geese. The filling-ornament recalls the Faliscan cup from Rignano Flaminio (*NSc.* 1914, 271: p. 111, o) and the Bowdoin stamnos (Pl. 35, 1–3: p. 153 no. 6). The row of white dots above the egg-pattern also recalls the Bowdoin vase. The exterior is plain black.

There are cups, too, that must belong to the Fluid Group. I regret that I do not know the unpublished pictures on the reverse of the cup which heads the following list: for they might have determined the exact relation of the 'Foro Group', as we shall call it, to Faliscan.

### THE FORO GROUP
### Cups

No relief-lines.

1. Villa Giulia, from Rignano Flaminio. I, *NSc.* 1914, 274. I, satyr seated playing with swan. A, athlete and woman; B, the like. See p. 155.

2. Rome, Museo del Foro, fr., from Rome (Cloaca Maxima). Ryberg pl. 23 fig. 124 a. I, satyr seated, beating tympanon.
3. Rome, Museo del Foro, fr., from Rome (Cloaca Maxima). Ryberg pl. 23 fig. 124 b. I, satyr seated.

The following are probably related to the three:

*Cups*

Rome, Palatine, fr., from Rome (Palatine). Ryberg pl. 23, 124 e. I, satyr with horn.
Rome, Palatine, fr., from Rome (Palatine). Ryberg pl. 23, 124 d. I (male: a foot, and part of a garment remain).

I cannot tell how close the following cup-fragment may stand to the Foro Group:
Rome, Palatine, fr., from Rome (Palatine). *NSc.* 1907, 202 fig. 23; Ryberg pl. 23, 124 c.

### THE GROUP OF ORVIETO 28

In this group of cups the insides are replicas one of another, while the outsides sometimes have figures and palmettes, but more often patternwork only. The subject of the interior is a naked maenad seated to left, bending forward, beating a tympanon, and the design of the figure—I cannot vouch for details—is the same as in the satyrs of the 'Foro Group'. Add that in Villa Giulia 1396, at least, the drawing of the 'soft' maeander is the same as in the Foro Group, and that in Orvieto 28 there is the same filling-ornament below the tympanon as in the Forum cup Ryberg fig. 124 a. I have not seen these cups and know them only from Ure's sketches and notes: I cannot say just how close they are to the Foro Group.

1. Orvieto 28, from Orvieto. Outside, in black, tendril with floral filling.
2. Orvieto 29 (1287), from Orvieto. Outside, in black, laurel as on the underside of the Oxford phiale 1925.670 (Pl. 31, 3–4, and p. 182 no. 2).
3. Orvieto 30 (1263), from Orvieto. Outside undecorated.
4. Villa Giulia 1396. Outside, in black, ivy, and under each handle a palmette.
5. Villa Giulia 1397. Outside, rf., on each half a rude figure of a woman, and, at each handle, palmettes. See below.

I should expect these cups to be without relief-line, but Ure's notes are not explicit on this point.
The Group of Orvieto 28 is unpublished: but a published cup is connected with it, and may belong to it:

Villa Giulia 7881, from the territory of Falerii. A, *Boll. d'Arte* 1916, 368; A, Giglioli pl. 278, 6. I, Nike. A, woman; B, the like.

There is no relief-line. Nike stands full-face, her arms down, holding a garment behind her with both hands: for the drapery motive see p. 164. The drawing of the maeander is the same as in the Foro Group. I have not seen the outside, but according to Ure it is in much the same style as the inside, and is like the outside of Villa Giulia 1397 (no. 5).

The brief description by Pellegrini (*St. e mat.* i, 317) makes one wonder whether another cup might not prove to find a place in this neighbourhood:

Siena, Marchese Chigi, 250. I, 'satyr, laying a tympanon down on a stone; in the field, a rosette of white dots'. A–B, 'spirals with palmette leaflets'; this sounds like the pattern on Orvieto 28 (above, no. 1).

The custom of decorating the outside of a cup with simple patterns is not limited to our group, or period, in Etruscan. A cup in the Vatican (p. 50) has tongues outside, Goettingen J 55 (p. 68) a tendril: inside, these cups use relief-line. From Ure I have word of a group that should be at least contemporary with the late cups of which we have been speaking. It consists of Louvre K 498, K 499, and K 500: the design inside is a female head, in a sakkos, to left, and outside a laurel-wreath in black.

A cup from Vignanello, in the Villa Giulia (43972: I, *NSc.* 1924, 191; I, Giglioli pl. 278, 7), since it has a female head inside, and outside, at the edge, wave-pattern, might be expected to resemble the three cups in the Louvre: but so far as I can tell it does not: it has an earlier look. No relief-line of course. There seems to be some restoration. Lastly, a cup in the Vatican has a dove inside, and outside, a band of palmettes and flowers. It may be worth mentioning that part of the relief-decoration in the Tomba dei Rilievi at Cervetri is a representation of a cup with a band of laurel or olive on the exterior, light against a dark background (Solari figs. 81–2.; Giglioli pl. 343).

Another cup (or stemless cup?) from Vignanello, in the Villa Giulia (I, *NSc.* 1924, 183; I, Giglioli pl. 276, 5), is related to the Fluid Group: inside, the head of a boy satyr; outside, on each half, 'a similar head'; palmettes at the handles; no relief-lines.

A very rough cup in Berkeley, 8.2302, from Falerii, has Eros holding a phiale and a situla, within a line border, and, outside, on each half a rude draped figure facing left. The handle-palmettes which occupy the greater part of the exterior resemble, I think, those of Villa Giulia 1397 (p. 159 no. 5), and the cup should belong to the same group.

A cup in the Louvre, K 497, known to me from Ure's notes, has a naked youth with a horn and a basket, moving to left, and, outside, 'apparently a central figure, in black, between palmettes, very faded'. There is much white detail. The pattern-squares inside are of the same type as in Louvre K 500 (see above). The figure inside recalls the Foro Group: might it perhaps go with the fragment Ryberg fig. 124 c (above, p. 159)?

Three skyphoi seem to go together and to be connected with the Fluid Group, if they do not actually belong to it:

1. Rome, Principe del Drago, from Nazzano. A, Helbig *Untersuchungen über die Campanische Wandmalerei* 367, whence Pl. 11, 9. A, a satyr playing with a goat: they butt each other. B, 'a bald bearded Triton, with a snub nose, holding a shield'. The 'shield' is doubtless a tympanon (cf. p. 158). For the subject of the obverse Helbig compares the Pan and goat on wall-paintings from Herculaneum (Helbig *Wandgemälde der vom Vesuv verschütteten Städte Campaniens* no. 449); see also p. 110.

    What appears in the upper left-hand corner of the picture is the end of a bud, part of the floral decoration at the handle.

Furtwängler mentions a second skyphos in the Drago collection, from Nazzano, as 'a companion to' that published by Helbig, 'but without special interest of subject' (*Annali* 1878, 85 = *Kleine Schriften* i, 216).

2. Copenhagen inv. 6577, from Ferento. A, *CV*. pl. 220, 4. A, satyr seated; B, the like. Debased style. The affected figures recall the Brussels calyx-krater (p. 154 no. 2).

3. Geneva MF 274. A, *Rev. arch.* 1916, ii, 253–4. A, satyr with sash; B, woman running, looking round. The satyr has a black tail, omitted in the reproduction.

All three skyphoi have a border above the pictures: the border below the pictures is the same in all. The handle-decoration of the Drago vase is barely indicated in the illustration: the handle-decoration of the Geneva skyphos is not very accurately reproduced, but must be very like that of the Copenhagen vase: in particular, they share the peculiar 'cauliflower' form of the lower tendrils, which is the same as in the beaked jug Michigan 2609 (Pl. 34, 5–6: p. 156 no. 10). Other examples of the cauliflower tendril are on the bell-krater Ny Carlsberg H 153, which is connected, as will be seen, with the Michigan vase (this page, below); on a skyphos published by Passeri (pl. 149: A, satyr; B, naked maenad) and said by him to be 'in Museo Vaticano', but his locations are not always exact; and on a stamnos in New York (see p. 301).

### THE PAINTER OF NY CARLSBERG H 153
These two vases are related to the Fluid Group.

#### Bell-kraters
1. Roman market. Gerhard *AV*. pl. 320, 3–4. A, Apollo on a swan, with satyr and maenads; B, satyrs and maenad.
2. Copenhagen, Ny Carlsberg, H 153. B, *Bildertafeln* pl. 53, 1. A, naked maenad seated, and satyrs; B, satyrs and maenad.

I cannot make out from the retouched reproduction of no. 2 whether relief-lines are used or not, but I should guess that both vases lacked them.

In no. 1 the swan must be white, although in Gerhard's plate it is shown as reserved. Apollo arrives, mounted on his swan and holding the lyre. He is greeted by two women, probably maenads. The reaction of the satyr is not so clear. Gerhard thought that the maenad on the left was beating a tympanon, and she on the right playing ball, but the gestures are simply those of greeting: the ball is a filling-ornament only, and the tympanon belongs to the satyr. The subject is like that of an Attic bell-krater by the Meleager Painter in London (1917.7–25.2: Tischbein 2 pl. 12; Tillyard pl. 26, 162; Cook *Zeus* ii, 461: *ARV*. 871 no. 11). See also p. 153, foot, no. 1.

The treatment of folds in our two vases is characteristic. It is similar in the beaked jug Michigan 2609 (*CV*. pl. 24, 4, whence Pl. 36, 5–6), which we placed in the Fluid Group (p. 156 no. 10). Moreover, the woman on the oinochoe recalls those on the Apollo krater; the maeander is very like that on the Ny Carlsberg vase; and I seem to make out, on the right of the small reproduction in *Bildertafeln*, the same unusual 'cauliflower tendril' as on the neck of the Michigan jug (see pp. 156 and 161). The jug looks later, but I think it must be connected with the two kraters.

The treatment of folds connects the Michigan vase and the two kraters with Faliscan: for a similar system may be recognized on the backs of Faliscan cups: Villa Giulia 26013 and Würzburg 818 (p. 108 nos. 1–2); Villa Giulia 3602 (p. 108 no. 1); Berkeley 8.2303 (Pl. 25, 1–3: p. 111, λ); Würzburg 820 (p. 112 no. 1): Vienna, University, 498, 497, 499, 500 (pp. 109–10, α–Ϡ). The drapery on a skyphos in Goettingen which we supposed to be Faliscan may also be compared (p. 106: Jacobsthal *Gött. V.* pl. 20, 58), and, later, the drapery on a bell-krater in Hamburg which belongs to the Fluid Group (p. 154 no. 1: *St. etr.* 11 pl. 45).

# CHAPTER IX
# LATER RED-FIGURE, III

Various vases will be examined here which could not find a place in either of the previous chapters

## THE STAMNOS VILLA GIULIA 27134

The drawing seems from the reproductions to be in flat lines without relief.

Villa Giulia 27134. *ML.* 24 (Cultrera) pl. 26 and p. 400; Giglioli pl. 276, 2–4. Battle-scenes (A, horseman and archer; B, horseman). Under each handle, a bird-woman ('siren'), seen from the front, standing between two boys and laying a hand on the head of each.

There is little to add to Cultrera's description in *ML.* 395–400. He observes that there is no reason to call the warriors Amazons; the archer is male like the others. The most interesting parts of the vase are the subsidiary pictures under the hands. Cultrera compares the Etruscan black-figured hydria Berlin 2157 (*Jb.* 1, 211–2: see p. 13) and a fragmentary clay antefix, of the fifth century, in the Villa Giulia (18002: *ML.* 24, 399; Giglioli pl. 188, 2; Ferri *Divinità ignote* pl. 44); add a later clay relief, from Orvieto, in Copenhagen, Ny Carlsberg, H 276 (*Bildertafeln des Etr. Museums* pl. 86). This bird-woman is doubtless a death-demon, and if so the stamnos must have been intended from the beginning for sepulchral use.

## TWO VASES FROM SETTECAMINI

A vase in Florence resembles those of the Alcsti Group (p. 133) in subject, and the figure of the woman somewhat recalls the Admetos of the Paris krater, but the style is different:

### Volute-krater

Florence, from Orvieto (Settecamini). A, Conestabile *Pitt. mur.* pl. 17; A, Milani *Mus. Top.* 49, iv, 2 = Milani *R. Mus.* pl. 92, iv, 2; A, *Ausonia* 10, 95. A, two demons seizing a woman. On the shoulder, A, panthers attacking bull.

This is akin to another vase from the same site:

### Neck-amphora

Florence 70529, from Orvieto (Settecamini). A, Conestabile *Pitt. mur.* pl. 18; A, Milani *Mus. Top.* 49, iii, middle = Milani *R. Mus.* pl. 92, iii, middle; detail, *St. etr.* 4 pl. 24, 3. Centauromachy. On the shoulder, A, female head, frontal, among floral.

The technique of the neck-amphora is very unusual, for in addition to white, a pink, a yellow, and a bright red are used freely for flesh and other parts: see Brunn in *Bull.* 1863, 2–3 and Conestabile op. cit. 165 ff.

J. A. Spranger has kindly examined the originals for me and writes as follows:

'The vase is ordinary red-figure (like its more fragmentary sister-piece, 4036) but it was painted over after completion, with superimposed paint which often covers the original body-details. Most of this paint has now worn off, but the nature of it is quite clear. It is white, pink, red, or yellow. The yellow is an applied paint like the others, not a diluted glaze. I suppose the vase must have been fired again after painting.'

Conestabile speaks of other Centauromachy fragments from the site, apparently of the same sort as the neck-amphora (op. cit. 168–9). I conjecture that Florence 4036, mentioned by Spranger, may have been made up out of these.

Albizzati (*Mél. d'arch.* 37, 175–6) describes the two Settecamini vases as related, in style and technique, to the three Faina vases published in *Mon.* 11 pl. 5: that is to say, nos. 1, 4, 5 in our Vanth Group (p. 169). The type of neck-amphora is much the same, the sclerotic of the eye is white, and the Settecamini Cerberus is inspired by the same kind of model as those in Orvieto: but beyond that I do not see any special resemblance.

### VOLUTE-KRATERS IN BERLIN

The two vases were found together, form a pair, and must be by the same hand. There is no relief-line.

1. Berlin 2959, from Bomarzo. Gerhard *TG*. pl. 29 and pl. 30, 13–14. A, Dionysos with satyr and maenads. B, chariot: the driver wears a helmet. On the shoulder, animals attacking each other. On the neck, satyrs and maenads.
2. Berlin 2958, from Bomarzo. Gerhard *TG*. pl. 30, 15–16. Chariots: the drivers wear helmets. On the shoulder, animals. On the neck, satyrs and maenads, and a youth.

The vases are described by Gerhard (*TG*. 49–51), and by Furtwängler in his catalogue. The picture on A of no. 1 is somewhat unusual, and recalls the Italiote volute-krater by the Painter of the Birth of Dionysos (Trendall *Frühitaliotische Vasen* 42 no. 92) in Naples (2411: FR. pl. 175 and iii, 344), or even Makron's cup in Berlin (2290: *WV*. A pl. 4, whence Hoppin *Rf*. ii, 41: *ARV*. 304 no. 37). There the Dionysos is an image: here he is not definitely characterized as an image, yet brings images to mind. He stands frontal, holding kantharos and thyrsus. In front of him is an altar, spread with a cloth and over that the skin of an animal (a swine according to Furtwängler: in the reproduction it looks like a fawn). In front of the altar a severed ox-head lies on the ground, remains of a sacrifice; to left and right, plants. Behind the god is a woollen fillet, tied at intervals, festooned, as if hanging on the wall of the sanctuary; compare, for example, the Attic calyx-krater, from Al Mina, in Oxford (1939.599 *JHS*. 59 pll. 2–3). Two votaries are dancing; to left of the god, a young satyr, holding two uncertain objects (perhaps a fork and a phiale according to Furtwängler); to right a maenad with thyrsus (whatever is in her left hand may be at least in part repainted). The naked maenad on the left of the picture may also be dancing. She holds a garment out behind her legs with both hands: on this motive see Rapp in Roscher s.v. Mainaden p. 2282: compare also, in figures that are not dancing, the Etruscan stamnoi in Perugia (p. 121 no. 1: *Annali* 1832 pl. G) and

the Cabinet des Médailles (948: p. 146, ε; de Ridder 568), a gem in Florence (Furtwängler
*AG.* pl. 42, 14); and p. 159.

The chariots are examined by Nachod *Der Rennwagen bei den Italikern* 80–2 no. 100.

### THE MONTELUCE KRATER

I do not know whether relief-lines are used, but I should conjecture not.

### *Calyx-krater*

Perugia, from Perugia (Monteluce, outside the city, to the East). *AZ.* 1856 pl. 90; *AZ.*
1879 pl. 16; B. Tarchi pl. 127, 2. Herakles in battle.

The surface of the vase is in bad condition, and much of the detail has perished. The
subject is obscure. Herakles in battle. His opponents have usually been taken for
Amazons: but two of the fallen on B are certainly male: it is possible, though unlikely,
that the subject of B is different from the subject of A, possible also that the fallen on B
are Herakles' companions and not his enemies. The opponents of Herakles on A are
probably male. Engelmann was of this opinion (*AZ.* 1879, 192–6), and he supposed
the subject to be Herakles quelling Erginos of Orchomenos. This is not out of the
question, but if the painter knew the story he ought to have clad Herakles in full armour
(see Robert *Heldensage* 625). A perplexing feature in A is that the falling warrior wears
a girdle of four intertwined snakes. There is no parallel to this, and it might lead one to
conjecture that the warrior was a giant: but the rest of the picture does not suit. The two
females to left and right of A are Furies or the like, and so probably is a third female who
grasps the arm of the falling warrior. It is odd that the second opponent of Herakles
should wear a long chiton from the waist down secured by cross-bands. The costume of
the kneeling figure on the right is the same. It is not clear what he is doing; Engelmann
thought that he was extending his arms to be bound: but there is no one to bind him.
He is turned towards the left-hand group on B, but can hardly be connected with it.

The motives on B are easier to make out. The left-hand pair has been quoted already
(p. 57): we spoke of a type of group in which a warrior flees, falls, is overtaken by
another who dispatches him: this is the 'frontalized' or three-quartered variety of that
group. The second pair is an example of another type: a warrior collapses and is supported under the armpits by a companion behind him: early examples of this may be
found in the frieze of the temple of Apollo at Phigaleia (slab 542; Stackelberg *Der
Apollotempel zu Bassae* pl. 9; slab 531, ibid. pl. 17) and in the large frieze of the Nereid
Monument (slab 857: Brunn-Bruckmann pl. 215, 1, whence Winter *Kunstgeschichte
in Bildern* 264, 6). Here, however, it is to be suspected that the painter intended the
woman for a demon of the same sort as the three on A, and that she is no friend—unless
Death, who takes the warrior in strong hands, be a friend. In the third group a warrior
turns and strikes at a fleeing horseman. The last figure on B is a naked warrior fallen
forward, dead, on forehead and knees. According to Engelmann he is pierced by an arrow
and a spear: neither is visible in the reproduction he publishes, but one of them seems
to be indicated in the earlier publication (*AZ.* 1856 pl. 90). This figure is akin to several
in ancient battle-scenes, for instance one in the Amazonomachy of the Mausoleum (slab

1021: Beazley and Ashmole fig. 133; *Jb.* 43, 46, below), one on a bronze relief from Thebes, Louvre 1712 (de Ridder *Bronzes du Louvre* pl. 79: phot. Giraudon 178, 2), and the fallen Gaul in a type of Etruscan urn (Bieńkowski *Darstellungen der Gallier* 130–2).

The painter has added plenty of ravenous birds.

### THE BOSTON SKYPHOS

Boston 97.372. Pl. 37. A, a man taking leave of his wife, in the presence of a death-demon. B, a youth slaying a man. Very large (ht. 0.385). A brief account is given in the *Annual Report* of the Museum for 189.

This is an extraordinary vase and I know nothing like it: in spite of the difference in style and subject, it has some affinity with the Fluid Group. The shape of the skyphos is much the same as there; compare, for example, the skyphoi in Hamburg (*St. etr.* 11 pl. 44, 1–2: p. 158 no. 2), Goettingen (Jacobsthal *Gott. V.* pl. 20, 58: p. 106, above), Brussels (*CV.* IV Be pl. 1, 7: p. 158 no. 1). The character of the patternwork is not unlike, especially the tendrils and the convolvuluses. For the drawing of the maeander compare the beaked jug in Michigan (*CV.* pl. 24, 4, whence Pl. 36, 5–6: p. 156 no. 10). The drawing gives the impression of an experiment, without preparation, in an unfamiliar kind.

There seems to be no incised sketch. There are no relief-lines. The 'eye-folds' of the himatia are filled in with brown. There is much use of hatched lines for the inner markings in the male figures: on this see p. 135. Where the hair is drawn against a reserved surface it is contoured by a continuous line as if the background were going to be filled in with black.

At first glance the group on the obverse reminds one of the Admetus and Alcestis on the volute-krater in the Cabinet des Médailles (Pl. 30, 1–2 and p. 133 no. 1), and after much reflection I am inclined to return to this as the most probable interpretation. Which of the two, the man or the woman, is about to depart, and which to stay behind? The drawing is so miserable that it is hard to be sure: but the direction of the demon's head and legs seems to couple him with the woman rather than with the man. Admetus is delivering his farewell speech (Eur. *Alc.* 327–68), and Alcestis is looking at him and listening quietly. Some may prefer to think of the pair as contemporary Etruscans, comparing a later work, the sarcophagus of Hasti, wife of Afuna, from Chiusi, in Palermo (Micali *Storia* pl. 60, whence Martha 359; Ducati *St.* pl. 274, 1), where Hasti is shown taking affectionate leave of her husband, while a winged goddess of death lays hands on her to lead her away; but the analogy is not conclusive. It is true that the characters in the Boston picture have an un-heroic everyday look, but that is the painter's manner; and it is the same on the other side of the vase, which represents, surely, not a contemporary murder, but a scene from heroic legend, Orestes slaying Aegisthus.

The man on the obverse wears a himation and boots, the woman peplos, himation, shoes, an elaborate head-dress, a heavy necklace, and huge ear-rings. The ear-rings are of a favourite fourth-century Etruscan type (Hadaczek *Ohrschmuck* 61–3; Marshall *Cat. Jewellery* 255–6 and pl. 44 nos. 2251–9). For the head-dress I have no exact analogy, but the head-dress of Malavisch on the London mirror 626 is not unlike it (Gerhard *ES.* pl.

213). Turan on the same mirror has a necklace with pendants some of which at least have the same leaf-shape as those of our Alcestis. Such pendants are shown in more detail on an Etruscan clay bust in Hamburg (*Anz.* 1917, 92 figs. 17 and 17a; Arndt and Amelung *Einzelaufnahmen* 2700, 2), there also in combination with other kinds. The demon has a workman's chitoniskos, sewn at the shoulders to make short sleeves, and bordered; it is bunched a little over the girdle.

There is no sign of the left arm below the shoulder, and where the right leg is we need not ask. Horse's or satyr's ears, hooked nose, wrinkled brow, sunken jaws and cheeks, small eyes with pointed brows, rough hair and beard; snakes in the hair, wings. This is probably not Charun himself, but some other Etruscan demon corresponding to Thanatos. To the left of the group stands a column supporting a conoid—a sepulchral monument (see p. 89); and to the right an altar with triangular parapet.

The incident on the reverse takes place in front of a house, the door of which is shown, and above it part of the roof with the rain-tiles and cover-tiles. There are no antefixes: everything is plain in this vase except the woman's jewellery. This indication of a house by door and tiles recalls an Attic oinochoe of about 430 B.C. in New York (37.11.19; *Bull. Metr.* 34, 231, right; Richter *Greek Painting* 15, 2). To right of the figures, a large horn. There is expression in our painter's faces, and in so far as he is able to draw heads that look quite like not very interesting people in real life he makes one think of later artists, the Nun Painter and other painters of Volaterrae column-kraters (p. 128).

## THE PAINTER OF BRUSSELS R 273

No relief-lines.

### Oinochoai

#### (shape VII: beaked jugs)

1. Brussels R 273. *CV.* IV Be pl. 1, 10. Youth, and woman with thyrsus, at altar. On the neck, satyr.
2. Brussels R 274. *CV.* IV Be pl. 1, 8. Replica of the last.
3. Florence, from Populonia. *NSc.* 1905, 58 fig. 5, right middle. Eros and two seated women; on the neck, woman.

#### (shape II ?)

4. Lost, from Orbetello. Inghirami pl. 127. Youth, woman, and seated woman; on the neck, woman seated and woman.

### Cup

5. Once Munich, Preyss. I, Pl. 38, 1. I, maenad. She moves past an altar, holding a thyrsus in one hand and a cushion in the other. A white dot in the middle of each pattern-square and each maeander. A white line runs down the black mid-band of the peplos, as in the two Brussels jugs.

It may be asked whether the following does not go with the Florence vase, no. 3 (the reproduction is one inch high and very dim):

*Oinochoe*

(shape III, but the handle higher; thin neck)

Florence, from Populonia. *NSc.* 1905, 58, fig. 5, part. Eros, and two seated women.

An oinochoe of shape VII in the collection of Prof. A. B. Cook, Cambridge, is perhaps to be connected with the Florence oinochoe no. 3 (Nike and a young satyr; on the neck, a seated woman).

## THE PAINTER OF WÜRZBURG 817

No relief-lines.

*Oinochoai*

(shape VII: beaked jugs)

1. Würzburg 816, from Vulci. Langlotz pl. 236. Satyr and maenad at column. On the neck, Eros seated at altar.
2. Würzburg 817. Langlotz pl. 236. Satyr and seated maenad. On the neck, Eros seated.

The thickset figures, and the dress of the women, connect these vases with those by the Painter of Brussels R 273; and two others are related to both groups:

*Oinochoe*

(shape VII: beaked jug)

Florence, from Populonia. *NSc.* 1934, 415 fig. 69. Woman seated, satyr, and woman; on the neck, seated woman.

*Stamnos*

Philadelphia 400. A, H. R. W. Smith *The Origin of Chalcidian Ware* 105. A, Nike. B, young satyr running with a thyrsus. No relief-lines. The foot of the vase is modern.

A pair of oinochoai, shape VII, from Umbria, at one time in the Paris market (*Catalogue des Objets d'Art et de Curiosité . . . 19–20 mai 1930*, 13, 38b and 38a) recall both the Painter of Brussels R 273 and the Painter of Würzburg 817. The pictures on the body—Eros and two women—seem to be exact replicas one of the other; on the neck, 38a has Nike running, 38b a woman seated, holding a basket and looking round.

Two other oinochoai of the popular shape VII may be placed, I think, in this neighbourhood:

Würzburg 815. Langlotz pl. 236. Women seated, and Eros; on the neck, woman seated. Some relief-lines (in the egg-patterns, and according to Langlotz, in the drapery).

Würzburg 814. Langlotz pl. 236. Women seated; on the neck, naked woman seated. 'Little relief-line' according to Langlotz: it seems to be used for the egg-patterns. Langlotz calls this vase and the last Faliscan.

## THE TORCOP GROUP

Torcop is short for Toronto-Copenhagen. No relief-lines. On each, two female heads, and another on the neck. Nos. 1–4 at least may be by one hand.

## Oinochoai
### (shape VII: beak-jugs)

1. New York 91.1.465. Pl. 38, 4.
2. Toronto 490. Robinson and Harcum pl. 86.
3. Florence, from Populonia. *NSc.* 1934, 416.
4. Copenhagen 300, from Volterra. *CV.* pl. 219, 5.
5. Civitavecchia, from Castrum Novum. *St. etr.* 11 pl. 59, 3, 3.
6. Toronto 491. Robinson and Harcum pl. 85.
7. Philadelphia MS 2513. Perhaps also Geneva MF 144 (see p. 302 no. 17).

### THE VANTH GROUP

These important vases cannot, I think, be Faliscan, although they are certainly akin to the Fluid Group, especially to the earlier members of it—the works of the Painter of Vienna O.449 and what else was placed in their vicinity. See, however, p. 303.

The nucleus of the group consists of three noted vases in the Faina collection (nos. 1, 4, and 5), two of which bear the inscription *Vanth*, the name of the goddess. The three are by one hand, and the others may be by the same: but I am not well informed about those in Chiusi. There are no relief-lines. The brush-lines are rather thick. 'Soft' maeander. The 'heart-loop' (p. 151) occurs in one of the palmettes on the volute-krater in Palermo (no. 2). Albizzati had already noticed the relationship between the three Faina pieces and the Villa Giulia stamnos 1660 (p. 152).

### Volute-kraters

In nos. 2 and 3 there is a plastic snake, head below, tail above, on each side of the handle; no. 1 also had plastic handles, but only the lower parts of them remain; they may have been as in nos. 2 and 3, but it is not certain.

1. Orvieto, Conte Faina, 20, from Orvieto. *Mon.* 11 pl. 4–5, 3, whence Ducati *Cer.* ii, 475, 1 and *Ausonia* 10, 96, 1; A, phot. Alinari 32478, whence Della Seta *L'It. ant.*[1] 381, Ducati *St.* pl. 253, 617, Giglioli pl. 279, 1, Ducati *L'Italia antica* i, 381, Tarchi pl. 121, 1. Hades in his chariot, escorted by Charun and Vanth; a dead man in a mule-cart. On the neck, A, sea-monsters (kētē). The plate in *Monumenti* shows what is restored.
2. Palermo, from Chiusi. A, goddess (Aphrodite?) in chariot. On the neck, A, Skylla. The foot of the vase is modern. The hearts of the palmettes have loops on them (see p. 151).
3. Chiusi 1852, from Chiusi. A, Levi *Mus. Civ. di Chiusi* 125, middle, 2. A, Zeus in chariot. B, fight (horseman and hoplite). On the neck, 'hounds attacking bull and fawn'. As the last.

### Neck-amphorae

The model is the same in all, a pointed-amphora-like shape; similar, though not the same, the Florence vase mentioned on p. 163. In no. 4 the handles are twisted and were probably each composed of a pair of serpents intertwined; in no. 5 the handles are missing, but may have been as in no. 4; in nos. 6–9 each handle is in the form of a sea-god holding a pair of dolphins (see below, p. 171); in nos. 10 and 11 of kētē.

4. Orvieto, Conte Faina, from Orvieto. *Mon.* 11 pl. 4–5, 2, whence Ducati *Cer.* ii, 475, 2 and *Ausonia* 10, 96, 2; B, phot. Alinari 32477, whence Giglioli pl. 279, 4. Old man, the dead, led by two demons; Persephone in a chariot drawn by snake-headed birds, escorted by Hades and Vanth. On the scroll held by Vanth, [*V*]*anth*, retr.

5. Orvieto, Conte Faina, 21, from Orvieto. *Mon.* 11 pl. 4–5, 1, whence Ducati *Cer.* ii, 475, 3 and *Ausonia* 10, 96, 3; the Vanth, *Charites F. Leo dargebracht* (Jacobsthal *Zur Kunstgeschichte der griechischen Inschriften*) pl. 1, 10; B, *Archiv für Religionswissenschaft* 29 (1931) pl. 1, 1. Replica of the last. On the scroll, *Vanth*, retr.

6. Orvieto, Conte Faina, from Orvieto. A and side, phots. Alinari 32485, 32485 a 1, and another, whence Giglioli pl. 280, 1 and 3 and Tarchi pl. 120, 2. A, Lasa, seated, embracing a naked youth; and a third person. Very much restored.

7. Orvieto, Conte Faina, from Orvieto. Phots. Alinari 32484, 32479, and 32485 a 2, whence (B) Tarchi pl. 120, 1, and (one handle) Ferri *Divinità ignote* 163. A, replica of the last. B, satyrs and maenad. Very much restored.[1]

8. Chiusi 1856, from Chiusi. A, fight (horseman and two foot-soldiers). B, satyrs and maenad.

9. Chiusi 1857, from Chiusi. Replica of the last.

10. Chiusi 1854, from Chiusi. Side-view, Levi *Mus. Civ. Chiusi* 125, middle. A, youth and woman, with Erotes. B, satyrs and maenad.

11. Chiusi 1855, from Chiusi. A, Levi *Mus. Civ. Chiusi* 125, middle right. Replica of the last.

The brief account of the three Faina vases given earlier (p. 9) was based on Gustav Körte's (*Ann.* 1879, 299–305), with some difference in the emphasis: here one or two additions. All three vases are much restored, but the figurework honestly, for the missing parts have been left plain, the fractures kept clean, and nothing repainted or touched up. The drawings in *Monumenti* are careful: only the black background must be thought in. They also show the vases before the non-figure parts—mouths, feet, handles—were supplied. There are no relief-lines. The drawing of the maeander is the same as in the Painters of Vienna 449 and of Villa Giulia 1660 (pp. 151–2), and in other vases of the Fluid Group. For the three chariots see Nachod *Der Rennwagen bei den Italikern* 72 no. 78; for Vanth's roll, Messerschmidt in *Archiv für Religionswissenschaft* 29, 60–9. Respecting the volute-krater there is little to add: the sceptre of Hades has a head like a pomegranate—the slight irregularity in the reproduction is due to a blot in the original. There is somewhat more to say about the neck-amphorae. In one of them the elderly demons who escort the dead are both white, and should therefore be female, as Körte holds: we have already spoken of Etruscan demons in the form of aged females (pp. 152–3). In the replica only one of the two is white: this would not prevent the other from being

---

[1] The neck-amphorae Faina 24 (phot. Alinari 32486, whence Giglioli pl. 280, 2), 25 (phot. Alinari 32487, whence Tarchi pl. 121, 2), 17 (phots. Alinari 32480, 32480a, 32481, 32481a), and 18 (phots. Alinari 32482, 32482a, 32483, 32483a, whence Tarchi pl. 120, 3–4) are almost wholly modern, and I do not know why writers reproduce them as representative specimens of Etruscan art.

female also, for female flesh is not always painted white: not, to take one example, on the stamnos Villa Giulia 1660 (p. 152). A somewhat similar figure on the nenfro sarcophagus of Vel Urinates, from Bomarzo, in London, is thought to be female (D 20, Pryce *Cat. Etr. Sc.* 186 and pl. 4). I confess, however, that I sometimes find it difficult to regard the four sturdy creatures on the Faina vases as female, and wonder whether the artist, when he painted them white, may not have meant to indicate the pale complexion of dwellers in a sunless world. The dead whom they escort is an aged man with scanty white hair, bent, and supporting himself on a stick. He is warmly clad, wearing a sleeved under-garment as well as chiton and himation. The sceptre of Persephone has a head like a pomegranate. The head of Hades' sceptre is much like a thyrsus-head (especially in no. 5, where the inner marking of it is better preserved than in no. 4, and the stem, like a thyrsus-stem, has a slight cast). Körte noticed this, but rightly attached little importance to it: his translator, however, made him say that it 'might be supposed to point to a mythological connexion between Pluto and Bacchus' (*Annali* 1879, 303, 1); and other writers seized on the thought and made much of it; some years after, Körte corrected the mistranslation (*AZ.* 1884, 86).

It should be observed that on the Faina volute-krater there are two plants, a large and a small, which have heads very like the head of Hades' sceptre on the neck-amphorae. One might almost call them 'thyrsus-plants', and fancy that the sceptre of Hades was part of such a plant. But there is no such thing as a thyrsus-plant: a thyrsus consists of a bunch of ivy fastened to the top of a stalk of giant fennel or some similar plant. If the plants on the volute-krater are not thyrsus-plants, then the sceptre of Hades on the neck-amphorae may not be a thyrsus either. Plants with foliage like thyrsus-heads are traditional in Etruria, and good early examples may be found on fifth-century vases with design in added red (p. 197 nos. 38 and 39).

The plastic sea-gods forming the handles of the Faina neck-amphorae nos. 6 and 7 in our list are of the same type as those painted on the Phuipa cup and all the others referred to in connexion with them (see p. 56). In style, I see a real resemblance between the Faina sea-gods and one of the fine clay figures that decorated the pediment of the temple near the Pozzo San Patrizio at Orvieto: I mean the hero illustrated in *Dedalo* 6, 155–6. Orvieto had a magnificent tradition of architectural terra-cottas, and many of them are of local clay and were doubtless made on the spot.

According to Doro Levi (*Museo Civico di Chiusi* 124) the following is from the same factory as the volute-krater Chiusi 1852 (our no. 3) and very like it:

*Volute-krater*

Chiusi 1853, from Chiusi. A, Levi *Mus. Civ. di Chiusi* 125, middle, left. A, fight (horse-man and two on foot); B, fight. On the neck: A, Helios in his chariot; B, two winged figures. I have no note of this and take the description from Levi.

Fragments in Orvieto, from Torre San Severo (*ML.* 24 pl. at p. 11, 10) are from two handles just like those of the volute-krater in Palermo (p. 169 no. 2): the heads of the dragons are lost. There are traces of colour, white and red. Four damaged fragments of a red-figured vase (ibid. p. 15: satyrs and maenads) are in one style, are probably from a volute-krater, and might belong, I suppose, to the handles. The style is not obviously the same as in the Vanth Group.

## THE GROUP OF THE SPOUTED HYDRIAI
### *Hydriai*

1. London F 487, 'from the Basilicata'. Pl. 34, 4. Above, to each side of the plastic lion-head spout, the head of a youth. Below, chariot-race.
2. Leningrad, from Vulci. Micali *Mon. ined.* pl. 40. Above, Grypomachy (griffin and youth, one figure to each side of the plain spout). Behind, a naked man seated watching, and a sphinx. Under the side-handle shown, a black palmette. Below, lion, boar, and wolf; and a naked woman, half seen.

De Witte, in his catalogue of the Durand collection (no. 692), gives the provenience of the London hydria as the Basilicata: but the vase seems to me Etruscan.

The London hydria is of an uncommon model: round body, broad base with simple torus foot; small side-handles; the neck marked off from the shoulder; a lion's-head spout in the middle of the shoulder. There are no relief-lines, and the greater part of the drawing is in thick, coarse, brown outlines; but the two large heads on the shoulder are fully shaded in brown, with white high-lights on the side of the nose, the nostril, the lips, the chin, the cheeks, and ear. The sclerotic of the eyes is also in white. The wreaths are white with yellow details. In the chariot-race the tiaras worn by the drivers are also white with yellow details. The sclerotic, the sleeves, two horses of each team, many particulars of chariot and ornament are also white. Most of the second chariot is modern, and of the acanthus from which the palmettes at the back-handle spring.

The charioteers have sleeves, as in the Newcastle fragment connected with the Alcsti vase (Pl. 30, 3, and p. 134); and instead of the woollen cap worn there, tiaras. In the Newcastle fragment the youth who precedes one of the chariots wears a tiara. The chariot or car of the London hydria, with its eight-spoked wheels, lanceolate spokes, row of black spots near the upper edge, bears a distinct resemblance to that of the Faina volute-krater from the Vanth Group (p. 169 no. 1); nor are the horses unlike.

The other hydria is from the same fabric as London F 487, and the drawing might be by the same hand as there, but one cannot be sure from the illustration. The cushion-like filling-ornaments recur. The subjects are odd. Micali took the naked woman who seems to be issuing from the ground in a rocky place, to be Circe: Jahn was baffled by her (*Arch. Beiträge* 407), and so am I; nor do I understand the seated man or the sphinx.

Grypomachies are not very common on Etruscan vases, but one has been described already (p. 67); another is on a bell-krater in the Vatican (*Mus. Greg.* ii pl. 95, v, 1), a fourth on the calyx-krater Berlin 2951, a fifth on an oinochoe in the Villa Giulia, 12351 (Della Seta *Mus. Villa Giulia* 72); and an Etruscan vase with 'Herakles fighting griffins', formerly in the Roman Institute, is mentioned by de Witte in *Anz.* 1867, 52[1] and Furtwängler in Roscher s.v. Herakles, p. 2241.

---

[1] 'Rothen etruskischen Stils.' Read 'rohen'?

VARIOUS OINOCHOAI OF SHAPE VII

α. Amsterdam inv. 2678, fr., from Falerii. *CV*. IV B pl. 2 (Pays Bas pl. 88), 4. On the neck, Dionysos. Carried out in relief-line. 'Fragment of a cylindrical vase' according to Scheurleer, but it must be part of a beaked jug. It is not late; and is probably Faliscan, as Scheurleer held, although I do not know anything just like it. It stands apart from the other oinochoai in this list.

β. Vienna, Oest. Mus., 452, from Cervetri. Masner 65. Satyrs and maenads. On the neck, lozengy. Some part at least would seem to be in relief-lines: I have no note of the original, which might be Faliscan.

γ. Frankfort, Hist. Mus. Schaal *F*. pl. 54, c. Maenad, satyr fluting (and no doubt another figure). On the neck, seated woman. Carried out in relief-line.

δ. Florence, from Populonia. *NSc.* 1905, 58 fig. 6, below, 2. Woman and Eros. On the neck, youth? The neck is rather thick; and there is less incurve than usual at the base.

ε. Florence, from Populonia. *NSc.* 1934, 415 fig. 68. Centauromachy. On the neck, naked woman. No relief-line? Slenderer than usual. The Lapith recalls the warrior on a Campanian skyphos, from Capua, in Frankfort (Schaal *F*. pl. 57, e).

3. Rome, Conservatori. *Bull. Com. Arch.* 1911, 69 and 71. Herakles and Athena, with a woman (Hebe?). On the neck, woman. No relief-line, it seems. Etruscan graffito ⴽ.

η. Würzburg 813. *Kunstbesitz* pl. 20, 830; Langlotz pl. 236. Orestes at Delphi. On the neck, a man sitting on a pointed amphora: originally a satyr? Heavily restored. The patterns above the main picture seem to lack relief-line. The figures are so much repainted that nothing can be said about the technique. Langlotz's date is too early.

θ. Vatican. Phot. Moscioni 8591, whence Giglioli pl. 277, 3. Satyrs and maenads. On the neck, woman (maenad?) in short chiton. No relief-lines. For the maenad in the arms of the satyr see p. 110; for the maenad bare from the waist up, p. 88.

ι. Rome, Palatine, fr., from Rome. *NSc.* 1907, 201 fig. 21; Ryberg pl. 24, 125 a. (Eros.) The grooves at the base show that the vase was a beaked jug, and not a stamnos (as Ryberg).

κ. Vatican? Passeri pl. 155. Satyr attacking Lasa. On the neck, naked youth with thyrsus and horn, and owl.

λ. Villa Giulia 19772, from Cervetri. Woman (or Nike?). On the neck, owl. No relief-lines.

μ. Villa Giulia 19773, from Cervetri. Nike. On the neck, owl. No relief-lines. As the last. My notes on these two vases are very scanty.

ν. Once Treben, Leesen. *Kat. Leesen* pl. 5, 13. Female head. On the neck, palmette.

ξ. Brussels R 381. *CV*. IV Be pl. 1, 2. Female head. On the neck, palmette.

ο. Brussels R 274 bis. *CV*. IV Be pl. 1, 4. Uncertain object. On the neck, palmette.

π. Rome, Conservatori. A round with a star on it. On the neck, palmette.

ρ. Philadelphia 2835, from Ardea. *Boll. st. med.* 4, 4–5, pl. 2, 24. 'Scrolls and leaves.' On the neck, palmette.

The last five seem interconnected and are perhaps related to the Fluid Group: compare Toronto 493 (p. 156 no. 11).

PLATE

Villa Giulia 2768 (part), from Todi. *ML.* 23, 642. Head of an old man (satyr?). On the rim, a wreath in black. No relief-lines.

The plate was found in the same tomb as a Clusian head-kantharos and a Clusian skyphos (see p. 117 D no. 1 and B iib no. 6). Underneath, it bears an inscription, in black (*NSc.* 1886, 359), which Bendinelli reads as *Viscamervns* (retr.) (*ML.* 23, 637). So does another plate of the same size found in the same tomb (*ML.* 23, 637 no. 47): it is decorated with a female head, and is said to be 'like' our plate, but is unpublished.

VARIOUS SKYPHOI

Hamburg 660. A, Mercklin *Hamburgisches Museum: Griechische und römische Altertümer* pl. 31, 2; *St. etr.* 11 pl. 43, 3 and 6. A, Eros and swan; B, Eros. This may perhaps be akin to the Fluid Group, but it must be restored and I do not feel sure.

Berkeley 8.3824. A, young satyr; B, seated maenad. No relief-lines.

VARIOUS CUPS AND STEMLESS CUPS

*Cups*

1. Copenhagen inv. 3799, from Orvieto. I, *CV.* pl. 219, 4. A naked woman admiring herself in a mirror. No relief-lines. The painter is probably imitating Clusian tondi; he translates a figure like those of the Vatican and London cups (p. 113 nos. 1–2) into his own artless style.

2. Perugia, from Perugia (Santa Giuliana, a hill in the neighbourhood). I, *NSc.* 1914, 136. I, Silenos, drunk, supported by a young satyr and a maenad. Degraded style.

*Stemless cups*

1. Vienna, Univ., 503.55, fr., from Orvieto. *CV.* pl. 23, 7. I, youth.
2. Sydney 61. I, female head.

A BOWL IN SYDNEY

Sydney 62 is not a cup, but a handleless bowl, of the same shape, generally speaking, as those mentioned on p. 209, a. Inside, within a maeander border, a naked youth bends over a rough three-legged table, holding something in each hand. In front of him an animal, fawn or hare, hangs upside down. It is not clear what the youth is doing, whether cleaning the table, or cooking, or what, and as the vase is much restored I do not pursue the question. The provenience given is Bomarzo. A very similar vase, from Bomarzo, was once in Rome, in the possession of the dealer Depoletti, and there is a drawing of it in the Berlin Apparatus, 21.81. Here, however, the youth wears a loin-cloth, and there are other differences. This may be a replica of the Sydney vase, but more probably the two vases are the same. The loin-cloth may have been part of an original restoration, which was afterwards cleaned off; head and shoulders of the youth were then repainted, great part of the animal, and other particulars. There are no relief-lines. One really cannot say much about the style.

## THE GENUCILIA GROUP

See p. 10. Small plates decorated either with a floral female head, or with a star, within a wave border. 'Genucilia' from the inscription, painted before firing, on Providence 27.188 (*CV*. pl. 29, 2, whence Pl. 38, 17–19: no. 2). A short account of them is given by Mrs. Ryberg (101–2). She thinks that they originated in Falerii, but were imitated elsewhere, in Rome among other places. I have not found any strong reason for supposing more than one fabric, but may be mistaken. The Oxford plates from Veii and 'from near Naples', and Toronto 464 (nos. 8, 9, 13, 20, 12) are very poor, and the two Todi plates (nos. 13 bis and ter) look like imitations, but I cannot be positive that they are not from the same fabric as the rest.

Many Genucilia plates have been found in Latium, but not a few are from Etruria. The Latin inscription on the Providence plate supports the case for Falerii or Latium, but is not sufficient to prove it.

In the Berkeley, Providence, Carthage plates (nos. 1, 2, 33), the wave-pattern is less sprawling than usual.

Relief-lines are very seldom used: at least the only instance known to me is on the careful plate in Berkeley (Pl. 38, 20: no. 1).

It is not always possible to tell from the reproduction whether the plate is stemmed or stemless—the appearance from above is the same. When the height is recorded as well as the diameter, that decides.

### STEMMED PLATES
#### (with a female head)

1. Berkeley 8.991, from Narce? Pl. 38, 20.
2. Providence 27.188, from Falerii? *CV*. pl. 29, 2, whence Pl. 38, 17–19. Underneath the foot, in brown glaze, *P. Cenucilia* (for Poplia Genucilia, *JHS*. 53, 312).
3. Harvard 2270. *CV*. pl. 39, 7.
3 bis. Todi 509, fr., from Todi. *CV*. pl. 12, 11.
4. Oxford 1925.618. Pl. 38, 22. Dm. 0.152.
5. Philadelphia 2841, from Ardea. *Boll. st. med.* 4, 4–5, pl. 2, 39.
6. Toronto 463. Robinson and Harcum pl. 84.
7. Oxford 454, from Cervetri. Pl. 38, 26. Dm. 0.141.
8. Oxford 1872.1242, from Veii. Pl. 38, 27. Underneath the foot, in brown glaze, a rough dipinto, V. Dm. 0.145.
9. Oxford 1872.1243, from Veii. Dm. 0.129. Same style as the last. The drawing has been reinforced in places with incised lines (by a modern hand, or an ancient? I cannot be sure which).
10. Brussels R 418. *CV*. IV Be pl. 1, 1. Underneath the foot, a dipinto (see text to *CV*.).
11. Baltimore, Univ., 1047. *CV*. Robinson iii pl. 29, 4.
12. Toronto 464. Robinson and Harcum pl. 84. Compare Philadelphia 2842 (no. 25).
13. Oxford 1872.1241, 'from near Naples'. Pl. 38, 24. Dm. 0.138.
13 bis. Todi 508, from Todi. *CV*. pl. 12, 12.
13 ter. Todi 93, from Todi. *CV*. pl. 12, 10. As the last.

(with a star)

14. Harvard 2286. *CV*. pl. 39, 6.
15. Warsaw, Majewski Museum. *CV*. pl. 4 (Pol. 100), 14; Bernhard pl. 13, 2.
16. Rome, Antiquarium, from Rome (Esquiline). *Bull. Com. Arch.* 3 (1875) pl. 6–8, 14; Ryberg pl. 20, 107c.
17. Florence, from Populonia. *NSc.* 1934, 417, 6.
17 bis. London market (Spink: ex Marshall Brooks).
18. Philadelphia 2997, from Ardea. *Boll. st. med.* 4, 4–5, pl. 1, 18.
19. Villa Giulia 5429.
20. Oxford 1872.1240, 'from near Naples'. Pl. 38, 23. Dm. 0.136.

(with a rosette)

20 bis. Cambridge, Museum of Classical Archaeology, 103.


### Plates (*stemmed or stemless*)

(with a female head)

21. Rome, Antiquarium, from Rome (Esquiline). Ryberg fig. 107b.
22. Rome, Palatine, from Rome. *NSc.* 1907, 204 fig. 25.
23. Rome, Antiquarium, from Rome (Esquiline). Ryberg fig. 107a.
24. Rome, Antiquarium, fr., from Rome (Esquiline). *Bull. Com. Arch.* 3 (1875) pl. 6–8, 10.
25. Philadelphia 2842, from Ardea. *Boll. st. med.* 4, 4–5, pl. 2, 35. Compare Toronto 464 (no. 12).

(with a star)

26. Florence, from Populonia. *NSc.* 1905, 56 fig. 2, middle.
27. Villa Giulia, from Veii. *NSc.* 1930, 56, a.
28. Geneva MF 111. *Rev. arch.* 1916, ii, 255.
29. Rome, Palatine, from Rome. *NSc.* 1907, 204 fig. 26.
30. Rome, Antiquarium, from Rome (Esquiline). *Bull. Com. Arch.* 1912, 81.
31. Florence, from Populonia. As the last.
32. Cervetri, fr., from Cervetri. *St. etr.* 10, 85, 3.
   On the rim of no. 32, in Greek letters, incised I think, HPA. The plate was dedicated to Hera in her sanctuary, supported by the Greek community of Pyrgoi, at Caere (see Mengarelli ibid. 84).


### Ordinary plates (*without stem*)

(with a female head)

33. Carthage, from Carthage. Delattre *Carthage: Nécropole punique voisine de Sainte-Monique*, 2^me *semestre des fouilles (juillet—décembre 1898*, 9 fig. 16, whence Pl. 38, 25; Lapeyre and Pellegrin *Carthage punique* pl. 7, iv, 4.

(with a star)

34. Copenhagen inv. 1243, part. *CV*. pl. 231, 7.

35. Copenhagen inv. 1243, part. *CV*. pl. 231, 6.
36. Bologna.
37. Oxford 1878.146, from Malta. Pl. 38, 21. Small (dm. 0.107).

The following fragment of a plate (whether stemmed or stemless) probably belongs to the Genucilia Group: Rome, Mus. del Foro, fr., from Rome (Temple of Vesta: *NSc.* 1900, 177 fig. 29; Ryberg fig. 128a).

I have not seen the following and they are not figured, but they would appear, from the descriptions, to belong to the Genucilia group; they are mostly stemmed plates, but there may be stemless plates among them:

### (with female head)

Villa Giulia, from Falerii (many: *NSc.* 1914, 275). Villa Giulia, from Rignano Flaminio (nine: ibid. 273). Villa Giulia, from Vignanello (*NSc.* 1924, 190). Villa Giulia, from Corchiano (many: *NSc.* 1920, 27 nos. 2–23, and 29 nos. 5–12). Florence, from Ferento *NSc.* 1905, 34, b). Florence, from Tuscania (ibid.). Florence, from Falerii (ibid.). Where? from Poggio Sommavilla (*NSc.* 1896, 486 nos. 5–6). Sydney 37. Sydney 38.

### (with a star)

Villa Giulia, from Falerii (many: *NSc.* 1930, 56). Villa Giulia, from Rignano Flaminio (two: *NSc.* 1914, 269; see also *NSc.* 1930, 56). Villa Giulia, from Corchiano (*NSc.* 1920, 27).

See also Ryberg 100.

## THE GROUP OF FERRARA T 785

A class of very late red-figured vases found at Spina are thought by Aurigemma to be local work, 'North Adriatic'. The character is Etruscan; I am not sure that they are local. No relief-lines.

### *Bell-kraters*

1. Ferrara T 785, from Spina. Aurigemma[1], 105, i, 3, and 106 = [2]123, i, 3 and 124. A, female head; B, the like.
2. Ferrara T 779, from Spina. Aurigemma[2], 131. A, female head; B, two satyrs. See p. 179, top.

Bell-kraters decorated with female heads are common in Apulian and Campanian: nearest ours, the Campanian by the Vitulazio Painter (see *JHS.* 63, 104).

### *Oinochoai* (shape III)

3. Ferrara T 647, from Spina. Aurigemma[1], 105, i, 5, and 107, 1 = [2]123, i, 5, and 125, 1. Female head.
4. Ferrara T 519, from Spina. Aurigemma[1], 107, 2 = [2]125, 2. Female head.

### *Lekane*

5. Ferrara T 898, from Spina. A, Aurigemma[1], 105, ii, 3, and 108 = [2]123, ii, 3, and 126. A, two female heads; B, the like?

Another vase is related to these, but more deboshed:

## Bell-krater
Ferrara T 369, from Spina. *NSc.* 1927, 173 fig. 12; Aurigemma[1], 111, below, middle, and 112=[2]133, below, middle, and 134. A, head of a youth (?), nearly frontal; B, female head. See p. 193.

A number of vases with rough floral decoration, from the same site, and doubtless from the same fabric, are mentioned on p. 186.

Another very late red-figured vase from Spina, in Ferrara, T 16 (A, Aurigemma[1], 105, i, 4, and 109, 2=[2]123, i, 3, and 127, 1: A, Eros seated), does not seem to be in the same style as the Group of Ferrara T 785: whether it comes from the same fabric I cannot be sure from the illustrations. It is a lidded pelike: but the lid found on it, or with it, looks like a makeshift, originally made for a small 'nuptial lebes' like Ferrara T 888 (Aurigemma[1], 105, iii, 3=[2]123, iii, 3).

Lidded pelikai are not common: here is a list. No. 1 is red-figured, the rest black.

## Attic
1. Once Raoul-Rochette. Jahn *Vb.* pl. 2. Manner of the Meidias Painter (*ARV.* 835 no. 9).
2. Rhodes 13887, from Chalki. *Cl. Rh.* 2, 141 fig. 19, 1.
3. Darmstadt 540.
4. Copenhagen 491, from Athens. *CV.* pl. 176, 2.
5. Copenhagen 490, from Athens. *CV.* pl. 176, 1.
6. Rhodes 10790, from Ialysos. *Cl. Rh.* 3, 207, right middle. Found with vases from the middle of the fifth century.
7. Athens, fr., from Athens (Royal Stables). The lid is missing.
8. London 56.12–23.77, from Sardinia. The lid is missing.
9. Rhodes 6613, from Ialysos.

## Uncertain fabric (Campanian?)
10. Naples, from Cumae. *ML.* 22 pl. 105, 5, 3. I do not know if this can be the vase from Cumae published in *NSc.* 1883 pl. 2, 10: if it is, the cut is inaccurate.

## THE PAINTER OF TUEBINGEN F 18
No relief-lines.
## Skyphos
1. Tarquinia 1928, from Tarquinia. *Scritti Nogara* pl. 2, 4–5. A, head of Athena; B, the like.
## Bowl
2. Tuebingen F 18. Watzinger pl. 45. I, head of young satyr; and rouletting.

The shape of the Tuebingen bowl must be very much the same as in the Volcani Group (see p. 210). The use of rouletting on it, otherwise confined to black vases, recalls the 'pre-impressed' designs on some of the Pocola (p. 210) and elsewhere (p. 223).

Technically these vases are unusual: there are white high-lights on nose, cheek, lips, and eyeballs. In the Tuebingen vase, the white details on the face are hardly visible in the reproduction, but are described by Watzinger in his text; the border-line, too, was reserved and then painted white.

A cruder version of the same technique—white high-lights—is used in a very late bell-krater, from Spina, in Ferrara (T 779: Aurigemma[2], 131): this belongs to the Group of Ferrara T 785 (p. 177 no. 2): the other members of that group are in the ordinary red-figure technique.  See also pp. 172 and 180.

### THE POINTED AMPHORA IN THE TORLONIA COLLECTION

Rome, Prince Torlonia, from Vulci.  Drawing in the Roman Institute, whence (part), *Bonner Jahrbücher* 120, 180, whence Pl. 11, 8.  Amazonomachy.

Two Greeks attacking an Amazon fallen at the foot of a tree; to the right, a trophy (on a base, a post with a cross-bar, to which a corslet and a helmet are attached); to the left, a mounted figure, but only a small piece of it is reproduced.  I know no more of the vase than may be learnt from the published illustration and Woelcke's note in *Bonner Jahrbücher* 120, 225 note 78.  There is no indication that the technique is anything but ordinary red-figure.  The vigorous, accomplished style is not quite like anything else on Etruscan vases, or indeed on vases at all: nearest, perhaps, some of the Panathenaic prize-amphorae from the later part of the fourth century.  The lean, sinewy figures, with their long legs and small heads, evoke the school of Lysippos.

### THE FOULD STAMNOI

I place these in this chapter, but with hesitation, for I have not seen them and do not know what the technique is: whether a modification of red-figure, or a variety of 'Gnathian': more of this later.

#### Stamnoi

1. Once Fould.  Jahn *Telephos und Troilos und kein Ende* pl. 3 (from a drawing by Braun), whence (the chief pictures) Roscher s.v. Troilos p. 1227, whence Séchan 216; Chabouillet *Cabinet Fould* pl. 19 (not accessible to me).  Achilles and Troilos; Ajax with the body of Achilles.  On the shoulder, Erotes and Nike, driving bigae: the chariots are drawn by lions, swans, griffins, and (lynxes?).
2. Once Fould.  Silenos, drunk, carried by two satyrs.

These stamnoi are said to be a pair.  They belonged to Joly de Bammeville by 1843, and were later in the Fould collection, sold in 1861.  The first to mention them was Braun. In *Bull.* 1842, 165 he said that they were from Vulci; in *Bull.* 1843 also he speaks of them as from Vulci, for although he does not name the provenience when describing them on p. 182, on p. 183 he goes on to speak of another vase as an 'anfora pure vulcente', that is to say, in the language of those times, found at Vulci.  To Welcker (*Alte Denkmäler* iii, 392) the vases were from Vulci: but Welcker took his facts from Braun.  It was not till 1859 that Jahn published them as 'found together in an Apulian grave' (*Telephos und Troilos und kein Ende* 11).  I do not know where Jahn got his information: but I think it unlikely that the stamnoi were found in Apulia.  The style certainly bears a resemblance to that of late Apulian vase-pictures, but it does not seem to be Apulian.  As to shape, there are very few Italiote stamnoi, and they are not like this: in Etruria, on the other hand, the Fould stamnoi fall into place.

The Fould stamnoi are not ordinary red-figured vases.  According to Jahn they 'show
the manner of the latest vase-painting, an effort to give expression and character by the
use of several colours and by developed shading'.  The technique would therefore appear
to be the same as in another stamnos, unknown to me, with which Albizzati has already
compared them:

Rome, private (Prince Torlonia ?), from Vulci. A, *Atti Pont.*, new series, 15, 260. A,
   Erinys attacking a naked youth. B, Eros riding a dolphin and playing the flute.

The painter of this vase, according to Albizzati (l.c. 259), 'has achieved an effective
chiaroscuro, using diluted glaze for the shadows in the hollows, and bringing out the
high-lights with brush-strokes of white; so that the ground of the figures is covered
nearly all over'.

He adds that other vases in the collection are of exactly the same style.  He does not
name the owner, and describes him merely as 'a Roman prince', which is vague: but the
provenience, Vulci, suggests the Torlonia collection.

Albizzati calls the technique unique, and I do not know how it stands to the 'Gnathian'
technique which flourished among the Greeks of south-east Italy, at Taranto, in the
fourth and third centuries B.C.  One might possibly gather from Albizzati's description
that the figures were first reserved, and then painted up: if so, it is not the Gnathian
technique (in which the whole figure is painted on top of the black background), but
another, of which a few examples have been given above (pp. 178–9).  On the other hand,
in a kantharos from Tarquinia (see p. 216), which Albizzati compares, for technique,
with the Prince's stamnos, the figures were certainly superposed on the black background,
as in Gnathian, and then worked up with high-lights.

To return to the Troilos stamnos.  Jahn was disturbed by the group of Ajax retrieving
the body of Achilles, and asked 'what Ajax was doing in the immediate neighbourhood
of Troilos?'  The fact is that there are two pictures here, a large and a small; and that
the painter did not intend his Ajax to be thought of as 'near Troilos', although the two
are near each other on the surface of the vase.

The person in Oriental costume to right of the fountain must be a servant of Troilos.
He holds a garment over his left forearm and a staff or spear in his right hand.  These
may belong to Troilos, but there is no reason to identify the garment as Mayer does
(in P.W. s.v. Troilos p. 1217), with the κατάρβυλοι χλαῖναι mentioned in the *Troilos*
of Sophocles (fr. 622), or to suppose that the holder is the eunuch of Sophocles' play.

Jahn was inclined to see in the flying dove an allusion to the love of Achilles for Troilos,
which is mentioned by Lycophron and which Welcker conceived to have found a place
in the *Troilos* of Sophocles: but it is generally admitted that there is little evidence for
this trait being Sophoclean; and the dove, bird of Aphrodite, is not an appropriate symbol
of Eros.

The attitude of Achilles recalls a warrior on the calyx-krater, of the Clusium Group,
in Volterra (*RM.* 30, 149: above, p. 120).  The small heads and long legs of all the figures
show the influence of the new 'Lysippean' proportions; and as for the youth on the
Prince's vase he is almost as 'Lysippean' in his way as the fighters on the Amazonomachy
amphora (p. 179).

# CHAPTER X
# VASES WITH PATTERNS OR FLORAL WORK ONLY

A GOOD many vases with patterns or floral decoration but no figurework have been dealt with already: the earlier ones in the chapter on black-figure (pp. 11–24); the later in the following places:

P. 46: oinochoe of shape VI in the Vatican; see also p. 297.

P. 48: pointed amphora in the Vatican.

P. 48: oinochoe of shape II, but with high handle, in Dresden, ZV 2889.

P. 48: skyphoi in the Vatican and London.

P. 102: amphoriskos in New York.

P. 105: phiale in Toronto.

Pp. 117–20: duck-askoi and head-kantharoi of the Clusium Group.

P. 117: phialai in Ferrara.

Pp. 156 and 158: epichyseis; ring-askoi.

Others will be found among the plastic vases (Ch. 11, pp. 187–94) or those with decoration in added colour (Ch. 12, pp. 195–229), and a few, in which the patternwork is very slight, among the black vases (Ch. XIII).

Some of the vases in this chapter are at present isolated; others fall into groups, some of which can be associated with red-figure fabrics already treated. The decoration is usually in silhouette, occasionally in red-figure, and sometimes it stands on the border between the two.

## A NECK-AMPHORA

Florence ?, from Saturnia. *ML.* 30, 683, above, second from the right.

This is a neck-amphora of ordinary fifth-century model. It was found in a chamber-tomb together with bucchero and with Attic red-figured vases of about 495 to 475 B.C., but I do not know if it can be established that there was only one interment. Two of the red-figured cups are in Berkeley (*CV.* pl. 34).

Relief-lines are no doubt used for the lines bounding the long tongues on the body.

## AN OINOCHOE (SHAPE VI)

Würzburg 647. Langlotz pl. 216. Red-figure. No relief-lines.

Langlotz calls this Boeotian, but it is doubtless Etruscan. There is no distinct foot. See p. 181, and for the shape p. 200.

## THE GROUP OF THE VINE-PHIALAI

A phiale in Oxford (1925.670: Pl. 31, 3–4) has no figure decoration, but the tongue-pattern on the omphalos, and the black wreath on the reserved band outside, are so like those of the Funnel Group (pp. 141–5) that the phiale also is probably to be counted as belonging to it. Warm buff clay; dark brown glaze with a somewhat metallic lustre; no relief-lines; at the omphalos, outside as well as in, the glaze has fired red.

The Oxford phiale is one of several in the same style. No. 1 in the following list has ivy-leaves inside, with berries; the rest vine-leaves and grapes. Outside, a wreath, always, I think, in black.

*Phialai*

1. Rome, Prince Torlonia, from Vulci?
2. Oxford 1925.670. Pl. 31, 3–4.
3. Vatican, from Etruria. *Mus. Greg.* ii pl. 95, v, 2 and vi, 2.
4. Rome, Prince Torlonia, from Vulci?
5. Rome, Prince Torlonia, from Vulci?
6. Tarquinia, from Tarquinia.
7. Tarquinia, from Tarquinia.

A thin stand in the Torlonia collection (from Vulci?) goes with these: it is decorated with the same vine as the phialai; below that, a row of birds, beaks open, in silhouette, with the eyes reserved; on the lip, egg-pattern; on the lower edge, wave.

At a distance, a fragmentary phiale from Tivoli (*NSc.* 1927, 227) recalls the vine phialai, but seen closer the resemblance reduces itself to very little.

Albizzati (*Mél. d'arch.* 37, 114 nos. 26 and 27) mentions two phialai, decorated with vine, in Viterbo, but connects them with the Vatican Biga (pp. 46–8), which would make them much earlier.

### THE GROUP OF TORONTO 495

In *RG.* 91 I put together a group of vases decorated with patterns only. The character of the floral work connects them, first, with the Turmuca Group (pp. 135–41) and, secondly, with the Geneva (pp. 147–8). (1) Turmuca Group: see especially the peculiar pattern, in black, above the pictures on the Paris vase (Pl. 31, 1–2: p. 136 no. 1): 'sprung' (or 'honeysuckle') palmettes alternate with unsprung, and are separated by sprung flowers: floral bands very like this form the chief decoration of the beak-jugs Brussels A 2666 (*CV.* IV Be pl. 1, 3), Toronto 495 (Robinson and Harcum pl. 86), Berlin 2966 (from Tarquinia), and of the 'nuptial lebes' Toronto 217 (Robinson and Harcum pl. 15). (2) Geneva Group: the female heads there are flanked by just such palmettes and flowers as decorate the Group of Toronto 495: the resemblance is not only in general character, but in details like the triangular palmette-heart, the dot on each side of the mid-petal, the 'sprung' flower, the use of wriggly lines and of white retouches. Many of the beak-oinochoai in the Toronto Group have subsidiary decoration in white on neck or shoulder; and Louvre K 480, which is a beak-jug of the Geneva Group, has a white branch on the neck.

Other red-figured vases with floral decoration which approximates to that of the Toronto Group are a calyx-krater in the Vatican (A, warrior and Nikai), and the calyx-krater in Trieste (p. 133 no. 2: *Ausonia* 10, 89-93).

Simple, common vases like ours might be made in more than one locality: but the vases I put together in *RG*. 91 had the appearance, I thought, when I could compare the originals, of a single fabric. The fabric was possibly situated in Vulci.

No relief-lines. The decoration on the body is usually in silhouette, but the palmettes are sometimes red-figure: see *RG*. 91.

The alternation of normal and sprung palmettes is commoner in Etruria and Latium than in Greek art: head-kantharos in the Villa Giulia (p. 117, no. 1: Clusium Group); calyx-krater in Volterra (p. 120: Clusium Group); clay sima in the Villa Giulia, from the Temple dei Sassi Caduti at Falerii (Giglioli pl. 333, 4: I owe this instance to Jacobsthal); Praenestine cista formerly in the Sarti collection (*Mon.* 10 pl. 45–6, 1; *Vendita Sarti* pl. 11); Praenestine cista in the Villa Giulia (*Boll. d'Arte* 1909, 189).

In Greek art examples are not easy to find. Sprung and unsprung palmettes are often used in the same floral design (e.g. FR. pl. 97; ibid. pl. 79, 1; ibid. p. 69): but in *bands* of pattern, although at first glance there may seem to be an alternation of unsprung and sprung, one of the two elements—usually the unsprung—turns out to be really a flower, and not a palmette: see the plates in Schede's *Antikes Traufleisten-Ornament*. A genuine Greek example is on a clay sima from Olympia (*Olympia* ii pl. 121, 5); another on a red-figured guttus, Campanian of the fourth century, in Oxford, 1934.285. See p. 304.

### Oinochoai
### (shape VII)

1. London 39.11–9.4 (ex Campanari). Large (0.36). The palmettes are red-figure, the flowers in silhouette. Red is used as well as white in the decoration of the neck. For the form of the flowers compare the Turmuca calyx-krater in the Cabinet des Médailles (Pl. 31, 1–2 and p. 136, no. 1); for the 'laurel' on the neck, the Charun krater in Berlin (p. 142, no. 10).
1 bis. Cambridge, Museum of Classical Archaeology, 60. On the neck, in yellowish-white, plants.
2. Brussels A 2666, from Falerii? *CV.* IV Be pl. 1, 3.
3. Toronto 494. Robinson and Harcum pl. 85.
4. Oxford 1920.320. Pl. 38, 3. Ht. 0.328. Warm light brown clay, poorish black glaze with a slight metallic lustre. The bottom of the vase is roughly painted brown. On the neck, in white, an ivy-leaf on a wriggly stem, between two half-palmettes.
4 bis. Oxford 1946.157.
5. Munich 3237.
6. Berlin 2966, from Tarquinia.
7. Villa Giulia, from Vulci. A row of black palmettes and flowers. On the neck, in white, a cross with dots between the arms.
8. Heidelberg. *St. etr.* 7 pl. 20, 2; Pfister *Die Etrusker* 22.
9. Vatican. Where neck meets shoulder, wave; on the shoulder, tongues, then dot-band, then palmettes. The small sketch in *Mus. Greg.* ii pl. 95, iii, 5 is possibly an inaccurate rendering of this vase.
10. Toronto 495. Robinson and Harcum pl. 86.
11. Dresden. Black palmettes and flowers.

12. Vatican G 114, from Vulci. *RG.* pl. 34. The palmettes are rf., the flowers 'bf.' Described in *RG.* 91.

13–17. Rome, Conservatori. Five of them.

18. Dresden. Black palmettes and flowers.

19. Orvieto, Conte Faina, from Orvieto. Known to me from Ure's notes. Black palmettes. On the neck, floral decoration in white.

### (shape II, with high handle)

20. Vatican, from Etruria. *Mus. Greg.* ii pl. 95, iv, 4. The shoulder is black, with a row of white dots and a white ivy-wreath.

21. Tarquinia, from Tarquinia. Rf. palmettes, with flowers in silhouette. On the shoulder a black wave-tendril.

22. Tarquinia, from Tarquinia. Much as the last.

23. Würzburg 802. Langlotz pl. 229.

24. Cracow, Technical Museum. *CV.* pl. 2 (Pol. pl. 95), 3.

### (shape II, with low handle and thin neck)

25. Rome, Prince Torlonia, from Vulci? Red-figured palmettes. Above them, on a black band, an ivy-wreath with white leaves and berries and incised stem.

### *Hydria*

26. Vatican. Black palmettes and flowers. On the shoulder white rosettes.

### *'Nuptial lebes'*

27. Toronto 217. Robinson and Harcum pl. 15.

### *Pyxides*
### (type of Würzburg 883, Langlotz pl. 250)

28. Louvre, old no. 521. Doubtful if the lid belongs.

29. Louvre, old no. 493.

30. Louvre, old no. 480–1.

31. Louvre, old no. 485.

32. Villa Giulia, from Capena. Egg-pattern, wave.

33. Villa Giulia (ex Aug. Castellani). Similar to the last.

34. Villa Giulia, from Capena. Black laurel.

### *Duck-askos*

35. Oxford 258, from Tarquinia. Pl. 38, 9. On the shape see p. 192.

The pyxis Würzburg 883 (Langlotz pl. 250) is of the same shape as those in the list, and may belong to the same group. The tongue-pattern on the top recalls the Funnel Group (p. 141). A small pyxis of the same shape that might also belong is Philadelphia 2854, from Ardea (*Boll. st. med.* iv, 4–5, 18 pl. 2, 11); the lid is missing. An oinochoe of shape II, with high handle, from Etruria, in the Vatican (new no. 1022: *Mus. Greg.* ii pl. 95, iv, 2) is very like the oinochoai of our group, but did not seem to be certainly from the same fabric.

An Etruscan oinochoe, shape VII, with red-figured palmettes on the body and white plants on the neck was in the Sheringham collection and is described in Sotheby's sale catalogue for July 11th 1927, no. 46, 1, but I have no particulars.

## OTHER VASES WITH BLACK PATTERNS ONLY: VARIOUS
### Phialai

Würzburg 888. Langlotz pl. 249.

Yale 126. Baur 84.

Langlotz counts the first Campanian; Baur, the second, Attic: they seem to me Etruscan.

The type of decoration is the same in both: inside, a band of tongues, with a black band above it and another below; the omphalos black. The style, however, is different, and so is the technique: in the Würzburg phiale the uprights of the tongue-pattern have relief; in the Yale, none. The drawing of the tongues on the Yale phiale recalls the Alcsti vase (Pl. 30, 1–2, and p. 133, no. 1).

I do not know anything like a third phiale in Hamburg (506: *St. etr.* 11, 373) which has a band of floral pattern, in black, between two black bands.

### Skyphoi

Boston F. 577, from Chiusi. A, Fairbanks i pl. 76.

Chiusi 1918, from Chiusi. Uprights (simplified tongue-pattern), then tendril, then the same sort of pattern as on the Perugia cup published in *NSc.* 1914, 136 (p. 174, no. 2), or the Copenhagen skyphos inv. 6577 (*CV.* pl. 220, 4: p. 161, above, no. 2). The lower part of the vase is black. I know the Chiusi skyphos from Ure's notes.

Ferrara T 288, from Spina. A, Aurigemma[1], 105, i, 2, and 109, 2 =[2]123, i, 2, and 127, 2. Later curve.

### Jars
#### (i)

Chiusi, from Chiusi. The shape is something like that of the black jar Leyden 207 (Holwerda 16: see p. 246, foot). May belong to the Group of Toronto 495 (p. 182).

#### (ii)

Villa Giulia 2772, from Todi. *ML.* 23, 638, 1. It must have had a lid, like the lidded pelikai (p. 178). From a single interment, with a skyphos and a head-kantharos of the Clusium Group (Villa Giulia 2781 and 2769: p. 117, no. 6 and p. 117, no. 1).

### Oinochoai
#### (shape VII, beaked jugs)

Philadelphia 2834, from Ardea. *Boll. st. med.* iv, 4–5, 18 pl. 2, 30.

Chiusi 1919, from Chiusi. Round the middle of the body a broad reserved band with black uprights (simplified leaves).

(shape II)

Ferrara, T 950, from Spina.  Aurigemma[1], 105, ii, 5=[2]123, ii, 5.  Large leaves on the lower part of the body.

(Sant' Anatolia shape)

Michigan 2646.  *CV*. pl. 38, 3.

Oxford 259, from S. Anatolia near Spoleto.  Pl. 38, 6.  Long tongues as in the Michigan vase, but with dots between the heads; above them, wave-pattern, inverted.

On the shape, common in bronze, less common in clay, see p. 263.

### THE FABRIC OF FERRARA T 785

These vases, with hasty floral decoration in black, must belong to the same fabric as the very late red-figured vases from the same site described on p. 177.

#### *Lekanai*

1. Ferrara, T 369, from Spina.  *NSc*. 1927, 173 fig. 13, 2; Aurigemma[1], 111, ii, 3 and 113, 1=[2]133, ii, 3 and 135, 1.

2. Ferrara, T 369, from Spina.  Aurigemma[1], 111, ii, 5, and 113, 2=[2]133, ii, 5 and 135, 2.

#### *Oinochoai*

(shape VII)

3. Ferrara, T 1060, from Spina.  Aurigemma[1], 105, iii, 2=[2]123, iii, 2.

(shape IX: with two handles, see p. 265)

4. Ferrara, T 1082, from Spina.  Aurigemma[1], 105, iii, 4=[2]123, iii, 4.

5. Ferrara, T 369, from Spina.  *NSc*. 1927, 173 fig. 13, 1; Aurigemma[1], 111, middle=[2]133, middle.

#### *Small 'nuptial lebes'*

6. Ferrara, T 888, from Spina.  Aurigemma[1], 105, iii, 3=[2]123, iii, 3.

A lekane of much the same shape as nos. 1 and 2, apart from the knob, and also decorated with floral patterns in black, is in the Villa Giulia.  It was found at Vignanello together with two epichyseis (p. 156), a ring-askos (p. 158), an oinochoe of shape II (p. 156), and is earlier than the two from Spina.

# CHAPTER XI

# PLASTIC VASES

FOR Etrusco-Corinthian plastic vases see the references on p. 11.

Some of the finest plastic vases have been dealt with already—the duck-askoi and head-kantharoi of the Clusium Group (pp. 117–20)—, and four small oinochoai in the form of a female head have been counted late Faliscan (pp. 156–7).

An archaic group of head-vases which has sometimes passed for Etruscan has been assigned by Riis, with good reason, to Campania (*From the Coll.* 2, 147). We may add to his list the kantharos Capua P 899, from Capua (Patroni *Museo Campano* pl. 16, 2), another in Oxford (335), a third in the Spencer-Churchill collection at Northwick Park, and an oinochoe in the Robinson collection, Baltimore (*AJA*, 1920, 15–7; part, Beardsley *The Negro* 28 fig. 8) which combines a bearded head with the head of a negress. In several of the kantharoi one of the two heads is painted red, the other left plain: they are probably meant as male and female. In the Hasselmann kantharos (*Kunstbesitz* pl. 17, 764) the handles are set on in the same way as in many Campanian black-figured neck-amphorae, for example New York 06.1021.42 and 06.1021.44 (see p. 11) or Würzburg 797 (Langlotz pl. 231).

## THE NEGRO-BOY GROUP

### (i)

1. Villa Giulia 16338. *ML.* 24 pl. 27 (Cultrera), 47; Giglioli pl. 281, 2; phot. Alinari 41151, 1, whence Pl. 40, 6. Ht. 0.145.
2. Boston 07.863. Ht. *c.* 0.160.
3. Boston 07.864. Pl. 40, 5. Ht. *c.* 0.160.

### (ii)

4. New York GR 615. Richter *Etr.* figs. 134–5; Pl. 40, 4.

Nos. 1–3 are replicas: they are drinking-vessels—mugs or one-handled kantharoi: round flaring mouth, concave handle: head-vases of this type appear in Attica before the end of the sixth century (e.g. Boston 50.332, Buschor *GV.* 142, Buschor *Das Krokodil des Sotades* 13 fig. 19, *ARV.* 892; Tarquinia, signed Charinos, Pfuhl fig. 269, Hoppin *Bf.* 65, *ARV.* 894, above, no. 2; Würzburg 624, *JHS.* 49 pl. 4, 1–2, *ARV.* 895). In our vases the mouth is very shallow and strongly curved, perhaps influenced by 'oinochoe' shape X.

No. 4 is an oinochoe: mouth and handle are borrowed from oinochoe shape VII.

Relief-lines are used in the egg-pattern, and also to border the rays in no. 4.

The negro-head is very good: not equal to the magnificent negro-heads of Attic plastic vases in the archaic period (*JHS.* 49 pl. 1, pp. 41–3 and 76–7) but superior to later Attic ones (ibid. p. 78).

I have used the term 'Negro-boy Group', but not all Etruscan negroes belong to this group. The following vase is a mug like nos. 1–3 in our list, but the type of negro is quite different and by an inferior plastes; the decoration on the mouth of the vase is also different, and lacks relief-line:

Berlin 2970, from Vulci. Panofka *Delphi und Melaine* (*Antikenkranz zum Winckelmannsfest, 1849*) pl. 1, 3–4; Neugebauer pl. 88, 1. Restored. The floral pattern somewhat recalls the Alcsti vase in the Cabinet des Médailles (Pl. 30, 1–2: p. 133, no. 1). Below the floral pattern, a degraded egg-pattern. No relief-lines.

I have no note of another negro-head in Berlin, inv. 4982.51, described by Neugebauer (*Führer* 166) as 'a beak-oinochoe with tall mouth-piece', words that make one think of the New York negro.

### HEAD-VASE IN NEW YORK

A plastic vase in New York, 06.1021.204 (A, Sambon *Can.* pl. 12, 150), seems to stand alone. It is janiform—a young satyr's head, and the head of a negro. The mouth of the vase most resembles those of bottles from various Italiote fabrics (e.g. Genick pl. 37, 2, and pl. 37, 6; Lau pl. 42, 3; Reggio, *NSc.* 1931, 648, b): but there is a handle. Relief-lines are used in the decoration of the neck (tongues, egg-pattern). See p. 305.

### VARIOUS HEAD-VASES

*Kantharos*: janiform, head of Herakles and female head

α. Florence, from Orvieto (Settecamini). Milani *Mus. Top.* 49, iii, left. I know nothing more of this than may be gathered from the tiny reproduction: I do not understand Albizzati's reference to it in *Atti Pont.*, new series, 14, 223.

*Oinochoe*: head of a young girl: the mouth of the non-plastic part is missing; the neck of it is thin.

β. Ferrara T 346, from Spina. *NSc.* 1927, 169; Aurigemma[1], 101, 9=[2]113, 9.

*Oinochoe*: janiform, head of a youth (Herakles? Dionysos according to Gozzadini), and female head; the mouth of the vase and the handle are those of an oinochoe shape I or II.

γ. Florence. *Gaz. arch.* 1879 pl. 6, 9. The whole vase is covered with black: it is possibly connected with the Malacena Group.

### THE MUNICH CHARUN

Munich. Hirth *Formenschatz* 1902 no. 2 (L. Curtius), whence Pl. 40, 1–2; *Atti. Pont.* 15 (1922) pl. 2a; Giglioli pl. 281, 1 and 3; side-view, Nogara 149. The reproductions are all from the same photographs.

This fine and strange vase has been studied by Albizzati (*Atti Pont.* 15, 242–6). He is probably right in thinking that it was not made for the tomb but for the table, as a *memento mori*: he is reminded of the demon on the Etruscan kottabos-stand from Montepulciano in Florence (*NSc.* 1894, 238; Ducati *St.* pl. 215 fig. 530; Giglioli pl. 312, 1–2), and the skeleton that was passed round at Trimalchio's feast; see also Zahn Kτῶ Χρῶ.

This type of plastic vase—a mug, or one-handled kantharos—is old (see p. 187). Round the mouth of the vase, in added colour, an ivy-wreath. At the base of the handle, in relief, a small head of Pan, snub-nosed, and horned: such heads, at this place, are common in bronze vases and clay imitations. Charun's moustache is long. The beard is an imperial, the cheeks being shaven, although the hair has begun to grow. I do not remember seeing just such a beard elsewhere in antiquity: the nearest I can think of are on Attic red-figured vases, for instance the early amphora by the Kleophrades Painter in Würzburg (507: FR. pl. 103: *ARV.* 120 no. 1), or early cups of the proto-Panaitian Group in the Louvre (G 25: Hartwig *Meisterschalen* pl. 9: *ARV.* 212 no. 12) and Boston (01.8018: Hartwig pl. 14, 2; *ARV.* 212 no. 14). An odd feature is the double ear: a human ear (with spots on it) is surmounted by the ear of an animal—horse (or satyr). The right ear is damaged. The lobes are pierced for ear-rings, as often in barbarians. The present ear-rings are said not to belong. The septum of the nose is also pierced for a nose-ring: Albizzati gives examples of the practice from Carthage and Cyprus. The hair rises over the forehead in a stiff frill, another satyr-like trait: compare, for example, the Etruscan bronze satyr in Munich (*Rendiconti Pont. Acc.* 3 pll. 7–8; Giglioli pl. 257 and pl. 258, 5).

Is it too fanciful to see a resemblance in expression between the Munich Charun and Etruscan bronze griffin-heads (*St. etr.* 9 pl. 40, 6–7, from Todi; C. Smith *Forman Coll.* pl. at p. 21, 162)?

Albizzati is inclined to associate the vase with the fabric of Clusium (*Atti Pont.* 15, 246): I should like to look at it again with that thought in mind, but at present I do not see definite points of resemblance, and I note that the vase terminates below, in the old manner, abruptly, without the mouldings seen in the Clusium head-vases (pp. 117–18).

## THE BRUSCHI GROUP

A puzzling plastic vase in Boston was found at Tarquinia and was formerly in the Bruschi collection (Pl. 40, 7–8). In *ML.* 36, 485 there is a brief mention of it by Pallottino, who knew it from a Roman Institute photograph and described it as lost: the photograph gave only the back of the vase, which is therefore said to represent 'a human head of grotesque savour, the type of which is evidently derived from ancient Punic masks'. As a matter of fact there are two human heads back to back. The front one is an ideal head of a bearded warrior wearing a Corinthian helmet, in late-fourth-century style; the back one is an extraordinary caricature, the face of a man with beard and long moustache, thick lips, crushed nose, slanting eyes, Semitic look. What appears above his forehead is not a head-dress, but simply the back of the warrior's helmet: what we have is a face merely. The beard is hollow: turn the vase round, and you have, below the warrior's chin, a scallop-like projection forming the mouth of the vase. There is a small spout on top of the helmet: the tip is missing. There are also two horizontal handles, setting off from the heads at the level of the ears. The mouth of the warrior is open and pierced; the right corner of it is chipped. Lastly there are a pair of warts on the 'Semite's' nose, and the vase will 'stand' on these and the beard. This is probably a drinking-vessel: the lips could be applied to the scallop, while the spout was blocked with finger or thumb:

but there must be more in it than that: one would expect it to be a trick-vase, but the excellence of the mechanism is not clear to me and could only be ascertained by experiment with the thing itself.

The only vase very like this is not a replica but is doubtless the work of the same modeller. It is in the Vatican: there are small drawings of it in *Mus. Greg.* ii pl. 89, middle, and a good photograph of the under head by Alinari (35817, 2, whence Pl. 40, 9). Here both heads are caricatured. The under head is even more Semitic than in the Boston vase. The upper head is wreathed, and clean-shaven, the nose pushed to one side, one eye half-closed as if blind: the wide-open mouth serves as the orifice of the vase and gives the impression of a comic mask. There is the same spout on top of the heads as before, and the tip seems again to be missing. There are no handles, and no warts on the nose of the 'Semite': the warts in the Boston vase are an improvement designed, or utilized, to protect the surface of the nose when the vase rests on it.

If these 'Semites' recall 'Punic masks', as Pallottino finds, it is not so much the large clay masks as the tiny faces in coloured glass that are often found in tombs. Amusing as these are, they are far removed from the powerful art of the Etruscan modeller.

The fragmentary Todi 487, from Todi (part, *CV.* pl. 9, 5), must be a third vase of the Bruschi Group. Two grotesque heads are set back to back: the one figured in the *Corpus* should be compared with the upper head of the Vatican vase (on the left in *Mus. Greg.* ii pl. 89, middle): one eye half-closed, a wart on the nose and another on the forehead above the right eye. The spout is the same as in the other two pieces. The fragments of the second head include the forehead, wreathed with ivy; one handle is also preserved. Thin wall, fine light yellow clay.

### SATYRS IN NEW YORK

New York 20.212 and 213, from near Orvieto. *Bull. Metr. Mus.* 24, 82–3; Richter *Etr.* fig. 138. Ht. 0.19.

The two vases make a pair, reversed. A satyr sits on the ground with one arm round a funnel-shaped vessel as if supporting it. He wears a panther-skin; and, like many Etruscan satyrs (for example Pl. 27, 1), slippers. The vessel with its flowing mouth recalls Attic calyx-kraters of the late fourth century; on the lip, egg-pattern, with relief lines. The restorations can be made out in the reproductions. The beard is chipped.

The head of the companion-piece (not figured), and much else, is wanting. In the Museo Civico of Orvieto there is a satyr-head of similar style, and I do not know if the possibility that it belongs to the second New York vase is excluded; reddish clay, with traces, I think, of dark paint.

The New York satyrs bring to mind a pair of objects represented, standing with other vases on a table, in the wall-paintings of the Tomba dell' Orco at Tarquinia (Weege *Etr. Mal.* 30): a naked man, kneeling, holds a pointed amphora: the man is bearded, and may be a satyr. The amphorae contained wine, which could be drawn with a ladle; unless indeed the human stand is in a separate piece, so that the amphora could be lifted off and the contents poured out. The purpose of the New York vases is not so clear. A plastic vase in London, Attic of the late sixth century (E 785: *CV.* IV Ic pl. 371), consists of a seated figure of Dionysos holding a big drinking-horn. This must have been a drinking-vessel, but the shape of the New York funnels is not suitable for drinking. Perhaps they contained perfumed water; or perhaps sprigs of fragrant herbs. On Attic vases by the Eretria Painter (onos in Athens, *Eph. arch.* 1897, pll. 9–10, *ARV.* 726 no. 27; pyxis in London, FR. pl. 57, 3, *ARV.* 726 no. 25) sprigs are seen standing in loutrophoroi and nuptial lebetes.

Miss Richter compares the New York satyrs with the bronze satyr in Munich (*Rendiconti Pont. Acc.* 3 pll. 7–8; Giglioli pl. 257 and pl. 258, 5).

## DUCK-ASKOI

The shape has a long history (Mercklin in *St. etr.* 11, 382).[1]

Most of the vases in our list are common work, very unlike the fine duck-askoi of the Clusium Group (pp. 119–20). No. 1, Würzburg 891, comes nearest to the Clusium askoi; then one of the Fainas, no. 18. Of the more formal askoi, Hamburg 504, no. 2, is perhaps the best, and Oxford 339, no. 16, is as bad as any. Some are deeper than others. No. 9 alone has figure decoration, the rest have patterns only, including black and sometimes red-figure palmettes. There are no relief-lines.

### (with bail-handle, and behind it a spout)

1. Würzburg 891. Langlotz pl. 251, 2.
2. Hamburg 504. *Anz.* 1917, 114, fig. 46; Giglioli pl. 278, 5; *St. etr.* 11 pl. 41, 1.
3. Boston (R. 470). Cf. nos. 4–6.
4. Vatican. Phot. Alinari 34715, 1.
5. Würzburg 892. Langlotz pl. 251. As the next.
6. Orvieto, Conte Faina, from Orvieto. Tarchi pl. 131, 4. As the last.
7. Vatican. *Mus. Greg.* ii, pl. 93, iv, 3. Near the two last.
8. Rome, Conservatori.
9. Rome, Prince Torlonia, from Vulci? Large, with red-figure decoration: on one side, a satyr reclining on a rock.
10. Rome, Prince Torlonia, from Vulci?
11. Rome, Prince Torlonia, from Vulci?
12. Louvre H 102. Deep.

[1] The askos published by Tischbein and quoted by Mercklin is Attic and belongs to the following group. (Nos. 1–10 have the ordinary spout; in no. 11 it is like the mouth of a trefoil oinochoe, in no. 12 like that of a squat lekythos; in no. 13 the duck's head is replaced by an askos-spout, and there is no spout above the tail.)
1. Goluchow, Prince Czartoryski, 191, from Italy. *CV.* pl. 45, 1.
2. Dresden ZV. 2866. *Anz.* 1925, 140. The wavy line on the base signifies water.
3. Once Hamilton. Tischbein 3 fig. F.
4. London B 665. Hancarville 4 pll. 34–5.
5. London B 664, from Nola.
6. Leningrad, from Olbia. *Anz.* 1909, 175, fig. 40.
7. Cambridge. *Friends of the Fitzwilliam Museum, Report,* 1934, 3, fig. 5.
8. Reggio, from Locri. *NSc.* 1913, suppl. 8, fig. 6 bis.
9. New York 41. 162. 185. *Coll. E.G.* pl. 2, 53; *CV.* Gallatin pl. 30, 6. Compare the last and the next.
10. Ferrara, from Spina. Aurigemma[1], opposite p. 1.
11. London B 663, from Magna Graecia. Inghirami pl. 351.
12. London B 662, from Vulci.
13. London B 667, from Nola.

Some of these were put together in *AJA.* 1921, 327, no. 10.

A duck-askos in the Petit Palais (416: *CV.* pl. 46 7–8), which Plaoutine counts Italiote, seems to me Attic, like the replica New York 06.1021.264 (Sambon *Can.* pl. 12, 155).

13. Louvre H 103. Deep.
14. Louvre H 105. Deep.
15. Louvre (old no. 1268). Deep.
16. Oxford 339, from Veii. Pl. 38, 5. Deep. Ht. 0.17, length 0.20. Warm buff clay, bad brown and red glaze. Behind, a black palmette; another, smaller, on the top of the head.

(same type, but the handle is kinked: see RG. 99)

17. Frankfort, Hist. Mus. Schaal F. pl. 1, d. Shallow.

(without handle)

18. Orvieto, Conte Faina, from Orvieto. Tarchi pl. 131, 3.
19. Leningrad (St. 832). Anz. 1929, 258, fig. 19. Deep.

(fragment)

20. Oxford, Beazley, fr., from Orvieto. It is from the head of a rough duck-askos: black, with the eye and the commissure of the beak reserved; the feathers on the neck are indicated by coarse incisions made before the black was applied; round the neck a reserved band.

The deep duck-askos Oxford 258 (Pl. 38, 9), attributed on p. 184 to the Group of Toronto 495, has a kinked bail like no. 17, but the bail is smaller and there is no tail apart from the spout.

THE GROUP OF THE LOUVRE DEER-ASKOS

JHS. 56, 90.
The vase is in the form of a deer, lodged. Bail-handle; small spout on the head. Details are in black or brown glaze. There is considerable variety.

1. Florence 4236. An Eros sits on the rump. Handle as in Louvre H 176.
2. Louvre H 176. Enc. phot. iii, 64, b. The deer has a collar. The horns are gilt. The handle is triple—a black bar between two reserved ones.
3. Florence 81908, from Populonia. NSc. 1905, 58, fig. 5, below, middle. The handle is concave, black in the middle, reserved at the sides. On the spout, tongues, and above them, simplified astragalus (pellets alternating with uprights); on the lip of the spout, simplified egg-pattern.
4. Ferrara, T 399, from Spina. Aurigemma[1], 97, ii, 5 = [2]107, ii, 5.
5. Vatican. Mus. Greg. ii pl. 93, v, 3.

Three other vases are of the same type as these and may be from the same fabric:

(i)

Louvre H 177. Pale buff clay. Gilt all over.

(ii) poorer

Ferrara, T 83, from Spina. NSc. 1924 pl. 13, 2; Dedalo 5, 411. See p. 193.
Boston F. 515 (R. 63). E. Robinson Cat. of Greek Etruscan and Roman Vases 63, above; Fairbanks pl. 49. In bad condition.

A fine Etruscan askos in the form of a lion, in the British Museum, E 803, from Vulci (Newton and Thompson *The Castellani Collection*, pl. 11, whence Pl. 40, 3), belongs, I think, to the same fabric as the deer. The spout, which is in a more usual place, behind the handle, has black patterns on it, without relief-lines. The rows of short strokes indicating the fur are in diluted glaze. The side of the base is black, with a nebuly pattern in added white. Martin Robertson has already attributed the lion to the same fabric as the Louvre deer H 176, our no. 2 (*JHS*. 58, 45).

### THE GROUP OF THE SPINA BULLS

*JHS*. 56, 90.

The Ferrara deer-askos no. 1 in the following list is evidently related to that in the Louvre, H 176 (p. 192, no. 2), after which we named the preceding group. The spout, however, has a different form and is situated not on the head but behind the bail; and there is little use of glaze (according to Negrioli it is used for the muzzle, the brows, the outline of the eye, the pupil, the circle of the iris); the coat is indicated by red brush-lines, the tongue-pattern on the spout is red, and traces of red remain on the handle. There are other differences too.

The two bulls, nos. 2 and 5, found in the same tomb at Spina as the deer no. 1, belong to the same fabric. They seem to have been painted white. According to Negrioli there is red on the handle of no. 5, and a trace of brown in no. 2 on the handle and on the tip of the spout. It is not stated that this brown is glaze, but even if it should be, there is little of the vase-painter in these vases, more of the terracotta-maker.

The contents of Tomb 83 at Spina are carefully described by Negrioli in *NSc*. 1924, 308: it contained, besides the deer no. 1 and the bulls nos. 2 and 5, another deer of a different type which goes more or less closely with the Group of the Louvre Deer-askos (p. 192); also some glass vases, a glass bracelet, and an iron spear-head which are unpublished and probably would not afford a very precise date. The finding of our three vases in association with an askos of the other group has a certain importance, as it suggests that there is no great interval between the two groups.

Another bull belonging to our group, no. 3, was found at Spina in Tomb 369, the contents of which have also been described by Negrioli (*NSc*. 1927, 173): they include an extremely late red-figure vase and a pair of extremely late skyphoi with decoration in added red. For the red-figured vase see p. 178, top; for the skyphoi, p. 208.

*Askoi*

(deer)

1. Ferrara, T 83, from Spina. *NSc*. 1924 pl. 13, 1; *Dedalo* 5, 413; Aurigemma[1], 97, ii, 3, and 99=[2]107, ii, 3, and 111. Spout behind the bail.

(bull)

2. Ferrara, T 83, from Spina. *NSc*. 1924 pl. 13, 4; *Dedalo* 5, 409; Aurigemma[1], 97, ii, 4=[2]107, ii, 4. Spout behind the bail.
3. Ferrara, T 369, from Spina. *NSc*. 1927 pl. 13, 2, whence *Anz*. 1928, 134 fig. 12;

Aurigemma[1], 97, ii, 1, and 111 below=[2]107, ii, 1, and 133 below. Spout in front of the bail.   See p. 262, foot.

4. Orvieto, Conte Faina, from Orvieto. Tarchi pl. 131, 1.  Spout in front of the bail.

5. Ferrara, T 83, from Spina. *NSc.* 1924 pl. 13, 5; *Dedalo* 5, 408; *Anz.* 1926, 35; Aurigemma[1], 97, ii, 2=[2]107, ii, 2.  The spout is missing: according to Negrioli it was behind the bail (*NSc.* 1924, 309).

(panther)

6. Ferrara, T 651, from Spina.  Aurigemma[1], 97, iii, 6=[2]107, iii, 6.  Spout in front of the bail.

7. London, 73.8–20.592, from Tarquinia.

An askos in the form of a satyr riding a goat (*Annali* 1884 pl. B, 1) was found in the same tomb at Vulci as the *Iunones pocolom* in Gotha (p. 210 no. 3): it does not seem to belong to any of our groups; is nearest, perhaps, to the Spina Bull Group, but not, so far as one can tell, near: no details are given in the text to the plate in *Annali*.

# CHAPTER XII
# VASES WITH DECORATION IN SUPERPOSED COLOUR

## A. THE PRAXIAS GROUP

*AM.* 48, 24–30 and *Anz.* 1925, 275–8 (Rumpf); *Jb.* 43, 331–59 (Dragendorff); *St. etr.* 8, 339–42 (Herbig); *Anz.* 1936, 75–88 (Dohrn); *RG.* 87.

I group under this heading a large number of vases belonging to the first half of the fifth century. *Praxias* is written in Greek letters on the mouth of a small amphora from Vulci in the Cabinet des Médailles (no. 12) and is possibly the name of the painter or the potter. The Paris amphora is one of four put together by Rumpf (*AM.* 48, 24–30 and *Anz.* 1925, 276–7: nos. 12–15): they are by one artist, the Praxias Painter as he may be called, and all bear Greek inscriptions. It is curious that these most Etruscan-looking vases should be inscribed in Greek.

The rest of the vases in our list come from the same fabric as the four amphorae, but show considerable variety of style. The Copenhagen stamnos, no. 37, resembles the Jena amphora, no. 6. Dragendorff saw that the three Munich amphorae, nos. 1–3, went together, and that no. 4 probably went with them. The Cassel stamnos, no. 38, is related to the column-krater in Freiburg, no. 44. The two neck-amphorae in New York, nos. 10 and 11, go together; and the two in Naples, nos. 27 and 28. Dragendorff has made some other combinations which I cannot check.

Dragendorff's list consists of our nos. 1–5, 7–8, 12–15, 17–19, 23–6, 30–1, 33–4, 36–7, 43–4, 46, 48, and 51–6. No. 6 was added by Herbig.

*Amphorae*

1. Munich 3171 (J 890), from Vulci. Gerhard *AV.* pl. 197, whence (A) Bulas *Les Illustrations antiques de l'Iliade* fig. 31, and (B, redrawn) Séchan 118; *Jb.* 43, 343–4. A, the Fight at the Ships; B, Achilles and Priam. Restored (the restorations are given by Dragendorff *Jb.* 43, 344).

2. Munich 3170 (J 895), from Vulci. Gerhard *AV.* pl. 209; *Jb.* 43, 345 figs. 15–16; part of A, *Anz.* 1936, 86. A, unexplained (a naked youth collapses at a sepulchral mound); B, men. Attached to the mound, halteres, sponge, strigil, aryballos, discus in bag (not 'ball' as Jahn), lyre, sandals: similarly in the askos by the Tyszkiewicz Painter in Boston (*ARV.* 188 no. 59), discus, acontia, halteres, and sashes are attached to the mound from which the dead hero rises.

3. Munich 3185 (J 903), from Vulci. Gerhard *AV.* pl. 217; *Jb.* 43, 345 figs. 13–14. A, Aeneas and Anchises. B, a woman in a mule-cart, driven by a youth (rescue from a sacked city?). Doubtful whether foot and mouth belong.

4. Philadelphia (lent by Miss Annie Hegeman: ex Basseggio), from Vulci. *Mon.* 5 pl. 56. Death of Aegisthus.

5. Louvre G 63. Fight.

6. Jena 210, from Vulci. *St. etr.* 8 pl. 40. A, satyrs and maenad. B, men and youth. Restored.

7. Altenburg, from Italy. A, *Jb.* 43, 352. A, three women; B, the like.

8. Munich 3172 (J 910). Gerhard *AV.* pl. 89, 3–4; *Jb.* 43, 349. Perseus and Medusa. Restored.

9. Vatican. A, naked youth between youths. B, man and youth.

10. New York 24.97.7. A, Richter *Etr.* fig. 119. A, athlete; B, the like.

11. New York 24.97.6. Richter *Etr.* figs. 122–3. A, man praying; B, man.

12. Cab. Méd. 913, from Vulci. De Ridder pl. 26; *Anz.* 1936, 78 figs. 1–2. A, Peleus and the infant Achilles; B, Chiron and the infant Achilles. On A, ΠΕΛΕΙ. On B, ΛΥΙΛΕΙ retr., ΨΙR[Ο]N. On the handle, ΑΔΝΟΕ retr., on the mouth ΓΔΛ+ΙΑΣ.

13. Cab. Méd. 914, from Vulci. A, de Ridder pl. 26; *Anz.* 1936, 78 figs. 3–4. A, Eros; B, Eros. On A, ΕROTO complete, retr. (see *JHS.* 56, 253).

14. Berlin inv. 3363, from Vulci. *Annali* 1852 pl. T; *Anz.* 1936, 82 figs. 5–6. A, man and dog; B, youth and dog. On A, ΜΕΛΙΤΛΙΕ retr. On B, ΙΟΟRΟΙ. Such is my reading of the inscription on B: I cannot interpret it. I did not see the P drawn above the man's head in the illustration, but will not swear it is not there. On A, an alpha is written by mistake for lambda. Some restoration on A (hair-reserve) and B.

15. Sèvres 3114, from Vulci. *CV.* pl. 46, 1 and 5. A, Amazon; B, Amazon. On A, ΛΝΔROMΛΨΕ, the first seven letters retr. (see *JHS.* 56, 253).

16. Villa Giulia, from Vulci. A, rider; B, Nike running with sash.

*Pelike*

17. Louvre G 64. A, naked youths dancing; B, the like.

*Neck-amphorae*

18. Berlin 2980, from Vulci. A, jumper and youth; B, discus-thrower and youth.

19. Munich 3179 (J 904), from Vulci. A, two youths; B, the like.

20. Florence, from Saturnia. A, *ML.* 30, 647, ii, 1. A, youth and woman; B, the like.

21. Cambridge (ex Mus. Ethn.). A, two discus-throwers; B, two (youths?). Restored.

22. Amsterdam, from Italy. A, two youths; B, the like. Much restored.

23. Munich (J 900), from Vulci. A, two youths; B, youth and woman.

24. Munich (J 902), from Vulci. A, two youths; B, the like.

25. Munich 3175 (J 894). A, woman dancing; B, the like.

26. Munich 3178 (J 909), from Vulci. A, *Jb.* 43, 347, fig. 19. A, youth (komast); B, youth and cock.

27. Naples inv. 82761, from Vulci. A, youth; B, the like.

28. Naples inv. 82755. A, komast.

29. Vatican. A, warrior (naked, from behind, the left leg drawn in back-view, with spear and shield). B, youth (same attitude, the right arm extended, a cloak on the left arm).

30. Munich 3177 (J 898), from Vulci. B, *Jb.* 43, 347, fig. 20. A, man; B, youth.

31. Munich 3182 (J 886), from Vulci. A, male; B, male.

32. Vatican G 108, from Vulci. *RG.* pl. 31. A, youth; B, youth.

33. Munich 3173 (J 268), from Vulci. A, *Jb.* 43, 353. A, a naked male on the back of a bull. B, warrior? and male? Restored.

34. Munich (J 267), from Vulci. A, rider. B, two youths?

35. Würzburg 806. A, Langlotz pl. 236. A, youth; B, youth.

### *Stamnoi*

36. Munich 3191 (J 899), from Vulci. A, *Jb.* 43, 346, fig. 18. A, satyr and maenad. B, two youths. The picture on A recalls early work by the Syleus Painter (*ARV.* 164–8 and 954); compare also the Attic column-krater Boston 22.677 (Gerhard *AV.* pl. 77; *Bull. MFA.* 20, 74 above).

37. Copenhagen inv. 3796, from Orvieto. A, *Jb.* 43, 346, fig. 17; *CV.* pl. 218, 3. A, satyr and maenad. B, two men.

37 bis. Boston 80.596 (R 485). A, youth leading ram to altar; B, youth with stick.

38. Cassel, Prince Philip of Hesse, from Montepulciano. Neugebauer *ADP.* pl. 72. A, two jumpers; B, youth and woman.

39. Lost. Drawings in the German Institute, Rome, blue 17. A, athletes and boy; B, athletes. On A, an athlete to right, holding a wreath in his right hand and an aryballos in his left; then a small boy to right, looking round, with a sponge in his left hand; then an athlete to left, his right arm extended with a strigil, in his left hand a wreath; on B, an athlete to right, looking round, with a discus, and another to left with halteres; between them, a plant with leaves like thyrsus-heads, as in the last.

40. Florence, from Chiusi. A, athletes and youth (a discus-thrower in the middle; a youth wearing a himation and holding a stick; a jumper to left). B, man between woman and youth.

41. Florence 4073. A, two athletes.

42. Florence (ex Vagnonville), from Chiusi or near. A, fight (two warriors).

43. Florence, from Chiusi. A, two youths. Restored I think.

### *Column-kraters*

44. Freiburg. *Jb.* 43 pll. 10–11 and pp. 331–5. A, two athletes; B, athlete and youth. On the neck: A, panther and bull; B, wolf (?) and boar.

45. Orvieto, Conte Faina, from Orvieto. A, athletes (jumper, seen from behind, and discus-thrower). B, warrior and woman at altar.

45 bis. Boston 80.595 (R 484). A, satyr turning a somersault over a skyphos; B, satyr chasing a cock. On the top side of the mouth, a wreath, and on each handle-plate a polypus as in no. 44.

45 ter. San Francisco, De Young Museum, 224.24865. A, two youths; B, the like. I owe my knowledge of this vase to the kindness of Miss Ethel Van Tassel.

### *Hydriai*
#### (of bf. shape)

46. Munich 3189 (J 889), from Vulci. Males and woman? On the neck, swans.

47. Cambridge (ex Mus. Ethn.). *C.A.H.*, Plates, i, 343, b. Two youths; between them a bird flying. On the shoulder, flower between eyes.

(kalpides)

48. Berlin 2981, from Vulci. Two women dancing.
49. Villa Giulia, from Vulci. Two youths.
50. Vatican G 109, from Vulci. Two youths. Much restored. Described in *RG.* 87 but not figured.

### Oinochoai (shape I)

51. Munich 3194 (J 897), from Vulci. *Jb.* 43, 342. Two warriors (dancing?).
52. Munich 3197 (J 906), from Vulci. *Jb.* 43, 348. Two youths. Restored?
53. Munich 3198 (J 908), from Vulci. Youth with spear, and youth.
54. Munich (J 893), from Vulci. Youth with lyre pursuing woman.
55. Munich 3195 (J 891), from Vulci. *Jb.* 43, 351. Youth with lyre pursuing woman. Restored?

### Kyathoi (one-handled kantharoi)

56. Munich 3200 (J 901), from Vulci. *Jb.* 43, 350. Warriors. On the front of the handle, plant.
57. Vatican G 107, fr., from Vulci. *RG.* pl. 31. On the front of the handle, youth.

### Fragments

58. Heidelberg E 51, fr. Naked women washing. Reserved inside. Rumpf (*BPW.* 34, 314) holds this to be Attic and by the Berlin Painter, but I cannot follow him.
59. Castle Ashby, the Marquess of Northampton. Two warriors. To the right, net-pattern.

Herbig, in *St. etr.* 8, 342, mentions an amphora in Altenburg as a pendant to no. 6.

The stamnos Munich 3192, published by Dragendorff in *Jb.* 43, 354–5, is not in our technique, it is a red-figured vase: see Mercklin in *St. etr.* 11, 374; and above, p. 32.

I keep apart from the Praxias Fabric a vase which belongs to the same period but differs in style and perhaps in technique also from the vases mentioned hitherto.

### Column-krater

Chiusi, private, from Chiusi. A, Noël Des Vergers pl. 12.

According to Noël Des Vergers's plate the picture would be either in red-figure or in added colour: but in the photographs which I owe to the kindness of Dr. Bianchi Bandinelli I do not find any difference of surface between figures and background. The figures are carried out in incision—thick for the master lines, thin for the minor. There is also a great deal of incised sketch, but no trace of added colour in the pictures. The pair of lines below the pictures, however, are added in colour; and so is the lotus-bud pattern on the neck of the vase, with incised details. It might be thought that the present state of the vase was due to over-cleaning: but I do not think this likely from such observations as I can make. The style is fairly good, and the date about 480 or not much later.

The subject on the side of the krater published by Noël Des Vergers is two youths with swords attacking a third who defends himself with a stone. The right-hand youth has a cloak over his shoulders, the others are naked. To the left is a plant with clumps of leaves resembling thyrsus-heads and recalling two stamnoi from the Praxias fabric (p. 197 nos. 38 and 39): I say a plant, although it looks more like a chandelier in the drawing: this part is obscure in the photograph. The same subject is probably represented on an Etruscan mirror in the Cabinet des Médailles (1312: Gerhard *ES*. pl. 58). The chief difference is that only one of the attackers uses a sword; the other catches the victim round the waist. Here also the youth attacked endeavours to defend himself with a stone. The attackers are inscribed: they are *Castur* and *Pultuce*. The name of their opponent is not given: but here a second mirror may possibly come in, London 629, from Chiusi (Gerhard *ES*. pl. 56, 1), on which two youths attack a third: the contest is not certainly the same, for neither sword nor stone is used; but there is a reasonable probability. *Pulutuke* and *Kasutru* are attacking *Chaluchasu*. This is not so helpful as it might be, for we do not know who *Chaluchasu* was: linguistically the name may be equivalent to *Chalchas* (Fiesel *Namen des griechischen Mythos im Etruskischen* 34, 36–7, and 91), who appears on an inscribed mirror from Vulci in the Vatican (Gerhard *ES*. pl. 223, whence Wolters *Der geflügelte Seher* 3; Ducati *Storia* pl. 213, fig. 523; Giglioli pl. 298, 1).

A lost Greek myth, in which Kalchas was forced to prophesy at the point of the sword? —'the reluctant prophet' is a well-known figure in legend. But this is no prophet.

The group on the column-krater, in its main lines, bears a certain resemblance to that on two mirrors in Berlin: Fr. 150, from Vulci (Gerhard *ES*. pl. 255), and its replica inv. 30480, from the neighbourhood of Rome (*Stephanos Wiegand* pl. 5; Giglioli pl. 5): but the subject is not the same: the youth in the middle promises to be victorious, and his opponents are bearded men with wings.

Noël Des Vergers says nothing about the picture on the other side of the vase. On the left, a man falls; of the youth or man in the middle, who strikes him down, hardly anything shows in my photographs; the right-hand figure is a woman, encouraging the champion.

In conclusion: a pair of early-fifth-century vases in the Villa Giulia have sometimes been stated to be in the technique of added colour: but from the careful description by Della Seta, who published them (*ML*. 23, 278–311), it is clear that this is not so. The painting is not superposed on the black background: the artist first drew the patterns and the figures (both contours and inner markings) in black lines, then filled the figures in with red, then blacked in the background and added a little white for the sclerotic of the eyes. There seem to be no other examples of this experimental technique.

### *Stamnoi*

1. Villa Giulia 22636, from Campagnano. *ML*. 23 pll. 1–2, whence (A) Ducati *St*. pl. 125 fig. 329 and (A) Giglioli pl. 205, 2. A, naked youths dancing; B, the like.
2. Villa Giulia 22637, from Campagnano. *ML*. 23, 290 and pll. 3–4. Same subjects as the last.

### B

### *Pelike*

Amsterdam inv. 4584, from Vulci? *Anz*. 1936, 82, figs. 7–8. A, warrior running; B, woman running with jug.

Dohrn places this with vases of the Praxias fabric, but it is later, and I prefer to keep it apart. The youth is imitated from some Attic vase of about 430–425 B.C.: compare for example the Helen oinochoe in the Vatican (FR. pl. 170, 1). He holds a spear and so is not a 'hoplitodromos'. The vessel in the warrior's hand looks like an oinochoe in the reproduction rather than a 'hydria'.

c

## *Oinochoe in Villa Giulia*

In *JHS.* 57, 26 I mentioned an oinochoe of shape VI, formerly in the collection of Augusto Castellani and now in the Villa Giulia, as imitating Attic work of about 425 or 420 B.C.: it reminded me of Aison, who has left us two oinochoai of this type (*ARV.* 799 nos. 9 and 10). I never saw the Villa Giulia vase close, but the figures (an athlete and a youth at an altar), with the band of double spirals above them, seemed to be in added colour, although the wreath of 'laurel' or olive below them seemed to be in red-figure.

An oinochoe of shape VI in Compiègne (918: *CV.* pl. 24, 2) is later. It is said to have been found at Chiusi, and may be Etruscan. On the shoulder, long upright lines, and dots, in white. Harvard 2302 (*CV.* pl. 39, 8) is decorated similarly (without the dots?), and might be from the same fabric, although it has a distinct foot and the Compiègne vase seems to have none (see p. 266). The upright lines are a summary version of tongue-pattern. Two Attic oinochoai of shape VI have tongue-pattern on the shoulder, fully carried out: London old cat. 1170; and Bologna 355 (Pellegrini *VF.* 175 fig. 107).

For other Etruscan jugs of this type, in various techniques, see pp. 46, 73, 181, 266, 282.

### D. ETRUSCAN GLAUKES
#### *Skyphoi* (type B: glaukes)

1. Vatican G 110, from Vulci. A, *RG.* pl. 31.
2. Cambridge, Prof. A. B. Cook. A, Cook *Zeus* iii, 787. The clay is of 'Corinthian' colour, the decoration in light red.
3. Cracow, Techn. Mus., inv. 9738. A, *CV.* pl. 2 (Pol. pl. 95), 5.

These three vases, decorated on each side with an owl between two sprigs of olive, are imitations of Attic red-figured glaukes (on which see Haspels *ABL.* 187–8; and *RG.* 87): I do not know of any Attic glaukes with decoration in added colour: phialai with owls on them yes (Athens Acr. 1078, Langlotz pl. 84, see Luschey *Die Phiale* 109). Though not by one hand, our three agree in two respects: first, they have no incised detail; secondly, beak, and dot and circle of the eyes, are reserved in black. The Vatican vase was perhaps dated too late in *RG.* 87: none of the Attic glaukes with human figures can be much later than the middle of the fifth century (Yale 160, Baur pl. 13): those with owls may not have lasted very much longer; Etruscan imitations may have lingered on but not for very long.

Other glaukes with added colour have been found on Etruscan and Italic sites, and may well be Etruscan, but I do not assume it. Such are the following:

Florence?, from Orvieto. A, *NSc.* 1939, 43, 2.

Rome, Palatine, fr., from Rome (Palatine). Ryberg, fig. 130 d.

Philadelphia 2934, from Ardea. A, *Boll. st. med.* 4, 4–5, pl. 1, 17.

Owl-and-olive decoration is used on Attic cup-skyphoi (of the type *CV.* Oxford pl. 48, 6, see also *BSA.* 41, 18 note 2) as well as on skyphoi: there are Italiote imitations of these, and I know of one Etruscan imitation:

Oxford, Beazley, fr., from Orvieto. Incision for details.

E

*Oinochoe* (shape VII: beaked jug)

London F 529. *CV.* IV Eb pl. 1, 9. Youth at altar. On the neck, owl between sprigs of olive.

'Oinochoe shape VII' suggests a *bird*, especially an *owl*; and this has affected the decoration. There are twenty-one Attic red-figured vases of this shape. Three of them have an owl on the neck (Vatican, and Mannheim, *ARV.* 661, Mannheim Painter nos. 7–8; and a lost vase, *ARV.* 662, lower middle), one a couple of owls (Erlangen, *ARV.* 662, near the Mannheim Painter), and one an owl on the body (Geneva 5764: komast with lyre, and flute-girl; between them, half-way up, an owl). Five others have the neck covered with *feathers*: Louvre G 442, *ARV.* 661 no. 6, by the Mannheim Painter; London E 564, *ARV.* 726, no. 20, by the Eretria Painter; Marseilles 2092 from Saint-Mauront (Clerc *Massalia* 313: about 425 B.C.); Bologna 872 from Monte Avigliano (*Atti Romagna* 21, 269 fig. 4); Ferrara, T 652, from Spina (end of the fifth century). Etruscan painters also placed an owl on the necks of their oinochoai shape VII: red-figure, Villa Giulia 19772 and 19773, from Cervetri (on the body of each, Nike; on the neck, an owl perched on a rock, to left, head in profile, white wings; no relief-lines used); added-colour, London F 529, Toronto 492 (Robinson and Harcum pl. 85), Amsterdam inv. 2664, fr., from Falerii (*CV.* IV B pl. 1 = Pays Bas pl. 87, 1), Sèvres 2046 (see p. 203, Sokra Group no. 32) and Zurich 424, from Tarquinia, described by Benndorf (*Die Antiken von Zürich* 172). Add the two red-figured vases, of the Fluid Group, with owls on the body, in the Villa Giulia and Toronto (see pp. 155–6 nos. 8 and 11). The neck-owls are the Attic bird, standing between two sprigs of olive.

The lines of the vase-shape are less mannered in London F 529 than in the Phantom Group (pp. 205–6) and most Etruscan beak-jugs, and recall fifth-century Attic: shorter neck, the lip less flaring, a single curve from belly to base. In Toronto 492 also (Robinson and Harcum pl. 85) the shape is comparatively pure; and so it is in the Sèvres vase which we have assigned to the Sokra Group (p. 203).

Pryce holds London F 529 to be Apulian. I do not know the shape in Apulian, and think our vase must be Etruscan.

F. THE SOKRA GROUP

The cup Villa Giulia 3676 (no. 5) bears on the underside of the foot the legend *Sōkra*, complete, in Greek letters and in the same colour as the designs. Sokra(tes) may be the painter's name, or the potter's (Giglioli in *NSc.* 1914, 277; Dragendorff in *Jb.* 43, 354): but this is uncertain. Strange, once more, that such an Etruscan-looking vase should be inscribed in Greek.

These are fourth-century cups. Some of them a little recall red-figured cups of the Clusium Group. Dragendorff believes that they were made at Falerii (*Jb.* 43, 354), but I should not think it likely.

Hauser saw (*Jb.* 11, 195) that no. 17 was a replica of no. 16, that no. 6 came from the same fabric, and that no. 1 was related; Mercklin compared no. 8 with no. 13 (*Anz.* 1928, 357); Dragendorff attributed no. 6 to the same hand as nos. 5 and 8 (*Jb.* 43, 354); Scheurleer compared nos. 5 and 8 with no. 21; Pryce nos. 3 and 20 with no. 16.

Smaller groups may be formed within the larger: Nos. 1 and 2. Nos. 16 and 17: these perhaps with the last. Nos. 3 and 7: cf. also no. 4. Nos. 5, 6, 7. Nos. 8 and 13. No. 25: cf. no. 21. Nos. 10 and 20. Nos. 14 bis and 14 ter. Nos. 15, 15 bis, 15 ter, 15 quater.

## Cups

1. Berlin inv. 3973. I *Annali* 1878 pl. S. I, Perseus. A, 'two draped figures'; B, the like.
2. Copenhagen ABc 782, from Volterra. *CV.* pl. 219, 3. I, youth; A, two youths; B, the like. By the same hand as the last.
3. Villa Giulia 3675, from Falerii. *CV.* IV Bq pl. 1, 1–3. I, Herakles. A, two youths; B, the like.
4. Volterra, from Volterra. I, phot. Brogi 13657, part. I, naked youth with pilos and thyrsus. Cf. the last. The border seems from the photograph to be red-figure.
5. Villa Giulia 3676, from Falerii. *CV.* IV Bq pl. 2, 1–2 and 6. I, two athletes; A, two athletes; B, the like. Underneath the foot, in the same colour as the designs, ΣΩΚΡΑ complete.
6. Munich 3206 (J 907), from Vulci. I, *Jb.* 43, 356. I, athlete and youth; A, athlete and youth; B, the like.
7. Copenhagen inv. 3797, from Orvieto. *CV.* pl. 219, 1. I, athlete and youth; A, two youths; B, the like.
8. Villa Giulia 17494, from Rignano Flaminio. I, *NSc.* 1914, 272; *CV.* IV Bq pl. 2, 3–5. I, naked youth with pilos and branch, and youth; A, two youths; B, the like. As no. 13.
9. Lost, from Chiusi. I, Inghirami *Mus. Chius.* pl. 160. I, athlete and youth.
10. Oxford, no number. I, athlete and youth; A, two youths; B, the like.
11. Villa Giulia?, from Gualdo Tadino. I, *NSc.* 1935, 163, 1. I, athlete and youth; A, 'two draped figures'; B, the like.
12. Chiusi, frr., from Chiusi. I, *NSc.* 1931, 220, b. I, athlete and youth. B (male).
12 bis. Boston 76.239 (R 486), from Chiusi. I, naked youth with phiale. A, two naked youths; B, the like.
13. Hamburg 1917.811. I, *Anz.* 1928, 355. I, naked youth running with pilos and garment. A, two youths; B, the like.
14. Villa Giulia, from Vignanello. I, *NSc.* 1924, 193. I, youth with a garment tied round his waist (not 'warrior with chitoniskos and corslet', as Giglioli). A, two youths; B, the like.
14 bis. Todi 490, from Todi. *CV.* pl. 10, 2. I, maenad.
14 ter. Todi 491, from Todi. *CV.* pl. 10, 3. I, maenad. As the last.
15. Chiusi, from Chiusi. I, *NSc.* 1931, 219. I, maenad. A–B, laurel.

15 bis. Todi 488, from Todi. *CV*. pl. 11, 3. I, maenad. As the last.

15 ter. Todi 495, from Todi. *CV*. pl. 10, 1. I, maenad.

15 quater. Todi 492, from Todi. *CV*. pl. 11, 1. I, satyr.

16. London F 541. *CV*. IV Eb pl. 3, 5 and pl. 4, 9; I, Cook *Zeus* iii pl. 65, 2. I, Pegasus. A, athlete and youths; B, the like. The bearded head below Pegasus is probably Medusa's, as Cook, iii, 853.

17. Leipsic, from Rome. I, Cook *Zeus* iii, pl. 65, 1. I, Pegasus. A, athlete and youths; B, the like. Replica of the last, by the same hand.

18. Volterra, from Volterra. I, phot. Brogi 13657, part. I, Pegasus.

19. Rome, Prof. Curtius, fr. I, Pegasus. A, (youth); B, (youth).

20. London F 540. *CV*. IV Eb pl. 3, 7. I, horse. A, two youths; B, the like.

21. Amsterdam inv. 3412, from Falerii. I and A, *CV*. Scheurleer IV B pl. 1 (Pays Bas pl. 87), 2 and 4. I, horse. A, two youths; B, the like.

22. Chiusi, fr., from Chiusi. I, *NSc*. 1931, 220, a. I, horse. According to Mingazzini two of the three horse-cups from Chiusi (nos. 22, 23 and below, p. 204) have laurel outside (cf. no. 15) while the third has 'rude draped figures and palmettes': but he does not say which.

23. Chiusi, fr., from Chiusi. I, *NSc*. 1931, 220, d. I, horse. See the last.

24. Oxford 1920.345. I, sea-horse. A, two youths; B, the like.

25. Volterra, from Volterra. A–B, phot. Brogi 13657, part. I, ?. A, two youths; B, the like.

26. Villa Giulia?, from Gualdo Tadino. I, *NSc*. 1935, 163, 3. I, 'a figure'. A, 'two draped figures'; B, the like.

27. Michigan 2615, fr., from Orvieto. *CV*. pl. 24, 2. I, (satyr): there were doubtless two figures.

### Stemless cup

28. San Giusto alle Monache (near Siena), Contessa Elisabetta Martini di Cigalà, from Monte Gallozzi (NE. of Siena). *NSc*. 1928, 427, fig. 5, c. I, youth.

### Skyphoi

29. Cambridge, Prof. A. B. Cook. A, athlete; B, youth. The added colour is almost white.

30. Boston 76.238 (R 483), from Chiusi. A, youth; B, the like.

31. Boston 76.233 (R 482), from Chiusi. A, youth; B, the like.

### Oinochoe (shape VII: beaked jug)

32. Sèvres 2046. *CV*. pl. 46, 3, 19, and 23. Two youths. On the neck, owl between olive-branches. For the drawing of the floral compare the cups nos. 5, 8, 20. The provenience of the vase is not given in the *Corpus*: according to de Witte (*Coll. Durand* no. 642) it is the Basilicata. The body curves in slightly towards the base, but in shape the vase is nearer to London F 529 (p. 201) than to the Phantom Group (p. 205).

### Column-krater

33. Philadelphia 2994, from Ardea. A, *Boll. st. med.* 4, 4–5, pl. 1, 19. A, youth; B, youth.

The maeander of the following cup is like that of no. 17: there is no trace of anything within it:

Philadelphia 2857, from Ardea. I, *Boll. st. med.* 4, 4–5, pl. 2, 38.

The following cups sound from the descriptions as if they belonged to the Sokra Group:

1. Berlin 2982. I, athlete and youth. A, two youths; B, the like. By the same hand as Munich 3206 (no. 6) according to Dragendorff (*Jb.* 43, 354, note 1).
2. Munich (J 892). I, athletes; A, three athletes; B, the like. From the same fabric as the Leipsic cup (no. 17) according to Hauser (*Jb.* 11, 195).
3. Chiusi, frr., from Chiusi. I, horse. Described in *NSc.* 1931, 219: see above on no. 22.

Perhaps also

Villa Giulia, from Corchiano. I, 'hippocamp'. Described by Bandinelli in *NSc.* 1920, 29, no. 16.

Becatti mentions, but does not figure, several cups from Todi, in Todi, which would seem from his description to belong to the Sokra Group: 493, with a satyr, said to be like 492 (our no. 15 quater); 494 and 496 with a 'naked maenad'; 489, 498, and 500, with a horse; 497 with a Tritoness. 489 and 497 have an olive-wreath outside.

## G. SUNDRY CUPS AND STEMLESS CUPS
### Cups

α. Villa Giulia (ex Augusto Castellani). I, youth. Copied from a work by an Attic painter of about 430 B.C.

β. Florence V 481, from Chiusi. I, two youths; A, three youths; B, the like. Imitated from an Attic cup of the Sub-Meidian Cup-group (see p. 28).

γ. Copenhagen inv. 3798, fr., from Orvieto. *CV.* pl. 219, 2. I, youth with branch. The line border is reserved. Perhaps connected with the Praxias Fabric?

ƛ. Bonn, fr. I, Scylla. A, three youths; B, the like. Formerly in the Roman market. This reminds me of a cup from Poggio Sommavilla described by Fossati in *Bull.* 1837, 211: 'la rarissima kylix che nel tondo interno ha Scilla, coronata, con angue barbato in ciascuna mano distesa, due cani le nascono dall' inguine e si slanciano, e l'infelice e truce donna finisce in pesce.' The description, as far as it goes, corresponds, but the Sommavilla cup is not expressly stated to be in our technique. Sokra Group?

ε. Philadelphia 2843, from Ardea. I, *Boll. st. med.* 4, 4–5, pl. 2, 36. I, two youths; A, two youths; B, the like. Sokra Group as I now see (p. 306).

ϛ. Villa Giulia 44561, from Vignanello. A–B, *NSc.* 1924, 253; *CV.* IV Bq pl. 1, 4–5. I, two youths; A, athlete and youths; B, the like. Cognate to the Sokra Group but not, I think, of it.

η. Chiusi, fr., from Chiusi. *NSc.* 1931, 220, c. A (satyr).

### Cups or stemless cups

θ. Florence?, from Citerna. I, *NSc.* 1936, 398, fig. 1, and 399. I, youth. See p. 306.

ι. Orvieto, from Orvieto. I, *NSc.* 1939, 43, 1 and pl. 31. I, lion.

*Stemless cups*

κ. Vienna, Univ., 503.1, from Orvieto. *CV*. pl. 32, 2. I, naked youth running (torch-racer).

λ. San Giusto alle Monache, Contessa Elisabetta Martini di Cigalà, from Monte Gallozzi (see p. 203). I, *NSc*. 1928, 427, fig. 5, b. I, naked youth running with stick.

### H. THE PHANTOM GROUP

Nos. 1–20 have a single draped figure on the body, whether male or female it is not always easy to tell; floral work at the handle and on the neck. In no. 21 the decoration of the body is the same, but there is a swan on the neck: nos. 23 and 24 have no figure on the body, but floral decoration instead.

The added colour is sometimes the normal reddish, but more often whitish.

Robinson (text to *CV*. Robinson iii pl. 38, 1) compared nos. 4, 6–8, 17 with no. 2; Miss Pease (text to *CV*. Harvard pl. 39, 2) nos. 8 and 17 with no. 10; Mrs. Ryberg no. 3 with no. 18. Robinson added vases in the Vatican and the Villa Giulia which I do not know.

*Oinochoai* (shape VII: beaked jugs)

1. Cambridge, Prof. D. S. Robertson. Three holding-marks on the foot.
2. Baltimore, Univ., from Palestrina. *CV*. Robinson iii pl. 38, 1.
3. London F 528. *CV*. IV Eb pl. 1, 10.
3 bis. Cambridge, Museum of Classical Archaeology, 67. Five holding-marks on the foot.
3 ter. Once London, Lt. Col. T. A. Ross (*Cat. Sotheby 14 May 1946*, no. 107, 1).
4. Würzburg 809. Langlotz pl. 236.
5. Civitavecchia, from Castrum Novum. *St. etr.* 11 pl. 59, 4, b.
6. Würzburg 807, from Basilicata. Langlotz pl. 236.
7. Würzburg 808. Langlotz pl. 236.
8. Toronto 497. Robinson and Harcum pl. 86.
9. Copenhagen inv. 7968. *CV*. pl. 218, 4.
10. Harvard 2253, from South Italy. *CV*. pl. 39, 2.
11. Harvard 2306. *CV*. pl. 39, 3.
12. Once Caylus. Caylus 4 pl. 38, 1.
13. Where? Jacquemart *Histoire de la céramique* 251, whence Jaennicke *Grundriss der Keramik* 22 fig. 6.
14. Volterra, from Volterra. Inghirami *Mon. etr.* 5 pl. 3, 3–4.
15. Rome, Conservatori.
16. Rome, Conservatori.
16 bis. New York 91.1.450.
17. Toronto 496. Robinson and Harcum pl. 86.
18. Rome, Antiquarium, from Rome (Esquiline). *Bull. Com.* 1875 pl. 6–8, 19; Ryberg pl. 21, 108.
19. Florence, from Populonia. *NSc*. 1905, 55, right=Ducati *Storia* fig. 369, right.
20. Copenhagen ABc 20. *CV*. pl. 218, 5.

21. Würzburg 810.  Langlotz pl. 236.
22. Berkeley, from Narce?
23. Philadelphia MS 4084.   24. Philadelphia L64.404.

A fragment, said to be of a skyphos, from Lanuvium, in Leeds (*BSA.* 11 pl. 28, 8) seems to belong to the Phantom Group; and Langlotz has already compared it with our no. 4.

Hoffmann (*Anz.* 1904, 53) speaks of a beaked jug in Colmar as the exact counterpart of no. 18.  According to Langlotz Munich 3214 is similar to Würzburg 807, our no. 6. Sydney 95 reads, in Louisa Macdonald's catalogue, like a member of the Phantom Group. A beaked jug in Florence, from Populonia, barely distinguishable in the reproduction (*NSc.* 1905, 56, right), may also belong, like the jug from the same site in our list, no. 19.

## J

The decoration of the following small vases is of the same nature as in the Phantom Group, and they may perhaps be related to it:

### Small pelikai

1. Boston 13.86 (R 482), from Chiusi.
2. Rome, Antiquarium, X 662, from Rome (Esquiline).  A, Ryberg, pl. 21, 112.
3. Harvard 3455.  A, *CV.* pl. 39, 5.  As the last.
4. Toronto 416.  A, Robinson and Harcum pl. 79.

### Squat lekythos

5. Toronto 488.  Robinson and Harcum pl. 79.
   Miss Pease has already compared no. 2 with no. 3.
   I do not know whether the following are connected with these, and am not even sure that they are Etruscan:

### Small hydriai

Toronto 425.  Robinson and Harcum pl. 79.
Toronto 424.  Robinson and Harcum pl. 79.  Same style as the last.

### Squat lekythos

Boston 13.78 (R 487).

### K. KANTHAROI: LATIN

From Minturnae.  *Boll. st. med.* 5, 4–5, pl. 5, 37, and pl. 6, 37, left.

This is a kantharos of a favourite fourth-to-third-century kind.  A fine assortment of such vases will be found figured in the Ensérune volume of the *Corpus Vasorum.*  The Minturnae potter has chosen the variety in which the handles have no ledge on top: compare *CV.* Mouret pl. 16, 12, pl. 17, 11, pl. 17, 7, pl. 18, 7, and Visedo Molto *Excavaciones en el monte 'La Serrata' próximo Alcoy (Alicante) (= Junta Superior de Excavaciones* 1921–2, i) pl. 6, a: contrast most of the other kantharoi in the Mouret fascicule.

The body is reeded.  On the neck, in added colour, 'vine-leaves'.  This very variety of kantharos is found in Gnathian, as Miss Lake observed (e.g. *CV*. London IV Dc pl. 4, 10, 14, and 17), but also in other fabrics, though not, so far as I know, in Attic.

Miss Lake groups variants of this shape under the same heading, 'type 37', and figures one of them on her pl. 6, 37, right.

A kantharos of the same *general* type as ours, but different in details, from Castrum Novum, is in Civitavecchia (*St. etr.* 11 pl. 59, 4, c); another, again differing, from Capena, in the Villa Giulia (*NSc.* 1922, 132).

An inscribed fragment is from a Latin kantharos either of the same type as ours or of an allied type:

Rome, Terme, fr., from Ardea. *Mél. d'arch.* 30, 101. On the neck, in added colours, ivy. On the lip, painted in white, . . . *omo · fameliai · donom · d* . . .

The inscription had already been published by Ritschl (pl. 10, h, and corrected p. 101), whence *CIL.*² 1, ii, 358. According to Picard (*Mél. d' arch.* 30, 101) the last letter is certainly a *d*: so *d*[*edit*], or *d*[*edet*]. The first letter of *fameliai* is Ⱶ (=*f*): ⌐ is a misprint.

### L. BOWL (flaring, without a distinct foot)

Copenhagen 495, from Volterra. A, *CV*. pl. 220, 5.

Inside, stamped, painted, and incised decoration. 'In the middle, an impressed rosette, from which leafy branches radiate, alternating with a bow-shaped motive; round this a dark red line; next the edge, between two white lines, a wavy line, incised, with a red dot in each bend. Brownish clay, dullish black glaze.'

The shape is the same as in Attic bowls of the West Slope class: see text to *CV*. Oxford pl. 47, 16 and 3. The models were such metal bowls as the silver vessel, parcel gilt, from Locris, in Athens (3736: *AM.* 26, 90).

For the decoration next the edge—a summary ivy-wreath—compare the mastoid from Monteriggioni (*St. etr.* 2 pl. 31, 88 bis: see p. 242).

### M. THE GROUP OF FERRARA T 585

These vases, decorated with palmettes in a special style, are very late.

#### *Skyphoi*

1. Florence, from Populonia. A, *NSc.* 1934, 417, 3.
2. Rome, Museo del Foro, fr., from Rome. Ryberg pl. 24 fig. 127.
3. Ferrara, T 585, from Spina.
4. Rome, Antiquarium, from Rome (Esquiline). A, Ryberg pl. 21 fig. 110.
5. Ensérune, Félix Mouret, from Ensérune. A, *CV*. pl. 18, 10.
6. Ensérune, Félix Mouret, from Ensérune. A, *CV*. pl. 18, 8.

#### *Askoi*

7. Villa Giulia, from Capena. Della Seta *L'It. ant.* 152 fig. 162, 1.
8. Rome, Palatine, fr., from Rome. Ryberg pl. 27 fig. 132 h.

The following represent a different type of skyphos:

1. Bologna 826, from Bologna.  *Atti Romagna*, 3rd ser., 5 pl. 5, 5; A, Pellegrini *VF*. 234.
2. Este, from Este.  *ML*. 10 pl. 5, 9.
3. Ferrara, T 369, from Spina.  A, *NSc*. 1927, 172, 3.  See p. 193.
4. Ferrara, T 369, from Spina.
5. Florence, from Populonia.  A, *NSc*. 1934, 417, 1.

The decoration of the Florence vase is invisible in the reproduction and is not des-cribed by Milani.  The Este vase and the Ferrara pair have a figure of a swan on each side, Bologna 826 'a bird'; and so has Bologna 827, which like 826 was found in a Gaulish grave at Bologna.  Negrioli, an accurate observer, connects the two Bologna skyphoi with a third, from Spina, T 156, in Ferrara, which has a swan on each side (*NSc*. 1924, 292 fig. 6): he reproduces the decoration but not the shape.  Ferrara T 156 was found together with a black kantharos of the Malacena Group (p. 232 no. 46).

I cannot say at present how close these skyphoi stand to the Group of Ferrara T 585, or whether they come, as I should guess, from the same fabric.

Albizzati says (*RM*. 30, 159) that in Volterra there are many skyphoi like Bologna 826.

There is little information about the skyphoi Bologna 828–30, which were also found in Gaulish graves at Bologna.  828 is decorated with palmettes; in 829 and 830 the decoration is said to be no longer recognizable.  Pellegrini implies that the shape is the same as in Bologna 826 and 827.

### N. THE HESSE GROUP

These four fine little vases were put together by Zahn (*Berl. Mus.* 1934, 1–11), assigned to one painter, dated in the first half of the fourth century, located in Southern Etruria or Latium.  The technique is that of superposed colour, but a subtle form of it: the warm brownish-yellow colour is not a mere flat wash, but is fully shaded with brown glaze, and enhanced by high-lights in white.  This technique was developed in South-east Italy, probably at Taranto, in the fourth century (Bulle in *Festschrift für James Loeb* 5–37; Bulle *Eine Skenographie*), and our painter borrowed it thence; unless indeed he himself, though settled in Etruria, was an Italiote from that quarter: for there is nothing essentially Etruscan in the style of the painting.

We can be brief here, since many of the questions raised by these vases are already dealt with by Zahn in his excellent article.

I was inclined, when looking at no. 2 in the Torlonia collection, to connect the Hesse Group with the 'Malacena' fabric (see pp. 229–30 and 236).

### *Kantharoi* (on the shape see p. 236)

1. Berlin (given by Prince Philip of Hesse), from Vulci.  *Berl. Mus.* 1934, 1–2, whence Pl. 39, 2–3.  I, little boy drinking out of an askos.
2. Rome, Prince Torlonia, from Vulci.  Messerschmidt *Die Nekropolen von Vulci* 99, left.  I, little boy reclining, drinking out of a phiale, which he fills from a rhyton.  The

shape of the kantharos is just the same as in the last. The esses of the border are brown flesh-colour, the bounding-lines are incised; the esses are separated by white dots, omitted in the reproduction.

### Bowl (phiale-like, but with a foot)

3. London F 542. I, *AZ.* 1870 pl. 28, whence (part) Rayet and Collignon 338, whence Ducati *Cer.* ii, 484; I, *CV.* IV Dc pl. 4, 3; I, *Berl. Mus.* 1934, 9. I, hunter (boy seated, holding a pair of spears, his hound beside him). For the attitude, see Zahn loc. cit., 4, who aptly compares the figure of Marsyas on an Attic krater-fragment in Sarajevo (*Wissenschaftliche Mitteilungen aus Bosnien* 12, 291 fig. 54, see p. 76); but the upward look of the hunter gives a different tone. As to the shape, the profile of the foot and of the underside are not the same as in the bowls of the Volcani Group (p. 210).

### Phiale

4. Villa Giulia, fr., from between Orvieto and Bolsena. *Annali* 1871 pl. A, whence *Berl. Mus.* 1934, 5. I, chariot-race: the drivers are Erotes.


### O. POCOLA, ETC.

The fifteen vases bearing the word *pocolom* preceded by the name of a deity in the genitive have often been studied (Jordan in *Annali* 1884, 5–20; Walters *HAP.* i, 489–91; Picard in *Mél. d'arch.* 30, 99–116; Wolters in *AM.* 38, 194–5; Lommatzsch in *CIL.* i, $2^2$ nos. 439–53; Karo in Daremberg and Saglio s.v. poculum; Zahn in *Berl. Mus.* 1934, 6–8; Bianchi Bandinelli in *Scritti Nogara* 11–20; Ryberg 135–40). They may be split up into the following batches:

(*a*) Seven small bowls (dishes) with figure decoration in added colours. These seem to be by one hand; by the same, but uninscribed, three small bowls and a plate. I call this the Volcani Group after one of the inscriptions. See pp. 210–11.

(*b*) A fragment of a bowl which may belong to the Volcani Group. See p. 215.

(*c*) A small bowl with simpler decoration—a wreath only and no figurework. The shape is the same as in the Volcani Group, but whether the painting is by the same hand or not can hardly be said. See p. 215.

(*d*) A lost bowl, not reproduced, and not to be placed. See p. 215.

(*e*) Two small oinochoai, black, striated, without figurework: they go together, but whether they are from the same fabric as the Volcani Group I cannot tell. See p. 216.

(*f*) Two small oinochoai: black and striated, like the last, but I have not seen them and do not know whether they are from the same fabric as the last couple or even of the same shape. See p. 216.

(*g*) A small oinochoe or mug of a different shape, black, without decoration: I cannot tell whether the fabric is the same as in any of the other vases. See p. 216.

The latest writer on these vases, Mrs. Ryberg (135–40), judges them to be 'probably a little earlier than the middle of the third century', and this date is not too early. The period of the first Punic War had already been suggested by S. Reinach (*Gazette des Beaux-Arts* 34 (1886), 248–9. The date assigned in *CIL.*, and repeated by Warmington

(*Remains of Old Latin* iv, 75) 'before the second Punic War', is correct so far as it goes, but perhaps implies that the vases are later than they really are. This is important for the study of Early Latin. Warmington gives only nine of the fifteen inscriptions.

The 'Pocola' were probably made in Latium; Bianchi Bandinelli (*Scritti Nogara* 18) and Mrs. Ryberg think that they may have been made in Rome, which had already occurred to Walters (*HAP.* i, 490) and is quite possible.

### (a) The Volcani Group
#### Bowls

1. Berlin 3634, from Chiusi or near? Ritschl, suppl. V pl. 5, A; *Annali*, 1884 pl. R. I, Eros. *Aisclapi· pocolom*. Furtwängler's description seems to interchange left and right. *CIL*. i, 2² no. 440.

2. Berlin 3635, from Vulci. Gerhard *Trinkschalen* pl. 18, 1–2, whence Ritschl pl. 10, c and C. I, Eros. *Volcani· pocolom*. *CIL*. i, 2² no. 453.

3. Gotha 298, from Vulci. *Annali* 1884 pl. A, whence Ducati *Cer*. ii, 483, and (redrawn) *Gazette des Beaux-Arts* 34 (1886), 244 = Rayet and Collignon 333. I, Eros standing on the back of a Maltese dog and driving it. *Iunonenes pocolom* (with dittography). An askos in the form of a satyr riding a goat (see p. 194) and a glass alabastron (*Annali* 7884 pl. B, 1 and 2) were found in the same tomb, and there is nothing against their belonging to the same interment. *CIL*. i, 2² no. 444.

4. Vatican, from Orte. Ritschl pl. 10, f and F. I, Eros. *Salutes· pocolom*. *CIL*. i, 2² no. 450.

5. Rome, Terme, 16107, from Rome. Ryberg fig. 153. I, Hermes.

6. Tarquinia 1960, from Tarquinia. I, *ML*. 36, 487, right; *Scritti Nogara* pl. 2, 1–3. I, Eros. The things on the platter seem to be two conical cakes, a round fruit, and three small fruits stuck on a skewer (see *AJA*. 1944, 357 and 361). The underside of the foot is reserved, with some black spilth of poor quality.[1]

7. Vatican, from Vulci (according to *CIL*.; from Orte according to Picard). *Mus. Greg.* ii pl. 88, 1, whence Ritschl pl. 10, d and D; I, *Mél. d'arch*. 30 pl. 3. Eros. *Keri· pocolom*. Four pre-impressed palmettes (see p. 223). *CIL*. i, 2² no. 445.

8. Vatican, from Orte. *Mus. Greg.* ii, pl. 88, 2, whence Ritschl pl. 10, e and E; I, *Mél. d'arch*. 30 pl. 2. Eros. *Lavernai· pocolom*. Four pre-impressed rosettes. *CIL*. i, 2² no. 446.

9. Louvre. I, Ritschl pl. 11, G; I, Pottier *Le dessin chez les grecs* pl. 15, 78. I, female head *Belolai· pocolom*. Belolai is simply a mistake for Belonai. I do not think there are any serpents in the hair: the head does not represent the goddess. The border is the usual red band between two white lines. The ivy leaves are white, the berries and the inscription yellow. *CIL*. i, 2² no. 441. The provenience is unknown: 'found at Florence' (Warmington *Remains of Old Latin* iv, 75) is due to a misunderstanding of certain words in *CIL*.

10. Cassel. I, Eros flying with torch and dish. The border is the usual red band between

---

[1] The stemless cup figured beside this (*ML*. 36, 487, left) and said to be in the same technique is really Attic red-figure of about 400 B.C., and has nothing to do with 'the best Faliscan and Etruscan vases'.

two white lines; outside this, a dancetty band, with invected outline, in yellow and red; white ivy-leaves, sideways, in the angles. There are patterns of the same type on Gnathian vases—a trozzella in Lecce (*CV*. IV Ds pl. 2, 2–3) and an oinochoe in Brussels (A 732: *CV*. IV Dc pl. 1, 2)—it is a variant of a common Gnathian pattern, in which the bands lie flat.

*Plate*

11. Villa Giulia 23949, from Capena. *CV*. IV Bq pll. 3 and 5; Ducati *L'Italia antica*[1] pl. 40; I, phot. Alinari 41116, whence Rostovtzeff *History of the Ancient World* ii pl. 11, 1, and Pl. 39, 1. War-elephant.

The ten bowls seem to be by one hand. The Laverna vase in the Vatican, no. 8, although perhaps not so characteristic as the rest, can hardly be separated from them. Of the uninscribed pieces, no. 10 was connected with the inscribed by Möbius, no. 6 by Bianchi Bandinelli (*Scritti Nogara* 11–13), no. 5 by Mrs. Ryberg (139). Zahn added the Elephant plate, no. 11 (*Bull. van de Vereeniging* 2, ii, 4). The patternwork shows that it belongs to the Volcani Group; but whether the figures are by the same hand as those on the bowls is another question.

The technique of the bowls is simpler than in the Hesse Group. White flesh; details in diluted glaze, yellow to brown. Little shading: sometimes on the wings; in the Tarquinia bowl, no. 6, the situla on the ground is fully shaded. The favourite border is a red band between two white lines. In no. 5 the chlamys of Hermes is red, except for a band at the edge. In no. 5 Hermes, though full-grown, has white flesh, like the woman and the children. This is the technique of the figures, heads, &c., on ordinary Gnathia vases.

The technique of the Elephant plate, no. 11 (Pl. 39, 1), is more elaborate: yellow (made by mixing diluted glaze with white), white, brown (for the flesh of the men), red (for the greater part of the saddle-cloth). The elephants have much detail in diluted glaze. The border next the picture is the usual red band between two white lines.

The red band between two white lines is not uncommon in Gnathian: Bianchi Bandinelli gives some examples (op. cit. 15), and others could be added. The sessile kantharoi are especially in point, because there, as in the Volcani Group, the band and lines border a tondo: London F 591, from Basilicata (A, *CV*. IV Dc pl. 4, 4); London F 593 (Hancarville 2 pll. 39–40; I, *CV*. IV Dc pl. 4, 2); London F 592 (I, *CV*. IV Dc pl. 6, 9); Munich (A, Lau pl. 34, 4); Oxford 1944.14; Princeton (inside, a swan; outside, rf. female heads in not the latest A.P. style).

The child Erotes are not interesting, nor is the Hermes, nor the female head on the Bellona bowl. The masterpiece of the group is the Elephant plate (Pl. 39, 1), which deserves attention.

On elephants in antiquity, see S. Reinach in Daremberg and Saglio s.v. elephas; Snijder in *Bulletin van de Vereeniging* 2, i, 9–11, and 2, ii, 4 (with contributions from Zahn); Bikerman *Institutions des Séleucides* 61–2; Bieńkowski *Les Celtes dans les arts mineurs* (abbreviated as *C.*) 141–50; Tarn *Hellenistic Military and Naval Developments* 92–100, and in *JHS*. 60, 84–9.

We begin with a list of ancient representations of elephants endorsed with towers, as in the Villa Giulia plate: πυργοφόροι ἐλέφαντες (Plut. *Parallela* 307b): the Elephant and Castle:

### Clay

α. Louvre. Fragment (relief from the interior) of a Calene phiale. Pagenstecher *Cal.* pl. 8, 46, whence *Mon. Piot* 21, 193; Bieńkowski *C.* 143. I cannot make out the position of the driver.

β1. Louvre, from Myrina. Figurine. Pottier and S. Reinach *Myrina* pl. 10, 1, whence Daremberg and Saglio, s.v. elephas, fig. 2623, and Winter *Typen* ii, 385, 3; Bieńkowski *C.* 142 fig. 212; Rostovtzeff *History of the Hellenistic World* i, pl. 52, 2.

β2. Athens. Bieńkowski *C.* 142 fig. 213. Replica of the last.

γ. Amsterdam, from Memphis. Lamp of red clay, covered with black glaze (Snijder). *Bull. van de Vereeniging* 2, i, 9 fig. 1; Bieńkowski *C.* 146, fig. 217. The attitude of the mahout, his head-dress, and the size of the saddle-cloth, connect this with B and C, although the fabric is different.

λ. Once Cairo, Fouquet, 384, from Memphis. Askos of black clay. Perdrizet *Les Terres cuites grecques d'Egypte de la collection Fouquet* pl. 95, 4, whence Bieńkowski *C.* 148 fig. 225. The upper part of the ring-handle is lost and the top of the tower which serves as the spout is damaged.

ε. Once Cairo, Fouquet, 386, from Benha. Lamp, of brown clay. Perdrizet op. cit., pl. 95, 1, whence Bieńkowski *C.* 148 fig. 226. There is said to have been a tower, but it is missing. There seems to be no driver.

ʒ. Naples inv. 124845, from Pompeii. Said to be a vessel. The left side, *NSc.* 1897, 25, whence Winter *Typen* ii, 385, 4, and *Mon. Piot* 21, 194; the right side, Alda Levi *Le terrecotte figurate del Museo Nazionale di Napoli* pl. 13, 1=Bieńkowski *C.* 144. Described by Sogliano in *NSc.* 1897, 26. The driver looks like a negro.

### Limestone

η. Amsterdam, from the Delta (Galiub?). Cake-mould. *Bulletin van de Vereeniging* 2, i, fig. 2.

### Silver

θ. Leningrad. Two 'phalerae'. One of them, Kondakov and Tolstoi *Antiquités de la Russie méridionale* 427; Smirnov *Argenterie orientale* pl. 170, whence Rostovtzeff *History of the Hellenistic World* i, pl. 53, 1, Trever *Monuments of Graeco-Bactrian Art* pl. 1. These seem to be later copies, from the Roman period, of a Hellenistic original.

ι. Formerly in the collection of Imhoof-Blumer. Silver (two-litra piece?), coined in Italy, most probably by Hannibal. Imhoof-Blumer and Keller *Tier- und Pflanzenbilder auf Münzen und Gemmen* pl. 4, 4.

### Lead[1]

κ. London, from France. Cut-out relief. Bieńkowski *C.* 145. The upper part of the tower is missing.

---

[1] The cut-out relief from Alexandria, formerly in the Fouquet collection (385: Perdrizet op. cit. pl. 95, 3; Bieńkowski *C.* 146 fig. 220), is also of lead (not clay, as Bieńkowski says), but as there is no castle it does not concern us here. The lead cut-out in Dresden (Bieńkowski *C.* 146 fig. 219) is not a replica.

We now return to the Villa Giulia plate. An Indian elephant. A baby elephant follows it, and according to Zahn (a very accurate observer) is tied to the mother's tail by a rope: I wish I could verify this particular. The end of the baby's trunk shows on this side of the mother's hind leg. The eyes of the animals are small as they should be, for the larger rings probably represent a fold of skin and not the outline of the eye. The saddle-cloth is coloured red, with a white border (there are not two cloths, one over the other, as Giglioli): this corresponds to the πόρφυραι mentioned by Plutarch, *Eum.* 14 . . . τὰς πορφύρας . . . ὅσπερ ἦν κόσμος αὐτοῖς εἰς μάχην ἀγομένοις. In the terracotta from Myrina (B) the cloth is also painted red.[1] The howdah is fastened by three bands attached to the base and passing round the animal: in the terracotta from Pompeii the bands are seen to be chains. The howdah is a crenellated tower (πύργος, Plutarch *Eum.* 14, Arrian *Tact.* 2, 4; θωράκιον, Aelian *HA.* 13, 9) (no doubt of wood, perhaps covered with skins), protected by a large shield on the near side (and naturally by another on the off side). The rim of the shield is clearly marked. These shields also occur in α, γ, 3, a pair of them in β; in the terracotta from Myrina (β1) they are painted blue, and the castle red. Two warriors are seen in the tower (οἱ πυργομαχοῦντες Polyb. 5, 84, 2), frontal, helmeted, spear in the right hand, shield on the left arm. The projection in the middle of the helmet is probably the crest in front-view, foreshortened, while the side-projections may be raised cheekpieces. We should doubtless think of two other warriors manning the off side of the tower, making a crew of four (Livy 37, 40, 'tergo impositae turres turribusque superstantes praeter rectorem quaterni armati'). These are occidentals: the mahout on the other hand is an Indian, as was usual in antiquity: so in the earliest recorded Greek representation of elephants, on the hearse of Alexander, ὁ δὲ δεύτερος πίναξ εἶχε τοὺς ἐπακολουθοῦντας τῆι θεραπείαι ἐλέφαντας κεκοσμημένους πολεμικῶς, ἀναβάτας ἔχοντας ἐκ μὲν τῶν ἔμπροσθεν Ἰνδούς, ἐκ δὲ τῶν ὄπισθεν Μακεδόνας καθωπλισμένους τῆι συνήθει σκευῆι, Diodoros 18, 27 (this means of course that each elephant had an Indian in front—the driver—and several Macedonians behind, the fighting crew). The mahout, as Della Seta noted, wears a 'Phrygian cap' (tiara), the flaps of which show at the nape. He rests his left hand on the back of the elephant, looks up, and raises his right hand with the goad. The head-dress of the mahout varies in the ancient representations: in Band γ it seems to be a sugar-loaf hat covering the ears; I do not know whether there is any indication of flaps; in α it is said to be 'an Oriental leather cap covering the ears so that only the face shows', in the terracotta Fouquet 387 (Perdrizet op. cit. pl. 95, 2, whence Bieńkowski *C.* 149) to be 'a sort of fez'; in the silver reliefs (θ) it has a more Indian look, like a kind of turban. The goad (ἄρπη, Aelian *NH.* 13, 9)[2] is regularly of the same boat-hook form as here, with crook as well as point: so in α and η, also on a Hispano-Carthaginian stater of

---

[1] In the Leningrad silver reliefs (θ) the cloth is elaborately ornamented: wave-pattern on the border; in the middle, lozengy; then a transverse border of circles within rectangles; then a large figure of a kētos. According to Rostovtzeff (op. cit. i, 433) 'the dragon which ornaments the rug is the forerunner of the Chinese and Sasanian dragons': but as it stands it is pure Greek.

[2] A Greek word κυσπίς with this meaning is known to S. Reinach (in Daremberg and Saglio s.v. elephas, 541) and also to Wellmann (in PW. s.v. Elefant 2257), but not to me. The Latin word *cuspis* is used by Silius Italicus, 9, 572, 'moderantem cuspide Lucas Maurum in bella boves'; but this does not show the word to have been a technical term for the mahout's goad.

the late third century B.C. (Imhoof-Blumer and Keller pl. 4, 1), a bronze coin of Tiberius (ibid. pl. 4, 5), a bronze coin of Nicaea, probably from the time of Elagabalus (Daremberg and Saglio s.v. elephas fig. 2627; Waddington *Recueil général* pl. 81, 32), a nicolo in Berlin, 6745 (Imhoof-Blumer and Keller pl. 19, 43), the late Antonine sarcophagus with the Triumph of Dionysos from the Via Salaria (*Mél. d'arch.* 8 pl. 12, whence *Jb.* 15, 217), an ivory diptychon in the British Museum quoted by Reinach and attributed by Delbrueck to the middle of the fifth century A.D. (Daremberg and Saglio s.v. diptychon fig. 2460; Delbrueck *Die Consulardiptychen* pl. 59 and p. 288: see also—I owe the reference to Dr. Otto Kurz—E. Weigand in *Kritische Berichte z. kunstgesch. Literatur* 1930–1, 51). In the terracotta from Pompeii (ξ) there seems to be a crook and no point; in some of the other figures the shape is not clear. The form has not changed in the last 2,200 years: it is the modern ankus, Sanskrit ankuça, and this was no doubt what Indians called it in the third century B.C.

So much I had written when Dr. Otto Kurz drew my attention to a recent article by R. Goossens, *Gloses indiennes dans le lexique d'Hésychius*, in *L'Antiquité Classique* 12 (1943), 52, which I quote:

Ἀγγόρπης· ᾧ τοὺς ἐλέφαντας τύπτουσι σιδήρῳ. ὄρπη· σίδηρος ἐν ᾧ τὸν ἐλέφαντα τύπτουσιν. γάνδαρος· ὁ ταυροκράτης παρ' Ἰνδοῖς.

'What connexion between ἀγγόρπης and ὄρπη, both designating "an iron instrument with which one strikes elephants"? The first element in ἀγγόρπης must be aṅka, "crook", or aṅkuśa, which in fact, according to the dictionaries, is specialized in the sense of "crook serving to excite the elephant". The second element is more enigmatic: one does not see to what Sanskrit term it could correspond, and on the other hand it bears a curious resemblance to ὄρπη. Now ὄρπη is a Greek word. It is an Aeolic form of ἄρπη, which is the very word used by Aelian (*Nat. An.* xiii, 22) to designate the goad serving to drive elephants. It is now clear that the compound ἀγγόρπη never existed: this monstrous form arose from the carelessness of a copyist who combined in a single word two glosses which Hesychius (or one of his readers?) had put together because their meaning was the same.'

Perhaps I may add that ἀγγόρπης (or ἀγγόρπη), from *ἄγγα (=aṅka) and ὄρπη, does not seem to me an impossible Greek compound of the ἰατρόμαντις, σακκοπήρα, type.

Oswald Couldrey and Dr. Otto Kurz have kindly informed me about representations of the ankus in early Indian art:

Bharhut (second half of the second century B.C.): Ramaprasad Chanda *Mediaeval Indian Sculpture in the British Museum* pl. 3a.

Sanchi (middle of the first century B.C.): Marshall and Foucher *The Monuments of Sanchi* 2 pl. 12, pl. 16, pl. 57.

Begram in Afghanistan (first century A.D.): Engraved ivory plaque: a mahout preparing to mount the elephant: he holds the ankus in his right hand: it has the same simple form as in our plate, but just below the spring of the heads there is a crosspiece or ring.

Gandhara relief in Boston (second or third century A.D. according to Coomaraswamy): *Art Bulletin* 9, 321.

Later representations are innumerable.

It will be noticed that the earliest of the Indian representations is much later than the

Villa Giulia plate. So are the earliest Persian, on embossed silver roundels assigned by Dalton to the second century A.D. (Dalton *Treasure of the Oxus*² pl. 28, 199 and 200).

The Begram elephant has a bell tied round his middle. A bell appears in several of the Western representations though not in the Villa Giulia plate, but it hangs round the neck.

The modern mahout rides astride the elephant's neck, with his legs behind its ears and often entirely concealed by them; and so in antiquity: in our plate, and in most of the ancient representations, the legs of the mahout disappear behind the elephant's ears. Aelian and Philostratos speak of the mahout as guiding the elephant with the goad (τὸν τὴν ἅρπην ἔχοντα Διὰ χειρῶν καὶ ἐκείνηι τὸν θῆρα ἰθύνοντα *NH*. 13, 9; εὐθύνειν αὐτὸ καλαύροπι, ἣν ὁρᾶις αὐτὸν ἐμβαλόντα τῶι ἐλέφαντι ὥσπερ ἄγκυραν *Vit. Ap.* 2, 11), but the modern mahout guides with his knees, and only uses the ankus if the animal is obstreperous; this was doubtless so in antiquity too, and the writers are at fault. On our plate the elephant is as quiet as can be, and the mahout is not striking it but waving his ankus. The presence of the baby would be odd, if the elephant were going into battle: this must be only a parade or march past.

This is one of the earliest European representatives of an elephant, and it is natural to follow Della Seta and connect it with the elephants brought to Italy in the army of King Pyrrhus, 280–276 B.C. The art of the Volcani Group, as of the Berlin kantharos and its companions (p. 208), is derived from 'Gnathia' models: there is nothing Etruscan in it, or at least in the painting: the vases were certainly made in Latium, but quite likely by Tarentine settlers. The painter either saw elephants, or a good representation of them: if he was an immigrant from Taranto, he may have seen them. Jacobsthal suggests to me that his chief model was a silver emblema similar to the original of the phalerae in Leningrad (p. 212, θ).

*b* (see p. 209)
*Bowls*

Rome, Antiquarium ?, fr., from Rome (Esquiline). I, *Annali* 1880 pl. R, 6. *Me*[nervai· pocolom]. Towards the middle of the interior, the usual red band between white lines. There was very likely a figure within this, but nothing of it is preserved. Nearer the edge, a yellow wreath of the same type as in no. 8 (p. 210), but not the same.

*c* (see p. 209)
*Bowl*

London F 604, from Vulci. I, Ritschl pl. 10, b and B; Walters *HAP.* i, 490; *CV.* IV Dc pl. 6, 8; phot. Mansell 778. I, wreath. *Aecetiai· pocolom*. Four pre-impressed rosettes. The underside of the foot is untidily covered with black. *CIL.* i, 2² no. 439.

*d* (see p. 209)
*Bowl?* (called a 'patera')

Once Rome, Secchi, from Orte. The decoration seems not to be recorded. *Coera· pocolo*. *CIL.* i, 2² no. 442: the first word is no doubt, as said there, Coerai (= Curae) with the *i* omitted by mistake: not Coera(s), as Lindsay, or a dative (Ryberg 135).

*e* (see p. 209)
### *Oinochoai* (shape XX)

1. Cab. Méd., from Terra di Otranto. *CIL.* x no. 258, whence *CIL.* i, $2^2$ no. 443 and Daremberg and Saglio s.v. poculum. The body striated. On the neck *Fortunai· pocolo·* with a stop at the end as well as between the words.
2. London, fr., from Lanuvium. *NSc.* 1895, 45, whence *CIL.* i, $2^2$ no. 452. As the last, but *Vestaipocolo* (complete). Lustrous black, with a greenish tinge.

Both vases are incomplete, the lip and the greater part of the handle being lost. The lip was probably flat, and the shape what we call 'oinochoe shape XX' (see p. 257).

*f* (see p. 209)
### *Oinochoai* (the exact shape not known: as in *e*?)

1. Tarquinia, from Tarquinia. Striated ('with gilt dots' according to Garrucci). *Veneres· pocolom. CIL.* i, $2^2$ no. 451.
2. Tarquinia, from Tarquinia. As the last, but *Menervai· pocolom. CIL.* i, $2^2$ no. 447.

Wolters pointed out (*AM.* 38, 194–5) that these are the vases of which Pagenstecher had given an inaccurate description (*Cal.* 15).

*g* (see p. 209)
### *Oinochoe* (mug, of special shape, with ring-handle)

Louvre L 604. Ritschl pl. 10, a and A. Plain black (rather bad greenish glaze). Buff clay. On the upper part of the body, *Saeturni· pocolom* in white. *CIL.* i, $2^2$ no. 449.

## P. A KANTHAROS IN TARQUINIA

We have already referred to a vase from Tarquinia, in Tarquinia (p. 180), with figures superposed on black background in clay-red and then worked up with high-lights. Unpublished: but half of it may be seen on the extreme right in Moscioni's photograph of the Sala Quinta in the old Corneto Museum (8259). It is a large kantharos of a special shape: in *RG.* 93 I gave a list of such kantharoi, which nearly all belong to a single third-century fabric, the 'Malacena Group' (see pp. 230–3). I mentioned the Tarquinia vase at the end of my list, but did not include it, as I am not sure that it is from the same fabric as the rest.

The handles are double and knotted, as in the Malacena Group. At the lower ends they turn into paws. The underside of the foot is reserved, not black as in the Malacena kantharoi. Below the picture, a broad band of lines criss-crossing to form diamonds, with a dot in the middle of each diamond; below that, in white, ivy, the leaves pointing downwards. On A, a woman running to left, looking round; a young satyr running to left, fluting; a satyr running to left, looking round. On B, a naked woman running, a woman dancing, a satyr dancing, all to left; on the right, a large vessel, like a pointed amphora, set in a stand.

Q

*Plates*

1. Villa Giulia 15321, from Capena.  I, *CV*. IV Bq pl. 4, 1.  Stamnos between two plants.
2. Villa Giulia 25923, from Capena.  I, *CV*. IV Bq pl. 4, 2.  Goose with serpent in beak.

The decoration is 'in white and yellow'.  There does not seem to be any special connexion between these and the Elephant plate (Pl. 39, 1 and p. 211) from the same site.

A third plate, with decoration in white, is mentioned by Della Seta (*Mus. di Villa Giulia* 348), but I have no further information about it:

Villa Giulia 23950, from Capena.  I, a bird approaching a bowl to drink; round, two wreaths of olive.

It would be worth looking at the following to see if they might prove to be from the same fabric as the two plates:

*Oinochoai*

(shape XX: see p. 257, foot)

1. Rome, Palatine, from Rome (Palatine).  *NSc.* 1907, 203, 1; Ryberg fig. 133a.
2. Rome, Palatine, from Rome (Palatine).  *NSc.* 1907, 203, 5.
3. Rome, Mus. del Foro, from Rome (Cloaca Maxima).  Ryberg fig. 133b.
4. Toronto 518.  Robinson and Harcum pl. 89.

(shape III)

5. Villa Giulia, from Capena.  Della Seta *L'Italia antica*[1] 152 fig. 162, 6.

(shape VII: beaked jug)

6. Villa Giulia, from Capena.  Della Seta *L'Italia antica*[1] 152 fig. 162, 4.  See below, under R, and compare, for the shape, the black beaked jug Copenhagen 539, from Volterra (*CV*. pl. 223, 3).

Perhaps the Van Deman askos and its companions in Cambridge and New York University (p. 273) might also be considered in such a context.

R

*Beaked jugs* (oinochoai shape VII) with simple decoration

(i) a group

1. Villa Giulia, from Capena.  Della Seta *L'It. ant.*[1] 152 fig. 162, 4.
2. Geneva.  Decoration as in no. 1.
3. Philadelphia MS 4050.
4. Castiglioncello, from Castiglioncello.  *NSc.* 1924, 164 fig. 5, 5.
5. London market (Sotheby, *Cat. 14 May 1946*, no. 107, 2, from the collection of Col. T. A. Ross).  On the body a band of olive or laurel; on the neck a wreath: both in white with yellow details.  Two nicks near the base.

(ii) sundry

1. Toronto 498 (bought from Pacini of Florence).  Robinson and Harcum pl. 86.
2. Arles, Musée Lapidaire.  Ivy.

3. London 1915.12–29.2. *CV*. IV Dc pl. 4, 19. According to A. H. Smith 'attributed to Altenburg near Cologne'; but should be Etruscan.
4. Würzburg 811. Langlotz pl. 236. Striated above and below the mid-band.

S. THE DEMONESS GROUP

*Oinochoai* (shape II, with high handle)

1. Vatican. *Atti Pont.*, new series, 15 pl. 2c, whence Giglioli pl. 372, 4 and 6. Bird-headed demoness.
2. London F 526, from Nola. Walters *BM. Cat. iv*, 222; *CV*. IV Eb pl. 4, 6. Youthful head in tiara.
3. Copenhagen inv. Chr. VIII 49, from Bari. *CV*. pl. 218, 2. Naked youth seated.
4. Toronto 452. Robinson and Harcum pl. 82. Young satyr.

The Vatican oinochoe has been published, with a commentary, by Albizzati (*Atti Pont.* 15, 252–6). He compares two bird-headed monsters, one on an Etruscan black-figured fragment, belonging to the Orvieto Group, in Goettingen (see p. 19: Jacobsthal *Gött.V.* pl. 2, 9), the other on a fragment of a small Attic red-figured pelike, by the Pan Painter, in Berlin (ibid. 9 fig. 10; *ARV*. 365 no. 48). He thinks that the hands of the Vatican creature are bound.

The vase is not easy to place. The subject suggests that it is Etruscan, although bird-headed monsters occur elsewhere too; and the floral work at the handle recalls, as Albizzati noted, Etruscan cups with decoration in added colour—our Sokra Group (p. 201); also, we may add, the Etruscan oinochoai of our Phantom Group (pp. 205–6). In shape, however, the vase resembles a pair of oinochoai, our nos. 2 and 3, which were not found, it seems, on Etruscan sites. The pair are evidently inseparable: if only they were both from Campania or both from Apulia: but while no. 2 is said to be from Nola, no. 3 is said to be from Bari.

In the fourth oinochoe, Toronto 452, the neck is not so sharply offset as in the others. The handle is like that of the Vatican jug.

Other vases with slight decoration in added colour are more appropriately treated among the black vases.

I think it may be worth while to say something about certain groups of *Italiote* vases in the added-colour technique, as these have sometimes been confused with Etruscan and are not always easy to distinguish.

A. THE XENON GROUP: APULIAN

This Apulian fabric begins in the late part of the fifth century.

*Kantharoids*

On the shape see p. 221. Nos. 1 and 2 are unusually elaborate, but not to be separated from the smaller and simpler pieces.

1. Frankfort. *Mél. Nicole* pll. 1–2 = Furtwängler *KS.* ii, 131–3. A, unharnessing a chariot. B, patterns. On A, +ΕΝΟΝ (= ξενών according to Furtwängler).
2. Berlin inv. 4500, from Canosa. A, Roscher s.v. Sternbilder 939; A, Moll *Das Schiff in der Bildenden Kunst* Bvib. 51. A, the constellations Ship Argo and Taurus; B, stars.
3. Once Englefield. Moses *Vases from the Collection of Sir Henry Englefield Bt.* pl. 33, 1.
4. Leyden GNV. 58.
5. Sèvres 197.1. A, *CV.* pl. 46, 25.
5 bis. Oxford 1945.67.
6. Naples. A, phot. Sommer 11018, viii, 10, whence *BCH.* 1911 pl. 9, 140.
7. Naples. Phot. Sommer 11018, ix, 6, whence *BCH.* 1911 pl. 9, 141.
8. Sèvres 196. *CV.* pl. 46, 14 and 29.
9. Sèvres 289. *CV.* pl. 46, 17 and 28.
10. Toronto 542. A, Robinson and Harcum pl. 91.
11. London, no number. A, *CV.* IV Eb pl. 4, 10.
12. London, no number. *CV.* IV Eb pl. 4, 4.

*Kantharoi* (sessile: imitations of the Attic kantharoi of the Saint-Valentin class[1])

13. Naples. A, phot. Sommer 11018, vi, 7, whence *BCH.* 1911 pl. 9, 128.
14. Copenhagen 337, from Bari. *CV.* pl. 272, 8.
15. Copenhagen 336. *CV.* pl. 272, 6.
16. Sèvres 212.1. A, *CV.* pl. 46, 18.
17. Toronto 468. A, Robinson and Harcum pl. 84.
18. Toronto 467. A, Robinson and Harcum pl. 84.
19. Naples. Phot. Sommer 11018, ix, 7, whence *BCH.* 1911 pl. 9, 154.
20. London (old no. 1253). *CV.* IV Eb pl. 2, 14.
21. Lecce 884, from Taranto. *CV.* IV Dr pl. 55, 1 and 4.
22. Lecce 883, from Taranto. *CV.* IV Dr pl. 55, 2 and 5.
23. Lecce 1593, from Rugge. *CV.* IV Dr pl. 55, 3 and 6.
24. Naples. A, phot. Sommer 11018, vi, 9, whence *BCH.* 1911 pl. 9, 129.
24 bis. Naples. A, phot. Sommer 11014, vi, 7.
25. Oxford 1874.398.
25 bis. Carshalton, Mrs. Landreth. Above, uprights; then, on A, floral—palmettes and flowers—, on B, ivy; then wave-pattern.
26. Copenhagen inv. 7971. A, *CV.* pl. 272, 7.
27. London 47.8–6.48. *CV.* IV Eb pl. 4, 2 and p. 5. ΕΥΠΟΛΙΣΚΑΛ complete.

[1] On the Saint-Valentin class, so called after the kantharos found at La Motte Saint-Valentin (A, Déchelette *Coll. Millon* pl. 31), see Zahn in Déchelette *Coll. Millon* 131, Jacobsthal and Langsdorff 62, Haspels *ABL.* 183–5. It includes (1) sessile kantharoi of the same shape as that from La Motte Saint-Valentin; (2) a small kantharos like the last but with a phallus substituted for one of the handles (Cab. Méd. 475; *CV.* pl. 68, 10–11); (3) a sessile kantharos of a different type (London 73.8–20.380: *CV.* III Ic pl. 32, 15); (4) skyphoi type A (e.g. Oxford 1945.66 and those mentioned below, p. 222); (5) skyphoi of Corinthian type (London 64.10–7.1675, *CV.* III Ic pl. 32, 14).

(1) and (4) had a long life, beginning before the middle of the fifth century and lasting into the fourth.

The sessile kantharos Todi 507 (*CV.* pl. 12, 8), called 'Etrusco-Campanian' in the *Corpus*, is Attic of the Saint-Valentin class.

## Skyphoi

28. Once Englefield. A, Moses *Vases from the Collection of Sir Henry Englefield Bart.* pl. 31, 4.
28 bis. Oxford 1945.53.
29. Naples. A, phot. Sommer 11018, ix, 2, whence *BCH.* 1911 pl. 9, 146.
30. Goettingen F 35.
31. Naples. A, phot. Sommer 11018, ix, 1, whence *BCH.* 1911 pl. 9, 174.

## *Dish* (like a stemless cup, but handleless)

32. London, no number. *CV.* IV Eb pl. 3, 3.

## Oinochoai
### (shape II)

33. Würzburg 831. Langlotz pl. 123.
34. Naples. Phot. Sommer 11018, vi, 11, whence *BCH.* 1911 pl. 9, 139.
35. London, no number. *CV.* IV Eb pl. 4, 8.
36. Sèvres 94. *CV.* pl. 46, 20.
36 bis. Hamburg. *Anz.* 1909, 1, 42.

### (shape I)

37. Ancona 1011.
38. Taranto, from Canosa.
39. Taranto, from Canosa. I seem to remember that there are many like nos. 38 and 39 in Taranto, from Canosa.

### (shape X)

40. London WT 152, from Bari. *CV.* IV Eb pl. 4, 5.
41. London 1915.4–15.1. *CV.* IV Eb pl. 4, 1.
42. Once Munich, Preyss.
43. Łańcut, Count Potocki. *CV.* pl. 1 (Pol. pl. 129), 12.
44. Brussels.
45. Ancona 5032, from Numana.
46. Once Munich, Preyss. A little squat.

### (shape VIII: mugs)

47. Ancona.
48. Würzburg 830. Langlotz pl. 239.
49. Naples. Phot. Sommer 11018, v, 10, whence *BCH.* 1911, pl. 9, 137.
50. Poznań, Miss Ruxer. *CV.* pl. 2 (Pol. 123), 13.
51. Leyden K 95.1.5.
52. Once Englefield. Moses *Vases from the Collection of Sir Henry Englefield Bart.* pl. 31, 1.
53. Oxford 1945.46.

## Bottle

54. London (old no. 1798). *CV.* IV Dc pl. 8, 4.

I noted kantharoi like nos. 13–27, and skyphoi like nos. 28–31, in the Museum of Taranto, but have no particulars.

A skyphos in Compiègne, 880, from Nola (A, *CV*. pl. 27, 13), would also seem to belong to the group.

According to Furtwängler (*KS*. ii, 131) a kantharoid, decorated with patterns, in Stuttgart, and three others in Bari have the same handles, mouth, belly, foot as the Frankfort Xenon vase, while Berlin 3664, from Nola, is different and rougher. Berlin 3666 and 3667 no doubt go with nos. 9–12 in our list.

The mugs Berlin 3668 and 3669 sound as if they belonged to the Xenon Group like nos. 47–53.

The kantharos Würzburg 622 (A, Langlotz pl. 216) is very like nos. 13–27 in our list, yet I do not feel quite sure that it belongs to the Xenon Group. Three small kantharoi go together and may belong to the group: Würzburg 829 (B, Langlotz pl. 123), Sèvres 212.2 (A, *CV*. pl. 46, 15), Cracow, Technical Museum, inv. 9733 (A, *CV*. pl. 2, Pol. pl. 95, 7); perhaps also Sèvres 212.3 (*CV*. pl. 46, 26), with a swan on each side.

A vase in London has the same shape, barring details, as the 'Xenons' in Frankfort and Berlin (nos. 1 and 2), but seems to stand somewhat apart from the Xenon Group:

London F 523, from Egnazia. *CV*. IV Eb pl. 4, 3. A, griffin. B, ivy. There were plastic masks at the lower spring of the handles, but they are missing.

Other vases of the same shape form a group distinct from the Xenon: the lower part of the body is reeded:

1. New York 41.162.39. A, *CV*. Gallatin pl. 63, 4.
2. Taranto, from Ceglie. On the shoulder, ivy in white.
3. Berlin 3665.

A reeded vase in Bari may go with these.

The shape is thought to be derived from Peucetian (Price in the text to *CV*. IV Eb pl. 4, 3): I do not know what is the relation between it and the late-fifth-century Attic kantharoids described in *V. Pol.* 70–1 (see also *ARV*. 782 and 855).

## B. OTHER IMITATIONS OF SAINT-VALENTIN VASES

### (i)

### *Kantharoi*

1. Bonn 160. A, *CV*. pl. 23, 6.
2. Baltimore, once Van Deman. A, *CV*. Robinson iii pl. 32, 1.
3. Florence, from Populonia. A, *NSc*. 1934, 417, 4.

These are imitations of Attic kantharoi of the Saint-Valentin Group (see p. 219). So were the Xenon Group kantharoi described on p. 219; but in our three the shape is a different model, with shorter cul, and a groove on the foot. The technique, too, is not the same. The Van Deman vase uses white as well as red; so, apparently, does the

Florence vase; while in Bonn 160 the dots and upright strokes instead of being in added colour are black on a reserved band, and the ivy-leaves are reserved.

It would not be strange if there were *skyphoi* that bore the same relation to those of the Saint-Valentin Group as our three kantharoi to the Saint-Valentin kantharoi: and such, I think, is the skyphos Toronto 526 (A, Robinson and Harcum pl. 90). Philadelphia 2830, from Ardea (A, *Boll. st. med.* 4, 4–5, pl. 2, 22) is akin to Toronto 526.

A kantharos in London, T 595 (A, *CV*. IV Eb pl. 2, 15), is nearer to our three than to the kantharoi of the Xenon Group, and seems to use two colours.

A kantharos formerly in the Schiller collection (Zahn *Sg. Schiller* pl. 36, 419) goes with the kantharoi of the Xenon Group in shape, but uses white as well as red, and can hardly belong to the group. A kantharos published by Caylus (4 pl. 38, 11) perhaps recalls the Schiller one, but is said to use white only.

A skyphos from Ferento, in Florence (?) (A, *NSc.* 1905, 34, f), is not quite like any of these kantharoi or skyphoi, but nearest to Toronto 526. Another from the same site (ibid., d) looks as if it might be comparable to the first, but according to Pernier the decoration is 'in brown on the light ground'.

I cannot say anything about the fabric of these skyphoi and kantharoi except that they are not Attic.

(ii)

The following group, on the other hand, can be placed: it is Campanian. The models are Attic skyphoi of the Saint-Valentin Group: compare specially, among these, London 90.7–31.32 (A, *CV*. III Ic pl. 32, 13), Copenhagen inv. 1414 (A, *CV*. pl. 159, 2), Bologna 513 (A, Zannoni pl. 83, 6, where the white wreath has been omitted by the draughtsman).

*Skyphoi*

1. Naples, from Cumae. A, *ML.* 22 pl. 109, 1.
2. Bremen, Focke Museum, 2520. A, Schaal *Brem.* pl. 26, c.
3. Amsterdam inv. 3442. A, *CV*. IV Dc pl. 2 (Pays Bas 46), 2.
4. Naples, from Cumae. A, *ML.* 22, pl. 109, 3.
5. Capua, from Capua. *CV*. IV Er pl. 45, 8–9. Mingazzini mentions another in Capua, unpublished.
6. Amsterdam inv. 3443. A, *CV*. IV Dc pl. 2 (Pays Bas 46), 2.
7. Naples 147985, from Frignano Piccolo. A, *NSc.* 1937, 119, 7.
8. Harvard 25.1908. *CV*. pl. 36, 7.
9. Naples. A, phot. Sommer 11016, iv, 12.

I cannot tell from the illustration whether a skyphos in Naples, from Castellamare di Stabia, belongs to our group or not (A, *NSc.* 1933, 344, 1, 3), or how it stands to the lekythos with decoration in added colour found in the same tomb (ibid. 1, 2).

## C. THE HANAU GROUP: APULIAN
### *Stemless cups (cup-skyphoi)*

On each side, an owl between olive-branches—the 'glaux' decoration referred to on pp. 200–1.

1. Taranto, from Taranto.
2. Cracow, Techn. Mus., inv. 9725. A, *CV*. pl. 2 (Pol. pl. 95), 6.
3. Hanau, from Rückingen near Hanau. Lindenschmit *Alterthümer unserer heidnischen Vorzeit* iii, part 7, text to pl. 1: fig. 2.

### D. APULIAN

Although I have nothing to compare with it, I draw attention to a vase in Berlin for three reasons: it is an unusually elaborate piece, it is well published, and its provenience is known:

#### *Volute-krater*

Berlin 3238, from Pomarico. A, *El.* 1 pl. 70; A and side, Jacobsthal *O.* pl. 114. A, Athena and Nike. B, centaur. On the shoulder, A, lion, griffin, and panther.

### E. THE RED-SWAN GROUP: APULIAN?

Stemless cups with, inside only, a lip. Half on the lip, half off it, a laurel-wreath. In the middle, usually within a pair of lines, a swan or goose (nos. 1–8), a palmette (nos. 9–10), a pair of palmettes (no. 11), a star (nos. 12–13). The central design is sometimes painted on top of an impressed design (small palmettes, or a rosette: see Wolters in *Mü. Jb.* 11 (1920–1), 116 and Mercklin in *Anz.* 1928, 346–7). Outside, laurel. No incision.
    None of these vases has the provenience recorded.

#### *Stemless cups*

1. London, no number. I, *CV*. IV Eb pl. 3, 8.
2. London, no number. I, *CV*. IV Eb pl. 3, 2.
3. Oxford 446.
4. Goettingen.
5. London market (Sotheby, ex Admiral Mark Kerr).
6. Naples 2650, 'from Etruria'. I, phot. Sommer 11018, vii, 2, whence *BCH*. 1911 pl. 9, 150. Pre-impressed.
7. Naples. I, phot. Sommer 11018, vii, 4, whence *BCH*. 1911 pl. 9, 151. The central design is obscure.
8. Hamburg 1917.991. I, *Anz.* 1928, 347. Pre-impressed.
9. London, no number. I, *CV*. IV Eb pl. 3, 9.
10. Sèvres 254. *CV*. pl. 46, 6 and 8.
11. London 59.2–16.79. *CV*. IV Eb pl. 3, 1.
12. Naples. I, phot. Sommer 11018, viii, 3, whence *BCH*. 1911 pl. 9, 152.
13. Naples. I, phot. Sommer 11016, vi, 4, whence *BCH*. 1911 pl. 8, 98. Pre-impressed?

London 67.5–8.1217 (*CV*. IV Eb pl. 3, 4) is a little different: the colour used is white not red, and the lip inside is decorated with ivy. It somewhat recalls the Paestanizing stemlesses (p. 226) and those associated with them (p. 227).
    An unpublished stemless in Copenhagen, Ny Carlsberg, H 157, would seem from Poulsen's description (*Katalog des Etruskischen Museums* 71) to be like nos. 1–8; one in

Naples (ex Santangelo) from Mercklin's description (*Anz.* 1928, 347) to be like nos. 9 and 10.  I do not know whether Naples inv. 80793, described by Mercklin (ibid.), is our no. 13 or another like it.  Mercklin also speaks (ibid. 346) of a 'handleless cup' in Bonn, 138, with the same decoration inside as the Hamburg stemless (our no. 8) but a tendril outside instead of a laurel-wreath.

A stemless in Catania, 757 (I, Libertini pl. 87: I, 'panther or griffin' according to Libertini; laurel; A–B, ivy), seems related to our group.  Mercklin (*Anz.* 1928, 347) mentions a stemless in Naples, Stg. 296, with a 'tiger' (panther?) over pre-impressed palmettes.

A pair of stemlesses are hardly to be separated from the Red-swan Group: inside, laurel, half on the lip, half off; and in the middle a rosette with *voided* petals:

### Stemless cups

1. Naples.  I, phot. Sommer 11018, vii, 1, whence *BCH*. 1911 pl. 9, 165.
2. Naples 1714.  I, phot. Sommer 11018, vii, 3, whence *BCH*. 1911 pl. 9, 149.

The same rosette with voided petals appears on another vase:

### *Plate* (the top side of the rim is flat)

Amsterdam inv. 3386, 'probably from Teano'.  I, *CV*. IV Eb–c pl. 1 (Pays Bas pl. 47), 5.  The rosette is encircled by a red band between two white lines.  The wreath is of 'wild olive'.

A plate of the same shape, formerly in the Preyss collection, Munich, is probably to be connected with the Red-swan Group.  It has a swan or goose inside, surrounded by a row of large V's set sideways, and outside that by a band of upright strokes.

Another plate of this shape is in London (no number: ex Durand 1027: from Nola: *CV*. IV Eb pl. 2, 3 and p. 4).  Inside, over a pre-impressed rosette, a palmette, surrounded by a tendril; on the topside of the rim, strokes; outside, a laurel-wreath.  A replica of this, but without pre-impression, is in Oxford (1945.50).  I do not know how close these two plates stand to the Red-swan Group.

A stemless cup in Taranto, from Francavilla Fontana (*NSc.* 1932, 402 fig. 4, 1), is decorated on the same principle as many of the stemlesses mentioned under this rubric, with a star in the middle of the interior and flowers near the edge, but between flowers and star there is a broad band of depressed striations, and the fabric is Apulian—late 'Gnathian'.

A small oinochoe of shape III, from Cumae, in Oxford, 1883.138, with a swan on it, may belong to the Red-swan Group.

### F. CAMPANIAN ?

### *Skyphoi*

1. Rome, Museo del Foro, from Rome.  A, Ryberg fig. 129a.  A, youths.
2. Rome, Palatine, fr., from Rome.  Ryberg fig. 129b.  (A piece of a himation and part of the floral decoration at the handles).

### F BIS.

Probably connected with the last, though not by the same hand as they:

#### Skyphos

1. Ensérune, Félix Mouret, from Ensérune. *CV.* pl. 13, 7–8, whence (part) Héléna *Les origines de Narbonne* 404. A, youth; B, (the like?).
2. Narbonne, fr., from Montlaurès. Héléna 405. A, youth holding a sash.

Héléna saw that the Narbonne fragment was in the same style as the fragmentary skyphos from Ensérune.

### G. THE GROUP OF LONDON F 525: CAMPANIAN

#### Hydria

1. London F 525. *CV.* IV Eb pl. 1, 8. Return of a warrior. A youth, wearing a chitoniskos with short sleeves, belted, his cloak hanging from his left arm, carries three spears over his left shoulder, and attached to them the spoils of a conquered enemy—pilos, chitoniskos, and wicker shield; he extends his right hand to take the vessel (phiale-like, but with two cup-handles) which the woman has filled from her oinochoe. Such subjects— the return of the warrior shouldering the spoils—are common in Campanian vases and wall-paintings: see Weege in *Jb.* 24, 99–162. The type of wicker shield shows that the vanquished was a Lucanian (Weege, ibid. 146).

The style of drapery, above all, connects two small vases with London F 525:

#### Squat lekythos

2. London F 533. *CV.* IV Eb pl. 1, 4 and pl. 2, 7. Mistress and maid (a woman seated with a phiale and a woman approaching her with a wreath).

#### Small pelike

3. London F 524, from Nola. *CV.* IV Eb pl. 1, 6 and pl. 2, 9. A, maenad. B, youth. Two other vases are also related:

#### Small nuptial lebes

Würzburg 812. Langlotz pl. 236. A, Eros. B, woman seated.

#### Skyphos (of Corinthian type)

London F 538, from Apulia. *CV.* IV Eb pl. 2, 13. A, warrior. B, woman with wreath and thyrsus. For the palmettes compare the squat lekythos London F 531 (p. 226 no. 8), the skyphos London F 536 (p. 226 no. 4), and the pelike London F 524 (above, no. 3). I should regard the provenience 'Apulia' as uncertain.

A comparatively important vase of which I owe photographs to the kindness of A. D. Trendall seems to form a link between the Group of London F 525 and the 'Paestanizing' Group described in the next section:

*Bell-krater*

Sydney 94. A, Dionysos seated, and a woman holding up a mirror. B, komos: a youth dancing along, beating a tympanon, and preceded by a youth holding a pail and a torch. Trendall counts the vase Paestan, and it certainly resembles Paestan red-figured vases, for instance, work by the Painter of the Boston Orestes: on the other hand attitudes, heads, palmettes, above all the style of the drapery connect it with the Group of London F 525.

## H. THE PAESTANIZING GROUP

The home of these vases may be Paestum itself, but I choose a more cautious designation. There is considerable difference of style among them, but they agree in being closely related to Paestan red-figure.

Pryce, in the *Corpus*, described nos. 4 and 8 as 'Campanian imitating Paestan', and Trendall nos. 4–6 and 8–9 as 'particularly near the style of Paestum' (*Paestan Pottery* 108 note 22).

*Stemless cups*

1. London F 539. *CV.* IV Eb pl. 3, 6. I, woman running with sashes and phiale. The costume, the plant on the right, the exergual band, the 'submerged' palmette in the exergue, the dot-rosette, all recall Paestan: compare, for example, the stemless by Python in Vienna, 602 (Trendall op. cit. pl. 20, c). For the pattern outside the cup— 'wild olive'—compare the stemless, by the Painter of Naples 1778, in Vienna, 103 (Trendall pl. 34, e).
2. Naples?, from Altavilla Silentina. I, *NSc.* 1937, 146. I, Eros. A–B, ivy.
3. Naples?, from Altavilla Silentina. I, *NSc.* 1937, 147. I, satyr. A–B, ivy. This goes with the last. The palmettes in the exergue, and the plants, are very Paestan.

*Skyphoi*

4. London F 536. *CV.* IV Eb pl. 2, 11. A, satyr; B, seated women. For the palmettes see p. 225, foot.
5. Madrid 11415 (L. 559). A, Leroux pl. 52, 2. A, satyr. B, seated women. By the same hand as the last.
6. London F 535. *CV.* IV Eb pl. 2, 10. A, satyr; B, woman. Recalls the Caivano Painter, on whom see Trendall op. cit. 84–91 and 126–7, and my notes in *JHS.* 63, 80–2.

*Squat lekythoi*

7. Sèvres 5335. *CV.* pl. 46, 2 and 4. Seated woman.
8. London F 531, from Nola. *CV.* IV Eb pl. 1, 7. Seated woman and woman. On the palmettes see p. 225, foot.

*Oinochoe* (shape II)

9. Naples 2069, from S. Agata (according to Macchioro). Patroni 151. Nike seated, and maenad. Especially near the Painter of the Boston Orestes: compare his oinochoe, shape II, Naples 946 (Trendall op. cit. pl. 32, b); for the Nike, his bell-krater Brussels

R 261 (ibid. pl. 30, a), for the maenad his bell-krater Vienna 622 (ibid. pl. 30, d). Compare also the oinochoe, shape III, Naples inv. 147867, from Aversa (*NSc.* 1937, 126). The seated figure is Nike and not a 'hermaphrodite Eros' (*BCH.* 1911, 208): cf. p. 119, middle.

### Small hydria

10. Capua 7533 (P. 32), from Capua. *CV.* IV Er pl. 17, 7 and 9. Naked youth running with sash and wreath. The attitude is like that of the satyrs on the skyphoi London F 536 and Madrid 11415 (above, nos. 4–5); the drawing of the palmette, too, is very much the same as there and in Sèvres 5335 (no. 7). In *CV.* pl. 17, 7 the foot of the vase has been mutilated by the doctoring of the background.

An unpublished vase would seem from the description to be very like the two skyphoi in London and Madrid, nos. 4–5, with which Lullies compares it (*Antike Kleinkunst in Koenigsberg Pr.* 44–5): Trendall, too, calls it 'similar in style and design to London F 536' (op. cit. 108 note 22):

### Skyphos

Koenigsberg 101, from Paestum. A, satyr; B, seated woman.

Other vases described by Trendall as particularly close to Paestan are a squat lekythos in Madrid (11545: L 549: Nike and seated youth) and a small hydria, also there (11156: L 557: naked youth dancing).

The drawing of palmettes and dot-rosettes inclines me to associate the following with the stemlesses in the Paestanizing list (nos. 1–3):

### Stemless cups

Naples. I, phot. Sommer 11016, vi, 1, whence *BCH.* 1911 pl. 8, 42.
Naples. I, phot. Sommer 11016, vi, 2, whence *BCH.* 1911 pl. 8, 46. As the last.

The wreath of 'wild olive', and the drawing of it, may perhaps connect the following with the London stemless F 539, no. 1 in our Paestanizing list:

### Stemless cup

1. Naples inv. 147872, from Aversa. *NSc.* 1937, 124, ii, 5.

### Cup-skyphoi

2. Naples. A, phot. Sommer 11016, iii, 10, whence *BCH.* 1911 pl. 7, 66.
3. Naples. A, phot. Sommer 11016, iii, 4, whence *BCH.* 1911 pl. 7, 65.

### Gutti

4. Naples. Phot. Sommer 11018, ix, 8, whence *BCH.* 1911 pl. 9, 178.
5. Naples. Phot. Sommer 11018, ix, 9, whence *BCH.* 1911 pl. 9, 179. In this and the last, straight leaves alternate with wilted, as in the stemless by the Painter of Naples 1778, Vienna 103 (Trendall op. cit. pl. 34, e: above, p. 226, middle).

### J. A CALYX-KRATER

The great 'garland-kraters' of the fourth century—black calyx-kraters with a garland, usually gilded, round the middle, though often found in Campania and often called

Campanian, are nearly all Attic: but a vase (in Naples?) published by Pernice (*HKP.* 4 pl. 13) is an Italiote, probably Campanian imitation. The ivy-wreath, white with brown details, is drawn in the same way on a small hydria from Campania which was formerly in the Bourguignon collection at Naples (*Vente 18–20 mars 1901* pl. 4, 63). Another ivy-wreath resembling these is on an oinochoe, shape I, in Toronto (523: Robinson and Harcum pl. 89). The three vases may come from a single fabric.

The lower part of the vase published by Pernice is squat, and the shape does not look right without the stand: so also in the Attic calyx-krater Berlin inv. 4983, where the stand is missing (*Amtl. Ber.* 30, 186; *Hauptwerke aus den Staatl. Museen* pl. 10; Neugebauer pl. 90), and in Berlin inv. 30017, from Teano (*ML.* 20, 115 fig. 88; *Stephanos* 13), which does not seem to me certainly Attic.

### K. THE SPECTRE GROUP: CAMPANIAN

Extraordinarily barbarous style.

#### (i) *The Painter of Madrid 11093*
##### *Skyphoi*

1. Capua, from Capua. A, *CV.* pl. 45, 1. A, youth with strigil between olive-branches; B, the like.
2. London F 537. A and side, *CV.* IV Eb pl. 2, 12. The like.
3. Sèvres 225. *CV.* pl. 46, 16 and 27. The like. Compared with the last by Mrs. Massoul.
4. Berkeley 8.2828. The like.
5. Once Pesaro, Passeri. Passeri pl. 100. The like.

##### *Special skyphos* (with spout)

6. London (old no. 1784). *CV.* IV Eb pl. 2, 6. Olive-branch; palmette; bud.

##### *Bell-kraters*

7. Berkeley 8.3829. A, replica of A on the next vase. The right-hand satyr, here as there, holds with both hands what ought to have been a wreath, but is actually a toy bow and arrow. B, the like, but the woman holds a sprig of ivy instead of olive.
8. Madrid 11093 (L 579). A, Leroux pl. 54. A, satyrs and maenad. B, flute-player, man, and another.

#### (ii)

Same fabric, but a different hand.
Capua, from Capua. A, *CV.* IV Er pl. 37, 3. A, youths; B, youths.

I owe photographs of the two vases in Berkeley to the kindness of Prof. H. R. W. Smith and his pupil Miss Ethel Van Tassel. Miss Van Tassel had already put together nos. 1–4 and 7, and associated the Capua krater with them.

According to Leroux (299 and 301–2) the unpublished bell-kraters Madrid 11036 (L 580), 11071 (L 581), and 11092 (L 582) are 'in the same style' as Madrid 11093. From Picard's brief description (*BCH.* 1911, 230 no. 156), a skyphos in Naples might belong to the Spectre Group. There may be a good many other vases of the same style stowed away in the darkest and dustiest corners of museum storerooms.

Another vase of the same type as the spouted skyphos, no. 6, is in London (old no. 1785: *CV*. IV Eb pl. 2, 8): it must be Campanian: the technique of the decoration is the same, but the style is not. The spouted skyphos may have been a Campanian speciality: at least the only other vase of the shape I know, in Naples, is from Cumae (*ML*. 22 pl. 109, 2): between handles and spout, sprigs of ivy, incised, with white leaves and yellow berries: 'Gnathia' technique, but not Gnathian, and doubtless Campanian.

## CHAPTER XIII

# BLACK VASES, ETRUSCAN AND LATIN

AN attempt is made here to distinguish the black vases made in Etruria and Latium from those made elsewhere, and in some manner to classify them. They have not received very much attention hitherto. A certain amount of material has been published in excavation reports. The collection of black Etruscan vases in Leyden is included in a useful work by J. H. Holwerda, *Het laat-grieksche en romeinsche Gebruiks-aardewerk uit het Middellandsche-zee-gebied in het Rijksmuseum van Oudheiden te Leiden*. Those in Copenhagen have been published by Blinkenberg and Johansen in the *Corpus Vasorum*. As long ago as 1824, Francesco Inghirami devoted three plates of his *Monumenti etruschi* to the types of black and unglazed vases discovered in his native city of Volterra. Of excavation reports and the like, the following deserve special praise: in Etruria, *La Tomba dei Calini Sepuś presso Monteriggioni* by Bianchi Bandinelli (*St. etr.* 2, 133–76); in Latium, *Vases from Ardea in the Pennsylvania Museum* by Mrs. L. A. Holland (*Boll. st. med.* 4, 4–5, 5–9), *Campana supellex: the Pottery Deposit at Minturnae* by Miss A. K. Lake (*Boll. st. med.* 5, 4–5, 97–114), *Il Santuario della Dea Marcia alle Foci del Garigliano* by P. Mingazzini (*ML.* 37, 693–955), and *An Archaeological Record of Rome* by Mrs. I. S. Ryberg. Lastly, I may perhaps mention my own publication of black and plain vases from Vulci in *RG.* 92–100.

Miss Lake dates the deposit at Minturnae about the middle of the third century, and gives good reasons for supposing that it consists entirely of potter's rejects, either from the workshop of one Valerios, or less probably from his workshop and one other. The majority of the black vases from Foci del Garigliano are also homogeneous. I regret that I have not seen any of the objects themselves: but I note that although both these Latin sites lie on the very border of Campania, the finds, viewed as a whole, have not the same aspect as those from Campanian sites. This cannot be wholly due to the fact that the Minturnae deposit is a dump, and Foci del Garigliano a sanctuary, whereas nearly all the controlled excavations in Campania have been in cemeteries.

It is natural that there should have been some export of vases from Campania into Latium and Etruria, and that Campanian influence should be stronger on the border between Campania and Latium than farther north: but this does not amount to much. Most of the vases to be dealt with in this chapter are what is commonly called 'Etrusco-Campanian': but as I do not believe in the idea I do not use the word. Campania had its own fabrics of black vases: some of ours are Etruscan, the rest Latin. Sometimes I cannot tell whether a vase is Campanian or Etruscan, especially if I have only a reproduction to go by—and the sort of reproduction that is generally thought sufficient for vases 'with nothing on them'—but this is no proof that the vase is 'Etrusco-Campanian'.

The date is the fourth century, and the third. The more elaborate vases, and many of the others, too, are strongly influenced by metal-work, and some of them are simply copies of bronze or silver originals. A large proportion of the better vases seem to be from one fabric, which in *RG.* 93–4 I named 'Malacena' after the site of the Tomba dei

Calinii Śepuś near Monteriggioni, which yielded a fine assortment of them. I do not know where the fabric lay: some would say Volterra. 'Malacena' vases often have a good or fair bluish-black glaze; and when one sees this one is inclined to ask whether the vase may not be from the 'Malacena' fabric. On the other hand, not all 'Malacena' vases are bluish.

The vases in this chapter will be arranged according to shape. The fabric to which they belong, when determinable, will be stated: but often it must remain open. A good many alien pieces will be adduced for the sake of comparison: but warning will always be given.

Plastic additions are common. Sometimes there is a little decoration in added colour.

## KANTHAROI

We begin with a type of kantharos (α.i) which I have already treated in *RG*. 93. It is widely distributed in Etruria, is a favourite piece of tomb-furniture, and a typical product of the Malacena fabric. α.ii and α.iii are different models from the same fabric.

### α.i. THE GROUP OF VATICAN G 116

1. Vatican G 116, from Vulci. *RG*. pl. 35. The glaze has a greenish tinge.
2. Vatican. *Mus. Greg.* ii pl. 94, ii, 6.
3. Vatican.
4. Vatican (ex Falcioni).
5. Villa Giulia, from Vulci (sporadico 48).
6. Villa Giulia, from Vulci (sporadico 49).
7. Villa Giulia (ex Augusto Castellani), from between Orvieto and Bolsena. *Annali* 1871 pl. C, 4.
8. Villa Giulia (ex Augusto Castellani), from between Orvieto and Bolsena.
9–10. Once Augusto Castellani, from between Orvieto and Bolsena. Two of them. Mentioned by Klügmann in *Annali* 1871, 26, together with the last pair.
11–18. Rome, Prince Torlonia, from Vulci? Eight of them.
19. Tarquinia 1975, from Tarquinia.
20. Tarquinia 1976, from Tarquinia.
21. Tarquinia RC 1928, from Tarquinia.
22. Tarquinia 1051, from Tarquinia.
23. Tarquinia 1120, from Tarquinia.
23 bis. Todi 510, from Todi. *CV*. pl. 13, 2.
23 ter. Todi 512, from Todi. *CV*. pl. 13, 5.
23 quater. Todi 514, from Todi. *CV*. pl. 13, 1.
24. Florence V 395, from Chiusi?
25. Florence V 422, from Chiusi? Blue-black glaze.
26. Florence V 423, from Chiusi.
27. Florence V 562, from Chiusi.
28. Florence, from Orbetello.
29. Florence, from Orbetello.

30. Florence 4501.
31. Florence 4582.
32. Florence 4505.
33. Florence 4506.
34. Florence 4545.
35. Florence 4544.
36. Florence 4500.
37. Florence 77192, from Sovana.
38. Florence 77191, from Sovana.
39. Florence 77193, from Sovana.
40. Florence, from Sovana.
41. Florence, from Sovana.
42. Florence, from San Miniato. *NSc.* 1935, 33, 2.
43. Castiglioncello, from Castiglioncello. *NSc.* 1934, 162, 1.
44. Arezzo 1259.
45. Arezzo 1249.
46. Ferrara, T 156, from Spina. *NSc.* 1924, 292 fig. 5.  See p. 208.
47. Ferrara, T 369, from Spina. Aurigemma[1] 111, i, 3 =[2]133, i, 3.  See p. 208.
48. Ferrara, T 369, from Spina. Aurigemma[1] 111, i, 8 =[2]133, i, 8.  See p. 208.
49. Chiusi, from Chiusi. Levi *Mus. Civ. di Chiusi* 125, ii, 4.
50. Chiusi, from Chiusi. Levi *Mus. Civ. di Chiusi* 125, ii, 7.
51. Ancona, from Montefortino. *ML.* 9 pl. 10, 6.
52. Naples.
53. Oxford 1936.619.  Pl. 38, 8.
54. Sèvres 4523.  *CV.* pl. 24, 12.  'Greenish black glaze.'
55. Berlin inv. 4005, from Monteriggioni. *St. etr.* 2 pl. 31, 109.
56. Berlin inv. 4070, from Monteriggioni.
57. Berlin 3728, from Bari.
58. Berlin, Dr. Philip Lederer.
59. Copenhagen 433, from Volterra.  *CV.* pl. 221, 14.
60. Leyden H 216, from Volterra.  Holwerda 20.  'Blue-black glaze.'
61. Leyden H 214, from Volterra.  Holwerda 20.  Graffito *Afnaś* (retr.) (ibid. pl. 12).
    'Blue-black glaze.'
62. Leyden H 215, from Naples.
63. Amsterdam inv. 1924.  *CV.* III pl. 4 (Pays Bas pl. 86), 5.
64. Cracow, Univ., inv. 637.  *CV.* pl. 15 (Pologne pl. 88), 8.
65. Leningrad (St. 612).  *CR.* 1880, 120.
66. Leningrad (St. 628).
67. Toronto 561.  Robinson and Harcum pl. 91.
68. Toronto 565.  Robinson and Harcum pl. 92.  Ex Pacini of Florence.
69. New York GR 473, from Bolsena.  Richter *Cat. Bronzes* 181, i, 4.
70. Harvard 2238.  *CV.* pl. 26, 10.
71. Florence, from Orbetello. *NSc.* 1885 pl. 1, 7, whence Martha 489, 325.

72. Florence, from Orbetello.
73. London CS 356.
74. Berlin 2886. Furtwängler *Beschr*. pl. 7. The provenience 'Smyrna' given by Furtwängler (p. 799) is cancelled by him on p. 1055.

The last four are unusually elaborate. The two Florences, and the London, have
rosettes (or rather a six-petalled flower) on the rim to left and right of the handles. In
the first Florence, and in London, the stem is reeded. In London and Berlin the cul is
reeded, and the body decorated with a band of vine-leaves and grapes in relief. The other
kantharoi differ little among themselves except in size. Some of them have a loop round
each handle.

I should doubt the proveniences given for nos. 57 and 62 ('Bari', 'Naples').

Todi 513 is said by Becatti to be like 512 (our no. 23 ter), and Todi 511 like 510 (our
no. 23 bis).

A kantharos in Leningrad (St. 703) must be of our shape or very near it: according to
Stephani it is of 'black clay': burned?

A black kantharos in Arezzo, 1261, has the same shape as ours, except that the stem is
a little different: the vase is of coarser make and does not come, I thought, from our fabric.

An important kantharos in Tarquinia is of nearly the same shape as ours, but the lip
differs, the stem is much as in Arezzo 1261, and there are painted patterns and figures:
it is not from the Malacena fabric: see p. 216.

I have left out the two large kantharoi from Chiusi figured in Levi *Museo Civico di
Chiusi* 125, ii, 2 and 6 because they may be not black but silvered: see pp. 290–1.

### α.ii. THE GROUP OF BERLIN INV. 4039

*RG.* 94.
1. Berlin inv. 4039, from Monteriggioni.
2. Florence, from Sovana.
3. Fiesole. Galli *Fiesole* 95 fig. 76, 2.
4. Florence 4449.
5. Florence, from Poggio Sala near Bolsena. Milani *Mus. Top.* 52, iii (to right of the
mirror).
6. Florence 4462.
7. Rome, Prince Torlonia, from Vulci?
8. Rome, Prince Torlonia, from Vulci?
(like these, but the handles closer to the mouth)
Leyden 213, from Volterra. Holwerda 20. 'Black, somewhat lacquer-like glaze'.
(another variant)
Vatican G 117, from Vulci. *RG.* pl. 35. Greenish-black glaze.

### α.iii. THE CASTIGLIONCELLO GROUP
(similar to the last group, but with ring handles)
1. Castiglioncello, from Castiglioncello. *NSc.* 1924, 164 fig. 5, 4.
2. Vatican, from Etruria. *Mus. Greg.* ii pl. 94, i, 2.

3. London.

4. London.

5. Florence 76598, from Poggio Sala near Bolsena. Milani *Mus. Top.* 52, iii (to the left of the mirror).

In nos. 3–5 the lower part is reeded. In no. 5 (as in Group α.iv) the ring-handles end below in snake-heads (compare pp. 258–9).

The three kantharoi that follow are somewhat similar in shape to these. I do not know that any of them are Etruscan. Nos. 1 and 3 are black; no. 2 is very like no. 1 in shape, but is painted 'matt yellow'. Nos. 1 and 2 have ring-handles, no. 3 not. The form of body and neck recalls handleless vases like Leyden 209 (p. 247 no. 6).

1. Philadelphia 2833, from Ardea. *Boll. st. med.* 4, 4–5, pl. 2, 23. Bad glaze.

2. Leyden 737. Holwerda 16.

3. Michigan 2630. *CV.* pl. 18, 34. 'Pale, dull orange clay; good glaze.'

A black vase from Teano, doubtless Campanian, corresponds roughly to these (*ML.* 20, 138, fig. 106, c).

Unglazed vases comparable to them, from Montefortino, are in Ancona (*ML.* 9 pl. 5, 12).

## α.iv. THE GROUP OF COPENHAGEN INV. 3817: SMALL KANTHAROID CALYXES

It is but a step from α.iii to α.iv, and I put α.iv here for convenience, but it can no longer be counted as a kantharos, for it is not a drinking-vessel: the mouth is that of a calyx-krater.

Mrs. Massoul has already compared nos. 1 and 7 with no. 2.

Nos. 1–6 have white decoration round the neck. In nos. 10 and 11 the body is reeded.

1. Goluchow, Prince Czartoryski, 183. *CV.* pl. 52, 1.

2. Sèvres 1163.1, from Volterra. *CV.* pl. 24, 11. The foot restored?

3. Yale 488. Baur 234.

4. Berlin, from Monteriggioni. *St. etr.* 2 pl. 31, 93.

5. Once Terrosi, from Monteriggioni. According to Bianchi Bandinelli just like the last.

6. Copenhagen inv. 3817, from Volterra. *CV.* pl. 221, 11.

7. Once Disney, from Volterra. *Mus. Disn.* pl. 127, 2.

8. Florence 4504.

9. Florence 4589.

10. London 47.8–6.40.

11. London 47.8–6.39.

The vase formerly in the Cinci collection at Volterra (Inghirami *Mon. etr.* 5 pl. 50, 18) may be our no. 7, which Disney had from Cinci. Inghirami also gives a one-handled version of the shape (ibid. pl. 49, 20).

## β.i. THE GROUP OF TODI 515

1. Florence. *Gaz. arch.* 1879 pl. 6, 3.

2. Florence. *Gaz. arch.* 1879 pl. 6, 8.

3. Copenhagen inv. 4985, from Cumae. *CV.* pl. 221, 10. The body is reeded, the stem fluted, as in nos. 1 and 2.

4. Todi 515, from Todi. *CV.* pl. 13, 4. As the last.

The fragmentary Todi 516 is said by Becatti to be like 515 (our no. 4).

Johansen saw that the Copenhagen kantharos was Etruscan, and cast doubt upon the provenience given by the dealer from whom it was acquired.

These four, or five, which may be from the Malacena fabric, are imitations of such metal kantharoi as the silver ones from the Crimea in Leningrad (*ABC.* pl. 38, 2) and from Taranto in the collection of Baron Edmond de Rothschild (*NSc.* 1896, 380–1; *Anz.* 1897, 63; Wuilleumier *Trésor* pll. 5–6). Another imitation is Berlin 2941, from Tanagra, in green 'fayence' (Furtwängler *Coll. Sab.* pl. 70, 3), which is said to have been found in the same tomb as the duck-vase London K 1 (Walters *Cat. Roman Pottery*, pl. 1, above). The kantharos held by the crone on the mosaic by Dioskourides of Samos, from Pompeii, in Naples (*Jb.* 26, 4; Herrmann *Denkmäler der Malerei* pl. 107; Pfuhl fig. 685; Curtius *Wandmalerei Pompejis* pl. 10) is also of this type: Bieber and Rodenwaldt had already compared the Berlin fayence vase.

A simpler and less slender version of the same type is the silvered vase from the collection of Augusto Castellani (*Annali* 1871 pl. B, 2: see p. 290).

The potters, for safety, bring the handles close up to the mouth.

I am accustomed to call a vase a kantharos only when the handles join the vase above as well as below; and when they do not rejoin the vase to speak of a kantharoid: but the distinction, though useful, is occasionally, as here, academic.

### β.ii.

Tarquinia RC. 627, from Tarquinia. *ML.* 36, 490, 2.

Akin to the preceding in shape, but there is no stem (I did not notice that there was anything missing at this point). The handles are largely modern. The body is reeded, the neck decorated with figures in relief. Malacena fabric, I was inclined to think. The relation of figures to background is much the same as in the krater Athens, Agora, P 3155 (*Hesp.* 3 pl. 3 and pp. 422–3: see Homer Thompson ibid. 422–6).

### γ.

From Minturnae. *Boll. st. med.* 5, 4–5, pl. 1, 38, pl. 5, 38, pl. 7, 38.

I do not know anything like this. The elements are much the same as in other kantharoi, for instance, those of the Saint-Valentin type (p. 219), but the proportions are different.

### λ.i. THE TORLONIA GROUP

1. Berlin, from Vulci. *Berl. Mus.* 1934, 1–2. Brown-black glaze. See below.
2. Rome, Prince Torlonia, from Vulci. Messerschmidt *Nekr.* 99, left. See below.
3. Berlin. I had taken this to be from Monteriggioni, but it must be the kantharos mentioned by Zahn in *Berl. Mus.* 1934, 10–11, as found at Poggio alla Città together with an askos of the tail-spout type (see p. 274 no. 4.).
4. Chiusi, from Chiusi (Tomba della Pellegrina). *Riv. Ist.* 4, 34, 1.

4 bis. Richmond, Cook.  Greenish glaze.  Cf. nos. 3 and 4.

5. Leyden 176, from Volterra.  Holwerda 16.  'Dull blue-black glaze.'

6. Leyden 177, from Volterra.  Holwerda pl. 2.

7. Vienna 2207 (ex Este).

8. Leyden 178, from Cortona.  Holwerda 16.

9. Leyden 179, from Volterra.  Holwerda pl. 2.  'Glaze fired matt brown.'

10. Leyden 180, from Volterra.  Holwerda 16.  'Glaze fired matt brown.'

11. Vatican, from Etruria.  *Mus. Greg.* ii pl. 94, i, 4.

Nos. 1 and 2 are not plain black: they are the two kantharoi decorated by the Hesse Painter with pictures in superposed colour: see p. 208, below, nos. 1–2.  I repeat them here because as far as shape goes they are hardly distinguishable from the plain black nos. 3–7.  In nos. 9–12 the foot is simpler, and the handle has no spur in the middle. It is possible that they all came from the Malacena fabric.  See also below, p. 239.

The dozen vases in our list form one species in a large family of kantharoi occurring in many fabrics and lasting down to Roman times.  Constant, the general shape of body and handles: the foot, and details, vary.  Another species, for example, Attic of the late fourth century, is represented by four vases in Alexandria (Breccia *Sciatbi* pl. 55, 113; 115; 111; 114); one in Providence (25.080: *CV.* pl. 27, 4); one in Sèvres (4166.13: *CV.* pl. 24, 6).  The prototypes were of metal.  Silver kantharoi of this great family: Leningrad, from the Taman peninsula (*CR.* 1880, 9); Amsterdam, from Kastel near Mayence (*Gids* pl. 42, 2); Saint-Germain, from Alise (*Mon. Piot* 9 pl. 16).

A black kantharos in the British Museum, known to me from the entry in the old catalogue, should belong to our group:

London, old cat. 226.  *Cat. GEV*. i, pl. 3, 87.  From the Campanari collection, so probably found in Etruria.

So should a kantharos in Brussels, which I know from a small photograph.

Another kantharos, in point of shape, belongs to the same *family* as the dozen vases in our list:

Once Rome, Dressel (now in Berlin?), from Rome (Esquiline).  *Annali* 1880 pl. R, 16 and 16b.

This is one of many vases, mostly plates and bowls, decorated inside with a small coin-like stamp representing Herakles holding kantharos and club: to left of him a star, to right the Latin inscription *aerar*.  On these see Dressel in *Annali* 1880, 292–4, Pagenstecher *Cal.* 15–17, Ryberg 123–5.  The provenience when known is nearly always Rome, and the vases were probably made there.

Type 26 at Minturnae (*Boll. st. med.* 5, 4–5, pl. 1, 26, and pl. 6, 26) might also be mentioned here.  It is decorated inside with impressed designs (see ibid. 101).

### λ.ii. THE GROUP OF BERLIN INV. 4077

Differs from λ.i in the handles, for the shape of which see no. 4.

1. Berlin inv. 4077, from Monteriggioni.  Greenish-black glaze.

2. Rome, Prince Torlonia, 220, from Vulci?
3. Rome, Prince Torlonia, from Vulci? As the last.
4. Leyden 181, from Volterra. Holwerda 16 and pl. 2 (the sketch to left of the section shows the double handle seen from above; the bar on top is part of the rim). 'Blue-black glaze.'
5. Leyden 182, from Volterra. 'Blue-black glaze.'
6. Leyden 183, from Volterra. Holwerda 16.
7. Florence, from Sovana. *NSc.* 1903, 221, 7.
8. Florence, from San Miniato. *NSc.* 1935, 33, 4.
9. Michigan 2920. *CV.* pl. 18, 23. 'Brownish-black glaze.' See below.
10. Leningrad. Stephani pl. 4, 180.

Nos. 1–3 go together. In nos. 4–6 and 9 the foot is a little different; in nos. 7–8 and 10 the exact shape of the foot is not known to me.

It seemed to me when I visited the Torlonia collection that nos. 2 and 3, as well as two pairs of kantharoid stemlesses (p. 239) were from the same fabric as the kantharos by the Hesse Painter (p. 235 no. 2 and p. 236). This group also will be Malacena.

No 9 was obtained from De Criscio at Naples, and is therefore said to be 'presumably from Pozzuoli or Cumae'. I cannot distinguish it, with what means I have, from the other vases in the list.

λ.iii

Certain black kantharoi, from Montefortino, in Ancona (*ML.* 9 pl. 11, 15) may perhaps be thought of as somewhat akin to λ.ii, but the belly is swollen and striated. Other black kantharoi from the same site (ibid. pl. 11, 16) have the same swollen belly, but not striated, and the handles have a ledge on top, as in λ.i.

ε. THE GROUP OF TORONTO 564

Small pelikoid kantharoi.

1. Toronto 564. Robinson and Harcum pl. 92. Ex Pacini of Florence. Bluish glaze.
2. Leyden 211, from Cortona. Holwerda 20. 'Black glaze.'
3. Leyden 212, from Cortona. Holwerda 20. 'Bluish glaze.'
4. Florence, from San Miniato. *NSc.* 1935, 33, 6.
5. Once Volterra, Cinci, from Volterra. Inghirami *Mon. etr.* 5 pl. 48, 13.
6. Oxford 1874.403. Pl. 38, 10. Ht. 0.091. Bluish glaze.
7. Oxford, Dr. F. P. Dickson, from Italy.

Berlin 4176 would seem from Furtwängler's cut to be of this shape (*Beschr.* pl. 7, 333).
In another the shape is similar, but the handles, which are fragmentary, seem not to have left the body at the lower end:
Bettona, from Bettona. *CV.* (Terni) pl. 9, 16.
Yale 507, from Rome (Baur 132) is a kantharos of somewhat similar type. The handles are double, with a sort of loop or crosspiece on top: that is, the same type of handle as in certain oinochoai (p. 257). Just under the mouth there is an ivy-wreath, the stalk incised,

the leaves white. I do not know the fabric. The curve of the body is much as in the Würzburg oinochoe 935 (Langlotz pl. 252); compare also the kantharos Leyden 212 (no. 3).

## SKYPHOI
### i. (type A)
Villa Giulia, from Capena. Della Seta *L'It. ant.*[1] 152 fig. 162, 2.

The glaze is probably the same as in the squat lekythoi described on p. 271, above, or some of them. I seem to make out in the illustration the same kind of horizontal ridges, due to turning, as in some of the squat lekythoi (see pp. 270–1).

There may well be other Latin or Etruscan black skyphoi, but they are hard to tell from Campanian in reproductions. Skyphos type A, in its later form with double-curved profile, is well represented at Minturnae (*Boll. st. med.* 5, 4–5, pl. 5, 34–6 and pl. 6, 34). Others are from Foci del Garigliano (*ML.* 37 pl. 36, 3 and pl. 35, 15). Leyden 184 (Holwerda pl. 2) is counted Etruscan by Holwerda. See also p. 116, ii. I cannot say whether a skyphos of Corinthian type, from Populonia, in Florence, is Etruscan or not (*NSc.* 1934, 418, iv, 2).

ii. A special type: very tall, with two ring-handles. Malacena fabric.
Vatican, from Etruria. *Mus. Greg.* ii pl. 94, iii, 2. Greenish-black glaze.

## STEMLESS CUPS
### i
Two stemless cups with impressed decoration, formerly in the Terrosi collection, from Monteriggioni (one, *St. etr.* 2 pl. 31, 108) have the same highly recurved handles as the Calene cups by L. Canoleios (Pagenstecher *Cal.* pl. 16) and perhaps the same raised ring near the middle of the interior—this is not clear from the reproduction. A stemless cup from Spina, in Ferrara (T 613: Aurigemma[1] 126, ii, 1 =[2]119, ii, 1) 3 has the ring and the recurved handles. The resemblance to Calene does not go further. I do not know whether our three cups are Etruscan or not. They are derived from some such metal models as the silver cup from Montefortino in Ancona (*ML.* 9 pl. 9, 1), which has a knob in the centre like the Calene cups.

### ii
A stemless cup from Monteriggioni in Berlin, inv. 4072, is very different. The handles, seen from above, form a sort of triangle. Inside, impressed, circles and the usual rows of short strokes. The inferior black glaze made me think of vases like Vatican G 120–2. (*RG.* pl. 35 and p. 95). Impressed stemlesses with similar handles are in Amsterdam (inv. 3382: I, *CV.* IV E pl. 3, 10=Pays Bas pl. 93, 10) and, from Sovana, in Florence (*NSc.* 1903, 220, 3). Another stemless with unusual handles is Copenhagen 401 (*CV.* pl. 222, 6), which Johansen classes as Etruscan, together with three ordinary stemlesses (499, 502, 500: *CV.* pl. 222, 2, 3, and 4), two of them from Volterra. In six Leyden stemlesses the exact shape of the handles is not clear from the publication: H 171, from Volterra (A, Holwerda 13); H 172, from Volterra; H 173 (I, Holwerda pl. 10); H 174

(Holwerda pll. 2 and 10); 175. The impressed palmettes and flowers of 173 resemble those of the strainer Copenhagen 440 (*CV*. pl. 222, 7: see p. 279, ii, 2).

I am disposed to think of these wretched stemlesses as Etruscan imitations of Campanian, but am willing to confess that I have not paid much attention to them hitherto.

### iii. KANTHAROID

1. Berlin inv. 4076, from Monteriggioni. Blue-black glaze.
2. Rome, Prince Torlonia, 218, from Vulci?
3. Rome, Prince Torlonia, from Vulci?

The body here is the same as in the kantharoi of Group Ⲗ (p. 235), and the foot is very nearly the same, but the handles are slender, recurved cup-handles. Two bronze stemlesses in the British Museum are very like this; another, from Galaxidi, in Amsterdam is shallower (Scheurleer *Cat.* pl. 15, 4; *Gids* pl. 38, 3); silver stemlesses in London, from Chalke (Walters *Cat. Silver* pl. 3, 14), and in Berlin (Furtwängler *Coll. Sab.*, text to pl. 145) are farther off.

### iv. KANTHAROID

1. Rome, Prince Torlonia, 216, from Vulci?
2. Rome, Prince Torlonia, from Vulci?

Body, foot, and handles are the same as in (iii), but there is a stem. The nearest approach to the shape is perhaps the Attic type of which Oxford 1927.654 (*CV*. pl. 65, 10), Sèvres 4166.11 (*CV*. pl. 25, 22), and a vase in Rhodes (*Cl. Rh.* 2, 147 fig. 25, 2) are examples: but the stem is different, and the resemblance is not close. A bronze vase in New York (Richter *Bronzes* 216 no. 596) and two like it in the British Museum are more remote.

All five vases, I think (iii and iv), are from the Malacena fabric: see p. 237.

### v. KANTHAROID

Ancona, from Montefortino. *ML.* 9, 695.

This black stemless belongs to the same *family* as (iii) and is evidently an imitation of metal stemlesses. I do not know the fabric, and cannot be certain that it is Etruscan.

## CUP

A vase found at Minturnae (*Boll. st. med.* 5, 4–5 pl. 1, 19 and pl. 4, 19) is a curious late version of the kylix.

## PHIALAI MESOMPHALOI
### i

1. Vatican G 118, from Vulci. *RG.* pl. 35. Black glaze, with a slight greenish tinge in places.
2. Berlin inv. 4006, from Monteriggioni.

3. Berlin inv. 4041, from Monteriggioni.
4. Berlin inv. 4276, from Monteriggioni.
5. Leyden H 290, from Volterra. Holwerda 26.

Fine make. Nos. 1 and 2 have rows of unusually minute strokes round the band of impressed palmettes and flowers within: the strokes are invisible in the reproduction *RG*. pl. 35. Just the same strokes and floral design recur on two strainers (p. 279, ii). Nos. 3–5 are very like nos. 1 and 2. Malacena fabric, I thought.

Leyden H 291, from Volterra, is grouped with H 290 by Holwerda, but not figured.

The black phiale Castiglioncello 1191, with a vine-tendril and small Erotes in relief (*NSc*. 1924, 164 fig. 5, 2; *St. etr*. 17 pl. 29, 1), though from an Etruscan site, Castiglioncello, is Calene, signed by L. Canoleius. A black phiale in Toronto (595: Robinson and Harcum 260 and pl. 95), with impressed decoration (including rows of little strokes), is from Cales, and Campanian.

I cannot tell whether the large phiale Todi 530, from Todi (side-view, *CV*. pl. 14, 25), decorated inside with ten impressed palmettes, has any connexion with our group. Becatti mentions four others like it in Todi.

ii

1. Orvieto, Conte Faina, 495, from Orvieto.
2. Orvieto, Conte Faina, 496, from Orvieto.
3. Heidelberg, fr.

These are replicas of the many Calene phialai decorated in relief with a chariot-scene representing the Entry of Herakles into Olympus (see p. 292): if I mention the three here it is on the authority of Pagenstecher (*Cal*. 71, λ and ε, and 73), who says that they are shown by the clay to be local Etruscan and not Calene.

## PHIALOID DISH

Florence, Terrosi, from Monteriggioni. *St. etr*. 2 pl. 33, 104.

This phiale is of the same type as the many silvered ones described on pp. 291–2: in the middle, a figure-scene in relief; round it, in relief, vine. The subject is not the same as in any of the silvered phialai, and the design of the vine is different. The fabric may be Malacena, but I am not positive.

## BOWLS

In shape these bowls are quite like certain dishies (p. 243), but they are shallower, and larger, have a different aspect, and no doubt served a different purpose, as drinking-vessels. They are slightly everted at the rim.

i

1. Leyden 272, from Volterra. Holwerda 13 and pl. 3. 'Purple-brown glaze.' Dm. 0.19.
2. Once Volterra, Cinci, from Volterra. Inghirami *Mon. etr*. 5 pl. 49, 11.

3. Leyden 279, from Montalcino. Holwerda 13 and pl. 3. 'Glaze fired purple-red, with black spots.' Dm. 0.17.

A similar bowl was found at Foci del Garigliano (inv. 1220: *ML.* 37 pl. 37, 18: dm. 0.173, ht. 0.072). I cannot tell whether it is Latin or Campanian. Another bowl from the site, which is said to be of the same shape as inv. 1220, has an impressed design of Campanian type (inv. 506: I, *ML.* 37 pl. 39, 1).

Type 17 at Minturnae is also like these, but deeper (*Boll. st. med.* 5, 4–5 pl. 1, 17 and pl. 3, 17: average dm. 0.17, ht. 0.08). Some of the Minturnae bowls have impressed decoration inside, a male figure moving cautiously forward (ibid. pl. 22, 3).

Somewhat similar bowls occur in Attic: Athens, Agora, P 4002 (*Hesp.* 3, 348, C 7, and 437, C 7), P 3394 (ibid. 415, E 117), P 3354 (ibid. 396, E 49); according to Homer Thompson, Agora P 3426 (*Hesp.* 3, 426, E 157) is not Attic.

## ii

A bowl in the Vatican, from Vulci (*Mus. Greg.* ii pl. 102, 3), is of the same general shape as Leyden 272 and those associated with it above, but more elaborate, for it is decorated inside with a fine female head, veiled, in high relief. The relief is no. 99 in Pagenstecher's list (*Cal.* 68): he believes it, and its replicas, though of what is called Calene type, to be probably Etruscan work. He figures one replica, a fragment with 'dull, bluish glaze' in Heidelberg (*Cal.* pl. 20, 99c): the others he mentions are in Heidelberg, Arezzo, and Tarquinia. His no. 99 f is a vase from Todi, known only from a brief reference in *Bull.* 1880, 19, where it is described as 'a very deep cup decorated with a female head, veiled, full front, in high relief'. I doubt if that is sufficient to establish it as a replica. I do not know if Todi 528 (*CV.* pl. 14, 27) could be the *Bullettino* bowl. Only the outside is figured in the *Corpus*; inside there is said to be, in relief, 'a bust' and 'two kymata'. The measurements are given as 0.185×0.075, against 0.19×0.085 in the *Bullettino*. As to shape, the bowl differs from the Vatican one in having no foot.

## MASTOI
### i (with ring-foot)

1. Leyden 208, from Volterra. Holwerda 16. 'Blue-black glaze.'
2. Florence, from Sovana. *NSc.* 1903, 220, 2.

Holwerda says that the Leyden vase has small feet (in the plural), but in the reproduction it seems to have a ring-foot or the like.

### ii

Castiglioncello 171, from Castiglioncello. *NSc.* 1924, 162, 2. The vase rests on three little feet, but I do not know the exact shape of them.

From Bianchi Bandinelli's description in *St. etr.* 2, 153 note 1, the bowl Florence 4591 would seem to be like this. The feet are satyr-faces. The glaze is said to be poor.

I do not know that these are Etruscan, but they may be.

Type 31 at Minturnae (*Boll. st. med.* 5, 4–5 pl. 6, 31) is another mastos of the same sort. The feet are cockle-shells.

These belong to a class of mastoi, from various fabrics, imitating metal, which stand on three tiny feet in the form of nipples, leaves, shells, or human heads. Such are the following:

1. Yale 508, from Apulia. Baur 132, 508; Hambidge *Dynamic Symmetry* 62 fig. 3. Leaves for feet.
2. Berlin 2866, from Crete. *AM.* 26, 76. Female heads for feet. Attic.
3. Athens, Pnyx, from Athens. *Hesp.* 12, 359, a. Shells for feet. Attic.
4. Amsterdam, Madame Six, 41, from Kalamata. Shells for feet.
5. Harvard 1895.242. *CV.* pl. 25, 2. Human heads for feet.
6. London G 33. Negro's faces for feet.
7. London 76.9–9.35. 'Nipples' for feet.
8. Catania 811, from Centuripe. Libertini pl. 92. Shells for feet.

The type of vase is also common in the class of 'Megarian' bowls.

According to Miss Lake (*Boll. st. med.* 5, 4–5, 101) type 31 at Minturnae (ibid. pl. 6, 31: top of this page) is but a variation on type 30 (ibid. pl. 6, 30), which has a proper foot and is usually decorated with patterns (ibid. pl. 22, 8). Type 32 (ibid. 101) is described as very similar to type 30, but having a lip projecting at right angles to the body. Type 33 is the same as 32, except that the place of the foot is once more taken by cockle-shells. Neither 32 nor 33 is reproduced: but from the account of 33 it would seem to resemble a vase from the Tomba dei Calinii Šepuś (*St. etr.* 2 pl. 31, 88 bis) which was found serving as a makeshift lid to a stamnos of the Malacena fabric. It ought to be possible, from the patternwork, to locate this whole group of mastoi and mastoids: they may be Campanian, but it does not seem certain.

## DISHIES

### i. ECHINOID

#### (i. a: stout make)

Attic potters made such dishies in great numbers and exported them widely. Proportions, curves, details vary. There are many local imitations, and the following will be among them, although it is seldom possible to tell from the reproductions alone whether they are Attic or not.

1. From Minturnae. *Boll. st. med.* 5, 4–5 pl. 3, 14 and pl. 5, 14. Many.
2. From Minturnae. *Boll. st. med.* 5, 4–5 pl. 3, 15 and pl. 15. Many.
3. Naples inv. 1239, from Foci del Garigliano. *ML.* 37 pl. 37, 3.
4. Civitavecchia, from Castrum Novum. *St. etr.* 11 pl. 59, 4, f.
5. Philadelphia 2853, from Ardea. *Boll. st. med.* 4, 4–5 pl. 2, 17.
6. Philadelphia 2851, from Ardea. *Boll. st. med.* 4, 4–5 pl. 2, 16.
7. Philadelphia 2852, from Ardea. *Boll. st. med.* 4, 4–5 pl. 2, 18. Shallower.

8. Villa Giulia, from Veii. *NSc.* 1930, 56, left, below. Found with a 'Genucilia' plate (p. 176 no. 27) and a dishie of different type (this page, foot, no. 1).
9. Naples inv. 73, from Foci del Garigliano. *ML.* 37 pl. 37, 5. Shallower.
10. Naples inv. 1671, from Foci del Garigliano. *ML.* 37 pl. 37, 7.
11. Naples inv. 1624, from Foci del Garigliano. *ML.* 37 pl. 37, 4. Shallower. Unusual curve.

In the dishie Rome, Antiquarium, 2388, from Rome (Ryberg fig. 120a) the mouth seems slightly everted.

### (i. b: thinner make; usually larger than in the last class)

1. Leyden 273, from Volterra. Holwerda pl. 3. 'Black glaze, here and there fired red.'
2. Leyden 274, from Volterra. Holwerda pl. 3. 'Dull black glaze fired brown.'
3. Leyden 275, from Volterra. Holwerda 13. 'Black glaze, fired matt.'
4. Leyden 276, from Volterra. Holwerda pl. 3. 'Black glaze, fired matt.'
5. Leyden 278. Holwerda 13 and pl. 13. 'Matt glaze fired red.'
6. Florence 8214, from Vetulonia. *CV.* IV Bz pl. 1, 18. I, impressed. Another, fragmentary, is mentioned in the text.
7. Philadelphia 2844, from Ardea. *Boll. st. med.* 4, 4–5 pl. 2, 14.
8. Philadelphia 2999, from Ardea. *Boll. st. med.* 4, 4–5 pl. 2, 5.
9. Philadelphia 2845, from Ardea. *Boll. st. med.* 4, 4–5, pl. 2, 27. Shallower.
10. Rome, Antiquarium, 2382, from Rome. Ryberg fig. 120b.

Type 13 at Minturnae is of this kind (*Boll. st. med.* 5 pl. 3, 13 and pl. 1, 13); so is Naples, from Foci del Garigliano, inv. 620 (*ML.* 37 pl. 37, 16 and pl. 39, 6). Holwerda thinks that Leyden 280 (Holwerda pl. 3) and 281 (ibid.) may be Etruscan, although one is said to have been found in Tripoli, the other near Naples.

It is impossible to tell all these from Attic without seeing them, or one fabric from another.

The shape of the *pocola* (p. 209, *a*) is a variety of this.

There are Greek dishies of the same general type: see, for example, *Hesp.* 3, 371, D 7–8.

The four echinoid dishies from the Tomba dei Calinii Šepuś (one, *St. etr.* 2 pl. 31, 83) are unglazed.

### (i. c: near i. b, but the mouth slightly everted)

1. Villa Giulia, from Veii. *NSc.* 1930, 56, b. Found with a 'Genucilia' plate (p. 176 no. 27) and a dishie of different type (this page, top, no. 8).
2. Philadelphia 2849, from Ardea. *Boll. st. med.* 4, 4–5 pl. 2, 32. 'Black clay, mottled in firing.'

An unglazed vase of this shape is Philadelphia 3001, from Ardea (*Boll. st. med.* 4, 4–5 pl. 2, 1).

A similar piece, from Sovana, in Florence (*NSc.* 1903, 220, 6), which is not black, but 'covered with a thick fat glaze of a dirty red colour', is shallower, and practically the shape of the 'bowls' described on p. 240. In fact it is not always easy to decide whether to classify such objects as 'bowls' or dishies.

## ii. with flaring body

1. Villa Giulia 19760, from Cervetri.  Dullish black glaze.  Inside, a small depressed circle.
2. Florence, from Sovana. *NSc.* 1903, 221, 1.

A similar type has been found at Minturnae (*Boll. st. med.* 5, 4–5 pl. 1, 18 and pl. 3, 18), sometimes with impressed decoration (see Lake, ibid. 100 under type 18, and 112; and pl. 22, 5).  It also occurs in Greek fabrics: for example, Athens, Agora P 3342 (*Hesp.* 3, 436, E 33, Homer Thompson); Samos (*AM.* 54, 45, 2).  I do not know whether the vase published in *Sg. Vogell* 40 fig. 17, b is Greek or not.  Not far from all these, a dishie in Rome, Antiquarium, 2386, from Rome (Ryberg fig. 120d).

## iii. Dishies or small bowls, with offset, torus-shaped lip

1. Leyden 255, from Volterra.  Holwerda 13 and pl. 2.  'Black glaze.'
2. Leyden 256, from Volterra.  Holwerda pl. 2.  I, impressed?  'Black glaze.'
3. Copenhagen 527, from Volterra.  *CV.* pl. 222, 1.  I, impressed.
4. Leyden 259, from Volterra.  Holwerda pl. 3.  'Blue-black glaze.'
5. Leyden 263, from Volterra.  Holwerda pl. 3.  'Dull black glaze.'
6. Leyden 264, from Volterra.  Holwerda 13.  'Dull black glaze.'
7. Leyden 268, from Volterra?  Holwerda pl. 3.  'Greyish-black glaze with lacquer-like lustre.'
8. Leyden 270, from Volterra.  Holwerda 13 and pl. 3.  'Lacquer-like glaze, in parts fired red.'
9. Leyden 271, from Volterra.  Holwerda 13 and pl. 3.  'Matt purple-brown glaze.'
10. Florence 8215, from Vetulonia.  *CV.* IV Bz pl. 1, 16.  Another, fragmentary, is mentioned in the text.
11. Leyden 266, from Volterra.  Holwerda pl. 3.  'Dull black glaze.'
12. Leyden 257, from Volterra.  Holwerda pl. 3.  'Black glaze.'
13. Leyden 258.  Holwerda pl. 3.  I, impressed.  'Blue-black glaze.'
14. Leyden 261, from Volterra.  Holwerda 13.  'Dull purplish glaze, partly fired red.'

Leyden 260 is said to be like 259; 269 like 268; and 262, 265, 267 like 263, 264 and 266: all from Volterra.

This variety of dishie appears to be Etruscan: at least in the Attic type that corresponds to it the lip is less prominent; and I have not found it in other Italian fabrics.  Gray bucchero examples are found in Etruria: so *ML.* 24, 871, 2 and 3, in the Villa Giulia, from a late-fifth-century tomb at Todi.

It will be noticed that two of our vases are said to have blue-black glaze.

This is also the shape of a Latin vase in Rome, Antiquarium, one of those decorated with a small impressed figure of Herakles and the inscription *aerar* (*Annali* 1880 pl. R, 16, c): on these vases see pp. 236 and 246.

## iv. with heavy overhanging rim

Rome, Antiquarium, 2387, from Rome.  Ryberg fig. 120e.

According to Mrs. Ryberg (ibid. 94 note 70) there are innumerable little dishes like this, with striated overhanging rim, from Rome, in the magazines of the Museo delle

Terme.  Similar dishes have been found at Foci del Garigliano (*ML.* 37 pl. 37, 9; and pl. 37, 21–2).  In type 45 at Minturnae (*Boll. st. med.* 5, 4–5 pl. 5, 45 and pl. 7, 45, above) 'the rim is usually stamped or incised'.  In Florence 8217, from Vetulonia (*CV.* IV Bz pl. 1, 14), the rim is decorated with 'incised zigzag lines interrupted at two points by a cross with six arms'.  In a dish from Minturnae (*Boll. st. med.* 5 pl. 5, 46 and pl. 7, 46) the rim-decoration consists of 'incised lines' (striations) and crosses.  Other dishes are like these, but the rim is plain: Philadelphia, from the territory of Falerii (*AJA.* 1942, 535 fig. 4: graffito, inside, *avii* or *ave*); Leyden 164, from Italy (Holwerda 22); Leyden 285, from Montalcino (ibid.); Leyden 287, from Montalcino (ibid.); Leyden 286, from Montalcino (Holwerda 22 and pl. 3); Todi 543, from Todi (*CV.* pl. 14, 6); Philadelphia 2850, from Ardea (*Boll. st. med.* 4, 4–5 pl. 2, 28); and a good many in Ancona, from Montefortino (*ML.* 9 pl. 11, 20; pl. 4, 16; pl. 11, 14; pl. 10, 18; pl. 11, 13).  The proportions vary.

The type is not confined to Latium and Etruria: a dishie, from Taranto, in Taranto may be counted as belonging to it (*Japigia* 9, 3 fig. 1).

A vase from Montefortino, in Ancona, is a stemmed version of the same (*ML.* 9 pl. 10, 8).

### v. 'SALT-CELLARS'

1. Oxford 1874.431.  Pl. 38, 11.  Blue-black glaze.  Ht. 0.056, dm. 0.093.
2. Florence 8950, from Vetulonia.  *CV.* IV Bz pl. 1, 9.
3. Florence 8949, from Vetulonia.  *CV.* IV Bz pl. 1, 20.
4. Florence, from Sovana.  *NSc.* 1903, 221, 9.  'Fine black glaze.'

No. 1 belongs to the Malacena fabric.

A Vatican vase, from Etruria (*Mus. Greg.* ii. pl. 94, vii, 2, below), ought to make a fifth.  The profile is much as in no. 1.  I assume that the object figured above it does not belong to it.

A vase from Bettona, in Bettona (*CV.* Terni pl. 9, 10), might be a sixth.  Todi 550, from Todi (*CV.* pl. 14, 2) has a different profile.

## STEMMED BOWLS OR DISHIES

These vary in detail, but share the thick stem.

1. Leyden 282, from Volterra.  Holwerda 13.  'Matt blue-black glaze.'
2. Leyden 283, from Volterra.
3. Leyden 284, from Volterra.  Holwerda 13.  'Blue-black glaze.'
4. Michigan 2636, from Chiusi.  *CV.* pl. 18, 4.  'Poor glaze, fired red in spots.'

The stemmed dish Philadelphia 2996, from Ardea (*Boll. st. med.* 4, 4–5, pl. 2, 6), though not Attic, is of a common Attic type (see *RG.* 65 on G 77).  I should guess that the black stemmed dish of the same type Villa Giulia 12562, from Falerii (*CIE.* 8050) was Faliscan.  It bears the Latinian graffito *sacra*, retr.

## PLATES

1. Vatican G. 122, from Vulci.  *RG.* pl. 35.  Small (dm. 0.118).
2. Villa Giulia, from Vulci.  Graffito, inside, retr., *Alfi.*  Small (dm. 0.17).

Poor glaze: in no. 1 black with a greenish tinge and fired to red-brown in parts; in no. 2 black and red. Not 'Malacena'. See p. 260, foot.

A black plate in Tarquinia, RC. 7586, from Tarquinia, resembles these, but the shape is not quite the same, the lip being flatter: in the middle of the interior, stamped, *Alf.* Tarquinia RC. 7585 is like RC. 7586, but I do not remember if it is stamped.

The inscription *Alfi* also occurs in 'in planta pedis' on a fragment of a 'large saucer' (plate?) found at Orvieto and mentioned in *NSc.* 1890, 210, whence *CIL.* xi. ii. 1, 6700, 22; *Alfi* and *Alf*, 'in planta pedis', on fragments, described as 'Arretine', from Rome (*CIL.* xv, 4946).

I cannot tell from the reproduction whether Copenhagen ABc 792 (*CV.* pl. 221, 13), from Volterra, is connected with nos. 1 and 2. The glaze is described as a lustrous greenish-grey. The rim is set off above by a groove. So also in Florence 8212, from Vetulonia (*CV.* IV Bz pl. 1, 15): 'black glaze turned brown in places'.

The following plates, of the same general type as Vatican G. 122, are said to have blue-black glaze:

1. Leyden 247, from Volterra. Holwerda pl. 2.
2. Leyden 248, from Volterra. Holwerda pl. 2.
3. Leyden 249, from Volterra. Holwerda 22.
4. Leyden 250, from Volterra.
5. Leyden 251, from Volterra.
6. Leyden 252, from Volterra. I. A, Holwerda 22.
7. Leyden 253, from Volterra. Holwerda pl. 2.

Another sort of plate, or dish, is represented by such as the following:

1. Leyden 243, from Montalcino. Holwerda 22 and pl. 2. 'Blue-black glaze.'
2. Leyden 231, from Volterra. Holwerda 22 and pll. 2 and 10. Inside, impressed, a small star. 'Lacquer-like blue-black glaze.'
3. Leyden 232, from Volterra. Holwerda pl. 2. 'Dull brown-black lacquer-like glaze.'
4. Leyden 244, from Volterra. Holwerda pl. 2. 'Dull blue-black glaze.'

This, in the main at least, is the shape of the plate in Rome, Antiquarium, from Rome (*Annali* 1880 pl. R, 16a), which is decorated with a small impressed figure of Herakles and the inscription *aerar*. I do not know whether this is the plate published by Ryberg fig. 136a, or a replica. On these and others like them see Ryberg 123–5; see also our p. 244.

## FISH-PLATE

Leyden 242, from Volterra. Holwerda 22 and pl. 2. 'Dull blue-black glaze.'

Not easily to be distinguished from the many black fish-plates made in Campania and elsewhere.

## SMALL JARS
### i

1. Leyden 206, from Cortona. Holwerda pl. 2. 'Blue-black glaze.'
2. Leyden 207, from Volterra. Holwerda 16. 'Blue-black glaze.' As the last.

ii

3. Leyden 210, from Volterra. Holwerda 16 and pl. 2. 'Blue-black glaze.'
4. Cracow, Univ., inv. 478, from Chiusi. *CV*. pl. 15 (Pol. 88), 23. 'Bluish glaze, fired to greenish yellow.' As the last.
5. Florence, from San Miniato. *NSc.* 1935, 33, 7. Compare the last two.

iii

(with large mouth)

6. Leyden 209, from Volterra. Holwerda 16 and pl. 2. 'Blue-black glaze.'
7. Once Volterra, Cinci, from Volterra. Inghirami *Mon. etr.* 5 pl. 50, 8. Just like the last, unless indeed it be the same.

A larger jar in Castiglioncello, from Castiglioncello (*NSc.* 1924, 164 fig. 5, 3), is shaped somewhat like (i) but flares towards the bottom.

A small black jar from Teano (*ML.* 20, 139 fig. 106, a), doubtless local, bears a general resemblance to (ii) and (iii). So does a black jar from Minturnae, but it has no foot (*Boll. st. med.* 5, 4–5 pl. 5, 39 and pl. 7, 39).

All these may be thought of as slightly smartened versions of kitchen pots; (ii) and (iii) also recall some forms of situla.

Pots similar to (ii) may be furnished with a pair of ring-handles: see under kantharoi, p. 234.

iv

1. Vienna (ex Este), from Volterra. Bluish-black glaze.
2. Vienna (ex Este), from Volterra. Bluish-black glaze.

These two little jars are shaped something like the oinochoai described on p. 262, η, but they have no handle and the lip is a little thicker. They may have served as pomade-pots. Malacena fabric.


CALYX-KRATERS

1. Once Disney, from Volterra. Disney *Mus. Disn.* pl. 126. Blue-black glaze.
2. Florence, from Monteriggioni. *St. etr.* 2 pl. 30, 89; Solari fig. 55.
3. Florence 4559. *Gaz. arch.* 1879, pl. 6, 4, whence Martha 489 fig. 330.
4. Todi 522, from Todi. *CV*. pl. 13, 3.

All four are from the Malacena fabric. They are calyx-kraters in the fourth-century tradition and derived from metal models: but there is nothing very characteristic about them. Plastic heads at the base of the handles are common in bronze calyxes (Pernice *HKP.* 4, 37–42). The wreath of vine or ivy round the middle doubtless occurred in metal calyxes, although I do not recall an example. Such wreaths are well known from clay vases, the Attic 'garland kraters' of the fourth century.

Bianchi Bandinelli mentions a fragment from Monteriggioni (*St. etr.* 2, 154 no. 89a) which is the handle of a calyx like no. 2.

## VOLUTE-KRATERS

1. Berlin, from Monteriggioni. *St. etr.* 2 pl. 31, 90. Separate stand. On the neck, floral, in red and white.
2. Once Terrosi, from Monteriggioni. According to Bianchi Bandinelli just like the last except for the pattern on the neck (*St. etr.* 2 pl. 31, 91).
3. Florence, from Orbetello. A, *NSc.* 1885, pl. 1, 6, whence Martha 491 and Milani *Mus. Top.* 111. The body is reeded, except for a strip round the middle, which is decorated in relief with griffins attacking fawns. Separate stand.

These are from the Malacena fabric.

No. 91a in Bianchi Bandinelli's list of finds in the Tomba dei Calinii Šepuś at Monteriggioni is the handle of a vase like nos. 1 and 2, but smaller (*St. etr.* 2, 154).

## STAMNOS, WITH STAND

Berlin, from Monteriggioni. *St. etr.* 2 pl. 31, 88, 1.

Malacena fabric: the date, therefore, left open by Jacobsthal (*ECA.* 1938), is the third century.

Bianchi Bandinelli (*St. etr.* 2, 153 no. 88, 2) mentions another similar stamnos with stand, formerly in the Terrosi collection, from Monteriggioni.

The attachments of the handles are heater-shaped, and each is decorated with the frontal head of a bald and bearded satyr, and above this a pair of tendrils. Handle-attachments of this shape are common in Etruscan bronze stamnoi, and are often decorated with frontal satyr-heads. I give a list of such handles, whether preserved sole, or on their stamnoi. Many of them have been mentioned by others; see Jacobsthal and Langsdorff 48 note 1; Ducati *Storia* 339 note 51; *Dedalo* 13, 281 (Marconi); *From the Coll.* 2, 167 (Riis); Hesp. 12, 100–111 (D. K. Hill); Jacobsthal *ECA.* 21–2 and 137–8.

I owe my knowledge of the handles in Berlin and Munich to Jacobsthal; photographs, also, of these and several others.

### A. THE FORMAL GROUP

The satyr-head is very formal. The handles are all from one fabric. Some of them have floral decoration instead of the satyr-head.

The Stuttgart stamnos (no. 7) was found in the same grave at Klein-Aspergle, in Wirtemberg, as an Attic red-figured cup, of about 450 or not much earlier, by the Amymone Painter (I, Jacobsthal and Langsdorff pl. 33; Ebert 7 pl. 1; *ARV.* 551 no. 18):[1] on the grave see Jacobsthal and Langsdorff 30–1. The stamnos from La Motte Saint-Valentin was found with a 'Saint-Valentin' kantharos (see p. 219) of the same period (Déchelette *Coll. Millon* pl. 31).

(satyr-head, with a pair of eyes above it)

1. Munich 191. Handle. Jacobsthal *ECA.* pl. 220, d.
2. Munich 192, from Vulci. Handle.

[1] I take the opportunity of correcting an error in my reference to this cup in *ARV.*: for 'Jacobsthal and Langsdorff pl. 33 and pl. 34, c' read 'I, Jacobsthal and Langsdorff pl. 33.' (The stemless cup figured on their pl. 34, c is not that by the Amymone Painter, but the black one found in the same grave).

3. Berlin Fr. 1389, from Tarquinia. Handle.
4. Vatican, from Vulci. Phot. Alinari 35553, 2, whence *Jb.* 55, 243, 2. Handle.
5. Carlsruhe 620. Wagner pl. 15, 2. Handle.
6. Louvre 2667–8, 'from Corinth'. De Ridder *Bronzes du Louvre* pl. 97. Pair of handles. As the last.
7. Stuttgart, from Klein-Aspergle. Stamnos. Lindenschmit 3, 12 pl. 4, 1; Déchelette *Coll. Millon* 121, 1; Ebert 7 pl. 2, a; Jacobsthal *ECA*. pl. 220, a.
7 bis. Bologna, from Bologna. *St. etr.* 17 pl. 17, 4, right.
8. Berlin inv. 6474–5, from Italy. Pair of handles. Advanced.
9. Carlsruhe 622. Handle.

(satyr-head, with floral instead of the eyes above it).

10. Vatican, from Vulci. *Mus. Greg.* i pl. 60, d. Handle.
11. Carlsruhe 621. Handle.
12. Bonn, Provinzialmuseum, from Weisskirchen. Déchelette *Manuel* 2, 3, 1068, 1–2; Jacobsthal *ECA*. pl. 220, b. Stamnos.

(plant, between eyes)

13. Saint-Germain, from La Motte Saint-Valentin (Haute-Marne). Déchelette *Coll. Millon* pl. 30 and p. 107. Stamnos.
14. Carlsruhe 616. Wagner pl. 11, middle; Schumacher pl. 9, 16 and 23. Stamnos, but it is said to be not certain that the handles, or both, belong.
15. Vatican, from Vulci or Bomarzo. *Mus. Greg.* i pl. 7, 5 and 5a. Stamnos.

(floral)

16. Carlsruhe 624. Wagner pl. 15, 5. Handle.

A pair of handles from Bologna, in Bologna, with a heart-shaped leaf surmounted by a palmette, and, above, a pair of eyes, bears some resemblance to the Formal Group, but is not certainly from the same fabric. Incision only, no relief.

### B. THE ASCOLI GROUP

The satyr-head is fine and bold, especially in nos. 1 and 2. Fifth century.

(satyr-head; above, floral)

1. Ancona, from S. Ginesio. One attachment, *NSc.* 1886, 45, G; one handle, *Dedalo* 13, 275. Stamnos.
2. Ascoli Piceno. One handle, *Dedalo* 13, 274. Stamnos.
3. Munich 3831. Neugebauer *Bronzegerät des Altertums* pl. 22, 1; Jacobsthal *ECA*. pl. 220, c. Stamnos.
4. Bologna, from Bologna. Part of a handle.
5. New York 50–1, from near Rome. Richter *Bronzes* 32 below. Pair of handles.

### C. VARIOUS, WITH SATYR-HEAD AND FLORAL ABOVE

1. Once Rome, Bonichi, from Capua. *Bull. Nap.* new series 2 pl. 7, 4–5. Stamnos. On the topside of the mouth, an Oscan inscription (Conway *The Italic Dialects* no. 99).

The exact style of the satyr-head is not clear from the cut, but seems nearer to the Formal than to the Ascoli Group.

2. Goettingen 74, said to be from near Mayence. Körte *Gött. Bronzen* pl. 16. Handle. The satyr-head has almost ceased to be human. The floral part recalls the Ascoli Group.

3. New York 249–50, perhaps from near Rome. Richter *Bronzes* 126, below; *Hesp.* 12, 102 fig. 4. Pair of handles. Later style: fourth century.

### D. OTHER HANDLES OF THE SAME SHAPE: VARIOUS

1. Louvre 2659. De Ridder *Bronzes du Louvre* pl. 97. Stamnos. The attachments are plain.

2. Florence, from Populonia. *NSc.* 1905, 35, i, 2. Stamnos. I cannot tell from the small reproduction whether the attachments are plain or decorated.

3. Carlsruhe 5623, fragment of a handle. All that remains of the decoration is 'part of a lotus-flower'.

4. Villa Giulia. A pair of handles. Floral.

5. Villa Giulia. A pair of handles. Floral. I owe my knowledge of this and the last to Jacobsthal.

6. Once Disney. Disney *Mus. Disn.* pl. 66, 1. Handle. Floral.

7–8. Florence, from Montepulciano. *NSc.* 1894, 289 fig. 4. Two stamnoi. On the attachments, debased eyes.

9. Ancona, from Montefortino. *ML.* 9 pl. 4, 8; Montelius pl. 152, 10; Dall' Osso 235, above; one handle, *Dedalo* 13, 276. Stamnos. On the attachments, 'tendril-goddess' flanked by goats: see Jacobsthal *ECA.* 138. The rest of the tomb-furniture belongs to the fourth century.

10. Cab. Méd. 1457. Babelon and Blanchet 586. Handle. On one attachment 'a satyr', on the other 'a maenad'; with these compare, perhaps, the bronze oinochoe of shape VI Louvre 2783 (de Ridder pl. 180: p. 283, ii no. 1), and the bronze handle, from a similar oinochoe, Gréau 222 (Fröhner *Coll. Gréau* 49–50: p. 283, ii no. 2).

### E. THE WORCESTER GROUP
(bearded head, horned, frontal: Acheloos?)

1. Worcester, Mass., 1434. *Hesp.* 12, 101 fig. 3. Pair of handles.

2. Louvre 2670. De Ridder *Bronzes du Louvre* pl. 97. Handle.

3. Goettingen. Körte *Gött. Bronzen* pl. 16, 75. Handle.

One fabric. The style of the Worcester Group is very Greek. For the floral above the head compare the handles of a Greek bronze calyx-krater in Berlin (Züchner *Der Berliner Mänadenkrater* pl. 7).

## SITULAE

### A. BELL-SITULAE

These situlae are closely interconnected. All but the last have a figure-relief of more or less rectangular form under each bail-attachment. In no. 12 the relief has a makeshift look. In no. 13 its place is taken by a large ivy-leaf. The fabric has usually been supposed

Campanian: so by Pagenstecher, Pernice, Sieveking. It will be noticed that the proveniences, when known, are always Etruscan. This would not be enough in itself to prove the vases native: but nos. 2, 4, 8 seemed to me to be from the Malacena fabric, and nos. 3, 5, 13 are connected with nos. 2 and 4 by the white pattern below the rim. I believe the fabric of all to be Etruscan.

Pagenstecher points out (*Jb.* 27, 149) that the chariot-groups in the reliefs of London G 30 (no. 1) are replicas of the corresponding groups on the 'quadriga phialai (see p. 292). Most of these phialai are Calene, but there seem to be Etruscan imitations as well (p. 240).

Our vases are imitated, of course, from Greek metal situlae. On bronze situlae of this type see Schröder *Griechische Bronzeeimer im Berliner Antiquarium* 5–11 ('type A'); *Jb.* 35, 84–93 (Pernice); *Mü. Jb.* 12 (1921), 122 (Sieveking); Pernice *HKP.* iv, 21–30; *Gnomon* 2, 472–3 (Neugebauer); *Anz.* 1936, 411–19 (Zontschev and Werner); Züchner *Der Berliner Mänadenkrater* (with other types); *Berl. Mus.* 59, 79 (Luschey); also p. 288.

1. London G 30, from Vulci: in one relief, Athena and Nike in chariot; in the other, Ares and Nike in chariot.
2. London G 31, from Vulci. In each relief, Dionysos with panther. Fine greenish and bluish glaze.
3. Berlin 4214, from Volterra. Schröder *Gr. Bronzeeimer* 8. In each relief, Pan attacking nymph.
4. Berlin inv. 30442. Schröder *Gr. Bronzeeimer* 9. In each relief, centauress and young satyr.
5. Florence 1060. B, Birch *Hist. of Ancient Pottery* (1873) 165 fig. 117. In one relief, satyr running with dog; in the other, satyr running with panther.
6. Florence 1059. In each relief, satyr running with dog.
7. Leyden H 292, from Volterra. Holwerda 26. In one relief, Artemis with hind; in the other, centaur and Lapith. 'Blue-black glaze.'
8. Louvre, fragment. The upper part remains, with the reliefs: in each, satyr pursuing maenad. This has been completed with fragments from the lower part of a calyx-krater (heads of maenads at the base of the handles). Malacena fabric.
9. Florence 75432, from Volterra. Milani *R. Mus. di Firenze* pl. 44. In each relief, satyr pursuing maenad.
10. Munich. A, *Mü. Jb.* 12, 121. In each relief, hunter.
11. Florence V 420 (ex Vagnonville: from Chiusi?). In each relief, hunter.
12. Florence, Terrosi, from Monteriggioni. *St. etr.* 2 pl. 32, 98. In each relief, a bearded figure, frontal. 'Greenish glaze.'
13. Copenhagen inv. 3816, from Volterra. *CV.* pl. 221, 9.

Schröder mentions (*Gr. Bronzeeimer* 10, foot) a fragment of a situla in Florence with a palmette in relief below the bail-holes: I have not seen this.

Copenhagen inv. 3816 (no. 13) is an imitation of just such a metal original as the bronze situla, a fragment of which has been found at Altavilla Silentina on the river Sele in Lucania (*NSc.* 1937, 145, fig. 2). Another bronze situla with a large ivy-leaf on it was found in the Tomba dei Calinii Šepuś at Monteriggioni (*St. etr.* 2 pl. 36, 144): it is fragmentary, and there would seem to be no trace of a bail. Compare also, for the ivy-leaf, a silver situla (of different type) from the Taman peninsula (*Anz.* 1913, 185, fig. 10).

### B. OVOID SITULA?

London G 32, from Vulci. *Cat. GEV.* ii pl. 10, 319. Below each bail-hole, in relief, a
　　Tritoness with raised arms.

The body of the vase is much restored, and I did not feel certain that there was evidence
for the lower part terminating as it now does. If there is, then the vase is copied from a
favourite type of metal object in Etruria: a small situla with egg-shaped body and a
single bail. If there is not, then the vase must have been a stamnoid situla of the same
type as those in the next section (c). In either case, it is very closely connected both
with them, and, as will be seen, with the bronze situlae of the ovoid type.

　　Malacena fabric.

　　Here is a list of ovoid situlae in metal:

#### (bronze)

1. Marzabotto, from Marzabotto. Gozzadini *Ult. scoperte* pl. 14, 6, whence Martha 94.
2. Carlsruhe 634, 1. Wagner pl. 12, 2; Schumacher pl. 9, 11.
3. Florence, from Populonia. Milani *Mon. scelti* pl. 5, 12. From the late-fifth-century
　　grave which contained the two hydriai by the Meidias Painter.
4. Carlsruhe 634, 2. Said by Schumacher to be like Carlsruhe S 634, 1, except that
　　the lip is decorated.
5. Vatican, from Vulci or Orte. *Mus. Greg.* i pl. 3, 3.
6. Berlin Fr. 1321. Schröder *Gr. Bronzeeimer* 14 fig. 11, 4.
7. Chiusi, from Chiusi. Levi, *Mus. Civ. di Chiusi* 119, left middle.
8. Florence, from Talamone. Milani *Mus. Top.* 101, right.
9. Louvre 2826, from Montefiascone. De Ridder *Bronzes du Louvre* pl. 102; phot.
　　Giraudon 153.
10. Berlin Fr. 1322, from near Vulci. Schröder *Gr. Bronzeeimer* 21.
11. Florence, from Bolsena. Heydemann *Ober* pl. 4, 3, whence (the reliefs only) Amelung
　　*Führer* fig. 42; Milani *Mus. Top.* 6.
12. Villa Giulia, from Vulci. *St. etr.* 11, 113–14. The bottom is missing, but the situla
　　must have been of this type.

#### (silver)

13. Boston 13.2861, from Chiusi. *AJA.* 1918, 267, fig. 10, a.
14. London, from Chiusi. *AD.* i p. 9 fig. 5; Walters *Cat. Silver* pl. 4. From the same
　　tomb as the sarcophagus of Seianti Thanunia (*AD.* i pl. 20).

Nos. 1–3 go together: the bottom is pointed. Nos. 9–12 have decoration on the body
in very low relief. The silver situlae, nos. 13 and 14, go together.

### C. STAMNOID SITULAE

Small, with a single bail.

1. Berlin inv. 4069, from Monteriggioni. *St. etr.* 2 pl. 32, 99. Below each bail-hole, in
　　relief, a Tritoness with raised arms.

2. Berlin, from Monteriggioni? As the last.
3. Louvre N 1847. The figures under the bail-holes are hard to make out, but may quite well be Tritonesses as in the others.
Malacena fabric.

Bianchi Bandinelli (*St. etr.* 2, 155 note 1) mentions a situla in S. Gimignano, from Poggio alla Città, as just like no. 1.

On stamnoid situlae see pp. 287–8. Our three are not very like any of the metal ones that have been preserved. The upper part is the same as in London G 32, described above, and in the bronze ovoids of the list just given. In fact the upper part of an ovoid situla is combined with the base and foot of the stamnoid situla in its later phase.

## NECK-AMPHORAE

### i

No. 1 is reeded.

1. Berlin, from Monteriggioni. *St. etr.* 2 pl. 31, 92.
2. Florence. *Gaz. arch.* 1879 pl. 6, 1.
3. Florence. *Gaz. arch.* 1879 pl. 6, 10, whence Martha 489 fig. 328. Like the last, but different foot.
4. Once Volterra, Cinci, from Volterra. Inghirami *Mon. etr.* 5 pl. 49, 13.

I should have thought that these were from the Malacena fabric, but no. 1 also recalls the oinochoe *St. etr.* 2 pl. 31, 95 (p. 256).

Bianchi Bandinelli (*St. etr.* 2, 154 no. 92a) describes a fragment found in the Tomba dei Calinii Sepuś at Monteriggioni as the foot of a vase like no. 1.

### ii

Ferrara, T 606, from Spina. Aurigemma[1] 126, 9=[2]119, 9.

I do not know any other neck-amphorae like this. I guess it to be Etruscan.

## PELIKAI

Types 10 and 11 at Minturnae (*Boll. st. med.* 5, 4–5, pl. 1, 10 and pl. 3, 10; ibid. pl. 3, 11) are small black pelikai. Mingazzini has already compared two black vases from Foci del Gargliano with them: inv. 680 (*ML.* 37 pl. 38, 6), and inv. 589 (ibid. pl. 35, 13).

## OINOCHOAI

First comes a large group of rather good Etruscan oinochoai, including several different shapes; then the rest of the oinochoai, Etruscan and Latin, arranged according to shape.

### THE GROUP OF VIENNA O. 565

Most of these belong to the Malacena Group: I felt doubtful about nos. 16–19.
(shape II, but high handle)

1. Copenhagen 405, from Volterra. *CV.* pl. 224, 10. 'Blue-black glaze.'
2. Copenhagen 402. *CV.* pl. 224, 9. 'Greenish glaze.'
3. Copenhagen 408. *CV.* pl. 224, 11. 'Black glaze.'

4. Copenhagen 414. *CV.* pl. 224, 14. 'Black glaze.'

5. London (cancelled number G 262). The handle is modern. The glaze where thin is brownish.

6. Berlin inv. 4056, from Monteriggioni.

7. Berlin inv. 4055, from Monteriggioni.

8. Berlin inv. 4026, from Monteriggioni.

9. Once Terrosi, from Monteriggioni. *St. etr.* 2 pl. 31, 96. On the shoulder, in white, ivy.

10. Lost? Jacquemart *Histoire de la céramique* 252, whence Jännicke *Grundriss der Keramik* 22 fig. 5.

11. Chiusi, from Chiusi. Levi *Mus. Civ. di Chiusi* 125, iii, left.

12. Copenhagen inv. 3818, from Volterra. *CV.* pl. 224, 12. Brownish-black glaze.

13. Leyden 185, from Volterra. Holwerda 10. 'Bluish-black glaze.'

14. Leyden 186, from Volterra. Holwerda 10.

15. Sèvres 1163.2, from Volterra. Ex Cinci. *CV.* pl. 24, 9. 'Bluish-black glaze.'

16. Louvre. At the lower attachment of the handle, plastic, a female head.

17. Louvre. Like the last.

18. Louvre. Like the last two.

19. Louvre. On the shoulder, in white, ivy. The handle is modern. At the base of the handle, a head of Silenus in relief. I could not say that this and the three preceding it belonged to the Malacena Group.

(the same, but the body reeded: nos. 20–2 are squat,
the others have normal proportions)

20. Vienna, Oest. Mus., 565, from Cervetri. Masner pl. 8.

21. Munich, Dr. Preyss. Seems to have a wreath in added colour on the shoulder.

22. Florence. *Gaz. arch.* 1879 pl. 6, 6.

23. Goluchow, Prince Czartoryski, 114, from Nola. *CV.* pl. 52, 8. Bluish glaze.

24. Toronto 545. Robinson and Harcum 252, below, and pl. 91. Acquired from Pacini of Florence. Bluish glaze.

25. New York 41.161.253 (ex Gallatin). *CV.* Gallatin pl. 32, 4.

26. New York GR. 472, from Bolsena. Richter *Cat. Bronzes* 181, above, 5. Found with a Malacena kantharos (see p. 232 no. 69). Slightly bluish glaze. Ivy-wreath on the shoulder.

27. Compiègne 924, from Chiusi. *CV.* pl. 24, 21. 'Greenish glaze.'

28. Florence ('585'). *Gaz. arch.* 1879 pl. 6, 2.

29. Once Pesaro, Passeri, from Todi. Gori *Mus. Etr.* part 2 class iv pl. 8, 1.

30. Vatican, from Etruria. *Mus. Greg.* ii pl. 94, vi, 2.

(shape I)

30 bis. Todi 523, from Todi. *CV.* pl. 13, 8.

(shape X)

31. Copenhagen inv. 3819, from Volterra. *CV.* pl. 224, 13.

32. Once Volterra, Cinci, from Volterra. Inghirami *Mon. etr.* 5 pl. 47, 4. At the lower end of the handle, a satyr-head, plastic.

(shape XX: see p. 257)

33. Leyden 187, from Volterra. Holwerda 20 and pl. 2. 'Blue-black glaze.'
34. Sèvres 1163.3, from Volterra. *CV*. pl. 24, 4.
35. Copenhagen 371, from Volterra. *CV*. pl. 224, 8. 'Dull brownish-black glaze.'
36. Once Disney, from Volterra. Disney *Mus. Disn.* pl. 127, 3.
37. Louvre N 1951. The same head at the lower attachment of the handle as in the last.
38. Berlin 2675. Bluish glaze.
39. Copenhagen 411, from Volterra. *CV*. pl. 224, 7. Blue-black glaze.
40. Leyden 188, from Volterra. Holwerda 20 and pl. 2. 'Blue-black glaze.'

(variant of the last shape)

41. Ancona. On the neck, plastic, a female head, and something else (grapes?).

(special shape, something like an oinochoe shape II, but the mouth round
instead of trefoil: the same principle, then, as in shape XX)

42. Oxford 1928.50. The handle ends above in the head of a young satyr, plastic, overlooking the mouth; below, in a head of Silenus. Bluish and greenish glaze. Ht. 0.264.
43. Todi 517, from Todi. *CV*. pl. 13, 7. Like the last, but the handle is double not triple, on the shoulder there is a vine-wreath in white, and the plastic head at the upper end of the handle is said to be female.

No. 144 on pl. 3 of Stephani's Leningrad catalogue is the shape of our nos. 23–30. According to Stephani his nos. 607, 622, 690, and 694 have this shape, but I do not know how close they are to the cut. No. 622 is said to be from Nola. No. 694 has a plastic head at the upper end of the handle as well as the lower, which suggests that it may go with the Brussels jug A 738, on which see p. 256.

I noted three black oinochoai, from Monteriggioni, in Berlin, inv. 4062, inv. 4020, inv. 4061, as of similar shape to nos. 33–40: at the lower attachment of the handle, a satyr-head. They are Etruscan, but I did not set them down as belonging to the Malacena Group.

An oinochoe in the Vatican, from Etruria (*Mus. Greg.* ii pl. 94, v, 2), to judge from the reproduction, is of the same shape as nos. 33–40, or nearly, and may go with them.

An oinochoe, from Monteriggioni, in the Terrosi collection (*St. etr.* 2 pl. 32, 101), may be of the same shape as nos. 33–40, but the mouth is missing, and the body is somewhat fatter.

The oinochoe Todi 521, from Todi (*CV*. pl. 13, 6), was probably of shape XX (the mouth is missing). It is doubtless Etruscan. The body is striated. The shoulder has the same plastic decoration as the Ancona vase, our no. 41: two bunches of grapes, and between them a female head (of Medusa according to Becatti). Todi 1444, fragmentary, is said to be like 521.

Todi 519, from Todi (*CV*. pl. 13, 9), probably belongs to our group. It is not unlike our nos. 42 and 43 in shape, but the base is narrower, the body is not reeded, the handle is different, and there is a spout on the shoulder. The Silenus-head at the lower extremity of the handle seems to be of the same type as in our group. Todi 520, unpublished, is said to be like 519.

Mercklin (in *RM*. 38–9, 116, a) compares a reeded oinochoe, which I have not seen, in the Museo Artistico Industriale, Rome, with Vienna Oest. Mus. 565 (no. 20).

In Brussels A 738 (*CV*. IV Dc pl. 2, 2) the shape is similar to that of nos. 23–30, but the handle is different and the reeding is reduced to striations. I do not know the fabric.

A black oinochoe in Ferrara, from Spina, T 995, (Aurigemma[1] 126, i, 2 =[2]119, i, 2) is not unlike nos. 1–19 in shape, but the neck is thicker, and the relation is uncertain.

Two reeded oinochoai found in the Tomb of the Calinii Šepuś (*St. etr.* 2 pl. 31, 95, a sort of shape I; and 2 pl. 31, 97, shape XX) are hard to separate from the Group of Vienna O. 565: on the other hand they seem to be connected with certain vases most of which must be not Etruscan but Italiote, probably Campanian. I have not seen the first oinochoe, and all I noted about the second (which is in Berlin) was that the glaze was greenish. Here is a list of various reeded oinochoai that recall them: they need not all be from one fabric.

(shape XX: see p. 257)

1. Oxford 344. Ex Henderson. Greenish glaze. At the base of the handle, the head of a young satyr, horned. Ht. 0.13. Greenish glaze.
2. Compiègne 928, from Chiusi. *CV*. pl. 24, 20. 'Greenish glaze.'
3. Edinburgh 1872.23.40, from Cumae. On the neck, ivy (clay-red, with white
4. Once Rome, Augusto Castellani, from between Orvieto and Bolsena. *Annali* 1871 pl. C, 3. On the neck ivy ('green stalks, white leaves, red berries').

(shape III)

5. Brussels A 737. *CV*. IV Dc pl. 2, 4.
6. Brussels A 736. *CV*. IV Dc pl. 2, 5.
7. Edinburgh 1881.44.25, from Nola. Round the neck, ivy in clay-red. At the lower attachment of the handle, a head of Medusa, plastic; overlooking the mouth of the vase, a ram's head. The handle is in three sections; a large ridged section, decorated with impressed scales, between two smaller tori. The ram's head, and the scales on the handle, connect the vase with Brussels A 736 (no. 6).

### THE GROUP OF OXFORD 412

The oinochoe Vienna, Oest. Mus., 563 is said to have been found at Cervetri: it seems, however, not to be Etruscan: it belongs to a group ('of Oxford 412'), which is probably Campanian:

*Oinochoai* (shape II: all reeded)

1. Vienna, Oest. Mus., 563, from Cervetri. Masner pl. 8. 'Metallic dullish glaze.'
2. Oxford 412, from Capua. Ex Fortnum 117. Metallic, bluish glaze. Ht. 0.226.
3. Mariemont 90. *Coll. Warocqué* i, 52 no. 90.
4. Naples, from Cumae. *ML*. 22 pl. 104, 5, 6. Found with Attic and Campanian vases

from the second half of the fourth century (see ibid. 648–9, tomb clxxxviii, pl. 104, 5 and pl. 106, 5).

5. Michigan 4663, from near Naples. *CV.* pl. 19, 11.
6. Once Zurich, Ruesch. *Sg. Ruesch* pl. 24, 48.

Other reeded oinochoai of very similar shape are from a different fabric or fabrics; bear no sign, so far as I know, of having been made in Italy; and might be Attic:

### (i: with gilt necklace or wreath)

Alexandria 10530, from Alexandria. Breccia *Sciatbi* pl. 49, 77. See the next.

Alexandria 10535, from Alexandria. Breccia *Sciatbi* pl. 49, 83. This and the last seem from the reproductions to be of the same group as the oinochoai shape III ibid. pl. 49, 76 and 79, the hydria ibid. pl. 50, 84, the kantharos ibid. pl. 53, 103.

### (ii)

Oxford 392 (375). Ex Henderson. Ht. 0.172.
Oxford 1939.7, from Melos. Ht. 0.189.
London 66.4–15.1.
London 66.4–15.2. As the last.
Leyden H 69, from Tripoli. Holwerda 10.
Cracow inv. 1460. *CV.* pl. 14, 3.

### α. OINOCHOAI SHAPE XX

I give this name to a type of oinochoe which is a great favourite in Etruria and Latium: the body is fairly like that of oinochoe shape III, but the side is usually less rounded and nearer a triangle in section, and the mouth, instead of being trefoil, is flat.

### *The Group of Harvard 3066*

(double handle, with a small crossbar—representing a loop—on top.
Nos. 1–6 are striated, perhaps also no. 7: nos. 8 and 9 are not.)

1. Rome, Antiquarium, from Rome. Ryberg fig. 115.
2. Harvard 3066. *CV.* pl. 24, 4. 'Steely black glaze.'
3. Civitavecchia, from Castrum Novum. *St. etr.* 11 pl. 59 fig. 3, 5.
4. Civitavecchia, from Castrum Novum. *St. etr.* 11 pl. 59 fig. 3, 8.
5. Vatican, from Etruria. *Mus. Greg.* ii pl. 94, ii, 5.
6. Rome, Antiquarium, from Rome. Ryberg fig. 119b. The body more rounded.
7. Civitavecchia, from Castrum Novum. *St. etr.* 11 pl. 59 fig. 3, 4.
8. Rome, Antiquarium, from Rome. Ryberg fig. 119c.
9. Civitavecchia, from Castrum Novum. *St. etr.* 11 pl. 59 fig. 3, 7.
10. Toronto 570. Robinson and Harcum pl. 92.

Like these, but without the crossbar, is a striated vase in Naples, from Foci del Garigliano, inv. 885 (*ML.* 37 pl. 36, 4).

Very like the Group of Harvard 3066 in shape, including the handle, are the four oinochoai, decorated with a wreath in added colour, which are described on p. 217.

Two of the striated jugs with *pocolom* inscriptions (p. 216, e) resemble some of those in the list, and also the vase from Foci del Garigliano—so far as they go: but the mouth is missing, and nearly the whole of the handle, the exact form of which is not ascertainable.

Type 2 at Minturnae (*Boll. st. med.* 5, 4–5, pl. 1, 2 and pl. 2, 2) also resembles the Group of Harvard 3066, but the crossbar is lacking; type 4 there has the crossbar, but is taller (ibid. pl. 1, 4 and pl. 2, 4); no. 5 replaces the crossbar or loop by a knot (ibid. pl. 1, 5).

An oinochoe, from Montefortino, in Ancona has the handle looped (*ML.* 9 pl. 11, 21). In another, from Spina, in Ferrara (T 224: *NSc.* 1927, 148, 3) it is knotted. The mouth in these is not quite the same as in our Group. The Ferrara vase was found together with a Clusium duck-askos and a red-figured Attic lekane of the fourth century: see p. 119 no. 6.

Other jugs, from various fabrics, resemble Type 2 at Minturnae: the handle is simple:

1. Naples, from Foci del Garigliano, inv. 590. *ML.* 37 pl. 35, 8.
2. Oxford 1939.9, 'from Pompeii'. Buff clay, poor black glaze.
3. Michigan 3244 e. *CV.* pl. 2, 11. 'Fine polished dark grey slip.'
4. Naples?, from Teano. *ML.* 20, 138 fig. 105, d.
5. Ancona, from Ancona. *NSc.* 1910, 344, 1.
6. Naples, from Foci del Garigliano, inv. 1172. *ML.* 37 pl. 35, 9. The body rounder.

Miss Van Ingen takes the Michigan vase to be 'Egyptian' (that is, Alexandrian?), and we might compare an oinochoe from Alexandria, in Alexandria (*Annuaire du Musée Gréco-romain* 1933–5, 136, 12).

The following oinochoe shape XX is not exactly like any of the above:
Vatican G 120, from Vulci. *RG.* pl. 35.

The glaze, black with a greenish tinge, is rather poor. The vase seems to be from the same fabric as the oinochoe Vatican G 121 (p. 260: *RG.* pl. 35) and the small plate Vatican G 122 (p. 245, foot: *RG.* ibid.).

### The Group of Copenhagen 505
#### (ring-handle, double)

1. Copenhagen 505, from Volterra. *CV.* pl. 224, 4. 'Dullish black glaze.'
2. Bettona, from Bettona. *CV.* (Terni) pl. 9, 25.
3. Copenhagen 507. *CV.* pl. 224, 3. 'Dull greyish-black glaze.'
4. Berlin inv. 4014, from Monteriggioni.
5. Berlin inv. 4036, from Monteriggioni.
6. Leyden H 224, from Volterra. Holwerda 20. 'Blue-black glaze mottled with dull brown.'

### The Group of Toronto 573
#### (like the last, but the ring-like, double handle ends in snake-heads)

1. Vatican. I cannot tell whether this is *Mus. Greg.* ii pl. 95, ii, 3, from Etruria.
2. Vatican.

3. Cracow, Univ., inv. 480, from Chiusi. *CV.* pl. 15 (Pol. pl. 88), 19. 'Lustrous black glaze.'
4. Florence, from Orbetello?
5. Toronto 573. Robinson and Harcum pl. 92. 'Lustrous black glaze.'

Another oinochoe shape XX with snake-handle is Würzburg 935 (Langlotz pl. 253): but the curve of the body is different, with an angle at the point of greatest breadth; and the handle is not quite the same.

The following are not unlike Würzburg 935 in shape, but there are no snakes:
1. Villa Giulia, from Capena. The neck is marked off from the body.
2. Villa Giulia, from Capena. The shape of the neck is different, and the body less angular.

An oinochoe quite like these is represented on *aes grave* (Haeberlin pl. 68, 25).

The following may count as an oinochoe shape XX, and is quite like those in the Group of Harvard 3066 (p. 257), but the handle sets off from the lip itself and not below it: I do not know the fabric:

Warsaw, Majewski Museum, 16257, from Rome. *CV.* pl. 6 (Pol. 102), 19. 'Poor matt glaze.'

An oinochoe from Foci del Garigliano, inv. 1171 (*ML.* 37 pl. 38, 10) is not unlike the Majewski vase, but taller.

Two other oinochoai in which the handle sets off from the lip are farther from shape XX, the body is fully rounded, and in the second of them the neck is very thin:

Leyden H 226, from Volterra. Holwerda 20. 'Glaze fired matt brown.'
Philadelphia 2988, from Ardea. *Boll. st. med.* 4, 4–5, pl. 1, 22.

Other oinochoai of shape XX will be found in the Group of Vienna O. 565 (p. 255), or in its neighbourhood (pp. 255–6), and among the vases with decoration in added colour (pp. 216–17).

Type 22 of Miss Lake's Black-on-buff ware at Minturnae (*Boll. st. med.* 5, 4–5, pl. 12, 22 and pl. 14, 22) differs from all these in having no foot. The shape reappears in unglazed ware at Foci del Garigliano (*ML.* 37 pl. 40, 12). Black-on-buff Type 21 at Minturnae is a variant (*Boll. st. med.* 5, 4–5, pl. 1, 21, pl. 12, 21, and pl. 14, 21), and Type 20 is also related (ibid. pl. 2, 20 and pl. 14, 20).

A black oinochoe in Florence, from San Miniato, (*NSc.* 1935, 33, 1) would seem from the very poor reproduction to have no foot: if so, it may perhaps be compared with a black vase from Foci del Garigliano, inv. 1053 (*ML.* 37 pl. 36, 5).

A black oinochoe in the Louvre, of the same general form as the last two, but more elaborate, seemed to me possibly Etruscan: no foot; triple handle with a plastic head of a satyr at the lower attachment and a comic mask at the upper.

β. OINOCHOAI: SHAPE XX, BUT WITH HIGH HANDLE

Leyden H 221, from Montalcino. Holwerda 20. 'Dull blue-black glaze.' The lip is said to form a small spout in front.

Two bronze oinochoai, from Montefortino, in Ancona give a somewhat handsomer version of the Leyden shape (*ML.* 9 pl. 5, 15; ibid. pl. 4, 19); another, from Etruria, in the Vatican (*Mus. Greg.* i, pl. 7, 1) differs in having no foot.

## γ. OINOCHOAI: OLPAI

These share the triangular form of the body with Oinochoe XX, but the vase is larger and the proportions different. The handle sets off from the mouth, not below it.

### (i) two replicas

1. Florence, from San Miniato. *NSc.* 1935, 33, 5.
2. Florence, from San Miniato. *NSc.* 1935, 33, 8.

### (ii) two replicas: unglazed

1. Florence, from Vetulonia. *NSc.* 1895, 307 fig. 21.
2. Florence, from Vetulonia. As the last.

### (iii)

1. Florence, from Orbetello. *NSc.* 1885, pl. 1, 13.

The vase from Orbetello, which is more elaborate than the others and has a head of Silenus in relief at the lower attachment of the handle, is an imitation of such metal originals as the bronze olpe from Montefortino in Ancona (*ML.* 9 pl. 5, 20; detail, *Dedalo* 13, 277). Four other bronze vases from Montefortino, and one from Chiusi, are less like it (*ML.* 9 pl. 9, 5, pl. 10, 15, pl. 11, 10, pl. 4, 14; *Riv. Ist.* 4, 34, 3).

A clay olpe that bears a general resemblance to those in our list is Harvard 1895.246 (*CV.* pl. 37, 12). Like the Orbetello vase it is a close imitation of a metal original. It seemed to me Etruscan, of the Malacena fabric.

An unglazed, 'metallizing' olpe in Michigan (2831: *CV.* pl. 39, 1) is 'presumably from Pozzuoli or Cumae' and is no doubt Campanian.

## λ. OINOCHOAI: OLPOID

Vatican G 121, from Vulci. *RG.* pl. 35. Pale light brownish clay, poor brown glaze.

Vases of this general sort—tall rough olpoid oinochoai—are very common in many fourth- and third-century fabrics. One or two examples only: Alexandria, from Alexandria (Breccia *Sciatbi* pl. 51, 91; Rhodes, from Chalki (*Cl. Rh.* 2, 145 fig. 24, 1; ibid. 2, 160, 1); Sèvres, from Benghazi (*CV.* pl. 25, 64; ibid. pl. 25, 65). The lower part of the vase is often left unglazed as here. But I do not know any other vase just like ours: nearest, perhaps, Florence 3704, but the shape is not quite the same: light pinkish clay, bad glaze covering the upper half only. Our vase comes from the same fabric, I thought, as the oinochoe Vatican G 120 (p. 258) and the plate Vatican G 122 (p. 245).

A rough unglazed oinochoe from Monte Padrone near Volterra, Copenhagen inv. 7135 (*CV.* pl. 221, 1), belongs to the same family as all these; and so, it seems, two others, from Poggio Sala near Bolsena, in Florence (Milani *Mus. Top.* 52, 1, 1 and 5).

## ε. OINOCHOAI
### *The Group of Copenhagen 509*
(round body, flat mouth, high handle)

1. Copenhagen 509, from Volterra. *CV*. pl. 223, 10. Dull blue-black glaze.
2. Oxford 1872.1269. Pl. 38, 12. Bluish-black glaze.
3. Florence, from Populonia. *NSc.* 1934, 418, 3.
4. Leyden H 218, from Cortona. Holwerda 20. 'Blue-black glaze, fired greenish-yellow in places.'
5. Berlin inv. 4029, from Monteriggioni. Blue-black glaze.
6. Leyden H 217. Holwerda pl. 2. 'Purple-black glaze.'
7. Leyden H 219, from Volterra. Holwerda 20. 'Dull glaze.'

   Leyden H 220, from Volterra, is said to be like 219.

   In nos. 1 and 2 (and 3?) the neck is set off from the body.

   The make is not fine, but the fabric is probably Malacena.

### 3. OINOCHOAI: NIPPLE-JUGS

Type 3 at Minturnae (*Boll. st. med.* 5, 4–5, pl. 1, 3 and pl. 2, 3) belongs to a large family of black oinochoai, comprising many varieties, which seem not to occur in Etruria, but flourish on the border of Campania, at Foci del Garigliano as well as at Minturnae, and also in Campania itself. There is often, though not always, a nipple on the breast of the vase, and often a swelling—corresponding to the loop found elsewhere (p. 257)—on top of the handle. The Group of Copenhagen 509 (above) might perhaps be thought of as the Etruscan equivalent of this family.

1. From Minturnae. *Boll. st. med.* 5, 4–5, pl. 1, 3 and pl. 2, 3. Nipple. The proportions are said to vary from vase to vase.
2. From Minturnae. *Boll. st. med.* 5, 4–5, pl. 1, 1 and pl. 2, 1. Taller, larger: cf. no. 15.
3. Toronto 568. Robinson and Harcum pl. 92. Nipple, handle-swelling. Metallic glaze, slightly greenish. The lower part of the vase unglazed.
4. Wilno, Society of Friends. *CV*. pl. 3 (Pol. 126), 3. Handle-swelling. The lower part of the vase unglazed.
5. Naples, from Caivano. *NSc.* 1931, 601, 6. Handle-swelling.
6. *vacat.*
7. Naples inv. 85553, from Cumae. *NSc.* 1883, pl. 2, 37. Handle-swelling.
8. Naples, from Caivano. *NSc.* 1931, 603, 1. The lower part of the vase unglazed. Found with fourth-century vases.
9. Naples, from Ponticelli. *NSc.* 1922, 268, g. Handle-swelling. No foot? Found with late-fourth-century vases.
10. Naples, from Foci del Garigliano, inv. 463. *ML.* 37 pl. 40, 14. Handle-swelling The lower part of the vase unglazed. Twenty others are mentioned ibid. 903.
11. Naples, from Foci del Garigliano, inv. 891. *ML.* 37 pl. 40, 5. Nipple (and two others near the root of the handle). Higher handle, with swelling. The lower part of the vase unglazed. Two replicas are mentioned ibid. 903.

12. Naples, from Foci del Garigliano, inv. 1473. *ML.* 37 pl. 40, 7. Nipple, higher handle. The lower part of the vase unglazed.

13. Naples, from Foci del Garigliano, inv. 710. *ML.* 37 pl. 35, 1. Nipple. Slight lip.

14. Naples, from Foci del Garigliano, inv. 28. *ML.* 37 pl. 35, 2. Lip.

15. Naples, from Foci del Garigliano, inv. 875. *ML.* 37 pl. 35, 7. Taller, larger: cf. no. 2.

16. Naples, from Foci del Garigliano, inv. 600. *ML.* 37 pl. 36, 1. Taller, larger.

To these we may perhaps add a tall oinochoe in Poznań (*CV.* pl. 5, Pol. 121, 4): the lower part is unglazed; for the handle compare no. 12.

Type 3b at Minturnae (*Boll. st. med.* 5, 4–5, pl. 1, 3b and pl. 2, 3b) is just like Type 3 (above, no. 1), except that the handle is replaced by a spout; there is no nipple.

One nipple-vase from Foci del Garigliano (*ML.* 37 pl. 40, 6) stands a little apart from the rest: the shape approximates to that of oinochoe XX (with higher handle). The lower part of the vase is unglazed.

The nipple is not recorded in vases from purely Campanian sites. At Foci del Garigliano nipple-vases seem to have been traditional from early times.

A shape of the same sort as in our list is found in Teanan oinochoai with the usual incised and painted decoration: Oxford 1911.89, from Teano; Oxford 1911.74, from Teano; Harvard 2391 (*CV.* pl. 37, 7).

## η. OINOCHOAI
### *The Group of Copenhagen 453*

The form is akin to 'Oinochoe shape VIII'.

1. Copenhagen 453, from Volterra. *CV.* pl. 224, 1.

1 bis. Bettona, from Bettona. *CV.* (Terni) pl. 9, 17.

2. Copenhagen 510. *CV.* pl. 224, 2.

3. London market (Spink).

4. Cracow, Univ., inv. 479, from Chiusi. *CV.* pl. 15 (Pol. pl. 86), 18.

5. Florence, from Saturnia. *ML.* 30, 658, i, 2.

6. Florence, from Saturnia. *ML.* 30. 658, ii, right.

7–9. Florence, from Saturnia. Three others like the last two: mentioned by Minto ibid. 660.

10. Florence, from Sovana. *NSc.* 1903, 221, 5.

11. Leyden H 225, from Volterra. Holwerda 20.

12–18. Ferrara T 369, from Spina. Seven of them. Aurigemma[1] 111, below =[2] 133, below. From the same tomb as a very late red-figured bell-krater (p. 178, top), a bull-askos (p. 193, foot), two Malacena kantharoi (p. 232, nos. 47–8), and other late vases.

These small, well-made, well-glazed vases may belong to the Malacena Group.

Leyden H 142, from Volterra (Holwerda 20), either goes with these, or is like them. The handle is missing. 'Lustrous black glaze.'

A rough vase is perhaps more like 'oinochoe shape VIII' than anything else, but has no connexion with our group:

Leyden H 222, from Volterra. Holwerda 20. The upper part is covered with 'grey glaze fired matt'.

In another rough jug the resemblance to 'oinochoe shape VIII' is merely superficial: Leyden H 227, from Volterra. 'Glaze fired matt brown.'

Todi 524, an oinochoe shape VIII, is counted 'Etrusco-Campanian' in the *Corpus* (*CV*. pl. 14, 9), but I cannot tell from the reproduction whether it is not Attic or Italiote.

### θ. OINOCHOAI: ARCISATE SHAPE

Leyden 223, from Volterra. Holwerda 20. 'Good blue-black glaze.'

Either this vase, or one just like it, is figured by Inghirami *Mon. etr.* 5 pl. 48, 18: formerly in the Cinci collection at Volterra.

A jug in Naples, from Foci del Garigliano, inv. 1008, is somewhat akin to Leyden 223 in shape (*ML*. 37 pl. 35, 3); so, it would seem, is a jug from Cumae, Naples inv. 85383 (*NSc*. 1883 pl. 2, 36); and so are silver vases of the Roman period, one for instance from the treasure of Arcisate (north of Varese) in London (Walters *Cat. Silver* pl. 17, 126), another formerly in the Ruesch collection at Zurich, from the neighbourhood of Lake Trasimene (*Sg. Ruesch* pl. 37, 173), a third formerly in the Gréau collection (Fröhner *Coll. Gréau* 80).

### ι. OINOCHOE

Philadelphia 2832, from Ardea. *Boll. st. med.* 4, 4–5, pl. 2, 20.

Mrs. Holland calls this black vase Campanian: and an oinochoe from Cumae, in Naples, might indeed be compared (*NSc*. 1883 pl. 2, 38).

### κ. OINOCHOAI: S. ANATOLIA SHAPE: VARIOUS

1. Roman market, from Narce?
2. Roman market, from Narce?
3. Leyden 229, from Cortona. Holwerda 20. Squat. 'Patchy purple-brown glaze.'

Nos. 1 and 2 are known to me from a collective photograph.

A fourth black vase of this type was found at Vitulazio in Campania (*NSc*. 1930, 550 fig. 3) with a very late red-figured bell-krater (see *JHS*. 63, 104, Vitulazio Painter no. 3).

Unglazed oinochoai of the same shape are in Philadelphia (2840, from Ardea: *Boll. st. med.* 4, 4–5 pl. 2, 19) and in Florence (from Populonia, five of them: *NSc*. 1905, 57, part: 'yellowish clay, originally coloured red'). Leyden 773, from Montalcino (Holwerda 20), which has a yellowish-white slip, is also of this shape (see p. 282). Two oinochoai with simple decoration in black have been mentioned above (p. 186). The shape is a great favourite with the Etruscans in bronze: good examples in New York (Richter *Cat. Bronzes* 206–9).

### λ. OINOCHOE (MUG WITH HIGH HANDLE AND NO FOOT)

Berlin, from Monteriggioni. *St. etr.* 2 pl. 32, 100.

Malacena fabric, I think.

This is imitated from a metal original: I do not know of any metal vase just like it, but the following bronze jugs belong to the same family: (1) Villa Giulia, from Todi (*ML*. 24, 863); Ancona, from Filottrano (*JRAI*. 67 pl. 25, 4); (2) Ancona, from Montefortino (*ML*. 9 pl. 4, 7; Dall' Osso 256); Ancona, from S. Ginesio (*NSc*. 1886, 45, F); and one formerly in the Ruesch collection at Zurich (*Sg. Ruesch* pl. 27, 101).

μ. OINOCHOAI: SHAPE IX

1. Copenhagen 531. *CV*. pl. 223, 9. 'Dull black glaze.'
2. Villa Giulia, from Capena.
3. Villa Giulia, from Capena.
4. Villa Giulia 23933, from Capena. The neck slightly offset.
5. Leyden H 189, from Cortona. Holwerda 10. 'Bad blue-black glaze.'

The shape of the handle varies. Nos. 2–4 are from the same fabric as the squat lekythoi from Capena (see p. 271).

Leyden H 190, from Cortona, is said by Holwerda to be like 189, but squatter.

Leyden H 767, from Volterra (Holwerda 54) is of similar shape, but is coated with a yellow slip (see p. 282). A vase in Orvieto, from Orvieto (Settecamini), is very like it, but unglazed (*NSc*. 1932, 94, d). Another unglazed vase in Orvieto, from Torre San Severo, is a ruder model (*ML*. 24, 14, 15, and 18, 1).

This shape of oinochoe has not received much attention, and I give a list of examples, from various fabrics, in clay and in bronze.

*Clay*

(i)

(black, except the first two)

1. Berlin 2414, from Locri. Pfuhl fig. 787; FR. iii, 317: Vorberg *Ueber das Geschlechtsleben im Altertum* pl. 4. Red-figured, Attic, by the Shuvalov Painter (*ARV*. 754, no. 29).
2. London (white no. 1166). Hancarville 1 pll. 107–8: the mouth is not given correctly, it is of the same type as in the last. On the mouth, in added clay-red, egg-pattern; at the base of the handle, a double palmette in the same.
3. London (white no. 1167: ex Hamilton).
4. Madrid.
5. Zurich 437. Benndorf *Die Antiken von Zürich* pl. 7, 80.
6. Naples. Phot. Sommer 11024, iii, 18.
7. Madrid.
8. Lyons 77. Cf. the last.
9. Toronto 577. Robinson and Harcum pl. 93.
10. Arles, Musée Lapidaire.
11. Toronto 576. Robinson and Harcum pl. 93. A different model.
12. Michigan 2817, from Cumae. *CV*. pl. 19, 9. Narrower.

Two unglazed vases may be added. Michigan 2839 is 'presumably from Pozzuoli or Cumae' (*CV*. pl. 39, 2): it is unglazed, except for two black lines on the mouth; at the lower junction of the handle, a rude bearded head.  An oinochoe from Vitulazio in Campania is quite like it, but plainer; on the shoulder, three incised lines (*NSc.* 1930, 550 fig. 4): among the vases found with it was a very late red-figured bell-krater (*JHS.* 63, 104, Vitulazio Painter no. 3; see also p. 263, κ).

On an Attic red-figured cup by Douris, Florence V 48, no. 57 in my list of his works (*ARV.* 284), the reclining man in the interior holds an oinochoe of the same shape as Berlin 2414 (no. 1), but with two handles, set close to one another.  Such vases exist:

(ii. with two handles, close to one another, but set lower than in i)

(black)

1. London.
2. Once Berlin, Prinz Albrecht.  *Verschiedener deutscher Kunstbesitz, Berlin 27–29 Mai 1935* pl. 84, 923.
3. Toronto 578.  Robinson and Harcum pl. 93.
4. From Minturnae, frr. of several.  *Boll. st. med.* 5, 4–5, pl. 3, 12.

A two-handled vase of much the same sort in Athens, Agora P 904, from Athens (*Hesp.* 3, 341, B 33) is reserved, with five brown lines: according to Homer Thompson a vase in Palermo, from Milocca, is very similar.  Compare also a vase from Cape Zoster (*Eph.* 1938, 26, 2).  Thompson compares Toronto 578, our no. 3.

Two others have rough floral decoration in black: these are the vases from Spina, in Ferrara, described on p. 186, nos. 4–5.

We now return to the one-handled oinochoai:

*Bronze*

1. Ferrara T 128, from Spina.  Aurigemma[1] 51, 2 and 179, left=[2]51, 2 and 209, left. From a fifth-century tomb.
2. Genoa, from Genoa.  *NSc.* 1898, 401.  Found with Attic vases of *c.* 450–400 B.C.
2 bis. Genoa, from Genoa.  *Ausonia* 5, 52, above.
3. From Al Mina.  *JHS.* 58, 138 fig. 18, 1.
4. Rhodes 12018, from Ialysos.  *Cl. Rh.* 3, 253.
5. Villa Giulia, from Vulci.  *St. etr.* 11 pl. 11 fig. 1, 2.
6. Villa Giulia, from Vulci.  *St. etr.* 11 pl. 11, 3, middle.
6 bis. Perugia, Museo del Palazzone, from Perugia.  *RM.* 57, 183 fig. 15, 1.
7. Bologna, from Bologna.  *Dedalo* 9, 342, 2.  Restored.  Found with Attic vases from the middle and the second half of the fifth century.
8. Vatican, from Vulci or Bomarzo.  *Mus. Greg.* i, pl. 7, below, 1, right.
9. Once Primicerio, from Nocera de' Pagani.  *Bull. nap.*, new series, 5 pl. 3, 11.

(a satyr-head at the base of the handle)

10. Munich 478, from Vulci.  Jacobsthal and Langsdorff pl. 31, a; *Jb.* 55, 235.
11. Naples market (Barone), from near Salerno.  *Bull. nap.*, new series, 4 pl. 10, 1–2.

(a gorgoneion at the base of the handle)

12. Carlsruhe 549.  Wagner pl. 12, 6.

13. Carlsruhe 551. Wagner pl. 15, 11. The handle remains. As the last.
14. Catania 474. Libertini pl. 60.

(a palmette at the base of the handle)

15. Tarquinia, from Tarquinia. *NSc.* 1907, 327, a, 3 and b, 1.
16. Oxford 1888.488b.
17. Catania 475. Libertini pl. 60.
18. Carlsruhe 550. Schumacher pl. 10, 9.
19. Reggio, from Locri. *NSc.* 1913, suppl., 19.
20. Vatican, from Vulci or Orte. *Mus. Greg.* i pl. 59, ii, 3. The handle remains.
21. Carlsruhe (F 322). Wagner pl. 15, 10. The handle remains. Compare the last.
22. Vatican, 'from Vulci, Bomarzo, or Orte'. *Mus. Greg.* i pl. 5, 4, right.

(an ivy-leaf at the base of the handle)

23. Stockholm, from Marion. *Sw.C.E.* 2 pl. 49, 1, 11.
24. Cairo 27744, from Edfu. Edgar pl. 8 and p. 28.

(a palmette at the base of the handle)

25. Vatican, 'from Vulci, Bomarzo, or Orte'. *Mus. Greg.* i pl. 5, 4, left. Fourth century.

(two palmettes at the base of the handle)

26. New York 505, from Teano. Richter *Cat. Bronzes* 192. Fourth century.
   A simpler version of the shape, in bronze, is in Bologna, from Bologna (Zannoni pl. 50, 16, whence Montelius pl. 103, 10): found with an Attic red-figured amphora of about 460 B.C.

v. OINOCHOE: SHAPE VI

Civitavecchia, from Castrum Novum. *St. etr.* 11 pl. 59 fig. 4, a.
   There are many Etruscan jugs of this shape in bronze, but few in clay. Another is the yellow-slipped Leyden H 766, from Montalcino (Holwerda 54), the model of which is different: see p. 282 no. 3.
   The Civitavecchia vase has a distinct foot, and so have most clay oinochoai of shape VI (as a precaution against chipping), whereas very few of the bronze ones have a distinct foot (Florence, from Populonia, Milani *Mon. scelti* pl. 5, 13 and p. 14 fig. 4; London WT 654, Jacobsthal and Langsdorff pl. 14, a).
   For red-figured jugs of shape VI, see pp. 46, 73 and 181; with added colour, p. 200.
   The lower part of our vase is unusually large compared with the upper, though not so large as in the Montalcino jug (p. 282). The handle rises high above the mouth, which is rare in this shape: the only other instances I know are in yellow-slipped vases of Canosan fabric, two in Yale (305–6: Baur 180), one in New York (06.1021.255).

OINOCHOAI: SHAPE VII (BEAKED JUGS)
I. The Group of Vatican G 119

A special model, small and neat: all from one fabric; probably the Malacena.
1. Vatican G 119, from Vulci. *RG.* pl. 35.

2. Vatican.

3. Vatican (ex Falcioni).

4. Villa Giulia 19732, from Cervetri.

5. Villa Giulia 19733, from Cervetri.

6. Villa Giulia 19778, from Cervetri.

7. Villa Giulia 19777, from Cervetri.

8–10. Rome, Prince Torlonia, from Vulci? Three of them.

11. Florence 4494.

12. Florence 4562.

13. Florence 4561.

14. Florence (ex Vagnonville), from Chiusi? The mouth is lost.

15. Florence V 396, from Chiusi?

16. Fiesole. Galli *Fiesole* 95 fig. 76, 3.

17. Chiusi, from Chiusi. *Riv. Ist.* 4, 10 fig. 3, 2.

17 bis. Bettona, from Bettona. *CV.* pl. 9, 15.

17 ter. Bettona, from Bettona. *CV.* pl. 9, 12.

18. Oxford 397.

19. Louvre H 300.

20. Louvre H 301.

21. Louvre H 299.

22. Louvre H 302.

23. Louvre H 305.

24. Louvre H 303.

25. Louvre H 304.

26. Berlin inv. 4045, from Monteriggioni.

27. Berlin inv. 4043, from Monteriggioni.

28. Berlin inv. 4028, from Monteriggioni.

29–31. Once Terrosi, from Monteriggioni. Bianchi Bandinelli (*St. etr.* 2, 156, no. 110) mentions six of them, one of which is figured ibid. pl. 31, 110; three of the six are our nos. 26–8.

32. Bremen, Focke Museum. Schaal *Brem.* pl. 29, a.

33. Leyden H 199, from Volterra. Holwerda 10 and pl. 2.

34. Leyden H 200, from Volterra. Holwerda pl. 2.

35. Leyden H 201, from Volterra.

36. Leyden H 202, from Volterra. Holwerda 10.

37. Leyden H 203, from Volterra.

38. Leyden H 204, from Volterra. Holwerda 10.

39. Copenhagen 535, from Volterra. *CV.* pl. 223, 6.

40. Copenhagen 534, from Volterra. *CV.* pl. 223, 8.

41. Copenhagen 538. *CV.* pl. 223, 5.

42. Copenhagen 537. *CV.* pl. 223, 7.

43. Boston (R 455). E. Robinson 166, foot.

44. Once Disney, from Volterra. Disney *Mus. Disn.* pl. 127, 1.

45. Once Carlsruhe, Vogell. *Sg. Vogell* pl. 6, 41.

These vary little. Nos. 12, 13, 15, 36, and 37 are squatter than the rest. Sometimes there is a distinct foot.

Berlin 2670, from Vulci, and 2671 might belong to this group, judging by Furtwängler's small cut, but I have not seen the originals.

## II. *Other oinochoai shape VII*

'Oinochoe shape VII' is a great favourite in Etruscan. As we have seen, there are many red-figured examples, many with black patterns, many decorated with superposed colours; and we have just pointed to a special black variety which we assigned to the Malacena fabric. There are other black oinochoai of shape VII, Etruscan and Latin, and to these we now pass. I include a few unglazed ones, but say nothing about those in bucchero (Magi in *RG.* i, 148–9) or in bronze (Jacobsthal and Langsdorff *Die Bronzeschnabelkannen*). It should be noted that in Italy the shape is rare outside Etruria and Latium. I know one Campanian example, the red-figured Capua 7551 (*CV.* pl. 46, 9 and 16). I do not know the fabric of a vase in Hamburg, decorated with white incised tongues, and white and red lines (*Anz.* 1909, 1, 51), or of a black one with a very thin neck in Naples (phot. Sommer 11023, ii, 7). In shape these two are not like any of the vases in our lists. The Hamburg vase is called Gnathian by Pagenstecher, but it is not that: I confess I cannot help thinking of Corinthian oinochoai like Oxford 1879.123 (*CV.* III C pl. 5, 15).

The black oinochoai of shape VII may be grouped roughly under two headings, A and B. In A there is no incurve towards the base, and the neck is shorter; there is usually a foot.

### A (i)
### *The Group of Leyden 192*

Heavy make, the glaze usually poor. Foot. These have an old-fashioned appearance, but I do not think that any of them are older than the later part of the fourth century.

1. Leyden H 192, from Volterra. Holwerda 10. 'Blue-black glaze with greenish-yellow spots.'
2. Oxford 381A. Pl. 38, 13. Buff clay. Dull black glaze.
3. Leyden H 194, from Volterra. Holwerda 10. 'Blue-black glaze.'
4. Oxford 1896–1908.G 520. Pl. 38, 14. Light buff clay, bad black glaze. The shoulder more pronounced. Compare nos. 3 and 10.
5. Leyden H 193, from Volterra. Holwerda pl. 2. 'Blue-black glaze.'
6. Leyden H 195, from Volterra. Holwerda pl. 2. 'Lacquer-like purple glaze.'
7. Leyden H 196, from Volterra. Holwerda 10. 'Glaze fired matt purplish-brown.'
8. Leyden H 197, from Volterra. Holwerda pl. 2. 'Glaze fired matt brown.'
9. Leyden H 205, from Volterra. Holwerda 10. 'Glaze fired matt brown.' Compare nos. 3 and 4. Very short.

Near these:

Harvard 2309. *CV.* pl. 39, 14. 'Matt black glaze.'

Todi 1684, from Todi (*CV*. pl. 16, 8), would seem from the description to be unglazed. In shape it goes with the black vase Leyden H 193, no. 5 in our list.

An unglazed vase in Naples, from Foci del Garigliano, inv. 693 (*ML*. 37 pl. 40, 4), is not far from these in shape.

### A (ii)

1. Leyden H 191, from Volterra. Holwerda 10.
2. Copenhagen 536. *CV*. pl. 223, 4. 'Dull brownish-black glaze.'

These two go together, and have the same character, generally speaking, as the Group of Leyden 192 (p. 268).

### A (iii)

Copenhagen inv. 8229, from Orvieto. *CV*. pl. 223, 1. 'Greyish-yellow clay; dull brownish-black glaze.' Foot.

### A (iv)

Castiglioncello 46, from Castiglioncello. *NSc*. 1924, 162, 4; *St. etr.* 16 pl. 29, ii, 4. Foot.

### A (v)

Miscellaneous, without foot
(black)

Naples, from Foci del Garigliano, inv. 607. *ML*. 37 pl. 35, 10.
Leyden H 198, from Volterra. Holwerda 10. Once glazed according to Holwerda, but the glaze has disappeared.

(unglazed)

Cracow, Univ., inv. 91. *CV*. pl. 16 (*Pol*. pl. 89), 33.

Harvard 2245 (*CV*. pl. 39, 17) looks black in the photograph, but according to Chase there are slight traces of a design in white. Nearest, but with a foot, Copenhagen 536 and Leyden 191 (see above).

A less ponderous version of the oinochoe shape VII is represented by Harvard 1925.30. 82 (*CV*. pl. 39, 15), which is black except for the lower part, and Harvard 2300 (*CV*. pl. 39, 16), which is reserved.

### B

The red-figured Etruscan oinochoai of shape VII, those with black patterns, and nearly all those with decoration in added colour (see pp. 201, 203, 205–6, 217–18), belong to a different type: the neck is longer, and the body curves in towards the base to give an S-shaped outline. This type also occurs among black vases:

1. Rome, Antiquarium, from Rome. Ryberg fig. 119a.
2. Rome, Antiquarium, 542, from Rome. Ryberg fig. 106a. The shape resembles that of the Phantom class (pp. 205–6).
3. Copenhagen 539, from Volterra. *CV*. pl. 223, 3. 'Dull black glaze.' For the shape compare Toronto 498 (p. 217, foot), which has decoration in added colour.
4. Poznań, Miss Ruxer. *CV*. pl. 2 (*Pol*. 123), 15. Bad glaze.

5. Harvard 2254. *CV*. pl. 39, 4. 'Glaze fired red on neck and body.'
6. Harvard 2256. *CV*. pl. 39, 1. 'Glaze fired red.' Compare the last.
7. Cambridge, Museum of Classical Archaeology, from Veii. Black, except the lower part, which is reserved. Dull buff clay; the glaze a bluish-black.

An unglazed oinochoe in London, 39.2–14.124, stands apart from these: the neck is shorter and there is less incurve at the base. The clay, fine, and 'Corinthian' in colour, recalls the *Ruvfies acil* askos in the Vatican (see p. 275). The vase was obtained from Campanari and was probably therefore found in Etruria.

All these 'S-curved' vases were footless. Copenhagen 530 (*CV*. pl. 223, 2) has a foot, and also a collar: 'greyish-yellow clay, brownish-black glaze.'

## SQUAT LEKYTHOI

Of the vases in this list, those found at Capena are from a single fabric: I am not sure whether the others are from the same as they, but think it likely. The shape is a kind of squat lekythos, heavily made. The mouth is usually compressed, often tulip-wise; sometimes the incurve is less pronounced, and sometimes the mouth may be said to be that of a normal squat lekythos.

Most of these vases are mentioned in *RG*. 98 on no. 142. None of them have blue-black glaze, and the fabric has nothing to do with the 'Malacena'.

(tulip-tops)
1. Villa Giulia 23466, from Capena. Slightly convex handle.
2. Villa Giulia, from Capena. Slightly convex handle.
3. Villa Giulia, from Capena. Concave handle.
4. Villa Giulia, from Capena. Concave handle. Fired red in parts.
5. Florence, from Populonia. *NSc*. 1934, 418, 7.
6. Once Berlin, Schiller, 428. Zahn *Sammlung Baurat Schiller* pl. 38. As the last.
7. Tarquinia RC 3864, from Tarquinia. Concave handle. Poorish black.
8. Philadelphia 2831, from Ardea. *Boll. st. med.* 4, 4–5 pl. 2, 21. Bad glaze.
9. Yale 461. Baur 228. Concave handle. Bluish glaze.
10. Villa Giulia, from Vulci (sporadico 76). Bad glaze.
11. Villa Giulia, from Capena. The body rounder, no incurve in the mouth. Handle slightly convex.
11 bis. Terni 1089, from Terni. *CV*. pl. 9, 2.
12. Compiègne 947. *CV*. pl. 24, 37. Said in the Compiègne *Corpus* to be from Nola, but many of the proveniences given there are false. No incurve in the mouth.
13. Villa Giulia, from Capena. The mouth has no incurve, but has a lip. Handle concave.
14. Villa Giulia, from Capena. As the last.

(similar, but squat)
15. Oxford 1936.620. Pl. 38, 15. Slightly convex handle.
16. Copenhagen inv. 8230, from Orvieto? *CV*. pl. 224, 6. No foot.

## (with squat-lekythos mouth)

17. Oxford 1937.680. Pl. 38, 16.
18. Villa Giulia, from Capena. Concave handle. Either this, or the next, will be the vase of this kind published in Della Seta *L'It. ant.*[1] 152 fig. 162, 5.
19. Villa Giulia, from Capena. Double handle.
20. Florence, from Populonia. *NSc.* 1934, 418, 10.
20 bis. Bettona, from Bettona. *CV.* pl. 9, 13.
21. Villa Giulia, from Capena. Flaring mouth, without lip. Convex handle.

No. 17 (Oxford 1937.680: Pl. 38, 16) has four brown 'holding-marks' on the side of the foot, where the fingers held the vase when painting or just after painting. In no. 15 (Oxford 1936.620: Pl. 38, 15) these marks are on the body and the neck, showing that the vase was held upside down. I noticed similar marks on no. 7 (Tarquinia RC 3864), but they are common on late black vases of many fabrics.

The attachment of the handle to the neck is the same in nos 18, 20, 6, and 17.

Nos. 15 and 17 are covered with slight horizontal ridges caused by the turning-tool: I notice the same in nos. 6 and 18. See also p. 238.

Black oinochoai (p. 264, μ nos. 2–4) are from the same fabric as those of our vases that come from Capena; and so, I think, is the skyphos from the same site (p. 238: Della Seta *L'It. ant.*[1] 152 fig. 162, 2).

A black vase, from Populonia, in Florence (*NSc.* 1905, 56 fig. 2, third row, right) makes one think of nos. 17–21, but the body is more like that of an oinochoe shape II.

Other black vases approximate in shape to the tulip-tops:

From Minturnae. *Boll. st. med.* 5, 4–5, pl. 2, 7. 'Thin fabric.' The mouth has no incurve.

From Minturnae. *Boll. st. med.* 5, 4–5, pl. 1, 8. 'Thicker fabric than the last.' The mouth has no incurve.

### (squat)

Naples from Foci del Garigliano, inv. 945. *ML.* 37 pl. 35, 5. The side of the mouth almost straight. The foot is missing.

Naples, from Foci del Garigliano, inv. 1110. *ML.* 37 pl. 36, 7. The mouth is missing. Compare also the unglazed vase Leyden H 872 (Holwerda 60), from Volterra.

The following vases, decorated with black, or rather brown, bands, have the same kind of shape as nos. 1–9, but need not be from the same fabric as they:

1. Vatican G 142, from Vulci. *RG.* pl. 35.
2. Florence. On the shoulder, graffito, *T. Volusio* (complete).
3. Villa Giulia, from Vulci (sporadico 75).

A slender olpe with black bands in Florence, 3653, seems to be from the same fabric as these three.

I do not know what the relation is between these black-band vases and the 'black-on-buff' ware found at Minturnae (Lakc in *Boll. st. med.* 5, 4–5, 103–5). One of these black-and-buff vases is not unlike our tulip-tops in shape: ibid. pl. 12, 21. So also the spouted vase ibid. pl. 16, 24.

A squat lekythos with brown bands in the Louvre (N 4089) approaches the peculiar shape of nos. 15 and 16 in our list.

## ASKOI

We distinguish two great types of Etruscan and Latin askoi: one tall, or deep; the other short, or shallow. The deep type is that which makes one think of a sitting hen: it divides into two sub-types, according to whether it has a spout at the tail (B) or not (A). Most of the Etruscan and Latin examples have the tail-spout. Besides these there are a few of other shapes (pp. 157–8, p. 148), and the plastic askoi, deep and shallow, decorated in red-figure or with black patterns: they have been dealt with already (pp. 119–20 and 191–4).

### DEEP ASKOI: TYPE A

Type A occurs in Apulian red-figure and in Gnathian;[1] in Italian black ware; and in Italian unglazed. Nor is it confined to Italy: unglazed examples have been found at Olynthos (Robinson *Olynthus* 5 pl. 28 and pl. 192), at Athens (*Hesp.* 3, 341, B 31), at Alexandria (Breccia *Sciatbi* pl. 59, 135), at Carthage (*Mus. Alaoui* suppl. i, pl. 102, 3). The askos from Carthage is local work, and so, probably, are the others: in any case they are not imports from Italy.

I give a list of black askoi type A; many of them are Campanian, but I cannot be sure that they all are.

1. Harvard 2308. *CV*. pl. 26, 2.
2. Oxford, Beazley.
3. Naples?, from Maddaloni. *NSc.* 1936, 56, i, 7.
4. Bremen, Focke Museum. Schaal *Brem.* pl. 29, e.
5. Naples inv. 85406, from Cumae. *NSc.* 1883, pl. 2, 23.
6. Naples, from Naples. *NSc.* 1935, 289 fig. 24, 42.
7. Naples. Phot. Sommer 11023, x, 2.
8. Warsaw, Majewski Museum, 16279, from Cumae. *CV*. pl. 6 (Pol. 102), 9.
9. Oxford 1911.72, from Teano.
10. Oxford 1932.129.
11. Once Hamilton. Hancarville 2 pll. 98–9.
12. Amsterdam inv. 3454. *CV*. IV E pl. 3 (Pays Bas 93), 4.
13. Naples, from Caivano. *NSc.* 1931, 601, v.
14. Naples, from Frignano Piccolo. *NSc.* 1937, 113, i, right.
15. Oxford, Beazley (ex Kerr).
16. London P 3.
17. Sèvres 111.1. *CV*. pl. 49, 36.

[1] Apulian red-figure: Ruvo, Jatta, 1402, from Ruvo (FR. pl. 80, 4). The rest 'AP. style': London F 414, from Ruvo (Walters *HAP*. pl. 44, 1); Cambridge 243 (*CV*. pl. 45, 4); Worcester, Mass. (*Worc. Ann.* 2, 25, 5); Harvard 2272 (*CV*. pl. 35, 8); Lecce 970, from Ruvo (*CV*. IV Dr pl. 42, 8); Oxford 485; where? (Genick pl. 32, 3); New York (*CV*. Gallatin pl. 32, 12); Brussels R 423 (*CV*. IV Db pl. 7, 5); Sèvres 109, from Basilicata (*CV*. pl. 40, 2–3); Toronto 457 (Robinson and Harcum pl. 82); Bologna PU 627 (*CV*. IV Dr pl. 32, 3); Bologna PU 628 (*CV*. IV Dr pl. 32, 4). Gnathian: London F 584, from Basilicata (*CV*. IV Dc pl. 5, 23); London F 585, from Basilicata (*CV*. IV Dc pl. 5, 19).

18. Sèvres 111.2. *CV*. pl. 49, 18.
19. Naples, from Foci del Garigliano, inv. 17. *ML*. 37 pl. 35, 14.
20. Civitavecchia, from Castrum Novum. *St. etr*. 11 pl. 59 fig. 4, e.
21. Würzburg 936. Langlotz pl. 253, 1.
22. Naples, from Caivano. *NSc*. 1931, 603, 2.
23. Wilno, Society of Friends. *CV*. pl. 2 (Pol. 125), 15.
24. Leyden 152, from Naples. Holwerda 16.

The askos decorated with a laurel-wreath in white, from Cumae, in the Majewski Museum at Warsaw (16278: *CV*. pl. 6, Pol. pl. 102, 11), is doubtless Campanian. I do not know the fabric of the Van Deman askos in Baltimore, which has a light red wreath (*CV*. Robinson pl. 32, 4): but I note that an exact replica of it, in the collection of Prof. A. B. Cook, Cambridge, is from Tarquinia. A third is in New York University.

An askos in the Villa Giulia, from Capena, is described in *NSc*. 1905, 304 no. 14 as having a wreath of olive or laurel in red: but I do not know what type of askos it is.

An askos of type A from Cumae, in Michigan (2913: *CV*. pl. 37, 8) is of 'red-orange clay, with a thin, pale buff slip'. This is also the shape of an unglazed askos, from Este, in Este.

An unglazed askos in Carthage, from Ard el-Kheraïb, is of type A, but has a spout setting out from the middle of one flank (Merlin and Drappier pl. 4, 29).

### DEEP ASKOI: TYPE B

Type B, the tall askos with tail-spout, is reported from Etruria and Latium. The only example found outside of Italy, so far as my lists go, is Oxford 1878.144, from Malta (below, ξ). I do not know this type of askos in Apulian or Campanian: I ought to say, however, that I cannot tell the fabric of the only two examples that have painted decoration: one in Amsterdam (*Mnemosyne* 1934 pl. 1 fig. 2), which has floral work on the shoulder as well as striations on the body; the other in Cambridge (210: *CV*. pl. 43, 21) with an ivy-wreath on the body and astragalus on the handle. In the Amsterdam vase the furrows on the topside of the mouth recall Calene askoi. There are tail-spout askoi in *native* Apulian (Mayer *Apulien* pl. 38, 9 and 10, pl. 38, 16, pl. 40, 13); see also *Jb*. 22, 219 figs. 15 and 16.

### (α: black)

1. Florence, from Saturnia. *ML*. 30, 657, 1, 1. The body is striated, and there is some impressed decoration on the back beneath the handle.
2. Florence, from San Miniato. *NSc*. 1935, 33, 3.
3. Berlin, from Monteriggioni? Bluish-black glaze.
4. Berlin inv. 4067, from Monteriggioni. Bluish-black glaze.
5. Ferrara T 1092, from Spina. Aurigemma[1] 105, iii, 5 = [2]123, iii, 5. A little shallower.
6. Rome, Antiquarium, from Rome (Esquiline). Ryberg fig. 106b. Sags a little.
7. Providence 16.600, 'from Pompeii'. *CV*. pl. 30, 2. ('Pompeii' as a provenience is often suspect.)
8. Berlin inv. 4011, from Monteriggioni. Bluish-black glaze. Sagging body.

9. Castiglioncello, from Castiglioncello. *NSc.* 1924, 163, 1. Sagging body.
10. Cambridge, Museum of Classical Archaeology, 1101. Dullish black glaze. Triple handle.

All these may well be Etruscan or Latin.

### (β: black; or unglazed: it is not stated which)

1. Once Volterra, Cinci, from Volterra. Inghirami *Mon. etr.* 5 pl. 48, 7.
2. Once Volterra, Cinci, from Volterra. Inghirami *Mon. etr.* 5 pl. 48, 9. Sagging body.

### (γ: 'Black-on-buff' ware)

From Minturnae. *Boll. st. med.* 5, 4–5, pl. 14, 26.

### (λ: unglazed: the Gallonios Group)

1. Berlin inv. 3117, from Rome (Esquiline). *Annali* 1880, pl. P, 3 and pl. R, 13; *Berl. Mus.* 1934, 3. Stamped on the handle, *C. Caloni.* The initial letter of the nomen curves round a little below, but I doubt if it can be intended for a *g. CIL.* xv, 6087. Same clay as Vatican G 143 (p. 275). The name is Gallonios (W. Schulze *Zur Geschichte der lateinischen Eigennamen* 171). The name *Caloni* is stamped on the handle of a vase from Chiusi which seems to have disappeared: it is described by Garrucci (*Syll.* no. 494, whence *CIL.* xi, 67054) as 'poculum ex creta tenuissima, quae caolina vocatur, ramis et foliis ornatum': Siebourg surmised (*RM.* 12, 47 no. 14) that this might be a bowl of 'Megarian' type, but so much is hardly to be got from the description. Pagenstecher thought that the inscription on Brussels A 760, a small 'Calene plate' with a relief of the Roman Wolf, gave the same name: it reads *Calo· cal* (Pagenstecher *Cal.* 33 no. 19, and 157: Calonus on p. 157 is a slip). The second word is indistinct: perhaps *Cal(enos)* according to Pagenstecher.
2. Rome, Prince Torlonia, from Vulci. Stamped on the handle, *P. Caisi.* Same clay as Vatican G 143 (p. 275). I take this to be the askos, from the Tomba François at Vulci, published by Ritschl (pl. xi, k and pl. xcvii, o and O), although that was said to be in the Museo Kircheriano: *CIL.*[2] 1, ii, i no. 435.
3. Tarquinia 1315A, from Tarquinia. Stamped on the handle, *Roma.* Same clay as the two last, but fired pink in places.
4. Berlin inv. 4109, from Poggio alla Città. Warm light-brown clay. Brown glaze at the end of the spout and on the mouth; on the handle, XII in brown. The body sags. According to Zahn the kantharos p. 235, λ, i no. 3 was found in the same tomb.
5. Louvre D 187. Very light yellowish clay (with an ochrous slip?).
6. Rome, Conservatori. Same colour as Vatican G 143.
7. Florence 4766. Same clay as Vatican G 143.
8. Perugia, Mus. del Palazzone, from Perugia. Galli *Perugia* 143 fig. 103, 2. Pale clay.
9. Ferrara, T 1059, from Spina. Aurigemma[1] 105, iii, 1 =[2]123, iii, 1. A little shallower.

### (ε: unglazed: these may belong to the Gallonios Group, but I am not sure)

1. Naples, from Foci del Garigliano, inv. 556. *ML.* 37 pl. 38, 15. The body sags.
2. Oxford 1877.35. Buff clay.
3. Poznań. *CV.* pl. 5 (Pol. 121), 12. The mouth seems different.

(3: white slip)

1. Oxford 1878.144, from Ben Gemmi, Malta. Very light buff clay. The body sags.
   Ht. 0.114.

It is from an askos of our Type B, as Zahn noted, that the little boy is drinking on the
kantharos of the Hesse Group in Berlin (p. 208, below, no. 1, and Pl. 39, 2–3).

Six of these askoi form a variety within Type B, distinguished by the sagging belly:
Berlin inv. 4011 (α, 8), Castiglioncello (α, 9), the second Cinci vase (β, 2), Berlin inv.
4109 (λ, 4), the Foci vase (ε, 1), the Oxford vase from Malta (3). In the Antiquarium
vase (α, 6) the belly sags, but less.

The blue-black glaze of the three askoi in Berlin (α, 3, 4, and 8) suggests that they
might be from the Malacena fabric, although the make is not fine. In many of the unglazed askoi, the clay seems to be the same as in Vatican G 143, which is a typical member
of the Ruvfies Group (below, no. 1). The signatures stamped on the handles are another
feature common to the two groups, although the language is Latin here and Etruscan
there.

London 39.11–9.6, from Etruria, unglazed, is a compound vase (*Mnemosyne* 1934, pl.
4 fig. 3): the upper part is an askos of type B; the lower part is roundish, with a spout:
there is no communication between the two parts, and the purpose is doubtful.

SHALLOW ASKOI

*The Ruvfies Group*

This is another type of tail-spout askos. There is often an Etruscan inscription stamped
on the handle. The inscription varies, and so does the technique: but the shape, and
much else, are the same, and all these vases must come from one Etruscan workshop.

The clay resembles that of the Gallonios Group, and is often indistinguishable from it.

I have already dealt with these vases in *RG*. 99–100, but make additions and corrections
here.

(unglazed)

1. Vatican G 143, from Vulci. *RG*. pl. 35. Stamped on the handle *Ruvfies*[:]*acil* (retr.).
   White clay. On the word *acil* see Olzscha in *Gnomon* 14, 359.
2. Tarquinia 1315B, from Tarquinia. Stamped on the handle *Ruvfies*[:]*acil* (retr.). Clay
   of 'Corinthian' colour.
3. Florence 72914, from Orbetello. *NSc*. 1885 pl. 1, 9. Stamped on the handle, *Ruvfies:*
   *acil* (retr.).
4. Florence 4663. Stamped on the handle, *Atrane* (retr.) and a little askos. *CIL*. xi. ii. 1
   no. 6700, 2, g.
5. Zurich 430. Benndorf *Die Antiken von Zürich* pl. 7 ,73. Bought in the Piazza Navona.
   Stamped on the handle, according to Benndorf, *A…rne* with a little one-handled vase.
   May this not be *A*[*tr*]*ane*? Yellow clay.
6. Florence 4462, from Sovana. Stamped on the handle, a dolphin, and *Pultuceśi* (retr.).
   Correct the description in *RG*. 99.

7. Florence 4674, fragment. The handle of an askos: stamped on it, *Precu* (retr.). Pale yellowish clay. On the name see Schulze 97–8.

8. Providence 14.434. *CV*. pl. 30, 1. Stamped on the handle, *Velnumnal* (retr.).

9. Florence, fragment. The lower part is lost. Stamped on the handle, *Velnumnal* (retr.).

10. Berlin inv. TC 3486. Stamped on the handle, *Velnumnal* (retr.).

11. Louvre. A little shallower than Vatican G 143. Very light buff clay.

11 bis. Vienna, Univ., 954A. *CV*. pl. 32, 9. 'White-grey, very fine clay.'

12. Florence 4666.

13. Florence 4664. Small. The handle is not kinked.

(red sigillata)

14. Vatican, from Vulci. *Mus. Greg.* ii pl. 93, 12. Stamped on the handle (retr.), *Atrane:* and a small mug. *CIL*. xi. ii. 1 no. 6700, 2, f.

15. Vatican. Stamped on the handle, an indistinct inscription which I could not read.

16. Perugia, Museo del Palazzone, from Perugia. Galli *Perugia* 144, 4.

17. Lost?, from Chiusi. Inghirami *Mus. Chius.* pl. 52, 1, whence Daremberg and Saglio s.v. askos fig. 574; Micali *Storia* pl. 101, 14. Stamped on the handle, *Atranesi* (retr.) between a horse and two ducks. 'Red clay' (i.e. sigillata?). *CIL*. xi. ii. 1 no. 6700, 2, a.

18. Louvre H 454. Stamped on the handle, *:Atrane* (retr.) and a small object (scarab? askos? mug?).

19. Florence 72912, from Orbetello. Stamped on the handle, *Atraneś* (retr.). Large (ht. 0.13).

20. Florence 72913, from Orbetello.

21. Yale 513. Baur 248. Stamped on the handle, *:Lethe:*. This may be the askos, found between Orvieto and Città della Pieve, formerly in the possession of Costa, Rome, mentioned in *CIL*. xi. ii. 1 under 6700, 1. See p. 277.

22. Florence, from Arezzo.

23. Florence, from Arezzo.

(black)

24. Tarquinia, from Tarquinia. Black glaze.

25. Oxford 1946.55, from Chiusi. Good black glaze.

26. Louvre D 189. Bad brownish-red glaze. Shallower than Vatican G 143. I think I took the glaze to be intended for black: if not, the vase may go under the next heading.

('slight red or brown slip')

27. Once Terrosi, from Monteriggioni. *St. etr.* 2 pl. 31, 80. Eight of them.

I am not sure whether an askos of this type from Capena, Villa Giulia 16592, belongs to the group or not: bad black glaze.

The following unpublished askoi may seem from the descriptions to belong to the Ruvfies Group:

1. Florence, from Orbetello. According to Milani *NSc.* 1885, 420 no. 102) this is just like the Ruvfies askos Florence 72914 (p. 275 no. 3), but the handle is lost. Unglazed.

2. Where?, from Rome (Esquiline). Described by Dressel in *Bull.* 1877, 87. Stamped

on the handle, between an askos and a horse, *Pultuceś* (retr.). 'Very pale clay; fine red glaze' [i.e. sigillata].

3. Where?, from Orvieto. Described by Fabretti (1st suppl. no. 452), whence Dressel in *Bull.* 1877, 87. Stamped on the handle, *Pultuceś* (retr.).

4. Once Rome, Pasinati. Described by Dressel in *Bull.* 1877, 87. Stamped on the handle, *Velnumnal* (retr.). 'Pale clay; yellowish glaze not much darker than the clay itself.'

5. Where?, from Sovana. Described by Gamurrini (*Appendice* no. 756). Stamped on the handle, *Velnumnal*.

6. Volterra, from Volterra. Described by Fabretti no. 357, whence *CIL.* xi. ii. 1 no. 6700, 2b. Stamped on the handle, *Atraneśi*.

7. Volterra, from Volterra. Described by Fabretti no. 357 bis, whence *CIL.* xi. ii. 1 no. 6700, 2c. Stamped on the handle, *Atraneśi*.

8. Once Pitigliano, Mancinelli, from Sovana. Described by Gamurrini (*Appendice* no. 757) as like no. 5. Stamped on the handle, *Atraneś*.

The inscription *Ruvfies acil* also occurs on a lamp from Vulci (Fabretti *suppl.* no. 352), *Atrane* on a lamp from Perugia (Fabretti no. 1918), *Lethe* on a fragment of a sigillata plate or plate-like dish (not Arretine) formerly in the possession of Vincenzo Funghini at Arezzo[1] (Funghini *Degli antichi vasi fittili arretini* pl. 1, 1: *CIL.* xi. ii. 1 no. 6700, 1a), and on three other sigillata vases:—once Arezzo, Gamurrini; once Chiusi, Brogi; and Fiesole (*CIL.* ibid. 1b–d). I do not know the shape of the three, but as the letters of the inscription are arranged in the same way as on the Funghini fragment—north, east, south, west—the vases are perhaps plates.

I append a list of tail-spout askoi which form another, later class: characteristic the 'Adam's apple' and the carinated back: various: I do not know the fabrics:

### The Class of Berlin inv. 4921

Berlin inv. 4921. Sigillata.

Baltimore (ex Van Deman). *CV.* iii pl. 37, 7. 'Orange clay and slip; very thin fabric.'

Leningrad. Stephani pl. 2, 78.

Leyden 685. Holwerda 49. Sigillata.

Bardo, Musée Alaoui, from Bulla Regia. La Blanchère and Gauckler *Mus. Alaoui* pl. 42, 216. 'Fine red clay glazed.' Two others are mentioned.

Naples inv. 85965, from Cumae. *NSc.* 1883, pl. 3, 113.

Yale 549. Baur 248. Sigillata.

Yale 551. Baur 248. Sigillata. Handle and spout restored.

Yale 550. Baur 248. Sigillata. The handle lost.

Michigan 2912A, from Cumae. *CV.* pl. 37, 7. 'Pale red clay; finer slip, pink to cream.' Different handle.

London 56.12–23. 225, from Sardinia. Red clay, unglazed. Handles as in the last.

Michigan 2912B, from Cumae. *CV.* pl. 37, 6. 'Pale orange clay.' Different handle.

---

[1] Miss Richter kindly sent me a photostat of the illustration in Funghini.

An askos, from Cumae, in Naples (*NSc.* 1883 pl. 3, 112) has the same shape as no. 6, except that the handle bestrides the back.

## PANS
### α. (with loop-handle)

1. Hamburg 1914.236. B, *Anz.* 1928, 358. 'Black glaze playing into brown.' Obtained in Florence.
2. Munich inv. 6527. Put with no. 1 by Mercklin (*Anz.* 1935, 144).
3. Louvre N 2252. Blue-black glaze. At the handle, as in no. 1, a head of Silenus in relief.
4. Oxford 1932.1158. 'Blue-black glaze. At the handle, a youthful head (maenad?) in relief.
5. Leyden H 299, from Volterra. A, Holwerda 22. 'Blackish purple glaze.'
6. Berlin, from Monteriggioni. The glaze is not blue-black.
7. Florence 4473.
8. Leipsic. The handle is lost.
9. London, old cat. 1845. *Cat. GEV.* ii pl. 10, 307. More elaborate. The bottom is moulded. Blue-black glaze.

All these go together and belong to the Malacena fabric.

A pan of the same general type, from Corchiano, in the Villa Giulia, has a stand-ring (*NSc.* 1912, 83 fig. 2): it is not from the Malacena fabric.

For yellow-slipped pans of our type, see p. 282. One in the Torlonia collection (from Vulci?) has neither glaze, I think, nor slip.

A simpler pan from Populonia, in Florence (*NSc.* 1905, 57, below, 2), is said to be of yellowish clay, originally coloured red; a strainer of the same fabric was found with it, or near it (p. 279, foot).

These are imitations of metal pans. I do not know of any exact equivalents in bronze: but the following group is of the same general type, and the palmette at the handle is like that of the Corchiano pan.

1–6. Vatican. Six of them. One is figured in *Mus. Greg.* i pl. 12, 2.
7. Orvieto, from Orvieto (Settecamini). *NSc.* 1932, 92, 2.
8. Ancona, from Filottrano. *JRAI.* 67 pl. 24, 4–5.

In another object from Filottrano, the pan has been modified to serve as a strainer or funnel: see p. 280.

The following bronze handles are either from pans like those in the Vatican, Orvieto, and Ancona, or from pans with statuette-handles (see below): or, of course, from strainer- or funnel-pans like the vessel from Filottrano:

Chiusi, from Chiusi. *NSc.* 1931, 208.
New York 727. Richter *Bronzes* 250.
Carlsruhe 468. Schumacher pl. 8, 34.
Vatican, from Vulci. *Mus. Greg.* i pl. 60, ii, 2.
Bologna.

Most of these have been quoted by Jacobsthal (*ECA*. 139).

A bronze pan in Bologna, from Bologna (Zannoni pl. 54, 3–4; Montelius pl. 111, 6) is a simpler model.

### β. (with statuette-handle)

The handle is in the form of a naked youth (nos. 1 and 2) or Eros (no. 3) with the left leg crossed in front of the right. The pan-part is much as in the preceding class.

1. Berlin inv. 4031, from Monteriggioni. *St. etr.* 2 pl. 32, 103 (right).
2. Florence 4474.
3. Florence, Terrosi, from Monteriggioni. *St. etr.* 2 pl. 32, 102 (misprinted 103, left).

Pans with statuette-handle are common in Etruscan bronzework: see for example *Mus. Greg.* i pl. 12, 1 and pl. 13, or Giglioli pl. 313. Nearest to ours, in some respects, New York 598, from Bolsena (Richter *Cat. Bronzes* 218).

### STRAINERS
### (with loop-handle)
### (i)

1. London, old cat. 1892.
2. London, old cat. 1891. *Cat. GEV.* ii pl. 10, 320. Bluish-black glaze.
3. Once Terrosi, from Monteriggioni. B, *St. etr.* 2 pl. 32, 107 (unless that is our no. 4).
4. Berlin inv. 4025, from Monteriggioni.
5. Copenhagen inv. 3820, from Volterra. B, *CV.* pl. 222, 9. 'Dullish black glaze, red in parts.'

No. 2 answers exactly to the *pans* of the Malacena Group (p. 278). No. 1 is also from the Malacena fabric, but the top side of the rim is broader than in no. 2 and has more mouldings. I do not know how this part is shaped in the other three. Nos. 3 and 5, like nos. 1 and 2, have a frontal female head in relief between the roots of the handle.

### (ii)

1. Volterra, from Volterra. Gori 3 pl. 34.
2. Copenhagen 440. A, *CV.* pl. 222, 7. 'Dullish black glaze.'

These two go together. The perforated part is smaller than in the last group, the shape of the handle is different, the top side of the rim is simple and nearly flat. The band of impressed palmettes and flowers, and the rows of tiny strokes encircling it, are just the same as in the Vatican and Berlin phialai described on p. 239, nos. 1–2. The two strainers must belong, like them, to the Malacena Group.

A strainer with loop handle and simple flat rim, from Populonia, in Florence (*NSc.* 1905, 57, below, left) is said by Milani to be of yellowish clay, originally coloured red. A pan of the same fabric was found with it, or near it (ibid. 57, below, 2: above, p. 278). A silvered strainer of similar type is in Chiusi (below, p. 293). Lastly, an unglazed strainer of pale yellow clay, in Berlin (3894: Furtwängler *Beschr.* pl. 7, 345) must be of this type in the main: I do not know the fabric.

All these, like the pans they resemble, are imitated from metal originals: I am not aware that any such models have been preserved: the nearest approach I can think of is a bronze strainer, or funnel rather, from Filottrano, in Ancona (*JRAI*. 67 p. 24, 3).

### γ. (with long straight handle)

Copenhagen inv. 3385. B, *CV*. pl. 222, 8. 'Dullish black glaze.'

Blinkenberg and Johansen are probably right in calling this Etruscan. I note that the arrangement of the holes is nearly the same as in the Terrosi strainer (*St. etr.* 2 pl. 32, 107: above, p. 279, middle, no. 3).

This must be an imitation of a metal strainer, but I do not know anything like it.

In conclusion, one or two objects that are not vases, but imitations, in clay, of metal.


## CANDELABRA

1. Florence, Terrosi, from Monteriggioni. *St. etr.* 2 pl. 33, 36. What remains is the foot, and the crowning statuette representing Herakles and Scylla. They are covered with black glaze. The rest of the candelabrum was probably of other material (wood?).
2. Florence, frr., from Monteriggioni. What remains, according to Bianchi Bandinelli (*St. etr.* 2, no. 37), is the foot, and part of the two figures forming the crowning statuette.

Foot and top of a clay candelabrum, including the statuette, were found at Populonia and are in Florence (*NSc.* 1905, 57, middle): but they are not glazed: 'traces of red (minium)' according to Milani.

These copies of bronze candelabra are far superior to other objects of the same sort, the statuette-lamps, of unglazed clay, from Perugia:

1. Perugia, Museo del Palazzone, from Perugia. Conestabile *Sep. dei Volunni* pl. 13, whence Martha 496; Galli *Perugia* 43; Tarchi pl. 36, 2; *RM.* 57, 191 fig. 19.
2. Perugia, Museo del Palazzone, from Perugia. Galli *Perugia* 42; Ducati *St.* fig. 674; restored after the last, Tarchi pl. 36, 1 and 3; *RM.* 57, 191 fig. 18.

## CHAPTER XIV

# THE GROUP OF VILLA GIULIA 2303; AND VASES WITH YELLOW SLIP

### THE GROUP OF VILLA GIULIA 2303

#### Volute-kraters

(The handle-protomai are kētē in nos. 1–4, dragons in no. 5; in no. 6 there are none. In no. 1 the set of the handles is unusual.)

1. Villa Giulia 2303, from Falerii. *CV*. IV Bt pl. 4, 4–5 and pl. 5, 3; A, phot. Alinari 41198, whence Giglioli pl. 372, 2.
2. Villa Giulia 2302, from Falerii. *CV*. IV Bt pl. 5, 1–2 and pl. 6, 1.
3. Villa Giulia 2301, from Falerii. *CV*. IV Bt pl. 5, 4–5 and pl. 6, 2.
4. Villa Giulia 2300, from Falerii. *CV*. IV Bt pl. 6, 3–5.
5. Toronto 612. Robinson and Harcum pl. 96.
6. Leyden 765, from Montalcino (23 miles W. of Chiusi). Holwerda 54.

#### Stamnoi

(The handle-protomai are kētē.)

7. Villa Giulia 2235B, from Falerii. *CV*. IV Bt pl. 1, 1–3; A, phot. Alinari 41195, whence Giglioli pl. 372, 1.
8. Villa Giulia 2235C, from Falerii. *CV*. IV Bt pl. 1, 4–5 and pl. 2, 3.
9. Villa Giulia 2308A, from Falerii. *CV*. IV Bt pl. 2, 1–2 and pl. 3, 1. The mouth modern.
10. Villa Giulia 2308B, from Falerii. *CV*. IV Bt pl. 2, 4–5 and pl. 3, 2.
11. Villa Giulia 2235A, from Falerii. *CV*. IV Bt pl. 3, 3–5. The foot modern.
12. Villa Giulia 2235D, from Falerii. *CV*. IV Bt pl. 4, 1–3. Mouth and foot modern.
13. Villa Giulia, from Vignanello. A, *NSc.* 1916, 62.

#### Neck-amphorae

(The handle-protomai are sea-horses or kētē.)

14. Copenhagen, Ny Carlsberg, H 162. *Bildertafeln des Etr. Mus.* pl. 56, 1.
15. Chiusi 1927, from Chiusi. Levi *Mus. Civ. di Chiusi* 125, lower middle, part.
16. Chiusi 1928, from Chiusi. Levi *Mus. Civ. di Chiusi* 125, lower middle, part.

These vases are to be kept well apart from the 'Bolsena' Group (p. 284) with which they have hitherto been confounded. I do not know of any evidence for their having been made at Orvieto or Bolsena.

The shapes are still fourth-century in character. The stamnoi recall Faliscan stamnoi, and the volute-kraters are not very far from the Faliscan volute-krater in the Villa Giulia (Pl. 20, 1 and p. 81 no. 1). The plastic handles are in the Faliscan and Etruscan tradition of the fourth century.

These are sepulchral vases, and some of them have holes in the bottom.

The clay is light brown (not grey, as Weege in Helbig and Amelung 372, 1800 c). In nos. 1–4 and 7–12 it is covered with a grey slip, which is thought to imitate silver—if so, tarnished silver. Floral decoration is added on top of this in white or yellowish-white, and there is sometimes a red band round the neck. The plastic handles are coloured with red, blue, white, yellow.

The volute-krater in Toronto, no. 5, is said to be covered with 'a golden-yellow colour over white'. The ivy-wreath round the neck is 'blue and rose over white'. The plastic handles are coloured blue, red, rose, and yellow.

There is little information about the colouring of the neck-amphora in Copenhagen, no. 14. The clay is stated to be yellow, the sea-horse heads of the handles to be painted red and blue. There is no reference in the catalogue to a slip on the body; or to the ivy-wreath painted on the neck, although it shows in the reproduction. As to the neck-amphorae in Chiusi, nos. 15 and 16, Levi does not mention any decoration on body or neck, but says that there are traces of yellow and red on the handles.

The volute-krater in Leyden (no. 6) is said by Holwerda to be of yellow clay with a yellowish-white coating. There seems to be no decoration on body or neck. Traces of red, white, and blue on the handles.

This leads on to the

### VASES WITH YELLOW SLIP

The volute-krater Leyden 765 (above, no. 6) was found at Montalcino. Other vases from the same site are said by Holwerda to be of the same clay and to have the same yellowish-white slip, and I therefore mention them here, although I do not know what relation they bear to the Group of Villa Giulia 2303:

#### Oinochoai
##### (shape III, but high, kinked handle)

1. Leyden 768, from Montalcino. Holwerda 54.
2. Leyden 769, from Montalcino. Holwerda 54. Replica of the last.

##### (shape VI)

3. Leyden 766, from Montalcino. Holwerda 54.

##### ('S. Anatolia' shape: see p. 263)

4. Leyden 773, from Montalcino. Holwerda 20.

##### (shape IX: see pp. 264–6)

5. Leyden 767, from Montalcino. Holwerda 54.

#### Pans (with loop-handle)

6. Leyden 772, from Montalcino. B, Holwerda 54.
7. Leyden 771, from Montalcino. A, Holwerda 54. Replica of the last.
   On this type of pan see p. 278.

To return to no. 3: there are many Etruscan *bronze* oinochoai of shape VI, and a whole group of them is characterized by a rectangular or trapezoidal figure-relief at the lower end of the handle. I give a list of these: but add that the proportions are not the same as in our vase, where the lower part is larger, compared with the upper, than in any other oinochoai of the shape, whether bronze or clay; and that in the bronzes the upper end of the handle is a ram's head whereas in the Montalcino vase it is a snake's (cf. p. 297). On the absence of a distinct foot see p. 266.

### (i)

The plaque has a different shape. Nos. 1 and 3 are complete: of the rest, only the handle remains. All these should be from one fabric.

1. Louvre 2782. De Ridder *Bronzes du Louvre* pl. 100 (the number misprinted 2702).
2. Vatican, from Vulci or Orte. *Mus. Greg.* i pl. 59, d.
3. New York 44.11.4. *AJA.* 1944, 8 figs. 20–2.
4. New York 43.11.5, from Orvieto. *AJA.* 1944, 8 fig. 19.
5. Once Gréau. Fröhner *Coll. Gréau* 47 no. 218.
6. Louvre 2801. De Ridder pl. 101.
7. Goettingen 25, from Palestrina. Körte *Gött. Bronzen* pl. 14.
8. Once Gréau. Fröhner *Coll. Gréau* 46 no. 216.
9. Once Gréau. Fröhner *Coll. Gréau* 48 no. 219.
10. Once Gréau. Fröhner *Coll. Gréau* 48 no. 220.
11. Once Gréau. Fröhner *Coll. Gréau* 48 no. 221.
12. Vatican, from Vulci or Orte. *Mus. Greg.* i pl. 59, e.
13. Florence, from Populonia. *NSc.* 1921, 336.
14. Once Gréau. Fröhner *Coll. Gréau* 47 no. 217.

### (ii)

No. 1 is complete, of no. 2 only the handle remains.

1. Louvre 2783. De Ridder pl. 100.
2. Once Gréau. Fröhner *Coll. Gréau* 49–50.

In a Vatican oinochoe of shape VI, from Vulci or Bomarzo (*Mus. Greg.* i pl. 8, 1, right), the handle ends in a ram's head above, but the lower termination does not seem, in the illustration, to be a plaque. In New York 494, from Falerii (Richter *Cat. Bronzes* 191) the upper end is a ram's head, but the lower end is plain: this vase, from the shape, would appear to be earlier than those with plaques.

Among the vases from Falerii in the Villa Giulia there are a good many yellow-slipped oinochoai of the same type as no. 4 ('S. Anatolia' shape); yellow-slipped pans, also, of the same type as nos. 6 and 7, but I do not know whether they have the vine-leaf at the handle. Other yellow-slipped pans are in Florence. In the Torlonia collection there is a similar pan, but without a slip (see p. 278).

Besides pans, there are yellow-slipped strainers in Florence, and others, from Falerii, in the Villa Giulia: but I have not noted the exact shape.

I cannot place the calyx-krater Leyden 764, from Volterra (Holwerda 54). According to Holwerda it seems related to the group of vases from Montalcino, but the slip is red. In some respects it recalls the calyx-kraters of the Bolsena Group (p. 286), but the shape is different as well as the technique.

# CHAPTER XV
# SILVERED VASES, ETC.

A LARGE class of late Etruscan vases, freely decorated with reliefs, are tawdry imitations of work in silver. Sometimes the silvering has disappeared; and sometimes it was never applied: of two vases alike in every detail of form, one may be silvered and the other not. There may be a whitish slip, perhaps intended as a priming for silver; or there may not even be a slip. All these vases are placed side by side in the following lists, irrespective of whether the silver coating has been applied or not.

The first to study these vases as a group was Klügmann (*Annali* 1871, 5–27). Many of them have been put together recently by Wuilleumier (*Trésor de Tarente* 81–115), but he does not separate them from works of similar technique found in South Italy and made there: indeed he believes that the style is the same, and that the argentata found in Etruria were either imported from Apulia, as Klügmann had already held (*Annali* 1871, 9), or perhaps rather made in Etruria by an Apulian immigrant: 'in any case', he proceeds, 'they enrich our knowledge of Tarentine toreutic, and furnish a precious element of datation' (*Trésor* 83). The hypothesis is not impossible: but I deem it more prudent to keep the two kinds of vase apart: they have little in common beyond a general resemblance in technique.

It is true that two of the neck-amphorae in our list (p. 289) are reported to have been found in South Italy: no. 6 in 'Magna Graecia', no. 2 in 'Apulia'. The provenience of no. 6 is a Campana provenience, and therefore somewhat suspect. That of no. 2 rests on the statement of the Neapolitan dealer Barone: it may be correct, but if so, export from Etruria is not ruled out. I doubt if much is gained by speaking of an 'Etrusco-Apulian' style, although of course these hyphenated words are attractive to many minds.

Most of the argentata dealt with in this chapter must come from one fabric: possibly all of them, but of that I am not sure. The provenience is nearly always the region of Orvieto and Bolsena, and it is very likely that the fabric was there too: Körte referred the argentata to Bolsena (*Annali* 1877, 95 ff., especially 177) and has been generally followed: I speak of 'the Bolsena Group' as a convenient term denoting the fabric to which most of our silvered vases belong: where the pertinence does not seem certain I say so. It is possible, as Zahn has suggested (*Berl. Mus.* 55, 7–8), that the argentata were made at Orvieto as well as Bolsena. Orvieto, Old Volsinii, was destroyed, and Bolsena, New Volsinii, founded, in 265 B.C.: the potters may have migrated from the one to the other. See, however, Galli in *ML.* 24, 13.

If the vase has been mentioned by Wuilleumier his number is given with a W. in front.

A find 'from between Orvieto and Bolsena', published by Klügmann in *Annali* 1871, 1–27, will often be mentioned in the following list. Some of the vases in it passed with the rest of Augusto Castellani's collection to the Villa Giulia: perhaps all of them, but I have not assumed it. Where I know the vase to be in the Villa I have said so: otherwise I have written 'once Augusto Castellani'.

Wuilleumier does not distinguish between the two brothers Castellani, Alessandro and Augusto, or between volute-kraters and calyx-kraters.

### Volute-kraters

1. New York GR 1014. A, Richter *Etr.* fig. 165. Restored.
2. New York GR 1015. (Mentioned by Richter *Etr.* 54.) Replica of the last, with slight variations. Restored. Nos. 1 and 2 were purchased from S. T. Baxter of Florence in 1896.
3. Once Gazzetta, Cozza, from Gazzetta near Bolsena. Parts, *NSc.* 1903, 594. (W. E 5a.)
4. Once Gazzetta, Cozza, frr., from Gazzetta near Bolsena. *NSc.* 1903, 595. (W. E 5b.)
5. Berlin 3897, from Orvieto. (W. E 14.)
6. London G 184, from Bolsena. This must be no. 237 in de Witte *Coll. Cast.* (1866). Not silvered. (W. E 15a and 15c.)
7. Once Augusto Castellani, from between Orvieto and Bolsena. *Annali* 1871 pl. C, 1. (W. E 11b.)
8. Once Gazzetta, Cozza, from Gazzetta near Bolsena. Part, *NSc.* 1903, 596. No traces of silvering. (W. E 2e.)
9. Florence, from Poggio Sala near Bolsena. (Described by Milani in *NSc.* 1896, 390 no. 3 and Pernier in *NSc.* 1903, 595, foot.)
10. Once Augusto Castellani, from between Orvieto and Bolsena. *Annali* 1871, pl. B, 5. (W. E 11a.)
11. Once Augusto Castellani, from between Orvieto and Bolsena. Described by Klügmann (ibid. 25–6) as the fellow of the last.
12. Chiusi 1890, from Chiusi. Levi *Mus. Civ. di Chiusi* 125, ii, 13 (rightmost but one); phot. Moscioni 10581, left.
13. Chiusi 1891, from Chiusi. Levi *Mus. Civ. di Chiusi* 125, ii, 9; phot. Moscioni 10581, right.
14. Berlin 3898, from Orvieto.

Bolsena Group. Nos. 1 and 2 go together; and nos. 3 and 4; no. 6 would seem from the description to go with no. 5, and both with nos. 3–4. All these have the body fluted, the neck and shoulder decorated with reliefs. The rest are plainer, have no reliefs above the fluted body. Nos. 7 and 8 have the same handles as nos. 1–2 and 3 (or 4); nos. 10–13, which go together, have a simpler handle, without the third volute.

No. 3, on the neck, has the same relief as the phialai p. 291 nos. 1–10.

Three silvered vases in the Faina collection would seem, from the brief descriptions by Cardella, to be volute-kraters:

1. Orvieto, Conte Faina, 369, from Castelgiorgio. (W. E 11d.)
2. Orvieto, Conte Faina, 369 bis, from Castelgiorgio. (W. E 11c.)
3. Orvieto, Conte Faina, 370, from Castelgiorgio. (W. E 15b.)

### Pseudo-volute-kraters

The general shape is that of a volute-krater, but the handle is in the form of two human figures, one above the other. Bolsena Group.

1. New York 06.1021.256, from Orvieto. A, *Vente 11–14 mai 1903* pl. 8, 3; A and handles, Richter *Etr.* figs. 167–9.
2. New York GR 1013. (Mentioned by Richter *Etr.* 53.) Part of the foot is modern.
3. Florence, from Poggio Sala near Bolsena. Milani *Mus. Top.* 52, i, 3.

No. 3 is a different model from nos. 1–2, and the body is reeded, not plain as there. The decoration on the neck of nos. 1–2 connects them with the dinos p. 286, foot and the situlae p. 287 nos. 2–7.

### Calyx-kraters

1. Florence, from Poggio Sala near Bolsena. (Described in *NSc.* 1896, 390 no. 1 and *NSc.* 1903, 589; W. E 3a.)
2. Florence, frr., from Poggio Sala near Bolsena. (Described in *NSc.* 1896, 390; W. E 3b.)
3. London G 180, from Bolsena. (Described in de Witte *Cat. Al. Castellani* (1866) no. 231, and by Walters; W. E 3c.)
4. Once Gazzetta, Cozza, from Gazzetta near Bolsena. *NSc.* 1903, 590–2. (Described in *NSc.* 1903, 589; W. E 4a.)
5. Once Orvieto, Ravizza, fr., from Bolsena. (Described in *Bull.* 1858, 189; W. E 4b.)
6. Chiusi 1889, from Chiusi. *NSc.* 1903, 589; Levi *Mus. Civ. di Chiusi* 125, middle, right; phot. Moscioni 10581, middle.
7. Once New York. *Cypr. Ant.* i, 80, 316. Purchased from S. T. Baxter of Florence in 1896.
8. Once New York, from Vulci. Ibid. i, 80, 317. Purchased from A. L. Frothingham in 1896.
9. Florence, from Bolsena. Ducati *St.* pl. 284 fig. 685, 3.
10. Orvieto, Conte Faina, 368, from Castelgiorgio. (Described by Cardella, 15; W. E 2d.)
11. Berlin 3896, from Orvieto. (W. E 2c.)
12. Once Augusto Castellani, from between Orvieto and Bolsena. *Annali* 1871, pl. B, 1, whence Martha 489 fig. 329. (W. E 2a.)

Bolsena Group. Nos. 1–6 go together; nos. 7–9 go together and are near 1–6; nos. 10–12 are simpler. No. 12 is a different model from nos. 1–9.

A vase from Gazzetta, described in *NSc.* 1903, 596 as a 'krater, smooth, with egg-pattern on the rim' is probably a calyx-krater rather than a volute-krater.

Klügmann speaks of a 'companion piece' to no. 12, but says that it never had a foot or handles (*Annali* 1871, 25: W. E 2b.)

### Dinos

Orvieto, Conte Faina, 438, from Orvieto. Phot. Alinari, whence Tarchi pl. 78, 2, above.

This goes with the stamnoid situlae p. 287, nos. 2–7 and the pseudo-volute-kraters pp. 285–6. The use of deep incisions to form a rough border connects it with the dishes pp. 291–2. Bolsena Group.

*Stamnoid situlae*

(i)

1. Once Augusto Castellani, from between Orvieto and Bolsena. *Annali* 1871 pl. C, 2. (W. H1.)

(ii)

2. Copenhagen inv. 2048, from Orvieto. *CV*. pl. 221, 2. No slip.
3. Once Gazzetta, Cozza, frr., from Gazzetta near Bolsena. Described, with the next, by Pernier in *NSc.* 1903, 595–6.
4. Once Gazzetta, Cozza, frr., from Gazzetta near Bolsena. See the last.
5. Florence, from Poggio Sala near Bolsena. Milani *Mus. Top.* 52, ii, 3. Described, with the next, by Pernier in *NSc.* 1903, 596.
6. Florence, from Poggio Sala near Bolsena. See the last.
7. Florence. Ducati *St.* pl. 284 fig. 685, 1. I do not know if this can be the same as no. 6.

All these belong to the Bolsena Group.

The Castellani vase, no. 1, is less ornate than the rest. Like them, it is a 'stamnoid situla' rather than a 'situla-stamnos' of the kind described by Jacobsthal in *ECA*. 138. There is no mouth or neck (the ledge at this point is merely a representation, I think, of bails lying on top of the vase). The body forms an S-curve from mouth to foot. The foot is set off from the base. The head of Herakles is perhaps the same as in the dishes p. 292, above. The bronze vessels nearest this are one in the Villa Giulia, from Todi (*ML*. 23, 650–1; Ducati *St.* figs. 606–7) and one in the British Museum from Bolsena (652: Hambidge *The Diagonal* 162). The chief difference is that the bronze vessels have a spout below one bail-attachment, whereas according to Klügmann the head of Herakles seen in the picture of the Castellani vase is repeated on the side not shown.

The following bronze situlae, from various sites and of various fabrics, are of the same type, although not so close to the Castellani situla as the two vases in London and Rome:

1. From Tsotylion in western Macedonia. *BCH*. 1935, 283. There seems to be no separate foot, but it should be said that there is evidently some restoration.
2. Vatican, from Vulci or Bomarzo. *Mus. Greg.* i pl. 8, 4. *Mus. Greg.* i pl. 8, 3a surely belongs to this and not to pl. 8, 3.
3. Berlin Fr. 681, from Chiusi. Schroeder *Gr. Bronzeeimer* 14 fig. 10.
4. Berlin. Schroeder *Gr. Bronzeeimer* 14 fig. 11, 1.
5. Cambridge. *Friends of the Fitzwilliam, Report,* 1934, 3, 6.

The following are fittings from such vases:

1. Carlsruhe 638. Wagner pl. 15, 7; Schumacher pl. 9, 24. Compare the Vatican situla, no. 2 in the last list.
2. From Tiriolo (Calabria). *NSc.* 1927 pl. 25, a and c and pl. 26.
3. Berlin inv. 7843, from Rome. Schroeder *Gr. Bronzeeimer* 18, 1.
4. Vienna, Oest. Mus., from Dodona? *AEM*. 6, 146 and pll. 1–2.
5. Berlin Fr. 1537. Schroeder *Gr. Bronzeeimer* 18, 3.
6. Berlin inv. 7484, from Locris. Schroeder *Gr. Bronzeeimer* 16 fig. 14, 1–2.

7. Berlin inv. 7167, from Lecce. Schroeder *Gr. Bronzeeimer* 16 fig. 14, 4.

8. Berlin Fr. 1465. Schroeder *Gr. Bronzeeimer* 18, 2.

9. Berlin inv. 1260. Schroeder *Gr. Bronzeeimer* 16 fig. 14, 3 and 5.

10. Berlin Fr. 1464. Schroeder *Gr. Bronzeeimer* 17.

This type of situla was also used by Italiote vase-painters—Apulian, Gnathian, Lucanian. Examples are given by Schroeder (op. cit.).

Nos. 2–7 in the list of silvered situlae go together. The shape is of the same type as in the Castellani vase, but there is a spout, and the human heads instead of being applied to the shoulder stand up from the top of the vase. Here also I take the ledge to be a garbled representation of bails. The character of the floral decoration on the shoulder connects these situlae with the silvered dinos and pseudo-volute-kraters described on pp. 285–6.

I cannot tell from the description (Levi *Mus. Civ. di Chiusi* 124) whether a silvered situla in Chiusi, 1898, from Chiusi, belongs to the same class as these.

A small, worn fragment of yellowish clay in Orvieto, from the tomb of the sarcophagus of Torre San Severo, should perhaps be mentioned here (*ML.* 24, 11, 9): Galli describes it (ibid. 18, g) as 'a rim-fragment with a female bust in relief, assignable to a small pelvis or wide-mouthed vase', and as 'the only piece from the tomb that may recall the Volsinian industry of silvered plastic vases'. The illustration certainly makes one think of the head on the Copenhagen situla (p. 287, above, no. 2), and the curved line below it may mark the spring of a spout: more cannot be said without seeing the original.

### Bell-situlae

1. Villa Giulia (ex Augusto Castellani), from between Orvieto and Bolsena. *Mon.* 9 pl. 26, 2; *AJA.* 1927, 283; Pernice *HKP.* 5 pl. 48, 1 and 4–5. (W. H 2a.)

2. Villa Giulia (ex Augusto Castellani), from between Orvieto and Bolsena. Replica of the last. (W. H 2b.)

These are the situlae with a relief of Socrates, Aspasia (rather than Diotima; see Fuhrmann in *RM.* 55, 78–86 and Schefold *Die Bildnisse der antiken Dichter, Redner und Denker* 162 and 215), and Eros, a replica of which, in bronze, decorates an iron chest, from Pompeii, in Naples (*Annali* 1841 pl. H, Jahn; *AJA.* 1927, 284, Amelung; *From the Coll.* 1, 28, Poulsen; Pernice *HKP.* 5, 79–86, pl. 48, 2–3 and pl. 49; *RM.* 55, 79; Schefold op. cit. 163, 2).

On this type of situla see pp. 250–2. I cannot tell whether ours are Bolsena Group or not.

According to Amelung (*AJA.* 1927, 284 note 2) 'the figure of Socrates alone recurs three times on the foot of a very richly decorated, formerly silvered vase from Orvieto in the Chiusi Museum. All the figures that appear on the foot, sides and lip of this vase were executed by means of moulds and then applied alternatingly.' I cannot identify this vase in Levi's *Museo Civico di Chiusi*. By 'from Orvieto' Amelung may mean 'of Orvietan style'.

Fragments of two silvered situlae 'in the form of a truncated cone' (that is, bell-situlae?) are known to me from Pernier's description only (*NSc.* 1903, 596 nos. 8 and 9):

Once Gazzetta, Cozza, from Gazzetta near Bolsena. Near the rim, sunk bands; rising from it, female heads; below them, leaves.

The pretty *bronze* situla (small, one-bailed) from the Tomba dei Calinii Śepuś (*St. etr.* 2 pl. 36, 160) belongs to none of the classes hitherto described: the following resemble it:

1. Carlsruhe 635. Schumacher pl. 9, 10.
2. Chiusi, from Chiusi. *NSc.* 1931, 214.
3. Florence 1491. *NSc.* 1931, 210, 1. The bail.
4. Ancona, from Filottrano. *JRAI.* 67 pl. 28, 3.
5. Florence 74798, from Todi. *St. etr.* 9 pl. 39, 1. Round bottom.

Doro Levi had already compared nos. 2 and 3 with the situla from the Tomb of the Calinii Śepuś.

## Neck-amphorae

1. Yale 347, from Orvieto. *Coll. Castellani* (1884) pl. 4, 2; Baur 204–5. Silvered. (W. F 1g.)
2. Naples market (Barone), from Apulia. *Bull. It.* 1 pl. 1, 1. Gilt. W. F 1a (but this is not the London vase G 185, our no. 7).
3. New York 06.1021.250, from Orvieto. A, *Vente 11–14 mai 1903* pl. 8, 5; B, Richter *Etr.* fig. 166. Ex 'Castellani' according to the sale catalogue.
4. Once Augusto Castellani, from between Orvieto and Bolsena. *Mon.* 9 pl. 26, 1. (W. F 1c.)
5. Once Augusto Castellani, from between Orvieto and Bolsena. Mentioned by Klügmann in *Annali* 1871, 14. (W. F 1d.)
6. Louvre, 'from Magna Graecia'. Ex Campana. Gilt. (W. F 1b.)
7. London G 185, from Bolsena. Not silvered. (De Witte *Coll. Cast.*, 1866, no. 236.) W. F 1j (see on no. 1).
8. Once Gazzetta, Cozza, from Gazzetta near Bolsena. Described by Pernier in *NSc.* 1903, 593. (W. F 1h.)
9. Florence 4641. (*NSc.* 1903, 593; W. F 1i, unless that be the next). The neck-amphora published by Solari (fig. 56, 1) is no doubt either this or the next.
10. Florence. (*NSc.* 1903, 593.)
11. Orvieto, Conte Faina, 365, from Castelgiorgio (between Orvieto and Bolsena). Phots. Alinari 32457–8, whence (A) Tarchi pl. 128, 1. (W. F 1e.)
12. Orvieto, Conte Faina, 366, from Castelgiorgio. Phot. Alinari, whence Tarchi pl. 128, 2. (W. F 1f.)

All these are replicas. Round the middle, in relief, Amazonomachy. No. 11 adds a seated figure on the shoulder. Bolsena Group.

## Oinochoai

### (shape III)

1. Once Augusto Castellani, from between Orvieto and Bolsena. *Annali* 1871 pl. B, 4. (W. B 3.)

2. Once Augusto Castellani, from between Orvieto and Bolsena.  Mentioned in *Annali*
   1871, 25 as like the last.
   Probably Bolsena Group.

### (shape I)

1. Florence, from Poggio Sala near Bolsena.  Milani *Mus. Top.* 52, ii, 2.  (W. B 5, part.)
2. Florence, from Poggio Sala near Bolsena.  Milani *Mus. Top.* 52, ii, 4.  (W. B 5, part.)
   These may be Bolsena Group, but it is difficult to be sure from the small reproductions.

The following should perhaps be added:

### Oinochoe

Florence, from Poggio Sala near Bolsena.  The shape is not clear from Milani's description: 'trefoil mouth; handle ending in ivy-leaves; yellowish clay with relief-decoration,
originally gilt or silvered.' (W. B 4.)

### Askoi
### (or perhaps to be called askoid oinochoai)

1. Florence, from Poggio Sala near Bolsena.  Milani *Mus. Top.* 52, i, 2; Ducati *St.* pl.
   284 fig. 685, 4.
2. Florence, from Poggio Sala near Bolsena.  Milani *Mus. Top.* 52, i, 4.
3. New York GR 1002, 'from South Italy'.  Brief mention by Richter *Etr.* 54.  Purchased
   from A. L. Frothingham in 1896.
4. Florence.  Brief mention by Milani *R. Mus.* 156.
5. London G 193, from Bolsena.  This must be no. 233 in de Witte's 1866 catalogue
   of Alessandro Castellani's collection.  Remains of 'black glaze' according to Walters.
   (W. B6.)
   Bolsena Group.  Nos. 3–5 sound like replicas of nos. 1 and 2.
   These 'askoi,' of a different type from those hitherto described, are imitations of such
metal originals as the bronze vases, from Todi, in Florence (*St. etr.* 9 pl. 39, 13 and pl.
40, 8); see also Pernice *HKP.* 4, 13–15 and *Gnomon* 2, 471 (Neugebauer).

### [Pyxis

A gilt pyxis of peculiar shape in Florence, 4646, mentioned by Milani among 'Volsinian'
vases (*Mus. Top.* 117; *R. Mus. Fir.* 156), is now published by Solari (fig. 56, 2).  The
Amazon relief with which it is decorated differs both from those of the silvered neck-
amphorae (p. 289), and from that of the hydria in the Villa Giulia (p. 294), and the fabric
is doubtful: I cannot see anything definite in the reproduction to connect the pyxis with
the Bolsena Group.  A replica in Boston (89.269: R 527: E. Robinson 191) is said to be
from Ruvo.]

### Kantharoid

Once Augusto Castellani, from between Orvieto and Bolsena.  *Annali* 1871 pl. B, 2.
   (W. G2).  On the shape and its metal original see p. 235.  Bolsena Group.

### Kantharoi (of Malacena shape)?

Levi, in *Mus. Civ. di Chiusi* 124, speaks of Chiusi 1103 and 1104 as silvered 'calyx-
kraters with double handles [anse a duplice bastoncello] well away from the body': are

these perhaps the large *kantharoi* of Malacena shape (p. 231, α, i) figured on his page 124, upper middle, left? If so, a link between the Bolsena Group and the Malacena.

Orvieto, Faina, 371, from Castelgiorgio, according to Cardella, is a 'silvered krater with knotted handles': I do not know what this can be: a kantharos perhaps?

### *Stemless cup*

Berlin 4219. I, female head.

Furtwängler (*Beschreibung* 1049), Pagenstecher (*Cal.* 20 note 2), Zahn (*Berl. Mus.* 55, 7, note 1) all agree in putting this with Berlin 3896–9: I do not know whether it is from the Bolsena Group or not.

### *Low dishes, phiale-like, but with a foot*

A special type: Bolsena Group.

At the centre, a figure-relief, which varies; near the edge, usually a broad band of vine. See also p. 240 and 292.

The relief of nos. 1–10 recurs on a volute-krater belonging to the Bolsena Group (p. 291).

### (Herakles seated, a woman seated, and Lasa between)

1. Once Augusto Castellani, from between Orvieto and Bolsena. *Mon.* 9 pl. 26, 3. (W. R 8a.)
2. Once Golini, from Bolsena. (*Annali* 1859, 352, Braun; W. R 8g.)
3. Once Golini, from Bolsena. (Braun, loc. cit.; W. R 8h.)
4. Boston 97.378. (Described in *Museum of Fine Arts, Boston, Report*, 1897, whence *Anz.* 1898, 141, 25: as stated there, this may be one of nos. 1–3.)
5–8. Florence, from Poggio Sala near Bolsena. Four of them. (*NSc.* 1896, 390 no. 9; W. R 8c–f.)
9. Once Hermann Weber. *Cat. Sotheby 22–23 May, 1919* pl. 2, 55. Not silvered. (W. R 8j.)
10. London G 187, from Bolsena. This must be no. 232 in de Witte *Coll. Al. Castellani* (1866). (W. R 8b and 8l.) Not silvered.

### (Herakles and two seated youths—Dioskouroi?)

Once Augusto Castellani, from between Orvieto and Bolsena. *Mon.* 9 pl. 26, 4. (W. R 9.)

### (Herakles and the Lion)

Once Augusto Castellani, from between Orvieto and Bolsena. *Mon.* 9 pl. 26, 5. (W. R 10a.)

Florence, from Orbetello. (*NSc.* 1885, 420 no. 96; W. R 10b.) The slip to take the silvering is said to be preserved, but no trace of the silvering itself.

### (Nereid riding a kētos)

Florence, from Orbetello. *NSc.* 1885 pl. 1, 8, whence Martha 495; Milani *R. Mus. Fir.* pl. 10, 8; Ducati *Cer.* ii, 532 = Ducati *St.* pl. 283, 684. The vine-border is in relief as well as the central design. (W. R 11.)

(head of Herakles)

Orvieto, Conte Faina, 439, from Orvieto. Phot. Alinari, whence Tarchi pl. 78, 1. (W. R 7a.)

Florence. Ducati *St.* pl. 284 fig. 685, 2. (W. R 7c.)

London G 188, from Bolsena. This must be de Witte *Coll. Al. Castellani* (1866) no. 235. (W. R 7b and 7d.) Not silvered.

New York GR 1147.

### Phialai

1–2. Once Augusto Castellani, from between Orvieto and Bolsena. Described in *Annali* 1871, 24; Pagenstecher *Cal.* 72, 3 and η, and 73 and 20.

3–5. Villa Giulia 2270, from Falerii. Described by Pagenstecher *Cal.* 71, q, r, and s, and 20. Tomb-dummies: the omphalos is not hollow.

Nos. 1 and 2 are silvered. Nos. 3–5 are silvered according to Pagenstecher; Weege (in H.–A. 372 no. 1800 d) says that they are 'without glaze'.

These are silvered examples of the many phialai decorated with a chariot-scene which represents the Entry of Herakles into Olympus (Pagenstecher op. cit. 70–3; Richter in *AJA.* 1941, 363–89). Most of the black-glazed ones are Calene: but according to Pagenstecher the two in the Faina collection at Orvieto (495 and 496, Pagenstecher 71, λ and ε) and a fragment in Heidelberg are shown by the clay to be local imitations (see p. 240). He considers the silvered ones to be Etruscan too. Two *silver* chariot-phialai from Eze (Alpes Maritimes) are in the British Museum (*Walters Cat. Silver* pl. 2); that in New York, from Spina (*AJA.* 1941, 364–8), is of the late fifth century.

Pagenstecher mentions (op. cit. 20) a silvered phiale mesomphalos in Athens, TC 13575, from Etruria, decorated with grapes in relief, and another in Chiusi, 1892, which according to Levi (*Mus. Civ. di Chiusi* 124) has vine-leaves and bunches of grapes. This recalls the subsidiary decoration of the dishes in the Bolsena Group (pp. 291–2), but I have no means of telling if the fabric is the same.

Pagenstecher also reports (ibid.) a silvered phiale mesomphalos, decorated with impressed ornaments, in Arezzo, and another from Falerii, in the Villa Giulia, with impressed leaves (ibid, 86, no. 133, x). The descriptions bring to mind the black phialai, with impressed decoration, of the Malacena Group (see pp. 239–40): but that is all one can say.

Lastly, there are silvered phialai mesomphaloi which would appear, from the descriptions, to be plain: four in Chiusi, 1894–7, mentioned by Levi in *Mus. Civ. di Chiusi* 124; one from Orvieto in Berlin, 3899 (found with nos. 3896–8, for which see pp. 285–6); and two from the neighbourhood of Orvieto in the Faina collection, 302 and 302 bis.

### Strainers

1. Orvieto, Conte Faina (433?; if so, from Orvieto). Phot. Alinari, whence Tarchi pl. 78, 2, below. (W. N 3b?)

2. Once Augusto Castellani, from between Orvieto and Bolsena. *Annali* 1871 pl. B, 3. (W. N 4a.)

Probably Bolsena Group. They are replicas, but in no. 2 the potter did not trouble to pierce the holes.

No. 1 may be 433 in Cardella's catalogue, described by him as a 'patera with a long handle'. He speaks of nos. 434 (from Copio near Baschi) and 435 in the same terms. His no. 432 must be different, for he describes it as a 'patera with handle' (not 'a long handle'), as less simple than the others, and as having the head of a maenad at the spring of the handle and vine-leaves and grapes under the rim. Wuilleumier treats the four as if they were replicas (Patères à manche, N 3 a-d), which does not square with Cardella's account.

Another 'handled patera', according to Wuilleumier (N 4 b) is no. 234 in de Witte's catalogue of Alessandro Castellani's collection (1866), found together with the London vases nos. 231-3, but not silvered: de Witte, however, calls it a strainer.

A silvered strainer of different type, with a *loop*-handle, is in Chiusi (1893, from Chiusi: Levi *Mus. Civ. di Chiusi* 125, left). On this kind of strainer see p. 279.

Wuilleumier speaks of a mastoid vase, from Montefiascone, in Berlin, 2896, as 'silvered', but according to Furtwängler it is simply a Megarian bowl burnt to grey.

# CHAPTER XVI
# LATE RELIEF VASES

A FEW lines, in conclusion, about certain miscellaneous Etruscan vases, mostly very late, which are not silvered or gilt, but equal the Bolsena Group, or even go beyond it, in the abundance of their plastic decoration.

### Hydriai

1. Villa Giulia 2320, from Falerii. Phot. Alinari 41303, whence Giglioli pl. 373, 1 and Nogara 150.
2. Villa Giulia, from Falerii. Replica, it seems, of the last.

On the polychromy see Cozza and Pasqui in *NSc.* 1887, 312–13. The subject of the chief zone is an Amazonomachy which is not the same as those of the Bolsena Group (p. 289).

### Volute-krater

Perugia, Museo del Palazzone, from Perugia. Conestabile *Sepolcro dei Volunni* pl. 57, whence Martha 493; Ducati *Cer.* ii, 533 = Ducati *St.* fig. 612; Galli *Perugia* 153; Tarchi pl. 130, 2. There seem to be no remains of colouring: according to Martha the decoration was in matt colours; Galli thinks that it was gilt or silvered.

### Kernoi (cluster-vases)

These are compound objects consisting of three or four small jars joined together and resting on a single ring or platform which is supported by a pillar-like stand and surmounted by an over-all handle. The simpler 'kernoi' (nos. 1–4) have a plastic female head between each pair of jars; in no. 5 the head is replaced by an Eros; in nos. 6–7 the decoration is freer, wilder.

This sort of composite is not confined to Etruria, but these are Etruscan, of various periods and fabrics. They have been collected and discussed by Messerschmidt in *RM.* 46, 48–53. On the purpose see ibid. 50–3. Our no. 5 was used to hold eggs.

1. Leningrad. Stephani pl. 6, 252.
2. Florence, from Orvieto (Settecamini). Milani *Mus. Top.* 49, foot, right; *RM.* 46 pl. 5, b; Tarchi pl. 25, 2.
3. Florence 73132, from Bolsena. Ducati *St.* pl. 284 fig. 685, 5; *RM.* 46 pl. 5, a; Solari fig. 56, 3.
4. Tarquinia, from Tarquinia. Phot. Alinari 26048.
5. London T.C. D 210, from Vulci. *Coll. Castellani* (1884) pl. 4, 1; *RM.* 46 pl. 3 and pl. 6, a; *CV.* IV Da pl. 20, 2. Polychrome.
6. London T.C. D 209. Walters *Cat. TC.* 340; *RM.* 46 pl. 4; *CV.* IV Da pl. 20, 1 and pl. 18, 2.
7. Louvre. Phot. Alinari 23734, whence *RM.* 46 pl. 6, b and Giglioli pl. 373, 2. The flowers somewhat recall the volute-krater in Perugia.

Messerschmidt mentions unpublished kernoi, from Conca and Falerii, in the Villa Giulia (*RM.* 46, 52–3).

# ADDENDA

## CHAPTER I

**P. 4,** six lines from the foot. In pictures of Zeus pursuing Ganymede, Ganymede usually holds the cock, but it is on the ground, in front of him, on an Attic rf. lekythos by the Pan Painter in Taranto (*ARV.* 366 no. 59), and on an Attic rf. column-krater, by the Harrow Painter, in Naples (3152: *ARV.* 180 no. 52) he drops it. In the unusual picture on a bf. amphora in Munich, with Greek (or Latinian?) inscription (834: SH. 95: above, pp. 56–7), where Ganymede is welcomed by Zeus, the cock is on the ground between them.

**P. 5,** line 4, 'sailed away'. In our literary record Amykos is either put to death, as in Apollonius, or as in Theocritus promises amendment: but according to the scholiast on Apollonius ii, 98, Ἀπολλώνιος μὲν ἐμφαίνει ὡς ἀνῃρημένον τὸν Ἄμυκον, Ἐπίχαρμος Δὲ καὶ ΠείσανΔρός φασιν ὅτι ἔΔησεν αὐτὸν ὁ ΠολυΔεύκης. It is not stated that the Argonauts then sailed away and left him to his fate, but Wolters reasonably infers that this was the sequel to the binding (*Der geflügelte Seher*, 17–18). He also compares the scene engraved on a Capuan bronze dinos of the sixth century, British Museum 560 (*Mon.* 5 pl. 25: no. 2 in Riis's list, *From the Coll.* ii, 157), where Herakles has tied a malefactor to a tree and is making off.

The representations of Amykos have been studied recently by Marchese in *St. etr.* 18, 45–81.

**P. 9,** foot, 'there is nothing . . .'. This is put crudely: but the fact is that while we *know* from their inscriptions that the Etruscans were interested in pedigrees and offices, in the loss or absence of their literature and in our slight and prejudiced record of their history we can know little about their moral theory and practice.

## CHAPTER II

**P. 11,** Ivy-leaf Group. The subject on B of the amphora in Zurich, Dohrn's no. 18, 'Bacchic procession' according to Dohrn, was seen by Brommer to be the Return of Hephaistos (*Jb.* 52, 201).

**P. 12,** 'Pontic' vases. Add the oinochoe (shape I) Edinburgh 1872.23.6, from Chiusi (sphinxes and panthers), and a neck-amphora in Reading with a unique representation, in a furious style, of Achilles carrying Troilos to the altar of Apollo.

**P. 12,** at the end of the 'Pontic' section. A pointed amphora in the Vatican (*Jb.* 24, 136) with a picture in the outline technique is said to have been found at Chianciano, but Weege must be right in treating it as Campanian (a naked man riding with a prisoner, a naked youth riding with spears). Other Campanian vases in the outline technique are an olpe from Cumae in Naples (*ML.* 22 pl. 70, 8: see p. 20) and a vase of curious shape, a sort of pelike, from Capua in Boston (10.8084: A, head of a man; B, head of a woman).

**Pp. 12–15,** Micali Group. Also by the Micali Painter, three neck-amphorae:
Washington 136617, from Orvieto. On the neck: A, sphinx and sirens; B, two sirens. The pictures on the body (A, Herakles and Eurystheus. B, olive-pickers) are modern, copied from an Attic vase by the Antimenes Painter, Berlin 1855 (Micali *St.* pl. 92).
New York GR 1080, from Umbria. Winged horses and a siren; on the neck, leaves between eyes.
Brooklyn 29.2. Three birds. On the shoulder, leaves between eyes.
A small neck-amphora in the Peabody Museum, Harvard University, 41.72.40, is a school-piece: sphinxes and birds; on the shoulder, A, leaves between eyes, B, large rays: white details, no incision. I owe my knowledge of this vase to Dr. George Hanfmann.

The neck-amphora Tarquinia RC 2803 (A, Romanelli *T.* 133: sphinxes) still belongs to the following of the Micali Painter; and a small neck-amphora in Geneva may be placed among the pattern-vases described in *RG.* 85 (on the shoulder, large roundels with dots set round the edge; below, large leaves pointing alternately up and down).

An important hydria in Dr. Hirsch's possession, New York, is near the Micali Group: two horse-hooved satyrs and a maenad dance between two sphinxes seated on large lavers.

No. 30 in my list of vases by the Micali Painter (*RG.* p. 78) is now published in *St. etr.* 16 pl. 48, 3–4; and no. 11 in my list of school-works (*RG.* 81) ibid. pl. 47, 1–2. The vase mentioned on p. 14, foot, was purchased at the Brooks sale by Mr. Costa Achillopoulos.

**P. 18,** lower middle. With Chiusi 577 compare also the neck-amphora Florence 73724, from Chianciano (*St. etr.* 16 pl. 47, 3–4: A, rider and youth; on the shoulder, panthers; B, the like), and another, in Tarquinia, from Tarquinia (A, Romanelli *T.* 134: A, fight).

**Pp. 19–20,** the Orvieto Group. Add a good neck-amphora in Washington (136419: on each side a satyr pursuing a maenad), and a stemmed dish (like Oxford 1933.1564 and Florence 76407) in Philadelphia, L 29.51.

**P. 21,** the Painter of Vatican 265. A fourth neck-amphora of the same group, and doubtless by the same hand, is Florence V 22, from Chiusi (*St. etr.* 16 pl. 42, 1–2: A, youth; B, youth). Compare also the neck-amphora formerly in the collection of Dr. A. H. Lloyd, Cambridge (A, *Cambridge Ancient History, Plates,* i p. 343, a: A, satyr dancing at a column-krater).

Geneva 15003 is a neck-amphora of the same curious type as Vatican 292, but the 'teeth' on the top are differently placed and the foot is in two degrees: on the body, bands and lines, with tongues at the shoulder; on the neck, one side, two satyrs and a maenad. The style is at least not far from the Painter of Vatican 265.

Not far, again, from this painter are three neck-amphorae in one style:
1. Florence V 23, from Chiusi. *St. etr.* 17 pl. 42, 3–4. A, satyr and maenad; B, the like.
2. Florence V 19, from Chiusi. *St. etr.* 17 pl. 43, 1–2 and p. 525. A, two youths; B, centaur.
3. Florence V 20, from Chiusi. *St. etr.* 17 pl. 43, 3–4. A, Eros; B, centaur.

**P. 23.** Add (after the Group of Vatican 246) a group of pattern-vases which is well represented in Washington by handleless chalices (136445, 136447, and others: the same sort of vase as in SH. pl. 41, but with shorter stem), oinochoai shape I (136422 and others), a two-handled jar (136418), and stemmed plates: decorated with palmettes, ivy-leaves, ivy-leaves ending in spiral tendrils, spirals, esses, all in black, without incision or added colour. One of the plates is of white clay like the Calò Group, but the other vases are a warm buff colour. Similar chalices in Florence are from Orvieto, and so is a stemmed plate in Oxford (1933.1563). A replica of the Oxford plate, with the same wave-pattern on the rim, is in Goettingen. A third stemmed plate of the same style, at one time in the London market (Sotheby), has a maeander on the rim. The date is no doubt fifth-century.

**P. 23,** foot, the Group of the Dot-wreath Plates. Add two stemless plates, and one stemmed, in Geneva; the stemmed plate Washington 1371; two plates in Washington (1372, and another said to be 'from Baiae or Pompeii'), and a plate in the collection of the Classical Faculty at Harvard.

**P. 24,** the Spurinas Group. Add, as nos. 11 bis, 21, and 22:
Boston (R. 561). *Vea* (Robinson 198). Stemmed plate.
Brunswick 561, fr. *CV.* pl. 33, 5. *Punie[s]a:* 'Flat dish.' Greifenhagen conjectures that the name may really be Apunies, quoting the graffito *Apuniesmi* on a plate from Pitigliano (*NSc.* 1892, 472, and 1898, 54): the writer having misplaced the interpoints.
Orvieto, fr., from Orvieto. *NSc.* 1934, 85, 11. . . . *car* . . . (?. . . *sar* . . . according to Minto). 'Coppa'.

No. 5 in my list is also published in *NSc.* 1934, 425, 4. Greifenhagen dates the Brunswick fr., and the five pieces he quotes, in the second half of the fifth century, but this does not follow from the find in the Tomba Ciarlanti: see p. 24.

## CHAPTER III

**Pp. 28–9.** The stemless cup Philadelphia 37.20.1 (I, youth in himation, standing to right) probably belongs to the end of the fifth century: no relief-lines. It occurred to me that the stemless cup Yale 341 (Baur 201: I, naked youth sitting on a rock) might be Etruscan rather than Italiote, and I was reminded for a moment of the Argonaut krater in Florence (p. 33). Trendall agrees with me that it does not seem to be Italiote. A stemless cup of a different type, deeper, with offset lip, Villa Giulia 49321, from Cervetri, should probably be dated near the beginning of the fourth century: inside, the head of a woman in three-quarter view, with relief-lines; outside, on each half, a woman standing to left, without relief-lines.

**Pp. 30–1**, note 1. One more example of the σεληνίς: Attic amphora of Panathenaic shape in Geneva, black with a gilt necklace, fourth century B.C.

**Pp. 33–5.** A of the Florence bell-krater 4026 is figured, after FR., in Buschor *Das Kriegertum der Parthenonzeit* (1943), 44, as 'Italic', and interpreted as 'warriors before battle'.

**P. 35**, foot, the London bell-krater 1927.10–10.1. The handful of crumpled drapery at the armpit of the left-hand figure on one side is a coarse version of a charming motive well seen in the Aphrodite from Gortyn (*ML.* 18, 266; Schrader *Pheidias* 270: replica of the 'Aphrodite of Daphne' in Naples, Brunn-Bruckmann pl. 673 right: from an Attic original of *c.* 430 B.C.) and in the helmet-cheekpiece influenced by the original statue (Brunn-Bruckmann, text to pl. 673 right, fig. 3; *Jb.* 41 pl. 5 and pp. 191–204, Rodenwaldt).

**Pp. 37–9.** The fragmentary cup London 1909.7–20.25, though far inferior to the calyx-kraters of the Sommavilla Painter, resembles them in style and might even be by the same hand. Inside, two males, the heads missing, both standing to right with the right leg frontal and bent at the knee, one wearing a chlamys, with the right arm akimbo and the left down holding the chlamys, the other wearing a himation. Outside: A, a youth pursuing a woman: she holds a thyrsus, but the youth (fragmentary) has a cloak and cannot be a satyr; B, a woman, holding a thyrsus (?) and a sash, running, looking round at a youth dressed in a himation who leans on his stick with his left arm extended and his right akimbo. The surface is much ruddled. The pictures are based on works of the sub-Meidian cup-group and the date must be late fifth century. The pubes is drawn in the peculiar fashion described on p. 39, top. This is one of many things that connect the Sommavilla Painter with the Perugia Painter and the Faina pelike. See p. 310.

**P. 40**, note 1. See also Picard in *RA.* 24 (1945), 133.

**P. 46.** The oinochoe, shape VI, London 42.4–7.24 is an almost exact replica, by the same hand, of the Vatican oinochoe published by Albizzati. The handle ends above in a ram's head instead of a snake's. Relief-lines. The surface well ruddled. According to Albizzati a replica of the Vatican oinochoe, but smaller, was once in the Roman market: it would be a third.

**P. 48**, third paragraph from the foot. Albizzati mentions two unpublished skyphoi in the Vatican (*Mél. d'arch.* 37, 113 nos. 22–3) as in the same style as *Mél. d'arch.* 37, 173, 2. It is not certain that the lid set on the published skyphos belongs.

**P. 55.** On groups like that of the Vatican Zeus cup see Kunze *Zeus und Ganymedes* in *Hundertes Winckelmannsprogramm* 38–41. Kunze points out (ibid. 39) that the figure in the arms of Zeus on the cup by Douris in the Louvre (G 123: see p. 4, note 2) is not certainly female: he thinks it is probably so, but the strong indication of the collar-bone seems to speak for male—so Ganymede.

**P. 56.** On representations of Zeus and Ganymede see Paul Friedländer in PW. s.v. Ganymedes, and Kunze *Zeus und Ganymedes* 38–9 and 48.

**P. 56,** no. 2 and **p. 57,** the Boston stamnos 07.862. The spout, the basin, the withy were white, and the white, as in the Oxford vase, was laid direct on the clay.

**P. 60,** foot. A good early example, as Jacobsthal reminds me, of a figure with one foot raised and the forearm laid foreshortened across the raised thigh is the Hermes on the Italiote volute-krater with the Birth of Dionysos in Taranto (*CV.* iv Dr pll. 19–20), the name-piece of Trendall's Painter of the Birth of Dionysos (*Frühit. Vasen* 42 no. 91). According to the *Corpus Vasorum* I attribute the krater, in *Vases in Poland,* to the Sisyphos Painter: what I said there (p. 73, right) was that it belonged to the same general group as the vases of the Sisyphos Painter and of kindred artists, but was not, so far as I could see, by the Sisyphos Painter. An instance, then, of the high standard of accuracy in quotation which as I have often pointed out (for instance in *ARV.* vii) has always been characteristic of the *Corpus Vasorum.*

On earlier figures leaning forward with one foot raised see Jacobsthal *Die melischen Reliefs* 190–2.

**P. 61.** On 'bell-pail' situlae in Attica see Amyx in *AJA.* 1945, 509 and 514–15.

**P. 65,** the stamnos Toronto 427. At the end of the inscription, two dots for punctuation.

**P. 66.** Another representation of Telephos and Orestes is on an Attic squat lekythos, decorated in relief, New York 28.57.9: fourth century.

**P. 68,** the London oinochoe F 100. I am now inclined to think that it may be Faliscan.

**Pp. 68–9,** various rf. cups. Add:

  Cambridge, Prof. A. B. Cook. I, youth and woman; A, youth and woman; B, the like. The couples stand facing one another, well wrapped up. Artless work, without relief-lines. Probably near the beginning of the fourth century.

  Toronto 272, fr. I, Robinson and Harcum pl. 84. I, Selene? A naked woman rides a horse side-saddle, preceded by a winged boy holding an alabastron (Hesperos?); behind her, the hand of a third figure is preserved, holding a spathē (?); this may be another winged youth. A, (the lower part of a male figure dressed in a himation, and the foot of another figure; part of the floral decoration at one handle also remains). Relief-lines are used inside, though not for the faces; no relief-lines outside.

  Boston 90.69, fr. What remains is the foot of the cup with the greater part of the interior picture. The rest of the cup is modern. On the left, a naked male with feet firmly planted holds Eros, who struggles, in his arms; a club, let fall, shows the figure to be Herakles. On the right, Athena watches, her right foot resting on an elevation, her right hand laid on her right knee. Fine style, unique subject.

## CHAPTER IV

**P. 70,** line 5. See below, addenda to p. 108.

**P. 73,** after the Nepi Group. Add:

  New York GR 999, from Falerii, is an important early Faliscan bell-krater. Height 0.416. On A, Dionysos, youthful, seated, is waited on by two maenads presenting him with fruit and wine; an old satyr sits on a pointed amphora and plays the flute; two satyrs beat tympana; a maenad dances or rushes, thyrsus in hand; another sits holding a lyre; there is also a fawn. On B, three large figures: a young satyr, horned, sits holding a thyrsus-like branch; a maenad approaches with phiale and oinochoe; a bearded satyr with a thyrsus, one foot raised, watches. The style is almost indistinguishable from Attic of the early fourth century, and the vase may have been painted by an Athenian soon after his arrival in Falerii. So the Nazzano Painter may have begun.

**P. 78,** no. 2. Part of the drawing in Conestabile, redrawn, is published by Saglio in D.S. s.v. 'acus' fig. 102 as from 'a Greek vase'.

**P. 80,** last paragraph. The votive offerings from Talamone are also figured in Montelius *Civ. prim. en Italie* pl. 205.

**P. 84,** paragraph 2. Jacobsthal adds another example of the use of small human faces or heads in decoration: wooden sarcophagus, from Anapa, in Leningrad (Minns *Scythians and Greeks* 326; Watzinger *Holzsarkophage* no. 12; *Bull. MFA.* 40, 53, Segall), found with a coin of Lysimachus.

**P. 89,** near the foot. Jacobsthal shows me drawings of three cippi in the Museum of Palestrina. The first resembles that published by Nogara. In the second the pigna is supported by a single row of acanthus-leaves. In the third it sits in a floral cup of just the same kind as on the Berlin stamnos.

**Pp. 96,** foot, **97.** The bird in the combat between Athena and Enkelados on an Attic bf. neck-amphora in Rouen (Gerhard *AV.* pl. 6) may be a bird of prey about to settle on the falling giant; and the bird on another Attic bf. neck-amphora with the same subject in the Walters Art Gallery, Baltimore (48.22: A, *Art in America* 29, July 1941, 156) certainly looks like one: these Attic birds are smaller and less obtrusive than the Etruscan.

**P. 100,** the Philadelphia stamnos MS 4854. An unusual feature is the band of rf. palmettes at the base of the vase.

**P. 102.** I cannot place the following Faliscan stamnoi exactly:

Philadelphia L. 64.228, 'from Lucania'. A, Dionysos and seated maenad (or Ariadne?); B, satyr and maenad. The stamnos is of the broad-based type described on p. 74. The woman on A sits to left, looking back, naked from the waist up, holding tympanon and thyrsus; Dionysos, youthful, approaches her, a kantharos in his left hand, a thyrsus over his right shoulder, his right hand extended towards a goose standing between the pair; on B, the satyr runs to right (the upper half restored), a horn in his left hand; the maenad stands facing left, with phiale and oinochoe. Good style. Relief-lines.

Princeton 45.192, fragmentary. Satyrs and maenads. Relief-lines on A but not on B.

Faliscan fragments in Bryn Mawr, with satyrs and maenads, may be from a stamnos. Relief-lines on A but not on B.

**P. 105,** examples of hydriai with no back-handle: Etruscan bf., Florence 4173 by the Micali Painter (*RG.* 79 no. 60); Attic rf., Vatican, by the Painter of the Woolly Satyrs (*Mus. Greg.* ii pl. 19, 2, *ARV.* 427 no. 5).

**P. 108,** the Group of Villa Giulia 1664. Add to the vases of the Group, or by the Painter, of Villa Giulia 1664, the skyphos:

New York GR 638. A, youth seated, and Eros. B, Nike. The youth, naked, sits to right; Eros, his right foot on a rock, bends and talks to him. Nike stands to left, looking back, with the left leg frontal and bent at the knee. Large (0.235). Relief-lines. The detail of Eros' wings largely repainted.

The skyphos also resembles the stamnos Villa Giulia 26017 (see pp. 101–2) and thus links, for a second time (see p. 70), Faliscan pot with Faliscan cup.

**Pp. 108–9,** the Painter of Villa Giulia 43800. The fragments Princeton 45.184 are from a Faliscan cup: I, satyr and maenad; A (the left leg of a woman, and the lower part of a male figure in a himation); B (the legs of a woman). Enough remains of I to show that it was a replica, in the same style, of the interior picture on Villa Giulia 43800 (*CV.* IV Br pl. 13, 1 and pl. 17, 3; better, *NSc.* 1924 pl. 5, a) and Villa Giulia 1614 (*CV.* IV Br pl. 12, 4)—nos. 1 and 2 in my list. I noted part of the rock on the left, the hand of the maenad holding an oinochoe at her side, enough of her head to show that it was turned to the right, the feet, in shoes, of the satyr, the upper part of his thyrsus, a piece of the olive on the right. Now the cup was unfinished: the background was never filled in. May not the Princeton fragments come from the same cup as the fragment Villa Giulia 1615 (*CV*. IV Br pl. 12, 5), our no. 3, an unfinished replica of Villa Giulia 43800 and 1614, which lacks just those portions which I happened to note at Princeton?

**Pp. 109–12.** Faliscan cups, unassigned. Add:

Philadelphia. I, Dionysos with maenad and satyr. A, two athletes and a youth. Dionysos, bearded, dressed in a thick garment with a panther-skin over it, head to left, walks in the middle with his feet far apart, supported by a bearded satyr on the right, and with his arm round the shoulder of a naked maenad on the left. He holds a branch of vine, which is also grasped by the maenad. The faces of both maenad and satyr are in three-quarter view to right. Ground-line with egg-pattern. This is a fine and uncommon piece. The packed composition is strangely like those of Clusine tondi, as if the Faliscan were imitating them; the conception of the god, too, is more like Clusium than Falerii.

Philadelphia MS 3444. I, Dionysos and a naked maenad. A, naked youth, woman, and youth. On I, both figures move to the right, embracing, their faces close.

Princeton. I, Herakles and a seated woman. A, a woman and two naked youths; B, the like; one of the youths holds a discus.

Washington 136388, fr., from Orvieto. A, a naked male seated to left; in front of him, an owl to left. Relief-lines, but none for the owl.

Bryn Mawr, fr. I (wings to left). A (the lower part of a naked youth to right, and the hand of the figure next him).

New York, New York University, fr. I (a stretch of the border, with part of an uncertain object cutting across it). A (the upper part of the left-hand figure, a youth in a himation; and part of a woman holding a tympanon).

Once Cologne, Niessen. I, *Sg. Niessen* pl. 107, 3141. I, a youth embracing a seated woman; both naked. A (lower part of a woman). The interior picture may be without relief-lines, so that the fragment should be placed among the cups on p. 112, β.

A small fragment of a Faliscan cup in the possession of Dr. George Hanfmann, Cambridge, Mass., is without relief-lines: I, (part of a male figure seated to right); little remains of the exterior: bought at Arezzo.

**P. 110,** ε. The group of satyr and maenad on the Munich cup is repeated, but reversed, and varied in details, on a Faliscan skyphos in the Museo Teatrale alla Scala at Milan (61: A, *Cat. Jules Sambon* pl. 1, 16: A, satyr pursuing maenad; B, 'naked youth with hoop'). This vase, to judge from the illustration, might be restored, but it is ancient in the main. It is not clear whether relief-lines are used or not, but I should guess that they were.

## CHAPTER V

**Pp. 117–18,** Clusium Head-vases. The Villa Giulia vase no. 1 is also figured in *Rend. Pont.* 17 (1941), 70, the Tarquinia vase no. 5 in Romanelli *T.* 137, 3. The Petit Palais mug 399 (*CV*. pl. 44, 6–7) should be scanned in connexion with the Clusium satyr-head vases.

**P. 118.** The two Ferrara head-kantharoi are also published by Mrs. Felletti-Maj in *Rend. Pont.* 17 (1941), 66–9.

**Pp. 119–20,** Clusium Duck-askoi. Add, as no. 16 bis, one in Tarquinia, from Tarquinia (A, Romanelli *T.* 137, 2; each side, a female head). The foot missing?

On this group see also Mrs. Felletti-Maj in *Rend. Pont.* 17 (1941), 75–80 and 82–3. Her list consists of our nos. 6, 11, 13, 16 bis, and 18, with three askoi not in our list: Würzburg 891 (see p. 191), Berlin 2969, of which I have no note, and an askos, from the collection of Augusto Castellani, in the Villa Giulia (*Rend. Pont.* 17, 79) which seems to belong to our group although the female heads on it are not recognizably of Clusium style. Mrs. Felletti-Maj figures both sides of our no. 6 on her pp. 76–7, and one side of our no. 11 on her p. 78.

**Pp. 121–2.** The finest column-krater of the Clusium Group, a recent discovery, should be added to our list as no. 1 bis:

    Florence, from Carmignano (near Poggio a Caiano). *St. etr.* 16 pl. 26. A, satyr laying hands on a naked woman (she holds an alabastron and a spattle, and has been engaged in her toilet); B, a young satyr, a satyr, and a woman dressed in a himation. No relief-lines. The vase is of great size (height 0.64), and the pictures are just like the tondi of the Clusium Group.

## CHAPTER VI

**Pp. 124–6.** I have not seen Weinreich's study of the Hesione krater in *Sitzungsberichte der Wiener Akademie* for 1942.

**Pp. 129–30.** Add to the list of unassigned Volaterrae column-kraters:

    Philadelphia L. 29.57, 'from the district of Volterra'. A, young satyr running with sashes; B, the like.

    Philadelphia L. 29.58. A, head of youth; B, the like. Much restored.

**P. 136,** foot. A new rerebrace from Olympia is figured in *Jb.* 56, Olympiabericht iii pl. 46 and pl. 47, 1; three fragments are mentioned (ibid. 15) but not figured.

**P. 145,** the Boston calyx-krater 08.201. Over each handle, the head of a woman at a window, recalling Italiote vases. As in the Trieste krater (p. 134, foot) the rf. palmettes on the cul give place to a black palmette, sprung, at each handle.

**Pp. 145–6,** late rf. stamnoi. Add, as α bis, γ bis, ε bis, ε ter:

    Boston. A, two naked youths. B, a woman. The vase is ancient, but the figures are almost completely modern, and the palmettes much restored. Relief-lines are used.

    Swindon, Mr. A. D. Passmore. A, two young satyrs and a maenad; B, a satyr and a maenad. I owe a photograph to the kindness of Mr. Passmore. No relief-lines. Very like London F 485 (our ƛ).

    Philadelphia MS 2521. A, woman running with a cushion to an altar; B, Eros with an alabastron. Restored. Same style as the oinochoe (shape VII) Philadelphia MS 2517 (p. 303).

    Geneva MF 164. A, satyr, with one foot on a rock, looking up; B, woman. No relief-lines. The stamnos is of the broad-based variety (see p. 74).

**P. 153.** Under vi add, as no. 9 bis, the small stamnos:

    New York 91.1.441. A, woman running, looking back; B, the like. No relief-lines. In the floral, the 'cauliflower' motive described on p. 161. The stamnos is of the broad-based type (p. 74).

**P. 153.** Add, before the calyx-kraters, the column-krater Geneva MF 254, with the head of a young satyr on one side, and a female head on the other. No relief-lines. The vase is of a peculiar model, and the upper side of the mouth, hard to see why, is pierced with eleven holes.

**Pp. 153–4,** calyx-kraters. The Florence calyx-krater mentioned on p. 154, near the foot, should doubtless be added to the list. Add also, at the beginning of it, for relief-lines are used on A though not on B, a calyx-krater in Princeton: little remains of A—parts of a satyr and of some female figures; on B, Dionysos, youthful, with two satyrs. A fragment in Bryn Mawr, from either a calyx or a bell-krater, is Faliscan, but I have not noted whether early or late: hair and hand, with phiale, of a woman;

Eros holding spathē and glass alabastron (see p. 78), a woman bending, with a male arm on her shoulder.

**Pp. 154–5,** bell-kraters. Add two fragments of a bell-krater, Geneva MF 253. On A, Dionysos seated to right, with kantharos, and a bearded satyr bringing a wineskin; On B, a bearded satyr to right, with one foot on a rock, and a maenad moving to right, looking back. Relief-lines on A but not on B. Above, a black wreath.

A small late Faliscan bell-krater, from Falerii, in the Villa Giulia, is known to me from Ure's note: on the front, a female head.

**Pp. 155–6,** oinochoai, shape VII. Add:

5 bis. Princeton 33.48. Satyr and woman; on the neck, maenad. The satyr runs to left, looking back, holding a swan by the neck; the woman stands with left arm akimbo; the maenad holds a thyrsus. Heart-loop.

6 bis. Philadelphia. Satyr pursuing maenad; on the neck, a young satyr.

7 bis. Washington 136408. I did not note the subject, but part of the decoration is a woman running with a tympanon.

10 bis. Philadelphia MS 3143, from Falerii. Swan. On the neck, a volute-krater. Very rough.

12. Philadelphia 99.158. Owl. On the neck, palmette. Cf. no. 11.

13. Geneva MF 315. Bird. On the neck, palmette.

14. London 1913.7–22.4. Female head. Compare Brussels R 274 bis.

15. Washington 154528, 'from Dali in Cyprus'. Female head? On the neck, palmette.

16. Brooklyn 27.729. Female head. On the neck, palmette.

17. Geneva MF 144. Two female heads. Compare the Torcop Group (pp. 168–9, and below).

I should now count the five oinochoai said on p. 173, foot, ν–ρ, to be 'perhaps related to the Fluid Group' (Treben; Brussels R 381 and R 274 bis; Conservatori; Philadelphia MS 2835) as belonging to it; nor can I well separate the Torcop oinochoai (pp. 168–9) from the Fluid Group and Faliscan. The early fragment in Amsterdam, p. 173, α, must also be Faliscan, but earlier than all these.

The pattern above the picture on Toronto 493 (no. 11), 'a band of thick chevrons', is a row of ivy-leaves.

**P. 157.** The small rough hydria Toronto 489 (Robinson and Harcum pl. 85: female head) seemed to me to belong to the Fluid Group.

**P. 158,** skyphoi of the Fluid Group. Add:

Geneva MF 289. A, Dionysos and maenad. Dionysos, youthful, is seated to left, the thyrsus in his left hand; a naked woman, with a garment hanging over her left forearm, bends towards him and offers him a large alabastron, which is decorated with groups of many diagonal lines and is probably of glass (see p. 78). Very large.

Geneva 12910. A, satyr and maenad: a bearded satyr sits to right, holding a sash; in front of him stands a naked woman holding a tympanon and a garment. Large. Like the last.

Princeton 45.90. A, woman seated on an altar. B, Nike. Large.

Bryn Mawr. A, head of young satyr. B, uncertain object.

Princeton 45.198. A, head of satyr; B, head of maenad.

Bryn Mawr P 120. A, head of youth; B, head of woman.

The following skyphoi may also belong to the Group, but I do not find it stated expressly in my notes:

Boston 12.1181. A, female head; B, bird.

Princeton 45.187. A, head of young satyr; B, head of woman. Rough.

Princeton 40.286. A, head of young satyr; B, head of woman. Very coarse.

I now think that the Boston skyphos 97.372 (pp. 166–7) must belong to the Fluid Group.

Now that I have seen the Geneva skyphos MF 274 (p. 161, above, no. 3) I feel that it belongs to the Fluid Group; and it doubtless takes the two others with it (Drago, and Copenhagen inv. 6577: pp. 160–1, nos. 1–2).

**P. 160.** A small cup in Philadelphia, MS 3445, belongs to the tail-end of late Faliscan and is much cruder than even Berkeley 8.2302: inside, a female head, reduced almost to a ball; outside, palmettes only, with nothing between them. No relief-lines. Even the glaze is bad.

**Pp. 160–1,** three skyphoi. See the addenda to p. 158, at the end.

## CHAPTER IX

**Pp. 166–7.** I now think that the Boston skyphos 97.372 must belong to the Fluid Group, late Faliscan.

**P. 167,** the clay bust in Hamburg. See also Jacobsthal *ECA.* 152 note 3.

**Pp. 168–9.** As I said above (p. 302), I cannot separate the Torcop Group from the Fluid Group, and must suppose it to be late Faliscan.

**Pp. 169–72,** the Vanth Group. Add, as no. 3 bis, the volute-krater:

Baltimore, Walters Art Gallery, 48.85. A, Zeus in his chariot; B, Zeus and others. The volute handles are plastic. The foot of the vase is modern. On A, Zeus drives to left, preceded by a naked woman who looks back at him, her face in three-quarter view: this group repeats, I do not know how closely, that on the Chiusi vase no. 3. B, Zeus, sceptred, sits to left, and a naked girl fills his phiale; on the left, a youth; on the right, a naked girl kissed by a youth; a naked maenad seated; and a satyr.

I observed on p. 169 that the vases of the Vanth Group were akin to the Fluid Group, but declined to call them Faliscan. After seeing the Baltimore krater I think they must be Faliscan. It is possible that the Faina Descents into Hades—the volute-krater no. 1, the neck-amphorae nos. 4 and 5—should be separated from the rest as non-Faliscan imitations: but I should like to see them again before deciding.

**P. 171,** middle. With the sceptre of Hades Jacobsthal compares Amphitrite's 'lady's trident' on the Sosias cup in Berlin (2278: FR. pl. 123, whence Pfuhl fig. 418: *ARV.* 21 no. 1); see also Jacobsthal *ECA.* 89.

I am not sure what the elder Philostratus meant by θύρσου 2ένΔρα (*Imagg.* i, 14, 3; i, 18, 1; cf. i, 23, 2 καὶ ὅθεν οἱ θύρσοι), but he may be referring to the giant fennel or one of the plants like it.

**P. 173,** various oinochoai of shape VII. Add:

Brooklyn 27.230. Nike (running, looking round). White flesh and wings. Relief-lines.

Philadelphia MS 2519. Woman seated, and young satyr. On the neck, maenad running (looking round, thyrsus in left hand). Compare, for example, the Painter of R 273 (pp. 167–8).

Philadelphia MS 2517. Eros (or Lasa) and a woman with a tympanon, both running and looking round; on the neck, a woman seated with a tympanon. Very coarse. Same style as the stamnos Philadelphia 2521 (p. 301).

On α and ν–ρ in this list see p. 302.

**Pp. 175–7,** Genucilia Group. Add the stemmed plates, with a female head: Philadelphia L. 64.405; Bryn Mawr P 121; Bryn Mawr P 126; New York, Prof. Karl Lehmann, fr. (compare, for example, the Providence plate, no. 2); Princeton 359 (poor); Harvard, Peabody Museum, 1413 (barbarized, but from the same fabric as the rest); and with a star: Philadelphia MS 3193; Yale 343; Brooklyn 44; Boston (no number); Harvard, Peabody Museum, 1414; Geneva MF 112. Eleven in London.

## CHAPTER X

**P. 181.** London 46.5–18.39, from the Rhodes collection (82), another Etruscan oinochoe of shape VI decorated with red-figure patterns and no relief-lines, resembles Würzburg 647, and at the same time harks back somewhat to the earlier vases of the same shape by the Painter of London F 484 (pp. 46 and 297). On the body a floral band and a maeander; on the shoulder, as in the Würzburg vase, long tongues and egg-pattern; above the tongues, rf. palmettes; much restored.

**Pp. 181–2,** Group of the Vine-phialai. Add, as no. 2 bis, the phiale Geneva I 526, from Italy: like no. 2.

**Pp. 182–5,** Group of Toronto 495. Add:

*Oinochoai* (shape VII)

2 bis. Berne 12519. On the neck, plants in yellowish white. The palmettes sprung and unsprung. Ht. 0.269.

3 bis. London, Greig. Plants in white on the neck.

6 bis. Geneva. The palmettes sprung and unsprung. Plants in yellow and white on the neck.

6 ter. Geneva. The palmettes sprung and unsprung. Black neck.

10 bis. Washington 1362 ('from Pompeii', but I distrust the provenience).

11 bis. Geneva. Sprung palmettes.

*Oinochoe* (shape II, with high handle)

22 bis. London (no number visible: ex Campanari). Black floral. On the shoulder, white leaves (reduced to upright strokes).

*Oinochoe* (of special shape)

25 bis. Geneva. Palmettes sprung and unsprung. The shape is rather like a squat neck-amphora (for example Toronto 508, Robinson and Harcum pl. 88). There must have been a slip-over lid, but the present lid is probably alien.

The following oinochoe, shape VII, probably belongs to the Group of Toronto 495:

Florence. Black floral on the body, plants on the neck. Known to me from Ure's note only.

An oinochoe, shape VII, in Geneva, squatter than usual, seemed related to the group; floral, and tendrils. See also p. 305, addenda to p. 185.

An oinochoe of special shape in Geneva, MF 327 (mug-like, but broadest in the middle; ring-handle) probably belongs to the Group; above, spirals; below, leaves reduced to upright strokes. Two oinochoai in Florence, 4169, and one from Orvieto, have a body quite like that of Geneva MF 327, but the mouth is different: 4169 has vine-leaves in black, the other has several rows of horizontal leaves, then an upright row: Etruscan of uncertain fabric.

The jar in Chiusi mentioned on p. 185 may belong to the group; so may a long-necked neck-amphora in Munich, 3236: black palmettes; on the shoulder, silhouette birds); compare also the neck-amphora Toronto 221 (Robinson and Harcum pl. 19) and the neck-amphora, of special type, originally lidded, Toronto 213 (ibid. pl. 15).

**P. 183,** sprung palmettes and unsprung. Both occur on the stamnos in Geneva, p. 147 foot and 148. Jacobsthal gives me another Greek example of sprung palmettes alternating with unsprung: column-base from the Temple of Apollo at Didyma, in the Louvre (*Enc. phot.* i pl. 223).

**P. 185**: add (after Skyphoi). The stemmed plate Toronto 499 (Robinson and Harcum pl. 86) seemed to me Etruscan. Stout stem, large turned-over lip like that of a fish-plate—larger even than in the Genucilia plates (pp. 175–7 and 303). The decoration consists of two rows of egg-pattern, without relief-lines. A similar plate in the Museum of Classical Archaeology, Cambridge, comes from Veii:

buff clay, the black glaze fired to red; two rows of egg-pattern, no relief-lines. A third such plate, Princeton 10.280, is plain black.

**P. 185,** foot, oinochoai shape VII. Another with similar decoration is Geneva MF 313. The three may perhaps be connected with the Group of Toronto 495 (pp. 182–5 and 304). An oinochoe shape VII in Geneva which has spirals on the shoulder as well as leaves on the body seemed to belong to the Group itself.

## CHAPTER XI

**P. 187,** Riis's class of Campanian head-vases. Add the oinochoe New York 06.1021.45, the janiform kantharoi New York 06.1021.41 and Harvard 27.144.

**P. 187,** the Negro-boy Group. The undersides of nos. 2–4 (I am not informed about no. 1) are well finished off with a black round, black bands, and a black moulding near the edge. (In the New York vase the resting-surface is painted red, as well as the upright edge of the foot.) The careful finish of this part connects the class with such of the Clusium head-vases and duck-askoi as I have seen from below.

Also of the Negro-boy Group a mug in Oxford (1947.147); and another, from Tarquinia, in Tarquinia (Romanelli *T.* 137, 1), where the negro boy wears a thick wreath of 'laurel', as in two other vases of the same type:—Louvre H 81, on which I have little information: it is much restored, and the handle modern; and Ferrara T 608 (Aurigemma[1] 101, 6, and 102=[2] 113, 6, and 114), mentioned on p. 118.

A finely executed head-vase in New York, GR 617, also makes one think of Clusium: it is in the form of a female head, with the upper part shaped as a round-mouthed oinochoe and decorated with lozenges and maeander. The underside is well finished off. The head is of late-fourth-century style.

**P. 188.** The New York head-vase 06.1021.204 was formerly in the possession of the Principe del Drago. The handle is double, knotted. The two heads were made from the same mould, but touched up differently—the back-head painted black and finished with frizzled hair to make it serve as a negro. The underside is flat and plain.

**Pp. 191–2,** duck-askoi. Nos. 3–8 form a 'standard' group; nos. 9–15 may well belong to it, but my notes are too scanty for me to be sure. Other duck-askoi of the standard group are:

Edinburgh 1872.23.19, from Tarquinia.
Philadelphia MS 1596.
Philadelphia L. 64.516.
Princeton.
Baltimore, Walters Art Gallery.
Boulogne? Panckoucke *Héracléide* pl. 1, 27.
A black askos in London, 1908.6–4.1, is of the same shape and doubtless belongs to the group.

Four of the vases in our list on pp. 191–2 are mentioned by Mrs. Felletti-Maj in *Rend. Pont.* 17 (1941), 80–1. I have not seen the Volterra askos, her no. 1.

**P. 191,** note 1, Attic duck-askoi. Add, as no. 4 bis, one in Mr. Joseph Brummer's collection, New York. Another, in Murcia, found at Cabezo del Tio Pio, seems to be an imitation. Five others, from Spina, in Ferrara, are mentioned by Mrs. Felletti-Maj in *Rend. Pont.* 17 (1941), 75.

**P. 194.** An Etruscan askos in Dr. Hirsch's possession, New York, is in the form of a lodged fawn, but does not belong, I think, to either of the groups described on pp. 192–4. The animal rests on a black base. There are no horns. The hide is scumbled with thinned glaze, spotted with dark brown and white. The spout is between head and tail.

Geneva MF 281 is an askos that should be Etruscan, but does not belong to any of our groups. It is in the form of a rudely modelled kētos, with a bail-handle, a hole in the mouth, and a spout beside the end of the tail. Pink surface, with large black spots.

The barrel-shaped askos Toronto 558 (Robinson and Harcum pl. 91) must count as a plastic vase. It is not Attic, and as it is said to have been found at Musarna near Viterbo it might be Etruscan. The shape is traditional in Etruria: Villa Giulia, from Veii (*NSc.* 1929, 50).

## CHAPTER XII

**Pp. 195–8,** Praxias Group. No. 4, the amphora in Philadelphia, is well preserved and free from restoration. The shape is just the same as in Munich 3171. No. 14 is published (after *Annali*) in *Jh.* 8, 243 fig. 56 and (A) Keller *Die antike Tierwelt* i 93 fig. 34: the inscription on A has led to the identification of the Maltese breed of dog. Add, as no. 16, an amphora in Worcester, Mass. (1125: A, satyr running with horn and wineskin; B, maenad dancing), and as no. 45 quater a column-krater in New York, GR 628 (A, komos—a youth with a kylix, and another dancing; B, two youths). Bothmer tells me of a column-krater in the New York market (Parke-Bernet, Dec. 10 1946, no. 227: three youths on each side), and Trendall of a hydria in Gotha (three men) in the same style as the Jena vase no. 6.

**P. 201,** E. Brunswick 672 (*CV.* pl. 46, 15–16) is part of another oinochoe shape VII with added colour and an owl on the neck. The owl is flanked by tendrils instead of olive.

**Pp. 201–4,** Sokra Group. Add the cups:

4 bis. Princeton 45.186. I, two youths; A, two youths; B, the like.

4 ter. Philadelphia MS 2843, from Ardea. I, *Boll. st. med.* 4, 4–5, pl. 2, 36. I, two youths; A, the like; B, the like. This is no. ε in my list of 'sundry cups' on p. 204.

4 quater. Princeton 43.135. I, youth (in himation; two big plants); A, two youths; B, the like.

5 bis. London 1947.1–15.1. I, athlete with strigil and athlete with akontion; A, two athletes; B, the like. Cf. no. 5.

12 ter. Washington 136381, fr. I, naked youth with wreath; A (legs of one of the two males); B (the like).

12 quater. Boston (old number 300), fr. I, naked youth with headband and garment; A (lower parts of two males); B (the like).

12 quinquiens. Washington 136394, from Orvieto. I, naked youth with staff or spear, and short sword; A–B, 'draped figures'.

27 bis. New York GR 910, from Orvieto. I (border of esses, and uncertain remains). A (part of the palmettes).

Add also, as no. 28 bis, the skyphos-fragment London 1908.7–24.1 (A, two athletes).

The cup from Citerna (p. 204, foot, θ) seems at least related to the Sokra Group.

**Pp. 205–6,** the Phantom Group. Add oinochoai shape VII in Washington (101837, from Chiusi; 136551; 136552), Philadelphia, Geneva (two), and one formerly in the Panckoucke collection (Panckoucke *Héracléide* pl. 1, 38: now in Boulogne?).

The oinochoai Philadelphia MS 4084 and L. 64.404 (p. 206 nos. 23 and 24) are said to be 'from Pompeii or Herculaneum', but these proveniences are always suspect.

**P. 210,** note 1. The Attic stemless cup in Tarquinia is also figured as 'Italic with added colour' in Romanelli *T.* 138, 2. See p. 72, note 3.

**P. 214.** The earliest representation of the ankus I have noticed is in the clay relief Philadelphia U. 18819, found at Digdiggeh outside the city of Ur, figured in *Bull. Univ. Mus.* 11 (April, 1946) pl. 9, 5 and to be published as no. 378 in *Ur Terracottas*. Legrain does not date it, but the title of his article implies that it belongs to the third millennium B.C.

**P. 217,** below. The Toronto oinochoe 498 may belong to the preceding group (i).

**Pp. 218–21,** Xenon Group. Add the sessile kantharos New York 06.1021.218, and another in Boston, the skyphos New York 09.192.2, the oinochoe shape II Washington 1353, from Italy, one in Geneva, and an oinochoe shape X formerly in the Niessen collection at Cologne (*Sg. Niessen* pl. 107, 3149). An oinochoe shape VIII (mug) in Bologna is figured by Laurenzi among red-figured vases (*CV.* IV Dr pl. 32, 10), but the decoration seems to be in added red and the vase to be of the Xenon Group, a replica of nos. 51–3; is it not PU. 771, in spite of the reported difference in height?

**Pp. 223–4,** the Red-swan Group. Add the stemless cups:

  2 bis. Yale 256. Swan.
  2 ter. Bari, from Ceglie. *Japigia* i, 257, 5. Swan.
  14. Yale 257, from Bari. Rosette.

The stemless cup Yale 255 probably belongs to the Red-swan Group: inside, a circle, quartered, with an ivy-leaf, pointing towards the centre, in each quarter.

**P. 224.** Here, under a heading E bis, one might mention a one-handled kothon in London (old cat. 1786: *CV.* IV Eb pl. 2, 4) with a laurel-wreath in added red. Yale 254 is a replica. Baur compares Berlin 3651, which I have not seen, with the Yale vase.

**P. 225,** F bis. The floral of the Narbonne fragment connects it with the skyphos-fragment London 1908.7–24.1, which we assign to the Sokra Group (p. 306).

**P. 225,** Group of London F 525. A small hydria in Philadelphia, 14.336, is to be compared with London F 525: sturdy shape, and, a rare feature, the back-handle twisted as there. The decoration consists of a large palmette, and a smaller one at the back, both in added red.

**Pp. 225–6,** the bell-krater Sydney 94. Trendall writes that it is in the style of such vases as Vienna 581 (Trendall *Paestan Pottery* pl. 14, 'Asteas Group') and some of the early work of the Painter of the Boston Orestes.

## CHAPTER XIII

**Pp. 231–3,** kantharoi, α. 1: the Group of Vatican G 116. Add as no. 58 bis the kantharos Geneva I 180, as nos. 69 bis, ter, and quater, the kantharoi New York 91.1.443, another in New York, and Boston 76.202, and as nos. 70 bis, 70 ter, 70 quater the kantharoi Philadelphia MS 1445, Philadelphia MS 1446, Washington 101686. The kantharos Philadelphia MS 1443 is of the same type, but the clay is ill levigated, the glaze poor, and the fabric cannot be Malacena. Round the body, two small fillets.

**P. 234,** kantharoi, under α. iii. Philadelphia MS 1439, from Toscanella, has the same shape as Philadelphia MS 2833, and may be from the same fabric. Philadelphia MS 1438 is like them, but the handles are different and more like those of Michigan 2630.

**P. 234,** kantharoids, α. iv, the Group of Copenhagen inv. 3817. Add, as no 7 bis, Geneva I 682, from Volterra.

**Pp. 234–5,** kantharoi, the Group of Todi 515. Philadelphia MS 3062 is a vase of the same shape, but plain black, without reeding or fluting. Poor glaze. Seems not to be Malacena.

**Pp. 236–7,** kantharoi, λ. ii, the Group of Berlin inv. 4077. Add, as nos. 3 bis and 3 ter:

  Toronto CA 269. Blue-black glaze, not fine.
  New York, New York University. Poor glaze.

**P. 237,** ε, the Group of Toronto 564. A small black Etruscan kantharos in Washington, 101859, has a similar shape, but the handles are different.

**P. 240,** upper middle. The Toronto phiale 595 has nothing to do with the Etruscan group.

**Pp. 240–1**, phialai. A phiale from Tarquinia, in New York, GR 651, may be Etruscan, but does not go with any of those mentioned. Inside, black with an ivy-wreath (incised stalk, white leaves) between two line-borders (a white band between two red lines; and a red band between two white lines). The glaze outside is slightly metallic.

**P. 241**, bowls, ii. The following are of the same shape and group as the bowl in the Vatican:
  Philadelphia MS 2580. The relief-head is a replica of the Vatican head (type Pagenstecher *Cal.* pl. 20, 99 c). Dullish black glaze.
  New York 06.1021.272, from Cervetri. Female head in three-quarter view to left.
  New York 06.1021.274, from Cervetri. Same head as the last.
  Baltimore, Walters Art Gallery, 48.119. Female head in three-quarter view to left.
  Baltimore, Walters Art Gallery, 48.120. Head as the last.
  New York GR 649, from Tarquinia. Veiled female head.
  Goettingen. Head of youthful Herakles. Fine black glaze.
  London old cat. 1973. Love-making. The glaze does not look very Etruscan. An unpublished bowl of the same shape, with a relief which reads like a replica of the London one, was in the possession of Augusto Castellani and was found between Orvieto and Bolsena (*Annali* 1871, 26).
The Etruscan provenience of the New York bowls will be observed.

**P. 247**, above, small jars, ii. A similar jar is in Philadelphia: black, reserved at the base, fabric resembling that of the 'kantharos' Philadelphia MS 1439 (p. 307).

**Pp. 248–50**, bronze stamnos-handles. The Bologna handle no. 7 bis in the Formal Group comes from the same tomb as four Attic vases:—two bf. Panathenaic prize-amphorae by the Achilles Painter (Peters *Studien zu den Panathenäischen Preisamphoren* 83–8; *AJA.* 1943, 448), datable about 440–430, a cup by the Painter of Agora P 5192 (*St. etr.* 17 pl. 20, 1: *ARV.* 611 no. 1) of about the same period, and a sub-Meidian cup-skyphos (*St. etr.* 17 pl. 20, 2: *ARV.* 864, vii no. 8) from the last decade or so of the fifth century.
  Our handle is no. 3a in the list *St. etr.* 17, 155 (the captions on the plate in *St. etr.* are confused).
  Add to the Ascoli Group, as no. 6, a pair of handles in the possession of Dr. Hirsch, New York: said to have been found at Populonia, and to have been in the Gréau collection (if so, perhaps no. 146 in *Coll. J. Gréau, Paris 1–9 juin 1885*).
  Add under C a stamnos-handle in Teplitz and a lost handle (formerly in Caylus's collection?: Caylus 4 pl. 46, 4). These seem to go with the Bonichi stamnos. All three are nearer to the Ascoli Group than to the Formal.

**Pp. 252–3**, stamnoid situlae. Add, as no. 2 bis:
  Geneva 14971. The upper parts of the bail-hole figures are missing, but the tails of the Tritons or Tritonesses remain. Malacena fabric.

**Pp. 253–6**, the Group of Vienna O. 565. Add, as nos. 15 bis–quater, oinochoai shape II, with high handle, in Geneva, New York (06.1021.103, from Orvieto), and Boston (98.201), and as no. 39 bis an oinochoe shape XX in Geneva (I 614, from Italy). An oinochoe shape II, with reeded body, in Geneva, goes with nos. 20–30 in almost all respects, yet seemed to me Campanian. In the reeded list (nos. 20–30), the only vases I have examined are nos. 24–6, which are Etruscan (Malacena fabric). It is possible, however, that some of the others are Campanian.

**P. 255**. An Etruscan oinochoe just like Oxford 1928.50 (no. 42), but reeded, is in the Gustav-Lübcke Museum at Hamm, inv. 1564: I owe my knowledge of it to Dr. Ludwig Budde. 'Ht. 0.21: yellow clay, blue-black glaze; on the neck, a white vine-wreath.'

**P. 255.** An unusually fine oinochoe of shape II, with high handle, in New York, GR 622, from Valdichiana, much resembles those from the Group of Vienna O. 565 in shape, and is Etruscan, but is not from the Malacena fabric. The body is reeded. The handle, triple, has a plastic palmette at its lower junction and a pair of plastic shells and rosettes at its upper. Good black glaze, slightly bluish to greenish.

**P. 258,** lower middle. Philadelphia MS 1455, 1456, and 1457, all from Toscanella, are black oinochoai, shape XX, no two just alike, but all resembling, in the main, Vatican G 120. Harvard 2257 (*CV.* pl. 26, 11) may be compared, for shape, with Philadelphia MS 1457.

**P. 262,** η, Group of Copenhagen 453. Add, as no. 19, Edinburgh 1881.44.3.

**P. 263,** κ, oinochoai of S. Anatolia shape. Add, as no. 4, a black oinochoe in the American Academy, Rome (*Mem. Am. Ac.* 17 pl. 6, 8).

**P. 263,** under κ. The oinochoe Philadelphia MS 2840 has a yellow slip: see p. 310.

**Pp. 264,** μ: oinochoai shape IX. A black oinochoe in New York, New York University, 40.86, most resembles Villa Giulia 23933, no. 4 in the list: offset neck and concave handle as there; poor black glaze. To the two-handled vases add Corinth C 34.946, from Corinth (*Hesp.* 6, 293, 151), plain with a few glaze bands; Corinthian. Miss Pease mentions three others in Corinth, C 34.947 and 948, C 31.238. A plain vase of this type is in Syracuse; more than one in Catania.

In the bronze list, add, as no. 4 bis, a vase in Florence, from Carmignano (*St. etr.* 16 pl. 25, a).

**Pp. 266–70,** black oinochoai of shape VII. Pp. 266–8, Group of Vatican G 119: add the black oinochoe Philadelphia L 64.36 and another in Yale.

**P. 268,** middle. Two black oinochoai, shape VII, very slender, with thin necks, in the London market (Spink) seemed Etruscan, and they may perhaps take the Naples vase with them, although they belong to type B.

**Pp. 268–9,** Group of Leyden 192. The oinochoe Philadelphia MS 3054, from Toscanella, may belong to this group, is at least near it. So is Geneva 14972.

**P. 269.** An unglazed oinochoe shape VII (type A, without foot), of whitish clay, was found, with other plain vases of the same fabric, in a tomb at Bolsena and is now in New York (Richter *Bronzes* 181, top, right). Among the objects found with it were a black kantharos of Malacena type (p. 232) and a reeded black oinochoe (p. 254). The unglazed oinochoe shape VII Harvard 2300 (*CV.* pl. 39, 16) is not unlike the New York one, but the neck is not so short. An oinochoe shape VII, that with its very short neck resembles the plain one from the Bolsena tomb in New York, is Oxford 1878.143, from Ben Gemmi in Malta: pinkish clay covered with a whitish slip. The clay is the same as in the askos from the same site, Oxford 1878.144 (p. 275, top, no. 1).

**P. 269,** foot, B. Add, as no. 3 bis, an oinochoe in Geneva.

**Pp. 270–1,** black squat lekythoi. Add, as no. 9 bis, the tulip-top:

Harvard 2291. Straight-backed handle. Has the turning-marks described on p. 271, middle.
   Add, on p. 271, as nos. 19 bis, 20 ter, and 21 bis:
New York, New York University. Concave handle. Poorish, slightly metallic glaze.
Washington 377365, from Italy. Convex handle.
Yale. Convex handle. Mouth as in no. 21. Metallic glaze.

**P. 272,** deep askoi, type A. Add a black one in Washington, 'from Cyprus', and an unglazed one from Naucratis (*JHS.* 25, 126 fig. 7).

**P. 273,** deep askoi, type B. Toronto C 41 is a black vase of this type.

**Pp. 275–7**, askoi, Ruvfies Group. Add, after no. 27 on p. 276: An askos in Geneva is of the same type as these. The mouth is replaced by the head of a griffin, which seemed, however, to be modern. Very bad black glaze.

**P. 277**, askoi, Class of Berlin inv. 4921. Add, after Berlin inv. 4921, the askos

Genoa inv. 1081. *CV.* V Bf pl. 1 (It. 937), 6. As Berlin inv. 4921. Sigillata ('orange glaze'). 2nd–3rd century A.D. according to Lamboglia quoted by Bernabò Brea.

Add, after Yale 550:

Toronto G 5025, from Carthage. I could not see whether unglazed red clay or sigillata.

Add, also, after Michigan 2912A, an askos in Winterthur, which, like the two Michigans, has no Adam's apple.

**Pp. 279–80.** Two plain black strainers, with loop handle, in Geneva, not of one make, are no doubt Etruscan, but do not belong to either of our groups.

## CHAPTER XIV

**Pp. 281–2**, Group of Villa Giulia 2303. Add, as no. 17, the neck-amphora Philadelphia MS 25, from Orvieto. The vase has a reddish-brown covering, apparently glaze. The handles (partly restored) are pairs of kētē intertwined, painted red and light blue; on the neck, an ivy-pattern; on the upper part of the body, two rows of floral decoration with a maeander below. The foot is modern. I did not leave myself much time to examine another vase in Philadelphia, I think a sort of neck-amphora, which may also belong to the group: light-coloured, greyish clay, covered with a white slip and over that with a yellow; kētos-handles as before, with red and light blue details.

**Pp. 282–3**, vases with yellow slip. A replica of no. 3 on p. 282, the Leyden oinochoe (shape VI) 766, is in Toronto, CA 265: pale clay, ochrous yellow slip; two replicas of no. 4, the Leyden oinochoe, of S. Anatolia shape, 773, in Princeton, 40.288 and 40.289: offset shoulder as there. The oinochoe of this shape in Philadelphia, 2840, from Ardea (p. 263, below, and *Boll. st. med.* 4, 4–5, pl. 2, 19) has a yellow slip and is like those in the Villa Giulia mentioned on p. 283, last paragraph but two.

## CHAPTER XV

**Pp. 291–2**, low dishes, phiale-like, but with a foot. Add, at the end, New York GR 1143, with a head of Silenus in relief; remains of blue and yellow. The usual vine-border, in this as in the other New York dish is replaced by a pair of wreaths. Both vases were formerly at Florence in the possession of Marchese Strozzi.

A rf. cup in the same style as London 1909.7–20.25 (see p. 297, addendum to pp. 37–8) is in the Cooper Union Museum, New York (1915.11–37: I, a youth seated, holding a spear, and a woman with her arm on his shoulder; A, two youths leaving home; B, the like). The pictures are again based on Attic work of the sub-Meidian cup-group. A skyphos-fragment in Oxford (1919.27: upper part of a youth with a thyrsus—Dionysos?) is also in the same style.

**P. 304**, note on p. 183: sprung and unsprung: see also Watzinger *Holzsarkophage* 46.

# GENERAL INDEX

*Inscriptions in italics*

acanthus, 45; acanthized leaf-hooks, 45, 51.
*Achilei*, 196.
Achilles: dead, 179; and Chiron, 196; and Priam, 52, 195; and Troilos, 179–80, 295; and the Trojan Prisoners, 8, 9, 88, 136–7.
Achilles Painter, 308.
*acila*, 131.
*acnaine*, 146.
acrobats, 2.
Actaeon, 136, 141.
Adamklissi, 98.
Admetos, 166.
Adonis, 82, 85.
*Aecetiai pocolom*, 215.
Aegisthus, 195.
Aelian, 115, 213, 213.
Aeneas and Anchises, 195.
*aerar*, 236, 244.
aes grave, 259.
Aeschylus, 38, 81, 86, 140.
Aesop, 159.
*afnaś*, 232.
ἀγγόρπης, 214.
Agora P 5192, Painter of, 308.
*Aiax viet*, 139.
*Aisclapi pocolom*, 210.
Aison, 200.
*Aivas*, 5, 59, 136, 138.
*Aivaś*, 53.
Ajax, 5, 8, 39, 42, 53–4, 136–41, 179.
*Akrathe*, 146.
Al Mina, 265.
alabastra, of glass, 78, 302, 302.
*Alacea?*, 68.
*Alcestei*, 134.
Alcestis, 8–9, 133–4, 166.
Alcmena, 5, 104.
*Alcsti*, 8, 133.
Alcsti Group, 133–5.
Alexander, hearse of, 213.
— sarcophagus, 57.
*Alf*, 246.
*Alfi*, 245, 246.
Alise, 236.
Altar, 50.
Altavilla Silentina, from, 226, 226, 251.
Amasis, 109.
Amazons, Amazonomachy, 49, 67, 126, 142, 150, 165, 179, 196, 289, 290, 294.
Amphitrite, 108.
*Amuces, Amucos, Amyche*, 58, 59, 80.
Amyklai, throne of Apollo, 82.
Amykos, 5, 35, 56–61, 78–80, 295.
Amymone Painter, 248.
Anapa, 299.
*Andromache*, 196.

ankus, 213–15, 306.
Antioch in Pisidia, frieze, 68.
Aphrodite, 7, 17, 46, 85, 86, 169; on goose, 37; Cnidia, 84; of Daphne, 296; from Gortyn, 296.
Apollo, 7, 43–4, 44, 44, 46, 49, 50, 68, 84, 92–4, 95, 127, 135; on swan, 153, 154, 161; with satyrs and maenads, 95; and Marsyas, 73–7, 107.
Apollodoros, 82.
Apollonios Nestoros, 80.
*Apunies, Apuniesmi*, 296.
Ara Pacis, 31.
araceae, 83.
archers, 49.
Arcisate, 263.
— shape, 263.
Ard-el-Kheraïb, 273.
Ardea, from, 173, 175, 176, 184, 185, 201, 203, 204, 204, 207, 222, 234, 242 (three), 243 (five), 245, 245, 259, 263, 263, 270.
Arethousa, 104.
Arezzo, from, 28, 29, 276, 276.
Argo, constellation, 219.
Argonauts, 34–5.
Ariadne, 7, 7, 36, 63–4, 77 (three).
*Arnthe*, 196.
Arrian, 213.
Artemis, 7, 44, 84, 108, 251.
aryballos, 59.
Ascoli Group, 249, 250, 308.
askoi, 272–8, drinking from, 208.
Astyanax, 7.
*Ataiun*, 136.
Atalanta, 42, 121.
Athena, 7, 17, 42, 56–7, 70, 71, 73, 111, 112, 112, 120, 142, 223, 251, 298.
*Atmite*, 8, 133, 134.
*Atrane, Atraneś, Atraneśi*, 275–7.
*aur*, 131.
Aurora Painter, 7, 80–5.
Aventicum, 116.
Aversa, 227.
*Avi*, 24, 245.
*Avlesvpinas*, 3, 25–6.

Babrius, 86.
bakchos-rings, 130.
balance, woman holding, 127.
bandages, 89.
Bari, from, 218, 219, 220, 232, 307.
bathing, 83, 84, 101.
battle-motives, 165–6.
beard, imperial, 185.
Begram, 214.
bell-situlae, 250.
Bellerophon, 37–8.

Bellona, 210.
*Belolai pocolom*, 210.
belts, 97.
Berkeley Hydria, Painter of the, 101.
Berlin inv. 4039, Group of, 233.
— inv. 4077, Group of, 236–7, 307.
— inv. 4921, Class of, 277, 310.
— Painter, 105.
Bettona, from, 237, 245, 260, 262.
Bharhut, 214.
bird-headed monsters, 218.
birds, big ugly, 2, 7, 8, 96–7, 299.
bird-woman, 163.
Birth of Dionysos, Painter of, 164, 298.
black patterns, 135, 143, 148, 154, 160.
—, patterns breaking into, 134, 135, 183.
Bologna, from, most of the vases in Bologna, q.v.
Bolsena, from, 232, 233, 234, 252, 254, 279, 284, 285, 286 (three), 287, 289, 290, 291 (three), 292, 294, 309; *see also* Poggio Sala.
— Group, 283, 286–93.
Bomarzo, from, 62, 68, 107, 116, 148, 164, 164, 174, 249, 265, 266, 266, 283, 287.
Bonn Faliscan, Painter and Group of the, 96–102.
Boston Orestes, Painter of the, 226, 307.
bow, toy, 228.
boxing, 2, 79.
Bruschi Group, 189–90.
Brussels R 273, Painter of, 147, 167.
bulla, 33–5, 50.
Bulla Regia, 277.

Cabezo del Tio Pio, 305.
Caecilia Metella, tomb of, 99.
Caivano, from, 261 (three), 272, 273.
— Painter, 41, 226.
Calene, 128, 240, 240, 251.
Cales, from, 240.
Calinii Śepuś, Tomba dei, 230–1.
Callimachus, 97.
*Caloni*, 274.
Campagnano, from, 199.
Campana reliefs, 84.
Campanizing Group, 63–7.
Canoleios, L., 238, 240.
Canosa, from, 219, 220.
Capena, from, 184, 184, 207, 211, 217 (six), 238, 259, 264 (three), 270 (seven), 273, 276.
Captives Group, 87–92.
Capua, from, 11 (four), 295; *see also* the vases in the Capua Museum.

Carmignano, from, 301, 309.
Carthage, from, 10, 176, 272.
Casale Val d'Elsa, from, 130.
Casalta (Val di Chiana), from, 30.
Castel Campanile, from, 2, 142, 145.
Castelgiorgio, from, 114, 131, 285 (three), 286, 289, 289, 291.
Castellamare di Stabia, from, 222.
Castiglioncello Group, 233–4.
Castrum Novum, from, 205, 242, 266, 273.
*Castur*, 199.
cauliflower tendrils, 161.
Ceglie del Campo, from, 221.
Centauress, 251.
Centaurs, Centauromachy, 15, 16, 17, 21, 22, 102, 121, 141, 163, 164, 173, 223, 251, 296; with satyrs and maenads, 100.
Centuripe, from, 242.
Cerberus, 9, 17.
Cerberus Painter, 143.
Cerotolo, from, 110.
Cervetri, from, 11, 18, 24 (two), 73, 118, 132, 142, 150, 152, 173 (three), 201, 201, 244, 254, 256, 267 (four), 297, 308, 308.
—, Tomba dei Rilievi, 59, 160.
*Chalchas*, 199.
Chalki, from, 260.
*Chaluchasu*, 199.
chariots, 82, 164–5, 170, 172; seen from front, 130; unharnessing, 29; drawn by wild animals, 179; chariot-race, 134, 135, 144, 172, 209.
Charun, 8, 9, 9, 9, 47, 62, 92, 132, 133–4, 136, 142, 188–9.
chests as seats, 111.
Chianciano, from, 295.
*Chiron*, 196.
Chiron and Achilles, 196.
Chiusi, from, 14, 15, 21, 21, 23 (three), 25, 28, 36, 39, 42, 56, 86, 113, 113, 114, 114, 114, 114, 132, 138, 153, 166, 169, 169, 170 (four), 171, 185 (four), 197 (three), 198, 200, 202, 202, 202, 202, 203 (four), 204 (three), 210, 231 (four), 235, 245, 247, 252 (three), 254, 256, 259, 260, 262, 267 (three), 274, 276, 276, 278, 281, 281, 286, 287, 288, 289, 295, 296, 296, 296, 296.
—, Tomba della Pellegrina, 235, 251; Tomba della Scimmia, 2, 49, 59.
— Pyxis Group, 19.
Christie Painter, 98.
Christodoros, 137.
Chrysis Painter, 40.
Circe, 54.
Citerna, from, 204, 306.
Città della Pieve, from, 120, 276.
club of Herakles, 142.
Clusium breasts, 116, 120, 122.
— Group, 6, 132, 174, 189, 300, 300–1, 305, 305.

*Coera· pocolo*, 215.
column-kraters, Attic, 50, 66.
Conca, from, 103, 294.
Copenhagen, 453, Group of, 262, 309.
— 505, Group of, 258.
— 509, Group of, 261, 261.
— ABc 1059, Group of, 22–3.
— inv. 3817, Group of, 234, 307.
— Painter, 138.
Corchiano, from, 71, 78, 85, 111, 157, 157, 177, 177, 204, 278.
Corfu, metope, 136.
Corinthian, Etruscan imitations of, 11.
Cortona, from, 126, 236, 237, 237, 246, 261, 263, 264, 264.
cuishes, 49.
Cumae, from, 178, 222, 222, 224, 235, 256, 256, 261, 263, 263, 263, 264, 272, 272, 273, 277 (three), 278, 295.
*Cupico*, 73, 74.
cushion-bearers, 121, 142.
Cypria, 5.

Danaid Painter, 146.
Danaids, 146–7.
dancers, 110, 196.
deer, plastic, 192–3.
Demoness Group, 218.
demonesses, 152, 165, 170–1, 218.
demons, 163, 166, 167, 170.
Didyma, Temple of Apollo, 304.
*[Die]spater*, 73.
Diespater Painter, 73–7; Diespater Group, 73–87.
Digdiggeh, 306.
Dike, 144.
Dinos Painter, 36, 60–1, 75.
Diodoros, 97, 98, 213.
Diomed and Aeneas, 17.
Dionysios I, 98.
Dionysos, *passim*; dancing, 109; drunk, 109; fat, 109; image of, 164; lord of the dead, 152; supported by satyr, 109, 124; with sceptre, 93; visiting poet, 129.
Dioskourides of Samos, 235.
Dirce Painter, 90.
Ditis Pater, 62.
Doidalses, 83.
Dolon, 90.
dolphins, 157, 170, 180; woman on dolphin, 153; satyr on, 112; as stamp, 275.
Dot-wreath Plates, 23, 296.
Douris, 3, 4, 26, 265.
drapery held out behind, 164–5; crumpled at armpit, 297; Faliscan, 162.
duck-askoi, 191–2, 300, 305.
dwarfs, 30, 31–2, 78, 129, 129; as Gauls, 128.

Ear, doubled, 187.

ear-rings, 166, 186.
*eca*, &c., 133.
egg, *see* Helen.
*Eivas Telmunus*, 140.
Electra, 66.
*Elinai*, 5, 53.
Eos, 126; carrying off youth, 81–2; and Tithonos or Kephalos, 7, 80–2.
epichyseis, 156.
Epigenes, 72.
Erbach Painter, 95.
Eretria Painter, 134, 191, 201.
Erinys, 144, 152, 179.
Eros, Erotes, *passim*; driving chariot, 179, 209; standing on dog, 210; on laver, 101; and Zeus, 74.
*Eroto*, 196.
Errera Painter, 66.
Etruscan-dancer hands, 114.
Euaion Painter, 60.
Euphorion, 63–4.
*Eupoliskal*, 219.
Euripides, 6, 55, 58, 66, 131.
Europe, 66.
Eurydice, 152.
expressive faces, 5, 59.

faces in ornament, 84, 299.
Faleria, from, 106.
Falerii, 6.
— from, 66, 73, 73, 77 (four), 88, 103 (three), 106 (two), 107 (three), 108 (four), 109, 111 (two), 112, 152, 153, 155, 156, 159, 160, 173, 175, 177, 177, 177, 183, 201, 202, 202, 203, 245, 245, 281 (ten), 283, 283, 283, 292, 292, 294 (three), 298, 302, 302.
Faliscan, 298.
fawn-bird, 15.
feather-vases, 201.
Ferento, from, 158, 158, 161, 177, 202.
Ferrara T 585, Group of, 207–8.
— T 785, Group of, 177–8, 179, 186.
Feuardent Marsyas, Painter of the, 75, 76.
Ficoroni cista, 5, 34–5, 58–61, 79–80, 84, 110.
Fight at the Ships, 195.
Filottrano, from, 264, 278, 278, 280, 289.
Fluid Group, 112, 149–62, 302, 303.
Foci del Garigliano, 230; vases from, *see under ML.* 37.
*Foied*, &c., 7, 106.
Foot set on an elevation, 60–1, 298.
Formal Group, 248–9, 250, 308.
Foro Group, 158–9.
*Fortunai pocolo*, 216.
Fountain scenes, 59, 79, 83, 103, 105, 108, 111, 127.
Fox and goose, 157.

Francavilla Fontana, from, 224.
Frignano Piccolo, from, 41, 222, 272.
*Fufluns*, 107.
'funeral masquerade', 62–3.
Funnel Group, 141–5, 181.

Gallonios Group, 274, 275.
*Ganumede*, 73.
Ganymede, 4, 56, 73–4, 295, 297, 298.
garland-vases, 227–8.
garment let down to the waist, 88.
Gauls, 7, 97–100, 128, 166.
Gazzetta, from, 285 (three), 286, 286, 287, 287, 289, 289.
Geneva Group, 147–8, 182.
Genoa, from, 70, 265, 265.
Genucilia Group, 10, 175–7, 303.
Gigantomachy, 2, 15, 56–7, 146.
gilt details, 55.
gladiators, 62.
glass, *see* alabastra; glass 'Semitic' heads, 190.
glaukes, 200.
Gnathian, 180.
goat and satyr, 160.
gorgoneion, 15, 48.
griffin, and grypomachy, 67, 80, 130, 145, 158, 172, 189, 221, 248.
Gualdo Tadino, from, 202, 203.

Hades, 9, 9, 47, 169–71.
hair, dressed high, 131, 137; of Gauls, 98; 'Z.' hair, 131.
Hanau, from, 223.
Hanau Group, 222–3.
Hands clasped, 137.
Harmonia, 134.
ἄρπη, 213.
Harrow Painter, 295.
Harvard 3066, Group of, 257–8.
Hasti, 166.
hatching, on the body, 67, 103, 122, 124, 126, 135.
head-vases, 300.
—, Campanian, 187, 305.
heart-loops, 151, 169.
heater-shaped handles, 248.
Hebe, 173.
Hector, Ransom of, 52.
Helen, the Egg of, 5, 5, 6, 39–42, 60, 115–16; Helen and Menelaos, 7, 94–6.
Helios, 37–8, 81–2, 126, 127, 130, 171.
helmet, tiaroid, 57.
Hephaistos, 29; Return of, 295.
Hera, 5, 7, 52, 94.
*HPA*, 176.
Herakleitos, 81.
Herakles, 2, 43, 46, 46, 56, 100, 118, 142, 146, 188, 188, 202, 236, 244, 287, 292, 295, 308; and Apollo, 127; and Athena, 111, 173; in battle, 165; and Cerberus, 17;
and Eros, 298; in Gigantomachy, 2; and griffins, 172; and Hesione, 124–6; and the Hydra, 16; and the kētos, 124; and the Lion, 140–1, 291; entering Olympus, 240, 292; pyre of, 103–5; resting, 70–2, 87; and Scylla, 280; and the Snakes, 5, 7, 52, 92–4; and Triton, 16; and woman, 291, 300; and youths (Dioskouroi?), 291.
'hermaphrodites', 119, 227.
Hermes, 5, 6, 7, 8, 47, 57, 60, 127, 152, 210; with infant Dionysos, 102; with the three goddesses, 17.
Hermonax, 27.
Hesione, 124–6, 301.
— Painter, 122–7, 131.
Hesperus, 298.
Hesse Group, 208–9, 236, 237.
Hesychius, 214.
high-lights, 178–9, 180, 216.
*hinthia Turmucas*, 9, 136.
Homer, 58, 82, 89, 91, 125.
horse-heads, 130.
howdah, 213.
hyacinth, 5–6, 53–4.
Hyades, 105.
Hyakinthos, 49–50, 142.
hydra, 16.
hydria, two-handled, 299; with twisted back-handle, 299.
Hypsis, 105.

Iguvium, aes grave, 99.
Iliupersis, 7, 92–6.
Incised drawing, 198.
*iooroi?*, 196.
Iphikles, 5.
Isidore, 62.
*Iunonenes pocolom*, 210.
Ivy on neck of vase, 27.
Ivy-leaf Group, 11, 295.

Jason, 34, 79, 125.
Jena Painter, 70, 101, 111.
Johannes of Gaza, 81.

Kadmos Painter, 37, 40, 74–5, 104.
Kaineus, 16.
— Painter, 16.
Kalchas, 199.
*kalnies*, 24.
kantharoid, 235.
kantharos, Sotadean, 72–3.
Kastel, 236.
*Kastur*, 116.
*Kasutru*, 199.
Kephalos, 81–2.
*Keri pocolom*, 210.
kernoi, 294.
kētos, 56, 82, 124–6, 133, 149–50, 152, 169, 170, 213, 281, 291, 310.
kētos-askos, 306.
Kiev Painter, 40.
Klein-Aspergle, from, 248.
knee-guards, 49.
kottabos-stand, 114.
Kronos, 95.
Kyknos, 16.
— Painter, 16–17.
kylix hanging at fountain, 59.
kynodesme, 58–9.

La Motte Saint-Valentin, from, 219, 248, 249.
La Tolfa Group, 111.
Lanuvium, from, 206, 216.
*Lap[·]nas*, 24.
*Larisal*, 24.
Lasa, *passim*.
*Lasna*, 147.
*Latva*, 116.
Laver-stands, 67.
*Lavernai· pocolom*, 210.
Leaky Jar, 146–7.
Lecce, from, 288.
Leda, 6, 39–42, 44, 53, 85.
*Lethe*, 276, 277.
Leyden 192, Group of, 268–9, 308.
— Kyathos, Group of, 23.
Lindian Chronicle, 95.
Lion, puppy-like, 27.
Livy, 63, 213.
Locri, from, 264, 266.
London F 64, Painter of, 70, 104.
— F 484, Painter of, 43–6, 297.
— F 525, Group of, 225, 307.
— Hydria, Painter of the, 105.
Lotus-bud Group, 18.
Louvre Deer-askos, Group of, 192–3.
— G 433, Painter of, 92.
Lucanian warrior, 225.
Lucian, 55.
Lucignano, from, 31.
Lysippos, 179, 180.

Maddaloni, from, 272.
Madrid 11093, Painter of, 228.
maenads, *passim*.
mahouts, 212–15.
Makron, 164.
Malacena Group, 208, 208, 230–1, 231, 235, 235, 236, 237, 238, 239, 240, 240, 241, 245, 247, 247, 248, 248, 251, 252, 253, 253, 260, 261, 262, 263, 266, 275, 278, 279, 279, 291, 292, 308, 308, 309.
Malta, from, 10, 177, 273, 275, 309, 309.
Maltese dog, 210, 306.
Manilius, 81.
Mannheim Painter, 201.
Marcellus Empiricus, 31.
Marcioni Group, 78–9.
Marsyas, 73–7, 107.
mattocks, 59, 60, 80.
Mausoleum, 165.
Medusa, 203.
Meidias Painter, 3, 36, 80, 178, 252; *see also* Sub-Meidian.

Meleager Painter, 93, 161.
*Melitaie*, 196.
Menelaos, 7, 95.
*Menerva*, 73, 140.
*Menervai· pocolom*, 215, 216.
Micali Painter and Group, 1–3, 12–15, 59, 295–6, 299.
Milocca, from, 265.
Minotaur, infant, 6, 54–5.
Minturnae, 230; vases from, *see under Boll. st. med.* 5, 4–5.
mirrors, Z Group, 130–2.
Montalcino, from, 241, 245 (three), 259, 263, 266, 281, 282 (seven).
Monte Cerretto, from, 106.
Montediano, from, 127.
Montefiascone, from, 154, 252, 293.
Montefortino, from, 232, 234, 237, 238, 239, 245, 245, 250, 260, 260, 264.
Monte Gallozzi, from, 203, 205.
Monteluce, from, 124, 127, 130, 165.
Monte Padrone, from, 260.
Montepulciano, from, 114, 130, 188, 197, 250.
Monteriggioni, from, 122, 124, 126, 127, 128 (twelve), 129 (four), 130, 130, 132, 232, 232, 233, 234, 234, 236, 239, 239, 240 (three), 243 (four), 247, 247, 248 (three), 251, 252, 255 (three), 256, 256, 258, 258, 261, 263, 267 (nine), 273 (three), 279 (four), 280, 280, 289.
Monte S. Savino, from, 115.
Monte Sannace, from, 136.
Montlaurès, from, 225.
Monzuno, from, 129.
Mound with athletic gear, 195.
Munich 872, Group of, 22.
— 878, Group of, 22.
— 886, Group of, 22.
— 891, Group of, 22.
— 912, Group of, 22.
— 980, Group of, 23.
Musarna, from, 306.
Mustilli, *see* S. Agata.

Naples, from, 273.
— Painter, 61.
— 1778, Painter of, 226, 227.
Narce, from, 84, 87, 100, 101, 107, 155, 175, 206, 263, 263.
Nazzano, from, 7, 36, 92, 160, 161.
— Painter, 9, 136–7, 144, 146–7, 152–3.
Negro-boy Group, 187, 305.
negroes, 118, 131, 187–8, 305.
Neoptolemos, 7, 94.
Nepi, from, 70.
— Group, 70–3.
Nereid, 291.
— Monuments, 165.
Nicaea, coin, 214.
Nijmegen, from, 31.
Nike, 2, 67, 79, 142, 146, 146, 147,

147, 153, 154, 154, 158, 158, 159, 179, 196, 201, 223, 226, 251, 303.
Nikias Painter, 36, 40.
nimbus, 38.
nipple-jugs, 261–2.
Nocera de' Pagani, from, 265.
Nola, from, 218, 221, 221, 225, 226, 254, 255, 256.
Nonnus, 82.
nose-ring, 189.
Novios Plautios, 5.
Numana, from, 220.
Nun Painter, 128.
Ny Carlsberg H 4153, Painter of, 161.

Odysseus, 54.
Oedipus, 38.
Oeta, 72.
oiling, 79–80.
Oinopion, 101.
olive, 201.
Olynthos, 272.
Orange, Arch of, 68, 98, 99.
Orbetello, from, 31, 43, 142, 146, 147, 154, 167, 231, 231, 232, 233, 248, 259, 260, 275, 276 (three), 291, 291.
— Group, 147.
Orestes, 173.
Orpheus, 40.
Orte, from, 210, 210, 215, 253, 266 (three), 283, 283.
Orvieto, from, 15 (four), 19 (many), 20 (many), 21, 23, 25, 29, 37, 37, 50, 52, 77, 77, 78, 89, 100, 109, 109, 110, 112, 114, 116, 116, 119 (three), 146, 150, 150, 159 (three), 163 (three), 169, 174, 174, 184, 188, 190, 191, 192, 197, 197, 201, 202, 203, 204, 204, 205, 246, 269, 270, 276, 277, 278, 283, 285, 285, 286, 286, 287, 289, 289, 292, 292, 294, 295, 308; *see also* Settecamini.
Orvieto, Tomba Golini, 155.
— Group, 19–20, 296.
— 28, Group of, 159.
'Orvieto and Bolsena, between', from, 209, 231 (three), 256, 284, 285 (three), 286, 287, 288, 288, 289 (three), 290, 290, 291 (three), 292, 292, 308.
Otranto, Terra di, from, 216.
outline technique, 12, 295.
Ovid, 5.
Owl-pillar Group, 46.
Owls, 7, 21, 30, 31, 69, 78, 94, 95, 107, 154, 155, 156, 157, 158, 158, 173, 173, 200, 201, 203, 222–3.
Oxford Ganymede, Painter of, 56–61, 298.
— 412, Group of, 256–7.
— 570, Group of, 112.

Paestanizing Group, 226–7, 307.

Paestum, from, 227.
'Palaestra Painter', 12.
Palamedes, 127.
Palestrina, from, 89, 131, 283.
palmettes sprung and unsprung, 183, 304.
Palmyrene, 31.
Pan, 3, 43, 100, 101, 189, 251; and goat, 160.
Pan Painter, 218, 295.
pans, 277–8; with statuette-handles, 278.
panthers conjoined in head, 20.
Pantoxena Painter, 81.
Papposilenos, 114.
Paris, Judgement of, 1.
— Painter, 1.
Parthenon, 111.
Pasiphae, 6, 54–5.
Patroklos, 8, 88–92.
Pausanias, 82.
*P. Caisi*, 274.
Pegasus, 203.
Peirithoos, 144.
*Pelei*, 196.
Peleus, Achilles, and Chiron, 196; and Thetis, 80, 83.
pelikai, lidded, 178.
penis, tied up, 58–9.
*Pentasila*, 9, 136.
Penthesilea, 9, 136–7.
Pentheus, 55.
Persephone, 9, 47, 170.
— Painter, 33.
Perseus, 38, 65, 196.
'Perseus Painter', 12.
Perugia, from, 36, 121, 124, 124, 127, 131, 165, 174, 265, 274, 280, 280.
— Painter, 36–7, 39, 297.
Pescia Romana, from, 13.
*P. Genucilia*, 10, 175.
Phaethon, 131.
phalerae, 49.
phallus, winged, 143.
phallus-bird, 143.
Phantom Group, 205–6, 218, 306.
Phersu, 32, 63.
phialai, 117.
Phiale Painter, 109.
Phigaleia, 165.
Philostrati, 50, 91, 95, 303.
Phoibe, 55.
*Phuipa*, 4, 55.
Pigmies, 129; and cranes, 101, 126 (three), 127, 127, 129, 129.
Pigmy Trumpeter, Painter of the, 127–8.
pigne, 89.
Pindar, 80, 140.
Pistoxenos Painter, 32.
Pitigliano, from, 24, 296.
Pitt Rivers Painter, 29.
planes, vague, 79.
Plato, 146; 'Plato' *Axiochus*, 146.
Plutarch, 212, 213.

Pocola, &c., 209–16.
Poggio alla Città, from, 235, 253, 274.
— Sala, from, 233, 234, 260, 285, 286 (three), 287, 287, 290 (five), 291.
— Sommavilla, from, 177.
Poine, 144.
pointed amphoriskoi, 103.
Polion, 40.
*Poloces, Polouces*, 58, 80.
Polybios, 97, 213.
polychrome, 163–4.
Polydeukes, 5, 5, 56–61, 78–80.
Polygnotos, wall-painter, 144, 146.
— vase-painter, and group, 27, 31, 109.
Pomarico, from, 223.
Pompeii, from, 212, 295.
'Pontic' vases, 1, 12, 295, 310.
Ponticelli, from, 261.
Populonia, from, 65, 66, 67, 67, 121, 121, 124, 139, 167, 168, 168, 169, 173, 173, 176, 176, 205, 206, 208, 221, 238, 250, 252, 261, 263, 266, 270, 278, 279, 280, 283, 308; coins of, 98.
Porano, from, 116, 131.
portrait-like heads, 10, 128–9.
Poseidon, 108.
Poseidonios, 97.
Pothos Painter, 75.
*Praxias*, 196.
Praxias Group, 195–8, 204, 306.
*Precu*, 276.
pre-impressed, 210, 215, 223, 224.
Premnousia, 104.
Priam, 1, 7, 52, 195.
*Prisis*, 131.
prisoner, 295.
Providence Painter, 43.
pseudo-red-figure, 3, 195.
pubes, peculiar rendering, 38–9, 297.
*Pultuce, Pulutuke*, 116, 199.
*Pultuceś, Pultuceśi*, 275, 277.
*Puniesa*, 296.
*Putnas*, 24.
Pyrgoi, 176.
Pyrrhus, King, 215.
Python, vase-painter, 38, 104, 226.

R, Group, 34.
red band between white lines, 211.
Red-swan Group, 223–4, 307.
relief-lines, 25.
rerebrace, 9, 91, 136–7, 301.
Riccardi Painter, 69.
Rignano Flaminio, from, 111, 155, 155, 158, 177, 177, 202.
*Roma*, 274.
Rome, from, 112, 157, 159 (five), 173, 176 (seven), 177, 200, 203, 206, 207 (three), 210, 215, 217 (three), 224, 224, 236, 237, 243, 243, 244, 244, 246, 246, 250, 257

(three), 259, 269, 269, 273, 274, 276, 287.
roof, 167.
rosettes with voided petals, 224.
rouletting, 178.
Rugge, from, 219.
*Ruvfies acil*, 275, 277.
Ruvfies Group, 275–7, 310.
Ruvo, from, 292.

*Śachus*, 24.
*sacra*, 245.
*Saeturni pocolom*, 216.
Saint-Valentin Class, 219, 221, 222, 248.
Sala Consilina, from, 19.
Salerno, from, 265.
*Salutes pocolom*, 210.
S. Galigano, from, 130.
S. Ginesio, from, 249, 264.
S. Giuliano, from, 24.
S. Miniato, from, 232, 237, 247, 259, 260, 260, 273.
San Severo, Torre, sarcophagus of, 8, 9, 117, 120, 171, 288.
Sanchi, 214.
Sant' Agata de' Goti, from, 226.
Sant' Anatolia, from, 186.
—, shape, 186, 263.
Sant' Oreste, from, 108, 111, 112.
Sardinia, from, 178, 277.
Saturnia, from, 181, 196, 262 (five), 273.
Satyr-and-Dolphin Group, 112.
satyr-plays, 37, 60.
satyrs, *passim*: satyr chasing cock, 197; and goat, 110, 160; on goat, 194; surprising women bathing, 36; turning somersault, •197; with pig's ears, 110.
Savona, from, 88.
sceptres, 171.
Scylla, 169, 204, 280.
sea-gods and Triton, 153, 170, 171, 303.
sea-horses, 82, 203, 281.
*Śech*, 24.
Seianti Thanunia, 252.
Selene, 298.
selenides, 30, 297.
Semele Painter, 76.
Semitic, 189–90.
*Semla*, 107.
σεμνότης, 4, 5.
Seneca, 126.
Sette Cannelle, from, 154.
Settecamini, from, 5, 52, 77, 150, 154, 163, 188, 264, 278, 294.
— Painter, 5–6, 52–5, 64.
shields, 49, 67–8, 98–9, 225.
Shuvalov Painter, 264.
Silenos, 310; drunk, supported, 174, 179.
Silius Italicus, 213.
'Siren Painter', 12.
sirens, 15, 163, 295.

Sisyphos Painter, 34, 61, 298.
situlae, 61, 250–3, 287–9; Attic, 298; bronze, 251–3, 289; situla-stamnoi, 287.
skyphoi, spouted, 228–9.
snake-headed birds, 170.
snake-tailed monster, 56.
*snenath*, 131.
Socrates and Aspasia, 288.
*Sokra*, 201.
Sokra Group, 201–4, 218, 306, 307.
Sommavilla Sabina, from, 37.
— Painter, 37–9, 297, 310.
Sophocles, 42, 58, 81, 140, 180.
Soracte, from, 36.
Sosias, 303.
Sotades of Maroneia, 86.
— Painter, 100.
— potter, 72.
Sovana, from, 232 (five), 233, 237, 238, 241, 243, 244, 245.
Sparta, comb from, 137.
spathai, 111, 135, 145, 298, 301, 302.
*Specas*, 24.
Spectre Group, 228–9.
sphinxes, 15 (four), 16, 16, 18, 20, 23, 23, 172, 295, 296, 296; the Sphinx and satyrs, 37–8.
Spina, *see* Ferrara.
Spina Bulls, Group of the, 193.
spots, 28, 51.
Spout-hydriai, Group of the, 172.
sprigs in vases, 190.
sprung palmettes, 182–3, 304.
Stabia, from, 106.
stag-headed woman, 65.
stamnoi, broad-based, 73–4; bronze, 248–50; represented, 217.
stamnoid situlae, 287.
Sub-Meidian Cup-group, 28, 297, 308.
Suessula Painter, 76.
Sun, 81–2; and satyrs, 37–8.
Sunium, Temple of Poseidon, 45.
swan, maenad on, 51; chariot drawn by swans, 49, 68.
Swing Painter, 134.
sword at left hip, 49–50, 97–8; bent sword, 140–1.
Syleus Painter, 74, 197.

*T. Volusio*, 271.
*Talamedes*, 127.
Talamone, from, 80, 252, 299.
*Talnithe*, 127.
Talos Painter, 36.
Taranto, from, 146, 219, 219, 223, 235, 245.
Tarquinia, from: the vases in the Tarquinia Museum, q.v.; also 15, 15, 24, 48, 57, 144, 183, 184, 194, 201, 249, 273, 308, 308.
—, Tomba degli Auguri, 32, 63; delle Bighe, 57; del Cardinale, 142, 144; delle Leonesse, 119; dell' Orco, 89, 190; dei Tori, 49.

Taurus, constellation, 219.
Teano, from 148, 224, 228, 234, 247, 262, 262, 266, 272.
Tecmessa, 139.
Telamon, 125.
Telephos, 54, 66, 298.
tendril-goddess, 250.
Tenos, pithos from, 96.
Terni, from, 270.
Tertullian, 62.
Thanatos, 42.
*Thenus*, 24.
*Thesan*, 81.
Theseum, 32.
Theseus, 144; and Periphetes, 31–2.
thyrsus, 152.
thyrsus-trees, 303.
Tiberius, coin of, 214.
*Tinthun*, 81.
Tiriolo, from, 287.
Titanomachia, 109.
*Titeles*, 24.
Tithonos, 81–2, 138.
Tityos, 97.
Tivoli, from, 182.
Todi, from: the vases in the Museum of Todi, q.v.; also 104, 117 (three), 119, 131, 131, 174, 185, 189, 244, 244, 254, 264, 287, 289.
— 515, Group of, 234–5, 307.
Tondo Group, 115, 117.
torch, racing, 143.
Torcop Group, 168–9, 302, 303.
Torlonia Group, 235–6.
Toronto 495, Group of, 182–5, 304, 305.
— 564, Group of, 237, 307.
— 573, Group of, 258.
tortoise in beak, 85–6.
Toscanella, from, 131, 177, 307, 309.
Trajan's Column, 99.
Trasimene, from, 263.
trefoil, 102, 150.
Triton, 4, 6, 15, 55–6, 68, 117, 153, 160, 308.
Tritoness, 6, 117, 204, 252, 252, 308.
*Tritun*, 56, 68.
triumphator, costume of, 49.
Troilos, 179–80, 295.
Trojan Prisoners, *see* Achilles.
trophy, 179.
trousers, 49.
Trysa, 57.
Tsotylion, from, 287.
Tuebingen F 18, Painter of, 178.
Tuebingen Faliscan, Painter of the, 107.
tulip-tops, 270, 309.
*Tuntle*, 115, 116.
*Turan*, 116.
*Turmś*, 115.
*Turms Aitas*, 47.

*Turmuca*, 9, 136.
Turmuca Group, 135–41, 182.
Tuscan Column, Painter of the, 128, 129.
Tuscania, *see* Toscanella.
tympanon in ornament, 84.

*Unas*, 24.

Val d' Elsa, from, 115.
Valdichiana, from, 309.
Valerios, potter, 230.
Vambrace, *see* rerebrace.
Vanth, 9, 169, 170.
Vanth Group, 9, 169–72, 230, 303.
*Vanth*, 169.
Vatican Biga, Painter of, 46–7.
— 238, Painter of, 16.
— 246, Group of, 23.
— 265, Painter of, 21, 296.
— G 111, Painter of, 39, 43, 48–50.
— G 113, Group of, 67–8.
— G 116, Group of, 231–3, 307.
— G 119, Group of, 266–8, 309.
*Vea*, 296.
*Vei*, 24.
Veii, from, 175, 175, 176, 192, 243, 243, 243, 270, 304, 306.
*Vel Urinates*, 171.
*Velnumnal*, 276, 277.
*Venelus*, 24.
*Veneres· pocolom*, 216.
*Vestai pocolo*, 216.
Vetulonia, from, 243, 244, 245, 245, 246, 260, 260.
Vienna 202, Painter of, 51.
'Vienna 318, Painter of', 19.
Vienna O. 449, Painter of, 149–51.
— O. 565, Group of, 253–6, 308, 309.
Viganello, from, 100, 100, 101, 101, 103, 103, 108 (three), 110, 111, 112, 155, 156 (three), 157, 160, 160, 177, 186, 202, 204, 281.
*Vile*, 5, 52.
Villa Giulia 1607, Group of, 103–5.
— — 1660, Painter of, 152.
— — 1664, Group of, 108, 299.
— — 1755, Painter of, 73, 77, 79.
— — 2303, Group of, 281–2, 310.
— — 3597, Group of, 107–8.
— — 43800, Painter of, 108–9, 299–300.
— — 43969, Painter of, 100.
*Vimarus*, 24.
Vine-phialai, Group of the, 181–2, 304.
Virgil, 79, 82, 89, 140.
*Viscameruns*, 174.
Viterbo, from, 104, 154.
Vitulazio, from, 263, 265.
— Painter, 177, 263, 265.
Volaterrae Group, 10, 123–32, 301.
Volcani Group, 209.
*Volcani· pocolom*, 210.

Volterra, from, 68, 113, 114, 116, 118, 120, 120, 121, 121, 122 (four), 124, 124, 126, 127, 129 (four), 130, 130, 147, 169, 202, 202, 203, 205, 217, 232 (three), 233, 234 (three), 236 (four), 237 (four), 238 (four), 240 (four), 241, 243 (four), 244 (seventeen), 245 (three), 246 (thirteen), 247 (six), 251 (three), 253, 253, 254 (six), 255 (six), 258, 259, 260, 261 (three), 262 (three), 263 (three), 267 (nine), 268 (seven), 269 (three), 271, 274, 274, 277, 277, 279, 279, 283, 301, 307.
Vulci, from, 1, 1, 2, 2 (six), 16, 17 (four), 22 (ten), 23, 24 (six), 25, 27, 28, 29, 43, 44 (three), 47 (four), 49, 53, 54, 55, 55, 67, 68, 114, 133, 136, 136, 138, 142 (four), 144, 145 (three), 146, 146, 156, 158, 168, 172, 179, 180, 182 (three), 183, 184, 184, 188, 191 (three), 193, 194, 195 (four), 196 (fifteen), 197 (four), 198 (ten), 199, 199, 202, 208, 208, 210 (three), 215, 231 (four), 233 (three), 235, 235, 237, 237, 239 (five), 245, 245, 248, 249 (three), 251, 251, 252 (four), 258, 261, 265 (four), 266 (four), 267, 268, 270, 271, 271, 274, 275, 276, 277, 278, 278, 283 (three), 286, 287, 294.
—, Tomba François, 90–1, 274.

Warrior, Campanian, with spoils, 225.
— dispatching another, 157.
Washing Painter, 30, 76.
Weisskirchen, from, 249.
West Slope bowls, 207.
Window, woman at, 301.
Withies, binding with, 58.
women washing, 111, 198.
Woolly Satyrs, Painter of, 299.
Worcester Group, 250.
Wreath of Dionysos, not ivy, 50; of Zeus, ivy, 76.
Würzburg 817, Painter of, 168.
— 818, Group of, 108.

*xenon*, 219.
Xenon Group, 218–21, 307.
Xenophon, 98.
Xenotimos Painter, 40.
XII, 274.

Z Group of mirrors, 104; 130–2.
*Zetun*, 4, 55.
Zeus, 5, 7, 46, 55, 70, 73, 74, 111, 111, 147, 169; carrying off a woman, 4, 55, 297; and Ganymede, 4, 56–7, 74, 295.

# INDEX OF COLLECTIONS

The classification in this index is a rough-and-ready one. 'Added' is short for 'with decoration in added (or superposed) colour'. 'Unglazed' includes, besides plain vases, those coated with silver, gold, yellow, matt red, or other colours. Some of the vases with very slight decoration in added colour may be found under 'black'. 'Patterned'—that is, 'with floral or geometric decoration but no figure-work'—includes some red-figured vases. 'Spurinas' means the inscribed plates and dishes collected on pp. 24 and 296–7: they did not seem to be quite 'patterned', so were given a heading of their own. The importance of duck-askoi in Etruscan led to a special heading 'ducks', although most duck-askoi might have been placed either among the red-figured or among the 'patterned' vases. Similarly 'head-vases'.

Etruscan and Latin vases head each list, then come Attic, Italiote, other, and 'uncertain' fabrics; then bronzes and 'varia'. A dash signifies that there is no museum number or that it has not been ascertained.

ALFEDENA, Museo:
armour   137
ALIOTTI (Arezzo), once:
rf. column-krater   31
ALEXANDRIA, Musée Gréco-romain:
*Attic*
*black*
kantharoi
—   236
—   236
—   236
—   236
skyphos
—   116
*uncertain*
*black*
oinochoai
—   257
—   257
—   257
—   257
—   258
—   260
kantharos
—   257
*unglazed*
askos   272
ALTENBURG, Museum:
*added*
amphora   196
  ,,   198
AMSTERDAM, Allard Pierson Museum:
*Bf.*
neck-amphora
1806   16
*Rf.*
oinochoe
2678, fr.   173, 302
cups
479   111
2674   110
3207, fr.   28
*black*
kantharos
1924   232

*added*
neck-amphora
—   196
pelike
4584   199
oinochoe
2664, fr.   201
cup
3412   203
*Italiote*
*added*
plate
3386   224
skyphoi
3442   222
3443   222
*uncertain*
*black*
askos
3454   272
stemless cup
3382   238
*added*
askos   273
*varia*
silver kantharos   236
lamp   212
cake-mould   212
AMSTERDAM, Mrs. Six:
*uncertain*
41, mastos   242
ANCONA, Museo Civico:
*black*
oinochoai
—   255
—   258
—   258
dish
—   245
kantharoi
—   232
—   237
—   237
*uncertain*
kantharos
—   234
*Attic*
rf. bell-krater   95

*Italiote*
*added*
oinochoai
—   220
—   220
—   220
*uncertain*
stemmed dish
—   245
kantharos
—   234
kantharoid
—   239
*bronze*
stamnoi
—   249
—   250
situla
—   289
oinochoai
—   260
—   260
—   260
—   264
—   264
—   264
pan
—   278
funnel
—   278, 280
*varia*
silver cup   238
ANN ARBOR (Michigan), University of Michigan:
*Rf.*
oinochoe
2609   156, 157
skyphos
2614   158
*patterned*
oinochoe
2646   186
*black*
stemmed dish
2636   245
kantharos
2920   237

*added*
cup
2615, fr.   203
*Italiote*
*black*
oinochoe
4663   257
*unglazed*
oinochoe
2831   260
*uncertain*
*black*
oinochoai
2817   264
3244 E   258
kantharos
2630   234
*unglazed*
oinochoe
2839   264
askoi
2912 A   277
2912 B   277
2913   273
ANTIOCH, Museum:
*Attic*
rf. volute-krater   74
AREZZO, Museo Civico:
*Rf.*
column-krater
—   31
cup
frr.   114
*black*
kantharoi
1249   232
1259   232
1261   233
*unglazed*
phiale   292
ARLES, Musée Lapidaire:
*Rf.*
squat lekythos   157
*added*
oinochoe   217
*uncertain*
black oinochoe
—   264

ASCOLI PICENO, Museo:
bronze stamnos   249
ATHENS, National Museum:
*Attic*
*Rf.*
  Nolan amphora
    Acr. 632, fr.   76
  calyx-krater
    14902   72
  oinochoai
    1218   109
    1219   109
  plastic
    10461, fr.   100
  pyxis
    Acr. 576   157
  onos
    1629   134, 191
  fragment
    Acr. 780   138
  cup
    Acr. 446   30
*black*
  pelike, fr.   178
*added*
  phiale
    Acr. 1078   200
*varia*
  stele, 715   45
  Aphrodite   31
  silver bowl   207
  clay figure   212
  relief pithos   96
ATHENS, Agora Museum:
*Attic*
*Rf.*
  kantharos
    P 9469   72
  skyphos
    P 8270   116
*patterned*
  oinochoe
    P 904   265
*black*
  krater
    P 3155   235
  bowls
    P 3354   241
    P 3994   241
    P 4002   241
  dishie
    P 3342   244
  skyphos
    P 1829   111
  kantharos
    P 9471   72
*added*
  kantharos
    P 2322   72
*uncertain*
*black*
  P 3426, bowl   241
*unglazed*
  askos   272

ATHENS, Ceramicus Museum:
*Attic*
  rf. calyx-krater   52
ATHENS, Pnyx:
*Attic*
  mastos   242
ATHENS, North Slope:
*Attic*
  plastic   109
ATHENS, private:
*Attic*
  rf. squat lekythos   45
BALTIMORE, Walters Art Gallery:
*Bf.*
  neck-amphora   2, 14
*Rf.*
  volute-krater
    48.85   303
  stamnoi
    48.61   142
    48.62   64–5
    48.63   145
*duck*
  —   305
*black*
  bowls
    48.119   308
    48.120   308
*Attic*
  bf. neck-amphora
    48.22   299
BALTIMORE, Johns Hopkins University:
*Rf.*
  1047, plate   175
*added*
  274, oinochoe   205
BALTIMORE, once Van Deman:
*uncertain*
*added*
  askos   273
  kantharos   227
  askos ('orange')   277
BALTIMORE, Prof. D. M. Robinson:
*duck*
  —   119
*Campanian head-vase*
  —   187
BARCELONA, Museu d' Arqueologia:
*Bf.*
  stamnos   21
BARDO, Musée Alaoui:
*uncertain*
  askos   272
  ,,   277
BARI, Museo Civico:
*Italiote*
*Rf.*
  bell-krater   41

*added*
  kantharoids   221
  stemless cup   307
*uncertain*
  bf. column-krater
    4305   17
BARONE (Naples), once:
  unglazed neck-amphora
       289
  bronze oinochoe   265
BARRE, once:
*Attic*
  white lekythos   72
BASSEGGIO (Rome), once:
  rf. calyx-krater   46
BENGHAZI, Museo:
  stone relief   134
BERKELEY, University of California:
*Bf.*
  neck-amphora
    8.201   13
  oinochoe
    8.920   20
*Rf.*
  hydria
    8.984   101
  oinochoai
    8.988   73
    8.989   73
    8.3399   143
    —   155
    —   155
  skyphoi
    8.997   84
    8.998   87
    8.999   100
    8.1000   158
    8.3824   174
    8.3825   143
  cups
    8.935   107
    8.2302   160, 303
    8.2303   111
  plate
    8.991   175
*added*
  oinochoe   206
*Italiote*
*added*
  bell-krater
    8.3239   228
  skyphos
    8.2828   228
BERLIN, Staatliche Museen:
*Bf.*
  amphora
    2154   16, 17
  neck-amphora
    inv. 3212   19
  hydria
    2157   13, 163
*Rf.*
  calyx-kraters
    2950   73–7

    2951   172
    2952   142
  volute-kraters
    2958   164
    2959   164
  column-kraters
    inv. 3986   122,124,131
    inv. 3987   128
    inv. 3989   10, 128
    inv. 3990   129
    inv. 3991   128
    inv. 3992   129
    inv. 3993   128
    inv. 3994   128
    inv. 3995   128
    inv. 3996   128
    inv. 3997   128
    inv. 3998   10, 128
    inv. 3999   129
    inv. 4000   129
    inv. 4001   128
    inv. 4002   129
    inv. 4003   129
    inv. 30042   66
  stamnoi
    2953   87
    2954   55, 61–2
    2955   145
    2956   145
    2957   146
    inv. 5825   8, 87–92, 299
    inv. 30459
       149, 150, 151
  'nuptial lebetes'
    2963   148
    2964   148
  skyphos
    4096   116
  cups
    2943   114
    2944   114
    2945   114
    2946   107
    2947   56
*patterned*
  2966, oinochoe   182–3
*Spurinas*
    4090   24
    4091   24
    4092   24
    4093   24
*added*
  amphora
    inv. 3363   196
  neck-amphora
    2980   196
  hydria
    2981   198
  oinochoe
    inv. 4029   261
  kantharos   208, 235
  bowls
    3634   210
    3635   210
  cups
    2982   204

BERLIN, Staatliche (*cont.*):
inv. 3973 202
*head-vases*
2970 188
inv. 4982.51 188
*black*
neck-amphora
— 253
volute-krater
— 248
stamnos
— 248
situlae
4214 251
inv. 4069 252
inv. 30442 251
— 253
oinochoai
2670 268
2671 268
2675 255
inv. 4014 258
inv. 4020 255
inv. 4026 254
inv. 4028 267
inv. 4036 258
inv. 4043 267
inv. 4045 267
inv. 4055 254
inv. 4056 254
inv. 4061 255
inv. 4062 255
— 263
askoi
inv. 4011 273, 274
inv. 4067 273
— 273
pans
inv. 4031 279
— 278
strainer
inv. 14025 279
mastoid bowl
2896 293
phialai
inv. 4006 239
inv. 4041 240
inv. 4276 240
kantharoi
3728 232
inv. 4005 232
inv. 4039 233
inv. 4070 232
inv. 4077 236
inv. 4176 237
— 235
— 236
kantharoid
inv. 4076 239
kantharoid calyx
— 234
stemless cup
inv. 4072 238
*unglazed*
calyx-krater
3896 286

volute-kraters
3897 285
3898 285
askoi
inv. 3117 274
inv. 4109 274
inv. TC 3486 276
strainer
3894 279
phiale
3899 292
stemless cup
4219 291
*Attic*
*Bf.*
neck-amphora
1855 295
*Rf.*
pelikai
2626 72
inv. 4283 218
calyx-krater
inv. 3974 66
bell-krater
2645 95
hydria
inv. 3769 111
oinochoai
2414 264
2418 76
lekythos
2430 40
squat lekythos
2691 45
cups
2278 303
2290 164
*black*
calyx-krater
inv. 4983 228
mastos
2866 242
*Italiote*
*Rf.*
panathenaic
3245 43
hydriai
3031 56
inv. 4533 41
*black*
oinochoe
— 256
*added*
volute-krater
3238 223
oinochoai
3668 221
3669 221
kantharoids
3664 221
3665 221
3666 221
3667 221
3668 221
3669 221
inv. 4500 219

*Cretan*
aryballos
307 30
*Boeotian*
bf. skyphoi
3159 101
— 61
*Sigillata*
inv. 4921, askos
277, 310
inv. 3130 64
*uncertain*
calyx-krater
inv. 30017 228
kothon
3651 307
'*fayence*'
2941, kantharos 235
clay acroterion 81–2
*bronzes*
cistae
inv. 3528 58
— 49
calyx-krater
— 250
situlae and parts
Fr. 681 287
Fr. 1321 252
Fr. 1322 252
Fr. 1464 288
Fr. 1465 288
Fr. 1537 287
inv. 1260 288
inv. 7167 288
inv. 7484 287
inv. 7843 287
— 287
mirrors
Fr. 150 199
inv. 30480 199
— 49
— 82
— 82
— 83
— 106
— 115
— 116
— 131
stamnos-handles
Fr. 1389 249
inv. 6474–5 249
*varia*
clay acroterion 81–2
gem 67.45 214
K 19, marble stele 45
BERNE, Historisches Museum:
*patterned*
12519, oinochoe 304
BETTONA, Museo Comunale:
*black*
oinochoai
— 258
— 262
— 267

— 267
salt-cellar
— 243
kantharos
— 237
BOLOGNA, Museo Civico:
*Rf.*
stamnos
824 31
column-kraters
825, fr. 130, 132
875 129
876 129
PU. 410 126
*patterned*
plate
— 177
*unglazed*
kantharos 31–2
*added*
skyphoi
826 208
827 208
828 208
829 208
830 208
*Attic*
*Bf.*
panathenaics
11 308
12 308
*Rf.*
calyx-kraters
288 bis 27
300 39
bell-krater
317 40
column-krater
197 66
oinochoai
355 200
872 201
kantharos
513 222
cup-skyphos
463 308
cup
437 308
*Italiote*
*Rf.*
askoi
PU. 627 272
PU. 628 272
*added*
oinochoe
— 307
*bronze*
stamnos-handle
— 249, 308
— 249
— 249
oinochoai
— 30
— 110
— 265
— 266

BOLOGNA, Civico (cont.):
pans
— 31
— 278
— 279
mirrors
— 61
— 132
BONICHI (Rome) once:
bronze stamnos
249, 308
BONN, Akademisches Kunstmuseum:
Bf.
neck-amphora
1226 20
stamnos
501 20
hydria
fr. 17
Rf.
calyx-krater
83 63–4
stamnos
1569 7, 96–100
Spurinas
— 24
— 24
added
cup 204
Attic
rf. bell-kraters
78, fr. 40
1216.1–14 40
1216, fr. 40
Italiote
added
'handleless cup' 224
uncertain
kantharos 221
BONN, Provinzialmuseum:
bronze stamnos 249
BORGHESI, once:
stemlesses?
— 28
— 29
BORGIA, once
mirror 46
,, 131
BOSTON, Museum of Fine Arts:
Bf.
neck-amphorae
F 550 11
F 571 18
Rf.
calyx-krater
08.201 145, 301
stamnoi
07.862
.4–5, 56–61, 298
— 301
phiale
80.539 158
skyphoi
97.372 166–7, 303

12.1181 302
cups
90.69 298
01.8114 111
01.8123 6, 114
patterned
plate
— 303
skyphos
F 577 185
Spurinas
10.8084 296
head-vases
07.863 187
07.864 187
— 189
duck
R 470 191
deer-askos
F 515 192
black
oinochoai
98.201 308
R 455 267
kantharos
76.202 307
unglazed
dish
97.378 291
added
stamnos
80.596 197
column-krater
80.595 197
pelike
13.86 206
squat lekythos
13.78 206
skyphoi
76.233 203
76.238 203
cups
76.239 202
old, 100 306
Attic
Rf.
askos
— 195
stemless cup
99.539 40
cup
10.193 139
Italiote
Rf.
bell-krater 77
added
kantharos 307
outline
10.8084, 'pelike' 295
uncertain
89.209, gilt pyxis 290
bronze
mirror 139–40
varia
alabaster sarc. 57
Gandhara 214

gem 38
,, 138
,, 138
BOULOGNE, Musée Communal:
duck
— 305
added
oinochoe 306
Attic
bf. amphora 137
BOURGUIGNON (Naples), once:
ducks
— 119
— 120
uncertain
hydria 120
BOWDOIN, see Brunswick, Maine
BREMEN, Focke Museum:
black
oinochoe 267
added
2520, skyphos 222
uncertain
black askos 272
BRESLAU, Museum:
bf. kyathos 13
BROOKLYN, Museum:
Bf.
neck-amphora
29.2 295
Rf.
oinochoai
27.230 303
27.729 302
patterned
plate
44 303
BROOKS (Tarporley), once:
bf. neck-amphora 14
BRUNSWICK, Herzog Anton Ulrich Museum:
Rf.
cups
268 64
— 28
Spurinas
561 296
added
672 306
BRUNSWICK (Maine), Bowdoin College:
Rf.
13.9 stamnos 153
cup 28
BRUSSELS, Musées Royaux du Cinquantenaire:
Bf.
neck-amphora
R 270 21
Rf.
calyx-krater
R 254 68, 154

oinochoai
R 273 167
R 274 167
R 274 bis. 173, 302
R 381 173, 302
skyphos
R 282 157
plate
R 418 175
duck
— 119
patterned
oinochoe
A 2666 182–3
black
kantharos
— 236
Italiote
Rf.
calyx-krater
— 76
bell-krater
R 261 226–7
askos
R 425 272
black
plate
A 760 274
added
oinochoai
A 732 211
— 220
uncertain
oinochoai
A 736 256
A 737 256
A 738 255, 256
bronze
greaves 49
mirror 82
BRYN MAWR (Pennsylvania), Bryn Mawr College:
Rf.
stamnos
fr. 299
krater
fr. 301
plates
P 121 303
P 126 303
skyphoi
P 120 302
— 302
cup
fr. 300
BUCCIOSANTI, once:
mirror 114

CABINET DES MÉDAILLES, see Paris
CAIRO, Museum:
bronze oinochoe 266
CAMBRIDGE, Fitzwilliam Museum:
Rf.

CAMBRIDGE, Fitzwilliam (*cont.*):
stamnoi
249     44, 99–100
AE 29     142
skyphos     6, 117
*Spurinas*
200     24
*added*
neck-amphora
AE     196
hydria
AE     197
*Attic*
rf. bell-krater
N 152, fr.     40
*duck*
—     191
*Italiote*
rf. askos
243     272
*uncertain*
210, askos     273
*bronze*
situla     287
CAMBRIDGE, Museum of Classical Archaeology:
*Bf.*
24 stamnos     21
*patterned*
60 oinochoe     183
103 plate     176
— plate     304
*black*
— oinochoe     270
1101, askos     274
*added*
67 oinochoe     205
CAMBRIDGE, Corpus Christi College:
mirror     131
CAMBRIDGE, Prof. A. B. Cook:
*Bf.*
neck-amphora
—     18
handled mastoid
—     15
*Rf.*
stamnos
—     142
oinochoe
—     168
cups
—     298
fr.     115
*added*
askos
—     273
skyphoi
—     200
—     203
*Attic*
rf. hydria     40
CAMBRIDGE, Prof. D. S. Robertson:
4912·1

*added*
oinochoe     205
CAMBRIDGE (Massachusetts), Harvard University, Fogg Museum:
*Rf.*
2270, plate     175
*patterned*
askos
2264     158
plates
2286     176
3122     23
*black*
oinochoai
2245     269
2254     270
2256     270
2291     309
2302     200
2309     268
3066     257
1895.246     260
squat lekythos
2291     309
kantharos
2238     232
*unglazed*
oinochoai
2300     269, 309
1925.30     269
*added*
pelike
3455     206
oinochoai
2253     205
2306     205
*Campanian head-vase*
27.144     305
*Italiote*
*Rf.*
2272, askos     272
*added*
2391, oinochoe     262
25.1908, skyphos     222
CAMBRIDGE (Massachusetts), Harvard University, Classical Faculty:
plate     296
CAMBRIDGE (Massachusetts), Harvard University, Peabody Museum:
*Bf.*
neck-amphora
41.72.40     295
*Rf.*
1413, plate     303
*patterned*
1414, plate     303
CAMBRIDGE (Massachusetts), Dr. George Hanfmann:
rf. cup, fr.     300
CAMPANA (Rome), once:
Bf. oinochoe     15, 139

CAMPANARI, once:
rf. calyx-kater     65
CANINO, once:
rf. stamnos     147
*Spurinas*     24 (four)
CAPUA, Museo Campano:
*Attic*
stamnos     27
*Italiote*
oinochoai
7551     268
—     156
skyphos
—     222
*added*
bell-krater     228
hydria     229
skyphos     228
*Campanian head-vase*
—     187
CARLSRUHE, Badisches Landesmuseum:
*Bf.*
neck-amphora
inv. 2592     11
*Rf.*
stamnos
348     142, 148
*Italiote*
*Rf.*
volute-kraters
258     144
388     147
*Bronze*
stamnos-handles
620     249
621     249
622     249
623     250
624     249
situlae and parts
634, 1     252
634, 2     252
635     289
638     287
oinochoai
549     265
550     266
551     266
F 322     266
pan-handle
468     278
CARSHALTON, Landreth:
*Italiote, added*
kantharos     219
CARTHAGE, Musée Lavigerie:
*Rf.*
plate     176
*uncertain*
askos     273
CASSEL, Hessiches Landesmuseum:
*added*
bowl     210

CASSEL, Prince Philip of Hesse:
*added*
stamnos     197
CASTELLANI, Alessandro (Naples), once:
strainer     293
CASTELLANI, Augusto (Rome), once:
*black*
bowl     308
kantharos     231
*unglazed*
neck-amphora     289
,,     289
calyx-krater     286
volute-krater     285
,,     285
,,     285
situla     287
oinochoe     289
,,     290
strainer     292
dish     291
,,     291
,,     291
phiale     292
kantharos     235, 290
kantharoid     290
CASTIGLIONCELLO, Museo:
*black*
46, oinochoe     269
jar     247
askos     274, 275
171, mastos     241
kantharos     232
,,     233
*added*
oinochoe     217
*uncertain*
1191, black phiale     240
CASTLE ASHBY, Marquess of Northampton:
*added*
fr.     98
CATANIA, Museo Civico:
*Italiote*
*added*
757, stemless     224
*uncertain*
*unglazed*
oinochoai     309
*black*
811, mastos     242
*bronze*
oinochoai
474     266
475     266
CAYLUS, once:
*added*
oinochoe     205
*bronze*
stamnos-handle     308

CHIUSI, Museo Civico:
*Bf.*
neck-amphorae
577 ... 18, 296
— ... 21
*Rf.*
neck-amphorae
1854 ... 170
1855 ... 170
1856 ... 170
1857 ... 170
volute-kraters
1852 ... 169, 303
1853 ... 171
cups
— ... 123
*patterned*
jar
— ... 185, 304
skyphoi
1914 ... 33
1918 ... 185
oinochoe
1919 ... 185
*black*
oinochoai
— ... 254
— ... 257
kantharoi
— ... 232
— ... 232
*unglazed*
neck-amphorae
1927 ... 281–2
1928 ... 281–2
volute-kraters
1890 ... 285
1891 ... 285
situla
1898 ... 288
strainer
1893 ... 279, 293
phialai
1894–7 ... 292
kantharoi
— ... 233, 290–1
— ... 233, 290–1
*added*
cups
— ... 202
— ... 203
— ... 203
— ... 204
— ... 204
*bronze*
situlae
— ... 252
— ... 289
pan-handle
— ... 278
*varia*
urns
— ... 57
— ... 63
— ... 67

CHIUSI, private:
column-krater ... 198
CINCI (Volterra), once:
*black*
neck-amphora ... 253
jar ... 247
oinochoe ... 254
    ,, ... 263
askos ... 274
    ,, ... 275
bowl ... 240
kantharoid calyx ... 234
kantharos ... 237
CIVITAVECCHIA, Museo Civico:
*Rf.*
oinochoe
— ... 169
*black*
oinochoai
— ... 257
— ... 257
— ... 257
— ... 257
— ... 266
*added*
oinochoe
— ... 205
kantharos
— ... 207
*uncertain*
askos
— ... 273
dishie
— ... 242
COLMAR, Museum:
rf. stamnos ... 153
oinochoe, *added* ... 206
COMO, Museo:
*bronze*
bottle ... 84
COMPIÈGNE, Musée Vivenel:
*black*
oinochoai
924 ... 254
947 ... 270
*added*
oinochoe
918 ... 200
*Italiote*
*added*
880, skyphos ... 221
COPENHAGEN, National Museum:
*Bf.*
neck-amphora
inv. 3837 ... 21
*Rf.*
calyx-krater
inv. 8179 ... 36
column-krater
inv. 3842 ... 30
oinochoe
300 ... 169

skyphos
inv. 6577 ... 161, 303
cup
inv. 3799 ... 174
*patterned*
neck-amphorae
ABc 1059, part ... 23
  ,,   ,, ... 23
— ... 23
plates
inv. 1243, part ... 176
  ,, ... 176
*black*
situla
inv. 3816 ... 251
oinochoai
371 ... 255
402 ... 253
405 ... 253
408 ... 254
411 ... 255
414 ... 254
453 ... 262
505 ... 258
507 ... 258
509 ... 261
510 ... 262
530 ... 270
531 ... 264
534 ... 267
535 ... 267
536 ... 269
537 ... 267
538 ... 267
539 ... 267
inv. 3818 ... 254
inv. 3819 ... 254
inv. 7135 ... 260
inv. 8229 ... 269
squat lekythos
inv. 8230 ... 270
strainers
440 ... 239, 279
inv. 3385 ... 280
inv. 3820 ... 279
dishie
527 ... 244
plate
ABc 792 ... 246
kantharoid calyx
inv. 3817 ... 234
kantharoi
433 ... 232
inv. 4985 ... 235
stemlesses
401 ... 238
499 ... 238
500 ... 238
502 ... 238
stamnos
inv. 3796 ... 197
oinochoai
ABc 20 ... 205
inv. Chr. VIII 49 ... 218
inv. 7968 ... 205

bowl
495 ... 207
cup
ABc 782 ... 202
inv. 3797 ... 202
inv. 3798 ... 204
*Attic*
black pelikai
490 ... 178
491 ... 178
kantharos
inv. 1414 ... 222
*Italiote*
*added colour*
kantharoi
336 ... 219
337 ... 219
inv. 7971 ... 219
*varia*
gem ... 139
COPENHAGEN, Ny Carlsberg Glyptotek:
*Bf.*
neck-amphorae
H 147 ... 19
H 148 ... 18
H 149 ... 21
*Rf.*
stamnos
H 152 ... 149, 150, 151
bell-krater
H 153 ... 135, 161
skyphos
H 159 ... 86
cup
H 156 ... 111
*unglazed*
neck-amphora
H 162 ... 281–2
*uncertain*
*added*
H 157, stemless ... 223
*Attic*
H 155, rf. pelike ... 87
*bronze*
H 244, mirror ... 154
*varia*
H 276, clay relief ... 163
H 212, tombstone ... 50
Lansdowne athlete ... 61
COPENHAGEN, Thorvaldsen Museum:
gem 41 ... 138
  ,, 64 ... 80
CORINTH, Museum:
*Attic*
bell-krater
C 34.379, fr. ... 109
*Corinthian*
*patterned*
oinochoai ... 309
CORTONA, Museo:
*Rf.*
column-kraters?
— ... 130
— ... 130

CORTONA (*cont.*):
— 130
cup
fr. 69
frr. 126
COZZA (Gazzetta), once:
*unglazed*
neck-amphora
— 289
calyx-kraters
— 285
— 286
volute-kraters
— 285
— 285
— 285
situla? 288–9
CRACOW, Czartoryski
Museum:
*uncertain*
*black*
1460, oinochoe 257
CRACOW, University:
*black*
oinochoai
479 262
480 259
jar
478 247
kantharos
637 232
*unglazed*
91, oinochoe 269
*Attic*
103, bell-krater 36
CRACOW, Technical
Museum:
*patterned*
oinochoe 184
*added*
9738, skyphos 200
*Italiote*
9725, cup-skyphos 223
kantharos 221
CUXHAVEN, Höhere Staat-
schule:
rf. frr. 155, 157

DARMSTADT, Hessisches
Landesmuseum:
*Attic*
black pelike 178
DENCI (Pitigliano), once:
*Spurinas* 24
DISNEY, once:
*black*
calyx-kraters 234
— 247
oinochoai 233
— 267
*bronze*
handle 250
DRESDEN, Albertinum:

*Rf.*
calyx-krater
395 142
*patterned*
oinochoai
ZV 2889 48
— 183
— 184
*Attic*
duck-askos
ZV 2866 191
*varia*
lead cut-out 212
DRESSEL (Rome), once:
black kantharos 236

EDINBURGH, Royal Scot-
tish Museum:
*Bf.*
oinochoe
1872.23.6 295
duck
1872.23.19 305
*black*
oinochoe
1881.44.3 309
*uncertain*
oinochoai
1872.23.440 255
1881.44.25 256
ENGLEFIELD, once:
*Italiote*
*added*
oinochoe 220
kantharos 219
skyphos 220
ENSÉRUNE, Mus. Com-
munal:
*Attic*
rf. cup 51
*uncertain*
kantharoi 206
skyphos, added colour
207
,, 207
,, 225
ERLANGEN, University
Museum:
*Rf.*
cup 28
*Attic*
rf. oinochoe 201
ESTE, Museo:
*added*
skyphos 207
*uncertain*
askos, unglazed 273
EVANS, Joan, once:
*Attic*
bf. stamnos 27
FERRARA, Museo di
Spina [T = tomb]:
*Rf.*
bell-kraters
T 369 178

T 779 177, 179
T 785 177
pelike
T 16 178
oinochoai
T 519 177
T 647 177
lekane
T 898 177
*patterned*
'nuptial lebes'
T 888 178, 186
oinochoai
T 369 186
T 369 186
T 950 186
T 1060 186
T 1082 186
phialai
T 1078 117
T 1078 117
head-vases
T 346 188
T 608 118, 300, 305
T 608 118, 300
duck
T 224 119
deer-askoi
T 83 192
T 83 193
T 399 192
bull-askoi
T 83 193
T 83 194
T 369 193
panther-askos
T 651 194
*black*
neck-amphora
T 606 253
oinochoai
T 224 258
T 369 262
askos
T 1092 273
kantharoi
T 156 232
T 369 232
T 369 232
*unglazed*
askos
T 1059 274
*added*
skyphoi
T 156 208
T 369 193, 208
T 369 208
T 585 207
*Attic*
*Rf.*
pelike
T 250 87
bell-krater
T 187 95
volute-krater
T 404 60

column-krater
T 597 66
oinochoe
T 652 201
kantharos
T 308 72
duck-askoi
— 191
— 305
*uncertain*
oinochoe
T 995 256
stemless cup
T 613 238
*bronze*
T 128, oinochoe 265
FIESOLE, Museo:
*black*
oinochoe 267
kantharos 233
*sigillata*
— 277
FILLON, once:
mirror 58
FLORENCE, Museo Archeo-
logico Etrusco:
*Bf.*
neck-amphorae
4168 18
4200 13
71005 13
73724 296
84819 11
V 19 296
V 20 296
V 22 296
V 23 296
— 11
— 11
— 20
pointed amphora
72711 21
pelike
78785 20
hydria
2173 299
oinochoe
— 20
fragment
— 20
*Rf.*
calyx-kraters
V 3 36
— 154, 301
bell-krater
4026 33–5, 297, 297
volute-krater
— 163
stamnoi
— 5, 52–3, 131
— 65
— 65
— 66
— 77
— 121
— 121

FLORENCE, Arch. Et.
(cont.):
— 146
column-kraters
4035   127, 129
4084   126, 130, 132
4090   129
4105   129
4108   129
4121   129
4122   129
4132   122
4136   129
88160   127, 130
— 67
— 130
— 301
neck-amphorae
4036   164
70529   163
75689   25
oinochoai
— 167
— 168
— 168
— 169
— 173
— 173
— 173
epichysis
2048   119
plates
— 177
kantharoi
— 29
— 29
— 29
skyphoi
— 116
— 158
— 158
cups
79240   6, 115
F, B3   28
PD 150, fr.   113
V 49   114
— 6, 41, 114
— 28
fr.   69
— 113
frr.   114
fr.   115
fr.   115
shape?
— 120
*patterned*
neck-amphora
— 181
oinochoai
3653   271
4169   304
— 304
'squat lekythoi'
— 271
— 271
chalices

— 296
stemmed dishes
75777   20
76407   20, 296
plates
— 176
— 176
skyphoi
4174   23
4185   23
V 78   23
V 80   23
*Spurinas*
— 24
— 24
*head-vases*
— 188
— 188
*ducks*
4231   119
4232   119
74690   119
*deer-askoi*
4236   192
81908   192
*black*
neck-amphorae
— 253
— 253
calyx-kraters
4559   247
— 247
volute-krater
— 248
situlae
1059   251
1060   251
75432   251
V 420   251
fr.   251
jar
— 247
oinochoai
3704   260
4494   267
4561   267
4562   267
V 396   267
V   267
— 254
— 254
— 259
— 259
— 260
— 260
— 260
— 260
— 261
— 262
— 262
— 262
— 262
— 262

squat lekythos
— 270
askoi
— 273
— 273
dishies
8214   243
8215   244
— 244
salt-cellars
8949   245
8950   245
— 245
pans
4473   278
4474   279
plate
8212   246
bowl
4591   241
mastos
— 241
kantharoid calyxes
4504   234
4589   234
kantharoi
4449   233
4462   233
4500   232
4501   232
4505   232
4506   232
4544   232
4545   232
4582   232
76598   234
77191   232
77192   232
77193   232
V 395   231
V 422   231
V 423   231
V 562   231
— 231
— 231
— 232
— 232
— 233
— 233
— 233
— 234
— 234
— 237
— 237
— 237
skyphos
— 238
stemless cup
— 238
candelabra
— 280
— 280
*unglazed*
neck-amphorae
— 280

— 280
calyx-kraters
— 286
— 286
— 286
volute-krater
— 285
pseudo-volute-krater
— 286
situlae
— 287
— 287
— 287
oinochoai
— 260
— 260
— 263
— 290
— 290
— 290
askoid oinochoai
— 290
— 290
— 290
askoi
4662   275
4663   275
4664   276
4666   276
4674   276
4766   274
— 276
fr.   276
pans
— 273
— 278
strainers
— 279
— 283
kernoi
73132   294
— 294
dishes
— 291
— 291
— 291
— 292
dishie
— 243
*sigillata*
askoi
72912   276
72913   276
— 276
*added*
neck-amphora
— 196
stamnoi
4073   197
V   197
— 197
— 197
oinochoai
— 205
— 206

FLORENCE, Arch. Et.
(*cont.*):
skyphoi
— 200
— 207
— 208
cup or stemless
— 204, 306
cup
V 481 204
*Attic*
column-krater
V 38
cup
V 38 265
*uncertain*
gilt pyxis
4646 290
kantharos
— 221
skyphos
— 222
*bronze*
situlae and parts
1491 289
74798 289
— 252
— 252
— 252
stamnoi
— 250
— 250
oinochoai
— 266
— 283
askoid oinochoe
— 290
mirrors
74781 131
77759 131
— 81
kottabos stand
— 188
statuette
— 139
*varia*
stone urn 89
gem 165
FLORENCE, Uffizi:
marble relief 99
FLORENCE, Terrosi:
*Rf.*
column-kraters
— 127
— 128
— 129
— 129
— 130
— 130
— 130
*black*
calyx-krater
— 234
volute-krater
— 248
stamnos

— 248
situla
— 251
oinochoai
— 254
— 255
— 267
dish
— 240
pan
— 279
strainer
— 279, 280
candelabrum
— 280
*unglazed*
askoi 276
*uncertain*
stemless cup
— 238
— 238
FLORENCE, private:
mirror 131
FOULD, once:
stamnos 179–80
,, 179
FRANKFORT, Historisches
Museum:
*Rf.*
oinochoe 173
*duck*
— 192
FRANKFORT (Liebig-
haus?):
*Italiote*
*added*, kantharoid 219
FREIBURG, University:
*added*
column-krater 197
FUNGHINI (Arezzo), once:
*uncertain*
'plate' 277

GAMURRINI (Arezzo),
once:
*uncertain*
'plate?' 277
GENEVA, Musée d'Art et
d'Histoire:
*Bf.*
neck-amphorae
15003 296
F 140 11
— 21
— 21
— 296
kyathos
— 23
*Rf.*
bell-krater
MF 253, frr. 302
column-krater
MF 254 301
stamnoi
MF 164 301
— 147–8, 304

oinochoai
MF 111 169
MF 144 302
MF 315 302
skyphoi
12910 302
MF 274 161, 303
MF 289 302
*patterned*
oinochoai
MF 313 305
MF 327 304
— 304
— 304
— 304
— 304
— 304
— 305
plates
MF 111 176
MF 112 303
— 296
— 296
phiale
I 526 304
*kētos-askos*
MF 281 305–6
*black*
situla
14971 308
oinochoai
14972 309
I 614 308
— 308
— 309
strainers
— 310
askos
— 310
kantharos
I 180 307
kantharoid
I 682 307
*added*
oinochoai
— 217
— 306
— 306
*Attic*
rf. oinochoe
5764 201
black panathenaic 297
*Italiote*
*black*
oinochoe 308
*added*
oinochoe 307
GENOA, Museo Civico:
*Rf.*
calyx-krater 70
*uncertain*
1081, askos 310
*bronze*
oinochoai
— 265
— 265

GOETTINGEN, University:
*Bf.*
neck-amphorae
J 4 11
J 5 11
J 8 14
fr. 218
oinochoe
J 6 14
*Rf.*
skyphos
J 54 106
cups
J 52 86
J 53 109
J 55 68
*patterned*
plate 296
*black*
bowl 308
*Italiote*
*added*
skyphos
F 35 220
stemless cup
— 223
*bronze*
stamnos-handles
74 250
75 250
oinochoe
25 283
GOLINI (Orvieto), once:
*unglazed*
dishes 291
GOLUCHOW, Prince Czar-
toryski:
*black*
114, oinochoe 254
183, kantharoid calyx
234
*Attic*
191 duck-askos 191
GOTHA, Museum:
*added*
hydria 306
bowl 210
*Attic*
rf. bell-krater 110
GRÉAU, once:
*bronze*
oinochoai and parts
216 283
218 283
219 283
220 283
221 283
222 250, 283
— 283
*varia*
silver oinochoe 283

THE HAGUE, Neder-
landsch Lyceum:
*Bf.*
neck-amphora 19

HAMBURG, Museum für
Kunst und Gewerbe:
*Bf.*
neck-amphorae
| | |
|---|---|
| 505 | 13, 15 |
| 1156 | 13 |
| 1157 | 14 |
| 1193 | 13 |
| 1224 | 14 |
| 1917.509 | 13 |

hydriai
| | |
|---|---|
| 462 | 49 |
| 511 | 17 |
| 512 | 13 |

*Rf.*
stamnoi
| | |
|---|---|
| 658 | 32–3 |
| 661 | 142, 146 |
| 662 | 142 |
| 1912.1909 | 141 |

bell-krater
| | |
|---|---|
| 659 | 154 |

oinochoe
| | |
|---|---|
| 1917.657 | 155 |

skyphoi
| | |
|---|---|
| 660 | 174 |
| 1220 | 154, 158 |
| 1221 | 154, 158 |

*patterned*
duck-askos 504    191
phiale    185
*black*
pan 1914.236    278
*added colour*
cup 1917.811    202
*Campanian bf.*
neck-amphora
1917.989    11
*Italiote*
*added colour*
oinochoe    220
stemless 1917.991    223
*uncertain*
oinochoe    268
*varia*
clay bust    167, 303
HAMILTON, once:
duck    191
HAMM, Gustav-Lübcke-
Museum:
*black*
1564, oinochoe    308
HANAU, Museum:
*Italiote, added*
skyphos    223
HARVARD, *see* Cambridge
(Mass.).
HASSELMANN, once:
rf. calyx    135
Campanian head-vase
187
HEIDELBERG, University:
*Bf.*
cup    13
fr.    19
*Rf.*

amphoriskos E 48    103
cup    143
*patterned*
oinochoe    183
*added*
E 51, fr.    198
*black*
phiale    249, 292
bowl    241
*Attic, rf.*
bell-krater 208    75
cup    28

JENA, University:
*added*
210, amphora 196, 306
*Attic*
rf. cup    50–1
,,    51
*Italiote*
101, skyphos, *added* 227

KARLSRUHE, *see* Carlsruhe.
KASSEL, *see* Cassel.
KOENIGSBERG, University:
*Italiote, added*
101, skyphos    227
ŁAŃCUT, Count Potocki:
*added*
oinochoe    220
LAUSANNE, Musée:
mirror    116
LECCE, Museo Provin-
ciale Castromediano:
*Italiote*
*Rf.*
neck-amphora
571    27
askos
970    272
*added*
trozzella    211
kantharoi
| | |
|---|---|
| 883 | 219 |
| 884 | 219 |
| 1593 | 219 |

LEDERER, once:
bf. hydria    13
black kantharos    232
LEEDS, Museum:
*added*
skyphos, fr.    206
LEESEN (Treben), once:
rf. oinochoe    173, 302
LEIPSIC, University:
*Bf.*
fr.    20
fr.    20
fr.    20
*Rf.*
column-krater
—    43, 49–50, 98–9
bowls
—    112
—    112

skyphos
—    116
*black*
pan    278
*added*
cup    203
*Attic, rf.*
bell-krater
T 655, fr.    40
*Italiote, rf.*
squat lekythos    76
*varia*
marble relief    104
LENINGRAD, Museum of
the Hermitage:
*Bf.*
hydria
inv. 3145    16
*Rf.*
hydria    172
*ducks*
| | |
|---|---|
| (St. 832) | 192 |
| (St. 834) | 119 |

*black*
oinochoai
| | |
|---|---|
| (St. 607) | 255 |
| (St. 622) | 255 |
| (St. 690) | 255 |
| (St. 694) | 255 |

kantharoi
| | |
|---|---|
| (St. 612) | 232 |
| (St. 628) | 232 |
| (St. 703) | 233 |
| — | 237 |

kernos
—    294
*Attic, rf.*
pelikai
| | |
|---|---|
| 852 | 40 |
| — | 76, 83 |

bell-kraters
fr.    76
fr.    76
stamnos
640    43
*Attic*
duck-askos    191
*Chalcidian*
neck-amphora    97
*Italiote*
volute-kraters
| | |
|---|---|
| (St. 424) | 147 |
| (St. 426) | 147 |
| — | 34 |

*uncertain*
askos    277
*bronze*
mirror    30
*varia*
silver kantharos    235
—    236
silver phalerae
212, 213, 215
gold helmet    83
gold plaque    138

wooden sarcophagus
299
LEYDEN, Rijksmuseum:
*Bf.*
amphora
K 94.9.5    11
kythos
K 10.2.11    23
*black*
situla
292    251
jars
| | |
|---|---|
| 206 | 246 |
| 207 | 246 |
| 209 | 247 |
| 210 | 247 |

oinochoai
| | |
|---|---|
| 142 | 262 |
| 185 | 254 |
| 186 | 254 |
| 187 | 255 |
| 188 | 255 |
| 189 | 264 |
| 190 | 264 |
| 191 | 269 |
| 192 | 268 |
| 193 | 268 |
| 194 | 268 |
| 195 | 268 |
| 196 | 268 |
| 197 | 268 |
| 198 | 269 |
| 199 | 267 |
| 200 | 267 |
| 201 | 267 |
| 202 | 267 |
| 203 | 267 |
| 204 | 267 |
| 205 | 268 |
| 217 | 261 |
| 218 | 261 |
| 219 | 261 |
| 220 | 261 |
| 221 | 259 |
| 223 | 263 |
| 224 | 258 |
| 225 | 262 |
| 226 | 259 |
| 227 | 263 |
| 229 | 263 |

pan
299    276
stemmed bowls or
dishes
| | |
|---|---|
| 282 | 245 |
| 283 | 245 |
| 284 | 245 |

plates or dishes
| | |
|---|---|
| 231 | 246 |
| 232 | 246 |
| 243 | 246 |
| 244 | 246 |

fish-plate
242    246
dishies
255    244

LEYDEN (*cont.*):
| | |
|---|---|
| 256 | 244 |
| 258 | 244 |
| 259 | 244 |
| 260 | 244 |
| 261 | 244 |
| 262 | 244 |
| 263 | 244 |
| 264 | 244 |
| 265 | 244 |
| 266 | 244 |
| 267 | 244 |
| 268 | 244 |
| 269 | 244 |
| 270 | 244 |
| 271 | 244 |

bowls
| | |
|---|---|
| 272 | 240 |
| 279 | 241 |

mastos
| | |
|---|---|
| 208 | 241 |

kantharoi
| | |
|---|---|
| 176 | 236 |
| 177 | 236 |
| 178 | 236 |
| 179 | 236 |
| 180 | 236 |
| 181 | 237 |
| 182 | 237 |
| 183 | 237 |
| 211 | 237 |
| 212 | 237, 238 |
| 213 | 233 |
| 214 | 232 |
| 215 | 232 |
| 216 | 232 |

skyphos
| | |
|---|---|
| 184 | 238 |

stemless cups
| | |
|---|---|
| 171 | 238 |
| 172 | 238 |
| 173 | 238 |
| 174 | 238–9 |
| 175 | 239 |
| 290 | 240 |
| 291 | 240 |

*unglazed*
calyx-krater
| | |
|---|---|
| 764 | 283 |

volute-krater
| | |
|---|---|
| 765 | 281–2 |

oinochoai
| | |
|---|---|
| 766 | 266, 282, 310 |
| 767 | 264, 282 |
| 768 | 282 |
| 769 | 282 |
| 773 | 263, 282, 310 |

pans
| | |
|---|---|
| 771 | 282 |
| 772 | 282 |

kantharos
| | |
|---|---|
| 727 | 234 |

*Campanian, bf.*
neck-amphora
| | |
|---|---|
| GNV. 4 | 11 |

*Attic, black*
| | |
|---|---|
| 118, skyphos | 116 |

*Italiote*
*added*
oinochoe
| | |
|---|---|
| K 95.1.5 | 220 |

kantharoid
| | |
|---|---|
| GNV. 58 | 219 |

*uncertain*
*black*
oinochoe
| | |
|---|---|
| 69 | 257 |

askos
| | |
|---|---|
| 152 | 273 |

dishies
| | |
|---|---|
| 164 | 245 |
| 273 | 243 |
| 274 | 243 |
| 275 | 243 |
| 276 | 243 |
| 278 | 243 |
| 280 | 243 |
| 281 | 243 |
| 285 | 245 |
| 286 | 245 |
| 287 | 245 |

*sigillata*
askos
| | |
|---|---|
| 685 | 277 |

LLOYD (Cambridge), once:
*Bf.*
neck-amphora              296
LONDON, British Museum:
*Bf.*
neck-amphorae
| | |
|---|---|
| B 64 | 2, 59 |
| B 67 | 13 |

hydria
| | |
|---|---|
| B 63 | 2 |

*Rf.*
pointed amphora
| | |
|---|---|
| F 482 | 45–6 |

stamnoi
| | |
|---|---|
| F 484 | 3–4, 26, 43–5, 304 |
| F 485 | 146 |
| F 486 | 142–4 |
| 1913.4–17.1 | 153 |

column-krater
| | |
|---|---|
| F 481 | 67 |

calyx-kraters
| | |
|---|---|
| F 479 | 7, 92–4 |
| F 480 | 136 |

bell-krater
| | |
|---|---|
| 1927.10–10.1 | 35, 297 |

hydria
| | |
|---|---|
| F 487 | 172 |

oinochoai
| | |
|---|---|
| F 100 | 68, 154, 298 |
| 1913.7–22.4 | 302 |

cups
| | |
|---|---|
| F 478 | 6, 113 |
| 1909. 7–20.25 | 297 |

*duck*
| | |
|---|---|
| G 151 | 119 |

*lion-askos*
| | |
|---|---|
| F 803 | 193 |

*panther-askos*
| | |
|---|---|
| 73.8–20.592 | 194 |

*patterned*
oinochoai
| | |
|---|---|
| 39.11–9.4 | 183 |
| 42.4–7.24 | 297 |
| 46.5–18.39 | 304 |
| — | 304 |

skyphos
| | |
|---|---|
| — | 48 |

*black*
situlae
| | |
|---|---|
| G 30 | 251 |
| G 31 | 251 |
| G 32 | 252 |

oinochoe
| | |
|---|---|
| — | 254 |

askos
| | |
|---|---|
| 1908.6–4.1 | 305 |

pan
| | |
|---|---|
| old 1845 | 278 |

strainers
| | |
|---|---|
| old 1891 | 279 |
| old 1892 | 279 |

kantharoid calyxes
| | |
|---|---|
| 47.8–6.40 | 234 |
| 47.8–6.43 | 234 |

kantharoi
| | |
|---|---|
| old 226 | 236 |
| CS 356 | 233 |
| — | 234 |
| — | 234 |

*unglazed*
neck-amphora
| | |
|---|---|
| G 185 | 289 |

volute-krater
| | |
|---|---|
| G 184 | 285 |

calyx-krater
| | |
|---|---|
| G 180 | 286 |

oinochoe
| | |
|---|---|
| 39.2–14.124 | 270 |

askoid oinochoe
| | |
|---|---|
| G 193 | 290 |

askos
| | |
|---|---|
| 39.11–9.6 | 275 |

kermoi
| | |
|---|---|
| T.C. D 209 | 294 |
| T.C. D 210 | 294 |

dishes
| | |
|---|---|
| G 187 | 294 |
| G 188 | 294 |

*added*
oinochoai
| | |
|---|---|
| F 526 | 218 |
| F 528 | 205 |
| F 529 | 201 |
| 1915.12–29.2 | 218 |
| fr. | 216 |

bowls
| | |
|---|---|
| F 542 | 209 |
| F 604 | 215 |

skyphos
| | |
|---|---|
| 1908.7–24.1 | 306, 307 |

cups
| | |
|---|---|
| F 540 | 203 |
| F 541 | 203 |

*Attic*
*Bf.*
neck-amphora
| | |
|---|---|
| E 210 | 101 |

hydria
| | |
|---|---|
| B 332 | 105 |

*Rf.*
pelike
| | |
|---|---|
| G 424 | 83 |

stamnoi
| | |
|---|---|
| E 447 | 111 |
| 98.7–16.1 | 98 |

dinos
| | |
|---|---|
| 99.7–21.5 | 57 |

bell-kraters
| | |
|---|---|
| F 64 | 40 |
| F 65 | 95 |
| F 74 | 72 |
| 1917.7–25.2 | 161 |

oinochoai
| | |
|---|---|
| E 564 | 201 |
| old 1670 | 200 |

squat lekythos
| | |
|---|---|
| E 701 | 45 |

pyxides
| | |
|---|---|
| E | 191 |
| E 782 | 45 |

plastic
| | |
|---|---|
| E 785 | 190 |

kantharoi
| | |
|---|---|
| 73.8–20.380 | 219 |
| 90.7–1.32 | 222 |

skyphoi
| | |
|---|---|
| old 1503 | 116 |
| 64.10–7.1675 | 219 |

cup
| | |
|---|---|
| E 83 | 35 |

*ducks*
| | |
|---|---|
| B 662 | 191 |
| B 663 | 191 |
| B 664 | 191 |
| B 665 | 191 |
| B 667 | 191 |

*black*
pelike
| | |
|---|---|
| 56.12–23.79 | 178 |

*Italiote*
*Rf.*
neck-amphora
| | |
|---|---|
| F 193 | 105 |

volute-krater
| | |
|---|---|
| F 279 | 144 |

bell-krater
| | |
|---|---|
| F 49 | 104 |

hydria
| | |
|---|---|
| F 210 | 146 |

epichysis
| | |
|---|---|
| F 397 | 156 |

askoi
| | |
|---|---|
| F 414 | 272 |
| F 584 | 272 |
| F 585 | 272 |

*added*
pelike
| | |
|---|---|
| F 524 | 225 |

LONDON, Brit. Mus.
(cont.):
hydria
F 525 ... 225, 307
oinochoai
WT 152 ... 220
1915.4–15.1 ... 220
— ... 220
squat lekythoi
F 531 ... 226
F 533 ... 225
kothon
old 1786 ... 307
bottle
old 1798 ... 220
dish
— ... 220
plate
— ... 224
kantharoi
F 523 ... 221
F 591 ... 211
F 592 ... 211
F 593 ... 211
old 1253 ... 219
47.8–6.48 ... 219
kantharoids
— ... 219
— ... 219
skyphoi
F 535 ... 226
F 536 ... 226
F 537 ... 228
F 538 ... 225
old 1784 ... 228
old 1785 ... 229
— ... 229
stemless cups
F 539 ... 226
59.2–16.79 ... 223
67.5–8.1217 ... 223
— ... 223
— ... 223

*East Greek*
amphora
B 21 ... 14
*uncertain*
*black*
oinochoai
white 1166 ... 264
white 1167 ... 264
66.4–15.1 ... 257
66.4–15.2 ... 257
askos
P 3 ... 272
mastoi
G 33 ... 242
76.9–9.35 ... 242
bowl
old 1973 ... 308
*unglazed*
askos
56.12–23.225 ... 277
*added*
kantharos

T 595 ... 222
'fayence'
K 1, duck ... 235
*bronze*
situla
652 ... 287
dinos
560 ... 49, 295
oinochoe
WT 654 ... 266
kantharoids
— ... 239
— ... 239
mirrors
623 ... 136
626 ... 166
627 ... 131
629 ... 199
700 ... 131
*silver*
situla
— ... 252
oinochoe
126 ... 263
phialai
— ... 292
*stone*
sarcophagi
D 20 ... 171
D 21 ... 57
D 22 ... 152
*gems*
211 ... 96
622 ... 104
635 ... 138
*varia*
ivory diptychon ... 214
lead cut-out ... 212
Persian silver ... 215
LONDON, Greig:
*patterned*
oinochoe ... 304
LONDON market (Spink):
rf. plate ... 176
black oinochoai ... 309
LOUVRE, *see* Paris.
LYONS, Musée:
*uncertain*
black oinochoe ... 264

MADRID, Museo Arqueo-
lógico:
*Attic, rf.*
11017, bell-krater 72
11039, column-krater
... 61
hydria 105
*Italiote*
*added*
bell-kraters
11036 ... 228
11071 ... 228
11092 ... 228
11093 ... 228
hydria
11156 ... 227

squat lekythos
11545 ... 227
skyphos
11415 ... 226
*uncertain*
black oinochoe ... 264
MANCINELLI (Pitigliano),
once:
askos ... 277
MANCINI (Orvieto), once:
mirror ... 44
MANNHEIM, Schloss-
museum:
*Attic, rf.*
oinochoe ... 201
MARBURG, University:
*Italiote, rf.*
epichysis ... 156
MARIEMONT, Musée
Warocqué:
*Italiote, black*
90, oinochoe ... 256
MARSEILLES, Musée
Borély:
*Attic, rf.*
oinochoe ... 201
MARZABOTTO, Museo
Aria:
*Attic, rf.*
cup ... 101
*bronze*
situla ... 252
*varia*
tombstone ... 89
MARZI (Tarquinia), once:
rf. skyphos ... 144
MICHIGAN, *see* Ann Arbor
MILAN, Museo Teatrale
alla Scala:
rf. skyphos ... 300
MINTURNO. *See under*
*Boll. st. med.* 4, 4–5, in
the index of publica-
tions. MUNICH, Museum
antiker Kleinkunst:
*Bf.*
neck-amphorae
821 ... 14
823 ... 14
825 ... 22
833 ... 11
837 ... 1
855 ... 12
856 ... 12
857 ... 13, 13
860 ... 12
870 ... 17
871 ... 14
872 ... 22
873 ... 13, 15
874 ... 12
875 ... 13
877 ... 22
878 ... 22
882 ... 13

883 ... 21
884 ... 22
885 ... 22
886 ... 22
887 ... 21
890 ... 22
891 ... 22
892 ... 18
3236 ... 304
amphorae
833 ... 11
834 ... 57, 295
stamnos
912 ... 22
hydriai
887 ... 17
911 ... 16
oinochoai
926 ... 14
929 ... 22
930 ... 22
kyathoi
958 ... 13
977 ... 13, 17
979 ... 23
980 ... 23
one-handled mastoid
985 ... 100
phiale
995 ... 14
frr.
— ... 15
— ... 18
— ... 20
*Rf.*
neck-amphora
3225 ... 87
stamnoi
3192 (J 1010)
... 32–3, 198
3227 (J 525) ... 3, 44
3228 (J 521) ... 44–5
(J 522) ... 145
(J 524) ... 145
calyx-kraters
3222 (J 523) ... 142
3224 (J 526) ... 29
oinochoe
inv. 7740 ... 156, 159
cups
inv. 8349 ... 143
S.L. ... 110, 300
*patterned*
oinochoe
3237 ... 183
*black*
pan
inv. 6527 ... 278
*head-vase*
— ... 188
*added*
amphorae
3170 (J 895) ... 195
3171 (J 890) ... 195, 306
3172 (J 910) ... 196
3185 (J 903) ... 195

MUNICH (cont.):
neck-amphorae
3173 (J 268) 197
3175 (J 894) 196
3177 (J 898) 196
3178 (J 909) 196
3179 (J 904) 196
3182 (J 886) 196
(J 267) 197
(J 900) 196
(J 902) 196
stamnos
3191 (J 899) 197
hydria
3189 (J 889) 197
oinochoai
3194 (J 897) 198
3195 (J 891) 198
3197 (J 906) 198
3198 (J 908) 198
3214 206
(J 893) 198
kyathos
3200 (J 901) 198
cups
3206 (J 907) 202
(J 892) 204
*Attic*
*Bf.*
neck-amphora 147
*Rf.*
2360, pelike 104
*Italiote*
*Rf.*
volute-kraters
— 34, 61
— 82
— 89
— 144
*added*
kantharos 211
*bronzes*
mirror 30
,, 76
stamnos
inv. 3831 249
stamnos-handles
191 248
192 248
oinochoe
478 265
satyr 189, 191
*varia*
stone relief 146
MURCIA, Museo:
*uncertain*
duck 305

NAPLES, Museo Nazionale:
*Bf.*
hydria
2781 18
oinochoai
2506 17
2508 13, 17
4912.1

*black*
kantharos
— 232
*added*
neck-amphorae
inv. 82755 196
inv. 82761 196
*Attic, rf.*
panathenaic
3235 80
volute-krater
3240 64
column-krater
3152 295
*Campanian bf.*
neck-amphora
inv. 81045 11
*Campanian outline*
oinochoe 20, 295
*Italiote*
*Rf.*
volute-kraters
2411 164
3222 89, 147
3253 84
3254 90
3255 84
3256 82
Stg. 709 144
bell-kraters
2293 66
— 38
— 41
panathenaic
3219 65
pelike
3231 74, 76
oinochoe
inv. 147867 227
*black*
oinochoai
inv. 85553 261
inv. 85383 263
— 256
— 258
— 258
— 258
— 261
— 261
— 261
— 263
askoi
inv. 85406 272
— 272
— 272
— 272
— 272
— 273
Black vases from Foci del Garigliano, see under *Mon. Linc.* 37 in the index of publications.
*added*
oinochoai
2069 226
— 220

— 220
lekythos
— 222
gutti
— 227
— 227
kantharoi
— 219
— 219
— 219
— 219
kantharoids
— 219
— 219
skyphoi
inv. 147985 222
— 220
— 220
— 222
— 222
— 222
— 222
— 228
cup-skyphoi
— 227
— 227
stemless cups
1714 224
2650 223
Stg. 296 224
Stg. 223
inv. 86793 224
inv. 14782 227
— 223
— 223
— 224
— 226
— 226
— 227
— 227
*uncertain*
pelike
— 178
oinochoai
— 264
— 268, 309
askos
inv. 85965 277
— 278
*varia*
bronze relief 288
R 140, marble relief 72
mosaic 235
NARBONNE, Musée:
*uncertain*
skyphos, *added* 225, 307
NEW HAVEN (Connecticut), Yale University, Museum:
*Rf.*
stemless cup
341 297
*patterned*
plate
343 303
phiale

126 185
*black*
oinochoe
— 209
squat lekythoi
461 270
— 309
kantharoid calyx
488 234
kantharos
507 237
*unglazed*
neck-amphora
347 289
*sigillata*
askos
513 276
*Attic, rf.*
bell-krater
129 92
skyphos
160 200
*East Greek*
bf. amphora
330 14
*Italiote*
*unglazed*
oinochoai
305 266
306 266
*added*
kothon
254 307
stemless cups
255 307
256 307
257 307
*uncertain*
sigillata, askoi
549 277
550 277
551 277
NEW YORK, Metropolitan Museum of Art:
*Bf.*
amphora
— 11
neck-amphorae
GR 517 21
GR 1080 295
*Rf.*
bell-krater
GR 999 298
stamnoi
91.1.441 301
GR 641 88
skyphoi
91.1.465 169
07.286.33 116
GR 638 299
*patterned*
amphoriskos
26.60.18 102
*head-vases*
GR 615 187
GR 617 305

NEW YORK (*cont.*):
06.1021.204    188, 305
*duck*
  19.192.14    10, 119
*satyrs*
  20.212 and 213    190
*black*
  oinochoai
    06.1021.103    308
    41.161.235    234
    GR 472    254, 309
    GR 622    309
  bowls
    06.1021.272    308
    06.1021.274    308
    GR 649    308
  kantharoi
    91.1.443    307
    GR 473    232, 309
    —    307
*unglazed*
  neck-amphora
    06.1021.250    289
  volute-kraters
    GR 1014    285
    GR 1015    285
  pseudo-volute-kraters
    06.1021.256    286
    GR 1013    286
  oinochoe
    —    309
  askoid oinochoe
    GR 1002    290
  dish
    GR 1143    310
*added*
  amphorae
    24.97.6    196
    24.97.7    196
  column-krater
    GR 628    306
  oinochoe
    91.1.450    205
  phiale
    GR 651    308
  cup
    GR 651    306
*Campanian bf.*
  neck-amphorae
    06.1021.42    11, 187
    06.1021.43    11
    06.1021.44    11, 187
*Campanian head-vases*
  06.1021.41    305
  06.1021.45    305
*Attic*
*Rf.*
  calyx-krater
    08.258.21    127
  bell-krater
    07.286.85    109
  hydria
    19.192.86    77
  oinochoe
    37.11.19    107
*relief*

squat lekythos
  28.57.9    298
*ducks*
  06.1021.264    191
  41.162.185    191
*Italiote*
*Rf.*
  askos    272
  skyphos    74
*added colour*
  kantharos
    06.1021.218    307
  kantharoid
    41.162.39    221
  skyphos
    09.192.2    307
*unglazed*
  oinochoe
    06.1021.255    266
*bronze*
  stamnos-handles
    50–1    249
    249–50    250
  pan and handle
    598    279
    727    278
  oinochoai
    206–9    283
    494    283
    505    266
    44.11.4    283
    44.11.5    283
  kantharoid
    596    239
  cut-out
    —    57
  mirrors
    799    83
    802    134
    —    30
*silver*
  phiale    292
*gems*
  31    55–6
  41.160.489    138
  —    137
Once NEW YORK, Metropolitan Museum:
*unglazed*
  calyx-kraters
    —    286
    —    286
NEW YORK, Cooper Union Museum:
*Rf.*
  1915.11–37, cup    310
NEW YORK, Morgan Library:
  bronze cista    131
NEW YORK, New York University:
*Rf.*
  cup    300
*black*
  40.86, oinochoe    309
  squat lekythos    309

kantharos    307
NEW YORK, Prof. Karl Lehmann:
  rf. plate, fr.    303
NEW YORK, Joseph Brummer:
  Attic duck    305
NEW YORK market (Hirsch):
*Bf.*
  hydria    296
*deer-askos*
  —    305
*bronze*
  stamnos-handles    308
NEW YORK market:
*added*
  column-krater    306
NEWCASTLE-UPON-TYNE, King's College:
*Rf.*
  neck-amphora, fr. 134–5
NIESSEN (Cologne), once:
*Rf.* cup    300
*Italiote, added*
  oinochoe    307
NÎMES, Maison Carrée:
  altar    99
NORTHWICK PARK, Capt. E. G. Spencer-Churchill:
*head-vase*    156
*Campanian head-vase*    187
ODESSA, Museum:
*Attic, rf.*
  pelike    72
OLYMPIA, Museum:
  rerebrace    136
  clay sima    183
ORVIETO, Museo dell' Opera del Duomo (Museo Civico):
*Rf.*
  stamnoi
    —    150, 153
    —    150, 153
  bell-krater
    —    154
  fragments
    —    171
  stemless cup
    —    29
  cups
    28    159
    29    159
    30    159
    598    113
*ducks*
  —    119
  —    119
  —    120
*satyr*
  —    190
*Spurinas*
  fr.    296

*patterned*
  skyphos
    175    23
  cup or stemless
    —    204
*black*
  skyphos
    —    117
*unglazed*
  situla?
    frr.    28
  oinochoai
    —    264
    —    264
*bronze*
  pan    278
*varia*
  sarcophagus from Torre S. Severo    8, 9, 89–91
ORVIETO, Museo Faina:
*Bf.*
  neck-amphorae
    332    15
    —    14
    —    15
    —    15
    —    15
    —    15
*Rf.*
  neck-amphorae
    17    170
    18    170
    21    9, 170, 303
    24    170
    25    9, 170, 303
    —    170
  pelike
    —    37, 39
  volute-krater
    20    9, 169, 303
  calyx-krater
    —    145
  cup
    —    143
*ducks*
  —    191
  —    192
*bull-askos*
  —    194
*patterned*
  oinochoe
    —    184
*black*
  phialai
    —    240, 292
    —    240, 292
*added*
  column-krater
    —    197
*unglazed*
  neck-amphorae
    365    289
    366    289
  volute-kraters?
    369    285

ORVIETO, Faina (cont.):
369 bis    285
370    285
calyx-krater
368    286
dinos
438    286
strainer
—    292–3
dish
439    292
phialai
302    292
302 bis    292
kantharos?
371    291
OXFORD, Ashmolean Museum:
Bf.
neck-amphora
1932.122    14
handled mastoid
1946.54    12
Rf.
stamnoi
1917.54    4, 56–7
1945.89    77, 92
fragment
1914.37    37
plates
454    175
1872.1241    175
1872.1242    175
1872.1243    175
skyphos
1919.27, fr.    310
cups
1927.4069, fr.    107
—    112
bowl
570    112
head-vase
1947.147    305
ducks
258    184, 192
339    192
patterned
oinochoai
259    186
1920.320    183
1946.157    183
stemmed dish
1933.1564    20, 296
plates
1872.1240    176
1878.146    177
1933.1563    296
phiale
1925.670    181–2
black
oinochoai
381 A    268
397    267
1872.1269    261
1896–1908 G 520    268
1928.50    255, 308

squat lekythoi
1936.620    270, 271
1937.680    271
askos
1946.55    276
pan
1932.1158    278
salt-cellar
1874.431    245
kantharos
1936.619    232
unglazed
askos
1877.35    274
added
cups
1920.345    203
—    202
Attic
Bf.
neck-amphora
208    64
Rf.
calyx-krater
1939.599    76, 76, 164
bell-kraters
529    34
G 138.31, fr    40
kantharos
1945.66    219
cups
1929.752    26
1931.11    28
1943.52    110
black
kantharoid
1927.654    239
Italiote
Rf.
485, askos    272
1934.285, guttus    183
added
oinochoai
1883.138    224
1945.46    220
plate
1945.50    224
kantharoi
1874.398    219
1944.14    211
kantharoid
1945.67    219
skyphos
1945.53    220
stemless cup
446    223
black
oinochoai
412    256
1911.74    262
1922.89    262
askoi
1911.72    272
1932.129    272
Campanian head-vase
335    187

Corinthian
oinochoe
1879.123    268
uncertain
oinochoai
344    256
392 (375)    257
1878.143    309
1939.7    257
1939.9    258
askos
1878.144    273, 275, 309
bronze
oinochoe
1888.488 b    266
varia
lamp 1884.642    157
slate palette    96
OXFORD, Pitt Rivers Museum:
Rf.
kantharos    29
OXFORD, J. D. Beazley:
duck-askos, fr.    192
cup-skyphos, fr.    201
Italiote askos    272
,,    272
OXFORD, Dr. F. H. Dickson:
black kantharos    237
PALERMO, Museo Nazionale:
Rf.
volute-krater    169
column-krater    25
stamnos    39, 61
Attic, bf.
lekythos    147
uncertain
striped oinochoe    265
varia
sarcophagus    166
PALESTRINA, Museo:
cippi    299
PARIS, Musée du Louvre:
Bf.
amphora
E 723    11
neck-amphorae
E 724    11
E 728    11
E 729    11
E 731    11
E 763    15
CA 1901    14
hydria
CA 2515    16
oinochoe
E 772    14
Rf.
stamnoi
K 415    148
K 416    148
oinochoe
K 480    148

cups
K 497    160
K 498    160
K 499    160
K 500    160
head-vases
H 75    117
H 76    118
H 77    117
H 78    117
H 80    118
H 81    305
ducks
H 97    119
H 98    119
H 99    120
H 100    6, 119
H 101    119
H 102    191
H 103    192
H 105    192
old 1268    192
deer-askoi
H 176    192, 193
H 177    192
patterned
squat lekythos
N 4089    272
pyxides
old 480–1    184
old 485    184
old 493    184
old 521    184
black
oinochoai
H 299    267
H 300    267
H 301    267
H 302    267
H 303    267
H 304    267
H 305    267
L 604    216
—    254
—    254
—    254
—    254
—    255
—    259
askos
D 189    276
pan
N 2252    278
situlae
N 1847    253
—    251
added
amphora
G 63    195
pelike
G 64    196
bowl
—    210
unglazed
neck-amphora
—    289

PARIS, Louvre (*cont.*):
askoi
D 187 274
— 276
kernos
— 294
*sigillata*
askos
H 454 276
*Attic*
*Bf.*
neck-amphora
F 60 134
hydria
F 287 74
*Rf.*
pelike
MN 734 72
hydria
CA 2260 40
oinochoe
G 442 201
— 42
statuette-vase
— 85
stemless cup
CA 2259 60
cups
G 25 189
G 123 7, 297
G 457 60
*Italiote, black*
phiale 212
*bronze*
stamnos and handles
2659 250
2667–8 249
2670 250
situla
2826 252
cista
1663 90
oinochoai
2782 283
2783 283, 250
2801 283
mirror
— 116
*varia*
clay statuette 242
stone sarcophagus 157
column base 304
PARIS, Cabinet des Médailles:
*Rf.*
neck-amphora
875 143
calyx-kraters
920 9, 90–1, 136–7, 183
921 142
volute-krater
918 8, 133–4, 166, 185, 188
stamnoi
947 5, 41, 53–4, 115

948 146
950 141
cup
1066 6, 54–5
*duck*
— 120
*Spurinas*
— 24
*added*
amphorae
913 196
914 196
oinochoe
— 216
*Attic*
*Rf.*
stamnos
388 33
skyphos
846 81
kantharos
475 219
*Italiote*
rf. hydria 59
*bronze*
1457, stamnos-handle 250
1312, mirror 199
*varia*
gem, 1820 bis 138
clay statuette 99
PARIS, Petit Palais:
*Bf.*
431, lekythos 19
*head-vases*
355 156
391 157
398 118
399 300
*Attic*
duck-askos
416 191
PARIS, Musée Rodin:
*Rf.*
cup 980 3, 25–7
*Attic, rf.*
bell-krater 72
PARIS, Fernand Chapou-thier:
*Attic, rf.*
hydria 40
PARIS, Baron Edmond de Rothschild:
silver kantharos 235
PARIS market (Feuardent):
*Attic, rf.*
calyx-krater
— 75
bell-kraters
— 36
— 101
PARIS market:
*Rf.*
oinochoe 155
cup 107

PARMA, Museo di Anti-chità:
*Rf.*
calyx-kraters
— 37–8
— 37–9
stamnos
— 54
*bronze*
mirror 146
PASINATI (Rome), once:
askos 277
PASSERI (Pesaro) once:
*black*
oinochoe 254
*Italiote, added*
skyphos 228
PATRIZI, Marchese (Montefiascone), once:
*Rf.*
column-krater 127
PEMBROKE, once:
*Chalcidian* 35
PERUGIA, Museo Civico:
*Rf.*
pointed amphora
— 3, 61
calyx-krater
— 165
column-krater
— 127, 130
stamnos
— 121
cup
— 174
*bronze*
mirrors
— 106
— 116
— 125
— 131
— 131
— 146
*varia*
sarcophagus 153
tombstone 89
urn 54
„ 58
PERUGIA, Museo del Palazzone:
*Rf.*
column-kraters
— 124–6, 301
fr. 130
*unglazed*
volute-krater 294
askos 274
*sigillata*
askos 276
*bronze*
oinochoe 265
*varia*
lamp 280
„ 280

PHILADELPHIA, University Museum:
*Rf.*
stamnoi
400 168
2521 301, 303
4854 100, 299
L 64.228 229
column-kraters
L 29.57 301
L 29.58 301
oinochoai
2513 169
2517 303
2519 303
2835 173, 302
3143 302
99.158 302
— 302
plates
2841 175
2842 176
L 64.405 303
bowl
1754 48
stemless cup
37.20.1 297
cups
3444 300
3445 300
— 300
*patterned*
oinochoe
2834 185
pyxis
2854 184
stemmed dish
L 29.51 296
plates
2997 176
3193 303
*ducks*
1596 305
L 64.516 305
*black*
oinochoai
1455 309
1456 309
1457 309
3054 309
L 64.36 309
squat lekythos
2831 270
jar
— 308
bowl
2580 308
dish
— 245
kantharoi
1438 307
1439 307–8
1443 307
1445 307
1446 307
2833 234, 307

PHILADELPHIA (cont.):
3062   307
*unglazed*
neck-amphorae
25   310
—   310
oinochoe
2840   263, 309
*added*
amphora
—   195, 306
column-krater
2994   203
oinochoai
4050   217
4084   206, 306
L 64.404   206, 306
—   306
skyphos
2934   201
cups
2843   204, 306
2857   204
*Attic, rf.*
stamnos   28
*Italiote*
*added*
14.336, hydria   307
*uncertain*
*black*
oinochoai
2832   263
2988   259
stemmed dish
2996   245
dishies
2844   243
2845   243
2849   243
2850   245
2851   243
2852   243
2853   243
2999   243
kantharos
2833   234
*unglazed*
3001, dish   243
*added*
kantharoi
2830   222
2833   236
*varia*
clay relief, Ur   306
PONIATOWSKI, once:
*Attic, rf.*
pyxis   88
POZNAŃ, Museum:
*unglazed*
askos   274
*Italiote, added*
oinochoe   220
POZNAŃ, Miss Ruxer:
black oinochoe   269
PREYSS (Munich), once:

*Rf.*
oinochoe   254
cup   167
*Italiote*
*added*
oinochoai
—   220
—   220
plate   224
PRIMICERIO, once:
bronze oinochoe   265
PRINCETON, University:
*Rf.*
calyx-krater
—   301
stamnos
45.192   299
oinochoe
vii.33.48   302
plate
359   303
skyphoi
40.286   302
45.90   302
45.187   302
45.198   302
cups
45.184   299
—   300
*duck*
—   305
*black*
plate
10.280   305
*unglazed*
oinochoai
40.288   310
40.289   310
*added*
cups
43.135   306
45.186   306
*Italiote, rf.*
kantharos   211
PROVIDENCE, Rhode Island School of Design:
*Rf.*
plate
27.188   10, 175, 303
*black*
askos
16.600   273
*unglazed*
askos
14.434   276

RAOUL-ROCHETTE, once:
*Attic, rf.*
pelike   178
READING, University:
*Bf.*
neck-amphorae
—   136–7
—   295
RAVIZZA (Orvieto), once:

*unglazed*
calyx-krater   286
*bronze*
mirror   131
REGGIO, Museo Civico:
*Attic*, duck-askos   191
*Italiote*, rf. situla   88
RHODES, Museum:
*Attic*
*Rf.*
fr.   72
*black*
pelikai
6613   178
10790   178
13887   178
kantharoid
—   239
*uncertain*
oinochoai
—   260
—   260
*bronze*
12018, oinochoe   265
ROME, Museo di Villa Giulia:
*Bf.*
neck-amphorae
3588   14
15539   16
M 409   11
frr.   11
stamnos
25153   14
column-krater
M 392   12
dinos
M 408   11
hydria
15538   16
oinochoai
—   97
—   97
kyathos
C   12
*Rf.*
stamnoi
1599   73–5
1600   73–5
1607   103
1609   103
1660   8, 152
1755   73, 77
1756   73, 77
2349   102
2350   102
3592   81, 84
3593   77, 78
3600   77
6152   78–80
15540   64, 65
26017   101–2, 299
27134   57, 163
43794   103
43795   103
43968   97, 102

43969   100
43970   100
—   59–60
volute-krater
2491   7, 80–4
calyx-kraters
1197   7, 92–6
8359   70–1
—   85
bell-kraters
6364   70–2
—   302
hydria
6369   157
oinochoai
12351   172
19772   173, 201
19773   173, 201
26053   155
—   155
—   155
—   155
—   156
askos
—   157
plates
2768, part   174
—   177
—   177
—   177
—   177
skyphoi
2775   117
2781   117
stemless cup
49321   297
cups
1396   159
1397   159
1614   108, 299–300
1615   109, 300
1664   108
1674   7, 106
1675   106
3594   107
3595   107
3596   108
3597   107
3602   108
6163   111
7881   159
17956   106
26013   108
43608   110
43609   78, 111
43791   101
43800   108, 299–300
43972   160
44500   111
44502   108
—   108
—   111
—   112
—   158
—   160

ROME, V. Giulia (cont.):
fragment
— 111
duck
— 301
head-vases
2769 117, 183, 300
16338 187
— 117
patterned
oinochoe
— 183
epichyseis
1761 156
— 156
— 156
jar
2772 185
squat lekythos
— 271
askos
— 158
pyxides
C 184
— 184
— 184
plates
— 176
— 176
— 177
— 177
— 177
black
oinochoai
19732 267
19733 267
19777 267
19778 267
23933 264, 309
— 259
— 259
— 264
— 264
squat lekythoi
23466 270
— 270
— 270
— 270
— 270
— 270
— 270
— 271
— 271
— 271
askos
16592 276
stemmed dish
12562 245
dishies
19760 244
— 243
— 243
pan
— 278
plate

— 245
skyphos
— 238
kantharoi
C 231
C 231
— 231
— 231
unglazed
volute-kraters
2300 281-2
2301 281-2
2302 281-2
2303 281-2
stamnoi
2308A 281
2308B 281
2235A 281
2235B 281
2235C 281
2235D 281
— 281
situlae
— 288
— 288
hydriai
2320 294
— 294
oinochoai
— 283, 310
pans
— 283
strainers
— 283
kernoi
— 294
— 294
phialai
2270 292
— 292
added
amphora
— 196
hydria
— 198
oinochoai
C 200
— 217
— 217, 217
askos
— 273
plates
15321 217
23950 217
25923 217
— 211-15, 306
phiale
C 209
kantharos
— 207
cups
3675 202
3676 202
17494 202
44561 204
C 204

— 202
— 202
— 204
— 204
Campagnano stamnoi
22636 199
22637 199
bucchero
dishies
— 244
— 244
Attic
Bf.
amphora
— 141
Rf.
bell-kraters
18543 95
11688, fr. 103
fragment
50328 100
cup
— 142
Italiote, rf.
situla
— 130
bronze
stamnos-handles
— 250
— 250
situla
— 287
cistae
— 49
— 58
— 183
see also Ficoroni cista
oinochoai
— 264
— 265
— 265
mirrors
— 60, 80
— 104
— 131
— 131
varia
clay, architectural
— 83
— 163
— 183
ROME, Città del Vaticano, Museo Vaticano:
Bf.
neck-amphorae
231 1
265 21
267 22
277 13
278 13
G 91 2
hydria
238 16
oinochoe
— 49

lydion
G 88 12
plates
233 12
G 87 12
Rf.
stamnoi
— 44
— 47, 48
— 142
— 150
G 113 67
volute-krater
— 4
column-krater
— 122
calyx-krater
— 142
— 182
bell-krater
— 172
'nuptial lebes'
— 148
hydria
— 47-8
oinochoai
G 111 49-50
— 45
— 147
— 173
— 296
cups
G 112 4, 55-6
— 4, 55, 297
— 50-1
— 113
— 160
head-vases
— 157
— 190
ducks
— 191
— 191
deer-askoi
— 192
patterned
neck-amphorae
292 21, 296
293 21
pointed amphora
— 48
hydria
— 184
oinochoai
G 114 184
— 183
— 184-5
— 184
squat lekythos
— 271
phiale
— 182
skyphoi
246 23
— 48
— 297

ROME, Vaticano (cont.):
*Spurinas*
— 24
*black*
oinochoai
G 119 266
G 120 258, 260, 309
G 121 260
— 254
— 255
— 257
— 258
— 258
— 267
— 267
salt-cellar
— 245
plate
G 122 245, 246, 260
phiale
G 118 238
bowl
— 241, 308
kantharoi
G 116 231
G 117 233
— 231
— 231
— 231
— 233
— 233
— 236
skyphos
— 238
*unglazed*
stamnos
— 52
askoi
G 143 275
— 270, 275
*sigillata*
askoi
— 276
— 276
*added*
neck-amphora
G 108 196
hydria
G 109 198
oinochoe
— 218
kyathos
G 107 198
bowls
— 210
— 210
— 210
skyphos
G 110 200
*Attic, rf.*
hydria
— 299
oinochoai
— 200
— 201

cup
— 26
*Italiote*
*outline*
pointed amphora 295
*bronze*
stamnoi and handles
— 249
— 249
— 249
situlae
— 252
— 287
cista
— 79–80
oinochoai
— 265
— 266
— 266
— 266
— 283
— 283
pans
— 278
— 278
mirrors
— 83
— 131
— 199
*varia*
statuette, Cand. 99 31
relief Croce, 574A 99
well-head 147
tomb 47

ROME, Antiquarium:
*Rf.*
plates
— 176
— 176
— 176
*patterned*
plates
— 176
— 176
*black*
oinochoai
542 257
— 257
— 257
— 269
— 269
dishies
2386 244
2387 244
— 244
plate
— 246
askos
— 273
*added*
pelike 206
oinochoe 205
bowl 215
skyphos 207

*uncertain*
dishes
2382 243
2388 243
ROME, Museo Barracco:
marble relief 72
ROME, Museo Capitolino:
Gaul 98
Leda 85
Celtomachy 99
ROME, Museo del Palazzo
dei Conservatori:
*Bf.*
neck-amphorae
150 11
— 18
*Rf.*
oinochoai
— 173, 302
— 173
*patterned*
oinochoai 184
*duck*
— 191
*unglazed*
askos 274
*added*
oinochoai
— 205
— 205
ROME, Museo del Foro
Romano:
*Rf.*
cups
fr. 159
fr. 159
plate
— 177
fr. 157
*black*
oinochoe 217
*added*
skyphos, fr. 207
*Italiote?*
*added*
skyphos 224
ROME, Museo Laterano:
marble frieze 84
ROME, Palatine:
*Rf.*
oinochoe, fr. 173
cups
fr. 159
fr. 159
— 159
plate
— 176
*patterned*
plate 176
*black*
oinochoai
— 217
— 217
*added*
askos 207

skyphos 200
*Italiote?*
skyphos, added 224
ROME, Museo delle
Terme:
*black*
dishies 244–5
*added*
bowl 210
kantharos 210
*varia*
marble Herakles 142
ROME, Villa Albani:
relief 157
ROME, Prof. Ludwig
Curtius:
*added*
cup 203
*Italiote*
*added*
calyx, fr. 143
ROME, Principe del
Drago:
*Rf.*
calyx-krater 7, 92–3
skyphos 160, 303
— 161
ROME, Marchese De Luca
Resta:
*Italiote, rf.*
volute-krater 104
ROME, Prince Torlonia:
*Rf.*
pointed amphora 179
cup 114
*patterned*
oinochoe 184
phialai
— 182
— 182
— 182
— 182
stand 182
*head-vase*
— 117
*ducks*
— 191
— 191
— 191
*black*
oinochoai 267
kantharoi
— 231
— 233
— 233
— 237
— 237
kantharoids
— 239
— 239
*unglazed*
pan 278, 283
*added?*
stamnos 180
*added*
kantharos 208, 235

ROME, Torlonia (*cont.*):
*unglazed*
askos 274
*Attic, rf.*
hydria 105
*varia*
wall-paintings 90
ROMAN market:
*Rf.*
calyx-krater 154
bell-krater 135
,, 161
stamnoi 46
cup 112
*patterned*
oinochoe 297
*black*
oinochoe 263
ROUEN, Musée des An-
tiquités:
*Attic, bf.*
neck-amphora 299
RUESCH (Zurich), once:
*Italiote, black*
oinochoe 257
*bronze*
oinochoe 264
*silver*
oinochoe 263
RUVO, Don Michele Jatta:
*Attic, rf.*
volute-kraters
1093 75
— 36
*Italiote, rf.*
askos
1402 272

SAINT-GERMAIN, Musée
des antiquités natio-
nales:
bronze stamnos 249
silver kantharos 236
SAMOS:
dishie, fabric? 244
SALONICA, Museum:
*Attic*
epichyseis
505 (R. 84) 156
8.41 (R. 92) 156
8.158 (R. 270) 156
*uncertain*
askoi 272
SAN FRANCISCO, De
Young Museum:
*added*
column-krater
— 197
SAN GIUSTO ALLE MO-
NACHE, Contessa Elisa-
betta Martini di Cigalà:
*added*
stemless 203
— 205
SAN GIMIGNANO, Museo:
bronze situla 253

SANT' AGATA DE' GOTI,
Dr. Domenico Mustilli:
*Attic, rf.*
bell-krater 40, 104
SARTEANO, Palazzo Bar-
gagli, once:
mirror 56
SARAJEVO, Museum:
*Attic, rf.*
krater, fr. 76, 209
SARTI, once:
*bronze*
cista 183
mirror 58
,, 58
SCHILLER, once:
*black*
squat lekythos 270
*uncertain*
*added*
kantharos 222
SECCHI (Rome), once:
bowl 215
SÈVRES, Musée Céra-
mique:
*Bf.*
frr.
1237.8 15
*black*
oinochoai
1163.2 254
1163.3 254
kantharoid calyx
1163.1 234
kantharos
4523 232
*added*
amphora
3114 196
oinochoe
2046 201, 203
*Attic, black*
kantharos
4166.13 236
kantharoid
4166.11 239
*Italiote*
*Rf.*
askos
109 272
*added*
oinochoe
94 220
squat lekythoi
225 228
5335 226
kantharoi
212.1 219
212.2 221
212.3 221
kantharoids
196 219
197.1 219
289 219
stemless cup
254 223

*uncertain*
oinochoai
9521.1 260
9521.2 260
askoi
111.1 272
111.1 272
SIENA, Museo:
rf. column-krater 130
SIENA, Marchese Chigi:
*Rf.*
column-krater 130
cup 160
SIGNORELLI (Rome), once:
bf. neck-amphora 15
,, 15
STUTTGART, Museum:
*Attic*
rf. stemless 248
black ,, 248
*bronze*
stamnos 248
SWANSEA, Lord, once:
rf. stamnos 144
SWINDON, A. D. Pass-
more:
rf. stamnos 301
SYDNEY, University,
Nicholson Museum:
*Rf.*
plates
37 177
38 177
bowl
62 174
stemless cup
61 174
*added*
oinochoe
95 206
*Italiote, added*
bell-krater
94 225-6, 307
SYRACUSE, Museo Nazio-
nale:
*Attic, rf.*
calyx-krater
17427 75
*Italiote, rf.*
bell-krater
— 90
*uncertain*
*unglazed*
oinochoe 309
TARANTO, Museo Nazio-
nale:
*Attic, rf.*
lekythos 295
*Italiote*
*Rf.*
volute-kraters
— 65
— 298
*black*
dishie 245

*added*
oinochoai
— 220
— 220
kantharoi
— 221
kantharoid
— 221
skyphoi
— 221
cup-skyphos
— 223
stemless cup
— 224
TARQUINIA, Museo
Civico:
*Bf.*
neck-amphorae
857 15
RC 2803 296
— 296
*Rf.*
calyx-kraters
— 109
— 142
bell-krater
— 51
oinochoai
RC 1644 67
RC 1645 67
skyphos
1928 178
*Spurinas*
— 24
*patterned*
oinochoai
— 184
— 184
phialai
— 182
— 182
*head-vases*
— 117, 300
— 305
*duck*
— 300
*black*
squat lekythos
RC 3864 270, 271
askos
— 276
plates
RC 7585 246
RC 7586 246
kantharoi
1051 231
1120 231
1975 231
1976 231
RC 627 235
RC 1928 231
*unglazed*
askoi
1315A 274
1315B 275

TARQUINIA (*cont.*):
kernos
— 294
*added*
oinochoai
— 216
— 216
bowl
1960 210
kantharos
— 180, 216
*Attic, rf.*
stemless cup
— 72, 210, 306
*bronze*
oinochoe 266
mirror 58
*varia*
stone relief 138
,, 138
sarc. of the Priest 89–91
TEPLITZ, Museum:
bronze stamnos-handle
308
TERNI, Museo Comunale:
*black*
squat lekythos 270
THEBES, Museum:
bronze kantharos 72
TODI, Museo Comunale:
*Rf.*
plates
93 175
508 175
509 175
head-vase
487 190
*black*
calyx-krater
522 247
oinochoai
517 255
519 255
520 255
521 255
523 254
1444 255
salt-cellar
550 245
bowl
528 241
phiale
530 240
kantharoi
510 231
511 233
512 231
513 233
514 231
515 235
516 235
*unglazed*
oinochoe
1684 269
4912.1

*added*
cups
488 203
489 204
490 202
491 202
492 203
493 204
494 204
495 203
496 204
497 204
498 204
500 204
*Attic*
507, kantharos 219
*uncertain*
oinochoe
524 263
dishie
543 245
TORONTO, Royal Ontario Museum:
*Rf.*
calyx-krater
410 153–4
stamnos
427 65, 298
'nuptial lebes'
471 148
hydria
489 302
oinochoai
490 169
491 169
493 156, 302
squat lekythos
487 157
plates
463 175
464 175
cup
272 298
*patterned*
neck-amphorae
213 304
221 304
'nuptial lebes'
217 182, 184
oinochoai
494 183
495 182–3, 307
plate
499 304
phiale
600 105
*black*
oinochoai
518 217
545 254
570 257
573 259
— 228
askoi
558 306
C 41 309

kantharoi
561 232
564 237
565 232
CA 269 307
*unglazed*
volute-krater
612 281–2
oinochoe
CA 265 310
*added*
oinochoai
452 218
492 201
496 205
497 205
498 217, 307
pelike
416 206
squat lekythos
488 206
*Italiote
Rf.*
457, askos 272
*black*
595, phiale 240, 307
*added*
kantharoi
467 219
468 219
kantharoid
542 219
*uncertain
patterned*
neck-amphora
508 304
*black*
oinochoai
523 228
568 261
577 264
578 265
*sigillata?*
askos
G 5025 310
*added*
hydriai
424 206
425 206
skyphos
526 222
TRIESTE, Museo Civico:
rf. calyx-krater
57, 133–4, 182, 301
TUEBINGEN, University:
*Bf.*
C 79, fr. 13
*Rf.*
column-krater
F 17 128
frr.
F 15 100
F 16 102
bowl
F 18 178

cup
F 13 107
*Attic, rf.*
F 12, cup, fr. 107
*uncertain*
F 36, askos 148
TYSZKIEWICZ, once:
gem 59

VATICAN, *see* Rome.
VIENNA, Kunsthistorisches Museum:
*Bf.*
hydria
406 16
*black*
jars
— 247
— 247
*Attic, rf.*
bell-kraters
869 40
1142 72
2000 40
— 95
squat lekythos
— 45
cup
202 51
*Italiote, rf.*
bell-kraters
581 307
622 227
stemless cups
103 226
602 226
VIENNA, Oesterreichisches Museum:
*Bf.*
fr. 13
*Rf.*
neck-amphora
449 150, 151, 155
stamnos
448 8, 152–3
oinochoe
452 173
*Spurinas*
451 24
*black*
oinochoe
565 254, 256
*Italiote, black*
563, oinochoe 256
*bronze*
situla-fittings 287
VIENNA, University:
*Rf.*
cups
497 109
498 109
499 110
500 110
stemless cup
503.55, fr. 174

VIENNA, Univ. (*cont.*):
*added*
   503.1, stemless  205
*unglazed*
   954A, askos  276
*Attic, rf.*
  calyx-krater
   551C      60–1
VILLA GIULIA, *see* Rome.
VITERBO, Museo:
*Bf.*
  neck-amphora  18
*Rf.*
  calyx-krater  154
  skyphos  158
   ,,      158
*patterned*
  phiale  182
   ,,      182
VOGELL (Carlsruhe), once:
*black*
  oinochoe  268
VOLTERRA, Museo Guarnacci:
*Rf.*
  calyx-krater
   —   120, 132, 183
  stamnos
   —     121
  column-kraters
   —     10
   —     30
   —     30
   —   121, 126
   —   121, 126
   —     122
   —     122
   —     124
   —   124, 132
   —     126
   —     127
   —     128
   —     128
   —     128
   —     129
   —     129
   —     129
   —     129
   —     130
  oinochoai
   —     118
   —     127
   —     147
  cups
   fr.     113
   fr.     114
*duck*
   —     305

*black*
  askoi
   —     277
   —     277
  strainer
   —     279
*added*
  oinochoe
   —     205
  skyphos
   —     208
  cups
   —     202
   —     203
   —     203
*varia*
  urns   54, 57, 84, 90–1
WARSAW, Majewski Museum:
*patterned*
  plate  176
*Italiote, added*
  askos  273
*uncertain*
  black oinochoe  259
  askos  272
WASHINGTON, National Museum:
*Bf.*
  neck-amphorae
   136419   296
   136617   295
*Rf.*
  oinochoai
   136408   302
   154528   302
  cup
   136328   300
*patterned*
  oinochoai
   1362     304
   136422   296
  jar
   136418   296
  plates
   1372     296
   —     296
   —     296
   —     296
  chalices
   136445   296
   136447   296
*black*
  squat lekythos
   377365   309
  kantharoi
   101686   307
   101859   307

*added*
  oinochoai
   101837   306
   136551   306
   136552   306
  cups
   136381   306
   136394   306
*Italiote*
*black*
  askos  309
*added*
  1353, oinochoe  307
WEBER, Hermann, once:
*unglazed* dish  291
WILNO, Society of Friends:
*uncertain*
  oinochoe  261
  askos  273
WINTERTHUR, Museum:
*uncertain*
  askos  310
WORCESTER (Massachusetts), Art Museum:
*added*
  1125, amphora  306
*Italiote, rf.*
  askos  272
*bronze*
  stamnos-handles  250
WÜRZBURG, Martin von Wagner-Museum:
*Bf.*
  amphora
   799     17, 49
  neck-amphora
   795     13
*Rf.*
  stamnos
   803     33
  column-krater
   804     129
  oinochoai
   813     173
   814     168
   815     168
   816     168
   817     168
  cups
   818     108
   819   143, 145
   820     112
*patterned*
  oinochoai
   647   181, 304
   802     184
  pyxis
   883     184

  phiale
   888     185
*ducks*
   891   191, 301
   892     191
*black*
  oinochoe
   935   238, 259
*added*
  neck-amphora
   806     197
  oinochoai
   807     205
   808     205
   809     205
   810     206
   811     218
*Attic*
*Bf.*
  265, amphora  109
*Rf.*
  amphora
   507     189
  calyx-krater
   523     93
*Campanian bf.*
  neck-amphora
   797     187
*Italiote*
*Rf.*
  cup     52
*added*
  'nuptial lebes'
   812     225
  oinochoai
   830     220
   831     220
  kantharoi
   622     221
   829     221
*uncertain*
  black askos
   936     273

YALE, *see* New Haven.

ZURICH, Eidgenössische Technische Hochschule:
*Bf.*
  amphora  295
*unglazed*
  askos  275
*added*
  oinochoe  201
*uncertain*
  oinochoe  264

# INDEX OF PUBLICATIONS

Where no references follow the title of a work, please look up the item under the museum number in the index of collections.

Albizzati *Vasi antichi dipinti del Vaticano.*
Alinari, photograph:
23734 — 294
26048 — 294
32457-8 — 289
32467 — 14
32471 — 143
32477 — 170
32478 — 169
32479 to 32487 — 170
32752 — 37
34712, 2 — 30, 120
34712, 1 — 128
34713, 3 — 122
34714, 1 — 121
2 — 122
3 — 121, 128
34715, 1 — 191
34715, 2 — 147
35553, 2 — 249
35812 — 113
35817, 2 — 190
35817, 3 — 190
35833 — 55
37482-3 — 18
41116 — 211
41151, 1 — 187
41161 — 130
41165 — 16
41178 — 16
41183 — 73
41200 — 106
41205 — 85
41207 — 80
41303 — 294
— 1
— 286
— 289
— 292
— 292
*Altertümer von Pergamon:*
2, pl. 46, 2 — 67-8
Ambrosch *De Charonte etrusco:*
pll. 1-2 — 142
2-3 — 62
Amelung *Führer durch die Antiken in Florenz:*
fig. 42 — 252
*American Journal of Archaeology* [AJA.]:
1909, 208 — 139
1918, 267, 10, a — 252
1920, 15-17 — 187
1927, 283 — 288
1927, 284 — 288
1938, 338-41 — 30

1939, 627 — 92
1942, 535, 4 — 245
1944, 8, 19 — 283
*Amtliche Berichte aus den Königlichen Kunstsammlungen:*
30, 86 — 228
38, 301 — 108
*Annali dell' Instituto di Corrispondenza Archeologica* [Annali]:
1832 pl. G — 121, 164
1841 pl. H — 288
1844 pl. H — 111
1845 pl. M — 68, 154
1848 pl. K — 39
1849 pl. A — 124
1850 pl. L — 40
1852 pl. T — 196
1859 pl. G-H — 43
1860 pl. N — 153
1862 pl. O — 36
1868 pl. B — 114
1871 pl. A — 209
B, 1 — 286
B, 2 — 290
B, 3 — 292
B, 4 — 289
B, 5 — 285
C, 1 — 285
C, 2 — 287
C, 3 — 256
1872 pl. A — 105
1878 pl. H — 63-4
S — 202
1879 pl. D — 77
E, 2 — 104
V — 152
1880 pl. P, 3 — 274
R, 13 — 274
R, 16 — 236
R, 16a — 246
R, 16b — 236
R, 16c — 244
1884 pl. A — 210
B, 1 — 194
R — 210
*Annuaire du Musée Gréco-romain:*
1933-5, 36, 12 — 258
*Annual of the British School at Athens* [BSA.]:
26 pl. 33 — 105
*Antike, Die:*
16 p. 25 — 60
*Antike Denkmäler:*
I pl. 20 — 252
p. 9, 5 — 252

2 pl. 8 — 105
41 — 49
3 pl. 12 — 97-8
35 — 146
*Antiquités du Bosphore Cimmérien* [ABC.]:
pl. 38, 2 — 235
*Archäologisch - epigraphische Mittheilungen aus Oesterreich* [AEM.]:
6 pl. 1-2 — 287
p. 146 — 287
15 p. 128 — 13
*Archäologische Zeitung* [AZ.]:
1844 pl. 13 — 147
1853 pl. 59 — 40
1856 pl. 90 — 165
1857 pl. 108, 1 — 50-1
1863 pl. 180, 3 — 133
1865 pl. 202, 2 — 95
203 — 95
1869 pl. 17 — 74, 76
1870 pl. 28 — 209
1871 pl. 46, 1 — 39
47 — 39
p. 61 — 15
1879 pl. 16 — 165
1883 pl. 6 — 144
1884 pl. 5-6 — 73-7
19 — 144
*Archäologischer Anzeiger* [Anz.] (part of the Jahrbuch):
1897 p. 63 — 235
1904 p. 54, 3 — 153
1909 p. 1, 42 — 220
175, 40 — 191
1913 p. 185, 10 — 252
1917 p. 92, 17 — 167
105 — 17, 49
114, 46 — 191
1925 p. 40 — 191
136 — 48
283-4 — 134
1926 p. 35 — 194
75 — 110
1927 p. 185 — 52
1928 p. 134, 12 — 193
347 — 223
354 — 155
355 — 202
1929 p. 258, 19 — 192
1936 p. 78, 1-2 — 196
78, 3-4 — 196
82, 5-6 — 196
82, 7-8 — 199
86 — 195

*Archiv für Religionswissenschaft:*
29 pl. 1, 1 — 170
Armoni, photographs:
— 113
— 119
Arndt and Amelung *Einzelaufnahmen antiker Sculpturen* (EA.):
527 — 72
2700, 2 — 167
*Art Bulletin:*
9, 35, 51 — 68
9, 321 — 214
25, 296, 2 — 133
*Art in America:*
29 p. 156 — 299
*Ashmolean Museum. Report of the Visitors:*
1943 pl. 1 — 110
*Athenische Mitteilungen,* see Mitteilungen.
*Atti della Pontificia Accademia Romana:*
14 pl. 10 — 117
p. 196-7 — 142
224 — 117
225, 3 — 120
226 — 117
231 — 157
15 pl. 2 a — 188
2 c — 218
p. 258 — 152
*Atti e memorie della R. Deputazione di Storia patria per la Romagna:*
5 pl. 3 — 40
5, 5 — 208
5, 7 — 130
Aurigemma *Il R. Museo di Spina* (ed. 1):
opp. p. 1 — 191
p. 51, 2 — 265
97, ii, 1 — 194
ii, 2 — 194
ii, 3 — 193
ii, 4 — 193
ii, 5 — 192
iii, 6 — 194
99 — 193
101, 6 — 118, 305
101, 9 — 188
102 — 118
105, i, 2 — 185
i, 3 — 177
i, 4 — 178
i, 5 — 177
ii, 3 — 177

Aurigemma (*cont.*):
ii, 5 — 186
iii, 1 — 274
iii, 3 — 178, 186
iii, 4 — 186
iii, 5 — 273
106 — 177
107, 1 — 177
107, 2 — 177
108 — 177
109, 2 — 178, 185
111, i, 3 — 232
i, 8 — 232
ii, 3 — 186
ii, 5 — 186
111 below — 194
111 below — 262
111 below, mid. — 178
112 — 178
113, i — 186
113, ii — 186
126, i, 2 — 256
ii, 1 — 238
9 — 253
205 — 60

Aurigemma *Il R. Museo di Spina* (ed. 2):
p. 51, 2 — 265
107, ii, 1 — 194
ii, 2 — 194
ii, 3 — 193
ii, 4 — 193
ii, 5 — 192
ii, 6 — 194
109 — 119
111 — 193
112, below, mid. — 178
113, 6 — 118, 305
9 — 188
114 — 118
119, i, 2 — 256
ii, 1 — 238
9 — 232
123, i, 2 — 185
i, 3 — 177, 178
i, 5 — 177
ii, 2 — 186
ii, 5 — 186
iii, 1 — 274
iii, 3 — 178, 186
iii, 4 — 186
iii, 5 — 273
124 — 177
125, 1 — 177
125, 2 — 177
126 — 177
127, 1 — 178
127, 2 — 185
131 — 177, 179
133, i, 3 — 232
i, 9 — 232
ii, 3 — 186
mid. — 186
below — 194
below — 262
134 — 178

135, 1 — 186
237 — 60

*Ausonia*:
2 p. 243, b — 41
252 — 41
257-9 — 41
5 pl. 5 — 88
p. 33 — 70
52, ab — 265
119 — 90-1
120-1 — 90-1
122, 4 — 88
127 — 90-1
145 — 90-1
7 pl. 2-3 — 130
p. 117 — 130
10 p. 89-93 — 133, 182
95 — 163
96, 1 — 169
96, 2 — 170
96, 3 — 170

Babelon and Blanchet *Catalogue des bronzes antiques de la Bibliothèque Nationale.*
Baur *Catalogue of the Rebecca Darlington Stoddard Collection of Greek and Italian Vases in Yale University.*
Baur *Centaurs*:
pl. 9, 176 — 16
Beardsley *The Negro*:
p. 28, 8 — 187
Beazley *Attic Black-figure: a Sketch* [*ABS.*]:
pl. 4 — 1
7 — 137
Beazley *The Lewes House Collection of Ancient Gems* [*LHG.*]:
pl. 3, 37 — 138
3, 41 — 138
9, 41 — 138
A, 3 — 4
A, 19 — 138
A, 20 — 138
Beazley and Ashmole *Greek Sculpture and Painting*:
fig. 57 — 4
Beazley and Magi *La raccolta Benedetto Guglielmi nel Museo Gregoriano Etrusco* [*RG.*]. See under the museum (G) numbers.
Behn *Die Ficoronische Cista*:
pl. 2, 2 — 33
Benndorf *Die Antiken von Zürich*:
pl. 7, 73 — 275
7, 80 — 264

Benndorf *Griechische und sicilische Vasenbilder*:
pl. 12, 7 — 157
Benndorf and Niemann *Das Heroon von Gjölbaschi-Trysa*:
pl. 10 — 57
*Berichte der Sächsischen Gesellschaft der Wissenschaften*:
1867 pl. 5, 5 — 47
*Berliner Museen*:
1934, 1-2 — 208, 235
3 — 274
5 — 209
9 — 209
Bernhard *Wazy Greckie w Muzeum Im. E. Majewskiego w Warszawie*:
pl. 13, 2 — 176
Bieber *Die Denkmäler zum Theaterwesen*:
pl. 80, 2 — 41
Bieber *The History of the Greek and Roman Theater*:
p. 271, 365 — 41
Bieńkowski *Die Darstellungen der Gallier in der hellenistischen Kunst* [*D.*]:
p. 30 — 128
Bieńkowski *Les Celtes dans les arts mineurs gréco-romains* [*C.*]:
pll. 8-9 — 67
p. 142, 212 — 212
213 — 212
143 — 212
144 — 212
145 — 212
146, 217 — 212
219 — 212
220 — 212
148, 225 — 212
226 — 212
149 — 213
*Bildertafeln des Etruskischen Museums*:
pl. 19, 1 — 87
19, 2 — 87
19, 3 — 87
20 — 87
21 — 87
22 — 87
23, 1 — 87
23, 2 — 87
24, 1 — 87
25, 1 — 87
25, 2 — 87
26, 1 — 87
26, 2 — 87
27 — 87
49, 1 — 19
49, 2 — 18

51, 2 — 111
52 — 149-51
53, 1 — 135, 161
53, 2 — 87
54 — 87
55, 1 — 86
55, 2 — 87
56, 1 — 281
83, 2 — 89
83, 3 — 50
108, 1 — 154
Birch *History of Ancient Pottery* (1873):
165, 117 — 251
*Bollettino d'Arte*:
1908 p. 368 — 159
1909 p. 189 — 183
1916, 352, part — 73
,, — 74
,, — 77
,, — 78
,, — 80
,, — 107
,, — 107
,, — 107
354-5 — 80
356 — 73
357 — 77
359, 1 — 106
359, 2 — 106
359, 3 — 106
360 — 107
363 — 70
364 — 78
365 — 92-6
368 — 159
1919 p. 179-83 — 49
1922-3, i, p. 23-5 — 127, 130
27, 5 — 127
28-9 — 124
31 & 34-5 — 124
1927 p. 320, 23 — 100
1935-6 p. 248, 1 — 118
1937-8 p. 149-51 — 97
*Bollettino dell' Associazione Internazionale degli Studi Mediterranei* [*Boll. st. med.*]:
4, 4-5 pl. 1, 17 — 201
1, 18 — 176
1, 19 — 203
1, 22 — 259
pl. 2, 1 — 243
5 — 243
6 — 245
11 — 184
14 — 243
16 — 242
17 — 242
18 — 242
19 — 263
20 — 263
21 — 270
22 — 222
23 — 234

*Bollettino d. Assoc. (cont.)*:
24 173
27 243
28 245
30 185
32 243
36 204
38 204
39 175
5, 4–5 pl. 1, 1 261
3 261
3b 262
8 271
10 253
13 243
17 241
18 244
19 239
21 259
26 235
38 236
2, 1 261
3 261
3b 261
7 271
20 259
3, 10 253
11 253
12 265
14 242
15 242
17 241
18 244
4, 19 239
5, 14 242
34 238
37 206
38 235
39 247
45 245
46 245
6, 26 236
30 242
31 242
34 238
37, 1. 206
7, 45 245
46 245
12, 21 259,271
22 259
14, 20 259
21 259
22 259
26 274
15 242
16, 24 271
22, 3 241
5 244
8 242
*Bonner Jahrbücher*:
120 p. 180 179
Brants *Description of the Ancient Pottery preserved in the . . . Museum of Archaeology of Leiden.*

Breccia *La necropoli di Sciatbi*:
pl. 49, 76 257
77 257
79 257
83 257
50, 84 257
51, 91 260
53, 103 257
55, 111 236
113 236
114 236
115 236
59, 135 272
*British Museum Quarterly*:
4 pl. 15, b 11
Brogi, photograph:
13657, part 126
,, 128
,, 128
,, 128
,, 129
,, 129
,, 130
,, 202
,, 203
,, 203
Brunn *I rilievi delle urne etrusche*:
1 pl. 32, 1 84
61, 2 90–1
(continued by Körte, q.v.)
Brunn *Kleine Schriften*:
iii p. 65 42
*Brunn - Bruckmann's Denkmäler griechischer und römischer Sculptur*:
pl. 673, A 297
Bulanda *Katalog der griechischen Vasen im . . . Museum zu Sarajevo*:
p. 39, 54 76
Bulas *Les Illustrations antiques de l'Iliade*:
fig. 24 90–1
27 88
29 90–1
30 90–1
31 195
*Bulletin de correspondance hellénique [BCH.]*:
1895 p. 98, 3 109
98, 4 109
1911 pl. 7, 65 227
7, 66 227
8, 42 227
8, 46 227
8, 98 223
9, 128 219
9, 129 219
9, 137 220
9, 139 220
9, 140 219
9, 141 219

9, 146 220
9, 149 224
9, 150 223
9, 151 223
9, 152 223
9, 154 219
9, 165 224
9, 174 220
9, 178 227
9, 179 227
1935 p. 283 287
*Bulletin of the Museum of Fine Arts Boston*:
20 p. 74, ab 197
26 p. 47, 9 138
40 p. 53 299
*Bulletin of the Metropolitan Museum of Art*:
6 p. 213, 6 57
7 p. 97, 5 74
20 p. 301 11
34 p. 231, r. 167
*Bulletin of the University Museum*:
11 pl. 9, 5 306
*Bulletin van de Vereeniging tot Bevordering der Kennis van de antike Beschaving te 's Gravenhage*:
2, i p. 9, 1 212
9, 2 212
1939 p. 7 16
13 12–13
*Bullettino degli Annali dell' Instituto.*
*Bullettino della Commissione Archeologica Comunale di Roma [Bull. Com.]*:
1875 pl. 6–8, 14 176
6–8, 19 205
1911 p. 69 and 71 173
1912 p. 81 176
*Bullettino Italiano*:
1 pl. 1, 1 289
*Bullettino Archeologico Napolitano [Bull. Nap.]*:
n.s. 2 pl. 7, 4–5 249
3 pl. 3 147
14 104
4 pl. 10, 1–2 265
5 pl. 3, 11 265
6 pl. 5, 1 42
*Burlington Fine Arts Club. Exhibition of Ancient Greek Art, 1903*:
pl. 100, M 27 138
Buschor *Das Kriegertum der Parthenonzeit*:
p. 44 297

*Catalogue des antiquités . . . le tout composant la Collection Théâtrale de M.*

*Jules Sambon, Paris, 1–3 mai 1911*:
pl. 1, 16 300
*Catalogue des objets d'art dépendant de la succession Alessandro Castellani. Rome, 17 mars–10 avril 1884*:
pl. 3, 1 118
4, 1 294
4, 139 289
p. 22 117
*Catalogue des Objets d'Art et de Curiosité . . . 19–20 mai 1930*:
p. 13, 38 168
*A Catalogue of the Contents of Singleton Abbey, Swansea, 13–19 October 1919*:
pl., no. 714 144
[Newton and Birch] *A Catalogue of the Greek and Etruscan Vases in the British Museum (1851–70)*:
i pl. 3, 87 236
10, 307 278
10, 320 279
ii pl. 10, 319 252
*Catalogue . . . Sotheby*, see Sotheby.
*Cambridge Ancient History*:
plate i p. 343, a 296
343, b 197
4 pl. 38, 1 205
38, 11 222
46, 4 308
Chabouillet *Description des antiquités composant le cabinet de M. Louis Fould*:
pl. 19 179
*Charites Friedrich Leo dargebracht*:
pl. 1, 10 170
*Clara Rhodos*:
2, 141, 19, 1 178
145, 24, 1 260
147, 25, 2 239
160, 1 260
3, 207, r. mid. 178
253 265
6–7, 176 73
Clerc *Massalia*:
p. 313 201
*Collection d'Antiquités Grecques de Monsieur E. G[eladakis], Paris 19–20 mai 1904*:
pl. 2, 53 191
*Collection du Dr. B[ourguignon] et de M. C[anessa], Paris, 19–21 mars 1910*:
pl. 24, 200 155

Collection Raoul Waroc-
  qué:
  i p. 52, 90          256
La Collezione Gagliardi:
  pl. 3, 1              58
Compte-rendu de la Com-
  mission Impériale Ar-
  chéologique [CR.]:
  1876 pl. 2, 1        83
  1880 p. 9            236
       120             232
Conestabile I monumenti
  di Perugia etrusca e
  romana:
  iii pll. 6–22        124
Conestabile Monumenti
  della necropoli del Palazzone circostanti al sepolcro de' Volunni:
  pl. 13               280
     57                294
Conestabile Pitture murali
  ... scoperte in una necropoli presso Orvieto:
  pll. 15–6            52
     17                163
     18                163
  p. 161               77
Cook Zeus:
  2 p. 461             161
  3 pl. 41             105
     65, 1             203
     65, 2             203
  p. 247               138
     258, 171          81
     424               146
     511               105
     513               104
     514               104
     516               104
     787               200
Corpus Inscriptionum
  Etruscarum [CIE.]:
  no. 8050             245
      8179             106
      8180             106
Corpus Inscriptionum Latinarum [CIL.]:
  1, 2² no. 435        274
         439           215
         440           210
         441           210
         442           215
         443           216
         444           210
         445           210
         446           210
         447           216
         449           216
         450           210
         451           216
         452           216
         453           210
  x no 258             216
  xi, ii, 1 no. 6700, 1  276
              1a       277

              1d       277
              2a       276
              2b       277
              2c       277
              2f       276
              2g       275
              22       246
  xi no. 67054         274
  xv no. 4946          246
         6087          274
Corpus Vasorum Anti-
  quorum [CV.].
Cultrera Una statua di
  Ercole:
  pll. 1–4             142
Curtius Die Wandmalerei
  Pompejis:
  p. 311               92
     313               92
Cypriote and Classical
  Antiquities, Duplicates
  of the Cesnola and other
  Collections, New York,
  Anderson Galleries,
  March – April 1928.
  [Cypr. Ant.]:
  i p. 80, 316         286
     317               286

Dall' Osso Guida illustrata
  del Museo Nazionale di
  Ancona:
  p. 235, ab.          250
     256               264
Dalton The Treasure of the
  Oxus²:
  pl. 28 p. 199–200    215
Daremberg, Saglio, and
  Pottier Dictionnaire des
  antiquités grecques et
  romaines [D.S.]:
  s.v. acus, fig. 102  299
      Alcestis, fig. 211  133
      askos, fig. 574  276
      Charon, fig. 1357  39
      diptychon, fig. 2460
                       214
      elephas, fig. 2623 212
        ,,      2627 214
      poculum          216
Dawkins The Sanctuary
  of Artemis Orthia:
  pl. 100              97
  pl. 130, 1           137
  pl. 131, 3           137
Déchelette La Collection
  Millon:
  pl. 30               249
  pl. 31          219, 248
  p. 107               249
  121, 1               249
Déchelette Manuel d'ar-
  chéologie préhistorique:
  2, 3, 1068, 1–2      249
Dedalo:
  5 p. 408             194

              409      193
              411      192
              413      193
  6 p. 26              153
    155–6              171
  9 p. 342, 2          265
  13 p. 274            249
     275               249
     276               250
     277               260
Delattre Carthage: Nécro-
  pole punique ... juillet–
  décembre 1898:
  pl. vii, 4, 4        176
Delbrueck Die Consular-
  diptychen:
  pl. 59               214
Della Seta L'Italia antica¹:
  p. 152, 162, 1       207
          2       238, 271
          4            217
          5            271
          6            217
  p. 243, 276          80
     381               169
Della Seta Museo di Villa
  Giulia.
Deltion, Arkhaiologikon:
  1 p. 24              45
Dempster De Etruria
  Regali:
  1 pl. 9, 1           58
Dennis Cities and Ceme-
  teries of Etruria:
  i p. 437             133
  ii, frontisp.        133
Deonna Délos xviii: le
  mobilier délien:
  pll. 21–5            67
Des Vergers, Noël L'Étru-
  rie et les Étrusques:
  pl. 4                42
     12                198
     15                13
     21                90
     28                90
Deubner Attische Feste:
  pl. 8, 3             109
     33, 1             109
Diepolder Die attischen
  Grabreliefs:
  pl. 6                45
Dinsmoor Observations on
  the Hephaisteion:
  p. 133, 59           72
     138, 22           72
Disney, see Museum Dis-
  neianum.
Dölger Ἰχθύς:
  pl. 135, 3           31
     136               31
Dohrn Die schwarz-
  figurigen etruskischen
  Vasen aus der zweiten
  Hälfte des sechsten Jahr-
  hunderts:

  pl. 2, 1             11
     2, 3              11
     2, 4              11
     3                 11
     5, 1              12
     5, 2              14
     6, 1              14
     6, 2              13
     7, 1              14
     7, 2              12
     7, 3              14
     7, 4              14
     8              2, 14
     9, 1              20
     9, 3              19
Ducati Storia della cera-
  mica antica [Cer.]:
  ii p. 466            88
     467               80
     470–1             120
     472               52
     473               124
     474               126
     475, 1            169
     475, 2            170
     475, 3            170
     483               210
     484               209
     532               291
     533               294
Ducati La Città di Misa:
  p. 13                89
     17, ab.           101
Ducati L'Italia antica:
  1 pl. 40             211
  p. 381               169
Ducati Pontische Vasen:
  pll. 1–2
Ducati Storia dell' arte
  etrusca [St.]:
  pl. 79 fig. 228      32
     104, 277–8        139
     129, 339          138
     142, 369, r.      205
     175, 447          47
     208, 516          57
     211, 520      50, 107
     213, 523          199
     215, 530          188
     215, 531          88
     216, 532          80
     217, 533          120
     217, 534          113
     218, 535          52
     219, 538          124
     220, 540          117
     224, 592          106
     244, 592          106
     250, 603      30, 110
     250, 605      30, 110
     250, 606–7        287
     251, 610          126
     251, 611, 1       128
     251, 611, 2       128
     251, 611, 3       122
     252, 612          294

Ducati *St.* (*cont.*):
252, 615 — 73
253, 617 — 169
260, 635 — 153
274, 662 — 166
278, 674 — 280
283, 684 — 291
284, 685, 1 — 287
2 — 292
3 — 286
4 — 290
5 — 294

Ebert *Reallexikon der Vorgeschichte*:
7 pl. 1 — 248
2, a — 249
*Elite des monuments céramographiques* [*El. cér.*], see Lenormant.
*Enciclopedia Italiana*:
Etruschi, pl. 95 — 80
96, 3 — 122
*Encyclopédie photographique de l'art: le Musée du Louvre* [*Enc. phot.*]:
iii. pl. 8, b — 60
64, a — 119
64, b — 192
103–7 — 90
223 — 304
Endt *Beiträge zur jonischen Vasenmalerei*:
pl. 1 — 17
pp. 29–31 — 17
*Ephemeris arkhaiologike*:
1897 pll. 9–10 — 134, 191
1938 p. 26, 2 — 265
Espérandieu *Recueil général des reliefs de la Gaule romaine*:
1 p. 199 — 68
297 — 99
Essen, van *Did Orphic Influence on Etruscan Tomb-paintings exist?*

Fairbanks *Catalogue of Greek and Etruscan Vases in the Museum of Fine Arts, Boston.*
Ferri *Divinità ignote*:
pl. 44 — 163
p. 163 — 170
Filow *Die archaische Nekropole von Trebenischte*:
p. 30 — 72
Fossing *The Thorvaldsen Museum. Catalogue of the Engraved Gems and Cameos.*
*Friends of the Fitzwilliam. Annual Report*:
1934 p. 3, 5 — 191
p. 3, 6 — 287

Fröhner *Collection de M. Albert B[arre]: Paris 16–18 mai 1878*:
p. 45 — 72
Fröhner *Collection Julien Gréau. Bronzes antiques*:
no. 80 — 263
nos. 216–21 — 283
no. 222 — 250, 283
*From the Collections of the Ny Carlsberg Glyptothek*:
1 p. 28 — 288
Funghini *Degli antichi vasi fittili arretini*:
pl. 1, 1 — 277
Furtwängler *Beschreibung der Vasensammlung im Antiquarium.*
Furtwängler *Die antiken Gemmen* [*AG.*]:
pl. 5, 34 — 96
16, 64 — 104
17, 32 — 138
19, 34 — 80
42, 14 — 165
61, 22 — 59
64, 38 — 139
Furtwängler *Kleine Schriften* [*KS.*]:
i pl. 7 — 92–3
8 — 63
ii p. 131–3 — 219
Furtwängler *La Collection Sabouroff*:
pl. 67 — 72
70, 3 — 235
Furtwängler *Olympia iv: die Bronzen.*
Furtwängler and Reichhold *Griechische Vasenmalerei* [*F.R.*]:
pl. 10 — 84, 89
21 — 1
38–9 — 36
41 — 36, 83
58 — 57
80, 4 — 272
87 — 76, 83
89 — 90
98 — 34, 61
103 — 189
109, 2 — 104
123 — 303
145 — 64
170, 1 — 200
172 — 83
175 — 164
177 — 33, 297
180, 2 — 38
i p. 51 — 82
ii p. 142, 43 — 84
142, 45 — 84
257, 90 — 40, 104
iii p. 57 — 56
317 — 264

Galli *Fiesole. Gli Scavi, il Museo Civico*:
p. 95, 76, 2 — 233
76, 3 — 267
Galli *Perugia: il Museo Funerario del Palazzone all' ipogeo dei Volumni*:
p. 42 — 280
43 — 280
143, 103, 2 — 274
144, 4 — 276
147 — 124
150–1 — 124
153 — 294
Gardiner, E. Norman *Athletics of the Ancient World*:
fig. 47 — 35
48 — 78–80
*Gazette archéologique*:
1879 pl. 3–5 — 6, 54
6, 1 — 253
2 — 254
3 — 234
4 — 247
6 — 254
8 — 234
9 — 188
10 — 253
*Gazette des Beaux-Arts*:
34 p. 244 — 210
Genick and Furtwängler *Griechische Keramik*:
pl. 25, 2 — 116
32, 3 — 272
Gerhard *Akademische Abhandlungen*:
pl. 5, 1 — 37
8, 4 — 138
19 — 43
Gerhard *Antike Bildwerke* [*AB.*]:
pl. 31 — 40, 104
Gerhard *Auserlesene Vasenbilder* [*AV.*]:
pl. 6 — 299
50 — 27
77 — 197
89, 1–2 — 65
89, 3–4 — 196
194 — 17
197 — 195
209 — 195
217 — 195
232–3 — 32
240 — 47
301 — 30
320, 1–2 — 154
320, 3–4 — 135, 161
321 — 3, 43–5
Gerhard *Etruskische Spiegel* [*ES.*]:
pl. 6–7 — 79
19, 3 — 121

19, 7 — 145
56, 1 — 199
58 — 199
64 — 59
66 — 61
68 — 146
74 — 76
80, 1 — 132
83 — 50, 106
111 — 131
117 — 46
118 — 49
119, 1 — 56
171 — 60, 80
180 — 82
189 — 116
196 — 131
213 — 166–7
223 — 199
224 — 59
240 — 47
255 — 199
257B — 131
290 — 81
362 — 82
363, 1 — 82
370 — 116
378 — 131
381 — 131
389 — 136
398 — 131
402 — 131
410, 2 — 116
supplement
pl. 31 — 106
34 — 131
35 — 114
60 — 61, 131
65 — 125
74 — 82
75 — 115
76 — 44, 116
77 — 116, 131
78 — 131
90 — 58
91, 2 — 58
96 — 59, 83
143, 2 — 146
151 — 131
154 — 83
p. 217 — 134
220 — 131
Gerhard *Festgedanken an Winckelmann*:
pl. 2, 1 — 47
Gerhard *Griechische und etruskische Trinkschalen des Königlichen Museums zu Berlin*:
pl. 16, 3–4 — 114
18, 1–2 — 210
C, 1 — 46
C, 4–5 — 46
C, 10 — 67
C, 13 — 46
C, 14 — 67

Gerhard *Trinkschalen und Gefässe des Königlichen Museums zu Berlin* [*TG.*]:
pl. 9, 1–2   56
10, 1–2   114
10, 3–4   114
29   164
30, 13–14   164
30, 15–16   164
Gervasio *Bronzi arcaici e ceramica geometrica del Museo di Bari:*
pl. 16, 1   136
Giglioli *L'arte etrusca:*
pl. 5   199
109–10   32, 63
130, 2   18
130, 3   14
130, 4   21
130, 5   16
131, 2   17, 49
131, 5   18
157, 2   136
188, 2   163
217, 1–2   139
218, 5   138
226, 4   59
237, 1   70
249, 4–5   32
257   189, 191
258, 5   189, 191
266–8   90–1
271   80
272, 1   106
272, 2   110
273, 2   92–6
274, 1   77
274, 2   77
274, 3   150
274, 4   78
275, 1   55
275, 2   114
275, 3   133
276, 1   113
276, 2–4   163
276, 5   160
277, 1   133
277, 2   124
277, 3   173
277, 4   147
278, 1   120, 154
278, 2   154
278, 3   154
278, 4   156
278, 5   191
278, 6   159
278, 7   160
279, 1   169
279, 2   136
279, 3   136
279, 4   170
280, 1 and 3   170
280, 2   170
280 4   37
280, 5   121
281, 1 and 3   188

281, 2   187
281, 4–6   117
284   57
291, 2   49
293, 2   49
296, 1–2   50, 106
298, 1   199
299, 2–3   131
299, 5   61
300   61
312, 1–2   188
313   279
314, 3   31, 110
333, 4   183
343   160
346, 2   153
348   90–1
372, 3   41
372, 4 and 6   218
373, 1   294
373, 2   294
Giraudon, photographs:
153   252
4005, c   23
4016, a   21
4016, b   21
4017F, b   147
8050–1   136
8147–9   133
16300   133
Goldscheider *Etruscan Sculpture:*
pl. 58   49
Gori *Museum Etruscum:*
ii, 4 pl. 8, 1   254
iii pl. 32   122
34   279
Gozzadini *Di ulteriori scoperte nell' antica necropoli a Marzabotto:*
pl. 14, 6   252
Graef and Langlotz *Die antiken Vasen von der Akropolis zu Athen.*
*Griechische Altertümer aus dem Besitze des Herrn A. Vogell, Karlsruhe* [*Sg. Vogell*]:
pl. 6, 41   268
p. 40, 17, b   244
Guthrie *Orpheus and Greek Religion:*
pl. 5   40

Hadaczek *Der Ohrschmuck der Griechen und Etrusker:*
35, 62   54
35, 63   117
Haeberlin *Aes grave:*
pl. 68, 25   259
Hagemann *Griechische Panzerung:*
p. 149, 162–3   49
Hambidgè *Dynamic Symmetry: the Greek Vase:*

p. 62, 3   242
162   287
Hamdy Bey and T. Reinach *Une Nécropole royale à Sidon:*
pl. 29   57
Hancarville *Collection of Etruscan Greek and Roman Antiquities from the Cabinet of the Honble Wm Hamilton:*
1 pll. 107–8   264
2 pll. 98–9   272
4 pll. 34–5   191
*Handbook of the Classical Collection,* see Richter.
Hartwig *Die griechischen Meisterschalen:*
pl. 9   189
26   139
68   4
73   26
*Harvard Studies:*
11 pl. 2   139–40
*Hauptwerke aus den Staatlichen Museen:*
pl. 10   228
Helbig *Untersuchungen:*
p. 367   160
Héléna *Les Origines de Narbonne:*
p. 404   225
405   225
Herrmann *Denkmäler der Malerei des Altertums:*
pl. 107   235
*Hesperia:*
3 pl. 3   235
p. 320, 6   116
341, B 31   272
348, C 7   241
371, D 7–8   243
396, E 49   241
422–3   235
426, E 157   241
436, E 33   244
437, C 7   241
4 p. 301, 49   109
480, 8   72
501   72
502, 8   72
6 p. 293, 151   309
12 p. 359, a   242
Heydemann *Mittheilungen aus den Antikensammlungen in Ober- und Mittelitalien:*
pl. 4, 3   252
p. 4   146
Hirschfeld *Athena und Marsyas:*
pll. 1–2   76
Hirth *Formenschatz:*
1902 no. 2   188
Holwerda *Het laatgrieksche en romeinsche*

*Gebruiksaardewerk . . . in het Rijksmuseum van Oudheden te Leiden.*
Hoppin *A Handbook of Attic Red-figured Vases:*
2 p. 41   164
123   105
477   40
Hoppin *A Handbook of Greek Black-figured Vases:*
p. 95   101

Imhoof-Blumer and Keller *Tier- und Pflanzenbilder auf Münzen und Gemmen:*
pl. 4, 1   213
4, 4   212
4, 5   214
19, 43   214
Inghirami *Etrusco Museo Chiusino:*
pl. 52, 1   276
88   114
103   25
160   202
161   14, 22
200–2   28
Inghirami *Monumenti etruschi o di etrusco nome:*
5 pl. 3, 1–285   118
3, 3–4   205
4, 1   29
4, 2 and 4   28
5, 3 and 5   130
47, 4   254
48, 7   274
48, 9   274
48, 13   237
48, 18   263
49, 11   240
49, 13   253
49, 20   234
50, 8   247
50, 18   234
55, 7   113
55, 8   56, 68
Inghirami *Pitture di vasi etruschi* [*Inghirami*]:
pl. 13   121
67   122
100, 1   129
100, 2   129
127   167
130   129
131   122
185   116
188   154
189   147
271   120
351   191
357   125
358   127, 129, 130
396–7   136
398–9   136

Jacobsthal *Aktaions Tod:*
p. 15    136
Jacobsthal *Die melischen Reliefs:*
pl. 7    82
p. 87    39
Jacobsthal *Early Celtic Art* [*ECA.*]:
pl. 219, c    84
220, a    249
220, b    249
220, c    249
Jacobsthal *Göttinger Vasen:*
pl. 1, 5–6    14
2, 3    11
2, 4    11
2, 9    218
3, 8    14
19, 56    86
20, 54    100
20, 58    106
21, 59    68
p. 9, 10    218
Jacobsthal *Ornamente griechischer Vasen* [*O.*]:
pl. 55, b    36
57, c–d    29
84    111
114    223
115, c–d    87
127, c    45
139, a    45
144, a    87
147    88
148    156
149    122
Jacobsthal and Langsdorff *Die Bronzeschnabelkannen:*
pl. 14, a    266
31, a    265
33    248
34, c    248
Jacquemart *Histoire de la céramique:*
p. 251    205
252    254
Jaennicke *Grundriss der Keramik:*
p. 22, 5    254
22, 6    205
Jahn *Archäologische Beiträge:*
pll. 3–6    37
Jahn *Telephos Troilos und kein Ende:*
pl. 1    66
3    179
Jahn *Vasenbilder:*
pl. 2    37, 178
3    37
*Jahrbuch des Deutschen Archäologischen Instituts* [*Jb.*]:

1 pp. 211–12    13, 163
3 p. 252    64
11 p. 194    77
196, 51    112
196, 52    112
197    116
15 p. 217    214
24 pl. 9    99
p. 136    295
25 p. 132    63
26 p. 4    235
27 p. 154    157
29 p. 240    13
34 p. 133    109
40, 157, 65    37
41 pl. 5    296
43 pll. 10–11    197
p. 331–5    197
342    198
343–4    195
345, 13–14    195
345, 15–16    195
346, 17    197
346, 18    197
347, 19    196
347, 20    196
348    198
349    196
350    198
351    198
352    196
353    197
356    202
45 p. 65    90–1
67, 3    90–1
67, 5    90–1
69, 6    88
52 p. 61    74
Bericht pl. 5, 1    136
55 p. 235    265
56 Bericht pl. 46    301
*Jahreshefte des Oesterreichischen Archäologischen Institutes* [*Jh.*]:
6 p. 140    49
7 p. 73    157
74    157
8 p. 145    38
243, 56    306
9 p. 100    55
10 pl. 7    144
p. 118    36
13 pll. 7–10    17
pp. 157–9    18
16 p. 167    52
28 p. 67    57
*Japigia:*
1 p. 257, 5    307
9 p. 3, 1    245
*Journal of Hellenic Studies* [*JHS.*]:
11 pl. 6    105
14 p. 117    11
25 p. 126, 7    309
43 pl. 6    16
pp. 171–2    16

50 pl. 1    3, 25
2    26
58, 138, 18, 1    265
59 pll. 2–4    76
*Journal of the Royal Anthropological Institute:*
67 pl. 24, 3    280
24, 4–5    278
25, 4    264
28, 3    289
*Journal of the Walters Art Gallery:*
3 p. 110    2, 14
134    64–5
136    145
138    142
*Junta Superior* see Visedo Molto.

*Katalog einer Sammlung griechischer und italischer Vasen aus dem Nachlasse des Freiherrn Ferdinand von Leesen:*
pl. 5, 13    173
Kekule *Die Geburt der Helena aus dem Ei* [*G.*]:
all    39–40
Kekulé *Ueber ein griechisches Vasengemälde im Akademischen Kunstmuseum zu Bonn* [*U.*]:
all    39–40
Keller *Die antike Tierwelt:*
i, 93, 34    306
Klumbach *Tarentiner Grabkunst:*
beil. A, 42    146
Körte *Göttinger Bronzen:*
pl. 14    283
16    250
Körte *I rilievi delle urne etrusche:*
ii pl. 3, 1    141
28, 3    54
29, 4    54
29, 5    54
29, 5a    54
30, 6    54
112, 5    63
114, 4    57
118    67
126, 8    57
Kondakov and Tolstoi *Antiquités de la Russie méridionale:*
p. 427    212
*Kunstbesitz eines bekannten norddeutschen Sammlers: München, Helbing, 22 Feb. 1910:*
pl. 17, 764    187
18, 819    84, 135

19, 774    23
20, 830    173
Kunze *Kretische Bronzereliefs:*
pl. 54, b    96

La Blanchère, du Coudray, and Gauckler *Catalogue du Musée Alaoui:*
pl. 42, 216    277
La Borde *Collection de vases grecs de M. le comte de Lamberg:*
1 pl. 56    95
60    72
2 pl. 26, 2    51
Lamb *Greek and Roman Bronzes:*
pl. 41, b    139
Langlotz, see Graef and Langlotz.
Langlotz *Martin von Wagner-Museum der Universität Würzburg: Griechische Vasen.*
Lapeyre and Pellegrin *Carthage punique:*
pl. 7, iv, 4    176
Lau, Brunn, and Krell *Die griechischen Vasen* [*Lau*]:
pl. 35    84
Leesen, see *Katalog.*
Lenormant and de Witte *Élite des monuments céramographiques* [*El. cér.*]:
1 pl. 15    147
88    146
90    223
2 pl. 66    75
68    95
102    136
3 pl. 25    107
4 pl. 81    68
Leroux *Vases grecs du Musée Archéologique de Madrid.*
Levi, Alda *Le terrecotte figurate del Museo Nazionale di Napoli.*
Levi, Doro *Il Museo Civico di Chiusi:*
p. 46    67
119, part    252
125, part    169
,,    170
,,    170
,,    171
,,    232
,,    233
,,    233
,,    254
,,    281
,,    281

Levi, *Civico di Chiusi* (*cont.*):
„  285
„  285
„  286
Levi, Doro *Il R. Museo Archeologico di Firenze nel suo futuro ordinamento:*
pl. 8, 4  154
Libertini *Il Museo Biscari.* See under the museum numbers (Catania).
Licht *Sittengeschichte Griechenlands:*
3 p. 92  101
Lindenschmit *Alterthümer unserer heidnischen Vorzeit:*
iii part 7, text to pl.
1, 2  223
iii, 12 pl. 4, 1  249
Lipperheide *Antike Helme:*
pl. 154  83
Lippold *Gemmen und Kameen:*
pl. 37, 8  104
Longpérier *Musée Napoléon III:*
pl. 59  11
Lücken *Greek Vase Paintings:*
pl. 26  61
29  101
Lullies *Antike Kleinkunst in Königsberg, Pr.*

Maiuri *La Casa del Menandro:*
pl. 14  83
Mansell, photographs:
778  215
3258  92
3271  144
Marshall and Foucher *The Monuments of Sanchi:*
2 pl. 12  214
Martha *L'art étrusque:*
p. 94  252
359  166
489, 325  232
489, 328  253
489, 330  247
491  248
493  294
495  291
496  280
Masner *Die Sammlung antiker Vasen und Terracotten im K.K. Oesterreich. Museum.*
Matthies *Die praenestinischen Spiegel:*
p. 73  58
79  58

87  82
113  83
Mayer *Apulien:*
pl. 38, 9  273
38, 10  273
38, 16  273
40, 13  273
*Mededeelingen van het Nederlandsch Historisch Instituut te Rome:*
7 pl. 2, 1  19
2, 2  14
*Mélanges d'archéologie et d'histoire:*
8 pl. 12  214
30 pl. 2  210
3  210
p. 101  207
37 p. 114  55
116  55
117  62
119  62
126  52
127  54
132  52
133  54
141–7  33
148  36
149  36
152–3  44
154–5  47
158  47
159  47
162–3  69
165  50–1
168  37
169  37
171  37
173, 1  48
173, 2  48, 297
175  46
*Mélanges Nicole:*
pll. 1–2  219
*Memoirs of the American Academy in Rome:*
17 pl. 6, 8  309
*Memorie della R. Accademia dei Lincei:* see Mingazzini.
Mercklin *Hamburgisches Museum: Griechische und römische Altertümer:*
pl. 31, 2  174
Merlin and Drappier *La Nécropole punique d'Ard-el-Kheraïb à Carthage:*
pl. 4, 29  273
Messerschmidt *Nekropolen von Vulci:*
pll. 27–39  90
p. 99, l.  208, 235
*Metropolitan Museum Studies:*
5 p. 125, 7  127

[Micacchi] *Sculptures antiques en Libye:*
pl. 14  134
Micali *Monumenti inediti:*
pl. 36, 2  15, 18
37, 1  18, 146
37, 2  46
38, 1–2  53–4
40  172
Micali *Storia degli antichi popoli italiani:*
pl. 60  166
92  295
101, 7, ab.  24
101, 7, below  24
101, 8  24
101, 9  24
101, 14  276
Milani *Monumenti scelti del R. Museo Archeologico di Firenze:*
pl. 5, 12  252
5, 13  266
p. 14, 4  266
Milani *Museo Topografico dell' Etruria:*
p. 6  252
p. 49, i, 1  78
i, 3  77
iii, 1  52
iii, l.  188
iii, mid.  163
iv, 2  163
foot, r.  294
p. 52, i, 1  260
i, 2  290
i, 3  286
i, 4  290
i, 5  260
ii, 2  290
ii, 3  287
ii, 4  290
iii, part  233
„  234
p. 101, r.  252
p. 111  248
Milani *Il R. Museo Archeologico di Firenze:*
pl. 10, 8  291
43, 2  33
44  251
92, iii, 1  52
92, iii, mid.  163
92, iv, 2  163
Minervini *Illustrazione di un antico vaso di Ruvo:*
pll. 1–2  80
Mingazzini *Le rappresentazioni vascolari del mito dell' apoteosi di Herakles:*
pl. 9, 1  70
Mingazzini *Vasi della Collezione Castellani:*
pl. 65  141

Minns *Scythians and Greeks:*
p. 326  299
391  83
Mirone *Mirone d'Eleutere:*
fig. 48  76
*Mitteilungen des Deutschen Archäologischen Instituts, Athenische Abteilung [AM.]:*
11 p. 87  96
92  96
22 p. 362  31
26 p. 76  242
96  207
39 pp. 163–4  136
54 p. 45, 2  244
62 pl. 25  72
28  45, 72
*Mitteilungen des Deutschen Archäologischen Instituts, Roemische Abteilung [RM.]:*
2 pl. 10  73
p. 234  73
3 p. 159  17
176  17
180, 9–10  13
30 p. 132  114
134  113
135  113
137  113
139  114
141  141
142  114
144  114
147–51  120, 132
152  122
154  131
155  10
157  132
158, 19  128
158, 20  129
Beil. 13  131
42 p. 120  125, 132
121  127, 129, 130
Beil. 24  51
43 p. 157  132
45 pl. 82  72
46 pl. 3  294
4  294
5, a  294
5, b  294
6, a  294
6, b  294
48 pl. 1–18  89
52 pl. 27, 1  122, 132
27, 2  128
28, 1  128
28, 2  128
29  128
30, 1  128
31, 1  128
31, 2  128
pp. 126–7  122, 132

*Mitteilungen* [*RM.*](*cont.*):

| | |
|---|---|
| 129 | 88 |
| 132 | 129 |
| 133 | 129 |
| 185 | 80 |
| 55 p. 79 | 288 |
| 57 p. 183, 15, 1 | 265 |
| 191, 18 | 280 |
| 191, 19 | 280 |

*Mnemosyne*:

| | |
|---|---|
| 1934 pl. 1, 2 | 273 |

Möbius *Die Ornamente der griechischen Grabstelen*:

| | |
|---|---|
| pl. 5, b | 45 |

Moll *Das Schiff in der bildenden Kunst*:

| | |
|---|---|
| Bvib 51 | 219 |

Montelius *La Civilisation primitive en Italie*:

| | |
|---|---|
| pl. 103, 10 | 266 |
| 111, 6 | 279 |
| 111, 8 | 130 |
| 152, 10 | 250 |
| 205 | 299 |
| 235, 7 | 114 |

*Monumenti antichi pubblicati per cura della Reale Accademia dei Lincei* [*M.L.*]:

| | |
|---|---|
| 1 pl. 9, 20 | 101 |
| 8 pl. 5 | 130 |
| 9 pl. 4, 7 | 264 |
| 4, 8 | 250 |
| 4, 14 | 260 |
| 4, 16 | 245 |
| 4, 19 | 260 |
| 5, 12 | 234 |
| 5, 20 | 260 |
| 9, 1 | 238 |
| 9, 5 | 260 |
| 10, 6 | 232 |
| 10, 15 | 260 |
| 10, 18 | 245 |
| 11, 10 | 260 |
| 11, 13 | 245 |
| 11, 14 | 245 |
| 11, 15 | 237 |
| 11, 16 | 237 |
| 11, 20 | 245 |
| 15 | 260 |
| p. 695 | 239 |
| 10 pl. 5, 9 | 208 |
| 13, a | 136 |
| 14 pl. 1 | 75 |
| p. 31 | 75 |
| 34 | 75 |
| 38 | 75 |
| 18 p. 266 | 297 |
| 20 p. 115, 88 | 228 |
| 138, 106, c | 234 |
| 139, 106, a | 247 |
| 471, mid. | 89 |
| 22 pl. 70, 8 | 20, 295 |
| 104, 5, 6 | 256 |
| 105, 5, 3 | 178 |
| 109, 1 | 222 |
| 109, 2 | 229 |
| 109, 3 | 222 |
| 23 pl. 1-2 | 199 |
| 3-4 | 199 |
| 3 | 131 |
| 4 | 117 |
| p. 290 | 199 |
| 635 | 117 |
| 638, 3 | 117 |
| 639 | 117 |
| 642 | 174 |
| 650-1 | 287 |
| 24 pl. 24, 42 | 16 |
| 24, 43 | 16 |
| 25, 43 | 16 |
| 25, 44 | 14 |
| 26 | 163 |
| 27, 46 | 64 |
| 27, 47 | 187 |
| p. 399 | 163 |
| 400 | 163 |
| 863 | 264 |
| 871, 2 | 244 |
| 871, 3 | 244 |
| 24 (Galli) pl. 1 | 90-1 |
| p. 11, 3, 7 | 120 |
| 11, 9 | 288 |
| 14, 15 | 264 |
| 17, 12 | 120 |
| 18, 1 | 264 |
| 35-50 | 90-1 |
| 38, 21 | 90-1 |
| 30 p. 495 | 18 |
| 647, ii, i | 196 |
| 683, ab. | 181 |
| 33 pl. 32, 60, 3 | 24 |
| 36 p. 482, 1 | 67 |
| 482, 2 | 67 |
| 486 | 117 |
| 487, l. | 72, 210 |
| 487, r. | 210 |
| 37 pl. 35, 1 | 262 |
| 35, 2 | 262 |
| 35, 3 | 263 |
| 35, 5 | 271 |
| 35, 7 | 262 |
| 35, 10 | 269 |
| 35, 14 | 273 |
| 35, 15 | 238 |
| 36, 1 | 262 |
| 36, 3 | 238 |
| 36, 4 | 257 |
| 36, 5 | 259 |
| 36, 7 | 271 |
| 37, 4 | 243 |
| 37, 5 | 243 |
| 37, 7 | 243 |
| 37, 9 | 245 |
| 37, 16 | 243 |
| 37, 18 | 241 |
| 37, 21-2 | 245 |
| 38, 10 | 259 |
| 39, 1 | 241 |
| 40, 4 | 269 |
| 40, 5 | 261 |
| 40, 6 | 262 |
| 40, 7 | 262 |
| 40, 12 | 259 |
| 40, 14 | 261 |

*Monumenti inediti pubblicati dall' Instituto di Corrispondenza Archeologica* [*Mon.*]:

| | |
|---|---|
| 2 pl. 8 | 136 |
| 9 | 136 |
| 35 | 34 |
| 37 | 80 |
| 49 | 147 |
| 50 | 17 |
| 55, a | 37 |
| 4 pl. 16 | 65 |
| 34 | 110 |
| 5 pl. 9, 2 | 124 |
| 12 | 34 |
| 15-16 | 2, 49, 59 |
| 25 | 49 |
| 41 | 54 |
| 56 | 195 |
| 6-7 pl. 61-4 | 90 |
| 70 | 36 |
| 8 pl. 2 | 157 |
| 9 | 89 |
| 31 | 49 |
| 42 | 75 |
| 9 pl. 15, 2 | 89 |
| 22-3 | 131 |
| 29 | 49 |
| 26, 1 | 289 |
| 26, 2 | 288 |
| 26, 3 | 291 |
| 26, 4 | 291 |
| 26, 5 | 291 |
| 10 pl. 51 | 92-3 |
| 11 pl. 4-5, 1 | 9, 170 |
| 4-5, 2 | 9, 170 |
| 4-5, 13 | 9, 169 |
| 1855 pl. 12-3 | 53 |
| 18 | 57 |
| 1856 pl. 20 | 60 |

*Monumenti della Pittura Antica scoperti in Italia:* [*MPAI.*]:

| | |
|---|---|
| Clus. i pll. 1-4, &c. | 49,59 |
| Tarqu. i p. 19 | 119 |

*Monuments des Nouvelles annales*:

| | |
|---|---|
| pll. 5-6 | 84 |

*Monuments et mémoires: Fondation Piot* [*Mon. Piot*]:

| | |
|---|---|
| 9 pl. 16 | 236 |
| 21 p. 193 | 212 |
| 194 | 212 |
| 29 pl. 5 | 38 |

Moscioni, photographs:

| | |
|---|---|
| 8259 | 143, 216 |
| 8590 | 150 |
| 8591 | 173 |
| 8591, 2 | 147 |
| 10581, 1 | 285 |
| 10581, 2 | 286 |
| 10581, 3 | 285 |
| — | 67 |
| — | 67 |

Moses *A Collection of Antique Vases*:

| | |
|---|---|
| pl. 13 | 72 |

Moses *Vases from the Collection of Sir Henry Englefield, Bart.*:

| | |
|---|---|
| pl. 31, 4 | 220 |
| 33, 1 | 219 |

*Münchener Jahrbuch der bildenden Kunst*:

| | |
|---|---|
| 12 p. 121 | 251 |

*Musée Alaoui: supplément i*:

| | |
|---|---|
| pl. 102, 3 | 272 |

*Museo Italiano*:

| | |
|---|---|
| 2 pl. 2 | 39 |

[Disney] *Museum Disneianum*:

| | |
|---|---|
| pl. 66, 1 | 250 |
| 126 | 247 |
| 127, 1 | 267 |
| 127, 2 | 234 |
| 127, 3 | 255 |

*Museum Etruscum Gregorianum* [*Mus. Greg.*]:

| | |
|---|---|
| i pl. 3, 3 | 252 |
| 5, 4, l. | 266 |
| 5, 4, r. | 266 |
| 7, 1 | 260 |
| 7, part | 265 |
| 8, 1, r. | 283 |
| 8, 3a | 287 |
| 8, 4 | 287 |
| 12, 1 | 279 |
| 12, 2 | 278 |
| 13 | 279 |
| 37, 1 | 79 |
| 40-1 | 57 |
| 59, d | 283 |
| 59, e | 283 |
| 59, 6 | 266 |
| 60, d | 249 |
| 60, ii, 2 | 278 |
| ii pl. 19, 2 | 299 |
| 63, 2 | 27 |
| 83, 2 | 55 |
| 88, 1 | 210 |
| 88, 2 | 210 |
| 89, mid. | 190 |
| 93, iv, 3 | 191 |
| 93, v, 3 | 192 |
| 93, 12 | 276 |
| 94, i, 2 | 233 |
| ii, 3 | 258 |
| ii, 5 | 257 |
| ii, 6 | 231 |
| iii, 2 | 238 |
| v, 2 | 255 |
| vi, 2 | 254 |
| vii, 2 | 245 |
| 95, ii, 3 | 142 |
| ii, 4 | 142 |
| iii, 3 | 48 |

**Museum Etruscum Gregorianum (cont.):**

| | |
|---|---|
| ii pl. 95, iii, 5 | 183 |
| iv, 1 | 148 |
| iv, 2 | 185 |
| v, 1 | 172 |
| v, 2 | 182 |
| v, 4 | 150–1 |
| vi, 2 | 82 |
| vi, 3 and 5 | 157 |
| vi, 4 | 47 |
| vi, 7 | 46 |
| vii, 3 | 65 |
| 99, 3 | 52 |
| 102, 3 | 241 |

**The Museum Journal [Mus. J.] (Philadelphia):**

| | |
|---|---|
| 5 p. 39 | 28 |
| 216 | 48 |
| 225 | 11 |
| 11 p. 65 | 100 |

Nachod *Der Rennwagen bei den Italikern.*

**Neugebauer *Antiken in deutschem Privatbesitz*:**

| | |
|---|---|
| pl. 71, 167 | 42 |
| 72 | 197 |

**Neugebauer *Bronzegerät des Altertums*:**

| | |
|---|---|
| pl. 22, 1 | 249 |

**Neugebauer *Führer durch das Antiquarium: Bronzen*:**

| | |
|---|---|
| pl. 57 | 49 |

Neugebauer *Führer durch das Antiquarium: Vasen.* See under the museum numbers.

**Newton and Thompson *The Castellani Collection*:**

| | |
|---|---|
| pl. 11 | 193 |

**Nicole *Meidias et le style fleuri*:**

| | |
|---|---|
| pp. 141–2 | 45 |

**Nogara *Gli etruschi e la loro civiltà*:**

| | |
|---|---|
| p. 54 | 89 |
| 58, 20 | 89 |
| 147 | 113 |
| 149 | 188 |
| 150 | 294 |
| 151 | 80 |
| 360 | 88 |

**Notizie degli Scavi di Antichità [N. Sc.]:**

| | |
|---|---|
| 1883 pl. 2, 10 | 178 |
| 2, 23 | 272 |
| 2, 36 | 263 |
| 2, 37 | 261 |
| 2, 38 | 263 |
| 3, 112 | 278 |
| 3, 113 | 277 |
| 1885 pl. 1, 6 | 248 |
| 1, 7 | 232 |
| 1, 8 | 291 |
| 1, 9 | 275 |
| 1, 11 | 31 |
| 1, 13 | 260 |
| 1886 p. 45, F | 264 |
| 45, G | 249 |
| 1887 p. 273, 2 | 106 |
| 1892 p. 472 | 296 |
| 1894 p. 289, 4 | 250 |
| 1895 p. 45 | 216 |
| 307, 21 | 260 |
| 1896 p. 380–1 | 235 |
| 1897 p. 25 | 212 |
| 1898 p. 54 | 296 |
| 401 | 265 |
| 1900 p. 177, 29 | 177 |
| 1903 p. 220, 2 | 241 |
| 220, 3 | 238 |
| 220, 6 | 243 |
| 221, 7 | 237 |
| 221, 9 | 245 |
| 276 | 24 |
| 589 | 286 |
| 590–2 | 286 |
| 594 | 285 |
| 595 | 285 |
| 596 | 285 |
| 1905 p. 34, a | 158 |
| 34, b | 158 |
| 34, f | 222 |
| 35, i, 2 | 250 |
| 55, r. | 205 |
| 56, part | 176 |
| ,, | 206 |
| ,, | 271 |
| 57, part | 65 |
| ,, | 65 |
| ,, | 278 |
| ,, | 279 |
| ,, | 280 |
| 58, 5, part | 168 |
| ,, | 168 |
| ,, | 192 |
| 58, 6, part | 66 |
| ,, | 67 |
| 1907 p. 201, 21 | 173 |
| 202, 23 | 159 |
| 203, 1 | 217 |
| 203, 5 | 217 |
| 204, 25 | 176 |
| 204, 26 | 176 |
| 327, a, 3 | 266 |
| 327, b, 1 | 266 |
| 345 | 138 |
| 1908 p. 207 | 139 |
| 1912 p. 74 | 106 |
| 83, 2 | 278 |
| 1913, sup., 8, 6 bis | 191 |
| 19 | 266 |
| 42, 55–6 | 88 |
| 1914 p. 136 | 174 |
| 243 | 130 |
| 271 | 111 |
| 272 | 202 |
| 273 | 155 |
| 274 | 157 |
| 275 | 155 |
| 1916 p. 55–7 | 155 |
| 58 | 101 |
| 59 | 108 |
| 60 | 108 |
| 61 | 108 |
| 72, 1 | 156 |
| 72, 2 | 156 |
| 72, 3 | 156 |
| 72, 4 | 157 |
| 1920 p. 22–5 | 85 |
| 1921 p. 336 | 283 |
| 1922 p. 132 | 207 |
| 268, g | 261 |
| 1924 pl. 5, a | 108–9, 299 |
| 6, b–d | 100 |
| 6, e | 100 |
| 7, a | 100 |
| 7, b | 103 |
| 9, a | 110 |
| 9, b | 111 |
| 13, 1 | 193 |
| 13, 2 | 192 |
| 13, 4 | 193 |
| 13, 5 | 194 |
| p. 162, 2 | 241 |
| 162, 4 | 269 |
| 163, 1 | 274 |
| 164, 5, 2 | 240 |
| 164, 5, 3 | 247 |
| 164, 5, 4 | 233 |
| 164, 5, 5 | 217 |
| 183 | 160 |
| 191 | 160 |
| 193 | 202 |
| 197 | 103 |
| 198 | 41 |
| 224 | 112 |
| 238 | 188 |
| 253 | 204 |
| 292, 5 | 232 |
| 330 | 108 |
| 331 | 112 |
| 1927 pl. 13, 1 | 119 |
| 13, 2 | 193 |
| 19, 2 | 60 |
| 25, a and c | 287 |
| 26 | 287 |
| p. 172, 3 | 208 |
| 173, 12 | 178 |
| 173, 13, 1 | 186 |
| 173, 13, 2 | 186 |
| 227 | 182 |
| 1928 p. 427, 5, b | 205 |
| 427, 5, c | 203 |
| 1929 p. 165, c | 126 |
| 165, h | 69 |
| 1930 p. 56, a | 176 |
| 56, b | 243 |
| 56, part | 243 |
| 550, 3 | 263 |
| 550, 4 | 265 |
| 1931 p. 208 | 278 |
| 210, 1 | 289 |
| 214 | 289 |
| 219 | 202 |
| 220, a | 203 |
| 220, b | 202 |
| 220, c | 204 |
| 220, d | 203 |
| 601, v | 272 |
| 601, 6 | 261 |
| 603, 1 | 261 |
| 603, 2 | 273 |
| 1932 p. 92, 2 | 278 |
| 94, d | 264 |
| 96, r. | 119 |
| 99, 1 | 150 |
| 99, 2 | 150 |
| 1933 p. 344, 1, 2 | 222 |
| 344, 1, 3 | 222 |
| 1934 p. 85, 11 | 296 |
| 162, 1 | 232 |
| 414 | 121 |
| 415, 69 147, | 168 |
| 416 | 169 |
| 417, 1 | 208 |
| 417, 3 | 207 |
| 417,·4 | 221 |
| 417, 6 | 176 |
| 418, 3 | 261 |
| 418, 7 | 270 |
| 418, iv, 2 | 238 |
| 425, 4 | 297 |
| 1935 p. 33, 1 | 259 |
| 33, 2 | 232 |
| 33, 4 | 237 |
| 33, 5 | 260 |
| 33, 6 | 237 |
| 33, 7 | 247 |
| 33, 8 | 260 |
| 163, 1 | 202 |
| 163, 3 | 203 |
| 1936 p. 56, i, 7 | 272 |
| 243, 2 | 130 |
| 398, 1 | 204 |
| 399 | 204 |
| 1937 p. 105, xv | 41 |
| 108 | 41 |
| 113, i, r. | 272 |
| 119, 7 | 222 |
| 126 | 227 |
| 145, 2 | 251 |
| 146 | 226 |
| 147 | 226 |
| 1938 p. 9 | 89 |
| 1939 pl. 31 | 204 |
| p. 10, 1 | 50 |
| 43, 1 | 204 |
| 43, 2 | 200 |

**Olympia:**

| | |
|---|---|
| ii pl. 121, 5 | 183 |

Alvarez - Ossorio *Vasos griegos . . . en el Museo Arqueológico Nacional.* See under the museum numbers.

Otchët Imperatorskoi Ar-
kheologicheskoi Kom-
missii:
1904 p. 68 ... 76
Overbeck Atlas der grie-
chischen Kunstmytho-
logie [KM.]:
pl. 18, 12 ... 55
18, 14 ... 47
25, 1 ... 73-7
26, 7 ... 44
Overbeck Gallerie heroi-
scher Bildwerke:
pl. 32, 1-2 ... 54

Pagenstecher Die cale-
nische Reliefkeramik:
pl. 8, 46 ... 212
16 ... 238
20, 99c ... 241, 308
99f ... 241
Panckoucke Héracléide:
pl. 1, 27 ... 305
38 ... 306
Panofka Antiques du
Cabinet du comte de
Pourtalès-Gorgier:
pl. 33, 3-4 ... 45
39 ... 119
Panofka Delphi und
Melaine:
pl. 1, 3-4 ... 188
Papers of the British School
at Rome [BSR]:
11 pl. 28, 8 ... 206
Passeri Picturae Etrus-
corum in vasculis:
pl. 42 ... 122
46, 1 ... 129
46, 2 ... 129
46, 3 ... 129
100 ... 228
139 ... 122
149 ... 161
216 ... 72
246-7 ... 21
Patroni Catalogo dei Vasi
del Museo Campano:
pl. 3 ... 27
16, 2 ... 187
Patroni La ceramica antica
nell' Italia meridionale:
p. 30, 26 ... 11
86 ... 66
151 ... 226
Pellegrini Catalogo dei vasi
antichi dipinti delle
collezioni Palagi ed Uni-
versitaria [VPU].
Pellegrini Catalogo dei vasi
greci dipinti delle necropoli felsinee [VF.].
Perdrizet Les Terres cuites
grecques d'Égypte de la
collection Fouquet:
pl. 95, 1 ... 212

2 ... 212
3 ... 212
4 ... 212
Pernice Griechische Pferdegeschirr:
Pernice Die hellenistische
Kunst in Pompeji:
4 pl. 13 ... 228
5 pl. 48, 1 ... 288
48, 2-3 ... 288
48, 4-5 ... 288
49 ... 288
p. 11, ab. ... 83
Pfuhl Malerei und Zeich-
nung der Griechen:
fig. 56 ... 30
163 ... 35
418 ... 303
467 ... 34
557 ... 27
561 ... 134
568 ... 109
579 ... 39
628 ... 5
685 ... 235
787 ... 264
Philippart Iconographie des
Bacchantes d'Euripide:
pl. 13, b ... 54
Pottier Le Dessin chez les
Grecs:
pl. 13, 40 ... 119
15, 78 ... 210
Pottier and S. Reinach
Myrina:
pl. 10, 1 ... 212
Pryce Catalogue of Sculp-
ture in . . . the British
Museum: Vol. I, Part
II: Cypriote and Etrus-
can Sculpture.

Raoul-Rochette Monu-
mens inédits d'antiquité
figurée:
pl. 45 ... 147
76, 3 ... 46
Rayet and Collignon His-
toire de la céramique
grecque:
p. 261 ... 117
324 ... 136
333 ... 210
338 ... 209
Rendiconti della Pontificia
Accademia Romana:
3 pll. 7-8 ... 189, 191
17 p. 66-9 ... 300
70 ... 300
79 ... 301
Revue archéologique [RA.]:
1916, p. 253-4 ... 161
255 ... 176
1927 p. 313, 77-9 ... 67
1941 p. 103 ... 72

de Ridder Catalogue des
vases peints de la Bibliothèque Nationale.
de Ridder Les Bronzes
antiques du Louvre.
Richter Ancient Gems from
the Evans and Beatty
Collections:
i no. 42 ... 138
141 ... 137
Richter Etruscan Art in the
Museum:
fig. 111-12 ... 11
113 ... 11
116 ... 11
117 ... 11
118 ... 14
119 ... 196
122-3 ... 196
134-5 ... 187
137 ... 10, 119
139 ... 102
140 ... 88
165 ... 285
166 ... 289
167-9 ... 286
Richter Greek Painting:
p. 15, 2 ... 167
Richter The Metropolitan
Museum of Art: Cata-
logue of Engraved Gems:
pl. 10 ... 4
Richter The Metropolitan
Museum of Art: Greek
Etruscan and Roman
Bronzes:
p. 181, i, 4 ... 232
i, 5 ... 254
r. ... 309
Richter The Metropolitan
Museum of Art: Hand-
book of the Classical
Collection (1930):
p. 186 ... 116
Richter and Hall Red-
figured Athenian Vases
in the Metropolitan
Museum of Art. See
under the museum
numbers.
Ritschl Priscae latinitatis
monumenta:
pl. xi, k ... 274
xcvii, o ... 274
sup. V pl. 5, A ... 210
10, A ... 216
10, B ... 215
10, C ... 210
10, D ... 210
10, E ... 210
10, F ... 210
11, G ... 210
Rivista del R. Istituto di
Archeologia e Storia
d'Arte [Riv. Ist.]:
4 p. 34, 1 ... 235

34, 3 ... 260
103, 2 ... 267
Robert, Louis Collection
Froehner, i: Inscriptions
grecques:
pl. 22, 50 ... 72
Robinson, D. M. Olyn-
thus V:
pl. 28 ... 272
192 ... 272
Robinson, D. M., Har-
cum, and Iliffe A Cata-
logue of the Greek Vases
in the Royal Ontario
Museum of Archaeology,
Toronto.
Robinson, Edward
Museum of Fine Arts,
Boston: Catalogue of
Greek Etruscan and
Roman Vases, see under
Boston.
Roemische Mitteilungen,
see Mitteilungen.
Romanelli Tarquinia:
p. 132 ... 15
133 ... 296
134 ... 296
137, 1 ... 305
137, 2 ... 300
137, 3 ... 300
138, 2 ... 306
Roscher Lexikon der grie-
chischen und römischen
Mythologie:
s.v. Danaiden, 951 ... 147
Herakles, 2241 ... 104
Kirke, 1195, 2 ... 54
Marsyas, 2454 ... 75
Olympos, 862 ... 80
Pygmaien,
3293, 2 ... 126
3294, 3 ... 127, 129
Sternbilder, 939 ... 219
Telephos,
298, 3 ... 54
305 ... 66
Tithonos, 1028 ... 81
1029 ... 138
Triton, 1170 ... 117
Troilos,
1227 ... 179-80
Tyndareos
1422, 5 ... 39
Rostovtzeff A History of
the Ancient World:
ii pl. 11, 1 ... 211
Rostovtzeff Social and
Economic History of the
Hellenistic World:
i pl. 52, 2 ... 212
53, 1 ... 212
Rumpf Chalkidische
Vasen:
pl. 12 ... 35
88 ... 97

Ryberg *An Archaeological Record of Rome:*
pl. 20 fig. 106a    269
        106b    273
        107a    176
        107b    176
        107c    176
    21 fig. 108    205
        110    207
        112    206
    22 fig. 115    257
        119a    269
        119b    257
        119c    257
        120a    243
        120b    243
        120d    244
        120e    244
    23 fig. 120e    244
        121b    157
        124a    159
        124b    159
        124c    159
        124d    159
        124e    159
    24 fig. 125a    173
        127    207
        128a    177
    25 fig. 129a    224
        129b    224
        130d    200
    27 fig. 132h    207
        133a    217
        133b    217
    29 fig. 136a    246
    34 fig. 153    210

Sambon *Vases antiques de terre cuite: Collection Canessa [Can.]:*
pl. 12, 150    188
    12, 155    191
*Sambon, Jules,* see *Catalogue.*
*Sammlung Niessen:*
pl. 107, 3141    300
        3149    307
*Sammlung A. Ruesch:*
pl. 24, 48    257
    27, 101    264
    37, 173    263
*Sammlung Vogell,* see *Griechische.*
Schaal *Griechische Vasen aus Frankfurter Sammlungen [F.]:*
pl. 1, d    192
    57, c    173
Schaal *Griechische Vasen . . . in Bremen:*
pl. 26, c    222
    29, a    267
    29, e    272
Schefold *Die Bildnisse griechischer Dichter Redner und Denker:*

p. 163, 2    288
Schefold *Kertscher Vasen [KV.]:*
pl. 18    76
Schefold *Untersuchungen zu den Kertscher Vasen [U.]:*
pl. 32, 4    76
fig. 59    76
Schrader *Pheidias:*
p. 270    297
Schreiber *Die hellenistischen Reliefbilder:*
pll. 37–40    109
Schröder *Griechische Bronzeeimer im Berliner Antiquarium:*
p. 8    251
    9    251
    14, 1–2    287
    14, 10    287
    14, 11, 1    287
    14, 11, 4    256
    16, 14, 3 and 5    288
    16, 14, 4    288
    17    288
    18, 1    287
    18, 2    288
    18, 3    287
    21    252
Schumacher *Beschreibung der Sammlung antiker Bronzen, Grossherzogliche Vereinigte Sammlungen zu Karlsruhe.*
*Scritti in onore di Bartolomeo Nogara:*
pl. 2, 1–3    210
    2, 4–5    178
    2, 6    128
Séchan *Études sur la tragédie grecque dans ses rapports avec la céramique:*
p. 118    195
    130    39
    216    179
    241    133
    511    66
Shepard *The Fish-tailed Monster in Greek and Etruscan Art:*
pl. 13, 82    56
Sieveking *Bronzen Terracotten Vasen der Sammlung Loeb:*
pl. 53, 2    110
Sieveking and Hackl *Die Königliche Vasensammlung zu München. I [SH.].*
*Singleton Abbey,* see Catalogue.
*Sitzungsberichte der Berliner Akademie:*

1851 pll. 1–2    121
Smirnov *Argenterie orientale:*
pl. 170    212
Smith (Cecil H.) *The Forman Collection:*
pl. p. 21, 162    189
Smith (Cecil H.) and Hutton *Catalogue of the Antiquities in the Collection of the late Wyndham Francis Cook, Esqre:*
pl. 2, 41    138
Smith (H. R. W.) *The Origin of Chalcidian Ware:*
p. 105    168
Solari *Vita pubblica e privata degli Etruschi:*
fig. 54    113
    55    247
    56, 1    289
    56, 2    290
    56, 3    294
    81–2    160
Sommer, photographs:
11104    84
11016, iii, 4    227
    iii, 10    227
    iv, 2    222
    vi, 1    227
    vi, 2    227
    vi, 4    223
11018, v, 10    220
    vi, 7    219
    vi, 9    219
    vi, 11    220
    vii, 1    224
    vii, 2    223
    vii, 3    224
    vii, 4    223
    viii, 3    223
    viii, 10    219
    ix, 1    220
    ix, 2    220
    ix, 6    219
    ix, 7    219
    ix, 8    227
    ix, 9    227
11023, ii, 7    268
    x, 2    272
11024, iii, 18    264
*Catalogue Sotheby Dec. 1 1913:*
pl. 2, 78    77
*Catalogue . . . Sotheby 22–23 May 1919:*
pl. 2, 55    291
    2, 103    119
Stackelberg *Die Graeber der Hellenen:*
pl. 24, 4    88
*Stephanos Theodor Wiegand zum 60. Geburtstag dargebracht:*
pl. 5    199

p. 13    228
*Studi e materiali:*
i, 137, 32, 74    80
*Studi etruschi [St. etr.]:*
1 pl. 70, 4    88
2 pl. 29, 41    127
        45    122
        60    129
    30, 52    128
        57    129
        67    130
        89    247
    31, 80    276
        83    243
        88    248
        88 bis    242
        90    248
        91    248
        92    253
        93    234
        95    253, 256
        96    254
        97    256
        104    240
        108    238
        110    267
    32, 98    251
        99    252
        101    255
        102    279
        103, r.    279
        107    279
    36, 144    252
        160    289
4 pl. 24, 3    163
        29    133
6 p. 465    24
7 pl. 15, 6    19
    16, 3    19
    17, 1–2    13
    20, 2    183
8 pll. 29–30    31
    34, 2    11
    40    196
9 pl. 11, 15    237
    37    131
    39, 1    289
    39, 13    290
    40, 6–7    189
    40, 8    290
    41, 5    119
11 pl. 11, 1, 2    265
    11, 3, mid.    265
    35, 1–2    13
    35, 3–4    13
    36, 1    14
    36, 2–3    14
    36, 4    14
    37, 1–2    13
    37, 3–4    13
    39, 1    13
    39, 3    19
    40, 1–2    17
    40, 3–4    14
    41, 1    191
    41, 3    143

Studi Etruschi (cont.):
41, 4–5 142
42, 1 142
42, 2 142
42, 3–4 141
43, 1–2 142
43, 3 and 6 174
43, 4–5 141
44, 1–2 154, 158
44, 3–4 154, 158
45 154
59, 3, 3 169
59, 3, 4 257
59, 3, 5 257
59, 3, 7 257
59, 3, 8 257
59, 4, c 207
59, 4, e 273
59, 4, f 242
p. 113–14 252
373 185
375 142
376 141
378 142
12 pl. 52, 1–2 16
52, 3 16
52, 4 16
53, 1–2 16
55, 4 20
55, 5 14
56, 2 18
56, 3 18
57 115
p. 293 115
16 pl. 25, a 309
26 301
29, ii, 4 269
42, 1–2 296
42, 3–4 296
43, 1–2 296
43, 3–4 296
47, 1–2 296
47, 3–4 296
48, 3–4 296
p. 525 296
17 pl. 17, 4, r. 249
20, 1 308
20, 2 308
29, 1 240
Sumbolae litterariae in honorem Julii De Petra:
pp. 166–7 66
The Swedish Cyprus Expedition:
2 pl. 49, 1, 11 266

Tarchi L'arte etrusco-romana nell' Umbria e nella Sabina:
pl. 25, 2 294
36, 1 and 3 280
36, 2 280
78, 1 292
78, 2, ab. 286

78, 2, below 292
103, 3 117
105 117
119, 3 37
120, 1 170
120, 2 170
120, 3–4 170
121, 1 169
121, 2 170
125, 4 143
127, 2 165
127, 3 124
127, 4 127, 130
128, 1 289
128, 2 289
130, 2 294
131, 1 194
131, 2 194
Thiersch Ependytes und Ephod:
pl. 11 31
Tillyard The Hope Vases:
pl. 19, 122 75
25, 150 36, 101
26, 162 161
27, 169 76
Tischbein Collection of Engravings from Ancient Vases now in the possession of Sir Wm. Hamilton:
1 pl. 59 36, 101
2 pl. 12 161
3 pl. 5 76
3 pl. 12 75
3 pl. 44 12
3 fig. F 191
Trendall Frühitaliotische Vasen:
pl. 11, c 74
19 34, 61
26 65
Trendall Paestan Pottery:
pl. 2, b 90
14 307
20, c 226
21, a 38
30, a 227
30, d 227
32, b 226
34, e 226, 227

Vendita Sarti:
pl. 11 183
12, 104 (107) 58
12, 105 58
Vente du 18 au 20 mars 1901:
pl. 4, 63 228
5, 78 120
5, 81 119
Vente du 11 au 14 mai 1903:
pl. 8, 3 286

8, 5 289
Vermiglioli Le Erogamie di Admeto e Alceste:
pl. 121
Verschiedener deutscher Kunstbesitz. Berlin 27–29 Mai 1935:
pl. 84, 923 265
Visconti Museo Pio-Clementino:
3 pl. 22 31
4 pl. 36 147
Visedo Molto Excavaciones en el monte 'La Serrata':
pl. 6, a 206

Waddington Recueil général des monnaies grecques d'Asie mineure:
pl. 81, 32 214
Wagner Antike Bronzen der Grossherzoglichen Badischen Alterthümersammlung in Karlsruhe:
pl. 12, 6 265
15, 7 287
15, 10 266
15, 11 266
Walter Beschreibung der Reliefs im Kleinen Akropolismuseum in Athen:
pp. 72–4 72
Walters Catalogue of the Bronzes in the British Museum.
Walters Catalogue of the Engraved Gems and Cameos in the British Museum.
Walters Catalogue of the Greek and Etruscan Vases in the British Museum, vols. ii and iv.
Walters Catalogue of the Roman Pottery in the British Museum.
Walters Catalogue of the Silver Plate in the British Museum:
pl. 4 252
17, 126 263
Walters Catalogue of the Terracottas in the British Museum:
p. 340 294
Walters History of Ancient Pottery:
pl. 44, 1 272
58, 2 136
i p. 490 215
Watzinger Antike Holzsarkophage:
no. 12 299

Watzinger Griechische Vasen in Tübingen, see under the museum numbers.
Weicker Der Seelenvogel:
p. 119, 44 11
Welcker Alte Denkmäler:
pl. 11 37
13 37
94, 2 124
Wiener Vorlegeblätter [WV.]:
1 pl. 2 75
A pl. 1 164
E pl. 1 144
2 89, 147
3 144, 147
4 147
6, 2 147
6, 3 144
9–10 49
1889 pl. 12, 1 5, 58
12, 4 58
12, 6 58
Winter Die Typen der figürlichen Terrakotten:
ii, 385, 3 212
385, 4 212
Wissenschaftliche Mitteilungen aus Bosnien und der Herzegowina: see Bulanda.
Wolters Der geflügelte Seher:
p. 3 199
Worcester Art Museum Annual:
2 p. 25, 5 272
Wuilleumier Le Trésor de Tarente:
pll. 5–6 235

Zahn Sammlung Baurat Schiller:
pl. 36, 419 222
38 270
Zannoni Gli Scavi della Certosa di Bologna:
pl. 24 31
50, 16 266
54, 3–4 279
83, 6 222
Zapiski Imperatorskago Odesskago Obshchestva Istorii i Drevnosteĭ (Odessa):
19 pl. 1, 3 and 1 72
Zoega Die antiken Basreliefe von Rom:
pl. 88 157
Züchner Der Berliner Mänadenkrater.
pl. 7 250

# ILLUSTRATIONS

PLATE I

1

2

3

4

PLATE II

2

1

2

1

PLATE III

1

2

3

4

PLATE IV

1

4

3

2

5

PLATE V

1

2

3

PLATE VI

1

2

3

4

5

PLATE VII

1

3

2

4

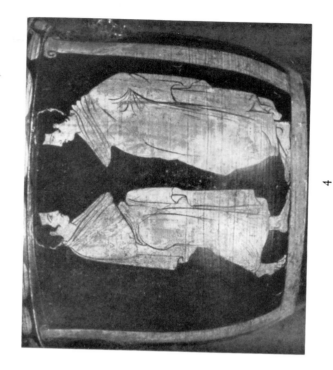

PLATE VIII

2

4

1

3

PLATE IX

1

2

PLATE X

2

4

5

1

3

PLATE XI

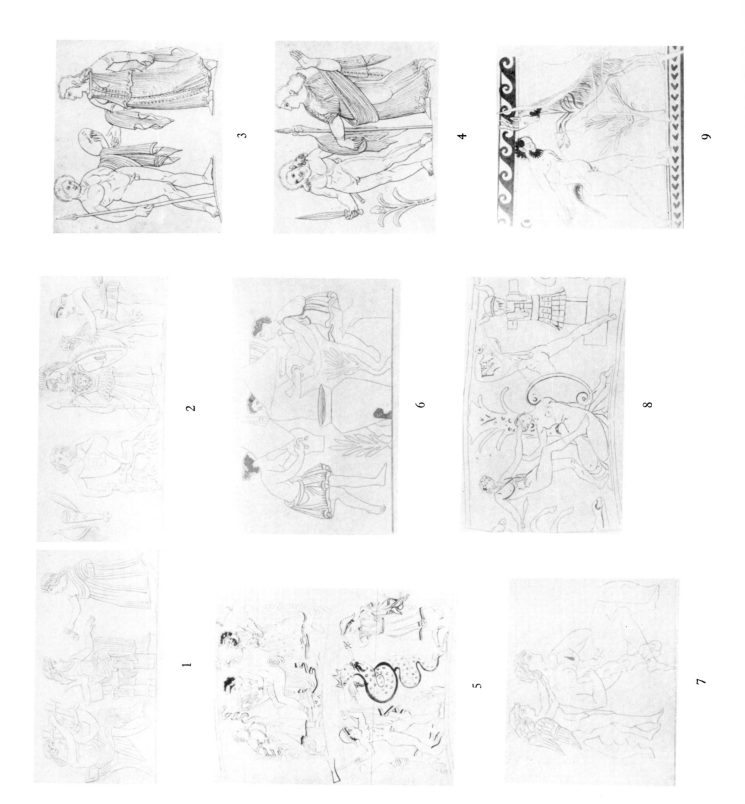

PLATE XII

1

2

PLATE XIII

1

2

3

4

2

1

PLATE XIV

1

2

PLATE XV

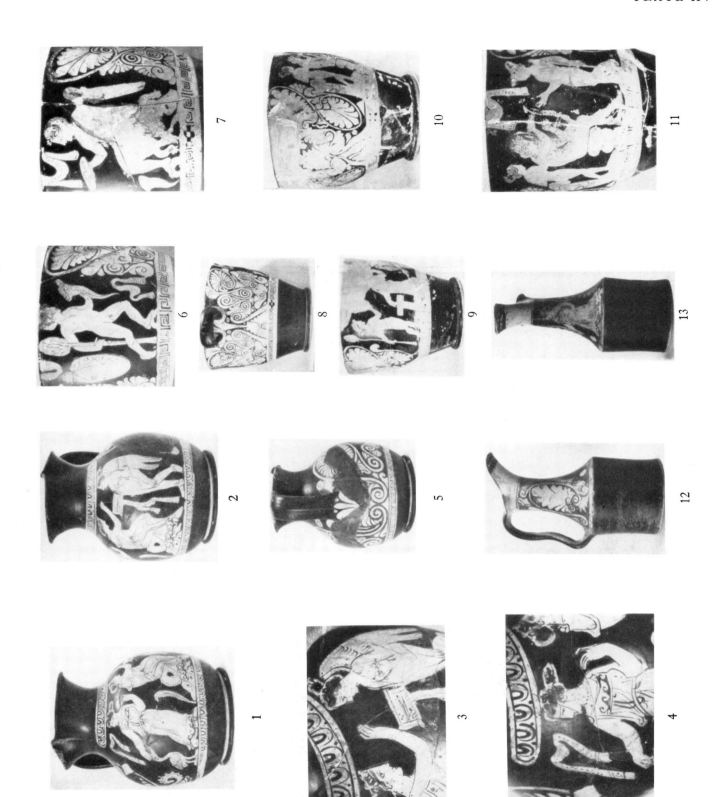

PLATE XVI

2

1

PLATE XVII

2

4

1

3

PLATE XVIII

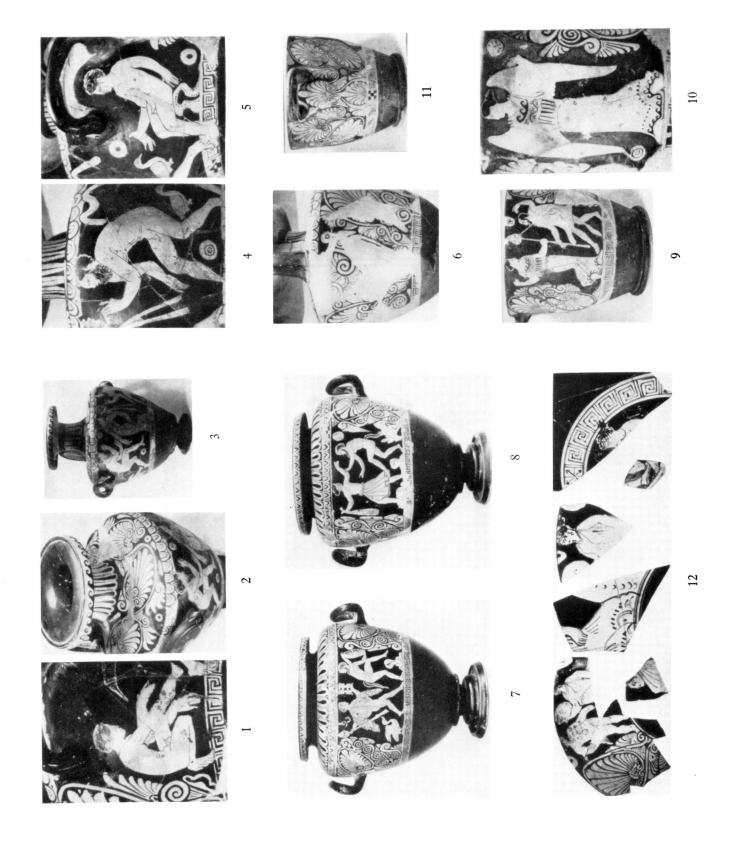

PLATE XIX

1

2

PLATE XX

2

3

1

PLATE XXI

3

6

1

2

5

4

PLATE XXII

1

2

3

PLATE XXIII

PLATE XXIV

2

4

1

3

PLATE XXV

1

2

4

3

5

6

PLATE XXVI

1

2

PLATE XXVII

1

2

3

4

6

5

7

8

9

PLATE XXVIII

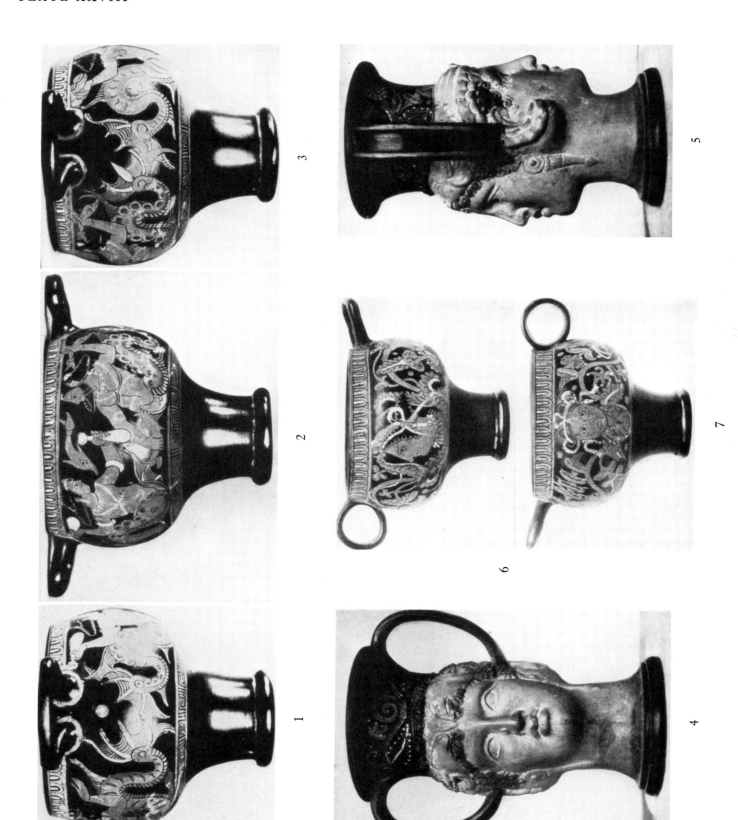

1

2

3

4

5

6

7

PLATE XXIX

1

2

3

4

5

6

7

8

9

10

PLATE XXX

1

2

3

PLATE XXXI

4

2

3

1

PLATE XXXII

3

6

5

4

7

2

1

PLATE XXXIII

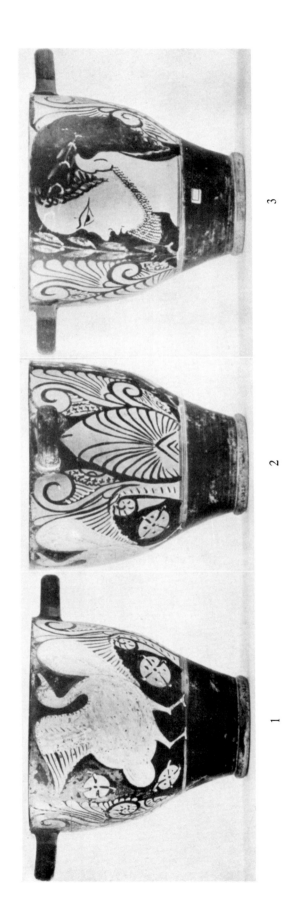

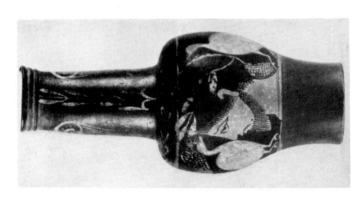

PLATE XXXIV

4

3

1

2

PLATE XXXV

3

7

2

6

5

1

4

PLATE XXXVI

1

2

3

4

5

7

6

PLATE XXXVII

1

2

PLATE XXXVIII

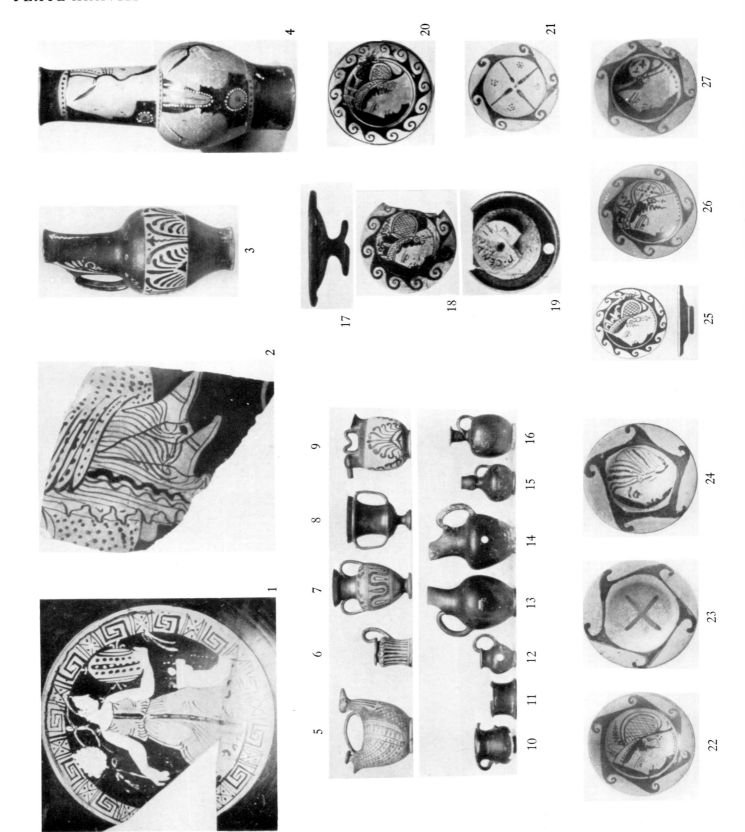

PLATE XXXIX

1

2

3

PLATE XL

1

3

2

5

4

6

7

8

9